SO-BII-807

Mastering
ASP.NET with C#

Mastering™
ASP.NET with C#™

A. Russell Jones

SYBEX®

San Francisco   London

Associate Publisher: Richard Mills

Acquisitions and Developmental Editor: Tom Cirtin

Editor: Gene Redding

Production Editor: Erica Yee

Technical Editor: Mike Gunderloy

Book Designer: Maureen Forys, Happenstance Type-O-Rama

Graphic Illustrator: Tony Jonick

Electronic Publishing Specialist: Jill Niles

Proofreaders: Nelson Kim, Laurie O'Connell, Yariv Rabinovitch, Nancy Riddiough

Indexer: Ted Laux

Cover Designer: Design Site

Cover Illustrator: Design Site

I dedicate this book to my friend Brenda Lewis, who cares not at all about its contents, but has nurtured its author since near childhood, and to my wife, Janet, who has—yet again—had the patience to endure a book's creation.

Acknowledgments

I WOULD LIKE TO acknowledge the considerable talents of the editorial staff at Sybex, who have been both patient and thorough, particularly Richard Mills, Tom Cirtin, Erica Yee, Gene Redding, Denise Santoro Lincoln, and Mike Gunderloy, and the many, often unrewarded people who spend time answering questions in technical newsgroups. You do make a difference.

Contents at a Glance

Contents

Introduction

FOR THE PAST 20 years, programming efforts have alternated between servers and clients. From mainframe batch processing to stand-alone applications to client-server to Internet, the focus of development shifts back and forth according to the current hardware, software, and communications model available. From teletypes to terminals, mainframes to minicomputers to modern servers, desktops to laptops to handheld devices, hard-wired direct connections to private networks to the Internet, programmers have concentrated their efforts either on improving the user interface or building the back-end systems that serve data to the devices that run the user interface. During the 1980s and early 1990s, the rapid evolution of microcomputers forced developers' attention toward the latter, which is why today's computer buyers enjoy high-resolution, deep-color displays; sound and voice capabilities; fast processors; a surfeit of data storage options; cheap memory; and powerful, graphical, interactive operating systems.

The rapid improvement in microcomputers caused a corresponding fragmentation of data; people worked with individual files on their own computers. Interestingly, that very fragmentation led to a rapid corresponding rise in networking capabilities, because businesses needed workers to be able to share information—and they also needed centralized, secure control of that information. Those needs drove the development of client-server computing, which couples the rich graphical user interface and fast processing of microcomputers with fast centralized databases.

Unfortunately, client-server computing, as it was initially conceived, caused several problems. The "fat" client programs were difficult to deploy, install, maintain, and upgrade. What companies needed was a different kind of client application: one that could accept data *and* application code from the centralized servers but display and let users interact with that data as with the desktop applications they had come to expect. The advent of the World Wide Web and browser technology seemed to promise an answer.

In the past several years, we've seen the resurrection of the "thin" client—typically a browser or small executable that retrieves data on demand from a central server much as mainframe terminals did back in the early days of computing. While the new thin clients have much more functionality than their mainframe-terminal counterparts did, they're still not completely satisfying to a public used to the richness of commercial applications such as Microsoft Office, Quicken, and thousands of custom client-server applications.

However, despite these shortcomings, browsers running HTML-based front-ends have changed the world. People and businesses are growing increasingly dependent on location irrelevance. They want to be able to reach any server, anywhere, anytime—and they're well on the road to realizing that desire. Location irrelevance trumps ease-of-use, so browsers and other remote clients are now ubiquitous.

Unfortunately, browsers haven't completely replaced the rich desktop client applications. They lea many people feeling as if they've been transported a couple of decades into the past. Browsers work extremely well when delivering static data, such as reports, documents, and images, but considerably les well when they're forced into client-server, form-driven, data-entry roles. The smooth, point-and-clic page transitions you experience when browsing the Web often stumble when the application suddenly requires you to enter data.

I believe .NET has the capability to change the situation. With the .NET framework, it's possibl to create more interactive and responsive centrally located software. At the same time, .NET improve the tools and simplifies the process for building rich clients. Finally, it bridges the two by making it extremely easy to provide both rich and thin clients (remember, you can't be too rich or too thin) with centrally located and managed data, meaning your users can have their familiar graphical controls and behavior, *and* you can manage the application centrally by having it dynamically update on demand.

What's in This Book?

This is a book of exploration (mine) as much as it is a book of explication. Microsoft's .NET frame work is extremely well designed for such a large and complex entity—but it *is* both large and complex The biggest problem I faced during the writing of this book wasn't what to include, but what to leave out, and that is a severe problem. There's so much material I would have liked to include, but time, space, the dramatic changes in the .NET framework and Visual Studio during the early portions of the writing and my own still-immature knowledge of the .NET framework prevented that.

The driving force behind this book was the idea that .NET provides a completely new model for building Web applications, as well as two brand-new languages for doing so (C# and VB.NET) and an expanded version of server-side JScript (JScript.NET).

For those of you who may be former VB programmers switching to C#, let me get something ou of the way. In my opinion, VB.NET is a brand-new language whose only connection to "classic" VE (all earlier versions) is a name and some shared syntax. Other than those elements, everything else ha changed. However, you'll find that C# is much closer to the spirit of VB than any other language that uses C-like syntax, and that Visual Studio .NET (VS.NET) makes using C# very straightforward. In fact, after using VB for many years, I came to detest having to code in case-sensitive languages, but due to the Intellisense technology in VS.NET, I haven't been bothered by that at all (yes, C# *is* a case-sensitive language).

If you've been building Web applications already, using any technology, you're *way* ahead of the average programmer, because you already understand how the Web works. Microsoft has made a huge— probably very successful—effort in Visual Studio and ASP.NET applications to hide how the Web works. Consequently, I've spent a considerable amount of time in this book trying to explain how ASP.NET applications make it so easy. In some ways, ASP.NET and C# are like classic VB—they make it easy to build moderate size, inefficient Web programs in much the same way that VB made i easy to build moderate size, inefficient Windows programs.

You see, while Visual Studio .NET and the .NET framework change Web programming, the Wel itself hasn't changed one iota due to .NET; it's still the same page-oriented, stateless communication mechanism it's always been. It's easy to forget that when you're building Web applications with C#. I think the biggest danger for Web programmers using .NET is that it *does* successfully hide complexity behind a rich programming model. However, complexity doesn't disappear just because it's been strained through the colander of Visual Studio. It's still there, hiding in the closet waiting to bite you when you're not looking.

Fortunately, .NET not only makes formerly complex tasks easier, but it also gives you the capability to open the closet, grab complexity by the ear, and drag it into the light, where you can see it clearly. After working with .NET for nearly a year during the writing of this book, I'm thoroughly convinced that .NET and similar systems constitute a great improvement in programming. Although you don't absolutely *have* to have Visual Studio to build the projects in this book, you'll be thoroughly dissatisfied with the book if you *don't* have Visual Studio.

Although Visual Studio combines most Web technology development into a single interface and assists and simplifies writing HTML and other file formats, the litany of technologies you need to know to be a complete Web programmer is still long, and none of them are simple. They are as follows:

C#   The language you use to build classes, retrieve and manipulate data, and handle events.

Hypertext Markup Language (HTML)   A formatting/layout language you use to design the user interface.

Cascading Style Sheets (CSS)   A robust, extensible, and hierarchical method for specifying the visual styles applied to page objects.

JavaScript/JScript/ECMAScript   A programming language you use to manipulate page objects within a client browser. JScript is Microsoft's proprietary version of ECMAScript. The name JavaScript was initially introduced by Netscape.

NOTE   *Don't confuse client-side JScript with Microsoft's new JScript.NET language. JScript is to JScript.NET as C# is to C++—the syntax is similar but the languages are different.*

Extensible Markup Language (XML)   A general-purpose markup language used throughout Visual Studio and .NET as a way to hold and manipulate data retrieved from a database; a format for specifying application configuration information; a way to persist data and objects; and a generic data container for passing messages, objects, and data from one component or tier to another.

Extensible Stylesheet Language (for Transformations) (XSL/XSLT)   An XML vocabulary created for the exclusive purpose of transforming XML documents from one state to another. That state can be from XML to XML, from XML to HTML, from XML to text, or from XML to any other form.

XML Schema (XSD)   An XML vocabulary created for the exclusive purpose of transforming XML documents from one state to another. That can be XML to XML, XML to HTML, XML to text, XML to PDF documents, or XML to anything else.

Document Object Model (DOM)   A model for manipulating objects created in a document tree structure. The document can be either XML or HTML. For example, you can use the .NET XML namespace classes to manipulate objects stored within an XML document, whereas you typically use JavaScript to manipulate the DOM objects that make up an HTML page. In some cases, you may even need to use the older COM-based MSXML parser to manipulate XML stored as data islands in Internet Explorer (IE). That parser also exposes DOM objects and methods, although they're slightly different than those in .NET.

Dynamic HTML (DHTML)   A name for the technology of manipulating objects created in the browser and responding to events raised by those objects or initiated by a user. DHTML-enabled browsers, such as IE and Netscape, let you specify the position, content, and display characteristics of every object within the page. In other words, DHTML lets you take an otherwise static HTML display and make it nearly as responsive as a stand-alone Windows application.

In Microsoft's previous Web programming systems (WebClasses in VB 6 and ASP with Visual InterDev), you still had to be able to write raw HTML. Although this version of Visual Studio makes a brave attempt at eliminating the need to know HTML, it hasn't succeeded entirely. Therefore, I've included a short tutorial on HTML because you'll need to know a minimum amount to be able to create C# Web applications. If you've been using FrontPage or Dreamweaver in an effort to *avoid* learning how to code raw HTML, I recommend that you study the tutorial thoroughly, because unless you're completely comfortable with writing HTML using a text editor, you will have a very hard time writing HTML indirectly using a programming language—and doing so is a requirement for many Web applications.

Who Should Read This Book?

This book is aimed squarely at beginning Web programmers who are minimally familiar with C# and the .NET framework. You don't have to be an experienced C# programmer to read this book by any means, but you shouldn't be a rank beginner, either. There's neither time nor space to explain the C# language or the frameworkitself other than as it relates to ASP.NET and Web programming. If you've taken an introductory C# programming course, built a couple of C# windows or console applications, or even read through a C#-specific programming book, you won't have much trouble with the code in this book.

Beyond a little C#, you don't have to know anything about the Internet, intranets, browsers, HTML, JavaScript, VBScript, XML, XSLT, the DOM, or any other Web-related technology to read this book. This is a beginner book. What you *will* find here is a thorough basic explanation of the principles of Web programming with C# and ASP.NET and a bit of exposure to each of the other Web technologies you'll need to build robust, scalable Web applications with C#.

Why Did I Write This Book?

I wrote this book because I'm fascinated with the processes of programming and writing. I've written two other Web programming books: one on WebClass programming with Visual Basic 6, *Visual Basic Developer's Guide to ASP and IIS* (Sybex, 1999) and one titled *Mastering Active Server Pages 3* (Sybex, 2000). Both books sold reasonably well, but that's not why I wrote them, nor is that why I wrote this one. The act of writing this book gave me both a reason and an excuse to explore the technology more broadly than if I had approached .NET simply as a tool to create Web applications—and that broad exploration provided a corresponding breadth and depth of information about the topic that I suspect is nearly impossible to obtain any other way. As I firmly believe that .NET and similar environments are the future of programming, I wanted to evangelize that belief as well as give myself an excuse to work with this technology from the first beta version through the final release.

I like learning computer languages. I've been programming for over 20 years now and programming for the Web since before classic ASP became available. Along the way, I've learned and worked with a large number of computer languages. While I am in no way an expert in any programming language or technology and don't pretend to be, I do have extensive experience with Visual Basic, databases, Web programming, XML, XSLT, and the other technologies discussed in this book.

My scholastic background is in science and biology, music, computer-based training (CBT), interactive video training (IVT), and most recently, Web-based training (WBT), database applications, and general purpose human resources (HR) Web-based applications. I was a premed student before deciding not to work in the medical field; instead, I worked at the Knoxville, Tennessee, zoo for several years, where I eventually became the head keeper of reptiles under curator John Arnett, working with (at that time) the tenth largest reptile collection in the world. But the strands of my herpetological curiosity eventually wore thin on the sharp edges of poor pay. My musical interests called, and I went back to college as a music major, studying piano and music theory.

I first became involved with computers in 1979 when I was an undergraduate piano student at the University of Tennessee and discovered Dr. Donald Pederson's music theory computer lab full of brand-new Apple II microcomputers with—believe it or not—8K of main memory. Back then, small was not only beautiful—it was imperative. My first program of substance taught people how to recognize and write musical chords—one facet of a class generally known as music theory.

That work sparked a fascination with computing that continues to this day. After completing a master's degree in music theory, I attended the University of Illinois to work on a doctorate in secondary education. The university was the site of the first important computer teaching system, called PLATO. As a research assistant, I worked with Dr. Esther Steinberg, author of *Teaching Computers to Teach*, investigating the relative importance of various interface features for beginning versus expert computer users. After graduating, I worked for InterCom, Inc. building computer-based training programs and HR applications for about 12 years. Toward the end of that time, I began writing technical articles, the first of which were for Fawcette's *Visual Basic Programmer's Journal* and *XML Magazine*, and then I began writing books for Sybex. Since 2000, I've worked briefly for the Playwear division of VF Corporation, one of the world's largest clothing manufacturers, and now work for DevX, Inc. (`www.devx.com`), initially as a Web developer and now as the Executive Editor, where I write, commission, and edit Web-related programming articles in all Web-related technologies.

What Will You Learn?

This book shows you how to use C# and the ASP.NET framework in a specific way—by using code-behind classes to build Web applications. In classic ASP, you could mix executable code and HTML in the same file. You can still do that in ASP.NET, but the technology described in this book is more like VB6 WebClasses, which used HTML templates in conjunction with a compiled VB-generated DLL. The DLL code could access the HTML templates to "fill" them with data, thus creating a very clean separation between the user interface (the HTML) and the code.

Code-behind classes in C# follow that same logic but are considerably easier to use. At the simplest level, you create an HTML template, called a Web Form, that contains the user interface elements. From the Web Form, you reference the code in a class in the code-behind file; finally, you program the contents of the HTML elements from the C# class. Like WebClasses, separating the code that activates the HTML templates from the templates themselves gives you a much cleaner separation. For example, it's very easy, after you have a defined set of user-interface elements, to let HTML designers build an interface and modify that interface by adding static elements or changing the positions and/or the look-and-feel of those elements without interfering with the way the page *works*. Similarly, you can reuse the user-interface templates, filling them with different data or copying them from one application to the next without having to rebuild the interface.

For these reasons, C# Web applications using the ASP.NET framework and code-behind classes are the base technology used in this book. I've devoted roughly half the book to explaining how to use and explore Web Forms, but as I've already mentioned, there are several ancillary technologies that you either *must* know, such as HTML and CSS, to build Web applications, or *should* know, or at least be aware of, such as database access with ADO.NET, Web services, caching data, writing components and services, XML, and transforming XML documents with XSLT.

How to Read This Book

Those who are truly Web beginners should profit from reading the first few chapters of the book, which discusses how the Web works, and has a short HTML tutorial. In contrast, those who already know HTML and CSS or who have classic ASP programming experience can skip sections covering technologies they already know without any problems.

Don't treat this book as a reference—it's not. It's a narrative exploration. As you progress through the book, you'll build a relatively large Web application and several related applications in which each individual chapter containing code becomes a subdirectory of the main project. There's no overarching plan to the application; it doesn't "do" anything other than provide a framework for exploration. When you're finished, you'll have a set of Web Forms, as well as some other .NET features such as User Controls, Composite Controls, and Web Services that contain the basic functionality you'll need to build similar features into your applications.

Although you can install the sample code from the Sybex website at www.sybex.com, I don't recommend you use the book that way. Instead, you should manually type in the code for each chapter. Copy the sample code if you get stuck or encounter problems or errors you can't solve. Along the way, you'll probably find shortcuts and better ways to solve a problem, and you'll discover your own way of working. You'll probably notice some changes in the book code as you go through it as well, where the code to accomplish something—a loop for example—changes during the course of the book. In some cases, those changes are intentional; there are many ways to solve problems, and I've included different examples in the code. There's not always a single most efficient method or the perfect syntax. Some people prefer one syntax; some another. In other cases, the changing code reflects my own changing and growing experience with the .NET framework and the C# language. In still others, the framework itself grew and changed while this book was being written.

What's Not in This Book?

This book is an exploration of a very specific technology—ASP.NET Web Forms using C# code-behind classes, and it's aimed squarely at the beginning Web developer. The code isn't always fully formed—it's not meant to be copied and reused in production applications; it's designed to teach you how .NET works, so you can build and debug your own production-quality code. Most of the code was written with specific learning points in mind.

You shouldn't expect a comprehensive listing of methods and properties. There are a few such lists, but not many. You can find those in the online .NET framework and Visual Studio documentation and in other books.

The amount of material that's *not* in this book would fill many other books—and probably already does. I've concentrated on the basics: building Web applications intended for browser clients. Even with that limitation, however, I have had to omit many interesting and pertinent topics. For example, if you're looking for advanced DataGrid-handling techniques or pointers on how to build commercial custom controls, you won't find it here. If you're looking for a book on using .NET for e-commerce or help with your Web design, this book isn't it. If you are seeking information on how to internationalize your Web application or deliver applications to mobile devices or you want a fully developed reusable application example, look elsewhere. If you want to know how to integrate other Microsoft .NET technologies, such as Passport and MyServices, this book doesn't tell you how. But if you want to explore .NET Web Forms from the code-behind class viewpoint, I hope you'll find this book both interesting and informative.

Part 1

Basic Web Programming

In this section you will find:
- ◆ Chapter 1: Behind the Scenes: How Web Applications Work
- ◆ Chapter 2: HTML Basics
- ◆ Chapter 3: Brief Guide to Dynamic Web Applications

Chapter 1

Behind the Scenes: How Web Applications Work

BEFORE YOU CAN UNDERSTAND much about what a C# application can do, you need to understand what happens with Web requests in general. Because a Web application is often a combination of simple informational HTML pages and more complex dynamic pages, you should understand how the server fulfills requests that don't require code. A considerable amount of background negotiation and data transfer occurs even before the user's request reaches your code.

A Web application is inherently split between at least two tiers—the client and the server. The purpose of this chapter is to give you a clearer understanding of how the client and the server communicate. Additionally, you will learn how C# integrates into this communication process and what it can do to help you write Web applications.

In this chapter:

◆ How Web Requests Work

◆ How a Client Requests Content

◆ How the Web Server Responds—Preparation

◆ How the Web Server Responds—Fulfillment

◆ What the Client Does with the Response

◆ Introducing Dynamic Web Pages

◆ What C# Can Do

◆ Summary

How Web Requests Work

A Web request requires two components, a Web server and a client. The client is (currently) most often a browser, but it could be another type of program, such as a spider (a program that walks Web links, gathering information) or an agent (a program tasked with finding specific information, often using search engines), a standard executable application, a wireless handheld device, or a request from a chip embedded in an appliance, such as a refrigerator. In this book, you'll focus mostly but not exclusively on browser clients; therefore, you can think of the words "browser" and "client" as essentially the same thing for most of the book. I'll make it a point to warn you when the terms are not interchangeable.

The server and the browser are usually on separate computers, but that's not a requirement. You can use a browser to request pages from a Web server running on the same computer—in fact, that's probably the setup you'll use to run most of the examples in this book on your development machine. The point is this: Whether the Web server and the browser are on the same computer or on opposite sides of the world, the request works almost exactly the same way.

Both the server and the client use a defined *protocol* to communicate with each other. A protocol is simply an agreed-upon method for initiating a communications session, passing information back and forth, and terminating the session. Several protocols are used for Web communications; the most common are Hypertext Transfer Protocol (HTTP), used for Web page requests; Secure Hypertext Transfer Protocol (HTTPS), used for encrypted Web page requests; File Transfer Protocol (FTP), used to transfer binary file data; and Network News Transfer Protocol (NNTP), used for newsgroups. Regardless of the protocol used, Web requests piggyback on top of an underlying network protocol called Transmission Control Protocol/Internet Protocol (TCP/IP), which is a global communications standard that determines the basic rules two computers follow to exchange information.

The server computer patiently waits, doing nothing, until a request arrives to initialize communication. In a Web application, the client *always* gets to send the initialization to begin a session—the server can only respond. You'll find that this can be a source of frustration if you are used to writing stand-alone programs. Session initialization consists of a defined series of bytes. The byte content isn't important—the only important thing is that both computers recognize the byte series as an initialization. When the server receives an initialization request, it acknowledges the transmission by returning another series of bytes to the client. The conversation between the two computers continues in this back-and-forth manner. If computers spoke in words, you might imagine the conversation being conducted as follows:

Client	Hello?
Server	Hello. I speak English.
Client	I speak English, too.
Server	What do you want?
Client	I want the file /mySite/myFiles/file1.htm.
Server	That file has moved to /mySite/oldFiles/file1.htm.
Client	Sorry. Goodbye.
Server	Goodbye.
Client	Hello?
Server	Hello. I speak English.

Client   I speak English, too.

Server   What do you want?

Client   I want the file `/mySite/oldFiles/file1.htm`.

Server   Here's some information about that file.

Client   Thanks; please send the data.

Server   Starting data transmission, sending packet 1, sending packet 2, sending packet 3…

Client   I got packet 1, packet 2 has errors, I got packet 3, I got packet 4.

Server   Resending packet 2.

The conversation continues until the transmission is complete.

Server   All packets sent.

Client   All packets received in good condition. Goodbye.

Server   Goodbye.

TCP/IP is only one of many computer communication protocols, but due to the popularity of the Internet, it has become ubiquitous. You won't need to know much more than that about TCP/IP to use it—the underlying protocol is almost entirely transparent. However, you do need to know a little about how one machine finds another machine to initiate a communications session.

How a Client Requests Content

When you type a request into a browser address bar or click a hyperlink, the browser packages the request and sends an important portion of the URL, called the *domain name* to a naming server, normally called a DNS server, typically located at your Internet Service Provider (ISP). The naming server maintains a database of names, each of which is associated with an IP address. Computers don't understand words very well, so the naming server translates the requested address into a number. The text name you see in the link or the address bar is actually a human-friendly version of an IP address. The IP address is a set of four numbers between 0 and 255, separated by periods: for example, 204.285.113.34. Each 3-digit grouping is called an "octet."

Each IP address uniquely identifies a single computer. If the first naming server doesn't have the requested address in its database, it forwards the request to a naming server further up the hierarchy. Eventually, if no naming server can translate the requested name to an IP address, the request reaches one of the powerful naming servers that maintain master lists of all the publicly registered IP addresses. If no naming server can translate the address, the failed response travels back through the naming server hierarchy until it reaches your browser. At that point, you'll see an error message.

If the naming server finds an entry for the IP address of the request, it caches the request so that it won't have to contact higher-level naming servers for the next request to the same server. The cache times out after a period of time called the Time to Live (TTL), so if the next request exceeds the TTL, the naming server may have to contact a higher-level server anyway, depending on when the next request arrives. The naming server returns the IP address to the browser, which uses the IP address to contact the Web server associated with the address. Many Web pages contain references to other files that the Web server must provide for the page to be complete; however, the browser can request only one file at a time. For example, images referenced in a Web page require a separate request for each image.

Thus, the process of displaying a Web page usually consists of a series of short conversations between the browser and the server. Typically, the browser receives the main page, parses it for other required file references, and then begins to display the main page while requesting the referenced files. That's why you often see image "placeholders" while a page is loading. The main page contains references to other files that contain the images, but the main page does not contain the images themselves.

How the Web Server Responds—Preparation

From the Web server's point of view, each conversation is a brand-new contact. By default, a Web server services requests on a first-come, first-served basis. Web servers don't "remember" any specific browser from one request to another.

Modern browsers and servers use version 1.1 of HTTP, which implements *keep-alive* connections. As you would expect, that means that the connection itself, once made, can be kept active over a series of requests, rather than the server and client needing to go through the IP lookup and initialization steps for each file. Despite keep-alive HTTP connections, each file sent still requires a separate request and response cycle.

Parts of a URL

The line that you type into the browser address field to request a file is called a Uniform Resource Locator (URL). The server performs a standard procedure to service each request. First, it parses the request by separating the requested URL into its component parts. Forward slashes, colons, periods, question marks, and ampersands—all called *delimiters*—make it easy to separate the parts. Each part has a specific function. Here's a sample URL request:

```
http://www.microsoft.com:80/CSharpASP/default.htm?Page=1&Para=2
```

The following list shows the name and function of each part of the sample URL.

http   *Protocol.* Tells the server which protocol it should use to respond to the request.

www.microsoft.com   *Domain name.* This part of the URL translates to the IP address. The domain itself consists of several parts separated by periods: the host name, www; the enterprise domain name, microsoft; and the top-level Internet domain name, com. There are several other top-level Internet domain names, including org (organization), gov (government), and net (network).

80   *Port number.* A Web server has many ports. Each designates a place where the server "listens" for communications. A port number simply designates one of those specific locations (there are 65,537 possible ports). Over time, the use of specific port numbers has become standardized. For example, I used 80 as the port number in the example, because that's the standard (and default) HTTP port number, but you can have the server listen for requests on any port.

CSharpASP   *Virtual directory.* The server translates this name into a physical path on a hard drive. A virtual directory is a shorthand name, a "pointer" that references a physical directory. The name of the virtual and physical directories need not be the same. One way to define virtual directories is through the Web server's administrative interface. Another way to create virtual directories is by creating a new Web application or Web service project in VS.NET. For example, VS.NET creates a virtual directory for you whenever you create a new Web application or a Web service project.

default.htm   *Filename.* The server will return the contents of the file. If the file were recognized as executable via the Web server (such as an ASP file) rather than an HTML file, the server would execute the program contained in the file and return the results rather than returning the file contents. If the file is not recognized, the server offers to download the file.

? **(Question Mark)**   *Separator.* The question mark separates the file request from additional parameters sent with the request. The example URL contains two parameters: `Page=1` and `Para=2`.

Page   *Parameter name.* Programs you write, such as ASP pages, can read the parameters and use them to supply information.

= **(Equals Sign)**   *Separator.* The equals sign separates a parameter name from the parameter value.

1   *Parameter value.* The parameter named `Page` has a value of `1`. Note that the browser sends all parameter values as string data. A string is a series of characters: A word is a string, a sentence is a string, a random sequence of numbers and letters is a string—text in any form is a string. Your programs are free to interpret strings that contain only numeric characters as numbers, but to be safe, you should *cast* or change them to numeric form.

& (Ampersand)   *Separator.* The ampersand separates parameter=value pairs.

Para=2   Parameter and value. A second parameter and value.

Server Translates the Path

You don't make Web requests with "real" or physical paths; instead, you request pages using a virtual path. After parsing the URL, the server translates the virtual path to a physical pathname. For example, the virtual directory in the URL `http://myServer/myPath/myFile.asp` is `myPath`. The `myPath` virtual directory maps to a local directory such as `c:\inetpub\wwwroot\CSharpASP\myFile.asp` or to a network Universal Naming Convention (UNC) name such as `\\someServer\somePath\CSharpASP\myFile.asp`.

Server Checks for the Resource

The server checks for the requested file. If it doesn't exist, the server returns an error message—usually `HTTP 404 -- File Not Found`. You've probably seen this error message while browsing the Web; if not, you're luckier than I am.

Server Checks Permissions

After locating the resource, the server checks to see if the requesting account has sufficient permission to access the resource. By default, Internet Information Server (IIS) Web requests use a special guest account called `IUSR_Machinename`, where `Machinename` is the name of the server computer. You'll often hear this called the "anonymous" account, because the server has no way of knowing any real account information for the requesting user. For ASP.NET pages, IIS uses the `SYSTEM` account or another guest account named `aspnet_wp_account` (ASPNET) by default.

For example, if the user has requested a file for which that account has no read permission, the server returns an error message, usually HTTP 403 -- Access Denied. The actual error text depends on the exact error generated. For example, there are several sublevels for 403 error messages. You can find a complete list of error messages in the IIS Default Web Site Property dialog. Web servers provide default error messages but usually allow you to customize them. By default, IIS reads error message text from the HTML files in your %SystemRoot%\ help\common\ directory, where the variable %SystemRoot% stands for the name of your NT directory, usually named winnt.

How the Web Server Responds—Fulfillment

Graphics files, Word documents, HTML files, ASP files, executable files, CGI scripts—how does the server know how to process the requested file? Actually, servers differentiate file types in a couple of different ways.

Internet Information Server (IIS) differentiates file types based on file extensions (such as .asp, .htm, .exe, and so on) just like Windows Explorer. When you double-click a file or icon in Windows Explorer, it looks up the file extension in the Registry, a special database that holds system and application information. The Registry contains one entry for each registered file extension. Each extension has an associated file type entry. Each file type entry, in turn, has an associated executable file or file handler. The server strips the file extension from the filename, looks up the associated program, and launches that program to return the file. IIS follows the same series of steps to determine how to respond to requests.

Other Web servers also use file extensions to determine how to process a file request, but they don't use Registry associations. Instead, they use an independent list of file extension–to–program associations. The entries in these lists are called MIME types, which stands for Multipurpose Internet Mail Extension, because e-mail programs needed to know the type of content included with messages. Each MIME type—just like the Registry associations—is associated with a specific action or program. The Web server searches the list for an entry that matches the file extension of the requested file.

Most Web servers handle unmatched file extensions by offering to download the file to your computer. Some servers also provide a default action if you request a URL that doesn't contain a filename. In this case, most servers try to return one of a list of default filenames—usually a file called either default.htm or index.htm. You may be able to configure the default filename(s) for your Web server (you can with IIS), either globally for all virtual directories on that server or for each individual virtual directory on that server.

The server can begin streaming the response back to the client as it generates the response or it can buffer the entire response and send it all at once when the response is complete. There are two parts to the response: the response header and the response body. The response header contains information about the type of response. Among other things, the response header can contain the following:

- A response code

- The MIME type of the response

- The date and time after which the response is no longer valid

- A redirection URL

- Any cookie values that the server wants to store on the client

Cookies are text strings that the browser saves in memory or on the client computer's hard drive. The cookie may last for the duration of the browser session or it may last until a specified expiration date. The browser sends cookies associated with a site back to the server with each subsequent request to that site.

NOTE *There's a lot of hype in the media about cookies. Some people have been so intimidated by these scare tactics that they use their browser settings to "turn off cookies." That means the browser will not accept the cookies, which can have a major impact on your site because you must have some way to associate an individual browser session with values stored on the server tier in your application. While methods exist for making the association without using cookies, they're not nearly as convenient, nor do they persist between browser sessions.*

What the Client Does with the Response

The client, usually a browser, needs to know the type of content with which the server has responded. The client reads the MIME type header to determine the content type. For most requests, the MIME type header is either `text/html` or an image type such as `image/gif`, but it might also be a word processing file, a video or audio file, an animation, or any other type of file. Browsers, like servers, use Registry values and MIME type lists to determine how to display the file. For standard HTML and image files, browsers use a built-in display engine. For other file types, browsers call upon the services of helper applications or plug-ins, such as RealPlayer, or Microsoft Office applications that can display the information. The browser assigns all or part of its window area as a "canvas" onto which the helper program or plug-in "paints" its content.

When the response body consists of HTML, the browser parses the file to separate markup from content. It then uses the markup to determine how to lay out the content on-screen. Modern HTML files may contain several different types of content in addition to markup, text, and images; browsers handle each one differently. Among the most common additional content types are the following:

Cascading Style Sheets These are text files in a specific format that contain directives about how to format the content of an HTML file. Modern browsers use Cascading Style Sheet (CSS) styles to assign fonts, colors, borders, visibility, positioning, and other formatting information to elements on the page. CSS styles can be contained within a tag, can be placed in a separate area within an HTML page, or can exist in a completely separate file that the browser requests after it parses the main page but before it renders the content on the screen.

Script All modern browsers can execute JavaScript, although they don't always execute it the same way. The term *JavaScript* applies specifically to script written in Netscape's JavaScript scripting language, but two close variants—Microsoft's JScript scripting language and the ECMA-262 specification (ECMAScript)—have essentially the same syntax and support an almost identical command set.

NOTE *Note that the JScript scripting language is distinct from JScript.NET—another, much more robust version of JScript that Microsoft released as an add-on to Visual Studio.NET.*

In addition to JScript, Internet Explorer supports VBScript, which is a subset of Visual Basic for Applications, which, in turn, is a subset of Microsoft's Visual Basic (pre-VB.NET) language.

NOTE *You can find the complete ECMA-262 specification at* `http://www.ecma.ch/stand/ecma-262.htm`.

ActiveX Components or Java Applets These small programs execute on the client rather than the server. ActiveX components run only in Internet Explorer on Windows platforms (roughly 60 percent of the total market, when this book was written), whereas Java applets run on almost all browsers and platforms.

XML Extensible Markup Language (XML) is similar to HTML—both consist of tags and content. That's not surprising, because both are derived from Standard Generalized Markup Language (SGML). HTML tags describe how to display the content and, to a limited degree, the function of the content. XML tags describe what the content *is*. In other words, HTML is primarily a formatting and display language, whereas XML is a content-description language. The two languages complement each other well. XML was first used in IE 4 for *channels*, a relatively unsuccessful technology that let people subscribe to information from various sites. IE4 had a channel bar to help people manage their channel subscriptions. With IE 5, Microsoft dropped channels but extended the browser's understanding of and facility with XML so that today you can use it to provide data "islands" in HTML files. You can also deliver a combination of XML and XSL/XSLT (a rules language written in XML that's similar in purpose to Cascading Style Sheets but more powerful) to generate the HTML code on the client. The XML/XSL combination lets you offload processing from the server, thus improving your site's scalability. Netscape 6 offers a different and—for display purposes—more modern type of support for XML. Netscape's parsing engine can combine XML and CSS style sheets to format XML directly for viewing. Unfortunately, Netscape doesn't directly support XSLT transformations, so you're limited to displaying the data in your XML documents without intermediate processing.

Introducing Dynamic Web Pages

The client-to-server-to-client process I've just described is important because it happens *each time* your client contacts the server to get some data. That's distinctly different from the stand-alone or client-server model you may be familiar with already. Because the server and the client don't really know anything about one another, for each interaction, you must send, initialize, or restore the appropriate values to maintain the continuity of your application.

As a simple example, suppose you have a secured site with a login form. In a standard application, after the user has logged in successfully, that's the only authentication you need to perform. The fact that the user logged in successfully means that he's authenticated for the duration of the application. In contrast, when you log in to a Web site secured by only a login and password, the server must reauthenticate you for each subsequent request. That may be a simple task, but it must be performed for every request in the application.

In fact, that's one of the reasons dynamic applications became popular. In a site that allows anonymous connections (like most public Web sites), you can authenticate users only if you can compare the login/password values entered by the user with the "real" copies stored on the server. While HTML is an adequate layout language for most purposes, it isn't a programming language. It takes code to authenticate users.

Another reason that dynamic pages became popular is because of the ever-changing nature of information. Static pages are all very well for articles, scholarly papers, books, and images—in general, for information that rarely changes. But static pages are simply inadequate to capture employee and contact lists, calendar information, news feeds, sports scores—in general, the type of data you interact with every day. The data changes far too often to maintain successfully in static pages. Besides, you don't always want to look at that data the same way. I realize I'm preaching to the choir here—you wouldn't have bought this book if you weren't aware that dynamic pages have power that static HTML pages can't match. But it's useful to note that even dynamic data usually has a predictable rate of change—something I'll discuss later in the context of caching.

How Does the Server Separate Code from Content?

In classic Active Server Pages (ASP), you could mix code and content by placing special code tags (`<% %>`) around the code or by writing script blocks, where the code appeared between `<script>` and `</script>` tags. Classic ASP uses an `.asp` filename extension. When the server receives a request for an ASP file, it recognizes—via the extension associations—that responding to the request requires the ASP processor. Therefore, the server passes the request to the ASP engine, which parses the file to differentiate the code tag content from the markup content. The ASP engine processes the code, merges the results with any HTML in the page, and sends the result to the client.

ASP.NET goes through a similar process, but the file extension for ASP.NET files is `.aspx` rather than `.asp`. You can still mix code and content in exactly the same way, although now you can (and usually should) place code in a separate file, called a *code-behind* class, because doing so provides a cleaner separation between display code and application code and makes it easier to reuse both. In ASP.NET, you can write code in all three places—in code-behind classes and also within code tags and script blocks in your HTML files. Nevertheless, the ASP.NET engine still must parse the HTML file for code tags.

How and When Does the Server Process Code?

The ASP.NET engine itself is an Internet Server Application Programming Interface (ISAPI) application. ISAPI applications are DLLs that load into the server's address space, so they're very fast. Different ISAPI applications handle different types of requests. You can create ISAPI applications for special file extensions, such as `.asp` or `.aspx`, or to perform special operations on standard file types such as HTML and XML.

There are two types of ISAPI applications: extensions and filters. The ASP.NET engine is an ISAPI extension. An ISAPI extension replaces or augments the standard IIS response. Extensions load on demand when the server receives a request with a file extension associated with the ISAPI extension DLL. In contrast, ISAPI filters load with IIS and notify the server about the set of filter event notifications that they handle. IIS raises an event notification (handled by the filter) whenever a filter event of that type occurs.

NOTE   *You can't create ISAPI applications with C#—or indeed in managed code—although you can create them in Visual Studio.NET using unmanaged C++ and the Active Template Library (ATL). However, you can override the default* HttpApplication *implementation to provide many of the benefits of ISAPI applications using C#.*

ASP.NET pages bypass the standard IIS response procedure *if* they contain code tags or are associated with a code-behind class. If your ASPX file contains no code, the ASP.NET engine recognizes this when it finishes parsing the page. For pages that contain no code, the ASP.NET engine short-circuits its own response, and the standard server process resumes. With IIS 5 (ASP version 3.0), classic ASP pages began short-circuiting for pages that contained no code. Therefore, ASP and ASPX pages that contain no code are only slightly slower than standard HTML pages.

How Do Clients Act with Dynamic Server Pages?

How do clients act with dynamic server pages? The short answer is this: They act no differently than with any other request. Remember, the client and the server know very little about one another. In fact, the client is usually entirely ignorant of the server other than knowing its address, whereas the server needs to know enough about the client to provide an appropriate response.

Beginning Web programmers are often confused about how clients respond to static versus dynamic page requests. The point to remember is that, to the client, there's *no difference* between requesting a dynamic page and requesting a static page. For example, to the client there's no difference between requesting an ASPX file and requesting an HTML file. Remember, the client interprets the response based on the MIME type header values—and there are no special MIME types for dynamically generated files. MIME type headers are identical whether the response was generated dynamically or read from a static file.

When Is HTML Not Enough?

I mentioned several different types of MIME type responses earlier in this chapter. These types are important because, by itself, HTML is simply not very powerful. Fortunately, you're getting into Web programming at the right time. Browsers are past their infancy (versions 2 and 3), through toddlerhood (version 4), and making progress toward becoming application delivery platforms. While they're not yet as capable as Windows Forms, they've come a long way in the past five years and are now capable of manipulating both HTML and XML information in powerful ways.

All of these changes have occurred because HTML is a layout language. HTML is not a styling language; therefore, CSS became popular. HTML is not a graphics description or manipulation language; therefore, the Document Object Model (DOM) arose to let you manipulate the appearance and position of objects on the screen. HTML is not a good language for transporting or describing generalized data; therefore, XML is rapidly becoming an integral part of the modern browser's toolset. Finally and, for this book, most importantly, HTML is not a programming language. You must have a programming language to perform validity checks and logical operations. Modern browsers are partway there; they (mostly) support scripting languages.

In Internet Explorer 5x and, to a lesser degree, Netscape 6x, all these technologies have become intertwined. You can work with XML through CSS or XSL/XSLT. You can use the DOM to change CSS styles and alter the appearance of objects dynamically. You can respond to some user events with CSS directly (like changing the cursor shape), and you can respond to or ignore almost all user events through script.

What C# Can Do

Since you're about to commit yourself to programming the latest server-side technology for creating dynamic Web applications, you should know what C# can do. Surprisingly, when you break Web programming down into its constituent parts, there's very little difference between Web programming and standard applications programming.

Make If/Then Decisions

If/Then decisions are the crux of all programming. C# can make decisions based on known criteria. For example, depending on whether a user is logged in as an administrator, a supervisor, or a line worker, C# can select the appropriate permission levels and responses.

Using decision-making code, C# can deliver some parts of a file but not others, include or exclude entire files, or create brand-new content tailored to a specific individual at a specific point in time.

Process Information from Clients

As soon as you create an application, you'll need to process information from clients. For example, when a user fills out a form, you'll need to validate the information, possibly store it for future reference, and respond to the user. With C#, you have complete access to all the information that clients send, and you have complete control over the content of the server's response. You can use your existing programming knowledge to perform the validation, persist data to disk, and format a response. Beyond giving you the programming language to do these tasks, C# Web applications provide a great deal of assistance.

C# Web applications use the ASP.NET framework to help you validate user input. For example, you can place controls on the screen that can ensure that a required field contains a value, and automatically check whether that value is valid. C# Web applications provide objects that simplify disk and database operations and let you work easily with XML, XSLT, and collections of values. With C#, you can write server-side code that *behaves* as if it were client-side script. In other words, you can write code that resides on the server but responds to client-side events in centralized code rather than in less powerful and difficult-to-debug client-side script. ASP.NET helps you maintain data for individual users through the Session object, reduce the load on your server through caching, and maintain a consistent visual state by automatically restoring the values of input controls across round trips to the server.

Access Data and Files

In most applications, you need to read or store permanent data. In contrast to previous versions of ASP, ASP.NET uses the .NET framework to provide very powerful file access. For example, many business applications receive data, usually overnight, from a mainframe or database server. Typically, programmers write special scheduled programs to read or parse and massage the new data files into a form suitable for the application. Often, major business disruptions occur when something happens so that the data files are late or never appear.

Similarly, have you ever written a program that created a file and later tried to access it only to find that the user had deleted or moved the file in the interim? I know—you're sure to have written defensive code so that your program could recover or at least exit gracefully, right?

Many applications would be much easier to write and maintain if the program itself could inter-operate with the file system to receive a notification whenever the contents of a specific directory changed. For example, if you could write code that started a data import process whenever data arrived from the mainframe, you could avoid writing timing loops that check for the appearance of a file or scheduling applications that run even though the data may not be available.

Similarly, if you could receive a notification *before* a user deleted that critical file, you could not only avoid having to write the defensive code but also prevent the problem from occurring in the first place!

You'll find that you can perform these types of tasks much easier using C# than you could in earlier versions of any programming language. You'll find that the most common file and database operations are simpler (although wordier) in C#. For example, one of the more common operations is to display the results of a database query in an HTML table. With VBScript or JScript code in a classic ASP application, you had to loop through the set of records returned by the query and format the values into a table yourself. In C#, you can retrieve a dataset and use a `Repeater` control to perform the tedious looping operation.

Format Responses Using XML, CSS, XSLT, and HTML

As I said earlier, you have complete control of the response returned by your application. Until recently, Web applications programmers needed to worry only about the browser and version used by the application's clients, but now an explosion of other Web client types has complicated things. Handheld devices, dedicated Internet access hardware, pagers, Web-enabled telephones, and an ever-increasing number of standard applications are raising the formatting requirements beyond the capability of humans to keep up.

In the past, for most pages with simple HTML and scripting needs, you could usually get away with two or three versions of a page—one for complete idiot browsers without any DHTML or scripting ability, one for Netscape 4, and one for IE 4 and higher. But as the number and type of clients expand, creating hand-formatted HTML pages for each new type of client becomes a less and less viable and palatable option. Fortunately, the wide and growing availability of CSS and XML is a step in the right direction.

Using CSS styles, you can often adjust a page to accommodate different resolutions, color depth, and availability. But CSS styles only affect the display characteristics of content—you can't adjust the content itself for different devices using CSS alone. However, through a combination of XML, CSS, and XSLT, you can have the best of both worlds. XML files hold the data, XSLT filters the data according to the client type, and CSS styles control the way the filtered data appears on the client's screen.

Visual Studio helps you create all these file types, and C# lets you manipulate them programmatically. The end result is HTML tailored to a client's specific display requirements.

Launch and Communicate with .NET and COM+ Objects

For the past year or two, the most scalable model for ASP has been to use ASP pages as little more than HTML files that could launch COM components hosted in Microsoft Transaction Server (MTS) or in COM+ applications. Microsoft termed this model *Windows DNA*. If you've been building applications using that model, you'll find that little has changed except that it's now much easier to install, move, rename, and version components. Of course, that's not such a small change.

Until .NET, you had to use C++ or Delphi to create free-threaded COM objects suitable for use in Web applications. (To be completely honest, some people *did* write code that let VB use multiple threads, but it wasn't a pretty sight, nor was it a task for programmers with typical skills.) Multithreading may not seem like such a big deal if you've been writing stand-alone applications. After all, most stand-alone and client-server applications don't need multithreading. However, in the Web world, it *is* a big deal. Web applications almost always deal with multiple simultaneous users, so for .NET to be a language as suitable for Web applications as Java, it had to gain multithreading capabilities. Many classic ASP programmers migrated from classic VB, and so they naturally tended to use that language to generate components. Unfortunately, VB5/6–generated DLLs were apartment threaded. Without going into detail, this meant that Web applications couldn't store objects written using VB5/6 across requests without causing serious performance issues.

C#-generated objects are inherently free threaded, so your Web applications can store objects you create with C# across requests safely. Of course, you still have to deal with the problems caused by multiple threads using your objects simultaneously, but you can mark specific code sections as critical, thus serializing access to those sections. But that's a different story.

C# also lets you access legacy COM DLLs, so you can use existing binary code without rewriting it in a .NET language. There's some debate over exactly how long you'll be able to do this. Personally, I think you have several years' grace to upgrade your COM DLLs to .NET. To use an existing COM DLL in .NET, you "import" the type library. One way to do this is by using the `TlbImp.exe` utility, which creates a "wrapper" for the class interface through which you can call the methods and properties of the class. Of course, there's a slight performance penalty for using a wrapper for anything, but that's often acceptable when the alternative is rewriting existing and tested code.

You can just as easily go in the opposite direction and export .NET assemblies for use with unmanaged C++, VB5/6, Delphi, or any COM-compliant language. To do that, you use the `TlbExp.exe` utility. This utility creates a type library but doesn't register it. Although `TlbExp` is easier to remember (it's the opposite of `TlbImp`), another utility, called `RegAsm.exe`, can both register and create a type library at the same time. Use the `/tlb` flag with `RegAsm.exe` to tell the utility to create the type library file. You can also use `RegAsm.exe` to create a REG (registration) file rather than actually registering the classes in your assembly, which is useful when you're creating setup programs to install application code on another machine.

Advantages of C# in Web Applications

C# is an extremely powerful tool for building applications for the Windows platform (and maybe someday soon for other operating systems as well). But it's certainly not the only tool for building applications. There's very little C# can do that older languages can't do if you're willing to delve deeply enough into the API or write enough code. However, by providing built-in support for certain kinds of applications, for memory management, and for object-oriented development, C# greatly reduces the effort involved in building them.

Web Services

A Web service is nothing more than a Web interface to objects that run on the server. Wait, you say, isn't that the same as Distributed COM (DCOM)? Not exactly, but it's similar. DCOM lets your applications launch and use remote applications and DLLs as if they were running on the local machine. It does this by creating proxy "stubs" on both sides of the transaction. DCOM wraps up the function, subroutine, method, or property call from your local application, along with any accompanying parameters, and forwards them over the network to a receiving stub on the server. The server stub unwraps the values, launches the object or application (if necessary), and makes the call, passing the parameters. The reverse operation occurs with return values. DCOM uses a highly efficient binary wrapper to send the data over the network.

DCOM was created in an era when remote calls came from machines that resided on a hard-wired proprietary network. As companies began to use the public Internet for business purposes, the network was no longer proprietary; instead, DCOM calls had to cross the boundary between the public network and the private corporate network. However, letting binary data cross that boundary is inherently dangerous because you can't know what the data will do. For example, the data may contain viral programs. Therefore, companies also put up firewalls that prevent binary data from crossing the boundary. Text data, like HTML, can cross the boundary unobstructed, but binary data cannot. Unfortunately, that had the side effect of preventing DCOM from operating easily through the firewall, because the firewalls are generally unable to differentiate between potentially unsafe public binary data and perfectly safe DCOM binary data.

Web services solve that problem. Web services perform exactly the same tasks as DCOM—they let you use remote objects. However, they typically use a different system, called the Simple Object Access Protocol (SOAP), to wrap up the call and parameter data. SOAP is a text file format. It uses XML to simplify the syntax for identifying the various types of data values needed to make generic remote calls. Because SOAP is a text file, it can cross firewall boundaries. However, SOAP is not a *requirement* for making remote calls; it's simply a standardized and therefore convenient method for doing so. In other words, you're perfectly free to write your own remoting wrapper—but if you do that, you'll need to create your own translation functions as well.

C# and Visual Studio have extensive support for SOAP. In fact, using SOAP in C# is transparent; the .NET framework takes care of all the value translation and transport issues, leaving you free to concentrate on building the applications themselves. The process for building a Web service is extremely similar to the process for building a COM DLL—or for that matter, writing any other .NET code, because all you need to do to expose a method or an entire class as a Web service is add attributes—bits of metadata that contain information *about* the code.

The biggest problem with Web services and SOAP is performance; it's simply not as efficient to translate values to and from a text representation as it is to translate them to and from a binary format like those used by DCOM and CORBA. Nevertheless, in a dangerous world, SOAP is a necessary evil, and I think you'll be pleasantly surprised by how fast Web services work. While the actual performance difference is certainly measurable, the perceived performance difference is negligible unless you're performing a long series of remote calls within a loop (and you should avoid that with any remote technology).

Thin-Client Applications (Web Forms)

C# works in concert with ASP.NET to let you build Web Form–based applications. A Web Form, as you'll see in Chapters 4, "Introduction to ASP.NET," and 5, "Introduction to Web Forms," is an HTML form integrated with C# (or any of the multitude of .NET languages sure to appear soon) code. If you're familiar with Active Server Pages (ASP), JavaServer Pages (JSP), or PHP Hypertext Processor (PHP), you'll quickly feel comfortable with C# Web applications and Web Forms. If you haven't written Web applications using one of these technologies, you're lucky to be entering the Web application field now rather than earlier, because C# makes building Web applications similar to building Windows applications.

You build Web Forms by dragging and dropping controls onto a form design surface. After placing a control, you can double-click it to add code to respond to the control's events. Web Forms support Web analogs of most of the familiar Windows controls such as text controls, labels, panel controls, and list boxes. They even support invisible controls such as timers.

The convenience of Web Forms aside, you're still building browser-based or thin-client applications, so you can expect to lose some of the functionality that you get with Windows clients. However (and I think this is the most important change you'll see with .NET), you're no longer limited to thin-client Web applications. By combining Windows clients with Web services, you can build rich-client applications almost as easily. In fact, the technology makes it simple to build both types of applications—and serve them both with a common centralized code base.

Rich-Client Applications (Windows Forms)

It may seem odd that I've included Windows Forms applications in a book about building Web applications, but I can assure you that it won't seem odd by the time you finish the book. The distinction between rich-client and thin-client applications is diminishing rapidly. As browsers add features, they get fatter, and as Windows Forms applications gain networking capability, they become more capable of consuming Web-based services. The result is that the only real decision to be made between a Web Form and a Windows Forms application is whether you can easily deliver the Windows Forms application code to the client base or if you must rely on the functionality of whatever browser or "user agent" is already installed on the client machines.

You'll build both types of applications in this book. You'll see the differences in application design and distribution, and then you can decide for yourself.

Summary

You've seen that clients communicate with the Web server in short transactional bursts. Client requests are typically made anonymously, so you must plan and code for security and authentication if your application deals with sensitive data. Between requests, the server "forgets" about the client, so unless you force the client to pass a cookie or some other identifying token for each request, the server assumes the client is brand new. Web applications use these identifying tokens to associate data values with individual browsers or (with secured sites) individual users. The strategy you select for maintaining these data values across requests is called "state maintenance," and it's the single most difficult problem in building Web applications.

C# helps simplify the process of building Web applications through Web Forms, Web services, robust networking abilities, and tight integration with ASP.NET, which provides the infrastructure for servicing Web requests.

Despite the existence of Visual Studio's Web Form editor, there's still an advantage to learning the underlying language used to create Web Forms—HTML. Fortunately, as a programmer accustomed to memorizing complex code operations, you'll find that HTML is straightforward and simple. You can learn the basics of HTML in about half an hour. In Chapter 2, "HTML Basics," you'll get my half-hour tour of HTML, which should be sufficient for you to understand the HTML code you'll see in the rest of this book. If you already know HTML, you can browse through this as a review or simply skip it and begin reading again at Chapter 3, "Brief Guide to Dynamic Web Applications."

Chapter 2

HTML Basics

THIS CHAPTER CONTAINS A half-hour tour to teach you the basics of the Hypertext Markup Language (HTML) structure and editing. If you already know HTML, you can probably skip this chapter and move directly to Chapter 3, "Brief Guide to Dynamic Web Applications." If you're not already comfortable with HTML, you should read this chapter and practice creating HTML files using the included files as a starting point. You should feel reasonably comfortable with HTML before you begin creating C# Web applications. HTML is a simple idea that, like many simple ideas, you can apply, combine, and extend to build very complex structures.

In this chapter:

- ◆ What Is HTML?
- ◆ Syntax: Tags and Attributes
- ◆ Formatting Text
- ◆ Including Images on Your Web Site
- ◆ Introduction to Hyperlinking
- ◆ Formatting Tables
- ◆ Using Image Maps
- ◆ Understanding Frames
- ◆ Controlling Element Position
- ◆ Cascading Style Sheets

What Is HTML?

HTML is a markup language, although the original intent was to create a content description language. It contains commands that, like a word processor, tell the computer—in a very loose sense—what the content of the document is. For example, using HTML, you can tell the computer that a document contains a paragraph, a bulleted list, a table, or an image. The HTML rendering engine is responsible for actually displaying the text and images on the screen. The difference between HTML and word processors is that word processors work with proprietary formats. Because they're proprietary, one word processor usually can't read another word processor's native file format directly. Instead, word processors use special programs called import/export filters to translate one file format to another.

In contrast, HTML is an open, worldwide standard. If you create a file using the commands available in version 3.2, it can be displayed on almost any browser running on almost any computer with any operating system—anywhere in the world. The latest version of HTML, version 4.0, works on about 90 percent of the browsers currently in use.

HTML is a small subset of a much more full-featured markup language called Standard Generalized Markup Language (SGML). SGML has been under development for about 15 years and contains many desirable features that HTML lacks, but it is also complex to implement. This complexity makes it both difficult to create and difficult to display properly.

HTML was developed as an SGML subset to provide a lightweight standard for displaying text and images over a slow dial-up connection—the World Wide Web. Originally, HTML had very few features—it has grown considerably in the past few years. Nevertheless, you can still learn the core command set for HTML in just a few hours.

HTML contains only two kinds of information: *markup*, which consists of all the text contained between angle brackets (<>), and *content*, which is all the text *not* contained between angle brackets. The difference between the two is that browsers don't display markup; instead, markup contains the information that tells the browser *how* to display the content.

For example, this HTML:

```
<html>
<head><title></title></head>
<body>
</body>
</html>
```

is a perfectly valid HTML file. You can save that set of commands as a file, navigate to it in your browser, and display the file without errors—but you won't see anything, because the file doesn't contain any content. All the text in the file is markup.

In contrast, a file with the following content contains no markup:

```
This is a file with no markup
```

Although most browsers will display the contents of a file with no markup, it is not a valid HTML file.

The individual parts of the markup between the brackets are *tags*, sometimes called *commands*. There are two types of tags—start tags and end tags, and they usually appear in pairs (although they may be widely separated in the file). The single difference is that the end tag begins with a forward slash, for instance </html>. Other than the forward slash, start tags and end tags are identical.

What Does HTML Do?

HTML lets you create semistructured documents. The heading commands separate and categorize sections of your documents. HTML also has rudimentary commands to format and display text, display images, accept input from users, and send information to a server for back-end processing. In addition, it lets you create special areas of text or images that, when clicked, jump—or *hyperlink*—from one HTML file to another, thus creating an interlinked series of pages.

The series of pages you create via hyperlinks is a program; however, it isn't a program like the ones you'll learn to create in this book because a series of pages has no intelligence and makes no decisions. All the functionality resides in the tag set selected by the HTML author (people whose primary task is creating HTML documents are called authors, not programmers). A series of pages linked together in a single directory or set of directories is called a *site*, or a *Web site*.

Despite the lack of decision-making capability, a Web site serves two extremely useful purposes:

♦ It provides a way for non-programmers to create attractive sites full of useful information. (Of course, it also provides a way for people to create unattractive sites full of useless information, but I won't pursue that.)

♦ In conjunction with the Internet, Web sites make that information available globally.

Why Is HTML Important?

Until HTML, it wasn't so easy to create screens full of information containing both text and graphics that anyone could read using any operating system. In fact, there was no easy way to display *anything* without either writing a program yourself or using a presentation program such as PowerPoint. This limitation meant that the output was available only to other people using the same operating system and the same program—often only to those using the same *version* of the program.

HTML is important because it provided millions of people with access to information online that they could not or would not have seen any other way. HTML was the first easy method for non-programmers to display text and images on-screen without limiting the audience to those who own or have access to the same program (or a viewer) that the author used to create the content. In a sense, browsers are universal content viewers, and HTML is a universal file format. In fact, HTML and plain text were the only universal file formats until recently; however, we have now added XML, which solves many problems with representing information that plain text and HTML do not address.

The Limitations of HTML

Despite its popularity, its availability, and the fact that it is a universal file format, HTML has some serious limitations as a way of creating structured documents, as a layout language, and as a file format. First, plain HTML has no way to specify the exact position of content on a page, whether horizontally, vertically, or along the z-axis, which controls the "layer" in which objects appear. Second, HTML, as I've said already, is not a programming language; it has no decision-making capabilities. Third, HTML is a fixed markup language. In other words, the tags are predefined, and you can't make up your own. The World Wide Web Consortium, a standards body more commonly known as the W3C, defines the tags that make up HTML. Unless the W3C extends the standard, the tag set never changes. This is both good and bad. It's good because most browsers can display most HTML. It's also bad, because the limited command set encourages—no, forces—companies to build proprietary extensions to perform more advanced functions.

Many of the useful concepts available in HTML today, such as forms, tables, scripts, frames, and Cascading Style Sheets (CSS), began as proprietary extensions but were later adopted and standardized by the (W3C) (see **www.w3.org** for more information). These extensions eventually became common usage, forcing the W3C to reevaluate and update the HTML standard. Through this extension and revisions process, many once-proprietary extensions have now become part of the standard HTML command set. Because of this, HTML has gone through several standard versions, the latest being HTML 4.01.

Syntax: Tags and Attributes

A valid HTML file has only a few requirements. Look at the following example:

```
<html>
<head>
<title>Hello World</title>
</head>
<body>Hello World
</body>
</html>
```

This example contains both tags and content. A *tag* is text enclosed in angle brackets (<>). If you look at the file in a browser, you'll see that it looks similar to Figure 2.1.

FIGURE 2.1

Hello World file
(`HelloWorld.htm`)

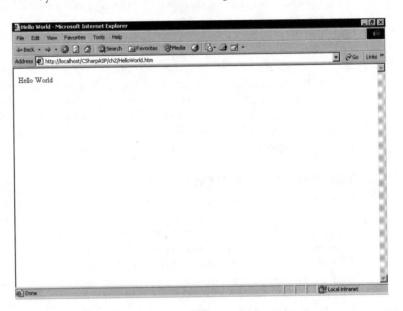

The `HelloWorld.htm` file is a short—but complete—HTML file. All HTML files begin with an `<html>` tag and end with a `</html>` tag (read "end html" or "close html"). Between those two tags are other tags as well as content, so `<html>` tags can contain other tags. Tags that contain other tags are called, appropriately enough, *containing tags*, or more properly, *block elements*. I'll use the term block elements in this book to mean a tag that can contain other tags. Note that the `<head></head>` tag is also a block element; among other things, it contains a `<title></title>` tag.

HTML tags have two parts—a start tag and an end tag. Although not all browsers require you to write the end tag in all cases, you should immediately get into the habit of doing so. As you move into XML (and you probably will want to move into XML at some point), the end tags *are* required in all cases.

At this point, I'm going to stop writing both the start and end tags in the text every time I refer to a tag. For example, rather than writing <head></head> every time I need to refer to that tag, I'll just write <head>. You can assume that the end-head tag is present.

NOTE   *HTML files are text files. They contain only two types of items: commands (also called tags or markup) and content. You can edit an HTML file with any text editor. I tend to use Notepad for small, quick edits and an HTML-aware text editor for larger files, such as the Visual Studio HTML editor, HomeSite, FrontPage, or Dreamweaver, because those editors color-code tags, insert end tags automatically, provide predictive syntax help via IntelliSense or tag/attribute lists, and provide many other helpful editing features.*

What Is a Tag?

You can think of tags in several ways, depending on your interest in the subject matter. For example, one way to think of a tag is as an embedded command. The tag marks a portion of text for special treatment by the browser. That treatment may be anything from "make the next character bold" to "treat the following lines as code." Another way to think of tags is as containers for hidden information. The browser doesn't display information inside the tags. In fact, if the browser doesn't understand the tag type, it ignores it altogether, which is extremely convenient if you need a place to hold information that you don't want the browser to display on-screen. Yet a third way to think about tags is as objects. A <p> tag, for example, contains a single paragraph. A paragraph has properties—an indent level, a word or character count, a style—I'm sure you have run across programs that treat paragraphs as objects when using a word processor.

What Is an End Tag?

The end tag simply marks the end of the portion of the document influenced by the tag. Computers aren't very smart—once you turn on bold text, it's on until you explicitly turn it off. Just a warning: Most browsers will allow you to skip some of the most common end tags, but take my advice and don't skip them. In the future, you're likely to want to convert some of those documents to XML— and in XML, the end tags are required.

Why Does HTML Look Like <*THIS*>?

The bracketed commands used in HTML have a long history. HTML inherited its syntax from SGML, but that's not the only use for bracketed commands. I first saw them used in XyWrite in the late 1980s. XyWrite was a word processor that was most popular with journalists precisely because it used HTML-like embedded commands. The reason it was so popular is bound up in bits and bytes, but it's an interesting story, so bear with me.

Each character you type on a computer is associated with a specific number. There are several different sets of these numbers for different computer systems, but the most common, even today, is called ASCII (American Standard Code for Information Interchange). For example, the ASCII value of a capital A is 65, the value of a space is 32, and the value of a zero is 48. The computer doesn't represent numbers as you do—it performs binary arithmetic. For historical reasons, most modern microcomputers work with bits in multiples of eight. Each set of 8 bits is called a *byte*—and a byte can hold 256 unique values, enough for the alphabet, the numbers and punctuation, some control characters, some accented characters, and a few lines suitable for drawing simple images.

All the visible characters have a value below 128. Most file types, including word processors of that time, use the upper range of characters as embedded commands. For example, a file format might use 157 as a marker for the beginning of a paragraph and 158 as the marker for the end of the paragraph. The reason for this is that files were much smaller if commands could be limited to one or two characters—and those characters weren't used in most text. You have to remember that at that time, memory was expensive and in limited supply. In contrast, the smallest possible XyWrite command was three characters long, and many people thought that was a waste of space.

Back to the story... Reporters were among the first to use electronic computer communications to send files over the telephone system. Early versions of the communications programs could use only seven of the bits for content—the last bit was a *stop bit*. It turned out that they couldn't use programs that needed the upper range of characters because they would lose the formatting if they transmitted the file electronically. But because XyWrite used the bracketed commands, which used common characters that fit into 7 bits, it was possible to transmit both the text and the formatting for XyWrite files. So XyWrite made its mark by being the first word processor to use bracketed commands.

OK, enough stories. The real reason HTML uses the bracketed commands is much less interesting—they were already present in SGML, they were easy for people to read and write, and they were also relatively easy for a program to *parse*—which means to separate into its component parts.

Attribute Syntax

Tags can contain one main command and an unlimited number of associated values, called *attributes*. Each attribute has a name and a value. You must separate the attribute from the command or any preceding attribute value with white space. White space includes spaces, tabs, and carriage return/line feed characters. The browser ignores this white space (except when it doesn't exist). White space, to a browser, is another form of command typically called a *delimiter*. A delimiter is any character or sequence of characters that separates one item from another. Using white space as a delimiter is completely natural because that's what we use between words.

Different types of delimiters mean different things. For example, in addition to using white space between words, we also use periods between sentences. In HTML, angle brackets separate tags, white space separates attributes, and an equals sign separates the name of an attribute from its value. Similarly, HTML uses quotes to delimit the value because an attribute value might contain any of the other delimiters: white space, equals signs, or angle brackets.

Here are some examples:

```
<font face="Arial" size=12>
```

The `<font>` tag has two attributes—`face` and `size`, each of which has a value. Not all values are that simple. Consider this tag:

```
<input type="hidden" name="txtPara" value="He was a
codeslinger, lean and nervous, with quick hands that
could type or shoot with equal accuracy.">
```

Once again, not all browsers require the quotes around every attribute value; and once again, even though they aren't required, you should school yourself to enter them every time. I can assure you that failing to enter the quotes around attribute values will cause problems for you at some point in your .NET programming career. Here are two versions of an HTML tag, one with and one without quotes:

```
<input type="text" value="This is my value.">
<input type=text value=This is my value>
```

In a browser, these tags show up as text input controls—the equivalent of the familiar single-line text boxes from Windows applications. The first input control will contain the text "This is my value." But the second version will contain only the word "This." That's because, without the quotes, the browser has to fall back on the next delimiter to mark the end of the attribute value. In this case, the next delimiter is a space. The browser then ignores the next three words in the sentence, *is, my,* and *value,* because they aren't recognizable keywords and aren't properly formed attributes either—they don't have an equals sign or a value.

You may use either single or double quotes to delimit the attribute value; in other words, both of the following are equally valid:

```
<script language='VBScript'>
<script language="VBScript">
```

You can embed quotes in a value three ways:

♦ Switch the outer enclosing quotes to the opposite type; for example, `value="Mary's socks"`, or `value='The word is "important"'`.

♦ Enter each inner quote twice: `'value=Bill''s cat'`.

♦ Use an *entity*—characters that substitute for characters that are otherwise not allowed. There are some special entities; for example, the entity for a quote character is the six characters `&quot;`. But you can display any character—including Unicode characters—in most browsers using an entity that consists of an ampersand followed by a number sign (`&#`), the decimal value of the character you want to display, and a trailing semicolon. You can use hexadecimal values instead by placing an `x` after the number sign. So the entity value for a single-quote character (ASCII 39) is `&#39;`, or using a hex value, `&#x27;`. Therefore, yet another way to embed a single quote is `"value='Bill&#39;s cat'"` or using a hexadecimal value, `"value='Bill&#x27;s cat'"`.

More HTML Syntax

Attribute values have the most involved syntax. The other syntax rules for HTML are straightforward.

White Space Is Optional   Unless you specifically include tags to force the browser to include the white space, the browser will ignore it. The sentences "Welcome to Visual C# and ASP.Net!" and "Welcome   to   Visual C#   and   ASP.NET!" both print exactly the same way on-screen when rendered by a browser.

Case Is Irrelevant   HTML parsers ignore case, so you can write tags in either uppercase (`<FONT>`) or lowercase (`<font>`). Having said that, you should try to be consistent (yes, case is relevant in

XML). There are two advantages to using lowercase. First, the W3C standardized lowercase tag commands for an XML-compatible version of HTML, called XHTML. Second, lowercase requires fewer keystrokes. Compatibility aside, choose either uppercase or lowercase for tags and practice writing them consistently. I typically write tags in lowercase, but I admit I'm not completely consistent about case.

The Order of Tags Is Important   An enclosing tag must completely enclose any inner tags. For example, `<font size=12><b>This is bold</font></b>` is an invalid HTML syntax because you must close the bold `<b>` tag before the `<font>` tag. The proper way to write the tags is `<font size=12><b>This is bold</b></font>`.
These simple rules will help you write perfect HTML every time.

Write the Ending Tag when You Write the Beginning Tag   For example, don't write `<html>` then expect to remember to type the end `</html>` tag later. Write them both at the same time, then insert the content between the tags.

Write Tags in Lowercase   They're easier to type.

Use Templates   Templates are prewritten files into which you place content. Templates save a lot of time because they already contain the required tags.

Indent Enclosed Tags   Set the tab or indent levels in your editor to a small value—I find three spaces works well. That's enough to make the indents readily apparent, but not so much that longer lines scroll off the page.

Use Comments Liberally
A *comment*, in HTML, is text enclosed in a tag that begins with a left angle bracket, includes an exclamation point and two dashes, and ends with two dashes and a right angle bracket: `<!--This is a comment-->`. Comments help you understand the content and layout of a file. They can also help separate sections visually. Browsers don't render comments, so you can use them whenever you like.

Creating a Simple Page

You should usually start a new file with an HTML template. The most basic HTML template contains only the required tags. You fill in the content as needed. Type the following listing into your HTML editor, then save it as `template.html`.

```
<html>
<head>
<title><!-- Title --></title>
</head>
<body>
<!-- Your content here -->
</body>
</html>
```

You'll use that file a great deal. If you're using a dedicated HTML editor, it probably loaded a similar file as soon as you selected New from the File menu.

Add a title between the title tags. Replace the comment <!-- Title --> with the title "HTML Is Easy." Move past the first <body> tag and add your content in place of the comment <!-- Your content here -->. The completed file should look similar to Listing 2.1.

LISTING 2.1: HTML IS EASY (ch2-1.htm)

```
<html>
<head>
<title>HTML Is Easy</title>
</head>
<body>
<h1 align="center">HTML Is Easy</h1>
<p>Although HTML has about 100 different tags, you'll
quickly find that you use only a few of them. The most
useful tags are the paragraph tag--the tag that encloses
this paragraph; the <b>bold</b> tag; the <i>italics</i> tag
(most commonly seen in Microsoft products as the <strong>
strong</strong> tag and the <em>emphasis</em> tag; the heading
tags; and the most useful of all--the table tags, used
to produce formatted tables, both with and without borders.</p>
<!--<p> </p>-->
<table align="center" border="1" width="50%">
<thead>
    <tr>
        <th align="center">Product</th>
        <th align="center">Price</th>
    </tr>
    <tr>
        <td align="left">Cap</td>
        <td align="right">$14.50</td>
    </tr>
    <tr>
        <td align="left">Boots</td>
        <td align="right">$49.99</td>
    </tr>
</table>
</body>
</html>
```

After you have entered the listing, save it as a file, and then view it in your browser. To do that, type **file://<drive><path><filename>** where *drive* is the drive letter where you saved the file, *path* is the directory or hierarchy of directories, and *filename* is the actual name of the file. In your browser, the page should look similar to Figure 2.2.

FIGURE 2.2

HTML is easy.
(`ch2-1.htm`)

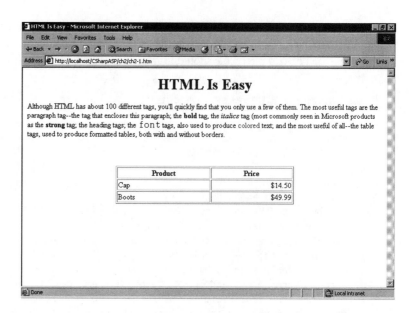

When you view Listing 2.1 in a browser, you should notice several features. The title appears in the title bar of the browser window, not in the body of the document. That's because the title isn't properly part of the document at all—it's part of the header, which is why the `<title>` tag is inside the `<head>` tag.

If you entered the text exactly as it's written, you should notice that the line breaks in the listing and the line breaks in the browser are different. Each line you entered (although you can't see it) ends with two characters called a *return* and a *line feed* (ASCII characters 13 and 10). The browser treats these as white space and ignores them. If you aren't willing to let the browser break lines for you, you'll need to break the lines explicitly yourself, using a `<br>` or break tag.

NOTE   *The `<br>` tag is one of several exceptions to the rule that you must always enter an end tag. The end break tag `</br>` is not required (although you can enter it if you like). However, even though your pages work fine without the end tags, get in the habit of writing them so that your pages will be XHTML and XML compatible.*

Another interesting feature is that the line breaks are relative to the area of the screen into which the browser renders content, called the *client area* of the window. Resize your browser window and watch what happens to the text. As you change the width of the browser window, the browser rerenders the text, changing the line breaks so that the text still fits inside the window—the text listing just gets longer.

NOTE   *What font did your browser render the paragraph text in? A serif font, such as Times New Roman, or a non-serif font such as Arial? What's the point size? As an HTML page designer, you should bear in mind that the default font face and the default point size are determined by the user through browser preference settings, not by your document. Both the default font face and the default size are user selectable in both Netscape and Internet Explorer (IE). If you want the text to appear in a specific face or size, you must include the appropriate font tags or (better) CSS styles. Even then, the results depend on exactly what the end-users have on their computers.*

Next, look at the `<h1>` tag. It has an attribute called `align="center"`, which forces the browser to display the content in the center of the page. There's another way to align content on the page. You could just as easily have written the following:

```
<center>
<h1>HTML Is Easy</h1>
</center>
```

In the browser, that construction would look identical. You would still see that type of syntax, although most HTML editors align each element separately. The `<center></center>` syntax is most useful when you want to force the alignment of many consecutive elements. In HTML 4.0, the `<center>` tag is deprecated but has been marked as shorthand for `<div align="center">`. Again, you should use the newer syntax except when required for older browsers.

The paragraph tag `<p>` encloses the entire paragraph. Try changing the paragraph alignment by adding an alignment tag. Add an `align="right"` attribute to the paragraph tag, then refresh the browser page.

TIP You should refresh the browser after making any change to an HTML file. I've seen numerous instances where people complain that their code changes aren't displaying properly, when the real problem is that they forgot to refresh the browser. The browser caches page content in a special folder. When you revisit a page, the browser first checks the cache to see if the content is already available. The browser can contact the server to see if there's a newer version of the page, but it doesn't do so by default. Refreshing the browser forces it to rerequest, reparse, and redisplay the page, thus incorporating any changes you've made since the last time the browser displayed the page. You can configure most browsers so that they always check for an updated page. That marginally slows down browsing remote files, but it does help ensure that you see the latest version. No matter how you configure the browser cache, when you don't see changes you just made, you should always refresh to force the page to update.

The `<b>` bold tag and the `<strong>` tag do exactly the same thing—they both produce bold text. The difference is that the `<b>` tag explicitly makes text bold, while the actual displayed result of a `<strong>` tag is not specified by HTML—that's up to the creators of the rendering engine. In practice, all the popular rendering engines make the text bold.

You'll find that a similar situation exists with the `<i>` tag. An `<i>` tag explicitly means to italicize the text, but many HTML editors use the emphasis (`<em>`) tag instead. Again, the displayed result of an `<em>` tag isn't specified by HTML—the rendering engine is free to emphasize the text in any fitting manner. In practice, all the popular rendering engines make the text italic.

You can use color names such as "red" or "blue," and most modern browsers will display the text in the intended color. Both IE and Netscape understand color names (although they understand different sets of color names). I'll show you a browser-independent way to specify colors in the upcoming section "Fonts and Colors," later in this chapter.

You can change the font using the `<font>` tag. Note that the command that changes the font is the face attribute. Most people misuse the word "font" when they actually mean *font face*. Also, the `size` attribute—specified as 5 in Listing 2.1, doesn't mean the point size, as is typical with word processors; it means the *relative* size of the text compared to the default size selected by the user. The standard sizes available range from 1 to 7, and the default text size is 3, so text enclosed in the tag `<font size="4">Larger text</font>` would show up in a larger point size than the surrounding text. Note that the font tag is *deprecated*, which means that you should avoid using it unless you have to, because the tag may not be supported in future versions. However, the <font> tag is still necessary if you must write HTML for *downlevel* browsers (obsolete, but still in use), so I've included it here.

At the end of the paragraph is a second, very short paragraph that contains only a single line: . That stands for *non-breaking space*. The starting ampersand and the ending semicolon are required. There are several of these commands, one for each non-alphanumeric character. You can use them to insert characters that the browser won't normally print, such as the left angle bracket (<) and right angle bracket (>), which stand for *less than* and *greater than*, respectively. The non-breaking space forces the browser to render the paragraph. Browsers ignore empty paragraph tags because they contain no content. A normal space won't work because it's white space, which browsers also ignore except where the white space functions as a separator—and then the browser collapses it into a single space character. The non-breaking space is an "invisible" character. You may know it as a "hard space" from working with word processors.

The table tag contains three attributes: an `align="center"` attribute, which forces the browser to align the table in the center of the screen; a `border="1"` attribute, which causes the browser to place a visible, one-pixel-wide border around each table cell; and a `width=50%` attribute, which causes the browser to render the table in half the available horizontal screen space (if possible). Again, resize your browser. Notice that the table width changes as the width of the window changes. Make the browser window so narrow that the table won't fit. You may need to scroll down to view the table as the browser window gets narrower. What happens? At some point, the table will no longer fit in half of the screen space. At that point, the browser gives up and simply renders the table in the center of whatever space is available. When that space becomes too small, the browser begins to clip the right edge of the table.

The table itself contains two separate sections: A <thead> section containing <th> tags makes up the head section of the table. Thead stands for table head. The <th> tags contain the column headers. You don't need a thead section, but if you use one in combination with the <th> tags, the browser automatically makes the column headers bold. The <tbody> section of the table contains the data. The <tr> (table row) tags delimit the rows, while the <td> (table data) tags delimit the individual cells in each column. The closing tags are required for all table-related tags except the column header (<th>) tags, for which closing tags are optional.

Now that you've seen a complete HTML file, I will spend a short amount of time explaining the use of each common HTML element more completely.

Formatting Text

HTML makes formatting text extremely easy, as long as you aren't too picky about how that text looks, where the lines break, or exactly where the text is, relative to other elements of the page. You control the appearance of text by the use of heading styles, fonts and colors, paragraphs, and lists.

List Styles

You've already seen how to use font tags and paragraph tags. HTML also contains tags to format bulleted and numbered lists. A bulleted list is an unordered list, one where the physical order of the items is unimportant. Therefore, in HTML, you use a `<ul>` tag, which stands for *unordered list,* to create a bulleted list. You place a `<li>` (*list item*) tag around each item in the list:

```
<ul>Things To Do
   <li>Go to the grocery store</li>
   <li>Pick up the dog from the vet</li>
   <li>Get a new computer</li>
</ul>
```

You create a numbered list when the order of the items in the list is significant. In HTML, you use `<ol>`, or *ordered list.* You still use `<li>` tags for the list items, just as in an unordered list.

```
<ol><b>Things to do--in order</b>
   <li>Go to the grocery store</li>
   <li>Pick up the dog from the vet</li>
   <li>Shop for a new computer</li>
</ol>
```

Figure 2.3 shows how these two list types appear in the browser.

FIGURE 2.3

List styles
(ch2-2.htm)

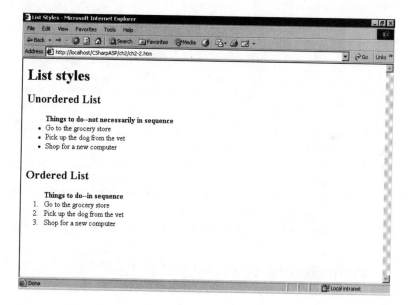

You can nest lists one inside another. The browser indents subordinate lists one level beyond the containing list tag indent level (see Figure 2.4):

```
<ol><b>Things to do--in order</b>
   <li>Go to the grocery store</li>
   <li>Pick up the dog from the vet</li>
   <ul><b>Remember these items</b>
      <li>Buy a new dog-tag</li>
```

```
        <li>Ask for new flea powder prescription</li>
    </ul>
    <li>Shop for a new computer</li>
</ol>
```

FIGURE 2.4

Nested lists
(ch2-3.htm)

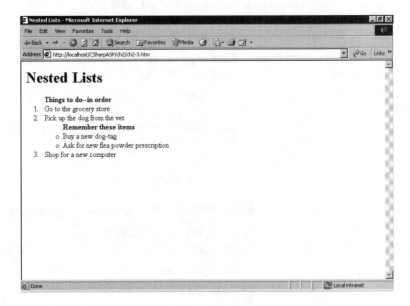

You can use several other text-formatting styles for special purposes. You'll find a complete list in Appendix A, "Quick HTML Reference." But a few are worth mentioning here.

As you've seen, the browser ignores line breaks. You can force a line break within a paragraph with the
 (break) tag. For example, look at Listing 2.2 in your browser (and see Figure 2.5). The first paragraph doesn't contain any line breaks, whereas the second paragraph contains a line break at the end of each line. The first paragraph resizes if you shrink the browser window. The second paragraph resizes the lines as well, but it always keeps the explicit line breaks intact.

LISTING 2.2: EXPLICIT LINE BREAKS (ch2-4.htm)

```
<html>
<head>
<title>Explicit Line Breaks</title>
</head>
<body>
<h1>Explicit Line Breaks</h1>
<p>This paragraph doesn't contain any line breaks.
The browser inserts the line breaks when it renders the
file on-screen. The browser will readjust the line breaks
```

```
if you resize the browser window.</p>
<p>This paragraph <i>does</i> contain line breaks.<br>
The browser breaks the lines at the &lt;br&gt; tags.<br>
when it renders the file on-screen.
The browser will <i>not</i> readjust the line breaks<br>
if you resize the browser window.</p>
</body>
</html>
</body>
</html>
```

FIGURE 2.5

Explicit line breaks
(ch2-4.htm)

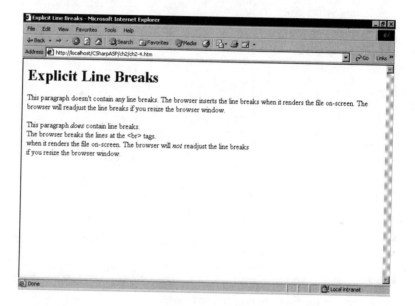

I'll end this formatting section with two short notes. First, many excellent HTML editors perform much of the tedious, low-level formatting for you, and I've seen many sites that use their advanced formatting features to great effect. However, until you're completely comfortable with basic HTML, you should avoid these advanced editors. The problem is that they do so much for you. The idea in this book is for you to understand HTML to the point where you are comfortable writing it with nothing more than a simple text editor. Therefore, I advise you to actually use a *simple* text editor until you're absolutely sure that you can edit any HTML that the advanced editors may insert.

Second, it's tempting to try to defeat the browser's default rendering of text, but you should avoid that temptation, again, until you have mastered the default renderings. I assure you that you can create very attractive and functional pages with nothing more than the default HTML commands. The more advanced HTML editors may actually inhibit your learning. You can specify the placement of text and images down to the pixel level in these editors. Keep in mind that they accomplish this absolute placement not through HTML commands, but instead with Cascading Style Sheets or embedded styles—both of which I'll cover briefly later in this chapter.

Heading Styles

HTML recognizes six heading levels, written as <h1> through <h6>. The number signifies the position of the heading content in a hierarchy, where the smaller numbers mean that the content is higher in the hierarchy, just like in most word processors. Figure 2.6 shows the six heading levels as rendered in IE 5.

FIGURE 2.6

Six HTML heading levels (`ch2-5.htm`)

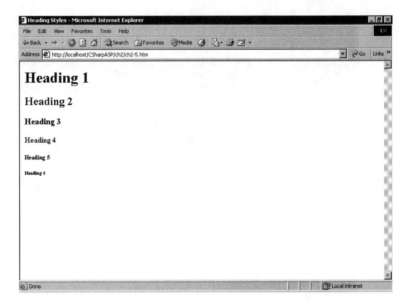

Again, the formatting of the displayed heading is browser specific. The heading levels will not appear identically in different browsers.

HTML is supposed to be a way of creating structured documents. You organize the document by heading levels like an outline. The top level <h1> might be the document title. Essentially, all other portions of the document would be subordinate to the <h1> level. You would then apply the <h2> style to each major subordinate level, and <h3> to each subheading inside the <h2> level. For example this chapter, structured in HTML, would look like this:

```
<h1>Chapter 2: HTML Basics</h1>
    <h2>HTML Is Just Markup and Content</h2>
        <h3>What HTML Does</h3>
        <h3>Why HTML Is Important</h3>
        <h3>HTML's Limitations</h3>
    <h2>Syntax: Tags and Attributes</h2>
        <h3>What Is a Tag?</h3>
```

```
<h3>What Is an End Tag?</h3>
etc...
```

Note that this is a relatively weak scheme for creating structured documents because there's no way in HTML to specify that the content for the subordinate tags "belongs" to the previous, higher-level heading level. That means that you can't, for example, select an <h2> tag and get all the <h3> tags and text associated with that tag. Instead, the association scheme is by position. The internal HTML parser rule is that all text following a heading level belongs to that heading level until it reaches the next heading level. Also, the browser doesn't format the content following a given heading level any differently from the text for a higher level. The only visual clue to the heading level is the format for the header itself; the renderer doesn't provide a visual clue such as indentation to help you differentiate content in the various levels.

Fonts and Colors

You've already seen a brief example of how to use the <font> tag. In this section, you'll explore it in more depth. Font tags by themselves are useless; they need one or more attributes to accomplish a change in the visual representation of the text enclosed by the tag (called the *tag text*). Font tags can take the following attributes:

face   Changes the tag-text font typeface to the specified face. If that face is not available on the client computer, the browser uses the default browser font. You can increase the likelihood that the browser will select a similar font by listing more than one face in the font tag. For example, the tag <font face="GreenMonster, Arial, Times New Roman"> specifies that your preferred font faces, in order, are GreenMonster (which, as far as I know, doesn't exist), Arial, and Times New Roman. The browser will first try to use GreenMonster. When that fails, it will use Arial, which should normally work on Windows platforms.

size   Changes the tag-text font size to the specified size. The size is a number, but you can append letters to define how the browser should interpret that number. By default, the browser interprets the font size number relative to the default text size (3).

color   Specifies the color for the tag text. IE and Netscape both understand a set of named colors. Unfortunately, they understand different sets, but all browsers understand a color representation called RGB (Red, Green, Blue). The RGB color values consist of three hex byte values, concatenated together to form a six-character string. Typically, you append a number sign (#) in front of the string. For example, the color #000000 signifies black. Even though the spaces don't appear, think of the string as if it were written #00 00 00. The first two zeros are the Red component, in this case, no red. The second two zeros are the Green component, and the third set of zeros is the Blue component. Since the value of each color component in this example is zero, the value defines the color black. Each component can have 256 values—from zero to 255. Unfortunately, you have to write them as hexadecimal values, not the more familiar decimals. See the following sidebar, "The Hexadecimal System and RGB Color Values," for more information about how to translate the values from decimal to hexadecimal.

THE HEXADECIMAL SYSTEM AND RGB COLOR VALUES

Humans tend to work with decimal (base-10) systems, probably because we have 10 fingers. Computers commonly work with several different bases: base-2 (binary), base-8 (octal), and base-16 (hexadecimal). Hexadecimal is usually called *hex* for short in programming terminology. Hex is convenient because a two-digit hex number can represent all the numbers from 0 to 255, which equates to the number of values one byte (8 bits) of information can hold. Another way to think of a byte is 28 power. Remember, each bit can hold only a zero or a 1, so a computer's "native" arithmetic base is base-2.

Each byte holds two *nibbles*. A nibble is four bits and can hold 16 unique values—from 0 to 15. Nibbles translate easily to hexadecimal, because each hex number can represent a single nibble. Just as the decimal system has 10 digits, the hex system has 16. The standard digits 0 to 9 represent the first 10 values, and we use the letters from A to F to represent the remaining five values. Just as in the decimal system, where each column is a multiple of 10, the columns in the hex system are multiples of 16. So the number 10 is A and the number 15 is F. After 15, you need to start a 16s column, so the value 16 can be represented as 10—meaning one 16 and no ones.

See the following list for some examples:

Decimal	Hex
0–9	Identical
10	A
11	B
12	C
13	D
14	E
15	F
16	10
32	20
64	40
81	51
255	FF

Each RGB color value is one byte, with a decimal value from 0 to 255; thus, you can represent each value with two hex digits, from 00 to FF. To translate between the two systems, use modulo arithmetic. Divide the decimal value you need by 16 to find the value for the first digit and use the remainder for the value of the second digit. For example, the hex representation of 17 is 11 (17 / 16 = 1, with a remainder of 1). The hex representation of 200 is C8 (200 / 16 = 12, with a remainder of 8).

To translate the other direction, simply multiply the leftmost digit by 16 and add the decimal value of the digit in the rightmost column. For example, B9 = ((11 * 16) + 9) = 185.

TIP   You don't really need to learn the hexadecimal system to write RGB color values (although it helps). One of the easiest ways to translate between decimal and hex comes with every Windows computer—the Calculator accessory. Click the View menu, then click Scientific. The calculator will change its appearance. Click the Dec (decimal) option, then enter a number and click the Hex button to translate from decimal to hex. Conversely, click the Hex button and enter a hex value, then click the Dec button to translate from hex to decimal.

As I mentioned earlier, `<font>` tags are deprecated in HTML version 4 and higher. When possible, you should use Cascading Style Sheets to apply formatting to text rather than `<font>` tags.

Paragraph Tags, Div Tags, and Spans

Paragraph `<p>` tags are block elements that surround paragraph text. They can contain "child" tags, such as text or image formatting commands, and they can also contain tables. You can force the browser to render a paragraph aligned left (default) or right, or centered by adding an alignment attribute; for example, `<p align="center">`.

A *div element*, often called a *layer*, is a way to divide your document into separate sections. You can think of a `<div>` tag as an artificial separation between areas of the document, just like heading levels. The primary difference is that `<div>` tags *are* block elements. You can retrieve all the text and HTML associated with a `<div>` tag by "asking" the `<div>` tag for its contents. By default, a `<div>` tag acts like a paragraph tag and accepts the same attributes. For example, you can right-align the contents of a `<div>` tag by adding an `align="right"` attribute to the tag. The W3C added the `<div>` tag to make up for the weak implementation of heading levels. Divs were originally implemented as `<layer>` tags (which are not supported in HTML 4.x or in Netscape version 6 and higher) in Netscape, where their main purpose was to help control where elements appear along the z-axis.

Spans have no default formatting. Their main purpose is to allow you to add specific formatting or actions, via style sheets or script, to sections of text smaller than a paragraph or a div.

You can see the difference in the following listing, Listing 2.3.

LISTING 2.3: DIV AND SPAN EXPERIMENTS (ch2-6.htm)

```
<HTML>
<HEAD>
<TITLE>Div and Span Experiments</TITLE>
</HEAD>
<BODY>
<span>This is a span.</span>
<span>So is this.</span>

<p> </p>

<div>
    <span>This is a span.</span>
</div>
<span>So is this.</span>
</BODY>
</HTML>
```

The file contains two copies of the sentences "This is a span." and "So is this.", each surrounded by a span tag. The only difference is that the first span (the indented line) in the second copy is part of a `<div>` tag. If you view the code in Listing 2.3 in your browser, it should look similar to Figure 2.7.

FIGURE 2.7

Div and span experiments (`ch2-6.htm`)

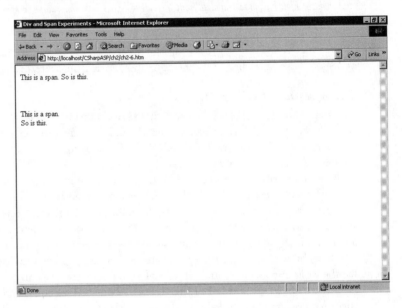

You'll see more about `<span>` and `<div>` tags when you work with individual elements on the page through the Document Object Model (DOM). Most modern HTML editors, such as FrontPage and Dreamweaver, use `<div>` and `<span>` tags extensively to isolate document elements in block tags over which you have z-axis control. You're likely to see a lot of them if you use an HTML editor.

The *<body>* Tag

The `<body>` tag accepts several attributes that can help improve the overall look of your pages by giving you control over the page background color and margins and even add background images to your pages. To add a background color, use a `bgcolor` attribute. For example, the following `<body>` tag changes the background color of the page to hot pink:

```
<body bgcolor="#FC00B3">
```

Here's a list of `<body>` tag attributes and their values.

alink   An RGB or named color value for selected hyperlinks. A hyperlink is selected and activated when a user moves the focus or the mouse to the link.

background   A URL that references an image.

bgcolor   An RGB or named color value that specifies the background color for the page.

bottommargin (**IE-only**)   A numeric value that specifies the number of pixels in the bottom margin of the page.

leftmargin (**IE-only**)   A numeric value that specifies the number of pixels in the left margin of the page.

link   An RGB or named color value for hyperlinks that have not been activated.

rightmargin (**IE-only**)   A numeric value that specifies the number of pixels in the right margin of the page.

scroll   Controls whether scroll bars can appear on the page.

text   An RGB or named color value that specifies the default color for text on the page.

topmargin (**IE-only**)   A numeric value that specifies the number of pixels in the top margin of the page.

vlink   An RGB or named color value for hyperlinks that the user has visited.

bgsound   A URL that references a sound file. The sound file downloads automatically and begins playing as soon as the download is complete. The requirement that the sound file download completely before the browser begins playing it makes the `bgsound` not particularly useful in practice.

Creating a Formatted Page with Fonts and Colors

There's nothing like practice to learn how to work with a technology. Try creating a page that contains a left margin of 100 pixels and a right margin of 100 pixels, and that uses at least three heading levels, a list, and assorted font color and formatting commands. Listing 2.4 contains a sample document for reference purposes.

LISTING 2.4: SAMPLE FORMATTED HTML PAGE (ch2-7.htm)

```
<html>
<head>
<title>Introduction to the DOM</title>
</head>
<body bgcolor="#ffffc0" leftmargin="100"
    rightmargin="100">
<font size=3>
<h1 align="center">Introduction to the Document
Object Model (DOM)</h1>
<h2>Differing Implementations in Netscape and IE

<p><font size=2 face="Verdana">
The World Wide Web Consortium (W3C) released a
specification for treating the various elements that
can appear on an HTML page as <i>objects</i>. The
purpose of the DOM is so you can programmatically access
the various elements on the page.</font></p>

<p><font size=2 face="Verdana">
Unfortunately, the two most popular browsers have
```

```
differing implementations of the DOM.
Microsoft's Internet Explorer (IE) browser has the most
complete implementation. Since version 3, both Netscape
and IE have exposed form and input elements to scripting
languages. Starting with version 4, IE now exposes almost
every tag, or element, to programmatic control. To do
this, Microsoft added some new attributes to every tag, the
most important of which is an ID that uniquely identifies
that element on the page. In contrast, Netscape's
(version 4) implementation is rather limited.
</font></p>

<h2>DOM Objects</h2>
<p><font size=2 face="Verdana">
Before you can understand DOM objects specifically, you need
to understand objects in general. An object is the computer
analogue of a "real" object.
</font></p>

<h3>Object Properties and Methods</h3>
<p><font size=2 face="Verdana">A ball makes a good example.
A ball has physical properties--it is (usually) round, it
has a color, it has a bounce factor, and to some degree, it
shares all these characteristics with every other ball.
You can represent these properties as characteristics
common to all balls--and you can also represent these
properties in program variables.</font></p>

<p><font size=2 face="Verdana">A ball can also act or
be the subject of action. For example, you can roll a
ball, throw a ball, or bounce a ball. These actions are
called "methods." All objects have properties and/or
methods. The properties are the intrinsic or acquired
characteristics of the object, while methods are actions.
In practice, there is some conceptual overlap between
the two. For example, a ball's color is clearly a
property, but the ball's velocity could be implemented
as a method as well as a property, e.g. &quot;The ball's
velocity is 0.&quot (property) or &quot;Change the ball's
velocity to 100.&quot;, which is the equivalent of
throwing the ball (property <i>or</i> method?).</font></p>

<p><font size=2 face="Times New Roman">
The following lists show some of the properties and methods
of a ball object.</font></p>
<h3>Ball Properties</h3>
<font color="#0000ff">
    <ul>
```

```
        <li>Shape</li>
        <li>Color</li>
        <li>Diameter (side-to-side)</li>
        <li>Diameter (front-to-back)</li>
        <li>Diameter (top-to-bottom)</li>
        <li>Composition</li>
        <li>Bounce factor</li>
        <li>Surface Texture</li>
        <li>Position</li>
        <li>Velocity</li>
        <li>Direction</li>
        <li>Acceleration</li>
      </ul>
    </font>

    <h3>Ball Methods</h3>
    <font color="#0000ff">
      <ul>
        <li>Roll</li>
        <li>Bounce</li>
        <li>Collide</li>
        <li>Move</li>
      </ul>
    </font></h2>
    </font>
    </body>
    </html>
```

The page is too long to show in a single image, but it's on www.sybex.com. To view the file in your browser, navigate to the CSharpASP\Ch2 directory and double-click the ch2-7.htm file.

Including Images on Your Web Site

It's hard to imagine a Web site without images. It's also hard to imagine a much easier way to get images onto a page than using HTML. With very little effort, you can mix images and text and even wrap text around the images. All your image work begins with the image tag, discussed in the following section.

The Image Tag

To place an image on a page, you use an `<img>` tag with an src=URL attribute that specifies which file you want to send. Interestingly, the server doesn't send the image file data with the rest of the page; instead, the browser parses the HTML and text in the page, then begins requesting associated content from the server, such as images. That's why you often see a page load, then the images begin to appear a few seconds later.

Sometimes the images don't appear in your browser window in sequence. The browser requests the images sequentially, but the server may not respond to the requests in the same sequence. That's something to keep in mind as you design your pages.

There are a few optional attributes for the `<img>` tag. The `width="number"` and `height="number"` attributes specify the width and height of the image, respectively. Both the `width` and `height` attributes are optional. If you don't include the attributes, the browser will show the image at its original size.

Optional tags are just that—optional. You can include them if you want or leave them off; but like most choices, there are consequences for either action you take. Because the default action of the browser is to show your images at the original size, leaving the `width` and `height` attributes off would seem to be a good choice most of the time—and it is, for small images. When you include the `width` and `height` attributes, though, the browser can reserve the screen area for the image before returning to the server to ask for the image file data. When you don't include the `width` and `height` attributes, the browser places a "missing image" icon in place of the image. Here's the problem. If the browser knows how big the image is going to be, it can complete the calculations for the layout of the remainder of the page. If the browser *doesn't* know how big the image is going to be, it has to delay the final layout until after it has retrieved the images from the server. It may even have to move text and images that have already been rendered. The end result is that your pages load more slowly when you don't include the optional `width` and `height` tags.

Most images placed in HTML pages are either Graphic Interchange Format (GIF) files or Joint Photographic Experts Group (JPEG) files, which are smaller than other image file formats because they're highly compressed. There's no technical impediment to using other file formats—although the client browsers may not be able to display them without special viewers. Netscape can natively display both GIF (pronounced "jiff") and JPEG or JPG (pronounced "j-peg") files. IE adds Windows bitmap (BMP) files to that list. Both browsers accept plug-ins or ActiveX extensions that provide viewers for other file formats. For example, Macromedia's Flash format requires users to download the Flash Viewer before viewing Flash content.

Unlike a standard executable program, missing resources don't bother a browser much—it simply ignores any resources that may be missing. If the resource would normally be visible, the browser may display the missing image icon in its place.

In addition to the `src`, `width`, and `height` attributes, you can specify how you want to align your image relative to the containing tag. For example, the containing tag for most images would be the `<body>` tag, so if you left align an image in the `<body>` tag, the image will appear aligned to the left edge of the page. If you were to place that same left-aligned `<img>` tag inside a table cell, the image would appear aligned to the left edge of the table cell, not the left edge of the page.

In addition to the `right` and `left` values you might expect, the `align` attribute may also take some less common values. Table 2.1 shows the result of certain alignment keywords.

TABLE 2.1: TABLE ALIGNMENT ATTRIBUTES

ALIGNMENT ATTRIBUTE	RESULT
ABSBOTTOM	Aligns the image at the lowest possible point relative to the text. ABSBOTTOM is the bottom of the longest descender of the text.

Continued on next page

TABLE 2.1: TABLE ALIGNMENT ATTRIBUTES *(continued)*

ALIGNMENT ATTRIBUTE	RESULT
ABSMIDDLE	Aligns the image in the absolute center of the text.
BASELINE	Aligns the image with the baseline of the text.
BOTTOM	Aligns the image at the bottom of the containing tag.
LEFT	Aligns the image at the left edge of the containing tag.
MIDDLE	Aligns the image in the horizontal center of the containing tag.
RIGHT	Aligns the image at the right edge of the containing tag.
TEXTTOP	Aligns the image with the top edge of the text.
TOP	Aligns the image at the top edge of the containing tag.
BORDER	An integer width that determines the width of the border. The default width is 1. A value of 0 means no border.
HSPACE	An integer value that determines the spacing between the left and right edges of the image and any surrounding items.
ISMAP	This attribute has no value. It may be present, in which case the image is treated as a server-side image map. An image map is one or more images that function like anchor tags—they hyperlink to an anchor tag in the current document, another document, or another URL. Server-side image maps are rarely used with modern browsers. When the user clicks an image defined as a server-side image map, the browser sends the mouse coordinates of the click event to the server. You have to process the click using ASP or a CGI script to initiate an action.
USEMAP	This attribute takes the name of a <map> tag as a value. It specifies that the browser should use the touch areas defined in the <map> tag to determine whether the user clicked in a hyperlinked area of the image. The <map> tag defines a client-side image map.
VSPACE	An integer value that determines the spacing between the top and bottom edges of the image and any surrounding items.

Placing Images on a Page

By default, the browser places the image on the page in the position where it is parsed. However, some actions change the default position. For example, if the first tag on the page is an <img> tag, the image will appear at the top-left corner of the *client area* of the browser window. The client area is the portion of the window where content appears. It excludes the border, status bar, and any toolbars. Any text following the image would appear starting at the bottom-right edge of the image, because placing the image on the page first moves the baseline to the bottom of the image (see Figure 2.8).

FIGURE 2.8

Default image
alignment
(ch2-8.htm)

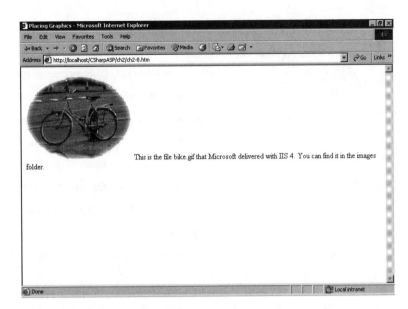

You can alter the `<img>` tag by adding an alignment attribute; for example, `<img src="someURL/ topImg.gif" align="right">` will align the image at the top-right corner of the client area. You might expect that adding text in the file after the image would then wrap the text so it would begin on the first line following the image and below the bottom edge of the image. But that's not how the browser renders the file. Changing the alignment renders the image on the right, as expected, but the browser begins plotting text at the top-left corner of the client area (see Figure 2.9).

FIGURE 2.9

Right-aligned image
(ch2-9.htm)

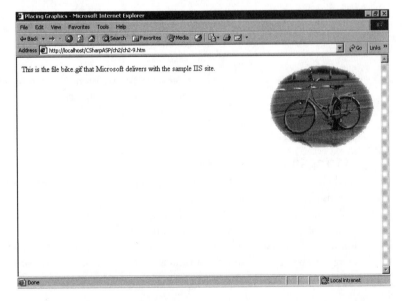

If you go back and explicitly add an `align="left"` attribute to the tag in the file displayed in Figure 2.8 (`ch2-8.htm`), the text will plot at the right top corner of the image rather than the bottom right corner.

You should spend some time experimenting with the various attribute settings for the `<img>` tag, because the results aren't always what you would expect.

Wrapping Text Around Images

HTML doesn't let you wrap text on both sides of images easily. You can wrap text around three sides of an image aligned to the left or right of the containing tag by adding an `align="left"` or `align="right"` attribute value to the `<img>` tag.

If you want to insert an image in a text line—for example, an icon or small image—you can place the image by centering it in the text line (see Figure 2.10).

FIGURE 2.10

Inline images
(`ch2-10.htm`)

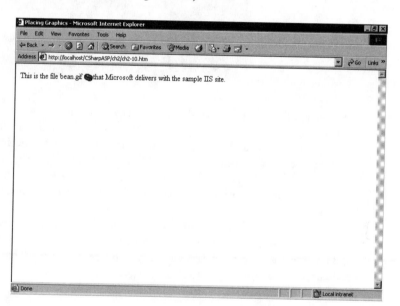

Background Images

Both IE and Netscape support background images. You specify the background image as an attribute to the `<body>` tag:

```
<body background="http://myserver/mysite/someimage.gif">
```

The image appears on the page as a background image, which means that any other content appears on top of the image—in other words, the z-order of the image is zero. As an example, I've plotted a list on top of an image in Figure 2.11.

FIGURE 2.11

Background image

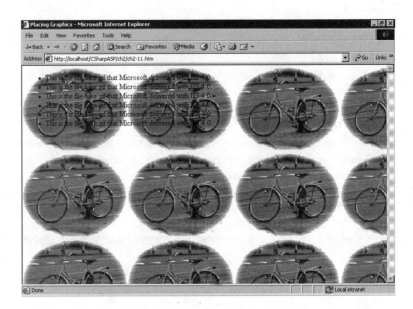

The first thing you'll notice about this image is that it's plotted multiple times. That's because the browser tiles the image across the entire background. *Tiling* an image means that the browser plots it at the upper-left corner and repeats the image across the horizontal width of the page. When it reaches the right edge, it begins plotting again at the left edge below the first graphic—the same pattern that people use when reading a book. The browser tiles the image because the technique was meant to make it easy to display a patterned or textured background image. If you need a single image, you should plot it explicitly.

IE makes it possible to plot a single background image as a *watermark*. A watermark image is *not* tiled. Like a watermark on paper, it's an image plotted one or more times, usually centered vertically and horizontally. Like a standard background image, a watermark has a z-order of zero, so all other content plots on top of the watermark image.

Introduction to Hyperlinking

Hyperlinks are the "Web" in World Wide Web. Hyperlinks give you the capability to aid or control where your application's users can go from any given location or screen in your application.

Hypertext is the brainchild of Ted Nelson, who envisioned the entire set of human knowledge as hyperlinked content. His Xanadu project worked toward this goal for many years. Today, the Internet is rapidly achieving his goal, albeit in an unstructured manner.

The goal of hyperlinking is to provide a way for people to move from one position, topic, or knowledge granule to a related position, topic, or knowledge granule. For example, if this document were in electronic form, I'd expect a hyperlink from every instance of a term related to ASP to a definition of that term and from every HTML tag to a definition of that tag. From the definition, I'd expect a link to one or more examples, any related terms, and perhaps other related technologies such as SGML, XML, or the W3C standards documents.

As a user moves among, or *traverses*, a set of links, the browser application maintains a history list that enables the user to traverse the visited pages in reverse order. Modern browsers maintain your history list—often for several weeks. Most modern browsers let you configure the length of time to maintain your browsing history. They also let you jump many steps backward at one time by formatting the entire history as a series of links.

You can think of the entire set of links as a Web, but in this book I'd prefer that you think of that set of links as an application. In an application, as opposed to a Web site, you have specific goals in mind: You want to guide the user from one logical point to another. In contrast, in a Web site, or on the Internet, the user may be simply browsing without any specific goal in mind. Therefore, in an application, links serve both as information connectors and as application action initiators. For example, a button on a form is a link—but its *function* is to initiate an action in the application. A navigation button is a link, but it doesn't necessarily link to related information—it may link to a menu, or it may exit the application altogether.

The Anchor Tag

In HTML, the primary means of linking one location to another is the *anchor*, or <a> tag. It's a very simple scheme that uses URLs to move between locations. You specify the URL as an href attribute value:

```
<a href="http://myserver/mysite/mypage.htm">
Go To My Page
</a>
```

The browser formats the text following the opening anchor tag as the link, so in the previous example, the only visible portion of the link is the phrase "Go To My Page." The browser continues to format text following the <a> tag as link text until it encounters the closing </a> tag. Everything between the start and end of the anchor tag, including spaces (an exception to the rule that browsers ignore white space), is the link text.

There are two types of anchor tags: links and bookmarks. Their functions are completely different.

A *link* is an anchor tag that acts as the *trigger* for a hyperlink—when you click on the link, it begins or triggers the linking action. *Bookmarks* are anchor tags that act as the *destination* for a link. You can jump to a bookmark, but bookmarks aren't visible, and you can't click them. The browser formats anchor tags that contain links as underlined, colored text—blue by default. Browsers generally change the link color after the user has visited the link target.

To create a bookmark, you must give the anchor tag a name attribute:

```
<a name="Bookmark1">
```

You can jump to a bookmark in the same document or in a different document. Basically, a bookmark is a way to jump to a place in a document other than the top of the document, which is the default link target. To jump to a different position in the same document, you would write a link tag like this:

```
<a href="#Bookmark1">
```

Note the pound sign (#)in front of the `href` attribute value. The pound sign informs the browser that the link target is a bookmark rather than a document. You can also link to bookmarks in other documents by appending the pound sign and the bookmark name to the end of the URL:

```
<a href="http://myserver/mysite/mypage.htm#Bookmark1">
```

You'll see many pages set up with links at the top of the page that jump to bookmarks farther down in the page. Typically, you'll also find that each bookmarked section has a link back to a bookmark at the top of the menu, so that after reading a section, you can jump back to the menu to select a different section. There are some good reasons to set up documents like this rather than as a set of linked pages. A single long document with a menu is less work to create and requires only a single trip to the server. A single long document is also easy to print. On the other hand, it's often more difficult to read long documents, because you have to scroll through them.

Listing 2.5 contains an example of a document with a menu and internal bookmarks for each section. The spacing (`<p> </p>`) paragraphs are just to put enough white space on the page to force the page to scroll—you wouldn't need them in a normal document. In the browser, the menu page looks like Figure 2.12.

FIGURE 2.12

A menu page with several sections (`ch2-12.htm`)

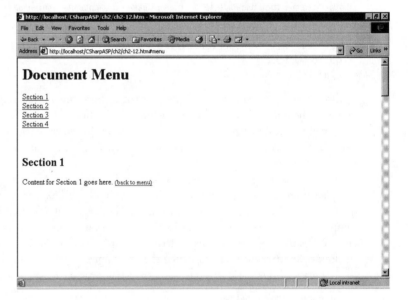

LISTING 2.5: A MENU PAGE WITH SEVERAL SECTIONS (ch2-12.htm)

```
<html>
<head>
<title></title>
</head>
<body>
<a name="Menu">
```

```
<h1>Document Menu</h1></a>
<a href="#Bookmark1">Section 1</a><br>
<a href="#Bookmark2">Section 2</a><br>
<a href="#Bookmark3">Section 3</a><br>
<a href="#Bookmark4">Section 4</a><br>
<p> </p>
<a name="Bookmark1">
<h2>Section 1</h2></a>
Content for Section 1 goes here.
<a href="#Menu"><font size="2" color="red">
    (back to menu)</font></a><br>
<p> </p>
<p> </p>
<p> </p>
<p> </p>
<p> </p>
<p> </p>
<p> </p>
<p> </p>
<p> </p>
<p> </p>

<a name="Bookmark2">
<h2>Section 2</h2></a>
Content for Section 2 goes here.
<a href="#Menu"><font size="2" color="red">
    (back to menu)</font></a><br>
<p> </p>
<p> </p>
<p> </p>
<p> </p>
<p> </p>
<p> </p>
<p> </p>
<p> </p>
<p> </p>
<p> </p>
<p> </p>
<p> </p>
<p> </p>
<p> </p>
<p> </p>
<a name="Bookmark3">
<h2>Section 3</h2></a>
Content for Section 3 goes here.
<a href="#Menu"><font size="2" color="red">
    (back to menu)</font></a><br>
```

```
<p> </p>
<p> </p>
<p> </p>
<p> </p>
<p> </p>
<p> </p>
<p> </p>
<p> </p>
<p> </p>
<p> </p>
<p> </p>
<p> </p>
<p> </p>
<p> </p>
<p> </p>
<p> </p>
<p> </p>
<p> </p>
<a name="Bookmark4">
<h2>Section 4</h2></a>
Content for Section 4 goes here.
<a href="#Menu"><font size="2" color="red">
    (back to menu)</font></a><br>
<p> </p>
<p> </p>
<p> </p>
<p> </p>
<p> </p>
<p> </p>
<p> </p>
<p> </p>
<p> </p>
<p> </p>
<p> </p>
<p> </p>
<p> </p>
<p> </p>
<p> </p>
<p> </p>
<p> </p>
<p> </p>
<p> </p>
</body>
</html>
```

So that you can see a different style, Listing 2.6 contains a multiple-choice question formatted as a set of short linked pages.

LISTING 2.6: A SET OF LINKED PAGES (ch2-13a.htm–ch2-13e.htm)

```
<!--*******************************************************
* This file (ch2-13a) contains the multiple-choice       *
* question. Each distractor is a link to another page    *
* that contains the feedback for that distractor.        *
*********************************************************-->
<html>
<head>
<title></title>
</head>
<body>

<p>Which of the following is <EM>not</EM> a valid anchor
tag type?</p>
<ol>
  <li><a href="ch2-13b.htm">A link to another document.</a>
  <li><a href="ch2-13c.htm">A link to a specific position in
  a document.</a>
  <li><a href="ch2-13d.htm">A link to a previous
  document.</a>
  <li><a href="ch2-13e.htm">A link to the Back button on the
  browser.</a>          </li></ol>
<p>Click on your answer.</p>

</body>
</html>
<!-- *******************************************************
* This file (ch2-13b) contains the feedback for the      *
* first (incorrect) distractor.                          *
*********************************************************-->
<html>
<head>
<title></title>
</head>
<body>

<p>Incorrect.</p>
<p>You selected: "1. A link to another document." That is a valid tag type.
Click <a href="ch2-13a.htm">continue</a> to try again.</p>

</body>
</html>
<!--*******************************************************
* This file (ch2-13c) contains the feedback for the      *
```

```
* second (incorrect) distractor.                          *
**********************************************************-->
<html>
<head>
<title></title>
</head>
<body>

<p>Incorrect.</p>
<p>You selected: "2. A link to a specific position in a document." That is a valid
tag type.
Click <a href="ch2-13a.htm">continue</a> to try again.</p>

</body>
</html>
<!--**********************************************************
* This file (ch2-13c) contains the feedback for the       *
* third (incorrect) distractor.                           *
**********************************************************-->
<html>
<head>
<title></title>
</head>
<body>

<p>Incorrect.</p>
<p>You selected: "3. A link to a previous document."
   That is a valid tag type.
Click <a href="ch2-13a.htm">continue</a> to try again.</p>

</body>
</html>
<!--**********************************************************
* This file (ch2-13c) contains the feedback for the       *
* fourth (correct) distractor.                            *
**********************************************************-->
<html>
<head>
<title></title>
</head>
<body>

<p>Correct.</p>
<p>You selected: "4. A link to the Back button on the browser."
   That is not a valid tag type.
</body>
</html>
```

If you look at this set of pages in a browser, you'll see the question first (see Figure 2.13).

FIGURE 2.13

Multiple-choice
question screen
(`ch2-13a.htm`)

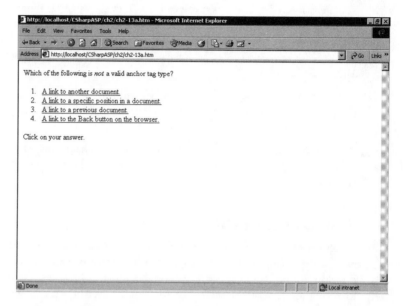

As you click each distractor, you'll see pages similar to Figure 2.14. I won't show them all, because you can download the code and view them in your browser. Figure 2.14 shows what happens if you select the first distractor.

FIGURE 2.14

Feedback for a
multiple-choice
question

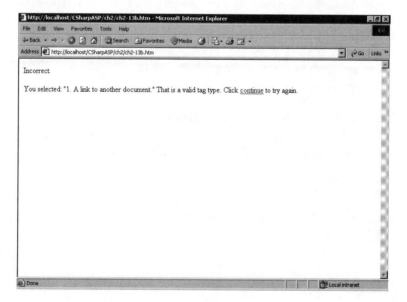

Anchor Tags and Images

You aren't limited to text links; you can use an image as a link source as well. For example, you could replace simple text links with custom icons for navigation. Users would click on a home icon rather than the word "home." You can make pages look much better with custom graphics for links than they do with text links. To create a hypertext link using an image, you simply surround the image tag with an anchor tag:

```
<a href="http://myserver/mysite/mypage.htm">
   <img src="http://myserver/mysite/home.gif" border=0>
</a>
```

By default, the browser places a border around clickable images. The border color inherits the link colors for the page. If you don't want the border, use the `border=0` attribute as shown in the previous example.

Formatting Tables

Tables consist of rows and columns. Because the browser ignores white space, which includes tabs, you usually use tables in HTML to display any items that you must separate with white space. Note that this does not necessarily apply to version 4 and higher browsers—you can use absolute positioning to force items to appear at specific pixel locations. Nevertheless, even with modern browsers, tables are useful for more than displaying columnar data.

The `<table>` tag contains several other tags that serve to delimit the columns and rows. Tables may have three sections—a header, a body, and a footer. The header and footer rows are "fixed" rows—they're not supposed to scroll (although they do in most browsers). The header and footer are optional; you don't have to include them to have a valid table. If you do include either a header or a footer, then you also need to include the body section. Tables may also have a `<caption>` tag. The browser formats the caption above the first row. Border settings for the table don't apply to the caption.

In addition, tables in IE can contain `<colgroup>` and `<col>` tags that can help simplify table formatting. The `<colgroup>` tag defines a set of columns, and the `<col>` tag defines an individual column within the column group.

Table, Table Row, Table Data Tags

Tables begin with a `<table>` tag. You delimit each row with a table row (`<tr>`) tag and each column with a table data (`<td>`) tag. The following HTML describes a simple two-row, two-column table:

```
<table>
   <tr>
      <td>
         Row 1, Col 1
      </td>
      <td>
         Row 1, Col 2
      </td>
   </tr>
   <tr>
```

```
        <td>
            Row 2, Col 1
        </td>
        <td>
            Row 2, Col 2
        </td>
    </tr>
</table>
```

WARNING *Be very careful to close all the table tags. Some browsers, such as IE, will close the tags for you and the table will be displayed properly, but others will not, and the table will not be displayed at all or will be displayed incorrectly. Microsoft's documentation states that the end tags are optional for most table elements, but the end tags are optional only if the rendering engine is IE. The rule is this: Don't rely on the rendering engine to close the tags for you; explicitly close all tags.*

As you can see from the previous code snippet, a table can contain an arbitrary number of rows, and each row may contain an arbitrary number of columns.

If you place the previous code snippet in a standard HTML template wrapper and view it in a browser, it's not particularly appealing—it looks like two tabbed columns (see Figure 2.15).

FIGURE 2.15

Simple HTML table
(ch2-14.htm)

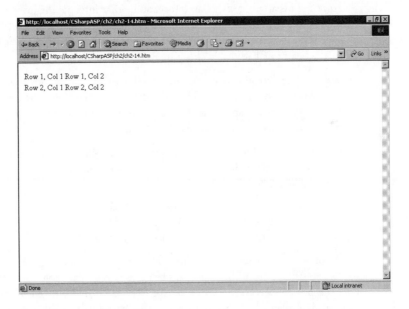

Fortunately, you can add attributes to the table tag to control its placement and improve its appearance. Attribute values for the table tag apply to all the columns and cells of the table unless you override them with attribute values for individual columns, rows, or cells. The following list contains the most common attribute values; you can find the rest in Appendix A.

align This attribute can take one of three values: left, right, or center. It controls the horizontal placement of the table on the page.

background   This attribute, like the `background` attribute for the `<body>` tag, accepts a URL that references an image file. The browser displays the image with a z-order of zero, so all the table data plots on top of the background image.

bgcolor   This attribute takes an HTML color value that controls the background color of the entire table. You can override the `bgcolor` value for any individual row or cell.

border   This attribute takes an integer value that controls the width of the border around the table and around each individual cell. The default value is zero: no border.

cellpadding   This attribute takes an integer value that controls the spacing between the contents of a cell and its border.

cellspacing   This attribute takes an integer value that controls the spacing between cells.

cols   This attribute specifies the number of columns in a table. It significantly increases the speed at which the browser renders a table. Without this attribute, the browser must parse the entire table to determine the maximum number of columns in a row, but with this attribute, the browser can begin rendering rows immediately.

height   This attribute takes an integer value that informs the browser of the final height of the area required to render the table. Like the `cols` attribute, including the height significantly increases the speed at which the browser renders a table. You may specify the height in pixels or as a percentage of the height of the visible client area.

width   This attribute takes an integer value that informs the browser of the final width of the area required to render the table. Like the `cols` and `height` attributes, including the `width` significantly increases the speed at which the browser renders a table. You may specify the width in pixels or as a percentage of the width of the visible client area.

If you take the table from the example at the beginning of this section, align it in the center of the page, specify the width and height, apply a caption, add a border, and pad the cells, the first two lines of the listing will look like this:

```
<table border="1" align="center" cellpadding="3"
   cellspacing="2" width="60%" height="80%">
<caption>Simple Table With Formatting</caption>
```

If you look at the altered table in a browser, it looks like Figure 2.16.

As you can see from the example, `<tr>` tags specify the table rows. You can use the `align` and `bgcolor` attributes with the `<tr>` tag. The `<tr>` tag can also take a `valign` attribute that controls the vertical alignment of the cell contents in that row. The possible values are `baseline`, `bottom`, `center`, and `top`.

FIGURE 2.16

Simple table
with borders
(`ch2-15.htm`)

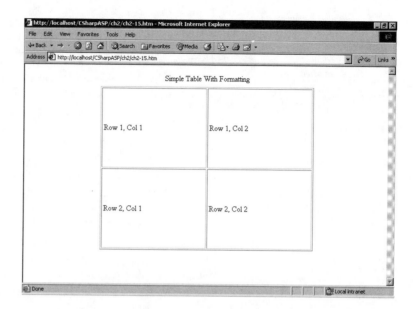

The `<td>` tag accepts `align`, `background`, `bgcolor`, and `valign` attributes. In addition, the `<td>` tag can take `colspan` and `rowspan` attributes. The values for `colspan` and `rowspan` are integers. They specify the number of columns and rows over which the cell extends. You need these attributes when you have a table in which rows contain differing numbers of columns. For example, if you wanted to add a third row to the table in Figure 2.16 that contained only one column or wanted to add a cell that was twice the height of the cells in other rows, you could specify the cells as follows:

```
<tr>
   <td colspan="2" align="center" valign="center">
      This is a double-width cell with centered contents.
   </td>
</tr>
<tr>
   <td rowspan="2" width="50%" align="center" valign="center">
      This is a double-height cell with centered contents.
   </td>
   <td width="50%" >Normal-height cell</td>
</tr>
<tr>
   <td width="50%" >Normal-height cell</td>
</tr>
```

After adding the new rows, the table looks like Figure 2.17.

FIGURE 2.17

Table using `colspan` and `rowspan` attributes (`ch2-16.htm`)

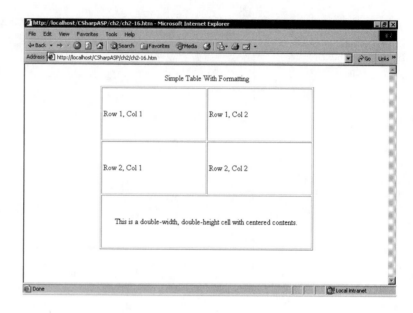

Table Header, Table Footer Tags

You can separate a table into three main functional parts—a header section, one or more body sections, and a footer section. The primary purpose of the header and footer sections is to duplicate th header and footer on each page when the user prints multipage tables. For tables without borders, you can separate sections in the body of the table with horizontal lines by placing the content into multiple body sections. You may have only one header and one footer section in a table.

To define the header section, use a `<thead>` tag. You may have multiple rows within the header section. You can also automatically format the header cells with bold text by using table header (`<th>`) tags in the header section rather than table data (`<td>`) tags.

You may have multiple table body (`<tbody>`) tags in a table. Each `<tbody>` tag defines one section of the table body. By default, a table has a table body section even if you don't define one explicitly. The browser separates multiple table body sections with horizontal lines.

You define the footer section with the table footer (`<tfoot>`) tag. The footer section may contain multiple rows. There's no corresponding `<tf>` tag for footer sections to parallel the `<th>` tag for the header section. However, you may use `<th>` tags in the footer section in place of the `<td>` tags just as you would in the header section to format the footer row(s) in bold text.

Using Tables for Layout

Because the browser normally renders and places content according to its internal rules, you don't have fine control over where a specific item will appear. In the more recent browsers (version 4 and higher), you can use absolute positioning to force items to plot at specific locations. In earlier browser (versions 3 and lower) as well as some less popular browsers, you still need to use tables to align and position items on the screen.

A second—and I think for most purposes, more important—reason to use tables for layout, even in modern browsers, is that you can specify table and cell widths in percentages rather than in pixels. It's important because several different common screen resolutions are in use: VGA (640 × 480), Super VGA (800 × 600), and XGA (1280 × 768). For example, adding a `width=60%` attribute to a table tag tells the browser to render the table at 60 percent of the width of the client area *regardless of the screen resolution* on the client computer. Sure, your text will wrap differently at different screen resolutions, but you know approximately how the page will look to different users because the table will take up the same percentage of screen real estate whether the user is running a VGA or an XGA display. In contrast, using pixel-based positioning sets the position of items without regard to the width and height of the screen.

Here's an example. Suppose I wanted to add custom numbered images instead of the numbers for the distractors in the multiple-choice question example in Listing 2.6, but I still wanted people to be able to click on the text of each distractor to answer the question. I could use two links rather than a single, all-text link. The first anchor tag would surround the custom image for each distractor. The second anchor tag would surround the text of the distractor. Both links would navigate to the same page. I would change the first page as follows:

```
<html>
<head>
<title></title>
</head>
<body>

<p>Which of the following is <EM>not</EM> a valid anchor
tag type?</p>
<a href="ch2-13b.htm"><IMG SRC="images/1.gif" border="0"></a>
<a href="ch2-13b.htm">A link to another document.</a><br>
<a href="ch2-13c.htm"><IMG SRC="images/2.gif" border="0"></a>
<a href="ch2-13c.htm">A link to a specific position in
  a document.</a><br>
<a href="ch2-13d.htm"><IMG SRC="images/3.gif" border="0"></a>
<a href="ch2-13d.htm">A link to a previous document.</a><br>
<a href="ch2-13e.htm"><IMG SRC="images/4.gif" border="0"></a>
<a href="ch2-13e.htm">A link to the Back button on the
  browser.</a><br>

<p>Click on your answer.</p>

</body>
</html>
```

Using Image Maps

An *image map* is similar to an image link except that you can define one or more clickable areas on the image. The clickable areas "map" to a bookmark or URL. For example, a map of the United States might show the outlines of each state, and each state would be a link to a different location. To create the complete image map with individual state images, you would need to create each image, then place the images on the page using absolute positioning so the images would align properly with each other. Alternately (and much simpler), you could use a single image and define the clickable areas for the states along the state boundary lines.

There are two kinds of image maps: server-side maps and client-side maps. *Server-side image maps* tell the browser that when a user clicks the image, the browser should send the coordinates of the clicked point to the server. A program (such as an ASP page) on the server must determine whether the coordinates are in a valid clickable area and, if so, hyperlink to the appropriate page. Server-side image maps were the only type of image maps available until version 3.*x* browsers appeared. Server-side image maps are still useful when you want to partition an image into many rectangular areas with script, or when your clients may be using older browsers. However, each click by the user forces the browser to send information to the server for processing, so server-side image maps are normally an inefficient use of resources.

NOTE   *You won't work with server-side image maps in this section, only client-side image maps. I'll return to server-side image maps later, when you work with the* **Request** *object in Part II.*

Client-side image maps define the clickable areas of the image and the URL associated with each area in client-side HTML. The client shoulders the burden of processing user mouse clicks, thus avoiding the round trip to the server generated by server-side image maps.

How Image Maps Work

To a computer, a screen is like a table with a single pixel in each cell. Each pixel has a column number and a row number. The first pixel is in the top-left corner of the screen in column 0, row 0. Usually, you specify pixels with two integer values separated by a comma; for example, 0, 0, or 100, 100. Another way of thinking about the computer screen, for those of you who remember plotting graphs in math class, is as an x-y grid. The column number of each pixel (the first number) is the x-axis value, and the row number (the second number) is the y-axis value. Any points you plot appear in quadrant 4, the area below the x-axis and to the right of the y-axis.

You use the same method to refer to pixels within an image rendered on a screen, except that the pixel locations are defined as offsets from the top-left corner of the image, not the top-left corner of the screen. So if you have a square image, 100 pixels on a side, and you plot that image at location 100, 100 on the computer screen, the actual top-left corner pixel of the image is 100, 100, but you would refer to pixels *within* the image as if that same pixel's location were 0, 0—the first row and first column of the image itself.

You can define any rectangle using the top-left corner and the bottom-right corner of the rectangle. I'll separate the individual pixel definitions with semicolons for clarity. For example, the rectangle covered by that image is 100, 100; 199, 199. From those two pixels, you can infer that the corners of the rectangle are top-left 100, 100, top-right 199, 100, bottom-right 199, 199, and bottom-left 100, 199.

If you were to divide that 100-pixel square image into four areas, you would define them as rectangles—in this case, squares—each 50 pixels per side. The points you would use are offsets from the top-left corner of the image. So, moving clockwise starting at the top-left corner, the first rectangle would be 0, 0; 49, 49, the second, 51, 0; 100, 49, the third, 51, 49; 99, 99, and the last, 0, 50; 49, 99.

You aren't limited to rectangles; you can also define circular areas and polygons. As you can imagine, figuring out the actual pixel values for rounded shapes or irregular polygons is rather difficult. Fortunately, you rarely have to calculate the values yourself. There are several image map editors available that let you trace or draw the borders of the mapped areas visually.

Creating Client-Side Image Maps

You create a client-side image map with the <map> tag. For example, Listing 2.7 shows the HTML to create the client-side image map described in the previous section—a square image divided into four equal-sized smaller squares, each of which is a hyperlink to a different document or bookmark.

LISTING 2.7: CLIENT-SIDE IMAGE MAP EXAMPLE (ch2-19a.htm)

```
<html>
<head>
<title>Client-Side Image Map</title>
</head>
<body>
<map name="fourSquares">
    <area shape=rect coords="0, 0, 49, 49"
          href="ch2-19b.htm#upperLeft" border="0">
    <area shape=rect coords="51, 0, 100, 49"
          href="ch2-19b.htm#upperRight" border="0">
    <area shape=rect coords="51, 49, 99, 99"
          href="ch2-19b.htm#lowerRight" border="0">
    <area shape=rect coords="0, 50, 49, 99"
          href="ch2-19b.htm#lowerLeft" border="0">
</map>
<IMG SRC="images/bluesquare.gif" usemap="#fourSquares" border=0>
</body>
</html>
```

The <map> tag is a named block element that contains a set of <area> tags, each of which defines a clickable area of the image. The map tag itself does not have to be in the same file as the <img> tag that uses the map coordinates. Using the United States map example, you could define the <map> tag containing the clickable areas for the states in one file, then reference that file from multiple pages, each of which might contain the same image map. That way, if you wanted to change one of the clickable areas, you would have to change only the file containing the image map definition.

The <area> tag defines the target URL for the link and the coordinates for the clickable region(s) of the image. You may create multiple <area> tags for a given image. Each <area> tag must have a shape attribute and a coords attribute containing the appropriate coordinates as a comma-delimited string. The shape attribute has three possible values:

- circ or circle
- poly or polygon
- rect or rectangle

When the shape attribute value is `circ` or `circle`, the coords attribute requires three values: the x and y coordinates of the center point and the radius. When the shape attribute value is `poly` or `polygon`, the coords attribute value is a list of x and y coordinates that define the polygon. When the shape attribute is `rect` or `rectangle`, the coords attribute value contains the x and y coordinates of the top-left and bottom-right corners of the rectangle.

Tools for Creating Image Maps

Several commercial-quality tools exist for creating image maps, and they all work similarly. You load an image into a map editor, then draw a rectangle, circle, or polygon over the image hotspots. The image map editing software outputs the HTML for the image map, sometimes just the map definition, but more often the link tags and the map definition.

Even if you only need to create simple rectangular hotspots on your images, image map tools can save you a significant amount of time.

Here are three popular resources; others are probably equally capable. Note that none of these solutions is free, and I don't recommend one over another. You can download MapEdit and JImageMap from many shareware sites on the Internet.

◆ Microsoft FrontPage 98 or FrontPage 2000

◆ MapEdit (shareware)

◆ JImageMap (Java solution)

Understanding Frames

To understand frames, you need to go back in time to the beginning of Windows itself. A window is an area of memory that contains a bitmap—a rectangular area of pixels. Each program "owns" one or more windows, and each window is either a top-level window or a child window. All windows are children of the desktop window—which you can think of as the screen itself.

For example, open up any program in Windows and look at the screen. You'll see a title bar, a window frame, and a client area. You may see additional items, such as a toolbar with buttons and other controls, and a status bar. Each of these items is a separate window. Each has specific properties, such as a height and width, and a background color. Now think about your screen if you open up multiple windows. If you think of the programs you open as items in a stack, one window is always on top. The z-order value controls the position of each window in that stack. The window on top (the active window) has a z-order of 0. All other windows appear behind the active window and have higher z-order values. Unless you maximize all the windows, each window probably appears in a slightly different position on-screen, meaning that each window has its own rectangle.

The programs' main windows are top-level windows. Each item, such as a toolbar button, is a child window. The child windows, although they are complete windows in their own right, appear and disappear with their parent window. If you minimize the program window, all the child windows disappear from the screen as well.

In the browser, you define child windows using a concept called *frames*. Frames are a sub-area of the main window, but you treat each frame as if it were a completely separate browser. Each frame can navigate independently to a page. To the computer, each frame is a child window with most of the capabilities of a stand-alone browser except that each frame is subservient to the top-level browser window. Frames must plot in the top-level browser window's screen area, and they minimize when you minimize the top-level window. You can think of frames as an easy way to divide the browser window into separate windows of varying sizes.

Frames can't exist by themselves—you must define them using a concept called a *frameset*. A frameset must be defined in its own page—you can't define a frameset and put content (other than a `<noframes>` tag) within a single HTML file; however, you may define more than one frameset in a single page. A frameset isn't visible—it's a containing tag for frames. A frameset contains one or more frames or framesets. The frames themselves are usually visible, although there are some good uses for invisible frames. For example, you can use invisible frames containing client-side script to control other frames on the page. You use the `<frameset>` tag to define a frameset and the `<frame>` tag to define a frame. For example, to create a frameset that divides the browser client area into two equal-sized frames, you would write a `<frameset>` tag as follows:

```
<frameset rows="50%, *">
    <frame name="topFrame" src="top_1.htm">
    <frame name="bottomFrame" src="bottom_1.htm">
</frameset>
```

For browsers that don't support frames (rare these days), you can add a `<noframes>` tag.

```
<frameset rows="50%, *">
    <frame name="topFrame" src="top_1.htm">
    <frame name="bottomFrame" src="bottom_1.htm">
    <NOFRAMES>You need a frames-enabled browser to view
        this site!</NOFRAMES>
</frameset>
```

Browsers that support frames ignore the `<noframes>` tag. Other browsers will display the text of the `<noframes>` tag, because it's the only HTML content in the file that does *not* appear between tags—remember that browsers ignore tags they don't support.

You define the sizes of the frames in pixels or in percentages. Note that you can use an asterisk in place of a value to define the last frame as "all the rest of the available area." In other words, I could have defined the frames as `rows="50%, 50%"`, and the results would be identical. The asterisk notation is particularly useful when you are defining frames in pixels. Often, you don't know the width of the browser screen, so it's difficult to define the last frame exactly. For example, suppose I want to divide the screen vertically into two frames. The left frame will contain a list of links, and I want it to be 200 pixels wide. I want to display content in the right frame—but I don't know whether the remaining available area is 440 pixels wide (VGA), 600 pixels wide (Super VGA), or 1,080 pixels wide (XGA). Therefore, I could define the frameset using the asterisk, as follows:

```
<frameset cols="200, *">
    <frame name="leftFrame" src="left_1.htm">
    <frame name="rightFrame" src="right_1.htm">
</frameset>
```

You can't use both the rows and the cols attributes within the same frameset, but you can nest framesets to accomplish the same result. For example, the following code defines a frameset with the screen divided vertically into two equal-sized frames. The frameset contains a second frameset that further divides the right frame horizontally into two equal-sized frames (see Listing 2.8).

LISTING 2.8: NESTED FRAMESETS (ch2-18a.htm-ch2-18d.htm)

```
**************************************************************
* This file (ch2-18b) contains the frameset definitions  *
**************************************************************
<html>
<head><title>Nested Framesets</title></head>
<frameset cols="50%, *">
   <frame name="leftFrame" src="ch2-18b.htm">
   <frameset rows="50%, *">
      <frame name="rightTopFrame" src="ch2-18c.htm">
      <frame name="rightBottomFrame" src="ch2-18d.htm">
   </frameset>
               <noframes>You need a frames-enabled browser to
                  view this page.</noframes>
</frameset>
</html>


**************************************************************
* This file (ch2-18b.htm) shows up in the left-hand       *
* frame. The other files (ch2-18c and ch2-18d.htm) are    *
* identical except for the title and text                 *
**************************************************************
<html>
<head><title>ch2-18b.htm</title></head>
<body>
   This is ch2-18b.htm
</body>
</html>
```

In the browser, Listing 2.8 looks like Figure 2.18.

FIGURE 2.18

Nested framesets
(`ch2-18a.htm`–
`ch2-18d.htm`)

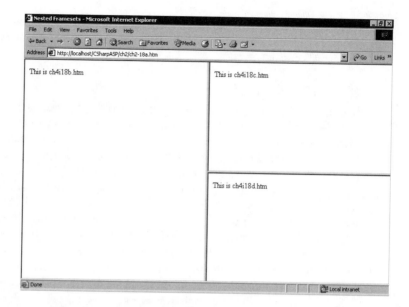

Advantages and Disadvantages of Frames

The primary advantages of frames are that they display content independently and can separate content visually. You can define a link in one frame that displays content or triggers an action in another frame without redrawing the entire screen.

Another, less important advantage of frames is that you can create resizable frames. A user can drag the frame border(s) to increase or decrease the viewing area covered by the frame. This feature can be useful. The easiest way to see it in action (if you're using IE) is to click the Search button on your browser's toolbar and perform a search. You can drag the right border of the Search frame to change the relative sizes of the search and the content windows.

The primary disadvantage of frames is that they are more difficult to create and control. To create the two-frame screen from the previous listing, you must create three pages: one that contains the frameset definition and one page for each of the frames.

Another disadvantage of frames is that they take longer to display. The browser's request for the frameset page requires one round trip to the server. The content for each of the frames requires at least one additional round trip. Consequently, displaying content in two frames can take up to three times as long as displaying the same content in a single page without frames.

Finally, frames often require some client-side programming in JavaScript or, if you have only IE users, VBScript. For example, if a user clicks a link in one frame that refers to an object—such as a button or link—in another frame, you must ensure that the target object actually exists, or the user will receive a script error message. The object won't exist until its page has been loaded. User actions while pages are still loading are a common cause of script errors. Because the primary reason to use frames is to have actions in one frame refer to objects or actions in another frame; this type of problem is ubiquitous.

I'm not going to spend a huge amount of time on client-side programming in this book, because it's primarily about server-side programming. However, I can tell you that it's more difficult to debug frames-based JavaScript than it is to debug server-side C# code. Despite the problems I've listed, if you're already comfortable with client-side scripting, frames can be an extremely powerful tool for organizing content.

How to Avoid Frames

If you don't use frames, you do have to repeat unchanging information—like a list of navigational links—on each page. Most servers have a mechanism for doing that; in IIS, you can use *include files* to place the content on each page. An include file is exactly what it sounds like—a reference to another file that the server "includes" with the response. The server replaces the include directive with the contents of the include file. For example, if you wanted to place a copyright notice at the bottom of every page, you could create an include file that contained the HTML for the copyright notice. You would place an include directive referencing your footer file on each content page. The server would include the HTML for the footer in the response. To the browser, the response appears just as if you had explicitly written the HTML for the footer into each page. In other words, the browser doesn't care (and doesn't know) whether the response contains HTML from one file or 100 different files as long as the response contains valid HTML.

In concert with include files, you can use tables to arrange elements in specific areas on the screen. Before absolute positioning of on-screen elements became possible in browsers, tables were the most common way to arrange content.

Controlling Element Position

There are two methods for positioning content on the screen. The first method uses absolute positioning with Cascading Style Sheet (CSS) styles and is by far the easiest method. Even though I haven't introduced you to CSS yet (described in the section "Cascading Style Sheets," later in this chapter), I promise that this technique is simple enough that you won't need much CSS knowledge to use it. The second method uses a mixture of tables and transparent images. I'll address each method individually.

WARNING   *The absolute positioning technique works only with browsers that can use CSS styles.*

Controlling Element Position with CSS Styles

First, a warning: Absolute positioning works only in version 4 and higher browsers and, unfortunately, the syntax and approach for Netscape and IE browsers is slightly different. Netscape 6 and IE 5.*x* are both considerably more compliant with the CSS specification than earlier browsers, although there are still some differences. IE treats each element on the screen—every paragraph, button, font tag—*every* HTML tag as an object. Therefore, each tag that you've seen so far can take several other attributes in addition to the ones I've listed. One such attribute is a style attribute. There are multiple values for styles. In this section, we're concerned with only the `position:absolute` value.

To position an object in IE, you add the `style` attribute, set the position to `absolute`, and specify the pixel location where you want the top-left corner of the object to appear. For example, to display an image at the point 50, 50, you would write the image tag as follows:

```
<img src="image/bike.gif" style="position:absolute; left:50; top:50">
```

This type of style usage is called an "inline" style, because you specify it inside the tag—in other words, in the line with the code. The value of the `style` attribute, like all attribute values, is a string. Within the string, you can specify multiple style settings. You separate the settings from each other with semicolons, and you separate the setting values from the setting names with colons. In this example, the words "Hello World" plot at the point 100, 100.

```
<div style="position:absolute; left:100 top:100">Hello World</div>
```

Controlling the Z-Order Position

Using styles, you can also control the z-order position of an element. All visible elements in a browser have a z-order value. Elements with higher values appear above elements with lower values. In standard HTML, the position of an element in the HTML stream determines its z-order position. In other words, elements toward the end of the HTML stream will appear above elements earlier in the stream. CSS supports a `z-index` attribute that controls the relative z-order position of each element. For example, to plot the text "Hello World" on top of the bike image element, you can write a page such as that seen in Listing 2.9.

LISTING 2.9: CONTROLLING THE Z-ORDER POSITION (ch2-20.htm)

```
<HTML>
<HEAD>
<TITLE></TITLE>
</HEAD>
<BODY>
<div style="position:absolute; left:100; top:100; z-index:0">
    <img src="images/bike.gif" border=1>
</div>
<div style="position:absolute; left:100; top:100; z-index:1">
    <b><font size="5" color="blue">Hello World</font></b>
</div>
</BODY>
</HTML>
```

The `z-index` value of 1 forces the browser to plot the text on top of the image, which has a `z-index` value of 0. Now, you may not be impressed, but I sure was when I saw this for the first time, because until that point, you had to use table cell background images to plot text on top of an image.

CSS styles support *relative* positioning as well, in which the browser determines an element's position relative to the position of its parent. You can express both absolute and relative positions in either pixels or percentages, using either positive or negative values. I'm a big fan of using percentages to specify positions whenever possible. If you use percentages, you isolate your page elements from dependence on the client's screen resolution. Also, the positions of display elements remain constant relative to the screen, even when the browser changes size.

For example, in Listing 2.10, the `<span>` tag containing the text "I'm Here!" plots above and to the left of its parent `<div>` tag.

LISTING 2.10: ABSOLUTE AND RELATIVE POSITIONING (ch2-21.htm)

```html
<html>
<head>
<title></title>
</head>
<body>
<div style="position:absolute; left:100; top:100; z-index:0">
   <img src="images/bike.gif" border="1" WIDTH="227" HEIGHT="179">
</div>
<div style="position:absolute; left:100; top:100; z-index:1">
   <b><font size="5" color="blue">Hello World</font></b>
   <span style="position:relative; left:-100%; top:-100%;
      z-index:2"><b><font size="5" color="red">
      I'm Here!</font></b></span>
</div>
</body>
</html>
```

Figure 2.19 shows how Listing 2.10 plots in a browser.

FIGURE 2.19

Absolute and relative
positioning
(`ch2-21.htm`)

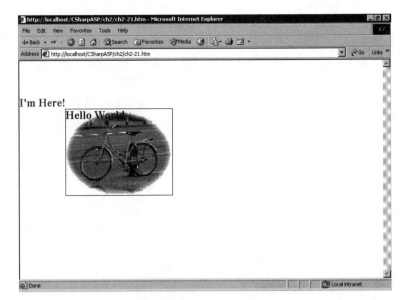

Controlling Element Position with Tables

You can accomplish similar results by using tables, although it's much more time-consuming and not as accurate. By varying the width and height of the table cells, you can place elements more or less where you want them to appear on the screen. For example, to place a graphic at the point 100, 100, you can create a table with two columns, no border, and four cells. By assigning the top-left cell a width and height of 99, you can be sure that the bottom-right cell area will start at 100, 100.

```
<table cols="2">
   <tr>
      <td width="99" height="99">
          
      </td>
      <td>
          
      </td>
   </tr>
   <tr>
      <td width="99" height="99">
          
      </td>
      <td>
         <img src="images/bike.gif" border="1"
            WIDTH="227" HEIGHT="179">
      </td>
   </tr>
</table>
```

I can place text on top of an image by setting the `background` attribute of the cell to the image. The browser will then place text content on top of the background image. Figure 2.20 shows the results. I've added borders to the table and some text to the top-left cell for clarity.

FIGURE 2.20

Controlling element
position with tables
(`ch2-22.htm`)

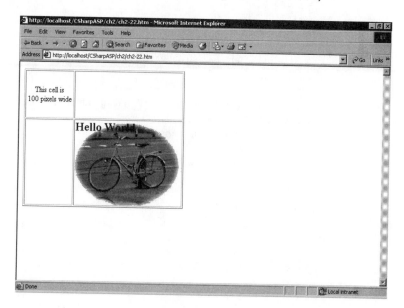

Controlling Element Position with Transparent Images

You are limited in the placement of text using the cell background image method. You may only assign the positions allowed by the align and valign attribute values of the <td> tag: left, right, center, and top, bottom, center, respectively. However, you can use a trick to place elements even more precisely.

Remember that you can control the width and height of an image using the width and height attributes of the <img> tag. That feature means that you can use a 1-pixel-wide image and size it to any width or height on the client. Thus, you can use a transparent image to force other content to plot either to the right or below it. Listing 2.11 shows the technique. I've changed the text color to white so it will show up more clearly on top of the image.

LISTING 2.11: CONTROLLING ELEMENT POSITION WITH TRANSPARENT IMAGES (ch2-23.htm)

```html
<html>
<head>
<title></title>
</head>
<body>
<table border="1" cols="2">
   <tr>
      <td align="center" valign="center" width="99"
         height="99">
         This cell is <br>100 pixels wide
      </td>
      <td>
          
      </td>
   </tr>
   <tr>
      <td width="99" height="99">
          
      </td>
      <td align="left" valign="top" background="images/bike.gif"
         WIDTH="227" HEIGHT="179">
         <img src="images/transparent.gif" width="50"
            height="50">
         <b><font color="white" size="5">Hello World</font></b>
      </td>
   </tr>
</table>
</body>
</html>
```

Cascading Style Sheets

Cascading Style Sheets (CSS) is too large a subject to cover in any reasonable depth here, so I'm just going to briefly cover the basics in this section and, hopefully, whet your appetite for more knowledge. Once you know the basics, you can use a CSS reference to improve your facility with CSS styles.

CSS evolved from the need to control the look of elements globally in a site or multiple sites. For example, if your company's marketing department decides that all public documents must use the Garamond font for standard text, how can you make the changes easily and ensure that you have changed all of the text? One way is to search every document for text content, then apply a <font> tag specifying the Garamond font for each occurrence—but that's terribly time-consuming and error-prone. It would be better if you could specify how an element appears once; changes to the specification would then "cascade" down to each occurrence.

What Cascading Style Sheets Do

CSS technology allows you to make global changes such as those described in the previous section much more easily. A Cascading Style Sheet defines attributes for element types. The style sheet definitions appear inside a <style> tag—usually placed in the <head> section of the document. This type of style definition is an *embedded* style sheet, because it's embedded into the document. CSS styles include the following capabilities:

- You can define styles that apply to all instances of an element type.

- Child elements "inherit" the style assigned to their parent.

- You can override the inherited style using other style sheets or inline styles.

- You can reference style sheets—the style definitions don't have to exist in each document.

For example, you can alter the font for all text in a document by defining a CSS style for the <body> tag:

```
<style type="text/CSS">
    body {font: 12pt Garamond;}
</style>
```

The style contains one *selector*, body, and one *rule*, {font: 12pt Garamond;}. The rule specifies that text in the selector will appear in 12-point Garamond. A document that contains this rule will render all text in the Garamond font.

Controlling Appearance with Styles

To see CSS in action, type or copy the code from Listing 2.12 into a file, save it, then open the file in your browser. Note that the text appears in your browser's default font—you'll change that in a minute.

LISTING 2.12: CASCADING STYLE SHEET EXAMPLE (ch2-24.htm)

```
<html>
<head>
<title>Cascading Style Sheet Example</title>
<!--<style type="text/css">
   body {font: 14pt Garamond;}
</style>-->
</head>
<body>
<h1>Cascading Style Sheet Example</h1>
<h2>Look at the face and size of the following text</h2>
<p>This is a simple HTML file. In the head section of
this file, there's a Cascading Style Sheet. When the
&lt;style&gt; tag is commented out, the text in the
document appears in your browser's default font. When you
uncomment the &lt;style&gt; tag, the text appears in
14-point Garamond (if you have the Garamond font
installed on your computer).</p>
</body>
</html>
```

Now, reopen the file and remove the comment tag around the `<style>` tag. Save the file, and refresh your browser. You should see the screen change. Figures 2.21 and 2.22 show the difference between the file with no style sheet and the file viewed with the style sheet in effect. Both files use the code from Listing 2.12, but I uncommented the `<style>` tag to create Figure 2.22.

FIGURE 2.21

Text without style sheet applied (ch2-24.htm)

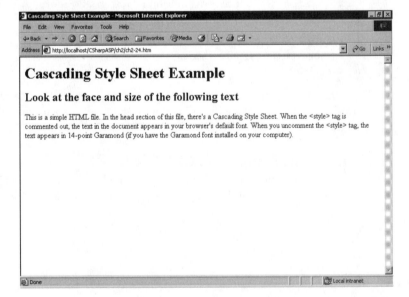

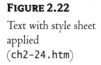

FIGURE 2.22

Text with style sheet applied
(`ch2-24.htm`)

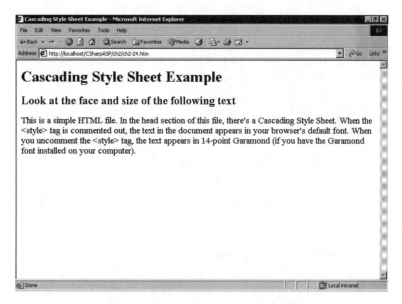

Types of CSS Styles

There are four types of CSS styles. You've seen two of them already, inline styles and embedded styles.

Inline Styles   Attributes of an element. You enter them using a `style="style definition"` attribute and value inside an element's tag.

Embedded styles   Are style tags embedded in the `<head>` section of a document.

Linked Styles   References to external style sheets. You enter them using a `<link>` tag in the `<head>` section of a document. The document containing the style sheet definition usually has an extension of `css`.

Imported Styles   External style sheets imported into an embedded or linked `<style>` tag. You import a style sheet using the `@import: url(someURL.css)` command syntax. The browser imports and processes imported style sheets rules *before* it processes rules that appear explicitly within the `<style>` tag.

The browser processes style rules in the order in which they appear, and rules that appear later take precedence over rules that appear earlier. Similarly, rules that apply specifically to an element take precedence over generic, inherited rules.

Overriding CSS Styles

It's nice to be able to define styles that apply globally to element types, but what about those instances when you don't want a global style to apply to a specific element? You can have multiple rules that apply to an element. Specific style rules override general style rules. For example, if you wanted the body text to appear in Garamond, but not the heading text, you could add a second rule to your `<style>` tag:

```
<style type="text/css">
    body {font: 14pt Garamond;}
    h1 {font: 24pt Arial;}
    h2 {font: 18pt Arial;}
</style>
```

You can always override styles defined in a `<style>` tag with inline style attributes. For example, suppose the following `<h1>` tag appeared in the same document as the `<style>` tag above:

```
<h1 style="font: 10pt Arial">
```

The heading would appear in 10-point Arial, because inline styles take precedence over more generic style rules.

Referencing External Style Sheets

You don't have to include the style sheet with each page; you can save the style sheet in a separate page and reference it from each file. Style sheets in other files are called *linked* or *external* style sheets. For example, the following `<link>` tag tells the browser to retrieve the style sheet definition from the file specified by the `href` attribute:

```
<link rel="stylesheet" type="text/css" href="mystyles.css">
```

You place the `<link>` tag in the head section of the document.

Another way to reference external style rules is to import them into an existing `<style>` tag. For example, suppose the following style rules exist in a document called `siteRules.css`.

```
<style type="text/css">
    body {font: 14pt Garamond;}
    h1 {font: 24pt Arial;}
    h2 {font: 18pt Arial;}
</style>
```

In your document, you can import the rules in the `siteRuless.css` file using an `@import` command inside the `<style>` tag:

```
<style type="text/css">
    @import: url(siteRules.css);
    li {font: 10pt Times New Roman;}
</style>
```

The effect of the preceding `<style>` tag is the same as if you had written the following:

```
<style type="text/css">
    body {font: 14pt Garamond;}
    h1 {font: 24pt Arial;}
    h2 {font: 18pt Arial;}
    li {font: 10pt Times New Roman;}
</style>
```

Using Classes in Style Sheets

In addition to defining styles for standard HTML elements, you can define your own styles by creating a selector name. Styles with selector names that you create are called *classes*, because you use them to subclass an element. The advantage of creating class styles is that you can apply them to any element using the `class` attribute. For example, if you create a style that turns the text red, you can easily apply it to any element in your document:

```
<style type="text/css">
    .redText {color:red;}
</style>
<p class="redText">
    This paragraph appears in red
</p>
<p>
    This paragraph appears in the default color
</p>
```

Control Hyperlink Appearance

In most static Web sites, the links change color when you click them, to show that you have visited that link destination. That behavior is not so desirable in applications, where a person may click the same link many times to accomplish a task. You can use CSS styles to control how your links behave. Links have three *pseudo-classes*, called `:link`, `:visited`, and `:active`. The `:link` pseudo-class controls how the link appears normally, when it's not either active (the user has clicked the mouse button on the link) or visited (the user has navigated to the link target). To keep visited links from changing color, set the same style for both the `:link` and `:visited` pseudo-classes:

```
<style type="text/css">
    a:link {color:blue}
    a:visited {color:blue}
</style>
```

Final Words about CSS Styles

You can do much more with CSS styles than just change fonts; however, you won't need advanced training in style sheets to work with the examples and projects in this book. Nevertheless, I urge you to begin learning and applying CSS styles now. As you build larger sites, CSS styles become increasingly important for controlling and modifying the look and feel of your pages.

Summary

Despite the existence of increasingly robust and powerful HTML editors, we're still in an era where developers need to understand how to read, write, and modify raw HTML. This is particularly true as you begin working with dynamically generated HTML, where you can't always simply substitute a value into a predefined HTML template. For example, imagine you had an HTML report template that contained a fixed page header and footer. The middle of the page contains the report itself. Your job is to generate the report by querying a database and displaying the results in a table.

The HTML template would look something like this:

```
<html><head><title>***ReportTitle***, ***ReportDate***</title></head>
<body>
<!-- Fixed HTML that defines the page header goes here -->
<table width="90%" align="center">
***ReportBody***
</table>
<!-- Fixed HTML that defines the page footer goes here -->
</body></html>
```

As the developer, you're supposed to replace the ***ReportTitle*** and ***ReportDate*** placeholders with the title and date of the report and replace the ***ReportBody*** placeholder with HTML table rows containing the report content. You could load this template into an HTML editor but that won't help you, because you need to build the rows dynamically. You could ask the template developer to provide a sample row, but you would still need to extract the content and replicate it once for each table row in the report body. That means you're going to have to create the HTML with script.

This type of operation—merging templated HTML with dynamic content—forms the basis of dynamic Web applications. Beginning with the next chapter, you'll explore dynamic Web applications in detail. Most dynamic applications consist almost entirely of operations like this simple example. The longer you work with dynamic Web content, the more you'll appreciate how a substantial investment in learning CSS styles, absolute positioning, and DHTML can simplify your life. Until you're thoroughly conversant with these simple technologies, creating them with script—where an HTML editor is useless except to view the output—will be a tedious and painful task. Therefore, if you haven't worked seriously in the past with HTML, CSS, and DHTML, you should take the time now to build several pages from the ground up—without the help of your HTML editor.

Chapter 3

Brief Guide to Dynamic Web Applications

NOW THAT YOU HAVE had some practice building HTML pages, you should have some idea of where and why HTML is not sufficient for building applications. HTML is entirely sufficient for building informational pages, but it's lacking the one thing that makes an application interesting to users—interactivity. Applications respond to user actions and input. HTML files can respond to certain kinds of actions—for example, clicking a link or an area of an image—but that's the limit of interactivity in HTML. If you want to go beyond that and respond to user actions and input in more complex ways, you need a programming language. HTML is not a programming language; it's a formatting language.

In this chapter:

◆   What Is a Dynamic Web Application?

◆   What Is the Data and Where Is It?

◆   How Can You Retrieve the Data?

◆   How Do You Package the Data?

◆   What Is the User Interface?

There are two places to interact with a user viewing a Web page in a browser. You can interact with the data whenever the user changes pages; you do that with code running on the server, generally called *server-side* code. You can also interact with the user by placing code within the browser itself. That is *client-side* code. Unfortunately, you can't always write client- and server-side code in exactly the same language (yet) because some browsers support only one scripting language—JavaScript. In contrast, using classic ASP, developers wrote most server-side code in VBScript; now, with ASP.NET, most people will use C# or VB.NET. You do have one option to help unify both client-side and server-side code: JScript. Unfortunately, JScript is a "second-tier" language in the .NET framework, meaning you can *consume* most Net resources, but you can't *create* them all.

TIP   In the future, as the .NET framework becomes common on client machines, you will probably be able to use C# for Internet Explorer (IE)-only applications.

As you learn to write dynamic Web applications, it's important to keep the distinction between client-side and server-side code in mind because it's one of the most common misconceptions of beginning Web programmers. I often read comments and questions about how "my browser won't work with my ASP.NET page!" as if the cause of the error were ASP itself. From the browser's point of view, there is no such thing as an ASP.NET page—there's only HTML and script, and it makes no difference to the browser whether that content was generated by an ASP.NET page, was produced by a CGI script, or simply comes from a static HTML file. If a browser doesn't work with your ASP page, your page generates invalid content for that type of browser—it's not the browser's fault.

It's also important to differentiate between the somewhat confusing terminology for Dynamic HTML (DHTML) and dynamic Web pages. Just remember that DHTML is a client-side way of changing the look or content of a Web page without contacting the server. In DHTML, you manipulate the elements on a page with script and with CSS styles, or—more likely—a combination of the two. In contrast, a dynamic Web page is a page in which part or all of the content does not already exist in HTML form; the server creates the page through code on demand. In other words, it creates the page dynamically. There's no magic about it. The browser expects a string of text characters with some combination of text, HTML tags, and script in response to every request, and as long as the string it receives contains valid text, HTML, and script, the browser is satisfied.

What Is a Dynamic Web Application?

A *dynamic Web application* is a set of programs that work together to produce the illusion that a user is working with a single program. For example, imagine a typical data-driven application. A user logs in and selects some parameters—perhaps a customer name from a list—to produce a report showing that customer's recent purchases. The user may be able to drill down into the data by selecting a specific order or product purchased by that customer to see details about the purchase, such as the purchase location, delivery type, or delivery date. When you create an application like this as a stand-alone Windows program, you might plan and write it as a single program. The program might have multiple modules or even multiple forms and classes, but it has a defined beginning and end—the user launches the application, works with it for a while, and then exits the application. While the user is working with the program, you—as the application's programmer—have control over what the user can do within the application.

For example, you may disable the Exit button during critical operations to ensure that a user doesn't quit your program at an inopportune time. After logging in, the user can't access the login form again without exiting and restarting the program because you simply don't provide access to the login form after the user is authenticated. In a data-entry application, after filling out a form, a user can't return to that form and change the data without going through a series of actions defined by the application designer—selecting a record and then electing to edit it. A user can't even quit the application without your knowledge unless he just turns off the power to the computer. In Windows applications, this kind of control is free—you don't have to work for it.

In a dynamic Web application, you don't have that luxury. User actions occur on a machine different than the one where your application is running. Therefore, your application doesn't know and can't control what users are doing at all times; you must learn to live without that level of control. You can use client-side script to watch and control some user actions, but others are beyond your control using script alone. For example, every browser has a Back button. Imagine that you have a form for users to fill out. A user fills out your form and clicks the Submit button, and you write the data to the database. You return the next logical page for the application.

Now imagine that the user presses the Back button. That doesn't send a message to your application (because the browser loads the page from its cache). Now the user changes something in the form and clicks Submit again. You certainly don't want to create another record and, depending on the application, you may not even want to overwrite the current record. This is *not* an uncommon scenario—you need to plan for and trap these types of events in your Web application.

Here's another common scenario. A user logs into your application and works for a while, but then he gets sidetracked and types the URL of another site into the browser window. Eventually, the user closes the browser and walks away from the computer. The question is this: How do you deal with this from an application perspective? Remember, you may have data stored on the server for that user. How can you know whether a user is still actively working with your application? The short answer is that you can't. Instead, for critical data, you store a user's data to disk whenever that data changes; for noncritical data, you discard it after a defined length of time—a value you can set on a per-user or per-application basis, called `HttpSessionState.Timeout`—usually called by its shorter name, `Session.Timeout`.

Finally, there's one last major difference between Web applications and standard executables. Suppose the user from the last paragraph bookmarks the current page in your application before closing the browser and walking away. Much later (after the `Session.Timeout` has occurred), the user logs back in and clicks the bookmark. How does your application respond? Again, this is an extremely common problem and one that you must anticipate or your application will definitely have problems. Unlike a standard application, you have no direct control over the problem—you can't prevent the user from creating the bookmark or from following it at any time. However, you can control what happens when your application receives an unanticipated request. For example, you can immediately route that user to the first page of the application. If your application is truly user friendly, you might restore that user's state immediately after he logs back in.

At the beginning of this section, I mentioned that a Web application is a *collection* of programs, not a single program. That's because in a transactional application, like a Web application, you can't rely on your traditional data storage techniques to build a cohesive application. Instead, you must learn to think in smaller chunks, each of which must be discrete. As you work with C# Web applications, you'll learn to view dynamic Web applications as a series of transactions between the browser and the server. Coding the individual transactions is fairly straightforward. Making the individual transactions behave as part of a larger, unified whole is the real challenge in Web application programming.

What Are Data-Driven Applications?

You've probably heard the term "data-driven site" often—I've used it myself in this chapter already. What does that mean exactly? Aren't all applications data-driven, in the sense that they take data from the server and deliver it to the browser? That's true, but it's also beside the point. A *data-driven application* provides users with data from a data source or sources external to the application itself. That means that the application must be able to read (and often write) to these external sources and introduces requirements for data validation, data caching, and data translation.

In addition, data-driven applications often tend to grow over time. Even a simple application that maintains a list of subscribers to a newsletter must be planned and written so that it works well not only with the initial set of data, which is likely to be small, but also with data accumulated over several years. It's relatively easy to write an application to deal with 100 records, but it's much more difficult to write an application that deals with either 100 or 100,000 records with equal aplomb. When you throw multiple simultaneous users into the mix, the application's complexity grows accordingly. Although this book isn't intended to address all the issues involved in building very large data-driven applications, you'll see how to plan and build data-driven interfaces, and you'll work with ADO.NET and SQL Server to create, deliver, and update information in an external relational database.

Why Should I Use HTML Templates and CSS?

Just as you've probably found that you tend to create the same types of forms repeatedly, you'll find that you tend to create the same types of HTML pages repeatedly. Also, one way to help give a cohesive feel to your Web applications is by carefully planning the user interface so that it doesn't change radically from page to page. You accomplish this by creating templates into which you "pour" data. Separating the user interface (the templates) from the data requires some careful planning, but it makes your site much easier to update and maintain.

For example, when building a corporate Web portal, you might decide to put the list of departments along the top of the page, each implemented as a drop-down menu of topics pertinent to the department. You could place the HTML, event-trapping code and data in each page of your application, but what happens when a department adds a topic or your company splits or combines departments? If you put the code into the individual pages, you'll have to change each page. This is a typical scenario for sites that start small and then grow. The developers, who could easily maintain 20 or 30 pages by hand using HTML editors or even a simple text editor, find that it's impossible to maintain the data and a consistent look-and-feel when the site grows to 200 or 300 pages.

The answer to this problem (as with so many programming problems) is to provide a layer of indirection by separating the top-of-page menu code into a single separate file. IIS supports an `#include` command that replaces the command itself with the contents of another file. For example, suppose the file `topmenus.asp` contains the HTML and client-side script for the menus. Rather than copying the contents of that file into each `.asp` page in your application, you need only to place a single line into each page. `#include` commands are written as HTML comments. Servers that don't understand the command ignore them, passing them through to the browser, which also ignores the commands because they're comments. For example, the following code would cause IIS to insert the contents of the file `topMenus.asp` into the page:

```
<!-- #include file="topMenus.asp" -->
```

In the `#include` command, the file `topMenus.asp` must be in the same directory as the requested file. An alternate version lets you reference a file in a common location on the server:

```
<!-- #include virtual="/includes/topMenus.asp" -->
```

The word `virtual` in the code tells you that the directory `includes` is a virtual directory on the Web server.

Taking the analogy a step further, the corporate portal designers go back through all the pages, rip out the menu code and data, and replace it with an `#include` command referencing a file that has all the functionality they need. But then (you guessed it), something else changes. The Marketing department issues a memorandum stating that all electronic company communications must use the Verdana font. Of course, the portal must change immediately because it has become such a visible part of the company information infrastructure. As the portal designer, you have a problem. How do you change all the myriad font tags within the HTML pages? You have a problem. It's relatively difficult to write accurate search-and-replace code to find and change all the possible ways someone can set fonts.

Before this happens to you, make plans to avoid this problem in the first place. Using CSS style sheets, create a set of class styles for your application. You should usually avoid the temptation to use inline styles or even embedded styles except when absolutely necessary. Use linked or imported style sheets. As you may remember from Chapter 2, "HTML Basics," you can link a style sheet using the `<link>` tag within the `<head>` section of a document; for example:

```
<link rel="stylesheet" type="text/css" href="mystyles.css">
```

I don't expect you to take this advice completely to heart and, in fact, I'm not going to follow my own advice for all the samples in this book. I'll let you in on a secret: The more "dynamic" your Web applications are and the more you encapsulate small bits of functionality in .NET classes, external CSS files, #include files, database data, and code, the easier they are to adapt when circumstances change. It's always easier and far less error prone to change code or data in a single location than in multiple locations.

Client Interaction

Dynamic Web applications imply that the contents change for a reason. One reason to build dynamic applications is so that database data displayed in its pages may change, but just as often, you build dynamic applications because you want your application to be responsive to individual users' preferences and actions. Each time a user requests a page from your site, you can consider it an opportunity for interaction. Each time the user types a key or moves the mouse, it's another opportunity for interaction. The fact that a user has visited a page before provides opportunities for interaction.

For example, if you visit www.amazon.com and buy one or more books, you'll find that the pages change subtly when you visit the site later. The folks at Amazon keep careful track of their clients' habits. By doing this, they can begin to predict your future purchases. If you purchase a Harry Potter book, experience shows that you're highly likely to buy another Harry Potter book and that you're also likely to pick a book from the list of books bought by other people who purchased the same Harry Potter book that you did. This technique is called *personalization*. Admittedly, this is an advanced example of personalization, but it's the same basic idea as greeting a user by name ("Welcome back, Mr. Jones") or saving a user's preferences.

I'm not recommending that you use personalization in every application you write; I'm saying that personalization and interaction are two sides of the same coin. The point of personalization is to increase interaction. You're more likely to buy another book when Amazon provides you with a list. Similarly, you're more likely to use an application if that application saves and applies your preferences each time you launch it. Web applications run on interaction. I'm sure you've visited Web sites that require you to fill out a long form. When you finally finish and submit the form, the site returns (after a delay) and gives you an error message (which you must often scroll to find) stating that you filled out some field or other improperly. That's an example of poor interaction, and you're unlikely to be very satisfied with the application. In contrast, an application that lets you know as soon as possible which field value is incorrect, gives you an informative message stating *why* the value is incorrect, and places your cursor in the invalid field—scrolling when necessary to bring the field into view—is much more likely to make you a satisfied client.

Until recently, providing a substantive level of interaction in browser clients was difficult because browsers simply didn't have the resources to let you interact with users other than at a simplistic level. However, IE, beginning with version 4 and significantly more so with version 5 and higher, provides a substantial subset of the events that you're familiar with from Windows programming. You can detect mouse movements (in fact, browsers provide `mouseEnter` and `mouseOut` events, which even the Windows API didn't provide directly), clicks, double-clicks, and drag-and-drop operations. In conjunction with DHTML, client-side script, and Web Services, you can build user interfaces that—while not the equal of Windows forms—are very serviceable. Finally, because .NET makes it so easy to communicate with a server, you can create C# applications that *do* use Windows forms.

Web Applications versus Web Sites

Although the terms *Web site* and *Web application* are often used interchangeably, there is a difference. Web applications are distinct from Web sites because they have a defined purpose. People browse Web sites, but they use Web applications to accomplish a task. Most Web sites are informational. Most Web applications are not.

When you look at the Sports area on Yahoo! (`www.yahoo.com`), you're not trying to accomplish a task; you're there to get information. Often you don't even have specific information in mind—you're just browsing. Sometimes it's difficult to tell applications from sites. For example, Expedia (`www.expedia.com`) is a site you can browse, looking for general travel information, fares, and flight availability, but it's also a place you can go to purchase a ticket. Expedia is an example of a site that contains embedded applications.

In contrast, most business applications are less ambiguous. When a user logs into a corporate application to fill out a purchase order, he's not interested in browsing; he wants to enter the order as fast and accurately as possible. The user's purpose is completely different for most applications than for most Web sites.

This difference is important, because it affects—or *should* affect—how you build the user interface, what types of assistance and error messages you provide, and how much data you're likely to store for individuals using your application.

What Is the Data and Where Is It?

Dynamic applications consume and store data. That data most often resides in databases so that you can provide up-to-date data on demand to clients. In a dynamic Web site, the data may also reside in cached HTML files, flat files, and, increasingly, XML files.

Databases

Relational databases are particularly convenient data repositories because they can store almost any type of data, from bit values to very large binary or text blobs (binary large objects—long sequences of text or binary data), and they also provide extensive sorting and filtering services.

Choose your database wisely. For example, don't use a file-serving database like Microsoft Access; use a full-scale relational database like SQL Server, Oracle, DB2, Sybase, MySQL, or Informix instead. If you don't have a full copy of one of these databases, you can use MSDE or Personal Oracle. These "light" versions function much the same as their full-scale parents except that they restrict both the database size and the number of simultaneous connections (MSDE is optimized for only five simultaneous connections). Therefore, they're perfectly suitable for application development with small numbers of developers and testers. I don't recommend deploying an application with these smaller databases, though—they don't support enough users.

HTML Files

While you *can*, with some work, store and retrieve data from HTML files, they're most useful for storing templates and cached data. For example, suppose you store the "real" data for a customer list in a database. You could run a query to retrieve that data each time a user requests the page that displays the list. That's the simplest way to ensure that you get the latest customer data. It's also a relatively poor use of resources. Customer lists don't change that often. Hitting the database to fulfill each request for the page means that you're using a database connection, server memory, and network bandwidth to provide the same data repeatedly.

Another way to provide exactly the same level of accuracy while using far fewer resources is to build the page dynamically during the first page request and then write the resulting HTML page to disk. For subsequent accesses, you can provide the page from disk.

But wait! As soon as the database changes, wouldn't that mean the page is out of date? Yes, but remember, you're building a dynamic application. If your application is the only one that changes the database, you can refresh the page whenever the data changes. If other applications can also change the database, you can write a trigger to refresh the data, write a change file, or change a flag in a table. If you refresh the cached data using a trigger, you would use an #include command in the page, which would then always read the most up-to-date data. If the trigger writes an entry to the change file, you can check the file time stamp to determine whether to refresh the data. If the trigger changes a flag in a table, you can use a stored procedure with a return value to determine when to refresh the data. Regardless of the method you use, the result is that you rarely need to retrieve the full customer list from the database to fulfill a request.

Flat (ASCII) Files

For many years, "flat files," or delimited ASCII files, were the method of choice for transporting data between disparate platforms and applications. Many business applications still receive data from mainframes in flat files, usually on a schedule. While they're less useful now than in the past because there are other alternatives, you still may find it easier to keep some types of data in flat files rather than in database tables. For example, it's often easier to append strings to an application log file than it is to build a database table, determine the fields you'll need, write stored procedures, and build a class and a collection class to handle reading and writing the log entries, especially because you may need to read the log only to help you pinpoint program errors.

Nevertheless, because so much data resides in flat files, they are a source for dynamic application data.

XML Files

XML files are the modern replacement for flat files. Although XML files are considerably less efficient than flat files due to the repeated tag entries in the files, they're also considerably easier to use. You don't have to write code to parse the file, determine field names and field lengths, and check for end-of-file or end-of-line markers. Also, you read an XML file containing any type of data in exactly the same way—

using an XML parser. But parser capabilities go far beyond simply breaking a file up into its constituent records and fields. Parsers can retrieve individual records or fields or sort and filter information like a database and, using Extensible Stylesheet Language Transformations (XSLT), they can transform data from one format into another. The .NET framework makes extensive use of XML, so you'll see more about it later in this book.

How Can You Retrieve the Data?

In conjunction with ADO.NET, C# has the best data-retrieval and data-handling capabilities of any general-purpose language yet created. From flat files to databases, from XML documents to custom file formats, you have complete control of how and where to store and retrieve data. You can even maintain data in memory when your primary consideration is performance. The following sections give a brief overview of the types of data retrieval available.

ADO.NET

Microsoft introduced ActiveX Data Objects (ADO) as an alternative to the Data Access Objects (DAO) technology that shipped with early versions of Visual Basic and Microsoft Access. ADO was an extension of the ideas introduced in an even earlier technology called ODBC: that you should be able to use a similar interface to access data, regardless of the specific back-end data storage technology. Like ODBC, ADO requires a different provider for each specific type of information store. Unlike ODBC, which was intended for use only with relational databases, ADO is a high-level interface that lets you retrieve data from various sources. As long as you have a provider for a particular data source, you can use the ADO objects in almost exactly the same way to read and write data. Eventually, ADO drivers became available for all the major relational databases, and you could often find drivers for file-serving databases and flat files as well.

ADO.NET is the newest incarnation of ADO. ADO.NET fixes several problems that ADO had, extends its capabilities, and is integrated into the .NET framework rather than being a separate add-on as ADO has been traditionally. In this book, you'll use ADO.NET extensively to retrieve relational data.

XML Parsers

There are many XML parsers available from both open source and commercial vendors. The parsers vary in their level of compliance with the World Wide Web Consortium (W3C) XML recommendation. The XML parser that ships with .NET is somewhat different from even Microsoft's recently released COM-based XML parser, `msxml4.dll`, but it's highly compliant with the W3C recommendations for both XML and XSLT. The .NET framework makes extensive use of XML for everything from passing parameters to SOAP to object persistence, so if you aren't already familiar with XML and XSLT processing, you will be by the time you finish this book.

NOTE   *You can find the W3C XML recommendation here:* `http://www.w3.org/XML/`.

C# File/Stream Processing

How new file and stream processing is in .NET depends entirely on which language you used before beginning C#. For example, programmers experienced with Java and C++ won't have any trouble with .NET's I/O classes and methods, but programmers using classic VB had an arcane and extremely outdated method for accessing files. There were several completely different commands to write data to a file, depending on how you opened it. For example, if you opened a text file, you could use the `Input` function to read data and the `Print` function to append data to the file. Alternatively, you could use `Read #` and `Write #` statements. In contrast, if you opened the same file for binary access, you used the `Get` method to read data and the `Put` method to write data.

Microsoft's release of the Microsoft Scripting Runtime library included the `FileSystemObject`, along with a set of objects that represented files and folders. When you used the `FileSystemObject` to open a file, it returned a `TextStream` object that you used to read from and write to the file. The `TextStream` object (as its name implies) worked only with text files, not binary or random-access files, but it made file access much more intuitive. Because Microsoft designed the object model to work with scripting languages like VBScript and JScript, which could only use `Variants`, it wasn't as efficient as typed-object or direct API file access; however, Microsoft included it in the VB6 release anyway (a preview of the direction taken with .NET). The objects weren't part of the VB runtime, but you could use them from VB by including a project reference to the Microsoft Scripting Runtime. If you are a former ASP programmer who used the `FileSystemObject` to perform file access, you'll feel right at home with the .NET methods of file access. The biggest difference is that the `FileSystemObject` could only read and write text files, whereas C#'s I/O capabilities deal equally well with binary files and can read and write to and from strings and memory blocks with equal aplomb.

C#, like most other modern languages, uses streams to read and write data. Streams usually have two forms—readers and writers—but some stream classes (through inheritance) provide both reading and writing services. Streams are ubiquitous in .NET. For example, the .NET `System.IO` namespace contains classes such as `StreamReader` and `StreamWriter`, `BufferedStream`, `FileStream`, `BinaryReader` and `BinaryWriter`, and `StringReader` and `StringWriter`, among others.

The advantage of streams is that, like ADO, they abstract the process for working with any kind of data. After selecting the appropriate `Stream` class, the methods you use to read and write data are very similar from one `Stream` class to another. For example, if you open a `FileStream` on a file, you use its `Write` method to write bytes to the file. Similarly, if you open a `StringWriter` stream on a `String` object, you write characters to the string using the `Write` method. You no longer need to memorize several different ways to open a file; instead, you create a `File` object and use its `Open` method to obtain the appropriate `Stream` type. Efficient file access is critical to most applications, and Web applications are no exception. C#'s file-handling support, string-handling improvements, and integration of regular expressions make most I/O operations very straightforward.

In-Memory Storage

No matter how you decide to store data long-term, you're likely to find a need for data cached in memory. Rather obviously, you do this because it's many times faster to retrieve data from memory than to retrieve it from a flat file or database on disk. Similarly, for maximum performance, it's often useful to cache objects in memory, where you can avoid the overhead required to create and initialize the objects for each request. In previous versions of ASP, you had to write such objects in C++ or Delphi. However, objects you create with C# are perfectly safe to cache on the Web server.

C#, in conjunction with ASP.NET, provides numerous options for server-side caching. You can cache objects, pages, the results of database queries, or even just parts of a page. You can refresh the data on a defined schedule, such as every 15 minutes or on demand. You can also drop data from the cache when it's no longer needed.

How Do You Package the Data?

No matter where you store the data—in memory, in a database, or in files—you need to package the data, format it, and send it to the client for display or use in client-side script. In Web applications, the very concept of *data* is often confusing, because programmers usually think of code as separate from data. Of course, that's true when the code is actually executing, but it's untrue when you're creating a client-side page that contains code. In that case, the client-side code *is* data to the server. It doesn't execute on the server, so until the code reaches the browser, it's just more text that you need to send to the client.

Before discussing the various types of data that you can send to client browsers, I want to make a recommendation. Think of the data you send to the browser as a single string of *text characters*. Forget about the type of data embodied in those characters. The most important thing you understand is that, for most pages, you're sending a single string of text characters. The reason I say this is because beginning Web programmers often get confused about exactly what happens where, particularly when dealing with client-side script. Therefore, it's simpler just to think of all responses as string values.

HTML to Client

Mostly, when writing Web applications, you're going to be sending HTML data to the clients. Even advanced browsers natively understand only a few kinds of files, such as HTML, CSS, text, a few image formats, XML files, and script. Less advanced browsers may understand only HTML and image formats. While most modern browsers accept plug-ins that extend the range of file formats they can use, other browsers don't. Therefore, the only thing that you can really rely on with browsers is that they can parse and display HTML 3.2.

NOTE *I could be wrong even about HTML 3.2, because there are more browsers out there than I have personally tested. Nevertheless, the Web industry generally accepts HTML 3.2 as the low-end standard.*

At any rate, you can forget sending file formats you create yourself to the client. Forget sending objects of almost any type. Unless you can shoehorn the data into one of the file formats the browser can parse, it won't be displayed. That's not always bad. Old browsers incapable of using JavaScript ignore the script if you place it within an HTML comment tag. For example, while IE 3.*x* and Netscape 3.*x* will show the `alert` box in the following code, other browsers won't.

```
<!-- Script that "down-level" browsers will ignore -->
<script language="JavaScript">
   alert("This browser can run JavaScript!");
</script>
```

Some non-browser types of clients, such as wireless devices, consume a special type of XML called the Wireless Markup Language (WML). These clients don't use the JavaScript language either; instead, they use a special variant of JavaScript, appropriately named WMLScript.

If you're lucky enough (or unlucky enough, depending on your point of view) to work in an intranet environment where the client browser is dictated by the IT department, you probably won't care about any of this discussion of which clients recognize which file formats. However, if you work in an industry that provides Web access to the public, to clients outside the company, to remote contract employees, or to employees who may not always use browsers, this discussion is entirely relevant.

The W3C's final recommendation for HTML is version 4.01, but recently another subset of XML, called XHTML (for Extensible HTML), has begun to gain prominence. The W3C is working on modules to extend XHTML, but the simplest version uses the same tag set as HTML, just in a "well-formed" manner. The term *well-formed* means that the document follows XML syntax rules—among other things, all opening tags have an equivalent closing tag, all attribute values are quoted, and tags are in lowercase. In contrast, standard HTML can contain unclosed tags such as `<p>` or `<br>`, attribute values do not need to be quoted unless they contain embedded spaces or other separator characters, and tags are case insensitive.

By making some relatively minor syntax changes to your HTML files, you can read the file's content with an XML parser. That's a major advantage because extracting content from HTML files is a time-consuming and error-prone process. It's also important to note that having made the transition to XHTML, you can use an XSLT processor to extract the data from your HTML files and transform it. Why is this important? Here's a scenario.

You've joined an e-commerce Web application to sell flowers. You have an enormous number of HTML files that contain arrangement, pricing, and delivery information. Some of these files are simply templates for dynamic information that comes from databases; others were hard coded when the application began. The application delivers a well-rounded set of choices to people who want to buy flowers, including arranging for delivery, payment, and order tracking. The Marketing department realizes that, with the increasing number of people carrying Web-enabled wireless devices, there's a brand new opportunity for them to purchase flowers while they're in transit. For example:

> *"Oops, it's Friday night, you're leaving the office, and you suddenly realize that it's your wife's birthday! No problem: access* `http://www.buyFlowersForYourWife.com/`. *They deliver within 30 minutes to any location in the city! Whew! A narrow escape."*

You've been brought in to add wireless e-marketing and e-commerce capabilities to the Web site. Probably the first thing you would want to do is to make all the pages dynamic. In the interim, you'll want to read the data out of the HTML files and turn it into WML data. But the "right" answer is something in between. The right answer is to get the data into a form that you can read with an XML parser. The simplest step is to reformat the data as XHTML. After you do that, you can use XSLT to transform the data into HTML, XHTML, WML, or into the client flavor of the week ML. Sure, that's going to take some work, but the end result is that next time a new client appears, it will take a lot less work, you'll be the first out the gate, and everyone will be happy.

XML Data to Client

XML is a very simple idea that has powerful repercussions. The idea is this: What if you wrapped your content in HTML-like tags but, rather than using tags like `<table>` and `<h1>`, you gave them names that described the content, such as `<person>`, `<employee>`, `<hotel>`, `<manufacturer>`, and so on? Taking the idea just one step further: Some HTML tags are block tags that can contain other tags. What if you were to use that capability so that rather than just being nested tags, the tags and their containers were considered to be in a parent–child relationship? That's XML in a nutshell. The difference is that HTML is a formatting language, whereas XML is a data-description language.

XML is more verbose, but it's considerably more convenient when you want to extract information programmatically. For example, consider a table in an HTML file. If you want to extract the column headers and values, you need to parse the file looking for `<td>` and `</td>` characters. That by itself is not difficult, but when the `<td>` tags contain other HTML markup, it's much more difficult. In contrast, extracting the same information using the XML Document Object Model (DOM) is easy. The DOM lets you use XPath queries to discover the content—the attributes of a tag or "node" in a document—and to determine the relationship of a tag to its children, siblings, or parent. The DOM also lets you use XSLT to transform documents from one form into another.

SOAP Requests/Responses

It's a small step from realizing that XML is a fairly robust data-description language to realizing that you can describe objects, methods, and parameters using XML. In fact, it's such a simple idea that almost every major database and e-commerce tool vendor adopted the Simple Object Access Protocol (SOAP) within two years after Microsoft first proposed it. If you know anything about the antagonistic relationships between some of the vendors, you'll understand how remarkable that is.

If you can persist objects and data to XML and use it to describe a method call and the associated parameters, then you can use XML as a transport mechanism to make remote method calls over HTTP that avoid the problems inherent in using binary data that performs the same function. Most firewalls block binary data because it may contain viral or malicious code, but they let text data through. Using the plain-text SOAP wrappers, you can pass a representation of the binary data through the firewall safely.

It's important for you to understand that SOAP is simply a standardized form of XML for making remote method calls and returning values. Other than the fact that it's a standard, there's nothing special about SOAP at all. In fact, you're perfectly able to bypass SOAP and use a customized, more streamlined version in your applications—but if you do that, you won't realize some of the built-in benefits of .NET.

When you create a Web Service project, the .NET framework takes care of the details of parsing SOAP-formatted requests and returning the values embedded in SOAP-formatted responses.

Custom Data Streams

Sometimes you have data processing needs that don't fit well into standard packages. For example, you may decide that for performance reasons, your application must maintain a constant open communication channel with a server. C# has much better built-in access to network communications than did classic ASP. In fact, you can write a custom HTTP server in C# without a great deal of effort. The `System.Net` classes contain `TCPClient`, `TCPListener`, and `UDPClient` classes that wrap the Windows Sockets interface in managed code. Using these classes, you can write custom data stream applications using a fairly high-level sockets interface. If you need even lower-level access, the `System.Net.Sockets` class provides base services for creating Internet connections.

What Is the User Interface?

Because .NET has such strong support for network communication built into the framework, it's much easier to build user interfaces that work with data stored on a Web server. In fact, it's so easy that .NET extends Web access to Windows applications. You've probably heard about this mostly in the context of Web Services, which are usually discussed as if they were irretrievably bound up with

SOAP—but they're not. You can generate a Web application that can serve data to a Windows front-end as easily as it can serve the same (or different) data to a browser front-end. These capabilities mean that, as a C# developer, you now face a choice. Which should you use: a browser (HTML) interface, a Windows interface, or both?

Browser-Based Interfaces

Browser-based interfaces (called Web Forms in .NET), while they've improved tremendously over the past few years, are still not the equal of Windows forms. The browser controls are subtly different and considerably less capable, and you typically have somewhat less control over the look-and-feel than you do with Windows forms.

The primary advantages of browser-based user interfaces are the capabilities to deliver an application to remote users with no installation and to update that application from a central location without requiring any changes to the client machines. Other advantages include the capability to run applications on multiple platforms, automatic form resizing (by using percentages for element sizes in HTML), automatic scrolling, automatic hypertext links, automatic Forward and Back buttons, and automatic bookmarking (although there's a good argument that these last two are not advantages at all).

.NET Windows Forms Interfaces

C# levels the playing field significantly. Windows Forms feature automatic resizing of controls, automatic scrolling, easy installation, the capability to automatically update the application based on version—in short, almost everything you need to dispose of the browser altogether and use Windows forms for all your front-end needs.

Client Capabilities

Of course, there are considerations other than the capabilities of the technology—specifically, the client capabilities. For one thing, a browser is .NET agnostic: You don't need the .NET runtime to deliver working browser applications. For another, no matter how easy it may be to create an install program with modern tools, you don't have to install anything on most clients to deliver a browser-based front-end. Most users already have a browser installed; therefore, as long as your application supports the user's browser type and version, your applications begin working as soon as the user browses to the starting URL. Finally, for some types of applications, a browser is simply better. For example, if your application doesn't have any special need for Windows control capabilities, it might be more convenient for users to click a desktop or "favorite" link to launch the application. That way, they don't need to close the program; they can just browse to a different location when they're done with your application.

On the other hand, browsers have some significant limitations when you need to save data or access the local filesystem for any reason. The browser's security restrictions prevent local file access. IE5 lets you save small amounts of data (64KB for restricted zones, 128KB for most zones, 512KB for the intranet zone) to the local computer. All browsers (depending on their settings) let you save even smaller amounts as cookies. You can work around the browser's security restrictions by creating signed components, but for most serious work, you'll find it's easier to create and install a Windows application than to deal with the security problems. Similarly, you'll find that for applications requiring complex drag-and-drop or drawing operations, you're generally better off with a Windows application.

Again, you can sometimes work around the browser limitations by creating Java applets or ActiveX or .NET controls that users can download and run in the browser, but if you can deliver an executable program to your audience, it's simply easier to avoid the problems. Finally, you program browsers with script. Almost all modern browsers can execute JavaScript or the standardized version called ECMAScript.

NOTE *The European Association for Standardizing Information and Communication Systems (ECMA) controls the ECMAScript standard. You can access the ECMA Web site at* http://www.ecma.ch/.

NOTE *Microsoft's proprietary version of ECMAScript/JavaScript is called JScript. I'll refer to all of these scripting flavors with the generic term "JavaScript" and use the term "JScript" for features that are proprietary extensions of the Microsoft version.*

The features available through script depend heavily on the browser version and the script version running on the client. The script itself may be visible via the View Source command on the browser's context menu, so if you have any sensitive or proprietary information in the script itself, you need to avoid using a browser for the user interface.

Summary

At this point, you should be comfortable with the idea of dynamic Web applications. Dynamic applications are data driven. Some are read-only, but almost all require user input. Before you tackle a dynamic application, you should decide how and where you're going to store the data, how you can partition the application so that you retrieve only the data you need at any given time, how you plan to display the data, and what type of interface is most suitable for the display and input requirements of the application.

No matter what you decide, C# Web applications work through a technology layer of the .NET framework called ASP.NET. The ASP.NET layer simplifies the process of writing code to respond to HTTP requests.

Part 2

Server-Side Web Programming with Visual C#

In this section you will find:

Chapter 4

Introduction to ASP.NET

ASP.NET IS THE .NET framework layer that handles Web requests for specific types of files, among those are .aspx and .ascx, and .asmx extensions as well as several others (you can get the full list by checking the Application Configuration properties for the Web site in the Internet Services Manager application). The ASP.NET engine provides a robust object model for creating dynamic content and is loosely integrated into the .NET framework. This integration makes it easy to change the implementation when the .NET framework migrates to platforms other than Windows.

In this chapter:

◆ What Is ASP.NET?

◆ Why Do You Need ASP.NET?

◆ What Does ASP.NET Do?

◆ Why Is ASP.NET in a C# Book?

◆ Creating Your First Web Form

What Is ASP.NET?

What is ASP.NET? This may seem like a relatively simple question, but I assure you that it's not. Because ASP.NET is part of the .NET framework, it is available on any server with the framework installed. In other words, it's not an add-on anymore; ASP has become legitimate. ASP.NET is implemented in an assembly that exposes classes and objects that perform predetermined specific tasks. If you are familiar with "classic" ASP (the versions of ASP that preceded .NET), you'll find that your approach to programming in ASP.NET is somewhat different, but the concepts behind building a Web application are much the same. If you're not familiar with classic ASP, so much the better—you won't have as much information to forget!

ASP.NET programs are centralized applications hosted on one or more Web servers that respond dynamically to client requests. The responses are dynamic because ASP.NET intercepts requests for pages with specific extensions, for example .aspx or .ascx, and hands off the responsibility for answering those requests to just-in-time (JIT) compiled code files that can build a response on-the-fly. Figure 4.1 shows how ASP.NET integrates with the rest of the .NET framework.

FIGURE 4.1

ASP.NET
integration
with the .NET
framework

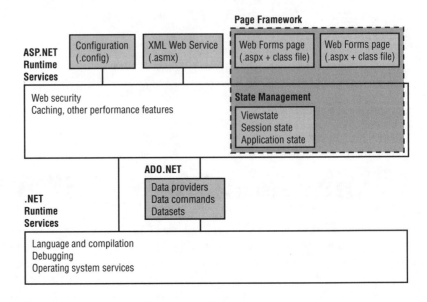

From looking at Figure 4.1, you can see that ASP.NET deals specifically with configuration (`web.config` and `machine.config`) files, Web Services (ASMX) files, and Web Forms (ASPX) files. The server doesn't "serve" any of these file types—it returns the appropriate content type to the client. The configuration file types contain initialization and settings for a specific application or portion of an application. Another configuration file, called `machine.web`, contains machine-level initialization and settings. The server ignores requests for Web files, because serving them might constitute a security breach.

This book concentrates on Web Forms and Web Services. Client requests for those file types cause the server to load, parse, and execute code to return a dynamic response. For Web Forms, the response usually consists of HTML or WML. For Web Services, the server typically creates a Simple Object Access Protocol (SOAP) response. While SOAP requests are inherently stateless and can thus execute immediately, Web Forms are stateful by default. Web Forms maintain state by round-tripping user interface and other persistent values between the client and the server automatically for each request. In Figure 4.1, the dashed rectangle titled Page Framework shows the difference—a request for a Web Form can use ViewState, Session State, or Application State to maintain values between requests. It is possible (but not the default) to take advantage of ASP.NET's state maintenance architecture from a Web Service, but for performance reasons, you should generally avoid doing so.

Both Web Forms and Web Services requests can take advantage of ASP.NET's integrated security and data access through ADO.NET and can run code that uses system services to construct the response.

The major difference between a static request and a dynamic request is that a typical Web request references a static file. The server reads the file and responds with the contents of the requested file. With ASP.NET there's no such limitation. You don't have to respond with an existing file—you can respond to a request with anything you like, including dynamically created HTML, Extensible Markup Language (XML), graphics, raw text, or binary data—anything. Capability, by itself, is nothing new—

you've been able to create CGI programs, JavaServer Pages, classic ASP pages, ColdFusion, and Net-Objects Fusion pages for quite some time. All these technologies give you the capability to respond to an HTTP request dynamically. So what are the differences?

- Unlike classic ASP, ASP.NET uses .NET languages. Therefore, you have access to the full power of any .NET assembly or class in exactly the same way as you do from any other Windows application written in C#. In this sense, ASP.NET is similar to early compiled CGI programs, but with CGI, a separate copy of the program had to be loaded and executed for each request. ASP.NET code exists in multithreaded JIT-compiled DLL assemblies, which can be loaded on demand. Once loaded, the ASP.NET DLLs can service multiple requests from a single in-memory copy.

- ASP.NET supports all the .NET languages (currently C#, C++, VB.NET, and JScript, but there are well over 20 different languages in various stages of development or deployment for .NET), so you will eventually be able to write Web applications in your choice of almost any modern programming language. In addition, there are open source groups working with Intel and Hewlett-Packard to support .NET on various flavors of Unix and Linux. JavaServer Pages support only Java, but because Java now has a wide support base, that's not much of a limitation. Java Servlets are more like ASP.NET but offer little support for state maintenance, Web Services, or XML. In addition, no Java design environment competes in features and quality to Visual Studio.

- Classic ASP supported several scripting languages, although in practice, VBScript and JScript were by far the most prevalent. Although the scripting languages you could use with classic ASP were untyped, interpreted, and not particularly powerful, you could extend ASP's basic functionality by writing DLLs in any COM-compliant language. Another ASP.NET competitor, Cold-Fusion, uses ColdFusion Markup Language (CFML) tags, which have a powerful but limited set of capabilities; however, you can extend CFML with custom programming in C++ or Java.

- Microsoft was able to draw on millions of hours of developer experience with classic ASP, so in addition to huge increases in speed and power, ASP.NET provides substantial development improvements, such as seamless server-to-client debugging, automatic validation of form data, and a programming model very similar to that of a Windows application.

Framework for Processing HTTP Requests

Microsoft's Web server, Internet Information Server (IIS), handles HTTP requests by handing off the request to the appropriate module based on the type of file requested. Note that IIS responds with one of only a few possible actions when it receives a request.

Respond with the File's Contents   The server locates and reads the requested file's contents and then streams the contents back to the requester. The server responds in this manner to `.htm` and `.html` file requests, as well as to all requests that have no associated application type—for example, EXE files.

Respond by Handing Off the Request   The server hands off requests for files that end in `.asp` to the classic ASP processor and files that end in `.aspx`, `.ascx`, or `.asmx` to the ASP.NET processor.

Respond with an Error   IIS responds with a customizable error message when a requested file does not exist, when the requesting client has insufficient permissions to authenticate or access the resource, or when an error occurs during processing.

Using the Internet Services Manager, you can change IIS's response to any particular file extension. For example, you could have the ASP.NET engine handle all requests for files with .htm or .html extensions, or you can create your own extensions and assign an action to them.

Classic ASP versus ASP.NET

In classic ASP, the server handed off file requests that ended in .asp to the ASP engine, an Internet Server Application Programming Interface (ISAPI) ASP DLL. Because there's a difference in the file extension (.asp versus .aspx, .ascx, and .asmx) for classic ASP and ASP.NET files, respectively, you can have both running on the same server simultaneously. However, that does *not* mean that both use the same back-end code—they don't, they're completely different. Fortunately for ASP programmers ASP.NET supports all the functionality available in classic ASP and a great deal more besides. Table 4.1 shows the major differences between the two technologies.

TABLE 4.1: COMPARISON OF CLASSIC ASP AND ASP.NET

CLASSIC ASP	ASP.NET	DESCRIPTION
Intercept client requests for files with an .asp extension.	Intercept client requests for files with the .aspx extension.	Provides the capability to create content on-the-fly—dynamic content.
Write server-side script in one of a small number of languages. Script languages are interpreted at runtime.	Write server-side code in any .NET language. .NET languages are compiled, not interpreted.	Compiled code is faster. The development environments and debug facilities are more powerful.
Extend ASP scripting functionality with COM objects.	Use any of the .NET System classes or call existing COM objects or .NET assemblies.	Provides the capability to extend ASP capabilities by writing custom code.
All processing happens *after* the server passes control to the ASP engine. Cannot take advantage of ISAPI services.	You can write code to intercept requests *before* the ASP engine takes control. You can write ISAPI services within the .NET framework.	Sometimes you want to respond to a request *before* the ASP engine parses the request. You can do that in .NET, but not with classic ASP.
Code and HTML are usually mixed inline within a page.	Code may be placed inline in ASP.NET pages, but is usually separated from the HTML in code-behind classes.	The .NET code-behind classes provide a cleaner separation of display and logic code and also simplify code reuse.

Continued on next page

TABLE 4.1: COMPARISON OF CLASSIC ASP AND ASP.NET *(continued)*

CLASSIC ASP	ASP.NET	DESCRIPTION
Developer responsible for implementing ways to maintain state data between pages.	Web Forms and Web Form controls act much like classic VB forms and controls, with properties and methods for retrieving and setting values.	While both classic ASP and ASP.NET render output in HTML, ASP.NET introduces ViewState, a scheme that automatically maintains the state of controls on a page across round trips to the server. Web Forms, Web Form controls, and ViewState simplify development and eliminate much of the gap between programming Web applications and stand-alone Windows applications.
Process submitted HTML form fields.	Process and validate submitted form fields.	Provides the capability to gather user input. Automatic validation takes much of the grunt work out of programming pages that require user input.
Settings stored in special ASP page that executes code for special events (such as application startup and shutdown).	Settings stored in XML-formatted files. Settings for subdirectories may override settings for their parent directories.	ASP.NET uses XML files to store settings, giving you programmatic access to configuration settings.
ADO.	ADO.NET.	ADO.NET is faster, more powerful, and much better integrated with XML for passing data between tiers.
MTS/COM+.	Same, through COM interoperability.	C# components can support object pooling, as did free-threaded C++ components. In contrast, VB6-generated COM components do not. Eventually, COM+ will be completely integrated into .NET.

Why Do You Need ASP.NET?

The first computer languages were little more than mnemonics substituting for raw machine code instructions, but as computers became more complex, each new language generation has supported an increasing level of abstraction. Visual Basic, for example, abstracted user interface design and construction into simple drag-and-drop operations (a model that VS.NET extends to all .NET-compliant languages). For the first time, you could create a working Windows application with very little effort.

Similarly, when Web programming first became widespread, there were few tools to help programmers write Web applications. To create a Web application, you initially had to write low-level socket communications code. Over the years, the abstraction level has increased for Web programming as well. First Common Gateway Interface (CGI) let you create executables that handled requests. Next, the Internet Server API (ISAPI) and its counterpart NSAPI (Netscape Server API) let you intercept requests and serve them from in-memory code components (DLLs), which was much faster. An ISAPI module, in turn, could host a scripting engine, a combination that became the basis for classic ASP and proved to be extremely popular with programmers. Microsoft extended the power of scripting language Web programming in classic ASP by providing several "intrinsic" objects. These represented the request, the server's response, the server itself, the user's session, and the "application." All together, they simplified and automated the process of parsing and encrypting the request and response data and made it easier to maintain global values and data for individual clients.

ASP.NET is the latest (and arguably the best) of these abstractions because it lets you work almost exclusively with rich high-level classes and objects rather than directly with raw data. Without ASP.NET, building a Web application is a chore. With ASP.NET, building a Web application is similar to building a Win32 application.

Client Changes

ASP.NET lets you build Web-based applications that interact with pages displayed remotely. Originally, classic ASP was designed to work with browsers, which at that time were capable of little more than displaying data and images wrapped in HTML markup. While the integration hasn't changed, the clients have changed dramatically. For example, modern browsers are much more capable than the version 3 browsers available when classic ASP was first developed. Not only can they display HTML and images, they also support Cascading Style Sheets (CSS), Dynamic HTML (DHTML), XML (to varying degrees), animations, complex image effects, vector graphics, sound, and video—and can run code, letting you offload appropriate portions of your application's processing requirements from your server to the client.

Centralized Web-Based Applications

It's not only browsers that have changed. Centralized Web-based applications have garnered a huge investment from companies that increasingly need to support mobile and remote clients. The cost of supplying private network connectivity to such clients is prohibitive, yet the business advantages of supporting such clients continue to rise. The only cost-effective way to supply and maintain corporate applications to these mobile and remote workers is to uncouple them from the network and build the applications to work over the public Internet via HTTP, WAP, and other advanced protocols. Therefore, Web-based applications are no longer the exclusive purview of Webmasters and specialist developers; they've become an integral part of the corporate IT operations.

Distributed Web-Based Applications

For all the advantages of centralized Web applications, they mostly ignore a huge reservoir of processing power that exists on the client machines. Recently, a new breed of application has begun to attract attention—the *point-to-point* program (often abbreviated as "P-to-P" or "P2P"). These programs typically use XML to pass messages and content directly from one machine to another. Most current implementations, such as Groove and Napster, use a centralized server as a directory service that helps individuals or machines contact one another. Peer-to-peer applications are often called *distributed* because the application runs at many points on the network simultaneously. In addition, the data used by distributed applications is usually (but not necessarily) stored in multiple locations. Finally, applications have begun to appear that run on multiple clients simultaneously, taking advantage of the enormous amount of unused processing power that exists on the "edge" of the Web. Unlike standard applications no one machine has to have the entire application; instead, each client processes data as requested and coordinated from a central server—in other words, the application uses the edge machines as nothing more than an extra CPU.

Functional Interoperability

As the client transition from stand-alone applications to browser-based interfaces occurred, another factor came into play: interoperability. IT departments have struggled with interoperability ever since programming escaped the confines of the mainframe. As the number of computers and computing devices within the business and entertainment worlds expanded, the problem grew. Today, computing is no longer limited to full-size desktop machines or even laptops. Handheld and notepad computers, telephones, and even pagers communicate with the Web servers and need to display data—sometimes even display the same data or run the same application as a desktop box. Similarly, IT departments now run critical applications on mainframes, minicomputers, and several different types of servers, from small departmental servers to server farms that supply computing power to the entire enterprise and beyond. These servers are made by different vendors and often run differing and incompatible operating systems, yet companies often need to transport and consume data between the various machines, databases, application tiers, and clients.

Companies have attacked the interoperability problem in several ways. They've tried limiting the hardware and software—creating tight corporate standards for desktop, laptop, and handheld computers. That approach hasn't worked very well—the industry changes too fast. They've tried and discarded the thin-client network computer approach. Too little benefit, too late. They've tried implementing Java as both the platform and the language—but performance issues, a lack of cooperation between the major software suppliers, and the lack of commercial-quality software have—at least temporarily—quelled that approach as well. Fortunately, a new interoperability standard has recently presented itself: Extensible Markup Language (XML).

Standardization, Verifiability, and HTTP Affinity

XML provides a possible solution to some of these interoperability problems. XML is not a panacea, but it does provide a standardized and *verifiable* text-based file format that can help ease the problems involved in moving data from one server to another, as well as accommodate displaying identical data on disparate clients. XML's standardization helps because the file format is universally recognized. XML simplifies programming because it can verify, by using a *document type definition* (DTD) or *schema*, that a file does indeed contain a specific type of content. Finally, XML's text-based format transfers very well over a plain HTTP connection, which helps avoid problems with firewalls and malicious code.

Web Services

These attributes—standardization, verifiability, and HTTP affinity—led to a new use for ASP: creating server-based code that delivers data without necessarily delivering HTML. In .NET, such pages are called Web Services. You can think of a Web Service as a function call or as an object instantiation and method call across the Web. Just as Web browsers and Web servers use a common protocol—HTTP—to communicate across the network, a Web Service uses a common XML structure called Simple Object Access Protocol (SOAP) to communicate with the calling application. You'll learn more about SOAP and Web Services in Chapter 21, "Web Services."

What Does ASP.NET Do?

What does ASP.NET do? Again, this is not a simple question. Classic ASP was limited to simple script languages that could respond to requests but provided no intrinsic direct access to system services other than those few required to read and respond to a request, such as writing output text. Although you could extend classic ASP through commercial or custom-built COM components, the relatively high overhead required to create COM objects and classic ASP's reliance on untyped interpreted scripting languages limited system performance. In contrast, creating .NET framework objects requires very little overhead, and ASP.NET lets you use fully object-oriented languages with seamless access to system services. Therefore, I'll describe just the primary tasks that ASP.NET accomplishes now, and I'll fill in the practical details in the remainder of this book.

Accepts Requests

All ASP.NET pages work essentially the same way. A client application makes an HTTP request to a Web server using a URL. The Web server hands off the request to the ASP.NET processor, which parses the URL and all data sent by the client into collections of named values. ASP.NET exposes these values as properties of an object called the HttpRequest object, which is a member of the System .Net assembly. An assembly is a collection of classes. Although an assembly *can* be a DLL, it may consist of more than one DLL. Conversely, a single DLL may contain more than one assembly. For now, think of an assembly as a group of related classes.

When a browser, or more properly a *user agent*, makes a request, it sends a string containing type and version information along with the request. You can retrieve the HTTP_USER_AGENT string via the HttpRequest object. For example, the following code fragment retrieves several items from the user agent and writes them back to the client. An ASP.NET Web Form Page object exposes the Http-Request with the shorter name Request that's familiar to classic ASP programmers.

```
Response.Write("UserAgent=" & Request.UserAgent & "<br>")
Response.Write("UserHostAddress=" & Request.UserHostAddress & "<br>")
Response.Write("UserHostName=" & Request.UserHostName & "<br>")
```

Builds Responses

Just as ASP.NET abstracts incoming data in the HttpRequest object, it provides a way to respond to the request via the HttpResponse object. Abstracting responses in this manner has been so successful that you'll find you need to know almost nothing about HTTP itself to use the HttpRequest and HttpResponse objects.

Assists with State Maintenance

Unlike a stand-alone or standard client-server application, Web applications are "stateless," which means that neither the client nor the server remembers each other after a complete request/response cycle for a single page finishes. Each page requested is a complete and isolated transaction, which works fine for browsing static HTML pages but is the single largest problem in constructing Web applications.

Classic ASP introduced the idea of a *session*, which begins the first time a client requests any page in your application. At that point, the ASP engine creates a unique cookie, which the browser then accepts and returns to the server for each subsequent page request. ASP used the cookie value as a pointer into data saved for that particular client in an object called the Session object. Unfortunately, because the client data was stored in memory on a single server, this scheme did not scale well, nor was it fault-tolerant. If the Web server went down, the users lost the in-memory data.

ASP.NET uses much the same cookie scheme to identify specific clients, but the equivalent of the Session object is now called the HttpSessionState object. ASP.NET addresses the session-scalability and data-vulnerability problems in classic ASP by separating state maintenance from the ASP.NET engine. ASP.NET has a second server application, called the session server, to manage session data. You can run the session server in or out of the IIS process on the same machine as your Web server or out of process on a separate computer. Running it on a separate computer lets you maintain a single session store across multiple Web servers. ASP.NET also adds the option to maintain state in SQL Server, which increases fault tolerance in case the session server fails.

Why Is ASP.NET in a C# Web Book?

VB6 had a project type called an IIS application—a technology more commonly known as WebClasses. I wrote a book about using WebClasses, called the *Visual Basic Developer's Guide to ASP and IIS* (Sybex, 1999). Using WebClasses, a VB programmer had access to the ASP intrinsic objects—Request, Response, Server, Application, and Session—and could use the compiled code within WebClasses to respond to client Web requests. But IIS applications required ASP to be installed on the server and, in fact, the project created DLLs that were called as COM components from an automatically generated ASP page. Therefore, a WebClass-based application in VB6 was really an ASP application that followed a specific track to instantiate and use VB COM components. Although the entire underlying technology has changed, that aspect has not.

TIP *A C# Web Application project is an ASP.NET application!*

ASP.NET, although advertised as if it were a separate technology, is not. It is part of and completely dependent on the .NET framework (refer to Figure 4.1). In fact, an ASP.NET project is *exactly the same thing* as a C# Web application project. You'll hear that you can write an ASP.NET application using Notepad—and you can! You can also write a C# application using Notepad. The big advantage of writing a C# Web application within the Visual Studio .NET (VS.NET) IDE is that you have access to a number of productivity tools, including syntax highlighting, IntelliSense, macros and add-ins, the Toolbox, HTML, XML, code editors, the Server Explorer, and so on, and so on, and so on. Remember that when you create a C# Web application project, you're really creating an ASP.NET project—you're just approaching the technology through a specific language and IDE.

C# Provides Code-Behind

In an ASP.NET application, you can either write code inline, as with classic ASP, or you can place the HTML code in a file with an .aspx extension and the code in a separate file with an .aspx.cs extension, called a *code-behind class* or *code-behind file.* There's little or no difference in performance between the two methods, but there's a fairly large difference in maintenance costs and reusability between the two approaches. For example, Listing 4.1 shows that you can still write code embedded in HTML in a manner very similar to the classic ASP style.

LISTING 4.1: CLASSIC ASP EMBEDDED CODE (ch4-1.aspx)

```
<%@ Page Language="C#"AutoEventWireup="false"%>
<html>
  <head>
    <meta name="CODE_LANGUAGE" content="C#">
  </head>
  <body>
    <%Response.write("Hello world")%>
    <form id="ch4-1" method="post" runat="server">
    </form>
  </body>
</html>
```

Alternatively, you can create exactly the same output using a code-behind class by placing the line Response.Write("Hello world") in the Load event for a Web Form (see Listing 4.2). Don't worry if that doesn't exactly make sense at the moment—it will at the end of this chapter.

LISTING 4.2: CODE BEHIND A WEB FORM EXAMPLE (ch4-2.aspx.cs)

```
// VS.NET autogenerated code omitted
private void Page_Load(object sender, System.EventArgs e)
{
    if (!IsPostBack) { // Evals true first time browser hits the page
        Response.Write("Hello World");
    }
}
```

.NET's Unified Platform for Design, Coding, and Debugging

You may already be familiar with the event model for Windows Form controls. One of the goals of .NET was to create that same sense of programmatic unity in working with Web applications. Therefore, even though there's usually a physical separation between the control in a browser and the application on a server, you can often develop pages as if that distance were not present. In .NET, HTML pages containing code are called Web Forms. Don't be misled by the name—both of the preceding code examples are "Web Forms," even though one looks exactly like an HTML page with two lines of code inserted and the other looks exactly like a C# method.

For those of you who might have used WebClasses (the class type from IIS Web application projects in VB6), a Web Form (with code-behind) is similar to the combination of an HTML template and a WebClass. The Web Form contains the HTML layout, while the code-behind class contains the program logic and exposes page-level events. But don't be confused—a Web Form is much more powerful than a WebClass.

In the VS.NET IDE, you design a Web Form in much the same way you design a Windows Form—by dragging and dropping controls from the Toolbox onto the Web Form drawing surface. When you add a new Web Form to your project in C#, you can elect to use the drag-and-drop metaphor or, if you're more comfortable editing HTML directly, you can click a tab and move into the HTML text-mode editor.

Because Web Forms aren't Windows Forms, you need to select a target client type. The first VS.NET release lets you target HTML 3.2–compliant clients (Internet Explorer (IE) version 3.x and earlier browsers, Netscape version 4.x and earlier) or HTML 4 ones (IE 4.x and 5.x, Netscape 6). Unless you have good reason to support the earlier browsers, you should make sure you target the HTML 4 clients. You can lay out a Web Form in either FlowLayout mode or in GridLayout mode. These two settings control how and where the browser places controls on the page.

When you select the FlowLayout option, the browser uses its standard internal HTML layout rules to place the controls. In other words, it places the controls linearly, from left to right and top to bottom, wrapping to the next line where necessary and exceeding the viewable width and height of the browser where wrapping is not possible, adding scroll bars as needed.

In contrast, GridLayout mode lets you place controls at fixed positions on the page. GridLayout mode is equivalent to writing an HTML `input` control where the `style` attribute specifies the `position: absolute` Cascading Style Sheet (CSS) style. In fact, that's exactly what it does—for example:

```
<input
type="text"
style="position: absolute;
left: 10;
top: 10">
```

After placing controls and content on the Web Form, double-click any control (if necessary, click OK in response to the prompt regarding conversion to a server-based control). VS.NET will open the code-behind class. If you insist on writing embedded code, click the HTML tab at the bottom of the Web Form window and VS.NET will switch to the HTML text editor. You can insert code by enclosing it between `<%` and `%>` tags or between `<script language="C#" runat="server"></script>` tags.

NOTE *Use the `<% %>` syntax only for inline code—code that you want to execute when the page is rendered. Code written in this manner is a code render block. To display a variable or the result of an expression, you can use the shorthand `<%=var or expression%>`. For all other embedded code, use the `<script></script>` syntax. You must declare page-level variables, subroutines, and functions within `<script></script>` blocks. You can reference external code using the `src` attribute of the `<script>` tag. You must include the `runat="server"` attribute for all server-side code.*

The ASP.NET engine treats all content on the page that is not between those tags as HTML content and streams it directly to the browser. You'll see a few examples of inline code and code within `<script runat="server">` blocks in this book, but not many, because this book discusses C#-generated code-behind classes almost exclusively.

Creating Your First Web Form

In this section, you'll create a Web Form that lets you enter some text into a textbox—nothing fancy here. You click a Submit button to send the text you enter to the server. But then I'll show you just a tantalizing glimpse of how C# exceeds any previously available Web technology in terms of power. The server will respond with a GIF image created on-the-fly containing the text you type into the text box.

Step 1: Creating a Project

Launch VS.NET. Click File ➤ New ÿ Project and select the item Visual C# Projects in the left pane of the New Project dialog (see Figure 4.2). In the right pane, select the Web Application icon (you may need to scroll to see the icon).

FIGURE 4.2

VS.NET New Project window

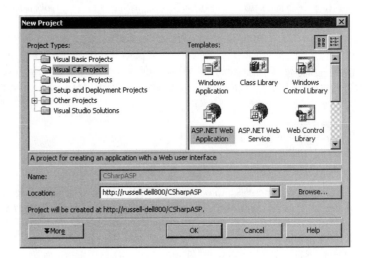

By default, C# names your Web application projects `WebApplication` with an appended number, for example, `WebApplication1`, but you should always enter a specific name. Click in the Name field and enter **CSharpASP**. Check the Location field; it should contain the name of the Web server you want to host this application. Typically, this will read `http://localhost`. However, you may create a project on any Web server for which you have sufficient permissions to create a virtual directory and write files.

Make sure the information you entered is correct, and then click OK. VS.NET will create the new project.

You should see the Solution Explorer pane (see Figure 4.3). If the Solution Explorer is not visible, select View ÿ Solution Explorer from the menu bar.

FIGURE 4.3

Solution Explorer pane containing a new project

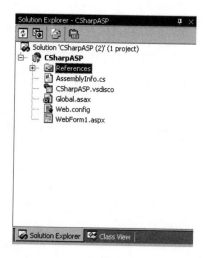

You'll use the **CSharpASP** project throughout this book. When C# creates a Web application project, it adds several items to the Solution Explorer pane. I'll explain all these in a minute, but first, create a new folder named **ch4**. Creating subfolders works exactly like creating subfolders in a Web site: You simply add the name of the folder to the root URL to view a page in that folder. To create the subfolder, right-click the **CSharpASP** virtual root in the Solution Explorer, click Add, and then click New Folder. Finally, type **ch4** for the folder name.

Select the **WebForm1.aspx** file and drop it on top of your new **ch4** folder. When you drop the file, VS.NET will move the ASPX file (and any associated files) into the **ch4** folder. If the file is already open, close it first and then move it. Your Solution Explorer pane should look similar to Figure 4.4.

FIGURE 4.4

Solution Explorer pane after creating the **ch4** folder

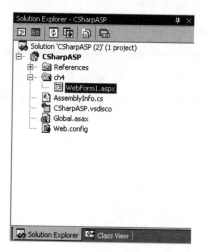

Step 2: Laying Out the Page

Select the WebForm1.aspx file and then right-click it to bring up the context menu. Select Rename from the menu and rename the file DynamicImage.aspx (don't forget or mistype the extension—it's required).

TIP *You can press F2 to rename a file, just as you can in Windows Explorer.*

Double-click the DynamicImage.aspx file to open it in the editing pane. By default, ASPX pages open in Design mode. If you're not in Design mode, click the Design tab at the bottom of the editing window to complete this example.

TIP *If you usually prefer to edit the HTML directly, you can change the default by clicking Tools ➤ Options and then selecting the HTML Designer item from the list of options. Change the Start Active Server Pages In option to Design View and then click OK.*

Right-click somewhere on the surface of the Web Form in the editing window and select Properties from the context menu. You'll see the DOCUMENT Property Pages dialog (see Figure 4.5).

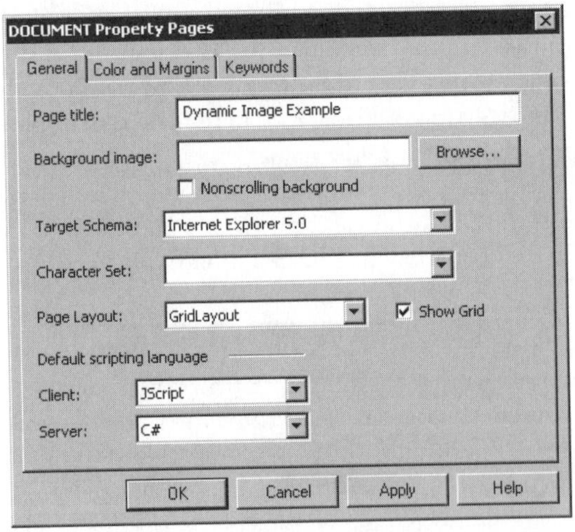

FIGURE 4.5

DOCUMENT
Property Pages
dialog

Enter **Dynamic Image Example** in the Page Title field. Set Target Schema to Internet Explorer 5.0 and the Page Layout setting to GridLayout. Hit OK when you are finished.

On the left side of your screen, you'll see a Toolbox tab. Move your mouse cursor over the tab; Visual Studio displays the Toolbox. Click the Web Forms bar, then click the Label Control item. Move your cursor back into the editing window and draw the Label control. You've just placed a Web Form label on the page. You should remember that Web Form controls are *not* the same as HTML controls, although they look identical; they have a different namespace from the equivalent HTML controls. Web Form Label controls and HTML Label controls (and most other controls that contain text) have a Text property like a Windows TextBox control rather than a Caption property like a classic VB Form Label control.

Next, drop a TextBox control next to the label. Your Web Form should look similar to Figure 4.6. That's it for page design—not elaborate, but functional. Next, you need to write a little code.

FIGURE 4.6

The DynamicImage .aspx Web Form after placing controls

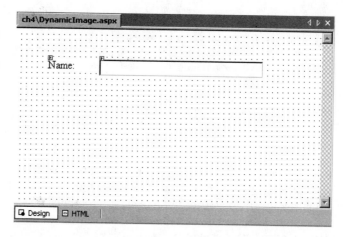

Step 3: Writing the Code Behind the Page

Right-click the surface of the Web Form and select View Code from the context menu. If you're not very familiar with C#, the code is somewhat intimidating, but don't worry, most of it is template code. The method you want to modify is the code for the Page_Load event.

A Web Form executes the Page_Load event each time it's requested; however, the event contains code to differentiate between an HTTP GET request and a POST request. The correct .NET terminology is IsPostBack, meaning that the Web Form has been submitted back to the server. In other words, when IsPostBack is true, the user has already seen the Web Form page at least once. IsPostBack is a Page object property. You can think of the Page object and the Web Form as essentially the same thing. When you need to, you can refer to the object that's running in C# using the keyword this, but you usually don't need to. Because the Page object is running when the Page_Load event executes, you don't have to use this keyword explicitly, as in this.IsPostBack, you can just write IsPostBack by itself.

In this sample page, you want to capture the text that the user enters into the text box, so your code will go into the bottom section of the If structure. For example, Listing 4.3 shows the code you need to add to the Page_Load event.

WARNING *Former VB programmers watch out! C# is case-sensitive, so, for example, the property* IsPostBack *and the word* isPostBack *are not the same.*

LISTING 4.3: THE DynamicImage Page_Load **EVENT CODE (DynamicImage.cs)**

```
using System.Drawing.Text;
// autogenerated code omitted
private void Page_Load(object sender, System.EventArgs e)
{
    if (IsPostBack) {
        Response.ContentType = "image/gif";
        getImage(TextBox1.Text).Save(Response.OutputStream,
            System.Drawing.Imaging.ImageFormat.Gif);
        Response.End();
    }
    Response.Write("Page before posting<br>");
}
```

I won't walk you through the entire code to create the image. However, because this is some of the first C# code listed in this book, I want to point out just a couple of things. First, the capability to create an image dynamically—any image—in memory simply wasn't available in classic ASP, in VB6, in C++, or intrinsically in any earlier Microsoft technology without extensive use of the Windows API. What you're seeing here is brand-new functionality or, at a minimum, a level of simplicity achieved by no other Microsoft language so far. Second, while the getImage function itself returns a Windows bitmap-formatted image, the DynamicImage.aspx Web Form returns a GIF-formatted image. In other words, C# has the power to transform an image from a BMP to a GIF image. Again, while that was possible in ASP by using externally compiled DLLs, it wasn't easy in earlier Web languages. Here's a function that creates a BMP file (yellow text on a black background) from the text entered by the user in the DynamicImage.aspx Web Form (see Listing 4.4).

LISTING 4.4: THE getImage FUNCTION (DynamicImage.cs)

```
private static Bitmap getImage(string s ) {
    Bitmap b = new Bitmap(1, 1);
    int width, height;

    //Create a Font object
    Font aFont = new Font("Times New Roman", 24,
        System.Drawing.GraphicsUnit.Point);

    // Create a Graphics Class to measure the text width
    Graphics graphics = Graphics.FromImage(b);

    // Resize the bitmap
    width = (int) graphics.MeasureString(s,aFont).Width;
```

```
    height = (int) graphics.MeasureString(s,aFont).Height;
    b = new Bitmap(b,new Size(width, height));

    graphics = Graphics.FromImage(b);
    graphics.Clear(Color.Black);
    graphics.TextRenderingHint = TextRenderingHint.AntiAlias;
    graphics.DrawString(s, aFont, new SolidBrush(Color.Yellow), 0, 0);
    graphics.Flush();
    return(b);
}
```

In the Page_Load method (refer to Listing 4.3), the page sets the Response.ContentType to image/gif because the browser needs to know how to interpret the response. Next, it calls the getImage method and transforms the resulting BMP to a GIF file. Finally, it writes the binary stream of bytes containing the GIF file to the browser, which displays the image.

Web applications don't have a defined beginning and end—users can request any page in the application at any time. To test a specific page, you need to tell VS.NET which page it should run at startup. In this case, you want the DynamicImage.aspx page to appear when you start the program. Right-click the DynamicImage.aspx file in the Solution Explorer and select the Set As Start Page item from the pop-up menu.

You can either build the project first or you can simply tell VS.NET to launch the program, and it will build the project automatically. To build the project, use one of the Build… options on the Build menu. To begin running, you can click the Run icon on the toolbar, press F5, or select Start from the Debug menu.

NOTE *You must be a member of the Debug Users account to debug ASP.NET applications.*

The first time you view the page, the Page_Load event fires. Because the browser requested the Web Form with the GET method (the first request for the Web Form), the Page.IsPostBack property is false, so you'll see the text Page Before Posting in your browser.

When you fill in some text and press the Enter key, the browser submits the form to the server. In IE, HTML forms with a single <asp:TextBox> or HTML <input> control submit automatically when you press the Enter key.

When you submit the form, the browser requests the DynamicImage.aspx page again, this time with the POST request method. The Page_Load routine fires again, but this time, the Page object's IsPostback property will have the value true (because it's a POST request), so the page performs the process to create an image.

Step 4: Viewing the Results in a Browser

Try it. Save the project and then press F5 to compile and run the project. The IDE opens up a new browser instance (see Figure 4.7).

FIGURE 4.7

The DynamicImage
.aspx Web Form
before posting

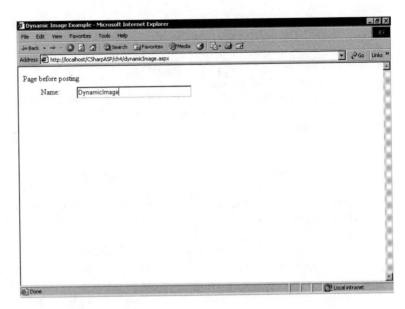

FIGURE 4.7

The DynamicImage
.aspx Web Form
before posting

Enter some text into the TextBox control and press Enter to submit the form. The server will respond with the text you entered in a GIF image sized appropriately to contain the text (see Figure 4.8).

FIGURE 4.8

The DynamicImage
.aspx Web Form
after posting

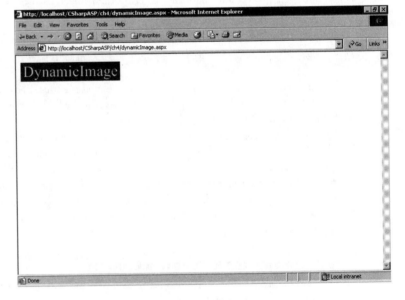

I don't know your level of experience with ASP, VB6, C++ or C#, or ASP.NET, but I can tell you—the first time I made this code run correctly, I was seriously impressed. Not only is the code that creates the bitmap only 13 (unwrapped) lines long, but there are no API calls, no handles, no special `Declare` statements, no memory management, no worries about memory leaks, and no DLLs to call or register. It just works. Now think of the hundreds of thousands of hours that people have spent doing exactly this kind of task for Web applications—drawing text in rectangles. I think this is a better way.

Summary

You've created a project and a Web Form, retrieved data from the client browser, and responded with custom code. At this point, you should begin to see how VS.NET has made the process of creating a C# Web application very similar to the process of creating a standard Windows application—you create a project, create forms, drag and drop controls onto the forms, and write code to activate the form in a code window associated with, but not tightly bound to, that form. This loose binding is an improvement on ASP because it facilitates code reuse. Just as you can create a generic Windows Form and use it repeatedly in multiple applications, you can do the same with Web Forms. You can reuse the user interface code of a Web Form by changing the code-behind class. Similarly, you can alter the look and layout of the user interface without recoding by changing the Web Form. Finally, you should realize that what you're really doing is using inheritance to customize generic classes to the needs of a specific application. The result is that you can now build a C# Web application with a familiar set of tools and operations.

Whether you've been programming in C++ or classic VB or building ASP applications, the examples in this chapter should show you the greatly increased ease-of-use and power of C# and its tight integration with ASP.NET; however, you've only begun to see the changes. In the next chapter, you'll explore Web Forms in much greater detail.

Chapter 5

Introduction to Web Forms

WITH VB6, MICROSOFT INTRODUCED a technology that used HTML templates in conjunction with an ASP page and a special type of dynamic link library (DLL) called a WebClass. Although the implementation had some serious problems, WebClasses clearly foreshadowed the direction that Microsoft has taken with .NET. WebClasses let you cleanly separate your code from the visual interface. Microsoft obviously learned a lot from the WebClass experiment, because Web Forms are like WebClasses on steroids.

In this chapter:

◆ Web Forms Are Server-Side Objects

◆ Form Validation

◆ Server-Side Validation

Web Forms Are Server-Side Objects

To create a C# Web application, click the New Project button from the Visual Studio (VS) start page to display the New Project dialog. Next, select C# Projects from the Project Types list, and then click the ASP.NET Web Application icon in the Templates pane of the dialog (see Figure 5.1). The fact that you must select the ASP.NET project type to create a C# Web application should reinforce the idea that C# Web applications and ASP.NET Web applications are the same thing.

When you first create an ASP.NET Web application project, C# adds a file called (by default) `WebForm1.aspx` to your workspace. This file is marked as the *startup page* and is the Web equivalent of a VB6 standard project's `Form1.frm`. You can compile and run the program, and C# will open a browser instance and call the `Web Form1.aspx` file. However, you won't see anything because the page has no content and no controls. By default, it's a blank page.

The key to working efficiently with Web Forms is to think of them as templates for content—and that content usually comes from the server, from the *code-behind* code. Therefore, while you *can* create and use Web Forms just as you may have built ASP pages in the past, it's not the most efficient way to use them. Instead, try to think of Web Forms in exactly the same way you think of Windows Forms—as templates to hold information. For example, consider the `MessageBox` class in C# (similar to the `MsgBox` function in VBScript—and similar to an alert in JScript). You can control the *content* of the message display, the title, text, and buttons, but you don't need to alter the window display to make efficient use of message boxes. Web Forms are similar. Try to build Web Forms that you can reuse for many different purposes.

FIGURE 5.1

Visual Studio New Project dialog: Create a C# Web application

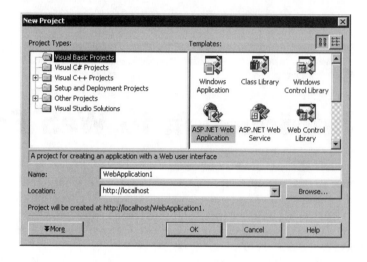

Creating Web Forms with Notepad

Despite the name and some very clever coding, there's nothing really new about Web Forms themselves. You can easily create a Web Form in Notepad or any other text editor as long as you include the required header information at the top of the page and name the file with the `.aspx` extension. Because .NET will compile changed or added Web Forms on-the-fly, you can simply place a file in a Web virtual directory and immediately request it from a browser; you're not required to perform an explicit compile step. In contrast, when you create the code for the application from within VS, you must compile the application before you can run it.

In the rest of this chapter, you'll work with the CSharpASP application you created in Chapter 4, "Introduction to ASP.NET," but within a new folder. Launch VS.NET, open the CSharpASP solution, and then right-click the CSharpASP entry in the Solution Explorer window. Click Add ➢ New Folder, and then name the new folder **ch5**. Press Enter to save the folder.

Next, open Notepad and type or copy Listing 5.1 into the editing window.

LISTING 5.1: CREATE A WEB FORM WITH NOTEPAD (notepadForm.aspx)

```
<%@ Page Language="C#"%>
<html>
  <head>
  </head>
  <body>
   <%Response.write("This form was created in Notepad");%>
  </body>
</html>
```

Click File ➤ Save and navigate to the folder referenced by the CSharpASP project (unless you specified a special location when you created the CSharpASP project, in most cases, the folder will be `C:\Inetpub\wwwroot\CSharpASP`). Expand the subfolder list for the `CSharpASP` folder and save the file as `NotePadForm.aspx` in the `ch5` folder. To force Notepad to save the file without a `.txt` extension, put double quotes around the filename in the File Save dialog, or change the file type to All Files.

Finally, open your browser and type the URL of your new file. Again, in most cases, you'll be able to reach the file using the URL `http://localhost/CSharpASP/ch5/NotePadForm.aspx`. You will see the line "This form was created in Notepad."

You may never need to create pages like this, but it's extremely useful to know that you don't need to have VS.NET installed to make minor changes to a file. I won't take you through the exercise, but you should know that you can change the code-behind C# class files using a text editor in exactly the same way—and .NET will also recompile those dynamically.

Code Render Blocks—Mix Code and HTML

You've seen how you can insert code directly into an ASP.NET page in the classic ASP manner. Now that you know it's possible, try your best to forget it for the rest of this book. There are times when it's convenient to place code directly into a page, but normally you should avoid the temptation. As soon as you place code into a page, it becomes isolated code. You can't inherit from classes defined inline in ASPX pages, so the practice is considerably less reusable than placing the same code in C# class files.

Web Forms' Compatibility with Existing ASP Pages

Despite being driven by a completely different technology than classic ASP, Web Forms have better backward compatibility with classic ASP pages than does C# with C++. For example, the only differences between the code in Listing 5.1 and the equivalent code in classic ASP written in VBScript are the language directive at the top of the page and the fact that, like JScript, the Response.Write method requires parentheses around the string argument in C#, and the closing semicolon, whereas no parentheses are required in VBScript.

For classic ASP pages written in JScript that use only the intrinsic ASP objects (such as the `Response` object), all you need to do is change a little of the syntax. However, many classic ASP pages use calls to external DLLs to add functionality, and .NET isn't directly compatible with COM-based DLLs. If you need to use an existing COM DLL in your C# application, you can add a special page-level attribute called `AspCompat`. You must add the `AspCompat` attribute to pages that call COM DLLs, or to call any code that requires access to any of the classic ASP intrinsic objects (`Request`, `Response`, `Session`, `Application`, or `Server`). Unfortunately, when you include the attribute `AspCompat=True` on a page, ASP.NET forces the Web Form to run in a single-threaded mode, which has an adverse performance impact. The `AspCompat` feature is intended to ease upgrades and let you begin to integrate ASP.NET pages into an existing site easily, without having to change the entire site at once, but it is not suitable for a long-term migration strategy.

Examples of ASP.NET Pages

The best way to understand an ASP.NET page is to walk through it in detail, examining what happens at each step.

WEB FORMS ARE HTML/XHTML/XML PAGES

As you just saw when you created a Web Form with Notepad, no magic is happening here. Web Forms really *are* just HTML pages—or more properly, they're Extensible Hypertext Markup Language (XHTML) pages by default.

NOTE *XHTML is a specific form of HTML that meets the XML 1.0 specification by requiring stricter syntax than does HTML. For example, all tags must be closed, case is relevant, and all attribute values must be enclosed in quotes. You can see the full XHTML 1.0 Recommendation at* `http://www.w3.org/TR/xhtml1/`.

When the ASP.NET engine reads the page content, it looks for tags with a specific namespace prefix, called `asp:`. Take a minute to go back and look at the `DynamicImage.aspx` file from Chapter 4. Load the file into the VS editor and then click the HTML tab at the bottom of the editing window. The Web Form has two controls: a label and a text box. Here's the code that the VS Web Forms design engine inserted when you placed the controls on the Web Form (note that the details may differ, depending on your settings, the order you placed the controls on the form, and their position):

```
<form id="Web Form1" method="post" runat="server">
<asp:Label id=lblName style="Z-INDEX: 101; LEFT: 48px; POSITION:
    absolute; TOP: 43px" runat="server" Width="78"
    Height="19">Name:</asp:Label>
<asp:TextBox id=TextBox1 style="Z-INDEX: 102; LEFT: 125px; POSITION:
    absolute; TOP: 43px" runat="server"></asp:TextBox>
</form>
```

This code contains several interesting features. First, whenever you place controls on a Web Form, VS.NET places them inside a `<form>` tag. That by itself is a major departure from simple HTML, where you could use input controls that were not part of a form. Note that the `<form>` tag uses the POST method rather than the GET method, that the form posts data back to the current page (it has no `action` attribute), and that it has a `runat=server` attribute.

Now run the page (use the context menu and select Set As Start Page) for the `DynamicImage.aspx` file. Don't enter any text into the text box; instead, right-click a blank space in the browser window and select View Source from the context menu. Here's the portion of the HTML code on the client that corresponds to the `<form>` tag on the server.

```
<form name="Web Form1" method="post" action="DynamicImage.aspx"
    id="Web Form1">
<input type="hidden" name="__VIEWSTATE"
    value="YTB6LTM3MDk3ODU5Ml9fX3g=ce6a788f" />
<span id="lblName" style="height:19px;width:78px;Z-INDEX: 101; LEFT:
    48px; POSITION: absolute; TOP: 43px">Name:</span>
<input name="TextBox1" type="text" id="TextBox1" style="Z-INDEX: 102;
    LEFT: 125px; POSITION: absolute; TOP: 43px" />
</form>
```

Viewstate—AUTOMATIC CONTROL STATE MAINTENANCE

Look at the code now! At first glance it looks the same, but there are several differences. First, the form now has an `action` attribute (it points back to the generating page, meaning the page posts data to itself). Second, there's a hidden input named __VIEWSTATE that contains a string of what looks like gibberish. Web Forms generate this hidden `viewstate` control as part of the Windows Forms–like event model on the server; when a user changes the content of a control on the client, the server must have the original value so it can compare the original contents with the changed contents and thus raise some sort of `changed` event. The string value is encrypted not so much to hide its contents from the user (after all, the user can see the "real" values in the controls on the page) as to minimize the size of the container. You can imagine how the `viewstate` control's contents can get fairly large when pages contain multiple-line text fields (`<input type="textarea">` controls in HTML) filled with text or entire tables containing data from a database.

Finally, you don't see the `<asp:Label>` and `<asp:TextBox>` tags that were present in the server-side code. That's because those tags are not HTML input controls—they're XML tags that represent the ASP.NET-specific server controls. At runtime, the server replaces these representations with HTML (or other output) rendered appropriately for the targeted client type. If you've been building Web applications with classic ASP, working with HTML input controls, and managing Viewstate yourself, you'll appreciate the time savings that automatic Viewstate management provides.

INTRODUCING SERVER CONTROLS

A *server control* is a class that specifies output and event behavior for the ASP.NET engine. The built-in ASP.NET Web controls render as XML-formatted elements. Remember that when the ASP.NET engine reads the page content, it looks for tags with the `asp:` namespace prefix. The `<asp:>` tags provide a layer of indirection. The tags "stand for" HTML but are not part of the HTML specification. Instead, you can think of the tags as a combination of standard HTML and script. The exact HTML/ script output generated by the ASP.NET engine depends on several page properties. For example, the `Page` property named `targetSchema` controls which version/type of HTML the ASP.NET engine generates in response to a page request. The default target is Internet Explorer 5.0, but you can target downlevel browsers by setting the `targetSchema` property value to a less capable browser version. When you do that, the output may change (depending on the controls you have placed on the Web Form). Similarly, you can control the client script language using the `defaultClientScript` property. At present, VS lets you select either JScript (the default) or VBScript. The number of client languages will likely expand to include C# and VB.NET in the future, as the .NET framework becomes more widely distributed.

Until the advent of server controls, it was the developer's responsibility to write HTML and script that would display and function properly on the range of clients using the site. Despite Internet Explorer's market dominance, several different types and versions of browsers are still used. Server controls let you bypass the difficulties involved in writing and testing different page versions on different browsers.

Browsers aren't the only clients, though. In the past couple of years, new types of HTTP clients have proliferated. Palm, palmtop, notepad, and telephone devices can all browse the Web (and your sites) to varying degrees, and all have special display requirements due to their small form factors and display area. Fortunately, as ASP.NET matures, it will support more devices. You can target any specific type of client by setting the `targetSchema` to an appropriate value for that client type. Out of the box, the available `targetSchema` types are as follows:

◆ Internet Explorer 3.02/Navigator 3.0

◆ Internet Explorer 5.0

◆ Navigator 4.0

The first two correspond roughly to HTML 3.2 and HTML 4.0 with CSS and DHTML support, respectively. The Navigator 4.0 option reflects the requirement to output Netscape-specific DHTML. However, if you need to target clients that have special output requirements (such as wireless devices), you can customize the ASP.NET engine through class inheritance. The salient point is that the mechanism is in place to target multiple device types from a single code base.

Therefore, one reason for the development of server controls is to let you concentrate more on the program and less on cross-browser or client-device issues.

HTML DISPLAY, EVENT-DRIVEN MODEL

Server controls have another purpose in addition to solving disparate client-device display requirements. They give you a server-side event-handling mechanism. For example, when a user clicks a button, you can "catch" and handle the `click` event on the server! That's a nice feature because it lets you develop, debug, and deploy centrally located and compiled code running in a known environment in response to user events, rather than distributed, interpreted client script running in unknown environments.

Because they run on remote machines, many server controls have *delayed* events: The client doesn't send a message to the server for *every* client action. For example, a text input control has an `onchange` event that fires when the control loses the focus. In classic ASP, to respond to the `onchange` event, you would have had to handle the event on the client. Now, you can wait until the user submits the form. At that point, the server can compare the stored `ViewState` values with the current values. If the contents of the text input control changed after the page was sent (in other words, the user changed the text), the values will differ, and the ASP.NET engine will raise the `onchange` event.

Of course, you're still completely free to trap and respond to events in client-side code as well. For example, you probably want to respond to invalid input as soon as possible—when the user enters the value—rather than waiting until the user submits the form. Checking input values is called *form validation*. ASP.NET can simplify validation as well, as you'll see later in this chapter.

ASP.NET Ships with 45 Web Controls

Windows users are spoiled. They're used to rich controls such as `TreeViews`, `ListViews`, `Coolbars`, `Toolbars`, splitters, and spinners. So far, browser-based HTML controls have been rather like poor relations—they often have the same names but bear few of the trappings. While ASP.NET doesn't exactly revolutionize client controls, it does give you a much wider assortment than you had with HTML, and if that's not enough, it also gives you the capability to create your own. Table 5.1 contains the 20 most commonly used server input controls that ship with ASP.NET.

TABLE 5.1: ASP.NET SERVER INPUT CONTROLS

CONTROL NAME	DESCRIPTION
`<asp:Button>`	A pushbutton, similar to a standard Windows PushButton or the CommandButton control in VB. The Text attribute is the equivalent of the VB Caption property. When clicked, the Button control submits the form to the server.
`<asp:Calendar>`	Provides a Calendar control in HTML. The level of functionality of this control (as of all Server controls) depends on the client's level of support for script and compliance with HTML specifications.
`<asp:CheckBox>`	Check box control. Unlike tristate Windows check boxes, these have only two values: true (checked) or false (unchecked).
`<asp:CheckBoxList>`	A grouped series of check boxes. Similar in function to placing a series of check boxes in a Windows Frame control.
`<asp:DataGrid>`	Probably the first of *many* grid controls. You can specify edit and sort options.
`<asp:DataList>`	Complex List control that lets you easily format data from a data set and even has options for letting the user edit the data.
`<asp:DropDownList>`	Single selection from an expandable drop-down list. Similar to a VB ComboBox with its Locked property set to true.
`<asp:HyperLink>`	The equivalent of a standard HTML anchor tag.
`<asp:ImageButton>`	The same effect as wrapping an <img> tag in an anchor (<a>) tag and giving it an href attribute. When clicked, the ImageButton control submits the form to the server.
`<asp:Image>`	Image display (GIF, JPG, etc.). The equivalent of a VB Image control.
`<asp:Label>`	Text-only, read-only display. The equivalent of a Windows Label control.
`<asp:LinkButton>`	Acts like a button—looks like a hyperlink. When clicked, the LinkButton control submits the form to the server.
`<asp:Panel>`	Just like a Windows Frame control, the Panel control serves to group or contain other controls except that, by default, a Panel control has no border and no label.
`<asp:RadioButton>`	A radio button control.
`<asp:RadioButtonList>`	A grouped series of radio buttons. Similar in function to placing a series of radio buttons in a Windows Frame control.
`<asp:Repeater>`	Used to format lists of items or entire rows from a data set. The Repeater control applies a custom format to the data in each row of the data.
`<asp:Table>`	Creates an HTML <table> tag.
`<asp:TableRow>`	Lets you control events, content, and display characteristics for any row in a table.
`<asp:TableCell>`	Lets you control events, content, and display characteristics for any cell in a table.
`<asp:TextBox>`	Single-line or multiline text input control. This control functions as a stand-in for both the <input type="text"> and <textarea> HTML controls.

You can bind all—yes, all—the server controls to data sources. Those sources, of course, can consist of data retrieved from a database, but they may also be XML documents, XML that you generate dynamically, or array data.

Your familiarity with some of these controls depends largely on your background. If you've been programming ASP pages, you should almost immediately feel comfortable with the controls that substitute for standard HTML input controls and tags, such as the `Table` or `HyperLink` controls. In contrast, if you've been programming Windows applications, you'll probably recognize that Microsoft has extended some of the most popular Windows controls to the Web by including the `DataGrid`, `DataList`, and `Calendar` controls. There are a few controls that have no direct single predecessor, such as the `CheckBoxList` control and the `Repeater` control.

runat="server"

Despite their similarity to common Windows controls and HTML input controls, server controls are considerably different. They run on the server, not on the client. To be more specific, by default, the events and data generated by the user on the client are posted back to the server, and you handle them there, not on the client as you would in a Windows application. The model is robust enough to let you perform many common operations with little or no code. For example, one of the most common operations on Web sites is to create a login/password security page to force users to authenticate before viewing the contents of a site. Most commonly, these pages have two text fields: one for the username that displays the user's entry in plain text, and one for the password, which typically displays asterisks rather than the characters that the user types. They usually have one or more buttons as well (see Figure 5.2 and Listing 5.2).

FIGURE 5.2

A simple login page

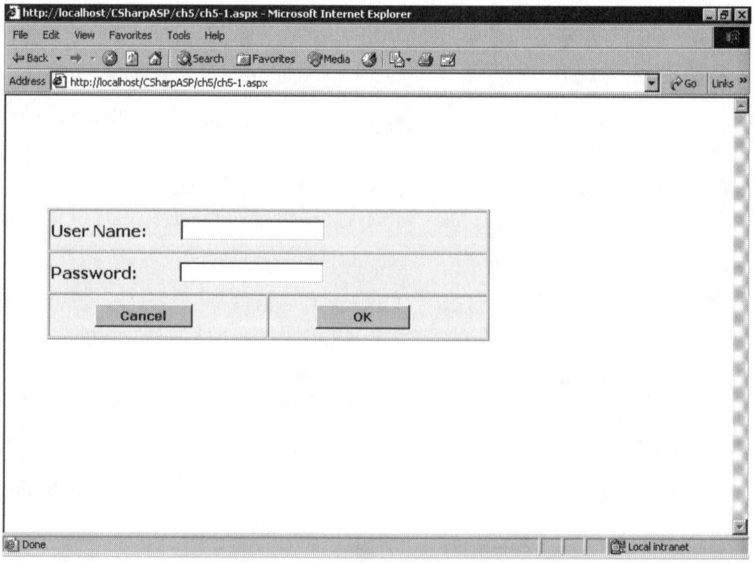

LISTING 5.2: HTML CODE FOR LOGIN FORM (ch5-1.aspx)

```
<%@ Page Language="c#" AutoEventWireup="false"
    Codebehind="ch5-1.aspx.cs" Inherits="CSharpASP.ch5.ch5_1" %>
<!DOCTYPE HTML PUBLIC "-//W3C//DTD HTML 4.0 Transitional//EN">
<HTML>
    <HEAD>
        <META http-equiv="Content-Type" content="text/html;
        charset=windows-1252">
        <meta content="http://schemas.microsoft.com/intellisense/ie5"
        name="vs_targetSchema">
        <meta content="Microsoft Visual Studio.NET 7.0"
  name="GENERATOR">
        <meta content="C#" name="CODE_LANGUAGE">
    </HEAD>
<body ms_positioning="GridLayout">
<form id=FORM1 method=post runat="server">
<table style="LEFT: 122px; POSITION: absolute; TOP: 106px" height=137
    cellSpacing=1 cellPadding=1 width=474 bgColor=#ffffcc border=1>
  <tr>
    <td colSpan=2><asp:label id=Label1 runat="server" Width="127"
    Height="18" font-size="Small" font-bold="True" font-
    names="Verdana"
    bordercolor="Transparent" borderstyle="None"
    backcolor="#FFFFC0">User Name:</asp:label><asp:textbox
    id=txtUserName runat="server"></asp:textbox></td></tr>
  <tr>
    <td colSpan=2>
      <asp:label id=Label2 runat="server" Width="127" Height="18"
      font-size="Small" font-bold="True" font-names="Verdana"
      bordercolor="Transparent" borderstyle="None"
      backcolor="#FFFFC0">
      Password:
      </asp:label>

      <asp:textbox id=txtPassword runat="server" textmode="Password">
      </asp:textbox>
    </td>
  </tr>
  <tr>
    <td align=middle width=200>
      <asp:button id=cmdCancel runat="server" Text="Cancel"
      font-bold="True" font-names="Verdana" commandname="cmdCancel"
      height="24" width="104"></asp:button>
    </td>
    <td align=middle width=200>
      <asp:button id=cmdOK runat="server" Text="OK" font-bold="True"
```

```
        font-names="Verdana" commandname="cmdOK" height="25"
        width="101"></asp:button>
      </td>
    </tr>
  </table>
  </form>
  </body>
  </html>
```

When you run this example, you can enter text into the fields, just like a standard HTML page. When you click one of the buttons, the browser submits the form data. But unlike a standard HTML form, *you get the entered data back.* By default, the server uses the ViewState hidden control to rebuild the state of the page and send it right back to the browser.

OK, you may not think that's exciting, but here are the steps required to perform the same operation by coding it manually in a classic ASP page:

1. Check to see if the page was reached via a GET (first display) or POST request.

2. If POST, then retrieve the form data from the request.

3. Using embedded code, rebuild the page. For each control, insert the value you just obtained from the POST operation to redisplay the values on the client side, for example `<input type="text" value= "<%=Request.Form("txtUserName")%>" id="txtUserName">`.

4. For each control, create hidden form variables to hold the current field values, such as `<input type="hidden" value= "<%=Request.Form("txtUserName")%>" id="txtUserName">`.

That's a considerable amount of work. Using ASP.NET, you didn't have to do anything but lay out some controls. But that's not all: You can perform complex input validation without writing any code.

Form Validation

It's been said that the only way to write a perfect data input program is to eliminate the users. While you probably don't want to go that far, you should recognize that the single greatest source of bad data is bad programs. The best data entry programs don't let users enter invalid data. Less elegant but still acceptable programs let users know when they *do* enter invalid data, but neither type accepts invalid data. In contrast, bad programs not only let users enter invalid data, they also skip the validation, invariably resulting in data integrity problems, expensive fixes, angry clients, and a lot of trouble all around.

To solve the problem, you *must* perform data validity checks. The general rule to follow is that the closer you perform these checks to the point of input, the more likely you are to get consistently good data. By checking the data at the point of input, you eliminate the need to check it during future operations, which both eliminates potential errors and provide an improved user experience. Unfortunately, I've seen programs that go far overboard by displaying annoying messages whenever a user types a single invalid key—something that even the best typists do occasionally. Similarly, many programs check field validity only after the user completes the entire form. In certain cases, that's acceptable, but more often, a better method is to check the fields when the user completes a defined part of the input task.

For example, on the login Web Form, you know that both the User Name and Password fields *must* contain a value, because you will be unable to authenticate the user without both values. Therefore you must ensure that both values have been entered. Beyond that, you should have rules for the contents of each field. For example, you might force passwords to be at least six characters, and you might not allow the username to contain any characters except letters and numbers.

Whenever a user submits the form without meeting the validation requirements, you want to redisplay the form and show a message stating what the problem is and how to fix it. In ASP.NET, you can perform many common data validation tasks without writing any code, using a set of server controls called *validators*.

Client-Side Validation

Here's an example that performs client-side validation using the `Validator` controls. Create a copy of the Web Form `ch5-1.aspx`. You can copy files within the Solution Explorer just as you do in the Windows Explorer. Right-click the `ch5-1.aspx` file in the Solution Explorer pane, then select Copy from the context menu. Next, right-click the `ch5` folder, and then select Paste from the context menu. That will paste a copy of the `ch5-1.aspx` file named `Copy of ch5-1.aspx` into the `ch5` folder. Rename the file `ch5-2.aspx` by selecting the new file and pressing F2 or right-clicking and selecting Rename from the context menu, and then typing the new name.

Copying and pasting a Web Form also pastes a copy of the code-behind file, `ch5-1.aspx.cs`. That can be a problem when you rename the ASPX file because, while renaming the file also renames the code-behind file, it does *not* rename the class created in the code-behind file. You must rename that manually. Double-click the `ch5-2.aspx.cs` file and rename the class `ch5_2.cs` (note the underscore rather than the dash).

Double-click the new Web Form to load it into the editing window. Click the Toolbox, and drag two `RequiredFieldValidator` controls onto the design surface. Place them just to the right of the two `TextBox` controls. Next, set the `ID` property of the new controls to `UsernameValidator` and `PasswordValidator`, respectively. Set other properties for the controls as follows:

Property	**UsernameValidator**	**PasswordValidator**
ControlToValidate	txtUserName	txtPassword
ErrorMessage	Username required	Password Required

When you finish, the Web Form should look like Figure 5.3.

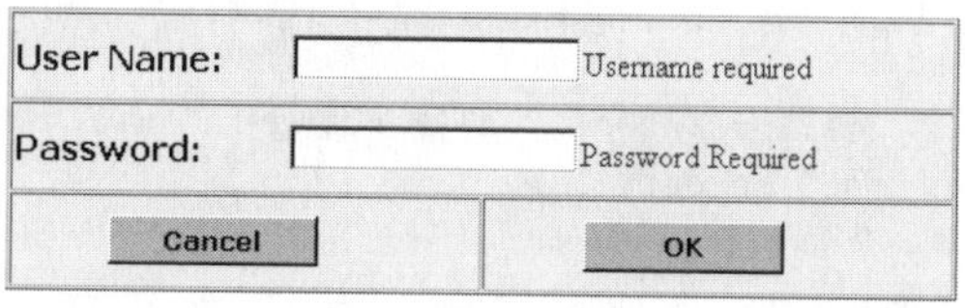

FIGURE 5.3

Simple login page with `Required-FieldValidator`s

Run the Web Form again. This time, submit the form without entering text into either the User Name or Password field. The submission triggers the validation check. The validation check fails for both controls, because the `RequiredFieldValidator` control performs only one check—it tests whether the control referred to by its `ControlToValidate` property contains a value different from the control's initial value. Stop the program and run it again. Enter some text into one of the two fields but not the other. You should see the error message appear for the empty field only.

Validators are "smart" controls. They follow the rule mentioned in the beginning of this section and perform the validation as closely as possible to the point of input. In this case, that point is heavily dependent on the browser. Using IE5 or higher, the controls generate client-side JavaScript or VBScript (depending on the setting of the `defaultClientScript Page` property). Using downlevel browsers, the controls generate no client script, and validation fires on the server when the user submits the form.

How does this all work? It's worth exploring a bit so that you'll understand the model. Using IE5, for example, with the `defaultClientScript` property set to `JavaScript`, the page generates the script in Listing 5.3. You can see the full HTML generated by the page yourself by running the program and then selecting View Source from the browser context menu. The highlighted sections show how ASP.NET translates the validation controls into HTML.

LISTING 5.3: HTML CODE AS SENT TO THE BROWSER FOR THE LOGIN FORM WITH
    `RequiredFieldValidator` (ch5-2.aspx)

```
<HTML>
   <HEAD>
      <META http-equiv="Content-Type"
         content="text/html; charset=windows-1252">
      <meta
         content="http://schemas.microsoft.com/intellisense/ie5"
         name="vs_targetSchema">
      <meta content="Microsoft Visual Studio.NET 7.0" name="GENERATOR">
      <meta content="C#" name="CODE_LANGUAGE">
   </HEAD>
<body ms_positioning="GridLayout">
<form name="FORM1" method="post" action="ch5-2.aspx"
   language="javascript" onsubmit="ValidatorOnSubmit();" id="FORM1">
<input type="hidden" name="__VIEWSTATE"
   value="dDwtMTYzMDIzNDQwMjs7Pg==" />

<script language="javascript"
   src="/aspnet_client/system_web/1_4000_2914_16/WebUIValidation.js">
</script>
<table style="Z-INDEX: 101; LEFT: 122px; POSITION: absolute;
   TOP: 106px"
   height="137" cellSpacing="1" cellPadding="1" width="474"
   bgColor="#ffffcc" border="1">
<tr>
<td colSpan="2">
<span id="Label1" style="background-color:#FFFFC0;border-
   color:Transparent;border-style:None;font-family:Verdana;
   font-size:Small;font-weight:bold;height:18px;
   width:135px;">User Name:</span>
<input name="txtUserName" type="text" id="txtUserName" />
```

```
<span id="UsernameValidator" controltovalidate="txtUserName"
   errormessage="Username required"
   evaluationfunction="RequiredFieldValidatorEvaluateIsValid"
   initialvalue="" style="color:Red;visibility:hidden;">Username
   required</span>
</td>
</tr>
<tr>
<td colSpan="2">
<span id="Label2" style="background-color:#FFFFC0;
   border-color:Transparent;border-style:None;font-family:Verdana;
   font-size:Small;font-weight:bold;height:18px;width:136px;">
   Password:</span>
<input name="txtPassword" type="password" id="txtPassword" />
<span id="PasswordValidator" controltovalidate="txtPassword"
   errormessage="Password Required"
   evaluationfunction="RequiredFieldValidatorEvaluateIsValid"
   initialvalue="" style="color:Red;visibility:hidden;">Password
   Required</span>
</td>
</tr>
<tr>
<td align="middle" width="200">
<input type="submit" name="cmdCancel" value="Cancel"
   onclick="if (typeof(Page_ClientValidate) == 'function')
   Page_ClientValidate(); " language="javascript" id="cmdCancel"
   style="font-family:Verdana;font-weight:bold;height:24px;
   width:104px;" />
</td>
<td align="middle" width="200">
<input type="submit" name="cmdOK" value="OK"
   onclick="if (typeof(Page_ClientValidate) == 'function')
   Page_ClientValidate(); " language="javascript" id="cmdOK"
   style="font-family:Verdana;font-weight:bold;height:25px;
   width:101px;" />
</td>
</tr>
</table>

<script language="javascript">
<!--
   var Page_Validators =  new Array(document.all["UsernameValidator"],
      document.all["PasswordValidator"]);
      // -->
</script>


<script language="javascript">
```

```
<!--
var Page_ValidationActive = false;
if (typeof(clientInformation) != "undefined" &&
    clientInformation.appName.indexOf("Explorer") != -1) {
        if (typeof(Page_ValidationVer) == "undefined")
            alert("Unable to find script library " +
            "'/aspnet_client/system_web/" +
            "1_4000_2914_16/WebUIValidation.js'." +
            "Try placing this file manually, or reinstall by running " +
            "'aspnet_regiis -c'.");
        else if (Page_ValidationVer != "121")
            alert("This page uses an incorrect version of " +
            "WebUIValidation.js. The page expects version 121. " +
            "The script library is " + Page_ValidationVer + ".");
        else
            ValidatorOnLoad();
}

function ValidatorOnSubmit() {
    if (Page_ValidationActive) {
        ValidatorCommonOnSubmit();
    }
}
// -->
</script>


</form>
</body>
</html>
```

The interesting and functional part here is the client-side script. First, note that the page includes a script file:

```
<script language="javascript"
    src="/aspnet_client/system_web/1_4000_2914_16/WebUIValidation.js">
</script>
```

That script file contains several utility functions for validating input. You should be able to find the file by following the path from your root Web directory. On my computer, the full path is as follows:

```
<script language="javascript"
    src="/aspnet_client/system_web/1_4000_2914_16/WebUIValidation.js">
</script>
```

The path may vary on your computer, because it's version dependent, but you should be able to match the value of the script's src attribute to a physical path on your server. Farther down in the file, you'll see a script that defines several variables and then checks whether the script was found and loaded by checking the `Page_ValidationVer` variable defined in the included script. The page displays message boxes (using the `alert` function in JScript) if either condition fails.

```
if (typeof(clientInformation) != "undefined" &&
    clientInformation.appName.indexOf("Explorer") != -1) {
        if (typeof(Page_ValidationVer) == "undefined")
            alert("Unable to find script library " +
                "'/aspnet_client/system_web/1_4000_2914_16/" +
                "WebUIValidation.js'. " +
                "Try placing this file manually, " +
                "or reinstall by running
                'aspnet_regiis -c'.");
        else if (Page_ValidationVer != "121")
            alert("This page uses an incorrect version of " +
                "WebUIValidation.js. The page expects version 121. " +
                "The script library is " + Page_ValidationVer + ".");
        else
            ValidatorOnLoad();
}
```

The real work occurs when the user clicks a button. Each operation that submits the form calls a function to check the data entered into the form. For example, here's the OK button definition. The `onClick` event checks to see whether a function called `Page_ClientValidate` exists; if so, it calls the function.

```
<input type="submit" name="cmdOK" value="OK"
    onclick="if (typeof(Page_ClientValidate) == 'function')
    Page_ClientValidate(); " language="javascript" id="cmdOK"
    style="font-family:Verdana;font-weight:bold;height:25px;
    width:101px;" />
</td>
```

The `Page_ClientValidate` function iterates through the `Validator` controls in the document, calling the `ValidatorValidate` function for each one.

```
function Page_ClientValidate() {
    var i;
    for (i = 0; i < Page_Validators.length; i++) {
        ValidatorValidate(Page_Validators[i]);
    }
    ValidatorUpdateIsValid();
    ValidationSummaryOnSubmit();
    Page_BlockSubmit = !Page_IsValid;
    return Page_IsValid;
}
```

The `ValidatorValidate` function fires the evaluation function bound to each validator, which in turn performs the appropriate test on the value of the control to which the validator is bound through its `ControlToValidate` property.

```
function ValidatorValidate(val) {
    val.isvalid = true;
    if (val.enabled != false) {
        if (typeof(val.evaluationfunction) == "function") {
            val.isvalid = val.evaluationfunction(val);
        }
    }
    ValidatorUpdateDisplay(val);
}
```

After iterating through all the validators, the `Page_ClientValidate` function calls a `Validator-UpdateIsValid()` function, which iterates through the page validators again, checking the `isvalid` property for each. If any of the `isvalid` properties returns `false`, the script sets a page-level variable called `Page_IsValid` to `false` and exits the loop.

So far, nothing's prevented the form from submitting, though. The `<form>` tag's `onsubmit` property calls another function called `ValidatorOnSubmit()`. That script checks to see if the validators are loaded and working properly by checking the value of a variable named `Page_Validationactive` that is set to `true` only when the `ValidatorOnLoad()` function executes properly. Finally, it calls the `ValidatorCommonOnSubmit()` function.

```
function ValidatorOnSubmit() {
    if (Page_ValidationActive) {
        ValidatorCommonOnSubmit();
    }
}
```

The common validation routine `ValidatorCommonOnSubmit` sets the event object's `returnValue` property to the inverse value of the `Page_BlockSubmit` variable that was set in the `Page_Client-Validate()` function. That's a little difficult to read, but if you translate it to English, it sounds better. "If the page should block submission, then return `false`, otherwise return `true`." If the `event.returnValue` is `true`, the form will submit the data to the server; otherwise, it won't do anything.

```
function ValidatorCommonOnSubmit() {
    event.returnValue = !Page_BlockSubmit;
    Page_BlockSubmit = false;
}
```

Finally, the function sets the `Page_BlockSubmit` variable to `false` to get ready for the next validation round (in other words, it clears the variable so the form will submit the next time if the user fixes the invalid input values). While all this client script is anything but simple, you usually won't need to think about it at all.

NOTE *There have been several versions of the client-side validation script file. I've used version 121 in this example. Your version may be different, but the differences should be slight.*

Now that you've seen a simple validation control, you can extend the validation a little. As I stated earlier, in addition to checking that the user has entered a value, you will want to perform a couple of other checks. The next example enforces a complex rule that usernames may contain only letters and numbers, that they must be between 3 and 10 characters long, and that passwords may contain any characters but must be between 6 and 10 characters long. You can perform these types of tests with a `RegularExpressionValidator` control. Make a copy of the `ch5-2.aspx` Web Form and rename it `ch5-3.aspx` (see the procedure listed earlier in this chapter to copy a Web Form). Drag two `Regular-ExpressionValidator` controls onto the Web Form. Place them under the table. Make them as wide as the table and two or three lines high. Set the `ID` property of the new controls to `UsernameRegExp-Validator` and `PasswordRegExpValidator`. Set other properties for the controls as follows:

Property	**UsernameRegExpValidator**	**PasswordRegExpValidator**
ControlToValidate	txtUserName	txtPassword
ErrorMessage	Invalid Username: Usernames must be between 3 and 10 characters, and may contain only letters and numbers.	Invalid Password
ValidationExpression	[a-zA-Z_0-9]{3,10}	.{6,10}
Display	Dynamic (or Static)	Dynamic (or Static)
EnableClientScript	True	True

The `ValidationExpression` property contains the regular expression that the validator uses to test the value of the control specified by the `ControlToValidate` property. The expression `[a-zA-Z_0-9]{3,10}` accepts alphanumeric characters and the underscore and limits the matched value to between 3 and 10 characters in length, inclusive. When you run the program, the same actions occur as before; the page generates client-side JavaScript to validate the control, and the validator checks the entered values using the regular expression. Try it. Enter two characters into the User Name field and then press the Tab key. The validation fires immediately. Your browser should look similar to Figure 5.4.

FIGURE 5.4

Regular-
Expression-
Validator
control example

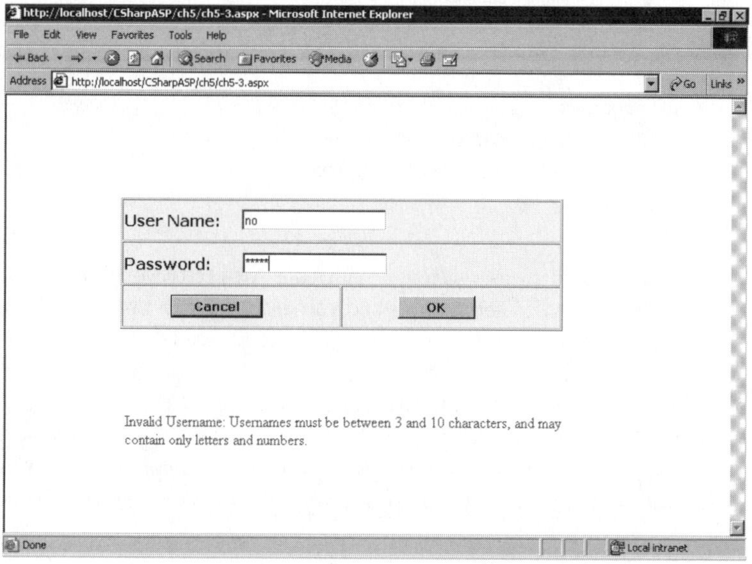

Server-Side Validation

Validation always fires on the server—even when validation has *already* fired on the client. This may seem odd, considering that you may have spent a lot of time making sure the client is unable to submit invalid values, but don't let that bother you. You may want to reuse the server-side code at some point—for example, you might inherit from your Web Form, or someone might submit a different form to your page. In any case, you don't have to let the controls validate on the client—you can force them to validate only on the server by setting the Web Form's `clientTarget` property to `Down-Level` or by setting the `EnableClientScript` property for any specific `Validation` control to `false`. Changing the `clientTarget` property prevents the page from generating any client validation script; instead, the Web Form submits all the values to the server, and the controls perform their validation tasks there. Changing the `EnableClientScript` property to `false` for a `Validation` control prevents only that control from firing client-side validation—again, the control still validates the data on the server when the user posts the form.

In some cases where you know the clients may consist of downlevel browsers, you may *have* to perform validation on the server. Another reason to validate on the server is when you want to closely control the position and content of the messages that appear. You can't easily alter the client-side validation code (although I'll show you how to work around that problem), but by writing a small amount of code in the code-behind class, you can change the messages that appear very easily.

Change the validation location to the server by entering **DownLevel** in the document `clientTarget` property field. You need to click the design surface to see the document properties. Next, double-click the OK button to open up the code-behind class. Double-clicking the control creates a `cmdOK_cClick` method stub—this is the event that fires each time the user clicks the OK button. Add the following code to the method stub:

```
private void cmdOK_Click(object sender, System.EventArgs e) {
    Page.Validate();
    if (!Page.IsValid) {
        foreach (BaseValidator val in Page.Validators) {
            if (!val.IsValid) {
                Response.Write(val.ErrorMessage + "<br>");
            }
        }
        lblErrors.Visible = true;
        lblErrors.Text = sb.ToString();
    }
}
```

Congratulations. Although the result isn't pretty, you've just coded a server-side loop that validates values entered on the client—and you didn't have to find the values, assign them to variables, or write any special validation code. By setting the `clientTarget` property to `DownLevel`, you turned off VS.NET's automatic client-side validation script generation. Therefore, when the user submits the form, the values return to the server—but you use the same validation controls to check the values. As I mentioned earlier, the server-side validation always occurs—even if you don't use it.

So when or why would you want to turn off client-side validation? First, you should turn it off when the target browser is not Internet Explorer. Ideally, in some utopian future state, all browsers would be equally capable of performing dynamic HTML operations and running the same version of client script code. Unfortunately, we haven't yet reached that state. Second, you may have noticed that VS.NET translates `Validator` controls into HTML `<span>` tags. Each `<span>` tag defines a specified area of the browser window where the `Validator` control can display its error messages. But the tags are transparent; therefore, you can't stack them on top of one another unless you're sure that only one `Validator` control can fire at a time—and as you've seen, you can easily create a form that fires multiple validation errors when submitted. Therefore, a third reason to validate on the server is to control the way the validators display error messages. Finally, with little effort, a malevolent user could post a request directly to the server.

NOTE *Microsoft chose to use a `<span>` rather than a `<div>` tag for the error messages because `<div>` tags always begin on a new line in downlevel browsers, whereas `<span>` tags do not necessarily begin on a new line. This lets you put the error messages on the same line as the control that contains the invalid input.*

The simple example you just created writes the error messages at the top of the screen, but you can easily change that. Drag a `Label` control onto the Web Form and place it underneath the table. Edit the label's `ID` property so it reads `lblErrors`, and set the `Color` property to `Red`, leaving the `Text` property blank. Next, change the code in the method so you concatenate all the error messages during the `cmdOK_Click` method and set the `lblErrors.Text` property to the concatenated string. Listing 5.4 shows the code. Finally, change the `Display` property for the two `RegularExpressionValidator` controls to `None` and change their `EnableClientScript` property to `false`.

LISTING 5.4: WEB FORM cmdOK_Click METHOD WITH SERVER-SIDE VALIDATION (ch5-3.aspx)

```
private void cmdOK_Click(object sender, System.EventArgs e) {
    System.Text.StringBuilder sb = new System.Text.StringBuilder();
    Page.Validate();
    if (!Page.IsValid) {
        foreach (BaseValidator val in Page.Validators) {
            if (!val.IsValid) {
                sb.Append(val.ErrorMessage);
                sb.Append("<br>");          }
        }
        lblErrors.Visible = true;
        lblErrors.Text = sb.ToString();
    }
}
```

I dimensioned the variable `val` in the `foreach` loop as a `BaseValidator` object. As the name implies, all `Validator` objects inherit from `BaseValidator`; therefore, you can assign any `Validator` object to a variable with the `BaseValidator` type. Of course, you could use `Object` just as well or iterate through the `Page.Validators` collection using an index variable, like the client-side code you saw earlier in this chapter. In this example, the code uses a `StringBuilder` object to create a string of error messages, so it needs to check the `IsValid` property for each `Validator` object separately. When your only interest is whether all values entered on the page are valid, you can test the `Page.IsValid` property, which will return `false` unless *all* the `Validator` controls validate successfully.

Finally, the user might click the Cancel button. In design mode, double-click the Cancel button and add this code to the autogenerated `cmdCancel_Click` event:

```
private void cmdCancel_Click(object sender, System.EventArgs e) {
    Response.Write("You cancelled the form. Click the Back " +
        "button on your browser to try again.");
    Response.End();
}
```

At this point, you've built a reasonably complicated form that

◆ Maintains user viewstate between pages

◆ Performs two different types of validation

◆ Displays customizable error messages when validation fails

And here's the interesting part—you've had to write only a few lines of code—and then only when you wanted to customize the validation error message display. After this short introduction to code, I'm sure you're eager for more, so let's move on.

Code-Behind Programming

VS.NET uses the code-behind model to separate user-interface components of Web applications from the logic components. In classic ASP, several *intrinsic objects* simplified the grunt work of parsing HTTP requests and delivering responses. VS.NET extends that model by encapsulating almost all the parts of a Web application. Of course, extending the model also meant that the number of objects you used had to increase as well. The .NET framework groups most of these objects in the `System.Web` namespace.

Page **Object**   The `Page` object is the base object for a Web Form. The `Page` object provides events, methods, and properties for a single page. You can think of a `Page` object and a Web Form interchangeably—although that's not entirely accurate. Web Forms inherit from the `System.Web.UI.Page` class. In object-oriented terms, you can say that a Web Form is a `Page` object. The `Page` object is your primary means of accessing the rest of the objects in this list because it exposes them all as properties. The `Page` object fires events you can hook to perform initialization and cleanup, as well as providing properties that help you determine the client type, the list of controls on a Web Form, the type and source of data bound to those controls, and (as you've already seen) the set of `Validator` controls.

HttpRequest **Object**   The `HttpRequest` object encapsulates the data sent by the client with each request. This object is similar to the classic ASP `Request` object. Each `Page` object exposes an `HttpRequest` object as a property called `Page.Request`. This book usually refers to the `HttpRequest` object as the `Request` object. For example, when a user submits a form, you can access the individual data values as items in the `Page.Request.Form` collection object.

HttpResponse **Object**   The `HttpResponse` object encapsulates the data returned by the server in response to each client request. This object is similar to the classic ASP `Response` object. Each `Page` object exposes an `HttpResponse` object as a property called `Page.Response`. You use the `Response` object each time you want to send data to the client. This book usually refers to the `HttpResponse` object as the `Response` object. For example, you've already seen the `Response.Write` method, which returns text data, and the `Response.BinaryWrite` method, which returns binary data.

HttpApplicationState **Object**   This is a container class for all objects in an ASP.NET application running on a single server. Values stored at Application scope are shared between pages in a single application, but not between applications or between servers or processes. Each `Page` object exposes an instance of this class as a property called `Page.Application`. This book usually refers to the `HttpApplicationState` object as the `Application` object. You'll use it in Web applications to store values common to the entire application—in other words, to store global variables.

HttpServerUtility **Object**   This object provides a set of methods and properties through which you can obtain information about the local server on which your Web application is running. These are similar to but more extensive than the set of methods available through the classic ASP `Server` object. Each `Page` object exposes an instance of this class as a property called `Page.Server`. This book usually refers to the `HttpServerUtility` object as the `Server` object. For example, you can obtain the local machine name with the `MachineName` property or encode/decode data via the `HtmlEncode`/`HtmlDecode` and `UrlEncode`/`UrlDecode`/`UrlPathEncode` methods.

HttpSession **Object**   `HttpSession` provides a container associated with a specific IP address. This object is similar to (but much more robust and scalable than) the classic ASP `Session` object. Each client has a unique IP address. Whenever the server receives a request from an unrecognized (meaning new) IP address, it creates a `Session` object and provides an in-memory cookie to the requesting client. If the client accepts the cookie, the client will send the cookie with each subsequent request to that server. The server can use the cookie value, called a `SessionID`, to associate data with that specific client. `Session`s are not required. In classic ASP, the `Session` object worked on only one server at a time; you couldn't use `Session`s for multiprocess or multiserver Web applications. Because classic ASP stored `Session` data entirely in RAM, you could easily lose the data if the Web server crashed. Classic ASP `Session`s were also slow. For these reasons, Web developers rarely used the `Session` object in classic ASP for large-scale Web applications, although `Session`s were widely used for smaller sites. ASP.NET has made many changes to the `Session` object that make it much more robust and scalable, so it's easier to write applications that must store state data for each client. Each `Page` object exposes an instance of this class as a property called `Page.Session`. This book usually refers to the `HttpSessionState` object as the `Session` object.

Cache **Object**   Unlike earlier versions of ASP in which, if you wanted caching, you had to implement it yourself, ASP.NET gives you fine-grained control over what to cache, how long to maintain the cache, and how often to refresh it. For example, you can cache an entire page, a portion of a page, the results of a database query, the contents of a file, or an object or collection of objects. The `Page` object exposes an instance of this class as the `Page.Cache` property.

Use of Any .NET Language

In classic ASP, you could write in any scripting language supported by the Microsoft Scripting Runtime model. The two most common scripting languages were VBScript and JScript, both of which shipped with ASP. In ASP.NET, you can write in any language that supports the Common Language Runtime (CLR) model. Initially, that means you can write in C# or JScript (which has been upgraded to a more full-featured, compiled language in its VS.NET implementation), but eventually your options may include over 20 different languages, including Perl, COBOL, Forth, FORTRAN, Eiffel, SmallScript (Smalltalk), and Scheme.

Scripting languages are interpreted, not compiled, and often use untyped variables. Although using interpreted languages has some advantages, it also means that operations written with script are usually slower than equivalent operations written in a compiled language. Scripting languages have grown more powerful over the past couple years, but they have a limited capability to interoperate with the operating system itself; most implementations have limited debugging facilities, and they don't use type-safe variables.

These limitations led to a complex model for creating Web applications in which Web developers used ASP pages primarily as collection points for **Request** and **Response** data and encapsulated most of the important operations in Common Object Model (COM) or ActiveX objects so they could get the benefits of compiled execution speed and deliver code encapsulated in ActiveX DLLs (hidden from clients).

You don't have to do that anymore. Although you still must learn a scripting language to write good Web applications, you need to use it only on the client (for now).

Only One Language per Page

As I mentioned in the previous section, the use of scripting languages in classic ASP had some advantages. One advantage was that you could mix routines written in more than one scripting language on a single page. You can't do that in VS.NET. You must choose and stick with a single language for each page, although you're perfectly free to use as many different .NET-compliant languages within an application as you wish. Frankly, mixing languages on a single ASP page was not a common practice anyway; most developers used VBScript for server-side code and JScript for client-side code. In larger groups, programming in multiple languages is somewhat more common, so I suspect that many applications in the future will contain code written in more than one language.

Display Separately from Data Processing

Another disadvantage of the classic ASP model was that the HTML code used to create the display and the logic code to power the application were often mixed into a single page. There's nothing wrong with doing this if you never plan to use the code again, but it promotes single-use coding, which is *not* the way to think if you're planning to make a long career out of programming. The more you program, the more you find that, with a little work, you can abstract most operations into classes with methods, properties, and events you can reuse in many different situations.

Page/Form Layout

If you were familiar with the Forms layout engine in VB6, you'll be instantly at home with the page layout capabilities of Web Forms. If not, it's similar to many other form-design packages or to many object-oriented drawing and presentation programs such as Visio and PowerPoint. Using the Web Form designer, you can drag and drop controls on a form using a familiar design model.

Designing HTML Pages

HTML pages have several advantages over the default form interface to most Windows development packages. First, they scroll automatically—and people are used to scrolling in Web pages—so you can take advantage of that feature in your own applications to give yourself a little extra vertical space when required. Also, you don't have to give HTML elements a predetermined size. By using percentages rather than fixed pixel widths, you can design pages that adapt to clients with different screen resolutions.

HTML pages also have built-in links, which makes it relatively easy to tie pages together visually and avoids some of the problems with using list boxes, drop-down lists, and rows of buttons (I'm sure you've all seen some of applications with a plethora of buttons).

By default, HTML pages refresh completely whenever the user browses to the page for the first time in a given browser session. That means you can change the page on the server, and most clients will see the updated version right away. In contrast, installed Windows COM–based applications must be uninstalled and then reinstalled for you to make updates or alter the program.

Inline versus *GridLayout*

Web Form layout is a little strange and awkward when you work in FlowLayout mode because the HTML rendering engine has final control over the placement and appearance of controls. When you drop a control on a Web Form, it doesn't stay where you put it; it moves into the next available standard layout position. However, if you ever worked with a WYSIWYG HTML editor such as Macromedia's Dreamweaver or FrontPage, you're familiar with the problems involved in laying out page elements in HTML.

When you work in GridLayout mode, though, things immediately feel much more familiar—especially if you're targeting an "uplevel" browser such as IE5. Controls stay where you put them; you can resize them, move them around the screen, and even overlay them on top of one another, much as you can in a standard IDE form designer.

However, being able to work in a familiar model can be misleading because the clients—typically browsers—don't work like Windows forms. If you're not familiar with HTML, you should study Chapter 2, "HTML Basics," carefully, because you'll need the knowledge to help you tweak the HTML produced by the Web Form designer.

Generated HTML Code

As presented earlier in this chapter, you can access the HTML that the Web Form designer generates by clicking the HTML tab at the bottom of the Web Form designer window, but by default, you don't have access to the HTML that ASP.NET generates automatically and sends to the browser. In most cases, that's a good thing because ASP.NET can generate fairly complicated code, and it's not always pretty. However, if you need to gain control over the generated HTML, you need to move up the object hierarchy and investigate the `WebControl` object. All `WebControls` inherit from this object. I won't go into much detail at this point, but it's worth pointing out several members that render the HTML for a control so that you'll know where to start when you want to create a customized control.

`WebControls` have most of the properties that you would expect from working with VB6 and Windows Forms controls. Properties such as `Height`, `Width`, `Font`, `ForeColor`, `BackColor`, `BorderStyle`, `BorderColor`, `BorderWidth`, `AccessKey`, `Enabled`, and `Visible` are fairly self-explanatory. However, several properties and methods are specific to Web applications:

Style **Property**   Most `WebControls` have a `Style` property that returns the `CSSStyleCollection` object. The `Style` property corresponds to the `style` attribute for HTML elements; in other words, it gives you programmatic server-side access to the Cascading Style Sheets (CSS) attributes for the control. For example, you can get the `Style` object for a `WebControl`, set its properties, and then merge the `Style` with another `Style` object using the `MergeStyle` method. This is essentially what happens when you set the `class` attribute to a CSS class. The element inherits the CSS style attributes *unless* those attributes are already defined locally within the element. In other words, merging styles adds attributes and values from the source `Style` object to the target `Style` object but does not overwrite any attributes or values that already exist in the target. You can also overwrite existing style attributes using the `ApplyStyle` method.

CSSClass **Property**   This property returns or sets the CSS class name with which the control is associated. Using this property, you can change the CSS class of a control programmatically on the server.

MaintainState **Property**   This property controls whether a control uses `ViewState` to maintain its properties across client page requests. By default, all `WebControls` use `ViewState`, but you will definitely want to disable it for specific controls. When you set the value of the `MaintainState` property to `false`, the control still appears and functions normally on the client, but values entered by the client during one page request will not reappear automatically after the user posts the form. For example, you may wish to disable this property for a Password field, forcing the field to appear empty whenever the login information submitted by a user is incorrect.

Page **Property**   Returns a reference to the page containing this `WebControl`.

Site **Property**   Returns a reference to the site containing this `WebControl`.

RenderBeginTag **Method**   Renders the HTML starting tag (`<div>`, for example) that represents this `WebControl`.

RenderControl **Method**   Renders the HTML tag attributes and values for this `WebControl`.

RenderEndTag **Method**   Renders the HTML tag attributes and values for this `WebControl`.

DesignTimeRender **Method**   This method takes an `HTMLTextWriter` object as a parameter. It uses the `HTMLTextWriter` object to render the HTML string representing the control during design time—this is what happens when you drop a control on a Web Form. If you create your own controls, you would use this method to create the HTML for those controls. Note that you would *not* need to use this method if you create custom a `WebControl` that is an amalgam of existing controls, only if you were to create a brand-new `WebControl`.

Summary

As you've seen, the ideas behind Web Forms, `WebControls`, and ASP.NET aren't new, but the implementation is. Specifically, the capability to treat a Web page as a single entity is revolutionary. By creating the .NET and ASP.NET objects, Microsoft has raised the level of abstraction in programming. For example, the Web programming model has become extremely similar to the Windows programming model. Similarly, by creating the CLR, Microsoft has raised the level of programming-language abstraction. Now, one .NET language differs from another primarily in syntax and degree of non-conformance with the CLR.

Still, to be an effective Web developer, you need some special knowledge about how the Web works, how to identify, maintain, and cache data for users and applications, and how to manipulate controls from both server and client code. You do that primarily by learning the methods, properties, and events of the `Page` object, as you'll see in the next chapter.

Chapter 6

Introduction to the System.Web Namespace

IN .NET, A *NAMESPACE* is a way of grouping related items together. The namespace prevents identical names from colliding by maintaining each set of names in a separate space. The namespace may or may not correspond to a single file. The class hierarchy in the System.Web namespace provides objects that are useful for these tasks:

- ◆ Accepting requests, including security and policy checks

- ◆ Getting information from a client

- ◆ Returning information to a client

- ◆ Storing and caching client (`Session`) and global (`Application`) values

- ◆ Designing and interacting with Web Forms

- ◆ Obtaining information about the current ASP.NET application and setting configuration values for it

- ◆ Tracing requests and error handling

Obtaining Information from the Client

There are two parts to the process of accepting an HTTP request. First, the client must have permission to make the request; then, if the client *does* have permission, the server attempts to fulfill the request. I won't go into the process of checking permissions right now; you'll work with permissions later in the book in Chapter 18, "Controlling Access and Monitoring." Although that process is not beyond your control, it has already occurred by the time your code-behind pages begin to execute in a Web application. Therefore, for the rest of this chapter, you can assume that the authentication step has been performed, the request has been accepted, and the client has permission to access the requested file.

Accepting Requests

The server "listens" for requests on an open TCP/IP port. There are 65,536 possible ports—more than enough for any purposes yet devised. The ports for the various common protocols are defined by convention, not by any physical restriction or logical reason. For example, Web servers usually accept HTTP requests on port 80, FTP requests on port 21, and Network News Transfer Protocol (NNTP) requests on port 119.

When the server receives a request, it determines how to process the request using a table of recognized file extensions. For example, the server handles .htm and .html requests directly, but it hands off requests for .asp files to the classic ASP engine and for .aspx, .asmx, and .ascx files to the ASP.NET framework.

As a C# programmer, you just need to be aware of the mechanism, not the details. In other words, if you make a request for an unrecognized file type, the server can't process the file. Similarly, different servers may handle requests for files with the same file extension in different ways. Just remember that the response mechanism depends on file extensions and that the action a Web server takes for any particular file extension depends on the associations it has for that extension.

A Brief Introduction to the *HttpResponse* Object

Although it's logical to discuss the common objects you need in the order in which a Web transaction happens, there is one object I need to introduce out of order: the HttpResponse object. It's impossible to provide meaningful examples without introducing the HttpResponse object—at least minimally—before discussing it in detail later in this chapter. For now, all you need to know is that the HttpResponse object (I'll abbreviate this to just the Response object from now on) exposes a method called Write by which you send content to the requesting client. The Write method is overloaded. The most commonly used version accepts a single String parameter, which contains the content to write to the output stream. For example, the following line writes "Hello World" to the client.

```
Response.Write("Hello World");
```

A similar and useful method is WriteFile. This is an overloaded method, but the simplest version accepts a String parameter containing the pathname of a file. The method opens and reads the file and immediately writes the content to the output stream. You can combine Response.Write and Response.WriteFile in a single response. For example, suppose you had detailed error messages stored in individual files. Based on the exception type, you could display a custom message followed by the complete generic detail information.

```
Response.Write("This application has encountered " +
    an error.<br><br>.");
Response.WriteFile(
"c:\inetpub\wwwroot\CSharpASP\Errors\MyCustomError.htm");
```

The overloaded methods for WriteFile let you write files to memory, use a file handle rather than a pathname, or write only part of a file.

Finally, the last concept you need to know about in advance is the process to write a cookie. The Response object has a Cookies collection that contains a set of HttpCookies. Remember, a cookie consists of two Strings—a key and a value. You'll explore the Response.Cookies collection in detail later, but for now, all you need to know is that to add a cookie, you create the cookie and then use the Add method to add it to the `Response.Cookies` collection.

```
System.Web.HttpCookie aCookie = null;
aCookie = New System.Web.HttpCookie("key","value");
Response.Cookies.Add(aCookie);
```

Now that you can write a little content back to the client, it will be much easier to introduce the HttpRequest object in more detail.

The *HttpRequest* Object

Most people think of a Web request as a URL that resolves to the location of a file—and a valid URL is mandatory for a successful request. However, clients send much more information than just the URL with each request. The request reaches the server as a stream of binary data. The part you're interested in consists of a set of delimited strings. You rarely need to know the values contained in these strings to fulfill requests for simple HTML pages, but you almost always need to know at least some of the values to fulfill requests for pages in a Web application. To simplify interaction with the values sent by the browser, the ASP.NET engine parses and stores the values as properties of an HttpRequest object.

In a Web Form, you access this HttpRequest object as a property of the Page object. As I said earlier, you can think of the Page object as the Web Form itself.

Because your Web Forms inherit from System.Web.UI.Page, they are Page objects. As long as you don't modify the generated code (and you shouldn't ever do that, because the Designer will overwrite your changes if you make any modifications to that code), you can rely on your Web Form to support the same properties and methods as its parent Page object.

All Web Forms are Page objects and, for your convenience, each Page object exposes properties containing instances of the System.Web classes you interact with most frequently. This simplifies your code considerably, because you don't need to refer to the Page object in code—it's automatically available. In addition, the Page object properties simplify the names of the objects. For example, rather than writing HttpContext.Current.HttpRequest each time you need to access client information, you can simply write Request. Now that you know this, I'll stop referring to the HttpRequest object by its full name while you're working with Web Forms, and I'll just call it the Request object instead.

NOTE *Within a Web Form code-behind class, you can access the* HttpRequest *object that contains client information via the* Page.Request *property. But because the Web Form is a* Page *object instance, you can drop the* Page *portion and simply write* Request *in your code. Finally, you can access the current object within a class with the keyword* this, *so you can also write* this.Request.

REQUEST OBJECT PROPERTIES

The first System.Web object you need on any given page (besides the Page object) is the Request object. The Request object exposes several properties. Each property contains a collection of values that hold the data sent by the client. These collections are your primary means of accessing client data directly, although you will often access the Form data through the properties of individual controls on the page. The collections and their base types are the following:

- `AcceptTypes` (String array)
- `Cookies` (HttpCookieCollection)
- `Files` (HttpFileCollection)
- `Form` (NameValueCollection)
- `Headers` (NameValueCollection)
- `QueryString` (NameValueCollection)
- `ServerVariables` (NameValueCollection)
- `UserLanguages` (Sorted String array)
- `Params` (NameValueCollection)

All `Request` object collections are read-only. You can't change the values because by the time you get to see `Request` values, the client has already finished sending them; therefore, it wouldn't do you any good to change them even if you could.

The Request.AcceptTypes Property (String Array)

The `Request.AcceptTypes` property contains a list of the MIME types the client can recognize. The following loop prints the MIME types accepted by the client:

```
Response.Write("<h1>Client MIME Types</h1>");
String [] arr1 = Request.AcceptTypes;
for (int i = 0; i <= arr1.GetUpperBound(0); i++) {
    Response.Write(arr1[i] + "<br>");
}
```

I've been unable to get IE5 and higher to list individual MIME types—when you view the result of the preceding loop with IE5 or higher as a client, the output is always */*. However, other browsers (and other clients) may provide results that are more useful. For example, the same loop accessed from Netscape 4x displays the following:

```
image/gif
image/x-xbitmap
image/jpeg
image/pjpeg
image/png
*/*
```

If you're sending special types of content, such as **text/xml** or Adobe PDF files, you can check the `AcceptTypes` list in advance to ensure that the client can render the response properly.

The Request.Cookies Property (HttpCookieCollection)

The `Request.Cookies` property contains a collection of key/value pairs that hold text values set by some page in your domain—but not necessarily in your application. By default, the collection is empty. The `HttpCookieCollection` class inherits from the abstract `NameObjectCollectionBase` class, which provides keyed access to objects in the collection. You can use the `Get` method to retrieve an individual cookie by name or by index number. You can also get an enumeration object to enumerate through the keys.

For example, assume that the browser sends a cookie named `lastItem`. You could display the cookie value by accessing the `Request.Cookies` collection using the `"lastItem"` key:

```
Response.Write(Request.Cookies.Item("lastItem").Value);
```

If you attempt to access a cookie that doesn't exist, an error occurs (see Figure 6.1).

FIGURE 6.1

The error message displayed for a null object reference

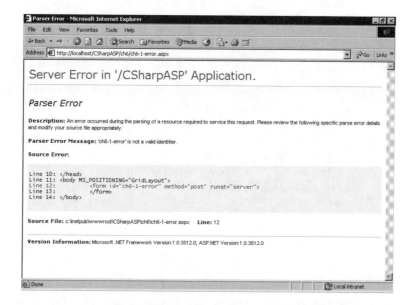

The null object reference error is a common error—perhaps the most common error you'll encounter while using VB.NET to build Web applications, and it's the equivalent of a VB6 "Object not set" error. It means that some object you tried to reference has not been initialized or doesn't exist.

To avoid this problem, you can check to see whether the key exists. Unfortunately, there's no `Exists` or `KeyExists` property, so you must retrieve all the keys and loop through them yourself. Fortunately, that's simple. The `keyExists` function shown in Listing 6.1 accepts a `String` and returns a `Boolean` value indicating whether the specified key exists in the `Request.Cookie` collection.

LISTING 6.1: TESTING WHETHER A COOKIE KEY EXISTS (ch6-1.aspx.cs)

```
bool keyExists(String aKey) {
    HttpCookieCollection cookies = Request.Cookies;
    System.Collections.IEnumerator e = cookies.GetEnumerator();
    while (e.MoveNext()) {
        if (e.Current.Equals(aKey)) {
            return(true);
        }
    }
    return false;
}
```

You can also retrieve the key values with the `AllKeys` property, which returns a `String` array containing all the keys. So another way to test whether a key exists is to retrieve all the keys and loop through the resulting array, as demonstrated in Listing 6.2.

LISTING 6.2: ALTERNATE TEST WHETHER A COOKIE KEY EXISTS (ch6-1.aspx.cs)

```
bool keyExists2(String aKey) {
    int i;
    String[] keys;
    keys = Request.Cookies.AllKeys;
    for (i = 0; i < keys.Length; i++) {
    if (keys[i] == aKey){
        return(true);
        }
    }
        return(false);
}
```

A cookie may have either a single key/value pair or a collection of pairs. (These subordinate key/value pairs are often called *subkeys*.) In other words, a cookie is a key/value pair in which the value can include a collection of other key/value pairs. You can retrieve the subkeys and values using the `Values` property. However, if you use the `Values` property and the target cookie doesn't have subkeys, you'll get an error. To solve the problem, you should first test to see if the cookie has subkeys, using the `HasKeys` property. If the cookie has a simple `String` value, `HasKeys` returns `false`. If it has a collection of subkeys, `HasKeys` returns `true`.

Listing 6.3 illustrates the process of creating and retrieving cookie subkeys. The code fragment writes a cookie with a key of `"Items"` and a null value; then it adds nine key/value pairs to its `Values` collection in a loop. Each subkey has a key from 1 to 9 and a value of `"Items"` concatenated with the key value, such as `Item1, Item2`, and so on.

LISTING 6.3: CREATING A COOKIE CONTAINING MULTIPLE VALUES (ch6-1.aspx.cs)

```
void makeCookie() {
    HttpCookie aCookie = new HttpCookie("Items", "test");
    int i;
    for (i = 1; i < 10; i++) {
        aCookie.Values.Add(i.ToString(), "Item" + i.ToString());
    }
    Response.AppendCookie(aCookie);
}
```

The first part of the code creates the cookie. To send the cookie, the last line appends it to the HttpResponse Cookies collection using the AppendCookie method. The next time the client requests a page from your site, it will send the cookie with the request. You can retrieve the cookie and use the Values and AllKeys properties to get a list of keys and then iterate through those keys to display the subordinate key/value pairs. The showCookie method (see Listing 6.4) retrieves the cookie from the Request.Cookies collection and prints out the subkey values.

LISTING 6.4: DISPLAYING A COOKIE THAT CONTAINS MULTIPLE VALUES (ch6-1. aspx.cs)

```
void showCookie() {
    HttpCookie aCookie;
    int i;
    String[] keys;
    HttpCookieCollection cookies = Request.Cookies;
    aCookie = cookies.Get("Items");
    if (aCookie.HasKeys) {
        Response.Write("This cookie has " +
            aCookie.Values.AllKeys.Length.ToString() + " keys.<br>");
        keys = aCookie.Values.AllKeys;
        for (i = 0; i < keys.Length; i++) {
            Response.Write(keys[i] + "=" + aCookie.Values[i] + "<br>");
        }
    }
    else {
        Response.Write("The cookie 'Items' has no keys.");
    }
    Response.Write("Cookie string value=" + aCookie.Value + "<br>");
}
```

The subkeys are actually stored like querystring parameters: An ampersand separates each key/value pair, and an equal sign separates the key from the value. The HttpCookie object parses this string into a collection when you access the subkeys via the `values` property. However, if you simply request the `Value` property of the cookie itself, you get a string constructed like this:

```
Cookie value=Items&1=Item1&2=Item2&3=Item3&4=Item4&5=Item5&6=Item6&
    7=Item7&8=Item8&9=Item9
```

That's a rather contrived example. Here's a better one. Suppose you visit an e-commerce site that has a shopping cart. The site chose to implement the shopping cart as a set of in-memory cookies. Therefore, when a user selects an item, the application needs to add it to the cart. When a user elects to view the cart or check out, the application needs to read and display the values.

Although you can do this with standard function calls, a better method might be to create a `ShoppingCart` class. The class needs three methods:

◆ `AddToCart`

◆ `DeleteFromCart`

◆ `GetCartContents`

In classic ASP, you had to use a `GetObjectContext()` method to get references to the ASP intrinsic objects from a COM class. In ASP.NET, you can simply reference the `HttpContext.Current` property to gain access to the current context. The `HttpContext` object exposes the set of ASP.NET objects associated with the current request; among those are the `Request` and `Response` objects, which you need to access the current request context from the `ShoppingCart` class. The `ShoppingCart` class takes advantage of .NET's capability to ferret out the current context. Each time you create an instance of the class, it creates a private class variable called `context` and sets its value to the current `HttpContext` object. By doing this, the class has complete access to the System.Web objects it needs to service the request. Of course, you could pass the required objects explicitly as parameters.

```
public class ShoppingCart {
  private HttpContext context;
  private HttpCookie aCookie;

  public ShoppingCart() {
     context = HttpContext.Current;
     aCookie = context.Request.Cookies.Get("cart");
     if (aCookie == null) {
        aCookie = new HttpCookie("cart", "cart");
     }
  }
// more code ...
  }
```

The class also attempts to retrieve the cookie called `cart`. Retrieving a cookie that doesn't exist does not raise an error—it simply sets the receiving variable to `Null` (or leaves it set to `Null`). Therefore, the `New` method in the class checks to see if the variable has been initialized; if not, it creates a new cookie.

You need a Web Form to consume the class. Figure 6.2 shows a simple Web Form that lets you add and delete items from ShoppingCart. In the figure, some items have already been added to the cart.

FIGURE 6.2

A simple Web Form to illustrate the ShoppingCart class methods

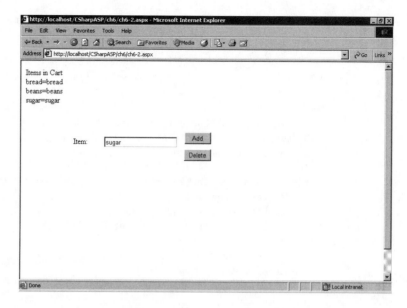

Listing 6.5 shows the complete code for the ShoppingCart class. Note that the class adds all values to the same key—cart. The AddToCart method uses the Response.Cookies.Values.Add method.

LISTING 6.5: THE COOKIE-BASED SHOPPINGCART CLASS (ShoppingCart.aspx.cs)

```csharp
using System;
using System.Web;
using System.Text;

namespace CSharpASP.ch6 {
    /// <summary>
    /// Summary description for ShoppingCart.
    /// </summary>
    public class ShoppingCart {
        private HttpContext context;
        private HttpCookie aCookie;

        public ShoppingCart() {
            context = HttpContext.Current;
            aCookie = context.Request.Cookies.Get("cart");
            if(aCookie == null) {
                aCookie = new HttpCookie("cart", "cart");
            }
        }

        public bool HasItems {
         get{
```

```csharp
            return keyExists(context.Request.Cookies, "cart");
      }
      set {
         // ignore
      }
   }

   public void AddToCart(String aVal) {
      aCookie.Values.Add(aVal, aVal);
      context.Response.AppendCookie(aCookie);
   }
   public void AddToCart2(String aVal) {
      deleteFromCart(aVal);
      aCookie.Values.Add(aVal, aVal);
      context.Response.AppendCookie(aCookie);
   }
   public void AddToCart3(String aVal) {
      aCookie.Value = aVal;
      context.Response.AppendCookie(aCookie);
   }

   public void deleteFromCart(String aVal) {
      if (aCookie.HasKeys) {
         aCookie.Values.Remove(aVal);
      }
      context.Response.AppendCookie(aCookie);
   }

   public string GetCartContents() {
      StringBuilder s = new StringBuilder(2000);
      int i;
      String[] keys;
      keys = aCookie.Values.AllKeys;
      // skip the first value-it's blank
      for (i = 1; i < keys.Length; i++) {
         s.Append(keys[i] + "=" + aCookie.Values[i] + "<br>");
      }
      return (s.ToString());
   }
   private bool keyExists
      (System.Collections.Specialized.NameObjectCollectionBase
      coll, String aKey) {
      System.Collections.IEnumerator e = coll.GetEnumerator();
      while (e.MoveNext()) {
         if (e.Current.Equals(aKey)) {
            return true;
         }
      }
```

```
        return false;
    }


  }
}
```

The Web Form ch6-2.aspx is a very simple Web Form that lets you type a name into a text field. The page then adds that name to the cart cookie's Values collection by calling the AddToCart method and displays the cart contents by calling the GetCartContents method. You can remove a value by clicking the Delete button, which calls the DeleteFromCart method (see Listing 6.6). Figure 6.2 shows the class after adding three items.

LISTING 6.6: WEB FORM UI METHODS TO ADD AND REMOVE ITEMS FROM SHOPPINGCART (ch6-2.aspx.cs)

```
private void Page_Load(object sender, System.EventArgs e)
   {
   if (IsPostBack)
      Response.Write("Items in Cart<br>");
   }
private void ButtonDelete_Click(object sender, System.EventArgs e) {
   ShoppingCart cart = new ShoppingCart();
   String item;
   item = txtItem.Text;
   cart.deleteFromCart(item);
   Response.Write(cart.GetCartContents().ToString());
}

private void buttonAdd_Click(object sender, System.EventArgs e) {
   string item;
   ShoppingCart cart = new ShoppingCart();
   item = txtItem.Text;
   cart.AddToCart(item);
   Response.Write(cart.GetCartContents().ToString());
}
```

Listing 6.6 doesn't show all the code in the class, just the three methods that return content—the Page_Load method and the methods for the two button clicks. The name of the text box is TxtItem, and the two buttons are ButtonAdd and ButtonDelete.

You should note that if you put some text in txtItem (perhaps the term bread) and then click the Add button several times, you'll see that the bread item simply gets longer with each click:

```
beans=beans
bread=bread,bread,bread,bread,bread
```

Apparently, when you supply the name of an existing key to the `Values.Add` method, it appends the new item, separating it from existing values with a comma rather than overwriting the existing value. This behavior seems odd to me, because it means that if you want to replace an existing value, you need to delete the subkey and then add it back with the `Add` method or check to see if the item exists and then set its value with the `Item` method. In other words, if you change the `AddToCart` method as shown in Listing 6.7, it works as you would expect.

LISTING 6.7: ALTERNATE WAYS TO IMPLEMENT THE AddToCart METHOD (ShoppingCart.aspx.cs)

```
public void AddToCart2(String aVal) {
   deleteFromCart(aVal);
   aCookie.Values.Add(aVal, aVal);
   context.Response.AppendCookie(aCookie);
}
public void AddToCart3(String aVal) {
   aCookie.Value = aVal;
   context.Response.AppendCookie(aCookie);
}
```

You may remember from Chapter 5, "Introduction to Web Forms," that the ASP.NET framework creates an `ASPSessionID` cookie in its response to the first request from any browser. It's worth checking to see what the ASP.NET system adds to the cookie collection. Create a new Web Form named `ch6-3.aspx`, place a button on the Web Form, and add the code in Listing 6.8 to the `Button1_Click` event.

LISTING 6.8: DISPLAYING ALL COOKIE KEYS AND VALUES (ch6-3.aspx.cs)

```
private void Button1_Click(object sender, System.EventArgs e) {
   String[] keys = Request.Cookies.AllKeys;
   foreach(String aKey in keys) {
      Response.Write(aKey + "=" +
         Request.Cookies.Get(aKey).Value.ToString() + "<br>");
   }
}
```

When you click the button, the server will loop through all the keys received from the browser and write each key and value back to the browser. Despite the fact that the Web Form contains no explicit code to add cookie values, you'll see one anyway (see Figure 6.3).

FIGURE 6.3

ASPSessionID
display example

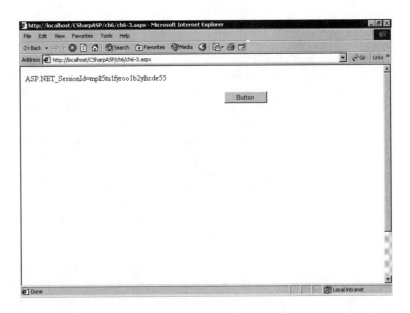

Leave the browser open, copy the URL, start a new browser instance, and paste the URL into the browser. Click the button. This time, the `ASPSessionID` cookie will have a different value. That `ID` is the `SessionID` cookie. It's a value guaranteed to be unique, and it identifies a specific browser instance. The value itself is otherwise meaningless, and it is not reused. Every time you open a browser instance, ASP.NET assigns it a new and different `ASPSessionID` value. In other words, there is no way to use the `ASPSessionID` exclusively to identify an individual user without gathering additional information— the `ASPSessionID` identifies only an individual browser instance.

ASP.NET can also use "munged" URLs to identify individual sessions; however, developers are responsible for inserting the values in each link. This is an onerous burden and is required only for users whose browsers are set to reject cookies. At one time, a large number of people did this, but it's become less common to reject cookies now. A munged URL looks like the following, although it would normally appear on a single line:

```
http://www.yoursite.com/yourApp/
    SESSIONID$0123456789ABCDEF/somefile.asp
```

Note that the `SessionID` value appears after the root application directory in the URL but before the pathname or filename of the requested file. By placing the `SessionID` in that position, the ASP.NET engine can parse the URL linearly, first to determine the application and then to apply the `SessionID` so it can retrieve the appropriate data in the requested page.

The Request Files Property (HttpFileCollection)

The `Request` object exposes a `Files` property that contains a collection of filenames uploaded by the client. Like the `HttpCookieCollection` class (and many other Web collections), the `HttpFiles-Collection` class inherits from `NameObjectCollectionBase`—which means it contains a list of key/value pairs.

The Request.Form Property (NameValueCollection)

The first thing I noticed about the Request.Form property was that it returns a NameValueCollection object. A NameValueCollection object inherits from NameObjectCollectionBase (like the HttpFile-Collection and HttpCookieCollection you've already seen) and consists of a set of keys, each of which may have multiple values.

When the browser requests a page, it also sends a header specifying the content type. You may remember that the <form> tag contains an attribute called method, which may be either POST or GET. When you send form data using the GET method, the browser sets the content type header to application./x-www-form-urlencoded; data sent using the POST method has a content type header of multipart/form-data. Typically, you'll use the POST method to send data; otherwise the form data is visible in the browser address bar, and the size of the data is limited to approximately 1,024 characters (the actual number is browser dependent).

A Web Form may contain only one form that executes on the server side (that has the runat="server" attribute), but forms typically contain multiple input values, one for each input control nested within the <form> tag. When the browser posts the form data, it includes the current value from each input control (unless that value is null). If the form contains more than one input control with the same name, the browser sends a comma-separated list containing the values of the identically named controls. Therefore, the form data is essentially a list of key/value pairs where the value may be either a single value or a list of comma-separated values.

The Forms collection gives you access to these values. For example, the Web Form ch6-5 contains several input controls (see Figure 6.4). The code in the Load event in the code-behind page retrieves all the form keys and values from the Request.Form collection and displays them in the browser. The loop is generic and works with any Web Form, so it can be very useful when you're trying to determine exactly what data the browser sent.

FIGURE 6.4

A Web Form with several input controls

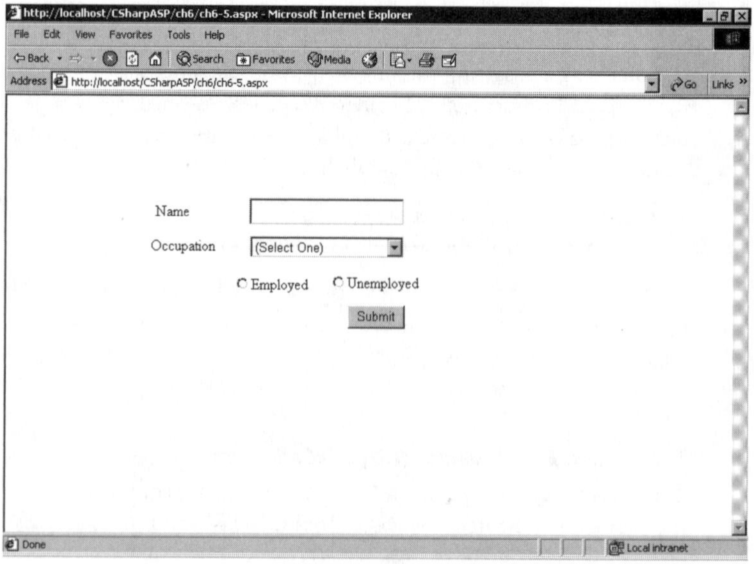

Listing 6.9 shows the control definitions. Note that the two radio buttons have a groupname property. This property "groups" the radio buttons so that they're mutually exclusive: Only one radio button in the group may be selected at any given time.

LISTING 6.9: A WEB FORM WITH SEVERAL INPUT CONTROLS (ch6-5.aspx)

```
<%@ Page Language="c#" AutoEventWireup="false"
    Codebehind="ch6-5.aspx.cs" Inherits="CSharpASP.ch6_5"  %>
<HTML>
    <HEAD>
        <meta name="vs_targetSchema"
            content="http://schemas.microsoft.com/intellisense/ie5">
        <meta name="GENERATOR"
            content="Microsoft Visual Studio.NET 7.0">
        <meta name="CODE_LANGUAGE" content="Visual Basic 7.0">
    </HEAD>
    <body ms_positioning="GridLayout">
        <form id="ch6_5" method="post" runat="server">
            <asp:TextBox id="txtName" runat="server" Width="165"
                Height="28" style="LEFT: 262px; POSITION: absolute;
                TOP: 106px"></asp:TextBox>
            <asp:Label id="Label3" runat="server" Height="19px"
                Width="84px" style="LEFT: 161px; POSITION: absolute;
                TOP: 110px">Name</asp:Label>
            <asp:Label id="Label2" runat="server" Width="83" Height="19"
                style="LEFT: 156px; POSITION: absolute;
                TOP: 146px">Occupation</asp:Label>
            <asp:DropDownList id="lstOccupation" runat="server"
                Width="164px" Height="22px" style="LEFT: 263px;
                POSITION: absolute; TOP: 146px">
                <asp:ListItem Value="">(Select One)</asp:ListItem>
                <asp:ListItem Value="Programmer">Programmer
                    </asp:ListItem>
                <asp:ListItem Value="Analyst">Analyst</asp:ListItem>
                <asp:ListItem Value="Other">Other</asp:ListItem>
            </asp:DropDownList>
            <asp:RadioButton id="optUnemployed" runat="server"
                Text="Unemployed" groupname="employmentStatus"
                style="LEFT: 346px; POSITION: absolute;
                TOP: 183px"></asp:RadioButton>
            <asp:RadioButton id="optEmployed" runat="server"
                Text="Employed" groupname="employmentStatus"
                style="LEFT: 244px; POSITION: absolute;
                TOP: 185px"></asp:RadioButton>
            <asp:Button id="Button1" runat="server" Text="Submit"
                style="LEFT: 367px; POSITION: absolute;
                TOP: 217px"></asp:Button>  
```

```
    </form>
   </body>
</HTML>
```

Load the Web Form `ch6-5.aspx` into your browser, enter some values, and then click the Submit button. You'll see the names of the various controls and their values appear in the response. Here's the code that displays the values:

```
private void Button1_Click(object sender, System.EventArgs e) {
   Response.Write("<b>Form data received</b>" + "<br>");
   foreach (String s in Request.Form.AllKeys) {
      if (s != "__VIEWSTATE") {
         Response.Write(s + "=" + Request.Form.Get(s) + "<br>");
      }
   }
}
```

As with other collections, the `AllKeys` property returns a `String` array containing the keys, which in this case are the IDs of the controls—except for the radio buttons, which use the value of the `groupname` attribute. The browser does *not* return the names of the grouped radio buttons and does not return any value for unchecked radio buttons. Therefore, code such as the following fragment will not work, because the value isn't present in the form data that the browser sends:

```
if (Request.Form.Get("optUnemployed") == false) {
   // Do something
}
```

Fortunately, there's a workaround. In the form value display example, the code explicitly excludes the `__VIEWSTATE` form value because it's present for all Web Forms by default and because the content is meaningless for the present purpose. However, the value does have a purpose—it lets the server compare the initial values of the controls with their present value; that's what raises change events. In other words, by the time the button-click (or any other control event) code runs, ASP.NET has already retrieved the form values and compared them with the initial control states stored in the `__VIEWSTATE` string. Therefore, despite the lack of `Request.Form` data for the unchecked radio buttons, you can still test their value directly:

```
if (optUnemployed.Value == false {
   // Do something
}
```

For those of you familiar with classic ASP Web programming, this marks a shift away from using the `Response.Form` values directly in favor of a control properties model. While you still can use the `Response.Form` values directly, there's less reason to do so if you let the page maintain `ViewState`. It's easier and takes less code to check the control values than to work with the raw `Response.Form` values.

In this particular instance, there's a second solution. You could use a RadioButtonList Web server control, which groups radio buttons, automatically lets users select only one item from the group, and has a `SelectedIndex` property that lets you detect which button (if any) a user selected.

The Request.Headers Property (NameValueCollection)

The browser sends a collection of headers with each request. Although you will not normally need to read the values directly, you can. I won't spend much time on this, but it's useful to know what type of information your application can use if necessary.

Like the `Request.Form` collection, the `Request.Headers` collection inherits from `NameValue-Collection`, so the loop to display all the request headers is essentially identical to the loop to display Form values. The Web Form `ch6-6.aspx` contains a single button with the text `Show Headers`. When you click the button, the following method executes on the server:

```
private void btnShowHeaders_Click(object sender, System.EventArgs e) {
    string s="";
    Response.Write("<b>Form data received</b>" + "<br>");
    foreach (String aHeader in Request.Headers.AllKeys) {
        s += aHeader + "=" + Request.Headers.Get(aHeader) + "<br>";
        switch (aHeader) {
            case "Content-Length" : {
                Response.Write("Request.TotalBytes=" +
                    Request.TotalBytes + "<br>");
                break;
            }
            case "Content-Type" : {
                Response.Write("Request.ContentType=" +
                    Request.ContentType + "<br>");
                break;
            }
            case "User-Agent" : {
                Response.Write("Request.UserAgent=" +
                    Request.UserAgent + "<br>");
                break;
            }
        }
    }
    Label1.Text = s;
}
```

You *could* use the `Request.Headers` collection to do the following:

◆ Determine the method used to send a form (`GET` or `POST`) by checking the `ContentType` header.

◆ Determine the type of client by parsing the `User-Agent` header.

◆ Determine the size of form data by checking the `Content-Length` header.

That's what ASP.NET does internally. But you don't have to. ASP.NET exposes most of the `Request.Headers` collection values in other ways. For example, you can determine the method used to send a form with the `Request.ContentType` property, the client type with the `Request.UserAgent` property, and the form data size with the `Request.TotalBytes` property. The `Request.Headers` collection becomes more important as you begin working with clients other than browsers, or with custom client applications that send specific, non-standard header values.

The Request.QueryString Property (NameValueCollection)

The values in the Request.QueryString collection are the parameters appended to the URL, which—in its entirety—is called the QueryString. For example, the following request contains two named parameter values:

```
http://myserver/myPage.aspx?Value1=Visual&Value2=CSharp
```

The names are Value1 and Value2, and the values are the strings Visual and CSharp. The Query-String collection works just like the other collections you've seen so far: To retrieve a value, use the Item method and provide the key as a parameter, for example:

```
Response.Write(Request.QueryString["Value1"]);
```

The preceding line would send the string Visual to the browser.

Here's an interesting question. You know that the default form method is POST, but what happens if you create a Web Form and want to use the GET method? You may recall that when a form uses the GET method, it appends the form data to the URL. The question is: When a form uses the GET method, is the form data available to the server in the QueryString collection and the Form collection, just the QueryString collection, or just the Form collection? It's an interesting question because if the form sends data via the request URL, how can the server differentiate between Form collection data and QueryString collection data? It turns out that the server *does* differentiate by checking the Request.ContentType property. When the property contains multipart/form-data, the form was sent using the POST method, and the server populates the Form collection. When the form uses the GET method, the property contains application./x-www-form-urlencoded, and the server populates the Query-String collection. In other words, you can't access data sent using the GET method with the Form collection; you must use the QueryString collection instead.

You can view all the QueryString values with a simple loop. Using the example query at the top of this section, the following loop returns Visual and CSharp:

```
foreach(String aKey in Request.QueryString.AllKeys) {
    Response.Write(aKey + "=" +
        Request.QueryString[aKey] + "<br>");
}
```

The Request.ServerVariables Collection (NameValueCollection)

The Request.ServerVariables collection contains a large number of useful values sent by clients with each request. The collection itself is a standard NameValueCollection, which should be familiar by now, so I won't go into more detail here. However, it's disconcerting to see how many of these values there are in each request and to discover how Web sites use these values to collect information about their clients, their clients' computers, and their clients' browsing habits.

Using a standard loop to return the keys and values from the ServerVariables collection, you'll see a list of items similar to those in Table 6.1. You can see the values applicable to your browser by loading the sample code Web Form ch6/ch6-7.aspx.

TABLE 6.1: *REQUEST.SERVERVARIABLES* KEYS AND VALUES

KEYS	VALUES
ALL_HTTP	HTTP_CONNECTION:Keep-Alive HTTP_ACCEPT:*/* HTTP_ACCEPT_ENCODING:gzip, deflate HTTP_ACCEPT_LANGUAGE:en-us HTTP_COOKIE:AspSessionId=545zs545ibax5tv12u21da55 HTTP_HOST:russell-dual HTTP_USER_AGENT:Mozilla/4.0 (compatible; MSIE 5.5; Windows NT 5.0)
ALL_RAW	Connection: Keep-Alive Accept: */* Accept-Encoding: gzip, deflate Accept-Language: en-us Cookie: AspSessionId=545zs545ibax5tv12u21da55 Host: russell-dual User-Agent: Mozilla/4.0 (compatible; MSIE 5.5; Windows NT 5.0)
APPL_MD_PATH	/LM/W3SVC/1/Root/CSharpASP
APPL_PHYSICAL_PATH	c:\inetpub\wwwroot\CSharpASP\
AUTH_TYPE	
AUTH_USER	
AUTH_PASSWORD	
LOGON_USER	
REMOTE_USER	
CERT_COOKIE	
CERT_FLAGS	
CERT_ISSUER	
CERT_KEYSIZE	
CERT_SECRETKEYSIZE	
CERT_SERIALNUMBER	
CERT_SERVER_ISSUER	
CERT_SERVER_SUBJECT	
CERT_SUBJECT	
CONTENT_LENGTH	0
CONTENT_TYPE	
GATEWAY_INTERFACE	CGI/1.1
HTTPS	off
HTTPS_KEYSIZE	
HTTPS_SECRETKEYSIZE	

Continued on next page

TABLE 6.1: *REQUEST.SERVERVARIABLES* KEYS AND VALUES *(continued)*

KEYS	VALUES
HTTPS_SERVER_ISSUER	
HTTPS_SERVER_SUBJECT	
INSTANCE_ID	1
INSTANCE_META_PATH	/LM/W3SVC/1
LOCAL_ADDR	192.168.0.5
PATH_INFO	/CSharpASP/ch6/ch6-7.aspx
PATH_TRANSLATED	c:\inetpub\wwwroot\CSharpASP\ch6\ch6-7.aspx
QUERY_STRING	
REMOTE_ADDR	192.168.0.2
REMOTE_HOST	192.168.0.2
REQUEST_METHOD	GET
SCRIPT_NAME	/CSharpASP/ch6/ch6-7.aspx
SERVER_NAME	russell-dual
SERVER_PORT	80
SERVER_PORT_SECURE	0
SERVER_PROTOCOL	HTTP/1.1
SERVER_SOFTWARE	Microsoft-IIS/5.0
URL	/CSharpASP/ch6/ch6-7.aspx
HTTP_CONNECTION	Keep-Alive
HTTP_ACCEPT	*/*
HTTP_ACCEPT_ENCODING	gzip, deflate
HTTP_ACCEPT_LANGUAGE	en-us
HTTP_COOKIE	AspSessionId
545zs545ibax5tv12u21da55	
HTTP_HOST	russell-dual
HTTP_USER_AGENT	Mozilla/4.0 (compatible; MSIE 5.5; Windows NT 5.0)

TIP *You'll find that you need some of these values more often than others. Following are the ones I use most often.*

APPL_PHYSICAL_PATH   The physical path of your application. The variable does not include the name of the requested file. This value is useful because you should never hard code a path in your application if at all possible. Another way to retrieve the physical path of your application is to use the `Server.MapPath(".")` method to map the current path. Chapter 8, "The *HttpServerUtility* Object," covers `Server.MapPath` in detail.

LOCAL_ADDR   The IP address of the server hosting your application. If you're developing with a Web server on the same machine as the browser requesting the file, the `LOCAL_ADDR` and `REMOTE_ADDR` values will be identical.

LOGON_USER   The network username for the person using the browser requesting this resource (applicable only if the IIS Allow Anonymous security option is turned off).

PATH_INFO   The full physical path to the requested file. This value is useful if you redirect but still need to know the name of the file originally requested.

SERVER_NAME   The name of the server as requested by the user. Note that all servers support the name `localhost`, which you may see if you're developing with a Web server on the same machine as the browser requesting the file.

SERVER_PORT   The IP port number—usually 80 for HTTP servers.

HTTP_USER_AGENT   The make and version of the requesting client. You use this value to determine the appropriate response. For example, you might need to send different content when the client is a WAP phone or a browser or if the browser is Netscape rather than IE.

As a final note, in previous versions of ASP, the `Request.ServerVariables` collection was slow, but that problem has been fixed in ASP.NET. You may use the collection just as you would any other ASP.NET collection.

The Request.UserLanguages Property (Sorted String Array)

The `Request.UserLanguages` property contains a `String` array listing the client's language preferences. The language preference strings are Locale ID (LCID) constants, each of which consists of a two-character language code usually followed by a dash and a two-character country code. By default, IE installs with a single U.S. English preference, so the only value in the collection is `en-us`, meaning English-United States. You can see the values applicable to your browser by loading the example Web Forms `ch6.aspx` and `ch6-7.aspx`.

The Request.Params Property (NameValueCollection)

The `Params` property returns a `NameValueCollection` that contains a combination of the items in the `QueryString`, `Form`, `ServerVariables`, and `Cookies` collections. Typically, you're better off specifying the collection than using the `Params` collection. You won't use the property in this book.

Other Request Object Properties

In addition to the collection and array properties you've seen so far, the `Request` object has several single-valued properties:

ApplicationPath   Retrieves the virtual path of your application. This is useful when you need to construct a URL dynamically. If you avoid hard-coding paths in your application, users may install it under a different name than you used to develop the application, so you need some way to determine the virtual path. Note that you can also obtain the path by stripping the filename from the `Request.ServerVariables("URL")` value.

ApplicationPoolID   The ASP.NET framework assigns each request to one of a pool of `Http-Application` object instances. If you need to know exactly which instance an IIS has assigned a specific request to, you can use the `ApplicationPoolID` property to find out. The `Application-PoolID` is a `String` value.

Browser   In previous versions of ASP, you had to use the `BrowserCapabilities` component (or third-party component) to determine the browser type, version, and related values. In ASP.NET, the `Browser` property returns an `HttpBrowserCapabilities` object, which in turn exposes properties you can use to determine the client's capabilities. Note that you can determine only a few of the values (such as the browser type, version, and operating system) using the `HTTP_USER_AGENT` string exposed by the `Request.ServerVariables` collection. In previous versions, the `Browser-Capabilities` component used an INI file to look up associated values for the various types of browsers. You can see the values applicable to your browser by loading the sample code Web Form `ch6/ch6-7.aspx`. (See Table 6.2 at the end of this section for a full list of the properties exposed by the `HttpBrowserCapabilities` object.)

ClientCertificate   Returns an `HttpClientCertificate` object containing information about the security certificate (if any) sent by the browser. `HttpClientCertificate` inherits from NameValue Collection. I've omitted those properties that are common to all classes based on the base `Name-ValueCollection` class. (See Table 6.3 at the end of this section for a full list of the properties exposed by the `HttpClientCertificate` object.)

ConnectionID   ASP.NET associates each request with a specific connection from a pool. Using this property, you can determine the connection associated with the current request.

ContentEncoding   Contains the character encoding set for the data supplied by the browser.

ContentType   Contains the MIME-type string for the data supplied by the browser.

FilePath   Returns a `String` value containing the full virtual path of the current request.

Filter   This property is *not* read-only. It retrieves or sets a `Stream` object containing the filter for the current request.

Form   Retrieves a collection of `Form` variables.

Headers   Returns a list of HTTP headers sent by the requesting browser.

HttpMethod   Returns the method used to request the file (`GET` or `POST`).

InputStream   Returns a `Stream` object that gives you direct access to the raw data sent by the browser.

IsAuthenticated   Returns a `Boolean` value indicating whether the client browser has been authenticated (applicable only if the IIS Allow Anonymous security option is turned off).

IsSecureConnection   Returns a `Boolean` value indicating whether the connection used for the current request is secure (uses HTTPS).

Params   This property returns a collection containing all the `QueryString`, `Form`, `ServerVariable`, and `Cookie` collection values.

Path   Returns a `String` value containing the virtual path of the request.

PathInfo   Contains additional path information when the request has a URL extension. For example, the `PathInfo` property for the request `http://www.myserver/myPath/myFile.htm/someExtension` would contain `/someExtension`.

PhysicalApplicationPath   Contains the physical path where the application is on the server.

PhysicalPath   Contains the physical path for the request.

RawURL   Contains the full URL as requested by the client.

RequestType   Another name for (and identical to) the `HttpMethod` property.

TotalBytes   Returns an `Integer` value containing the total number of bytes sent by the client.

Url   Contains the URL of the current request. This property differs from the `RawURL` property in that all replacements for the URL-encoded request have already been made. In other words, the request

    http://www.someserver/somePath/some page.aspx

(note the space in the filename) would be `URLEncoded` as

    http://www.someserver/somePath/some%20page.aspx

The %20 represents the hex value 32, the space character. For this URL, the `RawURL` property for a URL containing a space would contain the %20 character, whereas the `Url` property would not—it would return the URL with a true space rather than the encoded space.

UrlReferrer   Contains the last URL the browser requested *before* making the current request. This property may be blank. This is the equivalent of using the `Request.ServerVariables("HTTP_REFERRER")` value.

UserAgent   Returns the raw `USER_AGENT` string. This is the equivalent of using the `Request.ServerVariables("HTTP_USER_AGENT")` value.

UserHostAddress   Returns the IP address of the client. This is the equivalent of using the `Request.ServerVariables("REMOTE_HOST")` value.

TABLE 6.2: THE HttpBrowserCapabilities OBJECT'S PROPERTIES

PROPERTY	RETURN TYPE	DESCRIPTION
ActiveXControls	Boolean	Returns true if the browser supports ActiveX controls.
AOL	Boolean	Returns true if the client is an America Online (AOL) browser.
BackgroundSounds	Boolean	Returns true if the browser can play background sounds.
Beta	Boolean	Returns true when the client is tagged as a beta version.
Browser	String	This is confusingly named, but the property contains the string identifying the browser brand name, such as IE or Netscape.
CDF	Boolean	Returns true if the browser supports the Channel Definition Format (CDF).
ClrVersion	Version	Returns a Version object that represents the version number of the Common Language Runtime (CLR) installed on the client.
Cookies	Boolean	Returns true if the browser supports cookies.
Crawler	Boolean	Returns true if the requesting client is a program used by search engines to gather information about Web pages (a crawler).
EcmaScriptVersion	Version	Returns a Version object that represents the version number of the installed EcmaScript scripting language standard supported by the client browser.
Frames	Boolean	Returns true if the client supports the HTML <frame> tag.
JavaApplets	Boolean	Returns true if the client supports Java applets.
JavaScript	Boolean	Returns true if the client supports client-side script written in the JavaScript language.
MajorVersion	Integer	Returns the major version number for the client browser.
MinorVersion	Integer	Returns the minor version number for the client browser.
MsDomVersion	Version	Returns a Version object that represents the version number of the Microsoft HTML (MSHTML) supported on the client and that exposes Build, Major, Minor, and Revision properties.
Platform	String	Returns the name of the operating system hosting the client browser. The results aren't always what you might expect. For example, running on Windows 2000, the Platform property returns WinNT.
Tables	Boolean	Returns true if the client supports tables.
Type	String	Returns the browser client name as well as the major version. For example, IE. 5.5 returns IE5, while Netscape Communicator 4.76 returns Netscape4.

Continued on next page

TABLE 6.2: THE `HttpBrowserCapabilities` OBJECT'S PROPERTIES *(continued)*

PROPERTY	RETURN TYPE	DESCRIPTION
VBScript	Boolean	Returns `true` if the client supports client-side script written in the VBScript language.
Version	String	Returns the full major and minor version number. For example, IE 5.5 returns 5.5.
W3CDomVersion	Version	Returns a `Version` object that represents the version number of the World Wide Web Consortium (W3C) XML Document Object Model (DOM) (MSHTML) supported by the client.
Win16	Boolean	Returns `true` if the client is running on a 16-bit Windows OS (such as Windows 3.1).
Win32	Boolean	Returns `true` if the client is running on a 32-bit Windows OS (such as Windows 98 or Windows 2000).

TABLE 6.3: THE `HttpClientCertificate` OBJECT'S PROPERTIES

PROPERTY	RETURN TYPE	DESCRIPTION
BinaryIssuer	Byte()	Returns a byte array identifying the agency that issued the certificate.
CertEncoding	Integer	Returns a value indicating the type of encoding applied to the certificate.
Certificate	String	Returns the certificate content in ASN.1 format.
Cookie	String	Returns the `HttpCookie` containing the certificate.
Flags	Integer	Returns an `Integer` value consisting of a set of flags that provides additional certificate information.
IsPresent	Boolean	Returns `true` if the browser sent a certificate.
Issuer	String	Contains information about the agency that issued the certificate.
IsValid	Boolean	Returns `true` if the certificate is valid.
KeySize	Integer	Returns the size of the key used to encrypt the certificate.
PublicKey	Byte()	For certificates that use a public/private key encryption method, this property returns the public key required to decrypt the certificate.
SecretKeySize	Integer	For certificates that use a public/private encryption method, this property returns the size of the private key required to decrypt the certificate.

Continued on next page

TABLE 6.3: THE HttpClientCertificate OBJECT'S PROPERTIES *(continued)*

PROPERTY	RETURN TYPE	DESCRIPTION
SerialNumber	String	The certification serial number represented in ASCII as a series of digits separated by dashes.
ServerIssuer	String	Contains the value of the issuer field for a server certificate.
ServerSubject	String	Contains the value of the Subject field for a server certificate.
Subject	String list	Comma-separated list of values containing information about the subject of the certificate.
ValidFrom	Date	Date at which certificate validity begins.
ValidUntil	Date	Date at which certificate validity expires.

REQUEST OBJECT METHODS

In addition to the properties you've just seen, the Request object has several special public methods. (The methods that the HttpRequest object inherits from Object are common to all objects, so I've omitted them here.)

BinaryRead   When you receive binary content, such as an uploaded file or other binary stream, you use the BinaryRead method to retrieve it. The method returns a Byte array.

MapImageCoordinates   When a user clicks an ImageButton control in a Web Form, the browser sends the x- and y-coordinates of the point that was clicked. To retrieve the coordinates, you call the MapImageCoordinates method, passing the name of the image tag. The method returns the selected coordinates as an array of two Integers with the x-coordinate first and the y-coordinate second. For example:

```
private void imageButton1_Click(object sender,
   System.Web.UI.ImageClickEventArgs e) {
   int[] coords = Request.MapImageCoordinates("ImageButton1");
   Response.Write("Coordinates: ");
   for (int i = 0; i < coords.Length; i++) {
      Response.Write(coords[i].ToString() + ", ");
   }
   Response.Write("<br>");
   Response.Write(e.X.ToString() + ", " + e.Y.ToString());
}
```

MapPath   The MapPath method returns the physical path (but not the filename) of the virtual path passed as a parameter. To retrieve the path of the current directory, use the dot notation Request.MapPath("."). On my system, for example, requesting the URL

http://localhost/CSharpASP/ch6/ch6-8.aspx   and then querying the MapPath method with Request.MapPath(".") returns this path: c:\inetpub\wwwroot\CSharpASP\ch6.

SaveAs   The SaveAs method lets you save the contents of an HttpRequest to a disk file. The method saves all the data in the request. It accepts two parameters: a filename and an optional Boolean value specifying whether you wish to save the request headers in addition to the data. For example, the command Request.Save("c:\\request.txt", true); saves the current request to the file c:\\ request.txt and also saves the headers. The resulting file looks like this:

```
POST /CSharpASP/ch6/ch6-8.aspx HTTP/1.1
Connection: Keep-Alive
Content-Length: 110
Content-Type: application/x-www-form-urlencoded
Accept: image/gif, image/x-xbitmap, image/jpeg,
    image/pjpeg, */*
Accept-Encoding: gzip, deflate
Accept-Language: en-us
Cookie: AspSessionId=0nja1355ivdwztzc23yyag45
Host: localhost
Referer: http://localhost/CSharpASP/ch6/ch6-8.aspx
User-Agent: Mozilla/4.0 (compatible; MSIE 5.5; Windows NT 5.0;
    COM+ 1.0.2204)
// note that __VIEWSTATE appears one line in the saved file
__VIEWSTATE=YTB6LTIxMDUOMDg4NDFfX2F6SW1hZ2VCdXR0b24xX3hfeA%3D%3D5
    ffd0b70&ImageButton1.x=278&ImageButton1.y=168
```

WARNING   *The actual content saved may differ, depending on your server, the server and* web.config *settings, your browser, and your browser settings.*

Sending Information to the Client

Now that you've seen the information that clients send to the server in a request and how to retrieve it with the Request object, it's time to return to the Response object. As you've seen, you use the Response object to return data to the client. You've already used the Response.Write method to return text strings, but the object has several useful properties and some other methods as well. In classic ASP, the Response object was fairly simple; in ASP.NET, its capabilities are expanded, so don't skip this section even if you're an experienced ASP programmer.

The Charset property controls the character set used by the server to create the response stream. The ContentType property controls how the client will attempt to interpret the response data, and the ContentEncoding property controls how the client will translate the response byte stream into characters. English (Latin) characters are not a problem, but characters in other languages are. For example, by default, the browser translates a byte with the value 159 into the character Ÿ, but different encodings cause the client to translate the values differently. If you're working with languages other than English or with symbols or other special characters, you may need to change the ContentEncoding value for the characters to be displayed properly on the client.

HttpResponse **Object Properties**

The following sections explain the Response object's properties and provide some examples of their use.

THE *RESPONSE.BUFFEROUTPUT* PROPERTY

When you're creating a response on the server, you can elect to send the results immediately—every time you call the `Response.Write` method—or to buffer the results and send the completed response all at once after your code has finished processing the output. You control buffering with the `Buffer-Output` property. The property is read/write and takes a `Boolean` value. By default, ASP.NET buffers responses, which works well in most cases. You might wish to set the `BufferOutput` property value to `false` if you're sending a long response. For example, if you you're creating a report that might take several seconds to format, you could send the report headers first and then send each report section as you finish processing it. Sending the sections sequentially rather than storing them until processing for all sections is complete helps users know that your application is working. Giving users something to look at makes the application *feel* faster even when it isn't. You *must* set the `BufferOutput` property *before* you begin to write content—if you attempt to change the value after sending any content, ASP.NET raises an error.

The sample Web Form `ch6-9.aspx.cs` illustrates the difference between buffered and unbuffered output. The output is simple; the page writes `Item 1, Item 2, Item 3, Item N`. The code uses a `Timer` control to increase the processing duration of the page, thus simulating a busy server, or the process of creating a lengthy report, or any other server-intensive process. Listing 6.10 contains the relevant code—I've omitted the designer-generated code in the listing.

LISTING 6.10: AN EXAMPLE OF BUFFERED VERSUS UNBUFFERED RESPONSE (ch6-9.aspx.cs)

```
public class ch6_9 : System.Web.UI.Page {
    private int tickCount;
    private bool exitloop;
    protected System.Web.UI.WebControls.Button cmdBuffered;
    protected System.Timers.Timer timer1;
    protected System.Web.UI.WebControls.Button cmdUnbuffered;

    private void Page_Load(object sender, System.EventArgs e) {
        timer1.Interval = 10;
        timer1.Stop();
        timer1.Enabled = true;
    }

    private void cmdUnbuffered_Click(object sender,
        System.EventArgs e) {
        Response.BufferOutput = false;
        tickCount = 0;
        timer1.Start();
        while (exitloop == false){};
        // timer elapsed method shows output

    }

    private void cmdBuffered_Click(object sender, System.EventArgs e) {
        Response.BufferOutput = true;
        tickCount = 0;
```

```
      timer1.Start();
      while (exitloop == false) {};
      //timer elapsed method shows output


  private void timer1_Elapsed(object sender,
      System.Timers.ElapsedEventArgs e) {
      Response.Write("Waiting...tickCount=" +
         tickCount.ToString() + "<br>");
      tickCount++;
      if( tickCount > 100) {
         timer1.Enabled = false;
         timer1.Stop();
         exitloop = true;
      }
   }
}
```

When you view the Web Form in your browser, you'll see two buttons titled Buffered Response and Unbuffered Response. Clicking either button runs identical code on the server, except that one sets the `BufferOutput` property to `true` while the other sets it to `false`. Click the Buffered Response button. The code takes about 20 seconds to execute on the server. After you see the response, click the Unbuffered Response button. Which version takes longer? Which version *appears* to take longer? As a final note to encourage you to remember to disable buffering for long pages, research shows that even patient people rarely wait longer than 12 seconds for a Web page to begin to render. If the page takes longer than that, they leave.

THE *RESPONSE.CACHE* PROPERTY

ASP.NET has extensive caching capabilities that help solve several problems. One of the more intractable problems with classic ASP pages was that you had to include several header values with each page to prevent browsers from caching the file. Browser file caching isn't usually a problem with HTML pages because they don't change often; with dynamic pages, where the content may change continuously, you usually want the browser to load a fresh copy each time. The `Cache` property helps simplify the process.

Another problem is that while ASP.NET pages *are* dynamic, it may be overkill to build the full page for every request. Sometimes it's convenient to use a dynamic page even when the content changes once a day or less. The solution, of course, is to cache the page and thus reduce server load. In classic ASP, you had to write your own caching mechanism. Not anymore. The `Response.Cache` property returns an `HttpCachePolicy` object. You use this object's methods to adjust the cache settings. You'll see more about caching in Chapter 17, "State Maintenance and Caching."

THE *RESPONSE.CHARSET* PROPERTY

There are many different character sets, but no single set contains all the characters for all languages. For example, by default, IIS uses the UTF-8 character set, but if, for example, you need to output

Swedish characters, you'll need to change the character set to ISO-8859-1 or another character set that supports Swedish characters.

The Charset property is read/write. The page always writes a response header containing the value. When the Response.BufferOutput property is true, you can change the property value at any time, but the browser uses only the last setting. When the Response.BufferOutput property is false, you must set the Charset property before writing any content; otherwise you'll get the error message Cannot set content type after Http headers have been sent. The Web Form ch6-10.aspx contains an example.

THE *RESPONSE.CONTENTENCODING* PROPERTY

The ContentEncoding property controls the way the browser will attempt to convert the byte stream values back into characters. Unlike the Charset property, the ContentEncoding property returns a System.Text.Encoding object containing a specific encoding type. The default type is UTF8. You should not need to change this value unless you work with languages other than English.

THE *RESPONSE.CONTENTTYPE* PROPERTY

No matter how you like to think about your responses, the end result is that the Response object sends a string of bytes. The response you send may contain text, HTML, XML, image data, specific well-known file-type data—such as a Word, Excel, or PDF file—or a stream of custom binary or text data. The Response object includes a MIME type header that the client uses to determine the type of data contained in the response. The default response MIME type is text/html, but you can change that with the Response.ContentType property. It's important to get the ContentType setting correct, or the results on the client may be unpredictable.

The Web Form ch6-10.aspx has three buttons, with the IDs cmdShowEncoding, cmdGoodEncoding, and cmdBadEncoding.

When you click the cmdShowEncoding button, the server writes the Response object's Charset, ContentType, and ContentEncoding property values to the browser.

```
private void cmdShowEncoding_Click(object sender, System.EventArgs e) {
    // Enabling the following line causes an error
    //Response.BufferOutput = False;
    Response.Write("Charset=" + Response.Charset + "<br>");
    Response.Charset = "ISO-8859-1";
    Response.Write("Charset=" + Response.Charset + "<br>");
    Response.Write("ContentType=" + Response.ContentType + "<br>");
    Response.Write("ContentEncoding=" +
        Response.ContentEncoding.ToString() + "<br>");
}
```

The cmdBadEncoding button causes the browser to write an XML file mislabeled with the Content-Type of text/html. Despite the mislabeling, Internet Explorer displays the file (incorrectly) as XML rather than interpreting the tags as HTML and showing only the content between the tags.

```
private void cmdBadEncoding_Click(object sender, System.EventArgs e) {
    Response.ContentType = "text/html";
    Response.Write("<?xml version=\"1.0\"?>");
```

```
    Response.Write("<root><person><lastname>Brown</lastname>" +
      "<firstname>Joe</firstname></person></root>");
    Response.End();
    /* Note—this displays (improperly) in IE as XML,
       but may not be recognizable as XML
       in other clients due to the text/html header.
       If you change the content type to something unrecognizable, e.g.
       "x-application/csharpasp" the browser asks
       if you want to save or open the file
         (which is the correct behavior). */
  }
  private void cmdGoodEncoding_Click(object sender, System.EventArgs e) {
    Response.ContentType = "text/xml";
    Response.Write("<?xml version=\"1.0\"?>");
    Response.Write("<root><person><lastname>Brown</lastname>" +
      "<firstname>Joe</firstname></person></root>");
    Response.End();
  }
```

The cmdGoodEncoding button exhibits the same behavior as the cmdBadEncoding button in IE (see the note in the preceding listing). In Netscape 6, both the cmdGoodEncoding and cmdBadEncoding buttons display only content and not markup. If you're going to send XML directly to clients, be sure to test with all the anticipated client types for the application.

THE *RESPONSE.COOKIES* PROPERTY

The Response.Cookies property contains a collection of HttpCookie objects. You've already seen a little about the Response.Cookies collection—specifically, how to create a cookie. Now you can explore the process for creating cookies in a little more depth.

There are two types of cookies: in-memory or "transient" cookies exist only in the client's memory and exist only for the lifetime of the browser instance; disk-based or "persistent" cookies, which the browser writes to local storage, contain an expiration date and persist until that date. Here's the difference:

```
// write a transient cookie
HttpCookie transientCookie = new HttpCookie("transient", "transient");

// write a persistent cookie
HttpCookie persistentCookie = new HttpCookie("persistant",
  "persistant");

// set the expiration date to Dec. 31, 2010 at 11:59:00 PM
persistentCookie.Expires = new DateTime(2001, 12, 31, 23, 59, 59);

Response.Cookies.Add(transientCookie);
Response.Cookies.Add(persistentCookie);
Response.AppendToLog("This is a test from ch6-11");
```

The preceding code creates both a transient and a persistent cookie. Setting the expiration date (the `Expires` property) is the key to creating a persistent cookie. The browser writes persistent cookies (those where the `Expires` property is a valid date) to disk in the user's `Cookies` folder. The browser reads the cookies in that folder on startup and creates a cache. New persistent cookies and transient cookies are added to the cache. For each request, the browser checks the cookie cache to see if there's a cookie associated with the domain (and possibly path) of the request. If so, it sends the cookie data as part of the request header.

HttpResponse Object Methods

In addition to the `Write` method, which you've already seen, the `HttpResponse` object contains several other useful methods. (I've omitted the methods that the `HttpResponse` object inherits from `Object`, because they're common to all objects.)

AddFileDependencies   A response may depend on the existence and availability of one or more files. If the files are not available for any reason, the `Response` object raises an error. You can add files to the dependency list one at a time with the `AddFileDependency` method. The `AddFileDependencies` method lets you add several files at once by passing the method an `ArrayList` containing a list of filenames.

```
Array fList = new Array("file1.txt", "file2.txt");
Response.AddFileDependencies(fList);
```

AddFileDependency   A response may depend on the existence and availability of one or more files. If the files are not available for any reason, the `Response` object raises an error. The `AddFile-Dependency` method adds a single file to the dependency list.

AppendHeader   This method appends an HTTP header to the response. You must append new headers before writing any content; otherwise the `Response` object raises an error. For example, you can write a cookie using the `AppendHeader` method as well as with the `Response.Cookies` collection. The method accepts two strings; the first string is the header name, and the second string is the header value. To write a cookie with the `AppendHeader` method, you would write the following:

```
Response.AppendHeader("Set-Cookie",
  "myCookie=someCookieValue");
```

AppendToLog   The `AppendToLog` method lets you write information to the IIS log. For example, the line `Response.AppendToLog("This is a test");` causes IIS to write a line in the log like this (the entry appears in the log as a single line):

```
2001-04-05 04:45:09 127.0.0.1 - 127.0.0.1 80 GET
/CSharpASP/ch6/ch6-11.aspx This+is+a+test. 200
Mozilla/4.0+(compatible;+MSIE+5.5;+windows
+NT+5.0+COMM++1.0.2204   to the IIS log. By default, you can find the IIS log
in your %System%\Logfiles\W3SVC1 folder. See the example code for the Web Form
ch6-11.aspx for a more complete example.
```

BinaryWrite   You use the `BinaryWrite` method to write raw byte data to the browser. In classic ASP, this was the only method you could use to write binary data from a file. Other new methods, such as `WriteFile`, have made the `BinaryWrite` method less common in Web applications, but you can still use it to write raw file data. To try an example, open Notepad, enter some text in the default file, and save it as `c:\junk.txt`. Next, create a new Web Form called `ch6-12.aspx` and enter the code from Listing 6.11 in the code-behind class in the `Load` event. When you run the code, you will see the content you entered into the text file.

LISTING 6.11: EXAMPLE OF THE `Response.BinaryWrite` METHOD (`ch6-12.aspx.cs`)

```
if (!IsPostBack) {
    FileStream fs = File.OpenRead("c:\\junk.txt");
    BinaryReader br = new BinaryReader(fs);
    int size = 0;
    size = (int) br.BaseStream.Length;
    Byte[] b = new Byte[size];
    br.Read(b, 0, size);
    br.Close();
    fs.Close();
    Response.Write("<pre>");
    Response.BinaryWrite(b);
    Response.Write("</pre>");
    Response.End();
    Response.AddHeader("set-cookie", "me=me");
    Response.Write("Cookie written");*/
    Response.Write("<pre>");
    Response.WriteFile("c:\\junk.txt");
    Response.Write("</pre>");
}
```

Clear This method removes all content from the response buffer. The `Clear` method does not prevent content you may already have sent to the client (using the `Flush` method) from rendering, and does not stop the remainder of the page from executing, so the page may still send data to the browser after using the `Clear` method.

ClearHeaders `ClearHeaders` removes any existing header content from the response buffer. Using this method does not raise an error if you have already sent content to the client, but neither does it prevent the client from processing any headers already sent.

Close This closes the socket connection, but it doesn't terminate the response. For example, you might call the `Close` method for a response that initiates a long database operation. In that situation, you would respond to the client, flush the response, and then close the connection. After closing the connection, your application is unable to send any further response data to the client, but it can still perform processing initiated by the request—for example, updating a database, parsing files, or calculating report values. You might also use the `Close` method to ensure that buffered data is not sent (note that you can use the `Clear` and `ClearHeaders` methods instead). The `End` method sends buffered output to the client before terminating the response, so if you want to avoid that, you might call the `Close` method *before* calling the `End` method.

End   End sends any currently buffered content to the client and terminates the response immediately, closing the socket connection. Any code farther down the execution sequence in the same code-behind page that might otherwise have executed does not execute; however, event code in the `global.asax` file (such as `Application_EndRequest`) still executes.

Flush   Sends any buffered data to the client. For example, if you're building a large page, you can flush the data periodically so that the client can begin displaying the data before the response is complete. This speeds up the *apparent* time required to display the page, even though it slightly increases the *actual* time required.

Pics   Internet pages can supply a Platform for Internet Content Selection (PICS) header that clients use to determine the appropriateness of the content. The header is commonly known as a PICS label. A PICS label is nothing but a metatag containing the name `PICS-label` and a value supplied by one of a number of *label bureaus* (sometimes called *rating bureaus*). You can, of course, simply include the label in the HTML file for each Web Form, but the `Pics` method makes it easy to build dynamic pages that include the ratings. For more information see `http://www.w3.org/PICS/`.

Redirect   The `Redirect` method causes the client to rerequest the page or request another page. It takes one parameter—the URL of the page the client should request. It works by placing a redirect header in the response. For example, the header `<META HTTP-EQUIV="refresh" content="3">` refreshes the current page after 3 seconds. The `refresh` directive tells the client to request a page, and the content contains the number of seconds the client should wait before making the request. By adding a URL in the content, you can have the client request a different page. For example, the following line causes the client to request Microsoft's default page after 3 seconds:

```
<META HTTP-EQUIV="refresh" content="3;
URL=http://www.microsoft.com">
```

Writing the full HTML header using the `Response.AddHeader` method is more powerful than the `Redirect` method, which redirects immediately. Because the `Redirect` method requires a round trip to the client and back to the server, you should also see the `Server.Transfer` and `Server.Execute` methods (discussed in Chapter 8), which can often accomplish the same purpose without a round trip.

WriteFile   The `WriteFile` method writes the contents of a file to the client. It's overloaded so that you can write partial files by specifying the offset from the start of the file and the number of bytes. For example, the following code accomplishes the same result as the `Response.BinaryWrite` example shown earlier, but with less code. Comment out the code in the `Load` event for `ch6-12.aspx.cs` and enter this code instead:

```
if (!IsPostBack) {
    Response.Write("<pre>");
    Response.WriteFile("c:\\junk.txt");
    Response.Write("</pre>");
}
```

You will see the same result when you run the example, but it is accomplished with 3 lines of code rather than 10. This method is long overdue for ASP-based sites. For example, you might use this method to hide the filenames of `htm` or other files that are part of your application.

The *HttpApplication* and *HttpApplicationState* Objects

C# Web applications can have global values and objects, just as stand-alone Windows programs can have global variables containing values and objects shared between all classes. The `HttpApplication-State` object holds these values. Like most Web-based collections, it's implemented as a list of names and values in which the name is an indexed `String` array.

You can't access the `HttpApplicationState` object directly. Instead, you reach it through an `Http-Application` object. The ASP.NET runtime maintains a pool of `HttpApplication` objects. Each request receives an `HttpApplication` object instance from the pool. The runtime shuts down the application when the last session times out or when you explicitly close it via the `Session.Abandon` method. It raises events the first time any user requests any page from your application and immediately after the last active session times out or ends.

The ASP.NET framework creates a single `ApplicationState` instance for each application running on the server the first time any client makes any request for any page in the application. ASP.NET does not share `ApplicationState` objects across multiple machines, so you should never store information specific to a particular session at Application scope—use the SessionState class to store session-specific information. You'll see more about the `Session` and `SessionState` objects in the next chapter.

The `HttpApplication` object has a property called `Application` that exposes the `HttpApplication-State` object associated with a specific application. Web Form `Page` objects also expose that same instance as their `Application` property. Each application has one—and only one—`HttpApplication-State` object. Therefore, when you store objects at Application scope, you're actually storing them in the `HttpApplicationState` object. For those who are familiar with classic ASP the terminology is confusing, but there is a difference between the `HttpApplication` and `HttpApplicationState` objects. The way to remember them is that the `HttpApplication` object exposes the events you use to intercept `Application.Start`, `Application.End`, `Application.BeginRequest`, and `Application.EndRequest` events, while the `HttpApplicationState` object simply holds all the objects you store at Application scope. Both of these appear in code under the name `Application`.

From a practical point of view, there's little difference, which is probably why Microsoft chose to use the shorter term `Application` both for the events exposed by the `HttpApplication` object and to access objects stored at Application scope in the `HttpApplicationState` object. Therefore, I'll also use that shorter form from here on. Just remember that there are two objects, not one.

Web Applications Are Multiuser Programs

Because all requests share the `HttpApplicationState` object, and because IIS is a multithreaded multiuser program, multiple requests may try to access values stored in the `Application` object simultaneously. Therefore, you must be aware of the threading model of the objects you store there and take threading into account when you update Application scope information. If an object stored at Application scope is not thread safe, you must explicitly serialize access to that object; otherwise you'll have concurrency problems. The `Application` object won't warn you if you store an object that is not thread safe at Application scope (and most of the Collection classes are not thread safe for performance reasons), so be careful. If you must store collections at Application scope, be sure to pick thread-safe classes or handle the threading issues yourself.

Introduction to Threads—How IIS Handles Simultaneous Requests

IIS has a pool of threads that it uses in a round-robin fashion to service requests. For example, suppose (for simplicity) that IIS has five available threads in the pool. As long as only one request at a time arrives at the server, IIS will use the first thread in the pool for each request. When a second request arrives before the first request has finished processing, IIS allocates a second thread to handle the second request.

Now you have two requests being processed "simultaneously." Of course, they aren't really handled simultaneously; instead, the server uses time slicing to service the requests a little at a time. Each request gets a time slice. If the request finishes during any time slice, IIS returns the thread used for that request to the thread pool.

Despite the overhead involved in switching tasks from one thread to the next, this method improves overall Web server response time because it helps ensure that small, easy-to-process requests don't have to wait while a single long request executes.

When the number of simultaneous requests exceeds the number of available threads, IIS queues the requests and handles them in the order they arrived. If you find that IIS often runs out of threads (you can track thread usage with the Performance Monitor), you can increase the size of the thread pool. Increasing the thread pool size slows down the requests somewhat because of the increase in task-switching overhead required; however, by "tuning" your Web server, you can find a balance between the number of requests, the size of the thread pool, and the average time required to process requests.

Application Variables—Sharing Data between ASP.NET Instances

As you've seen, whenever a new client requests a file from an ASP.NET application, the ASP engine creates a `Session` object and a new `ASPSessionID` cookie for the response, thus creating a recognizable session for that client. Each session can have its own data stored specifically for that session, but all `Sessions` share data through the `Application` object. For example, suppose you have files stored in a folder named `userFiles`, and you want to serve those files to clients for your application.

You know that the folder is directly under your application root, but you don't necessarily know what the application root *is*, because someone else may install your application in a folder with a different name. Therefore, you want to get the application root physical folder path using the `Server.MapPath` method. Having done that once, you don't need to do it again because the path won't change during the lifetime of your application instance, so you can store it in the `Application` object (remember that this is actually the `HttpApplicationState` object) and share the value between all `Sessions`. Listing 6.12 shows an example.

LISTING 6.12: STORING A SIMPLE VALUE IN THE `Application` OBJECT (`ch6-13.aspx.cs`)

```
private void Page_Load(object sender, System.EventArgs e) {
    string rootpath;
    if (Application.Get("rootpath") == null) {
        Application.Lock();
        Application.Add("rootpath", Server.MapPath(".") + "\\");
        Application.UnLock();
        Response.Write("Stored the root path at " +
            "Application scope<br>.");
```

```
    }
    rootpath = (String) Application.Get("rootpath");
    Response.Write(rootpath);
}
```

The code first checks to ensure that the value stored in the `Application` object under the key `rootpath` is not `Null`; if it is, the code creates and stores the `rootpath` string under the `rootpath` key and writes a message stating that the string was stored. Finally, it writes the `rootpath` string to the client.

The first time you run this code, you'll see the string `"Stored the root path at Application scope."`, as well as the path itself. Refresh your browser. After refreshing, you'll see only the path. That's because for all subsequent requests, the server retrieves the path from the `Application` object—it doesn't need to store it again.

Note that the `Application.Item` method returns an `Object` variable, not the `String` variable that you assigned to it. You'll need to cast the `Object` variables to the correct types when you retrieve them.

In addition to simple objects such as `Strings` and `Integers`, you can store other objects, including collections. For thread-safe objects, you can simply access the values as shown in Listing 6.12. For objects that are not thread safe, such as collections, you need to serialize access to the objects. You do this by locking the `Application` object, retrieving (or updating) the value, and then unlocking the `Application` object. Note that locking the `Application` object prevents other threads from accessing *any* `Application` value until the object is unlocked; therefore, you should lock, process, and unlock `Application` as fast as possible.

For example, suppose you had an application in which several pages displayed a list of state codes. You want to keep a count of the number of times any person selects any state code, so you want to store the list as a collection, with the code as the key associated with an `Integer` value that you increment whenever a user selects that code.

To do this, it's most efficient to prebuild the collection, store it at Application scope, and then share it for all requests by all sessions. Listing 6.13 contains an example (omitting system-generated code).

LISTING 6.13: WORKING WITH COLLECTIONS AT APPLICATION SCOPE (ch6-14.aspx.cs)

```
using System;
using System.Collections;
using System.ComponentModel;
using System.Data;
using System.Drawing;
using System.Web;
using System.Web.SessionState;
using System.Web.UI;
using System.Web.UI.WebControls;
using System.Web.UI.HtmlControls;

namespace CSharpASP.ch6
{
    /// <summary>
```

```csharp
/// Summary description for ch6_14.
/// </summary>
public class ch6_14 : System.Web.UI.Page {
  protected System.Web.UI.WebControls.ListBox lstStates;
  String[] states= {
      "AL", "AK", "AR", "AZ", "CA", "CO", "CT", "DE", "FL", "GA",
      "HI", "IA", "ID", "IL", "IN", "KS", "KY", "LA", "MA", "MD",
      "ME", "MI", "MN", "MO", "MS", "MT", "NE", "NC", "NH", "ND",
      "NJ", "NM", "NV", "NY", "OH", "OK", "OR", "PA", "PR", "RI",
      "SC", "SD", "TN", "TX", "UT", "VT", "VA", "WA", "WI", "WV",
      "WY"};
  int[] statecounter = new int[51];

  private void Page_Load(object sender, System.EventArgs e) {
    if (!IsPostBack) {
      if (Application.Get("states")==null) {
        //states.Sort(states)
        Application.Lock();
        Application.Set("states", states);
        Application.Set("statecounter", statecounter);
        Application.UnLock();
      }
      lstStates.DataSource = states;
      lstStates.DataBind();
      showStateCount();
    }
    else {
      Trace.Warn("lstStates.SelectedIndex",
          lstStates.SelectedIndex.ToString());
      states = (String[])Application.Get("states");
    }
  }

  #region Web Form Designer generated code
  override protected void OnInit(EventArgs e) {
    InitializeComponent();
    base.OnInit(e);
  }

  private void InitializeComponent() {
    this.lstStates.SelectedIndexChanged += new
        System.EventHandler(this.lstStates_SelectedIndexChanged);
    this.Load += new System.EventHandler(this.Page_Load);
  }
  #endregion

  private void lstStates_SelectedIndexChanged(object sender,
      System.EventArgs e) {
```

```
    int selIndex=-1;
    String selState;
    try {
       selIndex = lstStates.SelectedIndex;
    }
    catch (Exception ex) {
       Response.Write(ex.ToString());
       Response.End();
    }
    if (selIndex >= 0) {
       selState = states[selIndex];
       // update the stateCounter list
       Application.Lock();
       statecounter = (int[]) Application.Get("statecounter");
       statecounter[selIndex]++;
       // re-store the stateCounter list
       Application.Set("statecounter", statecounter);
       Application.UnLock();
    }
    showStateCount();
    // clear the selection
    lstStates.SelectedIndex = -1;
}

private void showStateCount() {
    Response.Write("<table cellspacing=1 cellpadding=1
       width=300 align=left border=1>");
    Response.Write("<tr>");
    Response.Write("<td style=\"WIDTH: 75px\"
       bgcolor=#ccffff>State</td>");
    Response.Write("<td bgcolor=#ccffff>Counter</td>");
    Response.Write("<td style=\"WIDTH: 75px\"
       bgcolor=#ccffff>State</td>");
    Response.Write("<td bgcolor=#ccffff>Counter</td>");
    Response.Write("<td style=\"WIDTH: 75px\"
       bgcolor=#ccffff>State</td>");
    Response.Write("<td bgcolor=#ccffff>Counter</td>");
    Response.Write("</tr>");
    for (int i = 0; i < states.Length; i+=3) {
       try {
          Response.Write("<tr><td style=\"WIDTH: 75px\"
             bgcolor=#ccffff>" + states[i] + "</td>");
          Response.Write("<td bgcolor=#ccffff>" +
             statecounter[i].ToString() + "</td>");
          Response.Write("<td style=\"WIDTH: 75px\"
             bgcolor=#ccffff>" + states[i + 1] + "</td>");
          Response.Write("<td bgcolor=#ccffff>" +
             statecounter[i + 1].ToString() + "</td>");
```

```
                    Response.Write("<td style=\"WIDTH: 75px\"
                        bgcolor=#ccffff>" + states[i + 2] + "</td>");
                    Response.Write("<td bgcolor=#ccffff>" +
                        statecounter[i + 2].ToString() + "</td></tr>");
                }
                catch  {
                    Response.Write("<td style=\"WIDTH: 75px\"
                        bgcolor=#ccffff> </td>");
                    Response.Write("<td bgcolor=#ccffff> " +
                        "</td></tr>");
                }

            }
            Response.Write("</table>");
        }
    }
}
```

This example displays a table showing the number of times a user has clicked on each state on the left, and a list of state codes on the right. While there are better ways to accomplish the same task in a production application, the example does show how you should handle storing and retrieving collection data to an Application variable.

Although code such as that in Listing 6.13 can be useful if you don't want to store the value in advance, in many cases you'll want to store global resources on application start up and free them when the application shuts down. Although you might expect that application start up and shut down events would be exposed by the HttpApplication object, they're not; instead, you write code to handle those events in the global.asax file.

The *global.asax* File

Each C# Web application—and by now you understand that those are the same as ASP.NET applications—may have a global.asax file in the root directory of the site. The global.asax file is special: First, because it's global—variables and directives you set in the global.asax file are truly global to your application—much like setting the GlobalMultiUse property on a class module in VB6, or defining global variables. Second, the file is special because you can use it to write code for several special events. The file creates a class named Global, which inherits from System.Web.HttpApplication and exposes application-level events. During the lifetime of an application instance, the events fire in the sequence shown below.

Application_Start   The Application_Start event fires the first time any user requests any page in your application. Use this event to perform application initialization. For example, the Application_ Start event is a good place to set database connection strings, discover the physical path of your application, initialize arrays or collections, and check resource availability.

Session_Start The `Session_Start` event fires the first time any client requests any page in your application. Note that *client* does not imply *user*—a single user may have multiple client instances open at the same time, all requesting pages from your application. The first request from *any* client fires the `Application_Start` event, while the first request from *each* client fires the `Session_Start` event. Another way to think about this event is that ASP.NET raises the event for the first request to an application from any user without a `SessionID` cookie (or munged URL).

Session_End The `Session_End` event fires after a specific length of time has elapsed without a client making a request. For example, if a user closes the browser, begins browsing a different site, or simply walks away, the `Session_End` event will fire for that session after the definable timeout period (by default, 20 minutes) has elapsed. This is an extremely important concept for anyone writing client-server applications. From the server's point of view, there's no automatic way to know when a user is finished with an application other than to make a decision based on time. It's the equivalent of the server saying, "There's been no activity for X minutes—therefore that user must be finished." Users can end a session explicitly if you provide a button or link for them to click when they're finished. In the button or link code, you explicitly call the `Session.Abandon` method, which then fires the `Session_End` event. You should use the `Session_End` event to save persistent session data and to clean up, releasing unneeded objects and data.

Application_End The `Application_End` event fires when the last active session times out or ends due to a call to the `Session.Abandon` method. The server releases any objects stored at Application scope and shuts down the application. You should use the `Application_End` event to save persistent application data and release objects and data that you no longer need.

NOTE *To test the events in this and the next section, enable the code between the* START OF CH6-SPECIFIC CODE *comment and the* END OF CH6-SPECIFIC CODE *comment in the* global.asax *file on* www.sybex.com. *Making changes to the* global.asax *file automatically restarts your application and discards the current sessions; don't change the file in a running production application unless you are certain that you won't lose critical data by doing so.*

Other *HttpApplication* Events

In addition to the four main `Application` and `Session` events shown in the preceding section, the `HttpApplication` object exposes other events that are extremely useful and provide C# Web applications with capabilities that were unavailable with previous versions of ASP. Although you *can* write code for these events in the global.asax file, you don't have to—you can place code to handle the events in your Web Form class. For example, the `HttpApplication.BeginRequest` event fires whenever your application receives a client request. You can use this event to perform common request tasks.

Rather than using the #INCLUDE syntax to include a header, you could return the header during the `BeginRequest` event and would not have to remember to put the #INCLUDE line in each page of the application. Similarly, the `HttpApplication.EndRequest` event lets you perform common cleanup tasks, save request data, return a page footer, or perform any other action common to all the pages in your application. To handle these events on a global basis, write the code for them in your global.asax file. Alternatively, you may need to handle these events only in special cases, with specific Web Forms, in which case you should write the code in the code-behind class classes.

HTTPAPPLICATION.BEGINREQUEST AND HTTPAPPLICATION.ENDREQUEST

The `HttpApplication.BeginRequest` event fires immediately after the ASP.NET framework assigns an `HttpApplication` object to the request. Use this event for request initialization. Listing 6.14 contains an example.

NOTE *The following code exists in the* `global.asax` *file on* www.sybex.com, *but it is commented out. Uncomment the code to see the results.*

LISTING 6.14: THE `HttpApplication.BeginRequest` EVENT (`global.aspx.cs`)

```csharp
if (Application.Get("StartEventCount") != null) {
   int count = (int) Application.Get("StartEventCount");
   count++;
   Application.Lock();
   Application.Set("StartEventCount",(int) count);
   Application.UnLock();
}
else {
   Application.Lock();
   Application.Set("StartEventCount",1);
   Application.UnLock();
}
if (Application.Get("BeginRequestCount") != null) {
   int count = (int) Application.Get("BeginRequestCount");
   count++;
   Application.Lock();
   Application.Set("BeginRequestCount",(int) count);
   Application.UnLock();
}
else {
   Application.Lock();
   Application.Set("BeginRequestCount",1);
   Application.UnLock();
}

// Place the following code in the ch6-15.aspx.cs
// code-behind file for
// the Web Form ch6-15.aspx. Be sure to uncomment the code in the
//global.asax file first.
private void Page_Load(object sender, System.EventArgs e) {
   Response.Write("Application Start Event Fired " +
Application.Get("StartEventCount").ToString() + " times.<br>");
   Response.Write("Begin Request Event Fired " +
Application.Get("BeginRequestCount").ToString() + " times.<br>");
}
```

Set the Web Form ch6-15 as the startup page for the project, and then run the project. The Web Form Load event prints the values set in the global.cs class. The first time you run the page, you'll see this output:

```
Application Start Event Fired 1 times
Begin Request Event Fired 1 times
```

Now refresh your browser several times. Notice that the Begin Request count increments for each refresh, but the Application Start Event count remains the same. The Application Start Event fires only once—the first time you make a request to the application. Finally, open a second browser instance, paste the URL from the first browser into the second browser's address field, and press Enter to load the page. Notice that the Begin Request count increments, showing that both instances are sharing the value of the Application("BeginRequestCount") variable, but the Application Start Event count remains the same. Again, both instances share the value, but the Application Start Event does not increment because the application is already running.

By the way, the reason I showed you this code in a Web Form rather than simply writing the responses in the Application Start Event code in the global.asax.cs file is that the Response object doesn't exist yet when this event fires; therefore you can't use it to return a response. However, you *can* use the Response object in the Application_BeginRequest event code, because ASP.NET creates the Response object before the event fires.

The HttpApplication.EndRequest event fires immediately before the ASP.NET framework releases the HttpApplication object assigned to the request. Use this event for request cleanup or to write page footers. For example, the following code writes the current time to the client each time you refresh the page:

```
protected void Application_EndRequest(Object sender, EventArgs e)
{
    Response.Write("CSharpASP application ending request at: " +
        DateTime.Now.ToLongDateString());
}
```

You can't use the Response object during the HttpApplication.End event because it has already been destroyed, but you can log an entry to the event log if you need to know that it occurred. (You wouldn't normally do this in a production application because it will write an entry for every request.) For example:

```
protected void Application_End(Object sender, EventArgs e)
{
    System.Diagnostics.EventLog evtLog = new
        System.Diagnostics.EventLog();
    DateTime dTime = DateTime.Now;
    evtLog.Source = "Application";
    evtLog.MachineName = "."; // local machine
    evtLog.WriteEntry("CSharpASP application ending at: " +
        dTime.ToLongDateString());
}
```

Run the application again. In debug mode, when you close the browser, the .NET environment automatically ends the application as well. When you check the application event log, you'll see one entry for each time you ran the application.

The *HttpApplication.Error* Event

In classic ASP, you could trap errors (in VBScript) using the built-in On Error Resume Next statement. Beginning with JavaScript version 5, you could use try-catch blocks to trap errors. You could also intercept some types of errors with IIS itself and provide custom error display pages for users. Now, with .NET, you can use the error-handling capabilities of whichever language you select to trap errors on a page-by-page basis. In most cases, however, it's much more convenient to handle those errors on an application level, writing appropriate information to log or error files so you can track and fix errors, while displaying a different type of error message for the user.

Errors "bubble" up from the page level to the application level. You can intercept errors that have not been handled or resolved at a lower level when they appear at the application level by trapping them in the HttpApplication.Error event. To see this in action, create a Web Form that raises an error, and then add the code at the end of Listing 6.15 to your global.asax.cs file.

LISTING 6.15: APPLICATION-LEVEL ERROR-HANDLING AND LOGGING EXAMPLE (ch6-16.aspx.cs, global.asax.cs)

```csharp
// The following code goes into the ch6-16.cs code-behind class
// All the code does is raise an error
private void Page_Load(object sender, System.EventArgs e)
{
    Exception ex = new System.ApplicationException
        ("Error Raised on Purpose!!");
    throw ex;
}


// Add this code to your global.asax file

protected void Application_Error(Object sender, EventArgs e) {
    String sErr = "";
    sErr = "An error occurred on page " + Request.FilePath;
    sErr += " at " + DateTime.Now.ToString() + ".  ";
    sErr += "Error: " + Server.GetLastError().Message;
    sErr += System.Environment.NewLine;
    sErr += "Stack trace: ";
    sErr += Server.GetLastError().StackTrace;
    System.Diagnostics.EventLog.WriteEntry("CSharpASP", sErr);
}
```

Set the ch6-16 Web Form as the start page for the application and run the file. You will immediately get an error in the browser window (the error occurs on purpose). You'll see a by now familiar error display, but if you open the event application log, you'll also see a new entry that includes these items:

◆ The virtual path of the file in which the error occurred

◆ The date and time

◆ A description of the error

◆ A stack trace

Therefore, with very little work, you can add global error reporting to your application. At this point, if you ever worked on a production application with classic VB, you should be jumping with joy. Getting a stack trace in an error report was—to say the least—tedious with all earlier versions of VB. You had to code the stack trace manually, which was an error-prone task.

Of course, you can improve the error reporting considerably beyond the simple log entry shown in Listing 6.15 by exploring the System.Exception classes and the `Server.GetLastError` methods and properties by maintaining your own error log file, automatically sending error messages via e-mail, and gauging the severity of the error and responding accordingly.

Error Settings in the *web.config* File

I mentioned earlier that using application-level error trapping allows us to provide customized error messages. The preceding example omitted that feature for the sake of simplicity, so you can implement it now. You use settings in a file named `web.config`, located in your root Web directory, to control the error behavior. The `web.config` file is simply a place to hold settings for a specific Web application—much as INI files or Registry settings hold settings for Win32 applications. Unlike earlier settings files, `web.config` files are XML-formatted files, which have all the advantages of both INI files and the Registry. Like INI files, they are plain text and are easy to read, easy to modify, and easy to install. Like the Registry, they have a hierarchical tree structure with unlimited depth, and there's no arbitrary size limit on data values.

Sub-Webs (subdirectories) within a Web application can each contain their own `web.config` files. Local settings—in other words, settings within a sub-Web—can either inherit or override settings placed in a `web.config` file located higher in the application path, such as settings in the root directory of an application.

There's Always a web.config File

When Visual Studio .NET creates a new Web application project, the framework automatically creates a new `web.config` file in the root directory of the application. However, if you were to delete that file, the *system-level* `web.config` settings would still be in effect. You can find the system-level configuration file (`machine.config`) in your `%windows%\Microsoft.NET\Framework\(version)\CONFIG` folder. The settings in this file are the base settings for all the Web applications on a particular system. Therefore, most ASP.NET applications have at least two configuration files—the system-level configuration file and one in the application root directory.

Add a Custom web.config File

Select the ch6 folder in your CSharpASP project in the Visual Studio IDE, and then right-click to bring up the Shortcut menu. Select Add ÿ Add New Item, and then select Web Configuration File from the Add New Item dialog. Click the Open button to create the file. The IDE adds a file named web.config to the ch6 folder in your project and opens it in the editor window. By default, the file contains the XML version tag and a set of options within a <configuration></configuration> tag. Because the root CSharpASP web.config file applies the default settings, you don't need them in the ch6 subfolder, and you can delete everything but the XML version tag and the <configuration> </configuration> tags.

You want to override the settings for the <customerrors> section of the web.config file in the root CSharpASP folder. To do that, simply add a new <customerrors> tag in this web.config file. Edit the file until it looks like Listing 6.16 (remember that it is case sensitive).

LISTING 6.16: A CUSTOM web.config FILE FOR THE ch6 FOLDER (ch6/ web.config)

```
<?xml version="1.0" encoding="UTF-8"?>
<configuration>
   <customerrors
      mode="On" defaultRedirect="customError.aspx"
   />
</configuration>
```

NOTE   *The preceding file does not exist on* www.sybex.com, *because it interferes with the standard functionality of the subfolder. You will need to create it to test the* customerrors *tag in the subfolder.*

Save your changes. What you've just done is to tell ASP.NET that whenever any error occurs, it should redirect to the Web Form named customerror.aspx in the root application folder.

You could get much more specific than that. By adding <error> tags in the <customerrors> section, you can specify a particular redirection file for each type of error.

You need to create the customerror.aspx file. Add a new Web Form to the CSharpASP project in the root folder and name it customerror.aspx. For testing purposes it doesn't matter what you put in the file as long as you can see that the redirection occurred. The sample customerror.aspx file on www.sybex.com simply writes a "We are sorry…" message to the client. Don't set this file as the start file for the application. Instead, save the file and then launch the ch6-16.aspx file to force an error. You'll see your custom error page rather than the default error page.

NOTE   *Delete the* web.config *file in the* ch6 *subfolder before you continue.*

If you wanted to create a custom error redirection for the entire site, you could modify the custom-Errors tag in your CSharpASP root web.config file instead.

Sometimes, it's very useful to be able to show most users a custom error page but to show application maintenance personnel and administrators the default detailed error message. The mode attribute of the `<customerrors>` tag broadly controls this behavior. When `mode="On"`, all users see the custom error pages. Setting `mode="Off"` turns off custom error redirection altogether. Setting `mode="Remote"` turns on custom error redirection only for remote users. Users who access the machine locally (administrators and maintenance personnel) see the default error pages.

OTHER *HttpApplication* EVENTS

You've seen several of the most important of the events you can trap in the `global.asax` code-behind class file. The HttpApplication class (and through inheritance, the Global class defined in your `global.asax` file) raises several other events that you should explore. You can use the same procedures used in this chapter to handle the events. As you've seen, the ASP.NET intrinsic objects (such as `Response` and `Request`) are not always or not all available during global events. You should experiment thoroughly to discover which of the ASP.NET intrinsic objects you can use during any particular event.

When to Use *Application* Variables

Despite the free-threaded nature of most .NET objects, you should minimize your use of `Application` variables because each access forces a cast to a type and (if you think about how you'd write the accessing code) must check for locking. Therefore, while Application scope data access is much more robust than in classic ASP, you still pay some performance penalties for storing information at Application scope. Although you haven't seen the discussion about `Sessions` yet—that's in the next chapter—you can store information specific to each session in a `SessionState` object. Data stored at Session scope obviously carries less of a performance penalty. Because only one `Session` has access to the data, you don't have the locking issues with Session scope data that you do with Application scope data. As with most topics in programming, there are some tradeoffs. For each value you wish to store, consider these questions:

1. How many simultaneous users will the application serve? If the answer is small relative to the total load on the Web server, it doesn't matter much whether you use application variables or some other storage method.

2. How much data do you want to store? Even with today's memory prices, RAM is still a limited resource. You may gain some performance by caching that million-row database table in memory, but if it causes your Web server to run out of RAM to service requests, the net result is a loss in performance. Generally, you should minimize the size of data you store in RAM whenever possible.

3. Is the data truly applicable to all users of the application? If only a few users need the data, see if you can find another way to satisfy their requests.

4. What are the performance implications of not storing the data at Application scope? For example, you may find that the performance difference for opening a connection and running a stored procedure versus retrieving the data from an application-level variable containing a dataset is negligible. After all, modern databases cache table data in memory anyway so that they can service repeated requests. When you cache the data, you may be mirroring the database behavior and doubling the RAM storage requirements.

5. What are the resource implications of storing the data at Session scope? When you're storing small resources that change often, locking the `Application` object to modify the data (which blocks all other `Application` object data requests) may be worse for your application than redundantly storing the data at Session scope for each user or (better yet) as cookies.

6. Can you cache the data on disk? It's true that disk access speed is much slower than accessing data from memory, but modern operating systems also cache data. You can prove that to yourself by creating an HTML file (you can use `ch6\diskCacheTest.htm` as a test file), placing it in a folder of a Web application, and then browsing to the file and accessing it multiple times by holding down the Refresh button on your browser. Watch the disk access light. Does it light up for each request? No. The operating system checks to make sure the file hasn't changed and then serves the file from the disk cache. Maybe that's not a good test. Maybe explicitly reading the file would be a better test. It turns out that it makes no difference as far as disk access goes (you can test this using the Web Form `ch6-17.aspx`, which simply reads the file `diskCacheTest.htm`). Therefore, the more often your application uses the data, the more likely it is to be in the cache. Note that caching data on disk works beautifully for sequential data that rarely changes, but not nearly as well for random access data unless the file is small.

Summary

At this point, you should understand how requests and responses work in a Web application and be comfortable with the ideas of storing and retrieving data using cookies or the `HttpApplicationState` object. Using nothing but these techniques and objects, you can write quite powerful C# Web applications. While cookies are convenient, they must travel back and forth over the network. As the volume of data you must store for any individual user grows, cookies become a less palatable option. What you really need is a mechanism for storing user-specific data on the server. The mechanism should be robust enough to survive a Web server crash; it should be fast and flexible enough to accommodate many simultaneous users. Finally, the mechanism needs to work on both a single server and multiple servers connected in a Web farm. ASP.NET provides such a mechanism—called `Sessions`—which is the topic of the next chapter.

Chapter 7

The *SessionState* Object

THE `SessionState` OBJECT is an attempt to solve one of the biggest problems in Web applications—how to maintain application state between pages. HTTP's stateless model makes it very difficult to provide users with applications that remember user actions and input from one request to another. ASP.NET's `SessionState` object solves some of the major problems with maintaining state on individual servers, for multiple-server Web farms, and for browsers that refuse cookies.

In this chapter:

◆ Introduction to Session State

◆ Cookies, URL Munging, and the ASP.NET `Session` Object

◆ `Session` Variables

◆ Associating Data with Individuals

Introduction to Session State

One of the major weaknesses of VB6 IIS projects (WebClasses) was that they required you to turn on the Sessions option on your Web server—otherwise they wouldn't work. Why was that a problem? Because in classic ASP, using session data was relatively slow and unsafe (if the server crashed, your session data was lost), worked only on a single machine, and could only store free-threaded objects and scalar data. You *could* scale sessions up to several machines, but only by ensuring that each client was always routed to the same server for each request.

You'll be happy to know that ASP.NET sessions are much better. Not only are they faster, but you can store them in memory or in SQL Server by changing a configuration setting. They're no longer tied to a single machine. Microsoft built a separate `SessionState` server that can run on the same or a different machine than IIS—and several IIS servers can share a single `SessionState` server. The `SessionState` object can store data in memory on the local machine, out of process on a separate server, or in SQL Server. Using either of the last two options solves the Web farm problem. Because ASP.NET can store session data on a separate machine, you no longer have to route users to the same server for each request—all servers can share a single state server. The SQL Server option ensures that state data persists even across machine failures. In a Web farm situation, you can recover state data from a SQL Server machine even if the SQL Server crashes, which greatly reduces (although it doesn't eliminate entirely) the chances of losing user data permanently.

Those of you familiar with VB6 may be aware that it had an odd problem: it could consume free-threaded components but not create them. VB6 could create only apartment-threaded objects. That problem led to the peculiar situation where you could not create a VB component that you could safely store in a `Session` or `Application` variable. Fortunately, C# doesn't have that problem—in fact, .NET solves that problem generically—you can create free-threaded components with C# (and with VB.NET).

A short warning before you continue: Despite all these improvements, applications that use session state still don't perform or scale *as well as* sessionless applications. Before you simply skip this chapter, however, let me say that unless you're creating extremely busy, highly tuned Web sites that must serve hundreds or thousands of simultaneous users, you won't notice much—if any—difference in performance between applications that use session state and those that don't. If you don't want to use session state, you can turn it off for any specific application by changing a setting in the `web.config` file. You'll see how to do that in the section "Turning Off Session State," later in this chapter.

What Is a Session?

For the purposes of this chapter, a session (lowercase) is the length of time that a particular browser instance spends accessing a Web site. In contrast, I've used the word `Session` (capitalized) as a synonym for the `System.Web.SessionState.HttpSessionState` object because that's the name you use to reference it most of the time in the .NET framework from a Web Form.

A browser session and an `HttpSessionState` object are not the same thing, but they are related. An `HttpSessionState` object is a collection of objects associated with a specific `ASPSessionID`. As you saw in Chapter 5, "Introduction to Web Forms," each browser instance receives an `ASPSessionID` cookie (or munged URL) the first time it requests any page in your site. For subsequent requests (because the browser returns the `ASPSessionID` value to the Web server in the request header or as part of the URL), the server can use the `ASPSessionID` as a key associated with a collection of data specific to that instance. So in an ASP.NET application, you can use the `HttpSessionState` (or `Session`) object to store data specific to that browser instance—in other words, you can "maintain state" for that browser by maintaining data on the server side. This association between the browser and the server, via `ASPSessionID`, lasts as long as the browser returns to the site frequently enough to prevent the `Session` from "timing out," or until the user closes that browser instance.

The reason a browser session and the associated ASP.NET `Session` are not quite the same thing is because they can become disassociated. For example, if a user requests a page from your application, thus initiating a `Session`, and then closes the browser, the user has ended the browser session, but the ASP.NET `Session` remains in existence until it times out—you have no way of knowing when a user simply abandons your application by closing the browser or walking away. Similarly, if the user simply surfs to another domain or application, the ASP.NET `Session` containing that user's data is effectively orphaned and will eventually time out. After the `Session` times out, even if the user later returns to your application, ASP.NET will create a new `Session` and issue a new `ASPSessionID`. Finally, they can become disassociated if the user suddenly resets the browser to refuse cookies in the middle of a `Session` (seems unlikely, but I've seen it happen). Again, you lose the capability to associate that browser with already-stored `Session` data.

In Chapter 6, "Introduction to the System.Web Namespace," you built a cookie-based shopping cart. Using cookies for a shopping cart is a reasonable approach, but the shopping cart would be much simpler if you could simply store the shopping cart contents on the server. That way, you wouldn't need to send the cart data back and forth with each request; you could rely on the `ASPSessionID` cookie instead to let you find that particular browser instance's data.

Note that the `SessionID` isn't an identifier for anything except a single browser instance. The `ASPSessionID` cookie doesn't tell the server who you are, and it isn't persistent. Therefore, the server can't reuse the cookie value the next time you visit the site, and it contains pertinent data other than the `SessionID` value itself, which is simply a value guaranteed to be unique.

To sum up, although `HttpSessionState` is the "true" name of the class instance that stores session data, the `Page` object (that's the Web Form itself, remember?) exposes the `HttpSessionState` object using the shorter name `Session`. That's probably so it will be more compatible with classic ASP, where the object itself was named the `Session` object, but it might just be because the term `HttpSession-State` is too long to type comfortably. At any rate, for the rest of this chapter, I'll use the shorter name `Session` *object* with a capital "S" rather than the full `HttpSessionState` object name.

Why Do You Need State?

If you've ever built an application that uses global variables, you already understand why you might need stateful applications. Some types of applications consist of discrete operations. For example, an application that lets unauthenticated users browse a set of records in a database table never requires the server to know anything about the user. The tasks are as follows:

◆ Retrieve enough identifying row information so the user can browse the records.

◆ Retrieve all data for an individual row.

Each request to the server is complete—the server doesn't need to know which row the user browsed last—it only needs to know, or be able to discover, the *next* row that the user wants to view.

With that in mind, consider a more complex variation. Suppose the rows contain sensitive information, and each user is allowed to view only a subset of the rows in the table. In this configuration, you would need to add some sort of identity verification such as a login/password to the application. In a stateless application, you would need to verify the user's identity for each request. Displaying the set of rows viewable by that user would be no problem because you could build a database query that returned the set of viewable records. However, browsing forward or backward is a more expensive operation. When a user requests the next or preceding row, you would need to verify the user's identity and then retrieve that user's rowset again, find the current row, and scroll forward or backward to find the next or previous row the user is allowed to view. You can see that the process to return a row becomes much more complex. However, if you could store state for that user on the server, things might be simpler.

For example, suppose that you could store the set of row IDs for the rows viewable by the user. Now, having validated the user the first time, you could simply keep a pointer to the current row and increment or decrement the pointer to get the next or preceding row. For small recordsets, it would even be possible to store the entire recordset on the server, so that you could limit the interaction with the database.

There's more than one way to store state. You've already seen how to store state in cookies. Unfortunately, using cookies isn't always the best option because cookies must travel over the network for each request. A second way to store state is by persisting data in a database or in files. You would use a cookie to "connect" a user and the data. A third way is to maintain state data in memory. Again, you use a cookie to connect the user to that user's data. ASP.NET applications provide a transparent way for you to do this through the `ASPSessionID` cookie and the `Session` object.

One caution before you proceed: In general, the more complex your application becomes, the more it can benefit from storing state in memory. The corollary to that is this: The more your application must be able to scale, the greater the penalty from storing state in memory. Here's another way of looking at the problem. If you need to maintain 100KB of state data for each user, 100 users require 10MB of server RAM. If your application has 1,000 simultaneous users, you'll need 100MB of memory. The problem is worse than that. In a Win32 application, your app always knows exactly when the user exits. At that point, you can free resources. However, you can't force Web application users to quit the application explicitly, and without that power, the server has no way to know exactly when or if a user has quit. If a user closes the browser and walks away, any state data cached in memory on the server is now wasted. Therefore, `Sessions` "time out" after a certain period of time (by default, 20 minutes). The `Session` timer gets reset each time a user makes a request to the application; therefore, you can think of the timeout period as the duration that you're willing to "waste" the memory on the server. By definition, the user hasn't made any requests during the timeout period, or the `Session` wouldn't time out.

For applications where people enter, use the application rapidly, and then leave, you can reduce the `Session.Timeout` property value, thus recycling unneeded server memory more rapidly. However, for applications in which relatively long periods occur between server requests, such as applications that deliver long documents or where people work on data entry for an extended period—for example, newsgroup readers—you may even need to increase the `Session.Timeout` value. Of course, the larger the timeout value, the longer you're preventing the memory from being recycled, and therefore the more server memory you must add to cope with the increased load.

Here are some simple rules to follow:

◆ Don't use sessions unless you need them.

◆ Don't use sessions if you need to scale to very large numbers of simultaneous users.

◆ When you do use sessions, try to minimize the volume of data you store for each user.

◆ Give users a way to end the session explicitly; for example, by clicking a "close this window" button or link or logging out.

Cookies, URL Munging, and the ASP.NET *Session* Object

In this section, you'll explore the cookie and munged URL mechanisms that ASP.NET uses to associate browsers with `Session` data—and I'll briefly explain how you can use hidden form variables to maintain state yourself.

Associating Data with a Browser Instance

To maintain a session, the server must have some way of connecting all the requests from a single browser. As you saw in Chapter 5, when sessions are enabled, the server creates an `ASPSessionID` cookie for the first request from any browser that doesn't already have an `ASPSessionID`. When you create a new ASP.NET project using C#, sessions are turned on by default.

Associating Data with Cookies

A couple of problems arise when using cookies to match a browser with state data stored on the server. First, most—if not all—browsers have an option to refuse cookies. For example, you can turn off cookies in Internet Explorer (IE5) by clicking the Tools menu and then selecting Internet Options ➤ Security tab. You then select a zone—for example, Internet, Local Intranet, Trusted Sites, or Restricted Sites—and click the Custom Level button. That brings up the Security Settings dialog for the selected zone (see Figure 7.1).

FIGURE 7.1

Cookie options available through the Internet Explorer 5 Security Settings dialog

There are two types of cookies: those stored on your computer's hard drive, usually called *persistent* cookies, and those stored in memory, usually called *transient* cookies. The IE Security Settings dialog uses the terms "cookies stored on your computer" (persistent) and "per-session cookies" (transient). Regardless of the browser type, the basic options for each type of cookie are as follows (different browser versions implement different cookie options):

Disable   The browser won't accept that type of cookie, and the browser won't alert the user before rejecting the cookie.

Enable   The browser accepts that type of cookie and doesn't alert the user before accepting the cookie.

Prompt   The browser will alert the user whenever a site sends a cookie, and the user must accept or reject the cookie.

Other browsers have similar, although not identical, options. For example, Netscape 6 has enable, disable, and warn options, as well as letting you enable cookies for the originating Web site only—

meaning that the browser won't accept or return cookies from an associated Web site, such as an ad-generating site (see Figure 7.2). In reality, most people either accept or reject cookies—the act of providing a cookie has become so ubiquitous that selecting the Prompt option is just too annoying.

FIGURE 7.2

Cookie options available through the Netscape 6 Preferences dialog

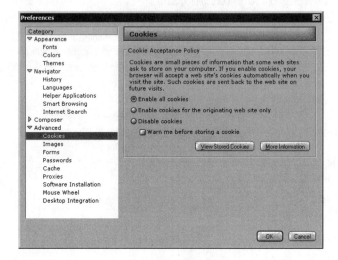

Cookies weren't originally meant to be "misused" by passing values among multiple domains, but data gathering by advertisers has made such use widespread. IE6 includes even more cookie options—an attempt by browser makers to let users regain control over their information (see Figure 7.3).

FIGURE 7.3

Cookie options available through the Internet Explorer 6 Internet Options Privacy dialog

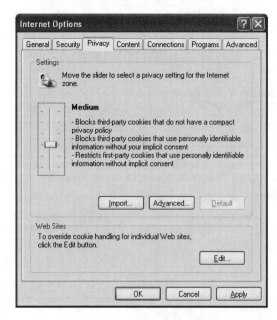

Second, users can see the cookie values. Windows stores persistent cookies for each user in a special `Cookies` directory, so users can always view persistent cookies, but they can see *any* cookie by temporarily selecting the Prompt (or equivalent) option in their browser. Being able to see the cookie isn't always helpful, though, because many sites don't send cookies in plain text form; instead, they send encrypted cookies or put binary information into the cookie that shows up as meaningless symbols in a viewer program, such as Notepad. It can be difficult to determine the purpose of even unencrypted, plain-text cookies. For example, here's the content of a cookie file from my computer:

```
BSESSIONID
g0owne23a1
www.cmlbiz.com/UDDIBrowser
0
4372144144
21419871
3073552328
39418852
*
```

NOTE *In Notepad, the cookie content shows up as one long string. I've separated the parts to show you that even when you know what the parts are, it's often difficult or impossible to tell what the data represents.*

With few recognizable dates or names, it's nearly impossible to tell exactly what the site is saving, which makes people nervous and often causes them to turn off cookies altogether—and that causes problems for server applications that need to maintain state data on the server. If the browser rejects the `ASPSessionID` cookie, the server cannot recognize that multiple requests from that browser represent the same browser instance. To the server, each request will appear to be the *first* request by that browser.

ASP.NET applications try to use cookies first, but if the browser won't accept cookies, your application can switch to inserting the `ASPSessionID` value into the URLs instead, a process called *munging* the URL.

Associating Data with Munged URLs

Munged URLs are standard URLs that have been altered by placing an identifying parameter value into the URL string. In practice, this value is exactly the same as the `ASPSessionID` cookie value. You can see this in action quite easily. Open the `web.config` file in your CSharpASP project. Scroll down until you see this tag:

```
<SessionState mode="InProc" stateConnectionString="tcpip=127.0.0.1:42424
sqlConnectionString="data source=127.0.0.1;user id=sa;password="
cookieless="false"
timeout="20"
/>
```

NOTE *The `SessionState` tag may appear in a slightly different form on your server, depending on other machine settings.*

For now, the important attribute is the `cookieless="false"` attribute. The attribute tells IIS to attempt to send a cookie for each new browser instance. Change the attribute so it reads `cookieless="true"`.

```
<SessionState mode="InProc"
    stateConnectionString="tcpip=127.0.0.1:42424"
sqlConnectionString="data source=127.0.0.1;user id=sa;password="
cookieless="true"
timeout="20"
/>
```

Next, create a new folder in the CSharpASP project called `ch7` . Add a new Web Form to the `ch7` folder. Name it `ch7-1.aspx` , change the default form ID to "Form1" and set it as the start page. In the `Page_Load` event, write the following code:

```
private void Page_Load(object sender,
    System.EventArgs e) {
    if (IsPostBack) {
        Response.Write("Postback<br>");
        Response.Write(LinkButton1.CommandName +
            "=" + LinkButton1.CommandArgument +
            "<br>");
        Response.Write("*******************<br>");
    }
    LinkButton1.CommandName = "ASPSessionID";
    LinkButton1.CommandArgument = Session.SessionID;
    Response.Write("ASPSessionID=" + Session.SessionID);
}
```

Now run the project. You'll see the screen in Figure 7.4.

The important part of the preceding URL appears just after the application name—CSharpASP. Because you changed the `web.config cookieless` attribute value, ASP.NET no longer attempts to send a cookie; it inserts the `ASPSessionID` value into the URL instead. You might think that doing so is fairly useless—after all, the page with the address currently shown in the browser window is one the browser *already has*. It isn't at all likely to be the *next* page that the browser requests—that's most likely to occur when a user clicks a link or button. Maybe ASP.NET inserts the `ASPSessionID` value into *all* the URLs on the page.

Here's a simple test. Add a link to the `ch7-1` Web Form. Open the `ch7-1` Web Form designer window and drag a `HyperLink` control from the Toolbox to the design surface. In the Properties window, change the `Text` property to `InterCom` and the `NavigateURL` property to `http://www.intercom-interactive.com`. The design surface should look like Figure 7.5.

Run the Web Form again. Did ASP.NET add the munged URL to the hyperlink? Move your cursor over it to see the link in the status bar. You'll see the hyperlink, but it hasn't been altered to contain the `ASPSessionID`. Of course, it wouldn't make any sense to add the `ASPSessionID` to an *external* link. You may be surprised by the fact that the `SessionID` shows up in the `Response.Write`.

How about an internal link? Close the Web Form to get back into edit mode. Add another `HyperLink` control. Set its `NavigateURL` property to `ch4-1.aspx` and its `Text` property to `ch4-1`. Now run the Web Form again. Does this *internal* link contain the `ASPSessionID` value? You may be surprised to find that it doesn't—I was. After all, how can ASP.NET maintain the `ASPSessionID` value if the link doesn't somehow return that value to the server?

FIGURE 7.4

The `ASPSessionID` cookie appears in the browser Address field when you set the session state **cookieless** attribute to **true**

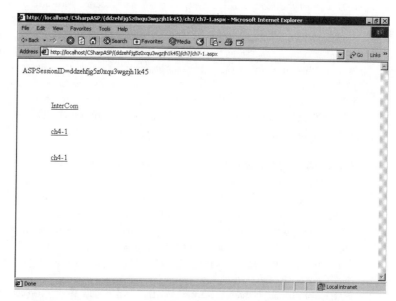

FIGURE 7.5

Visual Studio Web Form design surface after adding a `HyperLink` server control

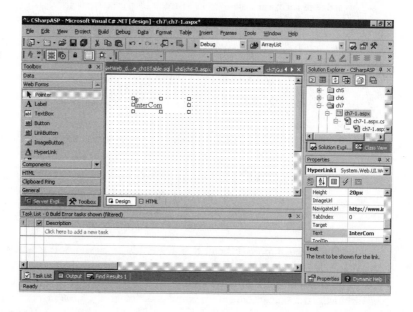

Although munged URLs work about as well as you can expect, they still have some problems. For example, if you have a Web Form with the URL `http://myserver/mypage.aspx`, and a user visits

your page, maybe rummages around in your munged site for a while, then leaves and goes to another site for a few minutes, it depends on how the user returns whether the session will "stick." If the user presses the Back button to get back to your site, the munged URL will maintain the session; however, if the user types your URL into the browser or reaches your site through a bookmark, the server can no longer connect the browser to the previous session, and the user's original session is orphaned. In contrast, if your site uses cookies, a user can leave and return as often as he likes. As long as he doesn't close the browser instance, the cookie will let the server connect the user to the existing session.

You have one more option for recognizing the browser instance during repeat requests. You can maintain state yourself by placing some recognizable value in a hidden form variable. Like munged URLs, this works only if the user stays within your site or returns to your site via the Back button. The only advantage of hidden form variables over munged URLs is that the user can't modify the hidden value—not much of a consideration in most cases.

Associating Data with Hidden Form Variables

Hidden form variables aren't really well hidden; they're just out of the way. A user can right-click the page, select View Source, find the `<form>` tag, and read the hidden value directly. Nonetheless, users won't usually change the value of a hidden form variable, so they're useful—but awkward to use—for maintaining state. The reason they're awkward is that you have to do the work to ensure the values move between the server and client for every page. If you miss a page or build the page so the user can return to the server without posting a form, you've lost the server-browser connection and all stored data for that connection.

It's not all bad, however. Remember that ASP.NET uses a hidden form variable itself—the _ViewState form variable—to keep track of the state of the controls in the browser. Here's the pseudocode procedure you use to maintain state with form variables:

1. When a browser requests a page with a GET method (as opposed to a POST method), you check for a specific identifying parameter (I'll call it BrowserID) in the URL. If you don't find a BrowserID parameter, you create a unique value and place it in a hidden form variable.

2. When a browser requests a page with a POST method, extract the BrowserID value from the Form collection.

3. Place all controls on each page within the form containing the hidden BrowserID form variable. That way, when the user selects a control, the value will post back to the server.

4. Build all links back to your application so they include the BrowserID parameter and value. For example, if the value of the BrowserID is 39d8210d9831, then to place a link on page1.aspx that links to page2.aspx, you would write the anchor tag as follows: `<a href="page2 .aspx?BrowserID=39d8210d9831">Page 2</a>`.

This is much more difficult than it sounds. In classic ASP, it wasn't as difficult because you automatically had complete control over the generated HTML. To be fair, you can *get* complete control in ASP.NET, but to do so, you have to either override the methods that render the ServerControls to HTML (the RenderContents methods), or forego the advantages of server controls altogether. Therefore, you should avoid using hidden form variables to save state. If you just want to pass a hidden variable to the client page, just use a Label control and set its EnableViewState property to true and its Visible property to false.

Session Variables

In this section, you can assume that Sessions are enabled and the requesting browser accepts cookies. When you want to store, retrieve, modify, or delete data for a specific browser instance, use the Session object.

Adding/Modifying *Session* Variables

The simplest way to store objects in the Session object is exactly the same way you store objects in the Application object—by creating a new String key value and setting Session[newKey] equal to the object.

For example, the code in Listing 7.1 creates a Session["counter"] variable and then increments it each time you refresh the page.

LISTING 7.1: CREATE A NEW Session VARIABLE (ch7-2.aspx.cs)

```
private void Page_Load(object sender, System.EventArgs e) {
    if (Session["counter"]!=null) {
        Session["counter"] = (int)Session["counter"] + 1;
    }
    else {
        Session["counter"] = 1;
    }
    Response.Write("Counter=" + Session["counter"].ToString() + "<br>");
}
```

The code checks to make sure the counter variable exists. If not, it creates the variable by setting it to 1; otherwise, it retrieves the value and increments it. Finally, it writes the value back to the browser. Note that to modify a Session variable, you don't need to perform any locking or unlocking as you do with the Application object, because the Session object stores data for only a single thread—data contention for session data is never an issue unless you explicitly spawn your own threads within a single request—and then you're on your own.

Load the ch7-2.aspx file into the IDE, set it as the start page, and then step through the code. Just to be perfectly clear, the browser doesn't send the counter value as a cookie—it stores the counter value on the server. To update the value, simply replace the variable with the new object.

You can store any object as easily as you can store simple value types. For example, the class GUID-Maker is a wrapper class for creating Globally Unique Identifiers (GUIDs). GUIDs were used widely in COM applications to identify classes and are extremely useful values, because they're virtually guaranteed to be globally unique—no other computer will generate the same GUID value, and your computer will never generate the same GUID twice. Here's the C/C++ struct definition:

```
typdef struct _GUID {
    unsigned long Data1;
    unsigned short Data2;
    unsigned short Data3;
    unsigned char Data4 [8];
} GUID;
```

Creating a GUID in previous Microsoft languages required an API declaration and a call. Using the API from C/C++ was easy. Having defined the GUID struct, you simply called `CoCreateGuid`, passing a pointer to a GUID structure, for example:

```
HRESULT CoCreateGuid (GUID *pGuid);
```

To turn the GUID into a string, you called the `StringFromGUID2` function and passed a pointer to the GUID structure, a pointer to a string buffer, and the length of the buffer.

However, creating GUIDs and turning them into strings using the API from VB6 was a little more involved. Listing 7.2 shows the VB6 code required to generate a GUID.

NOTE   *I've stripped the error-trapping code from Listing 7.2 for clarity. You can find the full code in the* `VB6CGUID-Maker.cls` *file on* www.sybex.com *in the* `ch7` *subfolder of the CSharpASP application.*

LISTING 7.2: VB6 FUNCTION TO GENERATE GUID VALUES (`ch7-VB6CGUIDMaker.cls`)

```
Private Declare Function CoCreateGuid Lib _
    "ole32.dll" (buffer As Byte) As Long
Private Declare Function StringFromGUID2 Lib _
    "ole32.dll" (buffer As Byte, ByVal lpsz As Long, _
    ByVal cbMax As Long) As Long
Public Function getGUIDString() As String
   Dim buffer(15) As Byte
   Dim s As String
   Dim ret As Long
   s = String$(128, 0)
   ret = CoCreateGuid(buffer(0))
   ret = StringFromGUID2(buffer(0), StrPtr(s), 128)
   getGUIDString = Left$(s, ret - 1)
End Function
Here's the equivalent code in C#:
public String getGUIDString() {
   return(System.Guid.NewGuid.ToString());
}
```

Now, suppose you want to create an instance of the GUIDMaker class and use it on every page in your application. Although you could share a single instance of the class at Application scope, you want to add a property to the class so it returns a new GUID the first time you call `getGUIDString` but returns the same GUID for each subsequent call. To do that, add a member `String` variable called `sGUID` to the class and change the `getGUIDString` function to a property that checks the `sGUID` string before returning a value. If `sGUID` is `Null`, the class creates a new GUID and stores it in `sGUID`; otherwise, it returns the existing GUID string stored in the `sGUID` member variable. Listing 7.3 shows the full code for the altered class.

LISTING 7.3: ALTERED GUIDMAKER CLASS THAT ALWAYS RETURNS A SINGLE, UNCHANGING GUID VALUE (GuidMaker.cs)

```csharp
public class GuidMaker {
   private String sGUID;
   public GuidMaker() {
      sGUID = GuidString;
   }

   public String GuidString {
      get {
         if (sGUID == null) {
            sGUID = (System.Guid.NewGuid()).ToString();
         }
         return sGUID;
      }
   }
}
```

Now, you can create an instance of the GUIDMaker class, store it in a `Session` variable, and access the `GUIDString` property whenever you need the value. For example, create a new Web Form in the `ch7` subdirectory of the CSharpASP application and name it `ch7-3.aspx`. Place the following code in the Page_Load event in the code-behind class file:

```csharp
private void Page_Load(object sender, System.EventArgs e) {
   GuidMaker gm;
   String[] arr = new String[10];

   for (int i = 0; i < arr.Length; i++) {
      arr[i] = "Item " + i.ToString();
   }
   Session["arr"] = arr;
   arr = (String[]) Session["arr"];
   for (int i = 0; i < arr.Length; i++) {
      System.Diagnostics.Debug.WriteLine(arr[i]);
   }
   if (!(Session["counter"] == null)) {
      int i = (int) Session["counter"];
      Session["counter"] = ++i;
   }
   else {
      Session["counter"] = 1;
   }
   Response.Write("Counter=" + Session["counter"].ToString() +
      "<br>");
   if (Session["guid"]==null) {
      gm = new GuidMaker();
```

```
         Session["guid"] = gm;
    }
    else {
        gm = (GuidMaker) Session["guid"];
    }
    Response.Write("The GUID value is: " + gm.GuidString + "<br>");
    // Uncomment the following code to see the Add method in
    // action. When you do that, the display will increment from
    // 1 to 2, but will then remain at 2 no matter how many
    // times you refresh the browser.
    // Session.Add("counter", 1)

}
```

Save the changes, set the **ch7.aspx** Web Form as the start page, and run the application. You'll see the **counter** value and a GUID in the browser—similar to Figure 7.6. Of course, the GUID that your server generates will be different. By refreshing the page, you can see that the counter changes each time the **Page_Load** method fires, but the GUID remains the same. If you launch a new instance of the browser or close the current browser and restart the application, the GUID will change, because it's stored at **Session** scope. Thus, the GUID is different for each browser instance.

FIGURE 7.6

Session("counter") and Session("guid") values shown in a browser

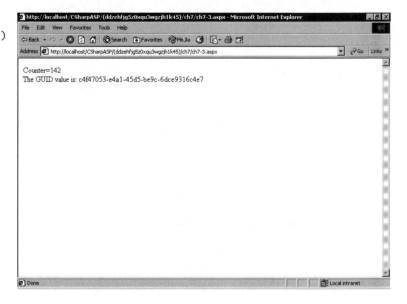

There's a second way to create **Session** variables. The **Session** object is a wrapper for a hashed name/value collection that contains objects, so, as with most collections, you can use the collection's Add method to add objects to the collection. The syntax is as follows:

```
Session.Add(name,value);
```

For example, rather than writing Session["counter"] = 1, you could write Session.Add-("counter", 1). The result is the same, regardless of which way you write the code. Note that the first method (except for the square brackets) is compatible with classic VBScript ASP code, while the second method is more like standard .NET collection code.

C# Is Free of Threading Issues

As you've just seen, you can store any object you create with C# in a Session variable. That's considerably different than was the case in VB6 and classic ASP, where you should never store VB6-generated objects in a Session variable. The apartment-threaded nature of VB6 objects prevented you from storing them at Session or Application scope, but C# objects (like all .NET framework objects) are free threaded, so if you're coming from a VB/ASP background, you don't have to worry about that anymore.

Clearing *Session* Variables

Just as there's more than one way to create a Session variable, there are several ways to destroy one.

Set It to *Null*   Session ["varname"] = Null

Use the *Remove* Method   Session.Remove("varname")

Use the *RemoveAll* Method   Session.RemoveAll

Use the *RemoveAt* Method   Remove an item by index; for example, Session.RemoveAt(3) would remove the fourth item in the collection because all .NET collections are zero based.

Determining Whether a *Session* Variable Exists

The simplest way to test whether a Session variable exists is to check if it is null.

```
if (Session["xyz"] == null) {
// do something here
}
```

Another way is to retrieve the keys or an enumerator and loop through the keys. Listing 7.4 shows an example:

LISTING 7.4: DETERMINING WHETHER A Session VARIABLE EXISTS (ch7-4.aspx.cs)

```
private void Page_Load(object sender, System.EventArgs e) {
   System.Collections.IEnumerator en;
   String aKey;
   Boolean foundKey=false;
   Session.Add("counter", 1);
   if (Session["xyz"] == null) {
      Response.Write("Session[\"xyz\"] is nothing." + "<br>");
   }
   else {
      Response.Write("Session[\"xyz\"] exists, and has a " +
         "value of: " + Session["xyz"] + "<br>");
```

```
        }

    if (Session.Count > 0) {
        en = Session.GetEnumerator();
        while (en.MoveNext()){
            aKey = (String) en.Current;
            if (aKey == "xyz") {
                foundKey = true;
            }
        }
        if (foundKey) {
            Response.Write("Found the xyz key in the SessionState " +
                "collection.<br>");
        }
    }
    else {
        Response.Write("There are no objects in the SessionState " +
            "collection.<br>");
    }
}
```

ASP.NET Session State

Now that you've seen *how* ASP.NET maintains state—by setting and retrieving an `ASPSessionID` cookie or URL value—there are several more topics to cover before you've explored `Sessions` thoroughly.

Associating Data with Individuals

Associating data with a browser is *not* always the same as associating data with an individual. For example, load the Web Form `ch7-3.aspx` into your browser. Leave that browser open and launch another browser instance. Navigate that browser to `ch7-3.aspx` as well. You'll see two different GUIDs and two different counter values. To the server, each browser is an entirely separate `Session`, even though the IP address of both browsers is the same. That's because the server doesn't look at the IP address; in fact, it doesn't know anything about you at all.

The reason I say "not always the same" is that browser instances running on the same machine share persistent cookies. For example, create a persistent cookie with an expiration date sometime in the future. Close the browser and then browse to the same page with two separate browsers at the same time. If you print the cookie value to the browser screen, you'll see the same value in both browsers. In contrast, transient, in-memory cookies (like the `ASPSessionID`) are *not* shared among browser instances, even on the same machine.

Similarly, if you browse to a site that stores data in persistent cookies on your local machine and then change machines, the server will provide the second machine with a different set of cookie values. Unfortunately, that's useless for identification purposes unless the cookie contains machine-specific information.

Therefore, keep these rules in mind when thinking about Web identification issues:

♦ You can't rely on transient cookies to identify individuals or machines. You *can* rely on transient cookies to identify a single browser instance reliably.

♦ You can't rely on permanent cookies to identify individuals or browser instances or machines. You can only rely on permanent cookies to identify individual machines if you use custom code to insert machine-specific values into the cookie—most users have their browser security level set to deny such information to Web pages.

♦ You can't rely on IP addresses to identify individuals, machines, or browsers. Not only are IP addresses relatively easy to "spoof," most people don't have a fixed IP address—they receive an IP address from an address pool when they connect to their Internet service provider (ISP).

Identifying Users via Username/Password or Another Recognition Mechanism

The only way to identify a specific user is to get that user to send you some information that could be known only to the user and to the server. Currently, the most common method for identifying individuals is a combination of a username and password. Personally, I think the era of passwords is rapidly drawing to a close; nonetheless, it's still your best bet for user identification. Smart cards—hardware devices that change passwords constantly—are a step up from passwords, because they prevent users from forgetting or writing down the passwords. Unfortunately, people can and do lose their smart cards. That's not so much a security risk as it is an unnecessary expense. In the not-too-distant future, biometric authentication mechanisms, such as fingerprint, voice, face, and retinal scan recognition engines, will completely replace passwords and smart cards. I have a fingerprint scanner sitting on my desk as I write this book.

You'll build a username/password form later in this book. For now, just remember that forgotten, lost, and stolen passwords are a major management problem, and you should avoid them if at all possible. If you're writing C# Web applications for an intranet, and your users all have IE, you can avoid managing the user information yourself by delegating security to IIS and Windows NT/2000. IE and IIS use Integrated Windows Security to transparently identify individuals connecting to the server. IE exchanges a hashed identification key with the server (it doesn't send the username and password over the network). After authenticating the user, the server runs requests using the user's security settings, which means your Web application security is as good as the network's. However, Integrated Windows Security can be a security hazard even worse than usernames and passwords if users routinely leave their machines running and unlocked.

ASP.NET Session State Security

ASP.NET supports several different types of security, including the following:

Forms Authentication This type uses the standard username/password dialog built into browsers. Browsers display the dialog when the server returns an access-denied message. If the user enters valid authentication information, the server sends a transient cookie that serves to identify the user during subsequent requests in the same browser instance.

Basic Authentication This is the oldest and least secure method for identifying a user. The user enters authentication information and the browser sends it to the server in plain text. That means the information is unencrypted, and anyone who can listen in on the wire can view the information. You should avoid this type of authentication if possible. Unfortunately, this is the only type that some older browsers can use. If you do have to use basic authentication, you should use it only with Web Forms that use content encryption, such as Secure Sockets Layer (SSL).

Digest Authentication This is a challenge/response type of authentication. The server challenges the browser for authentication information. The browser responds with a hashed value consisting of the requested URL, the username, the password, the request method, and a special value generated by the server during the initial challenge, called a *nonce*. You should prefer digest authentication over basic authentication because, unlike basic authentication, the browser doesn't send the username and password over the network. When supported by the client, digest authentication is completely transparent to the user. In other words, if all your clients support digest authentication, you can build security into your applications without the user ever having to enter a username or password.

ASP.NET Session State and Scalability

Microsoft has improved ASP.NET session state considerably by using a separate `SessionState` server. Four possible session state settings control the method ASP.NET uses to store session data:

Off The application does not use ASP.NET session state. That means the server will not try to send cookies or munged URLs to the clients, and you will not be able to maintain values across pages by creating `Session` variables. You *can* still create `Session` variables, but the server destroys them when request processing completes. Turning off session state gives you the most scalable version of ASP.NET but also requires you to implement any data-cacheing scheme yourself. There are only a few situations in which you might want to turn session state off in ASP.NET: when you already have a caching scheme in place, when you're building extremely high-volume applications, and when you don't need to cache data across requests.

InProc Sessions are in process (`InProc`) when the `SessionState` server runs in the same process as your application. When you create an application, session state is `InProc` by default. This setting works much like classic ASP session state. It's the least scalable and robust setting because the Web server and the `SessionState` server both run on the same machine, meaning you can't scale up to multiple servers with this setting. However, for applications without too many simultaneous users, it's also the fastest setting because the server can retrieve data directly from local memory without accessing the network.

StateServer ASP.NET has a second server application, called the `SessionState` server, that can run out of process on a separate machine. Using this method, you have most of the advantages of `InProc` session data, but because the session data is on a separate computer, you can scale your application across multiple Web servers, each of which queries the `SessionState` server for stored session data. Use this setting when you must run applications across multiple servers. Note that scalability and speed are two sides of the same coin. By running the `SessionState` server out of process, you gain scalability but lose performance because ASP.NET must send and retrieve stored session data across the network. Also, you should recognize that this version is no more robust than the InProc setting, because if the SessionState server crashes, users lose their data. However, running a separate SessionState server does provide data loss protection against any individual Web server crashing because the data doesn't reside on the Web servers.

SQLServer   Using this setting, ASP.NET stores session data in a SQL Server database. You don't have to do anything special to set this up—ASP.NET creates and expands the database automatically (although you are responsible for creating a backup and recovery plan). This version has the advantages of the StateServer setting (it uses a separate machine to store state, so you can scale your application across multiple Web servers) but is also robust because it uses SQL Server transactions to store the data. Therefore, if the server storing session state crashes, you can use SQL Server's recovery procedures to recover the data. Of course, this is also the slowest version.

Don't be too concerned about which setting you use for experimentation—nor should you be too concerned about performance differences between the various settings. As long as you have sessions turned on, you can switch between the various settings quite easily. You should be most concerned with whether you need to use sessions at all. In my opinion, unless your application serves a very large number of users, you won't see any performance degradation from using sessions if you use reasonable care in deciding how much data you store across requests and determine an optimum session timeout value.

Comparing Options for Storing State

In this book, you'll use the InProc SessionState setting for all the examples that use Sessions—and except for the example in this section, that will be *all* the examples in the book. My main goal in this section is to show you that the performance differences between the various options is negligible until your Web server is under a heavy load. The section uses SQL Server to retrieve a table and then stores the resulting data set in the Session object for future use. Don't worry about the database-specific code for now—you'll see more about database access later in this book. For now, just create or run the examples to see the performance differences.

NOTE   *You shouldn't build a real-world application like the one used in this section, because the data is duplicated for each* Session. *In a real application, store shared data at Application scope.*

This example retrieves the Customers table from the Northwind sample database and stores it at Session scope. Wait! How can you do this if you turn off session state? The answer is—you can't. If you turn off session state, you must retrieve the data from SQL Server for each request. I'll start with session state turned off.

First, create a new Web Form (ch7-5.aspx) and set the default form ID to "Form1". Click the View menu and select the Server Explorer item (see Figure 7.7).

This will display the Server Explorer window in VS.NET (see Figure 7.8).

FIGURE 7.7

The VS.NET
View menu

FIGURE 7.8

The VS.NET Server
Explorer window

Your Server Explorer will look somewhat different from mine because Server Explorer contains a list of items known to your server. Open the **Servers** folder (click the plus (+) sign) and then the SQL Servers item and select a SQL Server installation that has the Northwind database installed. If your Web server and your SQL Server are not on the same machine, you'll need to add another server. To add a server, right-click the Servers item in the Server Explorer window and select Add Server from the pop-up menu. Follow the Add Server Wizard directions to add the server.

Open the SQL Server item. You'll see the list of databases for the selected SQL Server instance. Select the Northwind database and open the Tables item (see Figure 7.9).

FIGURE 7.9

Server Explorer view of the Northwind database tables

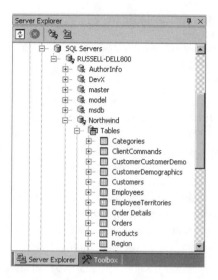

While you can drag-and-drop nonvisual controls such as `SqlConnection` and `SqlDataAdapter` from the Server Explorer, it's my opinion that normally you shouldn't do so. That's because the automatic code generation feature of ASP.NET often generates *too much code!* The reason is that ASP.NET, not knowing whether you want to perform read-only or both read and update operations, must generate all code as if you were performing updates. I know some of you won't care, but it seems wasteful to make the server process 50 automatically generated lines of code (much more for complex queries) rather than writing a few yourself. The basic process to get data from a SQL Server instance is as follows:

- Create a `SqlDataAdapter` object with a specified SQL query and connection string.

- Create a `DataSet` object.

- Use the `SqlDataAdapter`'s `Fill` method to retrieve the data.

You'll need to use the System.Data.SqlClient namespace to open a connection and retrieve data. Add this line to the top of the code-behind class file:

```
using System.Data.SqlClient;
```

For example, these three lines of code retrieve the contents of the Northwind Customers table into a data set:

NOTE Throughout this book, I've used the local SQL Server instance name `localhost` in connection strings, using the username `sa` (System Admin) and a blank password. I've also used SQL Server security (SQL Server usernames and passwords) rather than Windows security. If you're developing with a local instance of SQL Server or MSDE and you have a blank `sa` password, you will be able to copy most of the connection strings verbatim. However, if you are using a remote database server instance, you need to change the server name to the correct value for your server, and if you don't have access to the `sa` username or if the password is not blank, you will need to change those to the correct values for your database server as well.

```
SqlDataAdapter sda = New SqlDataAdapter
  ("SELECT * FROM Customers",
   "server=localhost;uid=sa;pwd=;database=Northwind");
DataSet ds = New DataSet();
sda.Fill(ds, "Customers");
```

Enter the preceding three lines into the `Page_Load` event. The code you just wrote opens the Northwind database using the connection string you entered as the second parameter to the `New SqlDataAdapter` method. After opening the connection, it runs the query you entered as the first parameter to the new `SqlDataAdapter` method. Finally, the `Fill` method populates the `DataSet` object with the retrieved data, stored under the key name `Customers`. Now that you have the data, you need to display it on the Web Form.

The easiest possible way to display a data set is to use a `DataGrid` control. Drag a `DataGrid` control from the Toolbox onto the Web Form design surface. It doesn't matter how you size the control—it will resize automatically to contain the data. You need to bind the control to the `DataSet control` you just created, so add these two lines to the `Page_Load` event:

```
DataGrid1.DataSource = ds.Tables["Customers"].DefaultView;
DataGrid1.DataBind();
```

Set the new Web Form as the start page and run the project. You'll see the table in Figure 7.10.

FIGURE 7.10

DataGrid control
filled with data from
the Customers table
in the sample
Northwind database

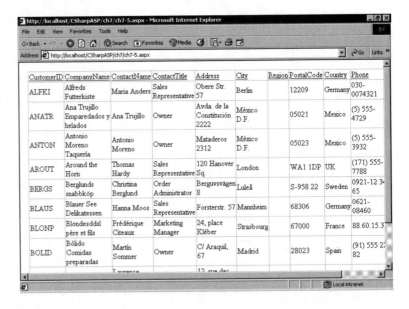

Not very pretty, is it? Don't worry; you can change that easily. Close the browser window to return to design mode. Select the `DataGrid` control. Under the Properties window, you'll see two links: `Auto Format` and `Property Builder`. Click the Auto Format link and select Colorful 3 from the Auto Format dialog (see Figure 7.11).

FIGURE 7.11

VS.NET `DataGrid` Auto Format dialog

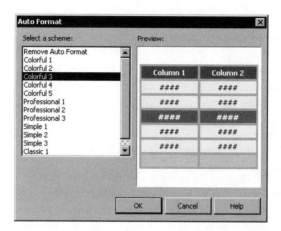

Click the OK button to close the dialog, and then run the Web Form again. The results might be more to your liking. Figure 7.12 shows the result after applying Auto Format to the table.

FIGURE 7.12

A `DataGrid` control with the Auto Format setting (filled with data from the Customers table in the sample Northwind database

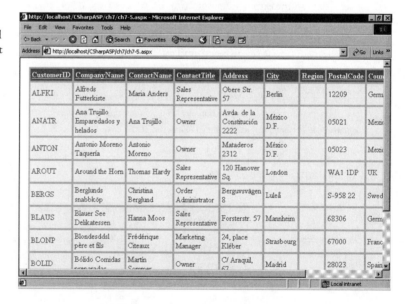

Even if you're a die-hard fan of some other language, you have to admit that this is an amazing result for writing five lines of code, adding a control, and setting one property. In case you're interested, click the HTML tab in design view, and you'll see how selecting Auto Format generates a large number of settings. If you can't find an Auto Format setting you like, you can click the Property-Builder link and create your own. And, of course, you can always create your own style sheet manually and apply it to the `DataGrid` control.

That's enough playing around with the display. The point is to use this page to compare the various options for storing session state.

TURNING OFF SESSION STATE

For baseline performance, the first test you'll make is to turn off session state. To do that, open your `web.config` file. Scroll down to the `<sessionState>` element and set the `mode` attribute value to `Off`.

WARNING *The* `web.config` *file, like other XML-formatted files, is case sensitive. Therefore, make sure you use the value* `Off`, *not* `off`; *otherwise, you'll get an error when you run the Web Form.*

Save the `web.config` file and then run the `ch7-5.aspx` Web Form you just created. After it loads once, refresh the browser several times—in fact, hold down the refresh key (F5 in IE). Fairly speedy—uncached, isn't it? Now set the `mode` attribute for the `<sessionState>` element back to `InProc`, save the `web.config` file, and repeat the browse-refresh operation. Do you notice any difference? No? You shouldn't, because we haven't cached the `dataset` yet. Of course, with a single machine, you're unlikely to be able to tell much difference unless you use some server tools to measure performance more precisely.

Try again. This time, you'll use the Performance Monitor application to help. The Performance Monitor can measure a huge selection of processor and server operations—and it graphs them nicely for you. In this case, you care far less about the actual numbers that you'll get than you do about the relative numbers. The actual numbers change according to many factors—your hardware, your SQL Server, the amount of memory available, and so on. Therefore, I'm not going to show my numbers either, but I will give you the rough relative results.

NOTE *The Performance Monitor ships as part of Windows 2000 and XP; if you're using Windows NT, you can use the Performance Explorer application, which works similarly, but some of the steps will differ. The rest of this section discusses the Performance application in Windows 2000 only.*

Click Start ➤ Programs ➤ Administrative Tools ➤ Performance. You'll see the Performance application (see Figure 7.13).

FIGURE 7.13

The Windows 2000 Performance application at startup

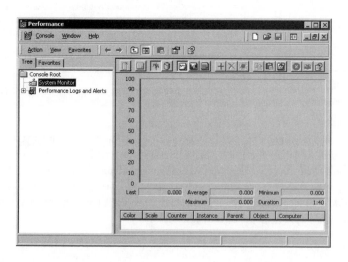

Select the System Monitor if it's not already selected (it is selected by default). The Performance application works by monitoring *counters*. You need to tell it which counters to monitor. In this case, you want to monitor the average number of Web requests per second. To add the counter, click the large plus (+) button on the toolbar. You'll see the Add Counters dialog (see Figure 7.14).

FIGURE 7.14

The Performance application's Add Counters dialog

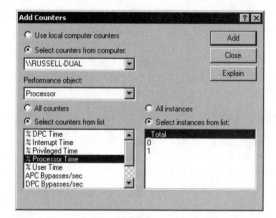

If your server is not already selected, select it. If your server and your development machine are the same computer, you can click the Use Local Computer Counters radio button.

Just below the computer name drop-down list is a Performance Object drop-down list. Click the drop-down arrow and then scroll to the top of the list and select ASP.NET Applications. Click the Select Counters from List radio button and select the Anonymous Requests/Sec counter. Finally, the Select Instances from List listbox contains the ASP.NET applications available on your server. Select the one that ends with CSharpASP. After making all the necessary selections, the dialog should look like Figure 7.15.

FIGURE 7.15

The Add Counters dialog set to monitor anonymous requests per second for the ASP.NET CSharpASP application

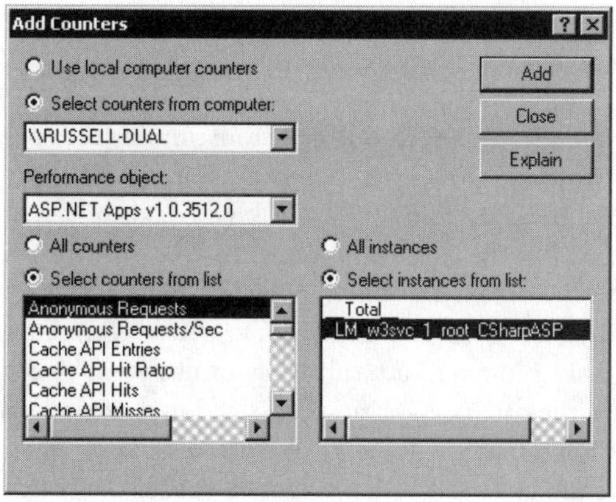

Click the Close button. The Performance application immediately adds and begins to graph the new counter. Browse to the ch7-5.aspx Web Form again and hold down the Refresh key. You'll see the graph rise as the server receives and processes requests. Remember, at this point you're running with session state set to InProc. You'll have to hold down the Refresh key for several seconds to get an accurate average. Make a note of the number. At this point, you should go back, turn off session state, and check the Performance application without session state, because you're about to store the DataSet in a Session variable. If you try to use Session variables in your application with session state turned off, you'll get an error. Make a note of that value as well. Is there any discernable difference? I can't see any difference on my hardware.

Next, stop the application and change the Page_Load code to match Listing 7.5.

LISTING 7.5: PERSIST A DataSet IN A Session VARIABLE (ch7-5.aspx.cs)

```
private void Page_Load(object sender, System.EventArgs e) {
    SqlDataAdapter dsc;
    DataSet ds = new DataSet();

    if (Session["ds"] == null) {
        dsc = new SqlDataAdapter("SELECT * FROM Customers",
            "server=localhost;uid=sa;pwd=;database=Northwind;");
        ds = new DataSet();
        dsc.Fill(ds, "Customers");
        Session["ds"] = ds;
    }
     else {
        ds = (DataSet) Session["ds"];
    }

    DataGrid1.DataSource = ds.Tables["Customers"].DefaultView;
    DataGrid1.DataBind();
}
```

Be sure to set session state back to InProc before running the code. When the page loads, the code in Listing 7.5 tests a Session variable with the key ds (for DataSet) to see if it is Null. If the Session variable doesn't exist, the code follows the track you've already seen—it creates a SqlDataAdapter, retrieves the data, and fills the DataSet. However, if the Session variable does exist, the code simply assigns the DataSet object reference stored in the Session variable to the local variable ds. The first time the page loads, the operation will be slightly slower than the preceding version because it has to test the Session["ds"] variable. However, each subsequent call should be considerably faster because the code doesn't have to query the database—it simply assigns an object reference to a local variable.

Save your changes and run the Web Form again. This time, you should see a considerable increase in the number of requests per second—in fact, if your Web server is on a different machine from the browser, you'll probably see at least a 50 percent improvement in speed. However, if your Web server and your browser are on the same machine, you'll see somewhat less of an increase because the browser uses up some machine resources as it starts parsing the response for each request.

Stop the project and change the `web.config` file `<sessionState>` mode attribute value to `StateServer`. The `StateServer` setting causes ASP.NET to maintain `SessionState` in a separate process. You may need to start the ASP.NET state service because the service doesn't start automatically when you boot your server. To start the service, click Start ➤ Programs ➤ Administrative Tools ➤ Services to start the Services dialog. Right-click the ASP.NET State entry in the Services list and select `Start` from the context menu (see Figure 7.16). After the service starts, you can close the Services dialog.

FIGURE 7.16

Starting the ASP.NET State service from the Services dialog

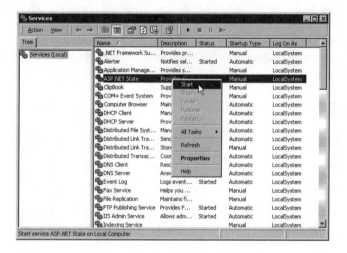

Save the `web.config` file, and rerun the application. Hold down the browser refresh key to repeat the performance testing procedure. You'll see a drop in the number of requests per second. Because the `StateServer` setting causes the `SessionState` server to run out of process, ASP.NET must marshal the data between processes, which is somewhat slower than running the server in process. With my setup, the average number of requests drops by about 30 percent, but that's a small price to pay for being able to scale your application—unchanged except for the `web.config` setting—from one machine to a multiserver Web farm.

The last session state setting, `SQLServer`, causes the `SessionState` server to maintain `Session` data in SQL Server. You don't have to create any tables or databases—ASP.NET takes care of that for you—but you do have to have a trusted login to SQL Server. This time, you may see a performance drop as compared to `StateServer`, depending on the amount of memory in your machine, whether any of that memory is dedicated to SQL Server, whether the SQL Server you're running is on the same or another server, the speed of the connection between the servers, and so on. With my setup, there's no apparent difference between the `SQLServer` setting and the `StateServer` setting after the first request (which is noticeably, but not irritatingly, slower). Again, a slight performance drop in exchange for the capability not only to scale across a Web farm but also to maintain your users' data in the event of a crash is a small price to pay.

Summary

You've seen how to store and retrieve data for a session—a browser instance by default, but possibly an identifiable user. ASP.NET associates objects stored in `Session` variables using a specific `ASPSessionID` value. If you turn off sessions using your `web.config` file (or programmatically), then you can't use the SessionState server to store data between requests; you must fall back on other methods, such as using cookies, hidden form variables, database tables, or files, or by implementing your own state maintenance methods.

Using the `web.config` `<sessionState>` element's `mode` attribute setting, you can turn off the `SessionState` server entirely, set it to run in process or out of process, or use SQL Server, giving you the capability to trade a little responsiveness for scalability and data recoverability by changing a single setting.

In the next chapter, you'll see how to use the `HttpServer` object to manage object creation, path mapping, and several other useful tasks.

Chapter 8

The *HttpServerUtility* Object

ALTHOUGH YOU CAN MANAGE most aspects of your Web application using the Request, Response, Session, and Application objects, sometimes you need to perform a few tasks that these objects cannot do, such as instantiate legacy COM objects from a ProgID or ClassID (the string or GUID stored in the Registry that identifies COM classes), map paths, transfer execution to another file, "escape" characters in strings destined to be used in a URL or in an HTML file, and execute code in other pages, as you'll see in this chapter. As with other commonly used ASP.NET objects, the Page object exposes an instance of the HttpServerUtility object under the shorter name Server; therefore, I'll use the shorter name in the rest of this book.

In this chapter:

- ◆ CreateObject and CreateObjectFromClsID Methods

- ◆ Executing External Code with Server Object Methods and the #INCLUDE Command

- ◆ The Server.HtmlEncode, HtmlDecode, UrlEncode, and UrlDecode Methods

- ◆ The Server.GetLastError and ClearError Methods

CreateObject and *CreateObjectFromClsID* Methods

In classic ASP, you needed the Server object to instantiate COM objects. For example, to retrieve an instance of a FileSystemObject from the Microsoft Scripting Library DLL, you used the following command in VBScript:

```
Set fs = Server.CreateObject("Scripting.FileSystemObject")
```

Using JScript on the server required a similar syntax:

```
fs = Server.CreateObject("Scripting.FileSystemObject");
```

In ASP.NET, you no longer need the Server.CreateObject method to create ASP.NET objects or to create COM objects for which you have a project reference, but you do still need it to create COM objects by ProgID, Type, or ClassID.

NOTE *You can create* Object *variables of any type using the* Server.CreateObject *method—whether you have a project reference or not—but you will not be able to compile code that uses the methods and properties of those objects, because C# can't use late-bound objects instantiated in this manner.*

For example, if you have a project reference to the Microsoft XML Library, version 3 (MSXML3.dll), you can create an early-bound DOMDocument object as you would a standard .NET object; for example:

```
MSXML2.DOMDocument domDoc;
domDoc = new MSXML2.DOMDocument.3.0();
```

The frequency with which you'll need to use the Server object is considerably less than it was in classic ASP, which is probably why it's now designated as a "utility" class.

When you must instantiate late-bound COM objects, you can use the Server.CreateObject or Server.CreateObjectFromClsID method. The CreateObject method uses COM ProgramID (ProgID) strings or .NET Types to create the object. A ProgID is a text string that identifies a class. Windows stores COM ProgIDs in the Registry database, in the HKEY_CLASSES_ROOT hive. To test this you'll need a COM object installed on the server that you can instantiate. Create a DOMDocument instance. Listing 8.1 creates a DOMDocument.3.0 object instance, loads it with an XML string, and then prints the text of the <item1> node.

WARNING *You must add a project reference to the Microsoft XML v3.0 component library to run the following code.*

LISTING 8.1: USING THE Server.CreateObject AND Server.HtmlEncode METHODS (ch8-1.aspx.cs)

```
private void Page_Load(object sender, System.EventArgs e) {
    DOMDocument30Class domDoc = new DOMDocument30Class();
    IXMLDOMNode N;
    domDoc = (DOMDocument30Class)
        Server.CreateObject("MSXML2.DOMDocument.3.0");
    // domDoc = (DOMDocument30Class)
        Server.CreateObjectFromClsid
            ("{f5078f32-c551-11d3-89b9-0000f81fe221}");
    // domDoc = (DOMDocument30Class)
        Server.CreateObject(System.Type.GetTypeFromProgID
            ("MSXML2.DOMDocument.3.0"));
    domDoc.loadXML("<?xml version=\"1.0\"?><root><item1>" +
        "This is a test</item1></root>");
    if (domDoc.parseError.reason != null) {
        Response.Write(domDoc.parseError.reason);
        Response.End();
    }
    Response.Write("<br />XML File loaded<br />");
    N = domDoc.selectSingleNode("//item1");
    if (!(N == null)) {
        Response.Write(N.text);
```

```
    }
    else {
        Response.Write("Could not get the node \"root/item1\".");
    }
    domDoc = null;
}
```

You can just as easily create the XMLDOM object using its `ClassID` (`ClsID`). A `ClassID` is just a GUID (see Listing 7.2 in Chapter 7, "The *SessionState* Object"). If you don't know an object's `ClassID`, you can find it by looking in the Windows Registry.

NOTE *Use the* `regedt32.exe` *or* `regedit.exe` *program to view the Registry to find* `ClassID`s *to use with the* `Server.CreateObjectFromClsID` *method.*

For example, the `ClassID` for the `DOMDocument.3.0` object is as follows:

```
{f5078f32-c551-11d3-89b9-0000f81fe221}
```

You can substitute the preceding `ClassID` and the `Server.CreateObjectFromClsID` method in the preceding example and it will run the same way (uncomment the code in the preceding listing to test it). The advantage of using the `Server.CreateObjectFromClsID` method is that it's slightly faster. The server always uses the `ClassID` to instantiate objects; when you use the `CreateObject` method, it must find the `ClassID` by checking the subkeys under the `ProgID` key, so using the `CreateObjectFromClsID` method saves a couple of Registry lookups.

If you have an existing `System.Type`, you can use that instead of the `ProgID` or `ClassID`. The third version retrieves a `Type` object representing an MSXML2.DOMDocument.3.0 class and instantiates that. Uncomment the code to test it.

Executing External Code with Server Object Methods and the *#INCLUDE* Command

ASP.NET has five methods for executing code in external files: the `#INCLUDE` command, the `Server.Execute` method, the `Server.Transfer` method, instantiating and calling class or object methods (other than those defined in the current `Page` object), and calling methods exposed by Web services. In this section, you'll deal with only the first three; you'll see more about executing class code and calling Web services later in this book.

Using the *#INCLUDE* Command in C# Web Applications

The `#INCLUDE` command is useful chiefly when you're writing ASP.NET code without code-behind classes, because you can group related functions and subroutines in separate files, include them, and then use them from a main page. In classic ASP, this was the only easy way to both include common code—such as headers, menus, counters, or copyright information—in multiple pages in your application and maintain that code in a single location rather than copying it into each page. However, in C# Web applications, you should typically create one or more classes and use object methods instead, because you have more control over when code loads than you do with the #INCLUDE command. The #INCLUDE command causes the server to perform a server-side include (SSI), which places the contents of the included file inline in the currently executing file, replacing the #INCLUDE command itself. The server inserts included files *before* it executes any code in the page.

You can't use the #INCLUDE command from your C# code-behind class; it's not a C# command. Instead, you write it into the HTML defined in the ASPX file. There are two forms of the command—one that loads a file from a virtual path, and one that loads a file from a specific physical path. You place the command between HTML comment tags. For example, the following command loads a file from the virtual directory called includes:

```
<!-- #INCLUDE VIRTUAL="/includes/scripts/fileops.inc -->
```

The VIRTUAL attribute value is the virtual path and filename of the file the server should include. A virtual directory reference always starts with a forward slash character (/). The advantage of using the VIRTUAL attribute is that if you ever need to change the location of the files, you can simply redefine the virtual directory to point to the new location.

The other form of the #INCLUDE command uses a FILE attribute instead of the VIRTUAL attribute in the preceding example. The attribute value is the path to the file. For example, if the fileops.inc file resides in the same directory as the executing page, you don't need to use a path.

```
<!-- #INCLUDE FILE="fileops.inc -->
```

NOTE   *Using the #INCLUDE command in ASP.NET is not as powerful as using Web Forms User controls, where you can apply output caching to the page fragments (see the section "Partial Page Cacheing and User Controls" in Chapter 23, "Build Your Own Web Controls," for an example).*

The Server.MapPath Method

When you need to know the exact location of a file, use the Server.MapPath method. The MapPath method accepts a String parameter containing a virtual path, a relative path, or a null string and returns the fully expanded physical path. The path does not have to exist. If the parameter does not contain any path information, the method returns the path of the executing file. For example, if you execute the file ch8-2.aspx, the following command returns the physical path of the executing file:

```
Server.MapPath("");
// returns "c:\inetpub\wwwroot\CSharpASP\ch8"
```

Note that the method does not end directory paths with a closing slash. If the parameter contains only a filename, the method appends the filename to the directory of the executing file:

```
Server.MapPath("madeUpFile.aspx");
// returns "c:\inetpub\wwwroot\CSharpASP\madeUpfile.aspx"
```

If the parameter contains a virtual directory, the method returns the path of the directory.

```
Server.MapPath("/scripts")
// returns "c:\inetpub\scripts"
```

You can use the shortcut "dot" notation with both the #INCLUDE command's FILE attribute and the Server.MapPath method. A single dot (.) refers to the current directory, and a double dot (..) refers to the parent directory. For example, suppose you want to include the file c:\inetpub\wwwroot\myApp\scripts\fileops.inc, and the currently executing page (login.aspx) is in a subfolder of that directory; for example, c:\inetpub\wwwroot\myApp\scripts\login\login.aspx. You can retrieve the full path of a file in the scripts parent directory using the parent path shortcut:

```
String pathToScripts = Server.MapPath("..");
// returns c:\inetpub\wwwroot\myApp\scripts
```

From the login.aspx page, you could include the file using the following:

```
<!-- #INCLUDE FILE="..\fileops.inc" -->
```

There are only two-dot notation shortcuts. You won't get the parent directory's parent directory by using three dots. Use this instead:

```
Server.MapPath("..\..");
```

You can, of course, use ASP.NET objects (such as the Server object) directly in HTML code as well (remember, you define code in ASP.NET files by placing it within a <% %> tag). You might think the following command would have exactly the same result as the #INCLUDE example in the preceding section that used the VIRTUAL attribute:

```
<!-- #INCLUDE FILE="<%=Server.MapPath("/includes/fileops.inc")%>" -->
```

However, if you run a Web Form where the HTML includes the preceding code line, it doesn't work, because the server inserts included files *before running code*. Therefore, when the server tries to include the file, it finds an invalid file path and can't include the file contents. If you can't use a variable to define the file location, how can you include files dynamically? The short answer is—you can't by using the #INCLUDE command. If you want to use a variable to define file locations or to execute code efficiently based on a logical decision, you need to use a different method. For example, this code doesn't work the way you would expect:

```
<%
Boolean b = true;
if(b) {
%>
<!--#INCLUDE FILE="onlyIfTrue.inc"-->
<%
}
else {
    %>
<!--#INCLUDE FILE="onlyIfFalse.inc"-->
<%
}
%>
```

Although the outcome of code such as the preceding fragment may work correctly, (depending on the code in the included files), the server will always include *both* files. The upshot is that by using the #INCLUDE command to include files selectively, you lose a measure of control over your code.

The *Server.Execute* and *Transfer* Methods

The Server.Execute method lets you execute code in another file as if it were in the current file. Unlike included files, you can't use the Server.Execute method to call a function and retrieve a result; instead, you use the Server.Execute method to execute entire files and return a result. The Server.Transfer method replaces the "old-style" Web technique of redirecting a browser to another location—as long as the new location is on the same server as the currently executing page. You can't use the Transfer method to transfer to a different server; however, you can transfer to a different site on the same server. For example, assuming you're running a page in the CSharpASP site, the following code won't work:

```
Server.Transfer("http://www.microsoft.com");
```

But this next example would work. I haven't created the file on www.sybex.com, but if you want to test it, create a new project called CSharpASP2, create a Web Form named transfer.aspx in the new project, compile it, and then add the following code to the ch8-2.aspx file in the Page_Load method. Make sure you add the code *before* the existing Server.Transfer command in the Page_Load method:

```
Server.Transfer("http://localhost/CSharpASP2/transfer.aspx");
```

It's easiest to see the difference between #INCLUDE, Server.Execute, and Server.Transfer with a few examples. Create three new Web Forms called ch8-2.aspx, ch8-3.aspx, set the default form ID for each page to "Form1", and ch8-4.aspx, and add the code in Listing 8.2 to the Page_Load event, which can be accessed by double-clicking the page in design mode. Also, create a file in the ch8 folder called ch8-2.inc.

> **LISTING 8.2: SIMPLE EXAMPLE FILE SHOWING THE DIFFERENCE BETWEEN THE #INCLUDE COMMAND AND THE Server.Execute AND Server.Transfer METHODS (CH8-2.ASPX.CS)**

```csharp
private void Page_Load(object sender, System.EventArgs e) {
    StringWriter tw= new StringWriter();
    Response.Write("The call to Server.MapPath(\"\") returned: " +
        Server.MapPath("") + "<br>");
    Response.Write("The call to Server.MapPath(\"madeUpFile.aspx\") " +
        "returned: " +  Server.MapPath("madeUpFile.aspx") +  "<br>");
    Response.Write("The call to Server.MapPath(\".\") returned: " +
        Server.MapPath(".") + "<br>");
    Response.Write("The call to Server.MapPath(\"..\") returned: " +
        Server.MapPath("..") + "<br>");
    Response.Write("The call to Server.MapPath(\"/scripts\") returned: "
        + Server.MapPath("/scripts") + "<br>");

    Response.Write("This code executed in ch8-2.aspx<br>");
    Server.Execute("ch8-3.aspx");
    Response.Write("This code executed in ch8-2.aspx after calling " +
        "the Server.Execute method.<br>");
    Session["footer"] =
        "This footer was written before the transfer to ch8-4.";
    Server.Execute("ch8-footer.aspx", tw);
```

```
Response.Write(tw.ToString());
//Server.Transfer("ch8-4.aspx");
//Throw new System.Exception()
}
```

NOTE *The last two lines of the preceding listing are commented out on* www.sybex.com. *Enable the* Server.Transfer *line before you continue.*

You won't see the #INCLUDE command in this code because it's C# code—but there's an #INCLUDE command in the HTML source for the ch8-2.aspx file. I won't show the entire file, but here's the relevant code line:

```
<!-- #INCLUDE FILE="ch8-2.inc" -->
```

Add the following code to the Page_Load event of the ch8-3.aspx.cs file:

```
Response.Write("This code executed in ch8-3.aspx via the " +
    "Server.Execute method.<br>");
```

Similarly, add the following code to the Page_Load event of the ch8-4.aspx file:

```
Response.Write("This code executed in ch8-4.asp via the " +
    "Server.Transfer method.<br>");
```

Set the ch8-2.aspx file as the start page. The code will write the line in the Page_Load event from the ch8-2.aspx.cs file, then the line from the #INCLUDE command in the ASPX file. At that point, it executes the ch8-2.aspx file, which writes another line. Finally, it transfers control to the ch8-4.aspx Web Form, which writes the final line. When you run the file, you'll see the output shown in Figure 8.1 in your browser.

FIGURE 8.1

Result of running the ch8-2.aspx Web Form with the Server.Transfer command enabled

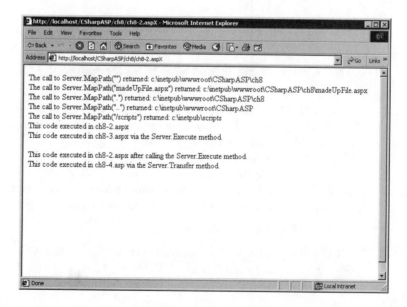

Add the following code to the `ch8-2.inc` file:

```
<%

Response.write("This code executed in ch8-2.inc<br>");

%>
```

What you should see from the output is that the `#INCLUDE` command didn't work. That's because the `Server.Transfer` command removes control from the `ch8-2.aspx` file *before* the form renders its HTML.

Disable (comment out) the `Server.Transfer` line and run the project again. This time, you'll see the message, `"This code executed in ch8-2.inc"` in the browser. Note that it appears *last* (see Figure 8.2). The `Page_Load` event executes before any code in an included file. This is one problem with placing code in included files—they're only useful, and only run, if the page gets a chance to render.

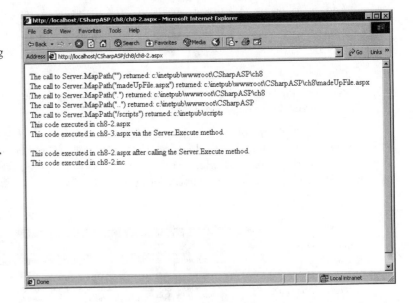

FIGURE 8.2

Output of simple example file showing the difference between the `#INCLUDE` command and the `Server.Execute` and `Server.Transfer` methods

Fortunately, C# fixes that problem by giving you several options. The `Server.Execute` option doesn't include unwanted code, and (unlike the `#INCLUDE` command) it works within code-behind classes, so you can call it directly from C#.

Next, you should understand that the `Server.Execute` method returns control to the original file. The `Server.Transfer` method causes ASP.NET to stop executing the `ch8-2.aspx.cs` code and immediately begins executing the `ch8-4.aspx.cs` code. You can prove this by uncommenting the last line in the `Page_Load` event code shown in Listing 8.1 and recompiling:

```
Throw New System.Exception()
```

Run the program again. Did you see the error? No, because ASP.NET stops executing the `ch8-2.aspx.cs` code at the point you called the `Server.Transfer` method.

Advanced Use of the *Server.Execute* Method

The Execute method isn't broadly useful for calling code in other pages because you can't specify a method; you must execute the entire page. However, it *does* have direct access to the ASP objects, including values sent by the browser in the Request object, and it *can* return values in a couple of different ways. To pass extra values (besides those in Request) to the page you want to execute, you can store values in one or more Session variables and then call the Execute method. Finally, you retrieve the values from the Session variables to use in the executed page. The first way to return values is to perform the same tasks in the opposite direction—store values in the second page and then retrieve them from the initial page.

One common use of the Execute method is to use external page files to build portions of a page. The main page returns all the page portions to the requesting client. Therefore, another way to return values is to use an overloaded version of the Execute method that accepts a Sytem.IO.TextWriter object. The executed page returns any output in the TextWriter object.

For example, suppose you want to display a formatted footer at the bottom of each page. The page that builds the footer (ch8-footer.aspx) expects the footer text to be in the Session("footer") variable. You can set the variable and then use the Execute method to build the footer, filling a TextWriter object with the result. To create the footer page, first create a CSS file named ch8.css and add it to your CSharpASP project in the ch8 folder. To do that, right-click the ch8 folder item in the Solution Explorer, select Add New Item from the pop-up menu, select the Style Sheet item from the Add New Item dialog, and then enter the name **ch8.css** in the Name field.

To use the new style sheet, you must define a CSS class (see Listing 8.3).

LISTING 8.3: CSS CLASS TO FORMATTING (ch8.css)

```
.footer
{
    border-right: black thin outset;
    border-top: black thin outset;
    display: block;
    font-weight: bold;
    font-size: 8pt;
    left: 0px;
    float: none;
    visibility: visible;
    page-break-after: always;
    overflow: visible;
    border-left: black thin outset;
    width: 100%;
    color: deepskyblue;
    direction: ltr;
    text-indent: 10px;
    border-bottom: black thin outset;
    font-style: italic;
    font-family: Verdana;
    position: absolute;
```

```
        background-color: #ffffcc;
    }
```

Add a Web Form named ch8-footer.aspx. Add a Panel Web Form control to the page, and then view the file's HTML and strip the code until the file looks like Listing 8.4. Note the script at the bottom of the page—more about that in a minute.

LISTING 8.4: THIS WEB FORM CREATES A FOOTER AND CENTERS IT NEAR THE BOTTOM OF THE PAGE (ch8-footer.aspx).

```
<%@ Page Language="c#" AutoEventWireup="false"
    Codebehind="ch8-footer.aspx.cs"
    Inherits="CSharpASP.ch8.ch8_footer"
%>
<HTML>
    <HEAD>
        <LINK href="ch8.css" type="text/css" rel="stylesheet">
    </HEAD>
    <body onload="setFooterPosition()">
        <asp:panel id="Panel1" style="DISPLAY: none" ForeColor="Red"
        HorizontalAlign="Center" runat="server" Width="490px"
        Height="16px" CssClass="footer"></asp:panel>
        <script language="JScript">
            function setFooterPosition() {
                ft=document.getElementById("Panel1");
                ft.style.pixelTop = (screen.availHeight - 150);
                ft.style.pixelLeft = (screen.availWidth -
                    ft.style.pixelWidth) / 2;
                ft.style.display="block";
            }
        </script>
    </body>
</HTML>
```

A Panel control is a container control; to make it useful, you need to place other controls inside it. You can do that dynamically when the page loads. Here's the code for the Page_Load event for the ch8-footer.aspx Web Form shown in Listing 8.4:

```
private void Page_Load(object sender, System.EventArgs e) {
    Label lb = new Label();
    if (!(Session["footer"]==null)) {
        lb.Text = (String) Session["footer"];
    }
    else {
        lb.Text = "This is the page footer.";
```

```
    }
    this.Panel1.Controls.Add(lb);
}
```

The preceding code creates a new `Label` WebControl, sets its `Text` property to the value of the `Session("footer")` variable, or to a default value if the variable doesn't exist, and then adds the new label to the `Panel`.

Note that the `Panel` control uses the "footer" class defined in the `ch8.css` file. The footer floats above the page because the style definition has a `position: absolute` property. The script I mentioned earlier uses client-side code to set the position of the footer after the page loads.

```
<script language="JScript">
    function setFooterPosition() {
        ft=document.getElementById("Panel1");
        ft.style.pixelTop = (screen.availHeight - 150);
        ft.style.pixelLeft = (screen.availWidth -
            ft.style.pixelWidth) / 2;
        ft.style.display="block";
    }
</script>
```

The script runs after the page is completely loaded because the `<body>` tag calls the `setFooter-Position` function:

```
<body onload="setFooterPosition()">
```

The subroutine obtains a reference to the `Panel` object (which renders as a `<div>` tag in HTML), and then places it 100 pixels above the bottom of the screen and centers it horizontally. The `pixel-Top` and `pixelLeft` properties take an integer pixel value. The `<div>` tag moves immediately when you set the position.

This short example could actually lead to all sorts of discussion about how the `Panel` control renders in HTML (run the project and select View Source in the browser to see) and about the relative efficiency of the various methods for running external code. However, the points I'd like you to remember from this section are these:

◆ There are multiple ways to run external code (code not in the Web Form itself) from a Web Form. Each has its purpose, and—if the code creates HTML—you may find that the different methods render differently in the browser.

◆ Internet Explorer supports displaying multiple complete HTML documents at one time. Run the project and view the source from your browser to see this—you'll see two complete HTML documents as well as the text written from the `Execute` and `#INCLUDE` commands that appear *before* the opening `<html>` tag.

◆ The `Server.Transfer` method is immediate and absolute—code you write after the command *will not execute*. I mention this one specifically because it's bitten me. As I was writing this example, I initially placed the client-side JScript to set the footer position in the `ch8-2.aspx` form HTML code—and it wouldn't run. Finally, I realized (by looking at the source in the browser) that *none* of the HTML appeared from the `ch8-2.aspx` file, which reminded me that the page was losing control because of the `Transfer` command before it had a chance to render the HTML.

Before leaving this topic, I want to be sure you understand the ramifications of the #INCLUDE method. Table 8.1 may help you decide which of these techniques to use.

TABLE 8.1: APPROPRIATE USES FOR #INCLUDE, Server.Transfer, AND Server.Execute

PROBLEM	TECHNIQUE	RECOMMENDATION
Call groups of related functions from multiple pages.	#INCLUDE	This works, but avoid the technique. You're better off creating classes or Web Form User controls and using the resultant object methods and properties in C#, because you can use the classes and cache the output from your C# code, whereas you have to embed the #INCLUDE command in an HTML file. You lose control over how and when code executes if you use included files.
Execute a function in another file.	#INCLUDE	Again, you should wrap the method in a class in C# rather than including files, for the same reasons given in the preceding recommendation.
Stop executing a file and begin executing another file.	Server.Transfer	When possible, prefer Server.Transfer over Response.Redirect because it avoids a round trip to the client.
Execute another page.	Server.Execute	Unfortunately, this is useful only for executing entire pages, not for executing methods in another page.

The *Server.HtmlEncode, HtmlDecode, UrlEncode,* and *UrlDecode* Methods

The HttpServerUtility object contains several other useful methods. The examples you've seen so far use the Response object to write text, but sometimes you need to write or read HTML-encoded or URL-encoded text. You may remember that you need to use *character entities* to force the browser to display angle bracket or ampersand characters because those are reserved characters in HTML. For example, to write the string AT&T to the browser, you must code it as AT&T. Similarly, URLs use characters such as the equal sign, the ampersand, and slashes, so if you want to use those in URL parameters, you need to escape them as well. To solve this problem, you replace the offending characters with a percent sign, followed by the hexadecimal value of the character. For example, some browsers (quite properly) won't recognize URLs that contain spaces:

```
http://www.badURL/This is a bad URL.htm
```

By replacing the spaces with %20 (a space character has an ASCII value of 32, or 20 in hexadecimal), the URL works in all browsers:

```
http://www.badURL/This%20is%20a%20valid%20URL.htm
```

You can, of course, write your own code to find and replace characters to encode them properly for HTML or URLs, but the HttpServerUtility object methods make that unnecessary.

Using the *Server.HtmlEncode* Method

Sometimes, you need to write HTML or XML to the browser. However, if you use the `Response` object to write HTML or XML code, the browser interprets it as HTML. To solve the problem, escape the text properly using the `Server.HtmlEncode` method before sending it to the browser.

The Web Form `ch8-5` contains two `Label` controls. In the `Page_Load` event, the Web Form assigns some HTML content to each `Label`. The code assigns "plain" unescaped HTML to the first label but uses the `Server.HtmlEncode` method to assign content to the second label (see Listing 8.5).

LISTING 8.5: USING THE `HtmlEncode` METHOD (`ch8-5.aspx.cs`)

```
private void Page_Load(object sender, System.EventArgs e) {
   String s;
   Label1.Text = "This HTML code <span class=\"redbolditalic\">" +
      "should appear</span> with the tags invisible";
   s = "This HTML code <span class=\"redbolditalic\">should " +
      "appear</span> with the tags visible";
   Label2.Text = Server.HtmlEncode(s);
}
```

The class definition for the `redbolditalic` style is in the `ch8.css` Cascading Style Sheet file. When the browser parses the HTML rendered for the `Label1` WebControl, it doesn't display the internal `<span>` tag because the browser also sees *that* as HTML. However, the `Server.HtmlEncode` method escaped the contents for `Label2`, so the browser displays the tags (see Figure 8.3).

FIGURE 8.3

Simple **Server .HtmlEncode** method call example

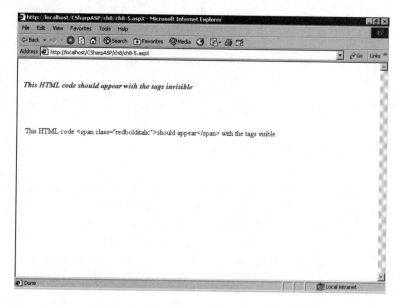

That's a fairly simple example; here's one that's more useful. Browsing the Internet, you may have seen tutorial ASP pages that have a button that, when clicked, can display the code for the executing page. C# Web Form files that use code-behind classes are slightly more complex because you need two buttons to display all the code—one for the `.aspx` file and one for the `.aspx.cs` file. Here are the steps to display the code for a file:

◆ Place code in the page that reads the text of the executing file.

◆ Apply the `Server.HtmlEncode` method to the text contents of the file.

◆ Place the code in a hidden `Label` control (or HTML `<div>` tag).

◆ Show the `Label` or `<div>` when the user clicks a button.

The Web Form `ch8-6.aspx` can display its own code and HTML files (see Figure 8.4).

FIGURE 8.4

A Web Form that displays its own code

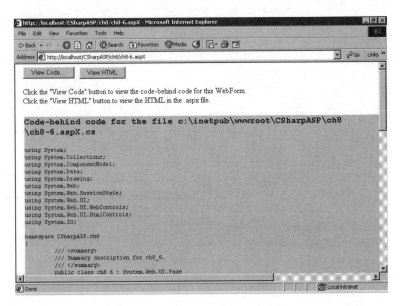

Listing 8.6 shows the code.

LISTING 8.6: THE WEB FORM `ch8-6.aspx` **DISPLAYS ITS OWN CODE-BEHIND CODE OR HTML IN A** `Label` **CONTROL WHEN YOU CLICK ONE OF THE BUTTONS ON THE FORM (**`ch8-6.aspx.cs`**)**

```
public class ch8_6 : System.Web.UI.Page {
    protected System.Web.UI.WebControls.Button btnCode;
    protected System.Web.UI.WebControls.Button btnHTML;
    protected System.Web.UI.WebControls.Label Label1;
    protected System.Web.UI.WebControls.Label Label2;
```

```csharp
private void Page_Load(object sender, System.EventArgs e) {
    Label1.Text = "Click the \"View Code\" button to view the " +
        "code-behind code for this WebForm.<br>";
    Label1.Text += "Click the \"View HTML\" button to view the " +
        "HTML in the .aspx file.";
    Label2.Visible = false;
}

private void btnCode_Click(object sender, System.EventArgs e) {
    String currFile;
    StreamReader sr;
    // get the name of the current file's code-behind file
    currFile = Server.MapPath(Request["SCRIPT_NAME"]) + ".cs";

    // create a StreamReader to read the contents
    sr = File.OpenText(currFile);

    // HtmlEncode the contents and place in Label2
    Label2.Text = "<h3>Code-behind code for the file " + currFile +
        "</h3><pre>" + Server.HtmlEncode(sr.ReadToEnd()) + "</pre>";
    Label2.Visible = true;
    sr.Close();
}

private void btnHTML_Click(object sender, System.EventArgs e) {
    String currFile;
    StreamReader sr;

    // get the name of the current file
    currFile = Server.MapPath(Request["SCRIPT_NAME"]);

    // create a StreamReader to read the contents
    sr = File.OpenText(currFile);

    // HtmlEncode the contents and place in Label2
    Label2.Text = "<h3>HTML code for the file " + currFile +
        "</h3><pre>" + Server.HtmlEncode(sr.ReadToEnd()) + "</pre>";
    Label2.Visible = true;
    sr.Close();
}
```

Listing 8.6 includes several of the Server methods discussed so far in this chapter. It uses the MapPath method to obtain the full physical path of the executing file:

```csharp
Server.MapPath(Request["SCRIPT_NAME"]);
```

The code `Request["SCRIPT_NAME"]` obtains the name of the current file from the `Request.Server-Variables` collection. Note that it would be more efficient to specify the `ServerVariables` collection by using this code instead:

```
Server.MapPath(Request.ServerVariables["SCRIPT_NAME"]);
```

The reason it would be more efficient is that by omitting the name, the server must search all the `Request` collections for a matching key rather than searching only the `ServerVariables` collection. Using a lookup to obtain the name of the current file makes the code much more generic—you can obtain the code or HTML for *any* executing file using this syntax. Be careful, though—if you use `Server.Execute` or `Server.Transfer`, the `Request.ServerVariables["SCRIPT_NAME"]` variable still references the originally requested file.

The code for the View Code… and View HTML… buttons is almost identical. The only difference is that when obtaining the filename, the code either uses the return value of the `Server.MapPath` method directly (see the `btnHTML_Click` code in Listing 8.6) or appends `.cs` to the returned filename, which references the code-behind file. (See the `btnCode_Click` event in Listing 8.6.) In either case, the code creates a `StreamReader` object to read the text from the file:

```
sr = File.OpenText(currFile);
```

Next, it sets the `Text` property of the hidden label using the `StreamReader` object's `ReadToEnd` method to read the file contents, and then it makes the `Label` WebControl visible.

```
Label2.Text = "<h3>HTML code for the file " + currFile +
   "</h3><pre>" + Server.HtmlEncode(sr.ReadToEnd()) + "</pre>";
Label2.Visible = true;
```

Using the `HtmlDecode` method has exactly the opposite result—you provide the method with encoded HTML, and it returns a string containing unescaped HTML. Both the `HtmlEncode` and `HtmlDecode` methods have an overloaded second version that stores the encoded or decoded text in a `TextWriter` object.

Using the *Server.UrlEncode* Method

The following example uses the Web Form `ch8-7 test.aspx`. Note that the file deliberately contains a space. Internet Explorer handles URLs containing spaces as if they were properly encoded, but you may need to replace the space with %20 to test the Web Form if you're delivering to other browsers (see Listing 8.7).

LISTING 8.7: USING THE `Server.UrlEncode` METHOD (`ch8-7 test.aspx.cs`)

```
public class ch8_7_test : System.Web.UI.Page
{
    protected System.Web.UI.WebControls.HyperLink HyperLink1;

    private void Page_Load(object sender, System.EventArgs e) {
        String href, thisFile;
        if (!(Request.QueryString["msg"]==null)) {
            Response.Write(Request.QueryString["msg"]);
```

```
            Response.End();
        }
        thisFile = Request.ServerVariables["URL"];
        href = String.Concat(thisFile, "?msg=", Server.UrlEncode
            ("This message = <h1>Hello! & How are you?</h1>"));
        HyperLink1.NavigateUrl = href;
        HyperLink1.Target = "_blank";
        HyperLink1.Text = "Click me!";
    }

    #region Web Form Designer generated code
    override protected void OnInit(EventArgs e)
    {
        //
        // CODEGEN: This call is required by the ASP.NET
        // Web Form Designer.
        //
        InitializeComponent();
        base.OnInit(e);
    }

    /// <summary>
    /// Required method for Designer support - do not modify
    /// the contents of this method with the code editor.
    /// </summary>
    private void InitializeComponent()
    {
        this.Load += new System.EventHandler(this.Page_Load);
    }
    #endregion
}
```

The Web Form contains a single anchor tag that, when clicked, displays a text message to the user in a new browser instance (see Figure 8.5).

The code in Listing 8.7 uses the `Request.ServerVariables("URL")` variable value to obtain the URL of the current request. It concatenates the current URL with a `QueryString` variable (`msg`) and the value `Hello! & How are you?` The text message itself contains several characters that can cause problems in URLs; therefore, the code uses the `Server.UrlEncode` method to encode the text before setting the `Hyperlink` control's `NavigateURL` property. For example, the equal sign, question mark, and ampersand are all special characters in URLs. The fully encoded URL looks like this (note that the URL appears in a single line when it appears in the browser's address bar):

```
"/CSharpASP/ch8/ch8-7 test.aspx?msg=This+message+%3d+%3ch1%3e
Hello!+%26+How+are+you%3f%3c%2fh1%3e
```

Like the `HtmlEncode` method, the `UrlEncode` method has a corresponding `UrlDecode` method, and both `UrlEncode` and `UrlDecode` have overloaded versions that can store results to a `TextWriter` object.

FIGURE 8.5

Clicking the anchor
tag in the leftmost
browser causes the
second browser to
appear and display
the message

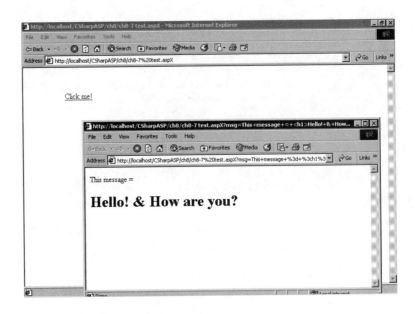

The *Server.GetLastError* and *ClearError* Methods

Early scripting languages had many problems. One of the worst was poor error handling. Fortunately, C#, with its Try-Catch blocks and structured exceptions, has gone a long way toward solving the problem. But there are still errors that you can't trap in code. For example, page preprocessing errors and compilation errors follow the default Internet Information Services (IIS) error-handling procedure. These errors don't (usually) crash ASP.NET—they can't—there may be many other applications that also depend on the server; therefore, Microsoft handles such errors by transferring execution to a default or custom ASP page. In Chapter 6, "Introduction to the System.Web Namespace," you saw how to define a global error page in the web.config file. You can also define custom error pages using the IIS management applet. In Windows 2000, click Start ➤ Programs ➤ Administrative Tools ➤ Internet Services Manager to launch the applet. The Internet Services Manager (ISM) applet runs as part of the Microsoft Management Console (MMC).

Without going into much detail on the ISM, here's the procedure to create a custom IIS error message:

1. Expand the item containing the name of your computer (there may be only one computer name visible).

2. Double-click the Default Web Site item.

3. In the resulting list of folders, find the CSharpASP application folder.

4. Right-click the CSharpASP application folder and select Properties from the context menu.

5. Click the Custom Errors tab.

You'll see a list of possible errors. Each entry in the HttpError column has a single number (for instance, 406) or an error number, a colon, and a suberror number (such as 500:15, read as "Error 500, sub-error 15"). Each error also has a type and an associated filename. You can replace the default file associated with an error with a custom ASP or ASPX file. Subsequently, IIS transfers execution to your custom file whenever the specified error occurs. If you're using a custom page, when an untrapped error occurs in your application, the server stores the error and transfers execution to the custom page. You can retrieve the error information using the Server.GetLastError method. For example:

```
Exception ex;
if (Server.GetLastError() != null) {
    ex = Server.GetLastError();
    Response.Write(ex.Message);
}
```

You can also clear any stored error that may have occurred using the Server.ClearError method.

Note that neither of these methods is of much use when you're developing an application, especially locally. They're much more useful for presenting users with less intrusive and technical error messages and for debugging and pinpointing problems in deployed applications, especially from a remote machine, where web.config settings might prevent the error message from being displayed.

You'll explore the debugging process and error-handling process in detail in the next chapter. As part of the error-handling discussion, you'll set up a custom error page. You'll see how to set up your ASP.NET applications for debugging, and you'll learn more about the machine.config and web.config files and how to avoid many common ASP.NET errors.

Summary

To review, you don't need the HttpServerUtility object as often as you needed the Server object in classic ASP pages, but it still provides some critical methods. The Page object exposes HttpServer-Utility under the simpler name Server. Use the Server object to transfer execution from one page to another (Transfer method), to execute another Web Form and return (Execute method), to encode and decode URLs and HTML (UrlEncode and UrlDecode methods), and to retrieve or clear otherwise untrappable errors.

Chapter 9

Debugging ASP.NET and Error Handling

VISUAL STUDIO PROVIDES ALMOST seamless end-to-end debugging for C# and ASP.NET applications. Unfortunately, the debugger included with C# is a read-only debugger—you can view and change the code, but you must stop the debugger and restart the program for any changes to code (but not to HTML) to take effect. If you're used to working in Break-Edit-Continue mode in classic VB, you'll find the loss of this feature debilitating. C# partially makes up for the loss of Break-Edit-Continue because its strong type checking, IntelliSense, syntax error markings, and compiler warnings reduce many of the most common errors that were endemic to classic VB.

In this chapter:

◆ Setting Up a Site for Debugging

◆ Using the Debugger

◆ ASP.NET Event Sequence

◆ Defensive Coding—How to Avoid Errors

◆ How to Approach Error Handling

◆ Writing Custom Error Pages

Setting Up a Site for Debugging

Three types of code occur in C# Web applications: standard C# code in code-behind classes and any other class written entirely in C#; ASP.NET embedded code that includes both inline and script block code embedded into the HTML in an ASPX page; and client-side script, which is VBScript or JScript code running in IE. You can't debug client-side code if you're using Netscape as your development browser.

Before you can debug any code in a C# application, you must enable the debugger. As you might expect, given the various locations and code types that you can debug, you should check the settings listed in the next several sections.

Check *web.config*

The `web.config` file contains a `<compilation>` element with a `debug` attribute. Make sure the `<compilation>` element (barring white space) looks *exactly* like the following line—remember that XML is case sensitive.

```
<compilation defaultLanguage="c#" debug="true" />
```

Check Debug Mode versus Release Mode

You can compile projects in two modes—Debug and Release. Debug mode inserts debug symbols into the resulting executable code, and the Release version does not. The easiest way to control the project compilation mode is through the configuration drop-down list on the main toolbar (see Figure 9.1).

FIGURE 9.1

Select the project compilation mode from the toolbar

Make sure the drop-down selection reads Debug before you run the project; otherwise, your application won't recognize any breakpoints you may have set. You should use Release mode only after you're finished debugging—but you *should* compile the application in Release mode before you deliver a program, because it runs significantly faster and creates smaller code than the Debug setting.

The toolbar drop-down affects only the active project. When you have multiple projects loaded, you can control the project compilation mode individually for each project through the Configuration Manager dialog. You can reach the dialog from the drop-down—select the Configuration Manager item from the list—or by right-clicking the Solution item in the Solution Explorer pane and selecting Configuration Manager from the context menu. The Configuration Manager lists each project in the current solution in a grid (see Figure 9.2).

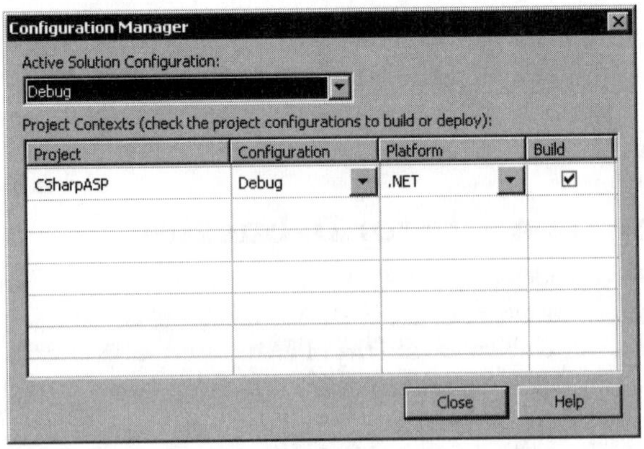

FIGURE 9.2

The Configuration Manager dialog

Configuration Manager

Active Solution Configuration:

Debug

Project Contexts (check the project configurations to build or deploy):

Project	Configuration	Platform	Build
CSharpASP	Debug	.NET	☑

Close   Help

You can also reach the Configuration Manager by right-clicking the Solution item in the Solution Explorer pane and selecting Properties from the context menu to display the Solution Property Pages dialog. Click the Configuration Properties item in the list portion of the dialog. The Configuration Manager appears in the right pane when you access it in this manner (see Figure 9.3).

FIGURE 9.3

The Configuration Properties dialog

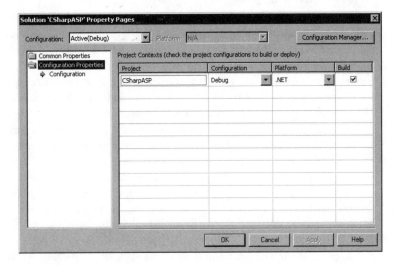

Enable Project Debugging

For each project, you must also enable debugging using the Project Property Pages dialog. Right-click the CSharpASP project item in the Solution Explorer pane and select Properties from the context menu to display the Project Property Pages dialog. Click the Configuration Properties item in the list portion of the dialog and then select the Debugging item. Make sure that the Enable ASP.NET Debugging item is set to True (see Figure 9.4). Depending on your project, you may want to enable other debuggers as well. Note that both the compilation mode Configuration drop-down list and the Configuration Manager dialog are also available from this dialog.

FIGURE 9.4

Enable ASP.NET debugging in the Project Property Pages dialog

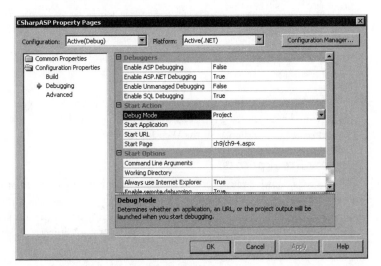

If you changed any settings, save them. Now you're ready to debug your application.

Keyboard Mapping

Visual Studio (VS) supports several different sets of predefined keyboard mappings. The keyboard mapping affects the set of shortcut keys in effect. By default, VS installs with keyboard mappings that are different than the keyboard mappings used in earlier Microsoft IDEs, Visual Studio 6, or Visual InterDev. Although I advise you to try to get used to the standard mappings so that you don't have to re-create them whenever you change computers or reinstall Visual Studio, those of you with a VB background may want to set your computers to use the Visual Basic 6 keyboard mappings.

If you don't like any of the available keyboard mappings, you can create your own. To select a different keyboard mapping, select Tools ➢ Options from the menu bar, and then open the Environment item in the Options dialog. Select the Keyboard item, and then you can change the keyboard mapping by selecting one of the predefined mappings from the Keyboard Mapping Scheme drop-down list. To change any item in any of the standard keyboard mappings to a key or set of keystrokes that suits you better, select a command from the command list and then move to the Press Shortcut Key(s) field and type the new shortcut key. Click the Assign button to assign the new shortcut. You can save your custom changes to one of the predefined keyboard mappings by selecting the mapping you want to alter using the Use New Shortcut In: drop-down list and then clicking the OK button. Alternatively, you can create a new keyboard mapping by clicking the Save As button and then entering a name. You can remove the keystroke mapping from any command by first selecting the command and then clicking the Remove button.

Using the Debugger

You can step through almost anything using the VS debugger—even generic files such as `Global.asax.cs`. For example, open the `Global.asax.cs` file from your CSharpASP project in the IDE. Find the `Application_BeginRequest` event stub and add a simple `Response.Write` line such as this:

```
protected void Application_BeginRequest(Object sender,
    EventArgs e) {
    Response.Write("<html><body>VBNetWeb<br></body></html>");
}
```

NOTE *The preceding code adds the text* CSharpASP *on the top line of each response in the application. Save the* Global.asax *file.*

Next, create a new folder named `ch9` in your CSharpASP project, and then create a new Web Form named `ch9-1.aspx` in the `ch9` folder. Change the default form ID attribute value to "Form1". You don't need to add code in the Web Form yet.

Setting Breakpoints

Reopen the `Global.asax.cs` file in the code editor, move your cursor to the `Response.Write` line in the `Application_BeginRequest` code, and press F9 to set a breakpoint. The line will turn red (the default breakpoint color). The gray Margin Indicator bar at the left side of the code window shows a red dot when the breakpoint is active and a red dot containing a question mark if VS does not recognize the breakpoint.

Pressing F9 with your cursor on a line toggles the breakpoint on or off. You can also insert or remove breakpoints by clicking the Margin Indicator bar or by right-clicking an *executable* code line (not a variable or method declaration) and selecting New Breakpoint from the context menu.

Press F5 to compile and run the code. VS will launch an instance of IE and attach to the IE and ASP.NET processes. You'll see the browser appear, and then VS will break in the `Application_Begin-Request` code with the cursor on the line where you set the breakpoint. Press F5 again to execute the breakpoint line and continue. Because there are no more breakpoints, the word `CSharpASP` appears in the browser.

Close the browser or click the stop button on the VS toolbar to halt the program and return to the development environment.

Breakpoint Properties

In the `Global.asax.cs` file, right-click the breakpoint line in the `Application_BeginRequest` code and select Breakpoint Properties from the context menu to view the Breakpoint Properties dialog (see Figure 9.5).

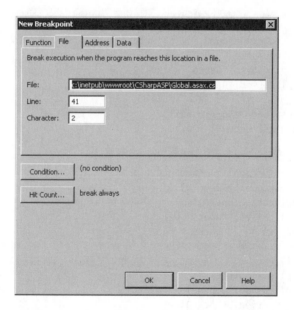

When you load the dialog with a breakpoint already selected, the File, Line, and Character fields are already filled in for you, but you should note that you can set them yourself. For example, if you receive an error message while running some code, you can create a new breakpoint and fill in the information that you obtained from the error message.

It's useful to explore this dialog's properties a little. First, you can set a condition. For example, suppose you want to break only when a variable has the value `true`. Click the Condition button to view the Breakpoint Condition dialog. Enter `Application["Debug"]` into the Condition field. Make sure the Condition check box and the radio button labeled Is True are selected (see Figure 9.6).

FIGURE 9.6

The Breakpoint
Condition dialog

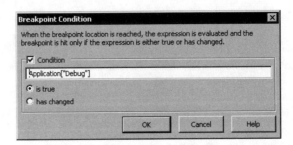

Close the dialog. Leave the breakpoint active in the `Application_BeginRequest` code and press F5 to run the application again. This time, it won't break on the line because the `Application["Debug"]` variable doesn't exist yet. Stop the application, load the `ch9-1.aspx` file into the design editor window, and add a button to the Web Form. Name the button `btnDebug` and give it a text value of `"Debug"`. Double-click the new Debug button and enter the code in Listing 9.1 into the `btnDebug_Click` event.

LISTING 9.1: TEST A BREAKPOINT CONDITION (ch9-1.aspx.cs)

```
private void btnDebug_Click(object sender, System.EventArgs e) {
    int debugCount;
    if (Application["Debug"]== null) {
        Application["Debug"] = false;
    }
    if (Session["Debug"]==null) {
        Session["Debug"] = 0;
    }
    debugCount = (int) Session["Debug"];
    Session["Debug"] = ++debugCount;
    if (debugCount % 2 == 0) {
        Application.Lock();
        Application["Debug"] = true;
        Application.UnLock();
    }
    else {
        Application.Lock();
        Application["Debug"] = false;
        Application.UnLock();
    }
    Response.Write("Session[Debug]=" + Session["Debug"] + "<br>");
    Response.Write("Application[Debug]=" + Application["Debug"] +
        "<br>");
}
```

This rather long example creates an `Application["Debug"]` variable if it doesn't already exist and a `Session["Debug"]` variable and then switches the value of the `Application["Debug"]` variable between `true` and `false` each time you request the page by clicking the button, causing the breakpoint to fire every other time. Run the application to test it.

You can also cause a breakpoint to fire based on the number of times a line executes. Right-click the breakpoint line in the `Application_BeginRequest` code again and select Breakpoint Properties from the context menu to reopen the Breakpoint Properties dialog. Click the Condition button and delete the condition. Next, click the Hit Count button and select the item that reads `Break When the Hit Count Is Equal To` from the When the Breakpoint Is Hit drop-down list (see Figure 9.7).

FIGURE 9.7

The Breakpoint
Hit Count dialog

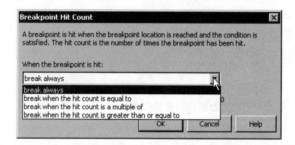

Enter the number **3** into the text field to the right of the drop-down list. Click OK to close the Breakpoint Hit Count dialog, and then click OK to close the Breakpoint Properties dialog. Run the project again. This time, don't click the Debug button, just refresh the form. The second time you refresh it (the third time the browser requests the page), VS will break in the `Global.asax.cs` file in the `Application_BeginRequest` event code.

Stepping Through Code

You don't have to set a breakpoint to debug your code. Often, it's useful to step through your code in the debugger. You have three main options: `Step Into` (F11), `Step Over` (F10), and `Step Out` (Shift+F11), which are the standard VS keyboard mappings for these functions. You can also place the cursor on a line that will execute in the future and select Run to Cursor (Ctrl+F10).

Stepping into code stops execution on each line. When a line calls external code, such as code in a class or another class, VS loads the appropriate code file and highlights the line currently executing. Stepping over code executes the current line without debugging through any called code. Stepping out code bounces you out of the current routine and breaks execution on the line in the parent routine following the call to the routine you were in when you began the step-out operation.

As you work with C# Web applications, you'll eventually write client scripts as well as server-side code. If you develop with IE5 or higher, you can set breakpoints inside client-side script code and step through that with the debugger just as you can with server-side code.

CODE IS READ-ONLY IN VERSION 1

You may be aware of this already, but for those who aren't, I'll mention it anyway. In this version of C#, you can view and even edit code while debugging an application, but any changes you make take effect only after you halt execution and recompile. People migrating to C# from other languages may find this behavior normal; however, if you have a Visual Basic background, you'll find it unnerving.

Read-only debugging is considerably different than the behavior of VB—unfortunately—but it's the price you have to pay, at least temporarily, for the increased power of the .NET framework and C#. The classic VB feature that lets you edit code while the program is executing is called Break-Edit-Continue, and it is sorely missed because the edit-compile cycle, while fairly quick, is not even close to the change time when you can edit running code. Fortunately, C# partially makes up for the missing feature because of its strong typing and better IntelliSense. Finally, Microsoft has promised to add the Break-Edit-Continue feature in the next version of the framework—as a core part of the framework—which means it may apply to C# and other .NET languages as well as to a future version of VB.NET.

I'm not trying to teach you how to debug just for the sake of debugging, but it's the best way to see how ASP.NET events occur. In the next section, you'll use the Step Into feature of the debugger to follow the ASP.NET event sequence in detail.

ASP.NET Event Sequence

You need to know exactly when events occur—and what events you can trap—to take full advantage of the ASP.NET environment. You've already seen that you can begin trapping errors even before code execution begins in your page by writing code and setting a breakpoint in the `Application_Begin-Request` event. But when you first begin an application, that's not the first event; in fact, it's not even the second. The only memorable way to discover how ASP handles events is to step through the code.

When you first create an ASP.NET application, VS creates a new `Global.asax` file and a code-behind file named `Global.asax.cs`. The file contains "stub" code for eight events:

◆ `Application_Start`

◆ `Session_Start`

◆ `Application_BeginRequest`

◆ `Application_EndRequest`

◆ `Application_AuthenticateRequest`

◆ `Application_Error`

◆ `Session_End`

◆ `Application_End`

There are many more events to which you can respond if necessary, but they're not implemented by default. Load the `Global.asax` file into the VS editor, and then click the Events button on the Properties pane toolbar. Next, click the arrow on the method drop-down list in the right pane. You'll see more than a dozen events that you can handle in code, but there are handleable events that don't show up in the VS.NET event method list. You'll see them in the code below.

The ASP.NET intrinsic objects such as the `Response` object and the `Session` object are not always available for every event, because some events (such as `Application_Start`) occur before the ASP.NET engine creates the objects. Therefore, the code in Listing 9.2 uses the `Debug.WriteLine` method to write event sequence data to the output window.

NOTE   *Most of the code in the* `Global.asax` *file on* **www.sybex.com** *has been commented out so that it doesn't interfere with running code in the rest of the project. To run the code in this chapter, uncomment the appropriate methods. When you finish this chapter, you should comment out the code again.*

LISTING 9.2: `Global.asax.cs` **FILE WITH ALL POSSIBLE EVENTS IMPLEMENTED**
             (`Global.asax.cs`)

```
using System;
using System.Collections;
using System.ComponentModel;
using System.Web;
using System.Web.SessionState;
using System.Diagnostics;

namespace CSharpASP
{
   /// <summary>
   /// Summary description for Global.
   /// </summary>
   public class Global : System.Web.HttpApplication
   {
      public Global()
      {
         InitializeComponent();
      }

      #region Web Form Designer generated code
      // autogenerated code omitted from this listing
      #endregion

      protected void Application_Start(Object sender, EventArgs e)
      {
         /* // Uncomment this code for Chapter 6,
            // Listing 6.13 (Web Form 6-15)
         if (Application.Get("StartEventCount") != null) {
            int count = (int) Application.Get("StartEventCount");
            count++;
            Application.Lock();
            Application.Set("StartEventCount",(int) count);
            Application.UnLock();
         }
         else {
            Application.Lock();
            Application.Set("StartEventCount",1);
            Application.UnLock();
         }*/
```

```csharp
        Debug.WriteLine("Application_Start");
}

protected void Session_Start(Object sender, EventArgs e)
{
    Debug.WriteLine("Session_Start");
}

private void Application_AuthenticateRequest
    (object sender, System.EventArgs e) {
    Debug.WriteLine(Request.ServerVariables["LOGON_USER"]);
    Debug.WriteLine("Global_AuthenticateRequest");
}


protected void Application_BeginRequest
    (Object sender, EventArgs e)
{
    /* // Uncomment this code for Chapter 6,
       // Listing 6-13 (Web Form 6-15)
    if (Application.Get("BeginRequestCount") != null) {
        int count = (int) Application.Get("BeginRequestCount");
        count++;
        Application.Lock();
        Application.Set("BeginRequestCount",(int) count);
        Application.UnLock();
    }
    else {
        Application.Lock();
        Application.Set("BeginRequestCount",1);
        Application.UnLock();
    }*/

}

protected void Application_EndRequest(Object sender,
    EventArgs e) {
    // Uncomment the following code line for the
    // Application_EndRequest example in Chapter 6
    // Response.Write("CSharpASP application ending " +
    //     "request at: " +
    //     DateTime.Now.ToLongDateString());
}

protected void Application_Error(Object sender, EventArgs e) {
    /* // Uncomment this code for Chapter 6,
       // Listing 6.13 (Web Form 6-15)
    String sErr = "";
```

```
        sErr = "An error occurred on page " + Request.FilePath;
        sErr += " at " + DateTime.Now.ToString() + ".  ";
        sErr += "Error: " + Server.GetLastError().Message;
        sErr += System.Environment.NewLine;
        sErr += "Stack trace: ";
        sErr += Server.GetLastError().StackTrace;
        System.Diagnostics.EventLog.WriteEntry("CSharpASP",
    sErr);
        */
    }

    protected void Session_End(Object sender, EventArgs e) {
        // Debug.WriteLine("Session_End");
    }


    protected void Application_End(Object sender, EventArgs e)
    {
        /* // Uncomment the following code for the
           // Application_End example in Chapter 6
        System.Diagnostics.EventLog evtLog =
            new System.Diagnostics.EventLog();
        DateTime dTime = DateTime.Now;
        evtLog.Source = "Application";
        evtLog.MachineName = "."; // local machine
        evtLog.WriteEntry("CSharpASP application ending at: " +
            dTime.ToLongDateString());
        */
    }


    private void Global_AuthorizeRequest(object sender,
        System.EventArgs e) {
        // Debug.WriteLine("Application_AuthorizeRequest");
    }
private void Global_AuthenticateRequest(object sender,
    System.EventArgs e){
    //Fires upon attempting to authenticate the user
    //Debug.WriteLine(Request.ServerVariables
        ["LOGON_USER "]);
    //Debug.WriteLine("Application_AuthenticateRequest ");
}
private void Global_Error(object sender,
    System.EventArgs e) {
    //Fires when an error occurs
    //Debug.WriteLine("Global_Error event occurred ");
}
```

```
private void Global_AcquireRequestState(object sender,
   System.EventArgs e) {
   // Debug.WriteLine("Global_AcquireRequestState");
}

private void Global_BeginRequest(object sender,
   System.EventArgs e) {
   // Debug.WriteLine("Global_BeginRequest");
}

private void Global_Disposed(object sender,
   System.EventArgs e) {
   // Debug.WriteLine("Disposed");
}

private void Global_EndRequest(object sender,
   System.EventArgs e) {
   // Debug.WriteLine("Global_EndRequest");
}

private void Global_PostRequestHandlerExecute(object sender,
   System.EventArgs e) {
   // Debug.WriteLine("Global_PostRequestHandlerExecute");
}

private void Global_PreRequestHandlerExecute(object sender,
   System.EventArgs e) {
   // Debug.WriteLine("Global_PreRequestHandlerExecute");
}

private void Global_PreSendRequestContent(object sender,
   System.EventArgs e) {
   // Debug.WriteLine("Global_PreSendRequestContent");
}

private void Global_PreSendRequestHeaders(object sender,
   System.EventArgs e) {
   // Debug.WriteLine("Global_PreSendRequestHeaders");
}

private void Global_ReleaseRequestState(object sender,
   System.EventArgs e) {
   // Debug.WriteLine("Global_ReleaseRequestState");
}

private void Global_ResolveRequestCache(object sender,
   System.EventArgs e) {
```

```
        // Debug.WriteLine("Global_ResolveRequestCache");
    }

    private void Global_UpdateRequestCache(object sender,
        System.EventArgs e) {
        // Debug.WriteLine("Global_UpdateRequestCache");
    }
  }
}
```

The code shown in Listing 9.2 is commented out in the CSharpASP project's `Global.asax.cs` file on **www.sybex.com**. Uncomment the code, set the `ch9-1.aspx` file as the start page, make sure you can see the Output window, and then run the application. The output will look similar to this (you may have additional symbol loading lines between the coded output lines):

```
Init
Global_BeginRequest
Application_BeginRequest
Global_AuthenticateRequest
Application_AuthenticateRequest
Global_AuthorizeRequest
Application_AuthorizeRequest
Global_ResolveRequestCache
Global_AcquireRequestState
Global_PreRequestHandlerExecute
Global_PostRequestHandlerExecute
Global_ReleaseRequestState
Global_UpdateRequestCache
Global_PreSendRequestHeaders
Global_PreSendRequestContent
```

As you can see, not all the trappable events are exposed directly through the VB.NET IDE. While I can't think of a good reason to implement both `Global_BeginRequest` and `Application_Begin-Request`—or any of the other dual implementations shown in Listing 9.2—doing so doesn't cause an error. Table 9.1 shows a description of each event.

TABLE 9.1: ASP.NET APPLICATION-LEVEL EVENTS

EVENT	EVENT FIRES WHEN ASP.NET ...
Init	Creates the `HttpApplicationState` instance for this request
Application_BeginRequest	Begins the request process
Application_AuthenticateRequest	Begins the authentication process
Application_AuthorizeRequest	Completes the authentication process

Continued on next page

TABLE 9.1: ASP.NET APPLICATION-LEVEL EVENTS *(continued)*

EVENT	EVENT FIRES WHEN ASP.NET ...
Global_ResolveRequestCache	Checks the cache to see if the page can be served from an existing in-memory copy
Global_AcquireRequestState	Retrieves the HttpSessionState object for this request
Global_PreRequestHandlerExecute	Begins to handle the request
Global_PostRequestHandlerExecute	Completes the handling of the request
Global_ReleaseRequestState	Releases the HttpSessionState object for this request
Global_UpdateRequestCache	Updates the in-memory cache for this request
Global_PreSendRequestHeaders	Begins sending the Response headers
Global_PreSendRequestContent	Begins sending the Response body

You need to set breakpoints in the events to step through them—simply pressing F11 doesn't help in this situation. Set a breakpoint on each `Debug.WriteLine` in the `Global.asax.cs` file, and then run the application. Watch the Output window for the results. When you're satisfied with the results, you should comment out the `Debug.WriteLine` statements and remove the breakpoints.

Using Trace Output

Implementing every possible event routine is useful for getting an overall picture of when events occur—and it's the only way to step through the `Global.asax` events, but it isn't very efficient. Another way to get a good overall picture is to enable tracing. *Tracing* collects internal execution data and formats it so that you can get a good picture of what's going on in your page or application. You can enable tracing for a single page or for an entire application, and you can control whether tracing occurs only when you run the application locally (on the server machine) or remotely (traces requests from any machine). Enabling tracing at the application level also enables page-level tracing.

Tracing is better experienced than described. Here's how to enable tracing for your entire application:

1. Open the `web.config` file and scroll down until you see this line:

   ```
   <trace enabled="false" requestLimit="10"
       pageOutput="false" traceMode="SortByTime"
       localOnly="true" />
   ```

2. Change the line so it reads as follows:

   ```
   <trace enabled="true" requestLimit="10"
       pageOutput="true" traceMode="SortByTime"
       localOnly="false" />
   ```

3. Save the `web.config` file.

The changes enable tracing throughout the application (`trace enabled="true"`) and tell the ASP.NET engine to format the trace output, append it to the page output (`pageOutput="true"`), and trace all requests, both those from the server machine itself and those from remote computers (`localOnly="false"`).

To test the output, create a new Web Form named `ch9-2.aspx` and change the default form ID attribute value to "Form1". Don't add any controls or code to the page, but set it as the start page. Tracing works regardless of which page you have set as the start page, but the output from a Web Form can interfere with the trace output (depending on the layout mode). Using a blank Web Form makes the trace information clean. Now run the application. You'll see output similar to Figures 9.8, 9.9, 9.10, and 9.11—tracing produces several screens of information.

NOTE *Tracing is a debugging operation. Unlike* **Debug** *statements, which are not included when you compile your application in Release mode,* **trace** *statements are compiled in Release mode. Trace operations execute at runtime, so tracing can slow down your application considerably. However, you can leave* **trace** *statements in your page and disable tracing, which causes the ASP.NET engine to ignore the statements.*

FIGURE 9.8

Trace output with tracing enabled in the **web.config** file (screen 1)

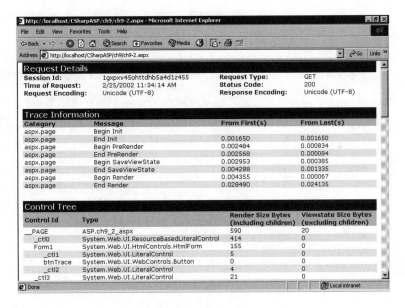

FIGURE 9.9

Trace output with
tracing enabled in
the web.config file
(screen 2)

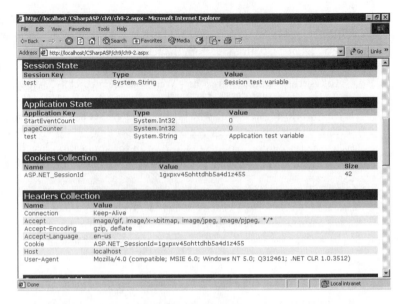

FIGURE 9.10

Trace output with
tracing enabled in
the web.config file
(screen 3)

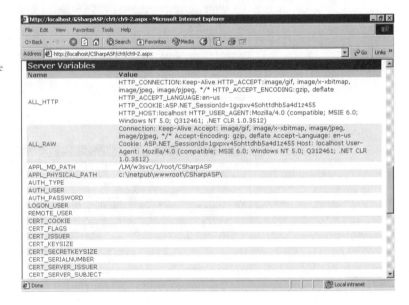

FIGURE 9.11

Trace output with tracing enabled in the `web.config` file (screen 4)

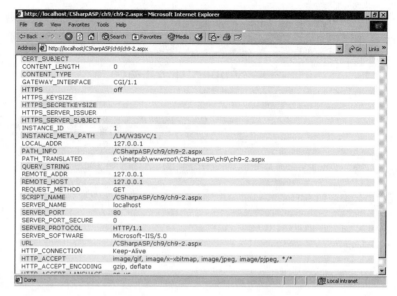

As you can see, tracing is much simpler than writing `Response.Write` statements or loops to display cookies, header variables, or `Request.Server` variables. For production applications, you should never enable tracing to remote machines; instead, set the trace attribute (`localOnly="true"`) to limit tracing to requests from the local (server) machine itself; otherwise, the trace information will appear on your users' screens.

While tracing output to the screen can be extremely useful, it doesn't work well with pages that have output formatted in GridLayout mode and that target CSS-enabled browsers. ASP.NET creates those pages using absolute positioning, which means the page output appears on top of the trace information (which is not formatted with absolute positioning). For these pages, which will probably represent the bulk of your ASP.NET Web Forms, set the `pageOutput` trace attribute to false (`pageOutput="false"`). Doing this doesn't disable tracing; it simply switches the trace output to a trace utility named `trace.axd` that ASP.NET creates in the root directory for your application. `Trace.axd` is an `HttpHandler` that intercepts the request and displays the trace results from memory.

The only way to view the trace data is to request it from a browser. For example, run your application with the Web Form `ch9-2`. Refresh the page several times and then type the URL **http://localhost/CSharpASP/trace.axd** into your browser (you may need to adjust the URL to point to your local CSharpASP application root). You'll see a page like that in Figure 9.12.

FIGURE 9.12

Viewing trace output via the `trace.axd` HttpHandler

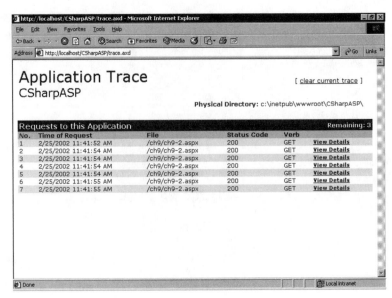

The trace listing has one entry for each traced request, up to the number of requests specified by the `requestLimit` attribute in the trace element in your `web.config` file.

```
<trace enabled="true" requestLimit="10" pageOutput="false"
    traceMode="SortByTime" localOnly="false" />
```

Click the `View Details` link to view the trace output for that request. The trace output itself is identical to the trace output shown earlier in Figures 9.8 through 9.11, so I won't repeat it here.

The tracing engine stops tracing after it reaches the limit set by the `requestLimit` attribute—tracing doesn't work in a round-robin fashion. Instead, the attribute value controls the total number of traced requests. After reaching the limit, you can clear the trace using the `Clear Current Trace` link in the upper-right corner of the `trace.axd` page.

You don't have to trace-enable your entire application. You can enable and disable tracing for any individual page by adding the trace attributes to the `@Page` directive. For example, restore the original `web.config` trace element settings to disable application-level tracing:

```
<trace enabled="false" requestLimit="10" pageOutput="false"
    traceMode="SortByTime" localOnly="true" />
```

Open the `ch9-2.aspx` file in the editor, and add a `trace="true"` attribute to the `@Page` directive.

NOTE   *The trace attributes* `requestLimit`, `pageOutput`, *and* `localOnly` *are not supported at the page level, only in the* `web.config` *file.*

Save and run the Web Form. You'll see the trace output in your browser. You can remove the `trace="true"` attribute or set the attribute value to `"false"` to disable tracing. You should experiment with tracing—especially if you've worked with classic ASP and have old debug code to look at, because tracing shows you many of the values that you had to code by hand in classic ASP. For now, leave tracing enabled for the `ch9-2` Web Form; you'll need it in the next section.

Tracing from Code

Enabling tracing at the application or page level gives you gross tracing information, but you can get fine-grained trace information by using the `Trace` object exposed by the `Page` object. You've already seen how to use the `Debug.WriteLine` method to write debugging information to the Output window. The Trace class works exactly the same way as the Debug class, except that, as I mentioned earlier, trace operations work even after you compile your project in Release mode. However, you can force ASP.NET to ignore `trace` statements by removing the `trace="true"` attribute or setting the value to `false`.

For example, suppose you want to know the value of a `Session` variable at a specific point in your code. Enabling tracing for the entire page may not show you the value at that specific point. Instead, use the `Trace` object to write trace output.

Add a button to the `ch9-2` Web Form. Name the button `btnTrace` and set its `Text` property to `Trace Test`. You should either set the Web Form's `pageLayout` property to `FlowLayout` or move the button to the right edge of the Web Form so that it doesn't interfere with the trace output. Add the following two lines of code to the `Page_Load` method:

```
Application["test"] = "Application test variable"
Session["test"] = "Session test variable"
```

Double-click the Trace Test button and add the following three lines to the `btnTrace_Click` event stub:

```
Trace.Write("Trace enabled on this page=" +
    Trace.IsEnabled.ToString());
Trace.Write("Trace test: " + Application["test"]);
Trace.Write("Trace test: " + Session["test"]);
```

Save your changes and, with tracing enabled in the `@Page` directive for the `ch9-2` Web Form, run the application. Click the Trace Test button to post the page back to the server, and then take a close look at the resulting trace output (see Figures 9.13 and 9.14).

NOTE *The remainder of the trace output for the Web Form* `ch9-2` *(not shown in Figures 9.13 and 9.14) consists of the Headers Collection section and the Server Variables section that you've already seen in Figures 9.9, 9.10, and 9.11.*

FIGURE 9.13

Trace output with explicit `Trace.Write` results (screen 1)

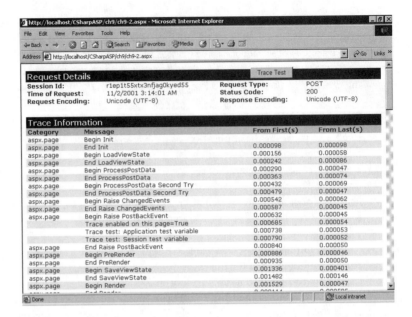

FIGURE 9.14

Trace output with explicit `Trace.Write` results (screen 2)

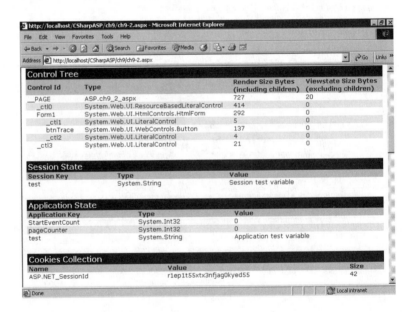

There are several interesting points in the output. First, notice that the Request Type is POST. All the preceding examples used the GET method. Next, note that the series of operations in the Trace Information section looks considerably different from the events you saw in the Global.asax file. However, they do follow the track you have probably intuited from working through the examples so far—the page initializes (Init); loads and parses the posted _VIEWSTATE data (LoadViewState);

processes any data posted by the user, comparing it to the existing _VIEWSTATE data to determine whether changes are made (`ProcessPostData`); and then fires control events (`PostBackEvent`). In this case, because you clicked the button, the page fires the `btnTrace_Click` event, which causes the `Trace.Write` statements to execute—they appear in the trace output a few lines from the bottom of Figure 9.13.

The point of all this (in addition to showing you the ASP.NET event sequence) is that you don't use the `trace.axd` "file" to view trace output generated by `Trace.Write` statements. Instead, they're placed directly into the page trace output. Note that by setting the `@Page` trace attribute to `true`, you generated trace output for the page even though the enabled attribute in the `web.config` file's trace element is `false`.

Also note that adding `Session` and `Application` variables caused the trace output to add `Session State` and `Application State` sections to the output.

Defensive Coding: How to Avoid Errors

The best approach to handling errors is to eliminate them. Unfortunately, as long as I've been coding, I haven't learned how to do that in all cases. In some cases, errors are beyond your control. Hardware breaks down, networks are sometimes unreliable, files get lost or moved, resource names change—the list of possibilities is endless. Even if such errors aren't your responsibility, it's your job to handle them insofar as it's possible for you to do that at the application level. You must realize that when you're working on your development machine, your program runs in the perfect environment; it's like a fledgling in a nest, "protected" by your knowledge and control of the environment. When you deliver the program, it leaves the nest; it has to stand on its own two feet, so to speak. The environment is likely to be different—sometimes very different—and the application will break unless you practice defensive coding.

Defensive coding is not the defining characteristic of a paranoid programmer but, rather, of an intelligent programmer. A lack of good error-handling examples is one of the worst things about many magazine articles and books on programming—including this one. Admittedly, there are good reasons for this omission. The volume of error-handling code sometimes visually overshadows the code that does the real work. Even more often, there's not enough room or time to add the error-handling code—yet programmers often copy the code into their applications and expect it to work perfectly.

You saw a brief example of validation in Chapter 5, "Introduction to Web Forms," where the `RequiredFieldValidator` controls prevented the user from submitting the form if it contained blank fields. That's one example of defensive coding. By preventing the problem from occurring in the first place, you don't have to handle the errors that inevitably arise if you don't prevent them.

In the real world, people enter numbers where they're supposed to write letters; they mistype dates; they leave out required information; and they unwittingly add spaces, carriage returns, and control characters to their input. For example, the passwords `"123456"` and `"123456 "` are not the same—the second password has a space at the end. In ASP.NET, you can use `RegularExpressionValidator` controls to solve many input problems, but sometimes you will still need to write validation code yourself.

Input validation is just one area where you need to code defensively. Any external resources used by your program make up another potentially large source of errors. External resources are files, directories, databases, COM DLLs, Web services, or any other source of information or code required by your program that doesn't reside within your program—in other words, anything you didn't code yourself and anything you don't control. You may think these resources are static, but they aren't. People move and rename files and directories—even executable files. A database location may change, newer (or sometimes older) installations may overwrite critical DLLs, and servers may change names. Permission levels may change when administrators change machines or when users move from one group to another. Even date formats may become obsolete—witness the enormous amount of money spent recently to upgrade systems that used two-digit years. You may not be able to control all these changes, but that really doesn't matter. Coding defensively is an attitude you use to force yourself to think about the potential for things to go wrong. Control those things you can, write good error messages for those you can't, but whatever you do, trap all errors, all the time.

In classic ASP, especially in the earlier versions, scripting languages had extremely weak error-handling capabilities. Fortunately, the ASP engine itself trapped errors; otherwise, an errant script could crash the server and potentially damage other applications.

With ASP.NET, the situation has improved considerably. Every language has strong error trapping, and one language can trap errors thrown by code written in another language. You still can't crash the ASP.NET engine (or at least, not easily). Unfortunately, even with all the improvements, there's no panacea—you'll be struggling with errors for your entire programming career—but in this chapter, you'll learn several ways to help you prevent errors and—failing that—find out where errors occurred.

Approaching Error Handling

One way to approach the understanding of a large subject is to categorize it into smaller chunks. There are five main categories of errors:

◆ Syntax errors

◆ Parameter/input errors

◆ Logic errors

◆ External code errors

◆ Resource errors

Your goals in trapping these types of errors should be, in order of importance, the following:

1. Keep your application from crashing.

2. Provide as much information as possible about the error.

3. Propagate errors back to a critical decision point.

4. Degrade gracefully.

In an ASP.NET application, it's very difficult to crash the application—the ASP.NET engine won't let that happen—but by default, any error that occurs on a page causes the ASP.NET engine to stop executing the code on that page. To your users, it doesn't matter whether your application crashed. If users can't accomplish their goals, then your program is broken, no matter what the reason. For error-handling purposes, each page of your application is a program unto itself. Therefore, the first goal is to make the page run properly.

If you can't fix an error in code, the second goal is to write an informative error message to the user, who in response may inform you of the error, and also to a log file or the Application event log. The more information you provide about the error, the easier it will be for you to find and fix it. You don't want your page to stop processing—even with good error messages—if you can work around the error, so you'll want to categorize errors based on how they affect your application. For example, input errors should never be fatal; you should trap them all and provide reasonable error messages so the user or programmer providing the information can solve the problem.

The third goal—to propagate errors back to a critical decision point—refers to the process of trapping errors in lower-level routines. When an error occurs in a low-level routine, the error is trapped and passes upward through the call stack until the error reaches a critical decision point. In an ASP.NET script, the critical decision point is usually the code running on that page.

During development, you should focus primarily on the first two goals. In some cases, you won't have enough information to do more than approach the third goal during initial development. Later in the development cycle, after several users have tested your application, you should be able to improve your error handling to solve common problems. Save the fourth goal until last. It does you no good to spend lots of time degrading gracefully if that causes you to miss fatal errors that crash the application.

ERROR HANDLING IN C#

Errors in the .NET framework and in C# throw *exceptions*. As you may expect by now, the framework uses classes derived from a base Exception class. The Common Language Runtime (CLR) common errors derive from a SystemException class, while any custom Exception classes you create should derive from ApplicationException. The basic error-trapping and -handling structure in C# is the `try-catch-finally` block. For example, the Web Form `ch9-3.aspx` code-behind file contains code that causes a divide by zero exception. Set it as the start page and run the application. You'll see the error message in Figure 9.15.

FIGURE 9.15

DivideByZero-
Exception error
message

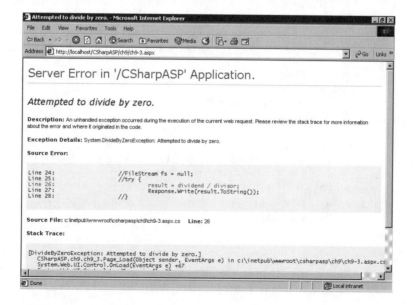

NOTE   *Causing an exception via dividing by zero in C# is more difficult than you might think. For example, writing the code* result = 5 / 0 *immediately underlines the* 5 / 0 *portion of the line, with the warning* This constant expression produces a value that is not representable in type 'Integer'. *Similarly, using the line* Response.Write((5 / 0).ToString()) *didn't produce the expected error—instead, the word "Infinity" appeared in the browser. In other words, watch out! You may not get the result you expect, even from this simple, if invalid, operation!*

TRY-CATCH-FINALLY EXCEPTION HANDLING

To trap the exception, you enclose the code in a try-catch-finally block. The finally clause of the block is optional. For example, in its simplest form—try-catch—the block looks like the following:

```
int result;
int divisor = 0;
int dividend = 5;
try {
   result = dividend / divisor;
   Response.Write(result.ToString());
}
catch (Exception ex) {
   Response.Write(String.Concat(ex.Message + "<br>"));
}
```

NOTE   *The* try-catch *block already exists in the* ch9-3.aspx.cs *file on* www.sybex.com *but has been commented out. Uncomment the* try-catch *block to handle the exception.*

The code attempts to execute the statements after the try statement. When the exception occurs, execution jumps to the catch statement. The variable ex "catches" the exception, and execution resumes with the Response.Write statement that displays the error message (ex.Message).

For added safety, you can include code that *always* executes, whether an error occurs or not. For example, suppose you want to display the HTML from a file named ch9-X.aspx in the browser, but the file doesn't exist. Ignore for a moment the fact that you should *always* test files before opening them, and—solely for example purposes—pretend that you might actually write code this bad:

```
FileStream fs = null;
try {
   fs = File.Open(Page.MapPath("ch9-X.aspx"), FileMode.Open);
   fs.Close();
}
catch (Exception ex) {
   Response.Write(String.Concat(ex.Message +  "<br>"));
}
finally {
   if (fs != null) {
      fs.Close();
   }
}
```

The attempt to open the nonexistent file causes an error. The code creates a FileStream object variable. The try block attempts to open the file, and the catch block displays the error, and then the finally block executes. However, if you simply write fs.Close(), you'll cause another error because the fs variable is Null—it never gets set. In other words, there's nothing special about code in finally blocks that prevents errors from occurring inside them. You must be just as careful with code in a finally block as you would be with any other code. Therefore, the finally block checks explicitly for a null reference before attempting to close the FileStream.

The code shown catches *any* exception, but you can filter exceptions so that you can respond differently to different errors. To do this, you would include multiple catch blocks, each of which would respond to a different exception or set of exceptions. For example:

```
FileStream fs = null;
try {
    fs = File.Open(Page.MapPath("ch9-X.aspx"), FileMode.Open);
    fs.Close();
}
catch (FileNotFoundException ex) {
    Response.Write(String.Concat(ex.Message +  "<br>"));
}
catch (Exception ex) {
    Response.Write(String.Concat(ex.Message +  "<br>"));
}
finally {
    if (fs != null) {
        fs.Close();
    }
}
```

NOTE *This code also exists in the* ch9-3.aspx.cs *file on* www.sybex.com *but is commented out.*

Although each exception has its own class, they all inherit from the base Exception class. While you could create a custom Exception class that implemented additional features, it would not be a good idea because an implicit cast from your custom Exception object to a base Exception object (as shown in the two preceding code examples—catch ex) would fail. Table 9.2 shows the properties and methods of the base Exception object; I've omitted properties and methods that the Exception class inherits from Object.

TABLE 9.2: PROPERTIES AND METHODS OF THE BASE Exception OBJECT

PROPERTY/METHOD	DESCRIPTION
HelpLink property	URL to an associated help topic.
Hresult property	Sets or returns an HRESULT—use to retrieve the error code returned from a Windows API call.
InnerException property	May contain an exception thrown by code lower on the stack. Exceptions raised from lower-level code often assign the preceding Exception object to the InnerException property, letting you track the progress of errors as they rise through the call stack.

Continued on next page

TABLE 9.2: PROPERTIES AND METHODS OF THE BASE Exception OBJECT *(continued)*

PROPERTY/METHOD	DESCRIPTION
Message property	A string containing a description of the error.
Source property	A string that describes the object or the application that caused the error. You can set this property explicitly, but by default, the Source property contains the name of the assembly where the error occurred.
StackTrace property	You should be ecstatic over this one—I know I am. The StackTrace shows the execution stack at the time the error occurred. In many languages prior to .NET, you had to code this feature yourself, which most programmers did not do.
TargetSite property	Returns the method (a MethodBase object) that encapsulates the method that threw the exception. This is extremely helpful because it can show you the parameter types and values for the method when the error occurred.
GetBaseException method	Returns the original (root) exception, thrown by the method returned from the TargetSite property.
GetObjectData method	Used to serialize an exception.
ToString method	You should override this method for custom Exception classes. The System Exception classes return a string containing the name of the exception, the error message, the name of an inner exception, and the stack trace—the information that you see by default in the browser when ASP.NET throws an exception.

THROWING EXCEPTIONS

You can throw exceptions as well as catch them. For example, suppose you build a Search class for your application. You want to differentiate between invalid search entries and searches that don't result in any hits; therefore, you can create an InvalidSearchEntry exception class and throw that exception when a user enters an invalid string. This particular application throws a custom InvalidSearchEntry exception whenever the user enters a blank search term or one that contains any spaces or capital letters. You must inherit your Exception classes from the System.ApplicationException class.

Listing 9.3 shows the code for the custom InvalidSearchEntry exception class.

LISTING 9.3: THE INVALIDSEARCHENTRY CUSTOM EXCEPTION CLASS

```csharp
using System;

namespace CSharpASP.ch9 {
    /// <summary>
    /// Summary description for InvalidSearchEntryException.
    /// </summary>
    public class InvalidSearchEntryException : ApplicationException {
        public enum InvalidSearchEntryEnum : int {
            InvalidSearchTerm=0,
            ContainsSpace=1,
```

```
            ContainsCaps=2
        }
        InvalidSearchEntryEnum m_invalidSearchEntry;
        public InvalidSearchEntryException(InvalidSearchEntryEnum
            invalidSearchEntry) {
            m_invalidSearchEntry = invalidSearchEntry;
        }
        public override String Message {
            get {
                switch (m_invalidSearchEntry) {
                    case InvalidSearchEntryEnum.InvalidSearchTerm :
                        return "The search engine encountered " +
                            "an invalid search term.";
                    case InvalidSearchEntryEnum.ContainsCaps  :
                        return "Search terms may not contain " +
                            "capital letters.";
                    case InvalidSearchEntryEnum.ContainsSpace :
                        return "Search terms may not contain spaces.";
                    default :
                        return "Unknown search error.";
                }
            }
        }

    public override String ToString() {
        System.Text.StringBuilder sb = new
            System.Text.StringBuilder(1000);
        sb.Append("<span style='color: red; font-size: 14px'>" +
            "<b>Invalid Search Term</b></span><br>");
        sb.Append(this.GetType().FullName +  "<br>");
        sb.Append("<b>Error Number</b>: " +  this.HResult +
            "<br>");
        sb.Append("Source</b>: " + this.Source +
            "<p> </p>");
        sb.Append("<b>Stack Trace</b>: " +  "<br>" +
            this.StackTrace);
        return (sb.ToString());
    }


    }
}
```

Note that the class overrides the Message and ToString methods inherited from Application-Exception, and that it has two constructors—a default constructor that takes no arguments and a second version that takes one of two InvalidSearchEntryEnum enumeration values: either Contains-Space or ContainsCaps. The passed enumeration value sets an internal flag that influences the Message property value, letting the error message be more explicit.

Run the ch9-4.aspx Web Form and enter some text into the Search In field. Enter a string to search for into the Search For field and then click the Search button. In the Result field the letters "et" in etudes will appear in red. Try the Web Form with both valid search terms (no spaces or capital letters in the Search For field—see Figure 9.16) and with invalid terms (see Figure 9.17).

FIGURE 9.16

The ch9-4.aspx Web Form after searching with a valid search term

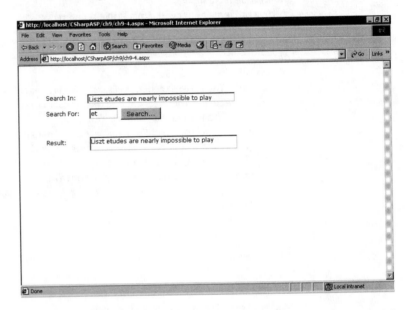

FIGURE 9.17

The ch9-4.aspx Web Form error display after searching with an invalid search term

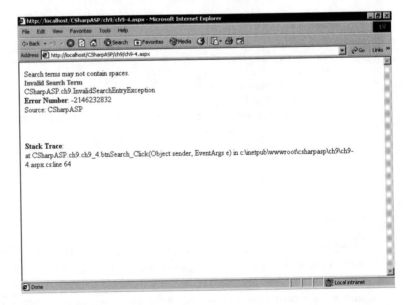

Listing 9.4 shows the code that executes when you click the Search button.

LISTING 9.4: CLICKING THE SEARCH BUTTON IN THE WEB FORM ch9-4.aspx **THROWS AN ERROR IF THE SEARCH TERM CONTAINS SPACES OR CAPITAL LETTERS**

```
private void btnSearch_Click(object sender, System.EventArgs e) {
    String srchIn, srchFor;
    int foundIndex;
    srchIn = txtSearchIn.Text;
    srchFor = txtSearchFor.Text;
    try {
        if ((srchIn == "") || (srchFor == "")) {
            throw new InvalidSearchEntryException
                (InvalidSearchEntryException.InvalidSearchEntryEnum.
                InvalidSearchTerm);
        }
        else if (srchFor.IndexOf(" ") > 0) {
            throw new InvalidSearchEntryException
            (InvalidSearchEntryException.InvalidSearchEntryEnum.
            ContainsSpace);
        }
        else if (srchFor.ToLower() != srchFor) {
            throw new InvalidSearchEntryException
            (InvalidSearchEntryException.InvalidSearchEntryEnum.
            ContainsCaps);
        }
        else {
            foundIndex = srchIn.IndexOf(srchFor);
            if (foundIndex >= 0) {
                lblResult.Text = srchIn.Substring(0, foundIndex) +
                "<b><font color='red'>" +
    srchIn.Substring(foundIndex,
                srchFor.Length) + "</b></font>" +
                srchIn.Substring(foundIndex + srchFor.Length);
            }
            else {
                lblResult.Text = "Search term not found.";
            }
        }
    }
    catch (InvalidSearchEntryException ex) {
        Response.Write(ex.Message + "<br>");
        Response.Write(ex.ToString());
        Response.End();
    }
}
```

In the next section, you'll see how to intercept the standard ASP error-handling mechanism so that you can handle errors yourself or customize the error display.

INTERCEPTING PAGE-LEVEL ERRORS

The Page class exposes an `Error` event, which the ASP.NET engine fires whenever an *untrapped* error occurs. Interestingly, this event does not show up in the event list in C# for the `Page` object. The event does *not* fire for trapped errors. To prove that, you'll override the event. Load the `ch9-4.aspx.cs` file into the editor and enter an event handler declaration for the `Error` event:

```
private void Page_Error(object sender, System.EventArgs e) {
    // error-handling code here
}
```

NOTE   *The `Page_Error` event code is commented out on www.sybex.com. Uncomment it to test the code in this section.*

At this point, it doesn't matter what the `Page_Error` subroutine does—it's just important to find out when it fires. Write anything you like into the `Page_Error` subroutine; for example:

```
private void Page_Error(object sender, System.EventArgs e) {
    Response.Write("An error event occurred.");
    Response.End();
}
```

You have to add a delegate for the new event. Although Visual Studio places automatically generated delegates in the `InitializeComponent` method, you should not alter that code, because changes to the Web Form may overwrite your modifications. Instead, create the delegate during the `Page_Load` method.

```
this.Error += new System.EventHandler(this.Page_Error);
```

Set a breakpoint on the first `Response.Write` statement in the `Page_Error` event (you *do* have to enter at least one executable line to set the breakpoint), and then run the application. Does the event fire? It shouldn't, because you trapped the errors using the `try-catch` block in the `btnSearch` click event code. Comment out the `catch` block (you'll need to add a `finally` block to get the code to compile) and then compile and run the page again. This time, the breakpoint should fire, and you should see the output in the browser. An alternate version (commented out in the code) uses the `Server.Transfer` method to transfer execution to a custom error file.

```
private void Page_Error(object sender, System.EventArgs e) {
    Response.Write("An error event occurred.");
    Server.Transfer("customErrors.aspx", false);
    //Response.End();
}
```

Note that you need either the `Response.End()` line *or* the `Server.Transfer` line, but not both. When you run this alternate version, IIS transfers program execution to the `customErrors.aspx` Web Form to write error information to the client.

The `customErrors.aspx` file uses the `Server.GetLastError` method to retrieve the error information for display:

```
private void Page_Load(object sender, System.EventArgs e) {
    Exception ex;
    ex = Server.GetLastError();
    if (ex != null) {
        Response.Write("Error Description: " + ex.Message);
    }
    else {
        Response.Write("No errors.");
    }
}
```

NOTE   *Comment out or delete the overridden* `Page_Error` *handler and the delegate in the* `Page_Load` *event before you continue.*

If you don't handle an error at the `Page` level, you can still trap it at Application scope.

INTERCEPTING ERRORS AT APPLICATION SCOPE

If an error slips past your `Page`-level error handling, you can intercept it in the `Global.asax.cs` file by implementing the `Global_Error` event handler. To intercept the errors, override the `Global_Error` event in the `Global.asax.cs` file just as you did to intercept `Page` errors in the preceding section. Because the process is identical, I won't repeat it here. The `Global_Error` event handler is your last opportunity to handle an error before ASP.NET passes it to the default error handler. At this point, you cannot recover from an error, but you can still make the error display a little friendlier—and you can still log errors (see Chapter 10, "File and Event Log Access with ASP.NET," for more information about logging errors and messages).

Writing Custom Error Pages

In addition to the various ways to handle errors you've already seen in this chapter, you may remember from the brief example in Chapter 6, "Introduction to the System.Web Namespace," that you can replace the default ASP.NET error display with a custom error page by setting the `<customErrors>` tag in the `web.config` file to point to a specific error-display file.

You're not limited to using a single Web Form to handle all errors. You can also create custom error displays for various *types* of errors by adding `<error>` child elements to the `<customErrors>` element. Each `<error>` element requires two attributes: `statusCode`, which contains an IIS error status code (use the Properties dialog for your IIS application and click the Custom Errors tab for a list of error codes), and a `redirect` attribute containing the URL for the custom error file you want to run when that error code occurs. For example, adding the following `<error>` element would redirect error output to a Web Form named `Err500.aspx`:

NOTE   *The* `Err500.aspx` *file is used as an example filename only—it is not on* **www.sybex.com**.

```
<customErrors mode="On"
   defaultRedirect="/CSharpASP/ch9/customErrors.htm">
   <error statusCode="500" redirect="Err500.aspx" />
</customErrors>
```

The `statusCode` number should be one of a standard set of HTTP status codes shown in Table 9.3. The list is by no means complete, but it contains the most common status codes.

TABLE 9.3: HTTP STATUS CODES

CODE	STANDARD MEANING	DESCRIPTION
200	OK	The request was successful.
301	Moved Permanently	The requested URL is no longer accessible, and the content has moved to a new location.
302	Moved Temporarily	The requested URL is temporarily inaccessible, and the content has moved to a temporary location.
304	Not Modified	Lets the client refresh from cache when a requested file or resource has not been changed since some specified date.
400	Bad Request	The request was improperly formatted.
401	Unauthorized	The request was denied because the resource requires the user to authenticate.
403	Forbidden	The requested resource is inaccessible.
404	Not Found	The requested resource cannot be found.
500	Internal Server Error	An error occurred while processing the request.
501	Not Implemented	The server does not know how to fulfill the request.
502	Bad Gateway	The server was unable to retrieve a valid response from an upstream server.

Summary

The end of this chapter marks the end of Part II of this book and also marks an important point in learning how to create C# Web applications. You've seen how Web requests work; how to create HTML to format data in a client application; how to use the standard ASP.NET objects and build Web Forms; how to cache application and user data in `Session` variables, `Application` variables, and cookies; and how to pinpoint errors in your code using the debugger and trace output. Now you just need some data to display. You can retrieve and store data from almost any type of file—text, binary, image, or XML—and from relational databases. In the next few chapters, you'll explore file I/O in C# Web applications, data access with ADO.NET, and XML file manipulations.

Chapter 10

File and Event Log Access with ASP.NET

HERE'S WHERE THINGS START to get interesting. Dynamic Web applications are all about data. The black art of Web programming has to do with how fast you can retrieve data, how up-to-date your displays need to be, how often you need to update data, and how fast you can manipulate data for display. One common source of data is files stored on disk, so you need to know how to access them, read them, save them, and write the content or selected portions of the content to the client. You also need to be able to accept files from clients and store them on the server. This chapter will show you how to do those things.

In this chapter:

◆ Accessing Files

◆ Checking Whether a File Exists

◆ Opening Files

◆ Writing Text to Files

◆ Reading Text from Files

◆ Reading and Writing Binary Files

◆ Simple FTP

◆ Sending and Receiving files

◆ Accessing the Windows Registry

Accessing Files

Web applications, by nature, are multiuser applications, so whenever you do anything, you need to consider resource management carefully. Holding resources exclusively for a single user affects scalability; therefore, the type of file access that is common in single-user Windows applications has catastrophic effects for a Web application. The multiuser requirement affects everything. For example, many applications let users store personalization data—settings—such as font and color choices, default folder paths, and so on. In a standard Windows application, you'd read the user's settings file and then keep the data in memory for the lifetime of the application so that you could refer to it as needed. Whether you can use the same strategy in a Web application depends heavily on how scalable you need the application to be. Suppose the maximum size of a user's settings file is 50KB. If you have 10 people using the application simultaneously, no problem; the data would require only half a megabyte of memory at most. But suppose you have 100 or 1,000 people using the application. Suddenly, the memory requirement for the settings data alone jumps to 50MB or 500MB, and that's without taking any working data into account.

Next, suppose you let users save a file. With a single-user application, you can generally let the person save the file with any name he wishes. But in a Web application, you're unlikely to let users select filenames at all because the chances of collision—two people selecting the same name—are too high. Simply denying users the capability to save a file because a file with that name already exists is an unpalatable option. Instead, you might implement a strategy whereby users *think* they get to select a filename, but your application creates the real filename using a machine-generated filename, so collisions can't occur.

Finally, if you've worked with almost any other modern language in addition to VB, file access using C# will be easy. If you worked with the Scripting FileSystemObject that shipped with classic ASP and VB6, you'll be comfortable with C# file access almost immediately, and you can skip quickly through the first part of this chapter. But if you're used to the standard VB `Open For Binary Access Shared` type of syntax, the model has changed. Fortunately, it's changed for the better.

In .NET, file access has been abstracted by one level. That means you should change the way you think about file access. Rather than "tell the operating system to open a file," the way to think about file access is in two steps: First, use the File class or create a `FileInfo` object. These operations return a Stream instance. Streams read from and write to files, memory locations, and strings. Then, you use the returned Stream to read and/or write data to the file. The reason it's better is that all the operations are similar—you'll see that writing data or reading data to/from a memory buffer, a file, or any object that supports an IStream interface is essentially the same. While the changes force you to change the way you think about files, they also immediately give you the capability to treat all types of I/O in almost exactly the same way.

Working with Files

Contrary to your probable expectations, you never need to create a new `File` object—all the `File` class methods are static, so they're accessible simply by creating a `File` variable. You can think of a file as a container for data, and you can think of the `File` object as a direct link to the container itself, a single file on a storage device, but only to the container, not to the contained data. For example, using the `File` object, you can get and set file dates and times, create files, open files, delete files, copy files, and read and set file attributes, but you can't read the contents using only the `File` object. You need a `Stream` object to access a file's contents.

In classic VB, it was easier to attempt to open a file and then trap the resulting error if the file didn't exist than it was to check for the file's existence. In .NET, it's easier to check first and avoid the error. I created a text file named `FileStaticMethods.txt` in the `CSharpASP/ch10` folder. The file contains a text-only copy of the MSDN System.IO.File class static methods that you can use to experiment. Table 10.1 shows the contents of the file in table form.

TABLE 10.1: System.IO.File Class Static Methods

METHOD	DESCRIPTION
AppendText	Creates a StreamWriter that appends text to a file on the specified path or creates the file if it does not already exist.
Copy	Overloaded. Copies an existing file to a new file.
Create	Overloaded. Creates a file in the specified fully qualified path.
CreateText	Creates a StreamWriter that writes a new text file on the specified fully qualified path.
Delete	Deletes the file specified by the fully qualified path. An exception is not thrown if the specified file does not exist.
Exists	Determines whether a file exists on the fully qualified path.
GetAttributes	Gets the FileAttributes of the file on the fully qualified path.
GetCreationTime	Gets the date and time the specified file was created.
GetLastAccessTime	Gets the date and time the specified file was last accessed.
GetLastWriteTime	Gets the date and time the specified file was last written to.
Move	Moves a specified file to a new location, providing the option to specify a new filename.
Open	Overloaded. Opens a FileStream on the specified path.
OpenRead	Creates a read-only file on the specified path.
OpenText	Creates a StreamReader that reads from an existing text file having the specified path.
OpenWrite	Creates a read/write Stream on the specified path.
SetAttributes	Sets the specified FileAttributes of the file on the specified path.
SetCreationTime	Sets the date and time the file was created.
SetLastAccessTime	Sets the date and time the specified file was last accessed.
SetLastWriteTime	Sets the date and time the specified file was last written to.

To illustrate how the File object allows you to read and change information about a file, the Web Form ch10-1.aspx lets you view and change the dates of text files on your server (see Figure 10.1).

The Web Form contains several germane features. To use the Web Form, set the file ch10-1.aspx to the start page and then run the CSharpASP application. Enter a filename into the File Name field. Select Physical Path or Virtual Path and then click the File Info button. If the file exists, you'll see the file's attributes and create, access, or modify date in the scrolling text field. Clicking the button calls a subroutine named showFileInfo (see Listing 10.1).

FIGURE 10.1

Example Web Form
ch10-1.aspx after
setting the last
access date

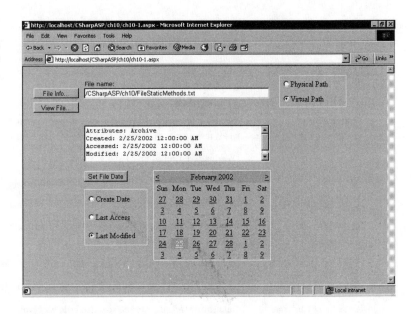

LISTING 10.1: THE showFileInfo SUBROUTINE RETRIEVES AND DISPLAYS INFORMATION ABOUT A FILE (ch10-1.aspx.cs)

```csharp
private void showFileInfo() {
    Boolean m_virtual;
    String m_filename;
    StringBuilder sb = new StringBuilder(1000);

    m_filename = txtFilename.Text;
    if (m_filename != null) {
        m_virtual = PathType.Items[1].Selected;
        if (m_virtual) {
            try {
                m_filename = Server.MapPath(m_filename);
            }
            catch (Exception ex) {
                lblMsg.Text = ex.Message;
                txtFileInfo.Text = "";
                return;
            }
        }
        if (File.Exists(m_filename)){
            sb.Append("Attributes: " +
                File.GetAttributes(m_filename).ToString() +
                System.Environment.NewLine);
```

```
                sb.Append("Created: " +
                    File.GetCreationTime(m_filename).ToString() +
                    System.Environment.NewLine);
                sb.Append("Accessed: " +
                    File.GetLastAccessTime(m_filename).ToString() +
                    System.Environment.NewLine);
                sb.Append("Modified: " +
                    File.GetLastWriteTime(m_filename).ToString() +
                    System.Environment.NewLine);
                txtFileInfo.Text = sb.ToString();
                lblMsg.Text = "";
            }
            else {
                lblMsg.Text = "The file does not exist.";
                txtFileInfo.Text = "";
            }
        }
    }
}
```

Assume that a user entered the filename /CSharpASP/ch10/FileStaticMethods.txt and then selected the Virtual Path radio button. The code in Listing 10.1 assigns the filename to a private String variable called m_filename, checks the path setting, and sets the Boolean variable m_virtual to true when the user selects the Virtual Path option or false when the user selects the Physical Path option. The File object requires a physical path; therefore, the code uses the Server.MapPath method to translate the virtual path to a physical path when necessary.

Checking Whether a File Exists

The highlighted line in Listing 10.1 shows how easy it is to check whether a file exists. If the file does not exist, the code writes the message "The file does not exist." below the File Name field by setting the lblMsg.Text property. If the file does exist, the listing creates a StringBuilder object and builds a string containing the file's attributes, create date, last modified date, and last access date.

You can use the calendar control that appears on the ch10-1.aspx Web Form to change any of the file dates—a task that was nearly impossible to perform cleanly in classic ASP without using an ActiveX control.

Reading Files

You can click the View File button to see the contents of any text file on your server that you have permission to access with your current ASP.NET security setup. You can view the contents of binary files as well, but you may not find the results satisfactory. Most of the View File button event code shown in Listing 10.2 duplicates code in the showFileInfo subroutine that you've already seen in Listing 10.1, but I've highlighted the pertinent lines that you need to open and read a text file.

LISTING 10.2: OPEN AND READ A TEXT FILE (ch10-1.aspx.cs)

```
private void btnView_Click(object sender,
    System.EventArgs e) {
    Boolean m_virtual;
    String m_filename;
    StreamReader sr;
    m_filename = txtFilename.Text;
    if (m_filename != null) {
        m_virtual = PathType.Items[1].Selected;
        if (m_virtual) {
            m_filename = Server.MapPath(m_filename);
        }
        if (File.Exists(m_filename)) {
            // try {
                sr = File.OpenText(m_filename);
                txtFileInfo.Text = sr.ReadToEnd();
            // }
            //catch (Exception ex) {
                // Me.lblMsg.Text = ex.Message
            // }
            //finally
                //If Not sr Is Nothing Then
                sr.Close()
                // }
        }
    }
}
```

You may notice that something critical is missing in the Listing 10.2 code. Yes, error-handling. If you were to place this code on a server, sooner or later it would crash when attempting to open the selected file, because someone would enter a filename for which he did not have read or change permission. For example, try changing the permissions on a text file—deny the Everyone group any access to the file—and then run the application again. You'll see a permission-denied error. Leave the file permissions set to deny access, replace the btnView_Click code with this improved version shown below, and then run the application. You'll still get an error, but this time, the code in the Web Form handles the error rather than relying on the default error-handling in the ASP.NET runtime.

NOTE   In the code on www.sybex.com, *the appropriate lines exist but are commented out. Remove the comments to run the code.*

```
private void btnView_Click(object sender,
    System.EventArgs e) {
    Boolean m_virtual;
    String m_filename;
    StreamReader sr;
    m_filename = txtFilename.Text;
    if (m_filename != null) {
```

```
    m_virtual = PathType.Items[1].Selected;
    if (m_virtual) {
        m_filename = Server.MapPath(m_filename);
    }
    if (File.Exists(m_filename)) {
        try {
            sr = File.OpenText(m_filename)
            txtFileInfo.Text = sr.ReadToEnd()
        }
        catch (Exception ex) {
            Me.lblMsg.Text = ex.Message
        }
        finally
            If Not sr Is Nothing Then
                sr.Close()
            }
        }
    }
}
```

The added try block catches any errors that occur and writes the error message under the File Name field on the Web Form.

This may seem rather obvious, but you should *always* trap for errors whenever you attempt to access outside resources of any kind, because you can't control them with your application. In Web applications it's particularly important because you may not be able to control *who* is accessing your application. I don't mean that in a personal sense—I mean that when you're developing an application on your own machine, you run with your own identity. But unless you're the server administrator, you may not have any control over the identity and permissions that your application must accommodate. You must assume that you may not be granted permission to access a resource or that the resource may not exist. I cannot emphasize this enough. Although you can find many input/output (I/O) examples in the documentation and in books and articles, very few of the examples contain error-trapping code.

Using the FileInfo Class

If you're going to perform several actions on a file, you should use the FileInfo class instead. The FileInfo class *does* have non-static methods; therefore, you use it differently, by creating an instance of the FileInfo class. The main reason to prefer the FileInfo class over the File class is that when you create an instance of the FileInfo class, the system performs security checks the first time you use the file and caches the results, whereas the File class must perform the security checks each time you call one of its methods. That's because the File class has only static methods; the class doesn't know if you're accessing the same file multiple times. The FileInfo class has all of the functionality of the File class and more, but because the FileInfo class is bound to a specific file, the syntax is slightly different. For example, you can almost—but not quite—substitute FileInfo for File in the ch10-1.aspx.cs code-behind class. Although slight, the syntax differences are enough to make it awkward to change your mind if you begin coding some functionality using the File class and later decide to switch to the FileInfo class to minimize the security checks.

The Web Form `ch10-2.aspx` is a functional duplicate of the `ch10-1.aspx` Web Form but uses the FileInfo class instead of the File class. However, I've abstracted the code that sets the filename by moving it to the `Page_Load` event.

LISTING 10.3: FUNCTIONAL DUPLICATE OF `ch10-1.aspx` USING THE FILEINFO CLASS (`ch10-2.aspx.cs`)

```csharp
using System;
using System.Collections;
using System.ComponentModel;
using System.Data;
using System.Drawing;
using System.Web;
using System.Web.SessionState;
using System.Web.UI;
using System.Web.UI.WebControls;
using System.Web.UI.HtmlControls;
using System.Text;
using System.IO;

namespace CSharpASP.ch10
{
    /// <summary>
    /// Summary description for ch10_2.
    /// </summary>
    public class ch10_2 : System.Web.UI.Page {
        protected System.Web.UI.WebControls.Button
            btnFileInfo;
        protected System.Web.UI.WebControls.TextBox
            txtFilename;
        protected System.Web.UI.WebControls.RadioButtonList
            PathType;
        protected System.Web.UI.WebControls.Label lblMsg;
        protected System.Web.UI.WebControls.TextBox
            txtFileInfo;
        protected System.Web.UI.WebControls.Button btnView;
        protected System.Web.UI.WebControls.Calendar
            Calendar1;
        protected System.Web.UI.WebControls.Button btnSet;
        protected System.Web.UI.WebControls.RadioButtonList
            FileDateType;
        protected System.Web.UI.WebControls.Label Label2;
        private FileInfo m_fileInfo;
        private String m_filename;
        private Boolean m_virtual;

        private void Page_Load(object sender,
            System.EventArgs e) {
```

```
      if (!IsPostBack) {
         Calendar1.SelectedDate =
            System.DateTime.Now.Date;
      }
      else {
         m_filename = txtFilename.Text.Trim();
         if (m_filename.Length == 0) {
            m_filename = null;
         }
         if (m_filename != null) {
            m_virtual = PathType.Items[1].Selected;
            if (m_virtual) {
               try {
                  m_filename =
                     Server.MapPath(m_filename);
               }
               catch (Exception ex) {
                  lblMsg.Text = ex.Message;
                  txtFileInfo.Text = "";
                  return;
               }
            }
         }
      }
   }

   #region Web Form Designer generated code
   override protected void OnInit(EventArgs e) {
      //
      // CODEGEN: This call is required by the ASP.NET
      // Web Form Designer.
      //
      InitializeComponent();
      base.OnInit(e);
   }

   /// <summary>
   /// Required method for Designer support - do not
   /// modify
   /// the contents of this method with the code editor.
   /// </summary>
   private void InitializeComponent() {
      this.btnFileInfo.Click += new
         System.EventHandler(this.btnFileInfo_Click);
      this.btnView.Click += new
         System.EventHandler(this.btnView_Click);
      this.btnSet.Click += new
         System.EventHandler(this.btnSet_Click);
```

```csharp
        this.Load += new
            System.EventHandler(this.Page_Load);

    }
    #endregion

    private void btnFileInfo_Click(object sender,
        System.EventArgs e) {
        showFileInfo();
    }
    private void showFileInfo() {
        Boolean m_virtual;
        String m_filename;
        StringBuilder sb = new StringBuilder(1000);
        FileInfo m_fileInfo;
        m_filename = txtFilename.Text;
        if (m_filename != null) {
            m_virtual = PathType.Items[1].Selected;
            if (m_virtual) {
                try {
                    m_filename = Server.MapPath(m_filename);
                }
                catch (Exception ex) {
                    lblMsg.Text = ex.Message;
                    txtFileInfo.Text = "";
                    return;
                }
            }
            try {
                m_fileInfo = new FileInfo(m_filename);
            }
            catch (Exception ex) {
                lblMsg.Text = ex.Message;
                txtFileInfo.Text = "";
                return;
            }
            if (File.Exists(m_filename)){
                sb.Append("Attributes: " +
                    File.GetAttributes(m_filename).ToString()
                    + System.Environment.NewLine);
                sb.Append("Created: " +
                File.GetCreationTime(m_filename).ToString()
                    + System.Environment.NewLine);
                    sb.Append("Accessed: " +
                    File.GetLastAccessTime(m_filename).
                    ToString() + System.Environment.NewLine);
                sb.Append("Modified: "
                    + File.GetLastWriteTime(m_filename).
```

```
                ToString() +System.Environment.NewLine);
         txtFileInfo.Text = sb.ToString();
         lblMsg.Text = "";
      }
      else {
         lblMsg.Text = "The file does not exist.";
         txtFileInfo.Text = "";
      }
   }
}

private void btnView_Click(object sender,
   System.EventArgs e) {
   StreamReader sr;
   if (m_filename != null) {
      m_fileInfo = new FileInfo(m_filename);
      if (m_fileInfo.Exists) {
         try {
            sr = m_fileInfo.OpenText();
            txtFileInfo.Text = sr.ReadToEnd();
            sr.Close();
         }
         catch (Exception ex) {
            lblMsg.Text = ex.Message;
         }
      }
   }
}

private void btnSet_Click(object sender,
   System.EventArgs e) {
   String m_datetype;

   m_datetype = FileDateType.Items
      [FileDateType.SelectedIndex].Value;
   if (m_filename != null) {
      m_fileInfo = new FileInfo(m_filename);
      if (m_fileInfo.Exists) {
         switch (m_datetype.ToLower()) {
            case "created" :
               m_fileInfo.CreationTime =
                  Calendar1.SelectedDate;
               break;
            case "access" :
               m_fileInfo.LastAccessTime=
                  Calendar1.SelectedDate;
               break;
            case "modified" :
```

```
                        m_fileInfo.LastWriteTime =
                            Calendar1.SelectedDate;
                        break;
                }
                showFileInfo();
            }
            else {
                lblMsg.Text = "The file does not exist.";
            }
        }
    }
    }
}
```

The first thing to note is that the constructor to create a new FileInfo instance fails if you pass it a null value. Therefore, you must check to ensure that the parameter you pass to the constructor contains some value.

```
if (m_filename != null) {
    m_fileInfo = new FileInfo(m_filename);
}
```

Next, notice that the Exists method doesn't take a filename parameter. In other words, the File class's implementation of Exists is generic—you can check for the existence of any file, whereas the FileInfo object's implementation is specific—you can use it only to check for the existence of the bound filename. That should immediately make you suspect that the filename you pass to the File-Info class constructor does not have to be a valid name—and you'd be correct. You can pass any string that contains characters to the FileInfo class constructor.

Despite the added code required to use the FileInfo class, it does have many useful features, and I recommend that you use the File class methods only for generic file existence and meta-information retrieval. Use the FileInfo class for everything else. I'm not going to show you examples of each of the FileInfo class methods here—they're fairly intuitive—but I will point them out when they appear in future examples.

Using the StringWriter Class

By now you're familiar with the StringBuilder class, but you don't have to use it directly. In fact, you can abstract almost all string writing operations by using a Stream class that reads from and writes to strings—regardless of the underlying implementation of that string. The .NET StringWriter class gives you that abstracted level. For example, several times in this book, you've seen code that creates a new StringBuilder, appends text and <br> tags, and then writes the resulting data to the browser using either the Response.Write method or by assigning the StringBuilder data to the Text property of a control on the page. Here's another way to accomplish much the same thing. The two operations shown in Listing 10.4 produce identical output.

LISTING 10.4: STRINGBUILDER VERSUS STRINGWRITER (ch10-3.aspx.cs)

```
private void Page_Load(object sender, System.EventArgs e) {
    StringWriter sw = new StringWriter();
    StringBuilder sb = new StringBuilder();
    sw.NewLine = "<br>";
    sw.WriteLine("StringWriter: This is a test.");
    sw.WriteLine("StringWriter: This is another test.");
    Response.Write(sw);
    sb.Append("StringBuilder: This is a test<br>");
    sb.Append("StringBuilder: This is another test<br>");
    Response.Write(sb);
    //// Uncomment the code below to see the results of
    //// calling Response.Write with a COM object variable
    //// parameter
    // MSXML2.DOMDocument doc;
    //doc = new MSXML2.DOMDocument();
    //Response.Write(doc + "<br>");
    //// Retrieve the fully qualified type name of a COM
    //// object variable
    //Response.Write(Type.GetTypeFromHandle
        (Type.GetTypeHandle(doc)).FullName);
}
```

The Web Form ch10-3.aspx on www.sybex.com contains the code. Note that the StringWriter section of Listing 10.4 uses an extra line to set the NewLine property: sr.NewLine = "<br>". But the line defines the line termination character—one of the main differences between writing text to a browser and writing text to other devices. The default NewLine property is a carriage return/linefeed (vbCrLf for those of you used to the VB6 intrinsic constants, \r\n for the C-proficient). By setting the NewLine property to "<br>", you can write to the StringWriter (and thus the browser) using the WriteLine method without having to concatenate the <br> tag for each line.

When you create a StringWriter using the default constructor, you get a StringBuilder object by default. If you want access to the underlying StringBuilder object, you can retrieve it with the GetStringBuilder method. Using one of the overloaded constructors, you can create a StringWriter object attached to a specific StringBuilder instance by passing the StringBuilder object to the constructor:

```
StringBuilder sb = new StringBuilder(1000);
StringWriter sw = new StringWriter(sb);
```

Listing 10.4 contains one more item of interest. Notice that you don't have to use the ToString method when you write the data using the Response object. Instead, you can pass the StringBuilder and StringWriter objects themselves as parameters to the Response.Write method:

```
Response.Write(sb);
Response.Write(sw);
```

One of the overloaded `Response.Write` methods accepts an object variable—and then calls the `toString` method. Because all objects inherit a default implementation of `toString` from `Object` and overload it, you can pass the `Response.Write` method any .NET object and get *something* back. You should be sure you understand what that something is because, by default, it's a string containing the class name of the object, not necessarily a string representation of the object's data.

Interestingly, this works with both .NET objects *and* COM objects, so you can use it freely with any object. For example, suppose you create a new instance of the `MSXML2.DOMDocument` object (the CSharpASP project references the MSXML2 library) and pass it to the overloaded `Response.Write` method as follows:

```
MSXML2.DOMDocument doc = new MSXML2.DOMDocument;
Response.Write(doc);
```

The preceding code snippet writes the string `MSXML2.DOMDocumentClass` to the browser. In response to the `ToString` call issued by the overloaded `Response.Write(ByVal obj as object)` method, a COM object returns just its name, but .NET objects may overload the `ToString` method and return a more useful string.

Using the Directory and DirectoryInfo Classes

Just as you use the File and FileInfo classes to manipulate files, you can use the Directory and Directory-Info classes to manipulate directories. The relationship between the Directory and the DirectoryInfo classes is similar to the relationship between the File and FileInfo classes. For example, the Web Form `ch10-4.aspx` uses the Directory class static method `Exists` to show that the current directory exists (rather obvious, but guaranteed to work). Listing 10.5 shows the code from the `ch10-4.aspx.cs` code-behind `Page_Load` method that lists the current directory contents.

LISTING 10.5: USING THE DIRECTORY AND DIRECTORYINFO CLASSES (`ch10-4.apsx.cs`)

```
private void Page_Load(object sender, System.EventArgs e) {
    DirectoryInfo di;
    Response.Output.NewLine = "<br>";
    Response.Output.WriteLine("<h3>Using Directory</h3>");
    Response.Output.Write("The path " +
        Server.MapPath(".") + " exists=");
    Response.Output.WriteLine(Directory.Exists
        (Server.MapPath(".")).ToString());
    foreach (String s in
        Directory.GetFiles(Server.MapPath("."))) {
        Response.Output.WriteLine(s);
    }
    Response.Output.WriteLine
        ("<h3>Using DirectoryInfo</h3>");
    di = new DirectoryInfo(Server.MapPath("."));
```

```
    Response.Output.Write(("The path " + di.FullName +
        " exists="));
    Response.Output.WriteLine(di.Exists.ToString());
    foreach (FileInfo fi in di.GetFiles()) {
        Response.Output.WriteLine(fi.FullName);
    }
}
```

The example shows you how to use the basic methods of the Directory and DirectoryInfo classes. In addition, the code in Listing 10.5 shows you how to overcome the rather unfortunately missing `Response.WriteLine` method by using the `Output` property to gain access to the `Response` object's underlying `Stream` object—which, as you saw in the preceding section, has a `NewLine` property and a `WriteLine` method. As with StringWriter, you can combine these to write lines of HTML without manually concatenating the `<br>` tag to each line. This is convenient when you need to write several lines in a row. Be careful when you use this technique, because it appends the `<br>` tag to every `Response.Write` statement until you reset the `NewLine` property to its default. On my machine, the output from Listing 10.5 looks like Figure 10.2.

FIGURE 10.2

Directory listing: output from the `ch10-4.aspx` Web Form

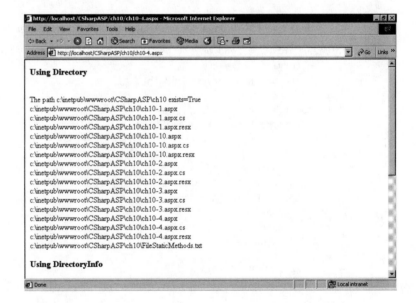

As a nice bonus, the `FileInfo` object performs tasks for you that you used to have to perform manually. For example, how many times have you written code to strip the file extension from a filename or to find just the filename or path? You don't have to do that anymore. As an example, here's the output from an alternate directory listing (see Figure 10.3).

FIGURE 10.3

Directory listing:
output from the
`ch10-4.aspx`
Web Form

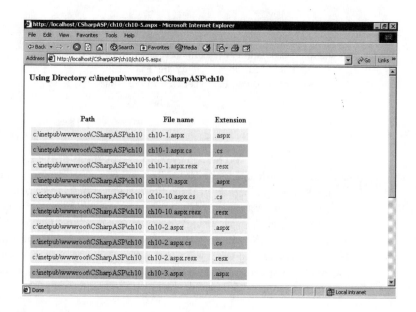

The Web Form `ch10-5.aspx` contains the code that generated this output:

```
private void Page_Load(object sender, System.EventArgs e) {
   DirectoryInfo di = new
      DirectoryInfo(Server.MapPath("."));
   Int32 counter=0;
   Response.Write("<h3>Using Directory " +
      Server.MapPath(".") + "</h3>");
   Response.Write("<table cellpadding='4' " +
      "cellspacing='5'><tr><th>Path</th><th>" +
      "File name</th><th>Extension</th></tr>");
   foreach (FileInfo fi in di.GetFiles()) {
      Response.Write("<tr");
      if (counter % 2 == 0) {
         Response.Write(" style='background: " +
            "lightyellow'>");
      }
      else {
         Response.Write(" style='background: lightblue'>");
      }
      Response.Write("<td>" + fi.DirectoryName + "</td>");
      Response.Write("<td>" + fi.Name + "</td>");
      Response.Write("<td>" + fi.Extension + "</td>");
      Response.Write("</tr>");
      counter += 1;
   }
}
```

Although this example is much better looking than the `ch10-4.aspx` Web Form, it is *not* a good example of using Web Forms or code-behind classes to generate output. Why not? Because the HTML is bound up in the code; in other words, writing HTML output in this manner defeats one of the primary purposes of Web Forms—to *separate* code from the user interface. It would be much better to use one of the intrinsic ASP.NET server controls and bind it to the data. You'll see more about that in Chapter 14, "Accessing Data."

Using the Directory or DirectoryInfo class, you can perform tasks such as creating new directories or subdirectories. You'll see an example in the next section.

Creating Files and Directories

So far, you've only seen how to read existing files and directories. Using the DirectoryInfo and FileInfo classes, you can create new directories, subdirectories, and files.

Page Counter Example

Suppose you want to create a counter for your page that lets you know how often it is visited. The question is, where can you store the count information? If you store it at Session scope, you need to keep the data in memory for every client instance accessing your application. If you store it at Application scope, the count will start over every time your application starts up. If you're going to create a counter that will persist across application instances, you need to store the data in a file or a database, and unless you precreate the file, you'll need to create it at runtime. You don't want to access the file for each page request because page requests occur on multiple threads; therefore, you would need to serialize access to the file to prevent collisions or access contention. Instead, you should create the file when the application starts and write the data when the application ends. While the application is running, you can store the information in memory, in an `Application` variable. You can serialize that process by using the `Application.Lock` method. For each page you want to count, the process is as follows:

1. Lock the `Application` object.

2. Retrieve the counter value from the `Application` variable.

3. Increment the counter value by 1.

4. Save the updated counter value to the `Application` variable.

5. Unlock the application.

You also need to decide where to write the counter file. It may be best not to write the file in the master directory so that you don't pollute the files that make up the application with files generated by the application. Therefore, the application will create a subdirectory called `counters` and place the counter file in that folder. The Web Form `ch10-6` shows how to create such a counter.

In your `Global.asax.cs` file, add the following code to override the `Init` event and define the counter variable. The `Init` event is one of the "hidden" Application-level events in C#, so you should just enter the code below manually:

```
public override void Init() {
    Debug.WriteLine("Init");
```

```
          Application["pageCounter"] = 0;
      }
```

Inside the Web Form, retrieve the counter variable and increment it:

```
private void Page_Load(object sender, System.EventArgs e) {
    int pageCounter=0;
    if (Application["pageCounter"] == null) {
        Application.Lock();
        Application["pageCounter"]=0;
        Application.UnLock();
    }
    else {
        pageCounter = (int) Application["pageCounter"];
        pageCounter++;
        Application["pageCounter"] = pageCounter;
        Application.UnLock();
    }
    lblCounter.Text = "Counter: " + pageCounter.ToString();
}
```

Always remember to use the `Application.Lock` and `UnLock` methods to prevent requests running on other threads from attempting to access and update the variable value simultaneously.

Finally, when the application ends, you want to write the counter value to a file. The ASP.NET framework calls the `Application_Start` method the *first* time a client requests a page from your application and calls the `Application_End` method after the *last* session times out or is abandoned. There are some restrictions, however. You can't use the **Request**, **Response**, **Server**, and **Session** objects while handling **Application Start, End, Init,** or **Dispose methods** because they either haven't been created (**Start, Init**) or have already been finalized (**End, Dispose**) before the events occur.

The code must create the **counters** subdirectory if it doesn't already exist. I've used the `Application_OnStart` event to create the subdirectory, but you could just as easily write this code into the `Application_Start` event handler. Remember that you can bind a `FileInfo` object to a file path even if the file doesn't exist yet. You can do the same with the `DirectoryInfo` object. The application creates the **counters** subdirectory when the application starts.

NOTE *The following code is commented out in the* Global.asax.cs *file on* www.sybex.com. *Uncomment the code to test it. You will have to hard-code the path to your CSharpASP application. The example code shows the default IIS path on drive C. You must change the path if IIS is installed on a different drive or path on your server.*

```
using System.Diagnostics;
using System.IO;

public void Application_OnStart() {
    EventLog.WriteEntry("CSharpASP",
        "CSharpASP application Starting");
    DirectoryInfo di = null;
    try {
        di = new DirectoryInfo
            (@"c:\inetpub\wwwroot\CSharpASP\ch10\counters");
```

```
        if (!di.Exists) {
            di.Create();
            EventLog.WriteEntry("CSharpASP",
                "counters folder created");
        }
    }
    catch (Exception ex) {
        EventLog.WriteEntry("CSharpASP", ex.Message);
        EventLog.WriteEntry("CSharpASP", ex.StackTrace);
    }
    if (Application["StartEventCount"] == null) {
        Application["StartEventCount"] = 0;
    }
}
```

WARNING *The* System.Diagnostics.EventLog.WriteEntry *calls are not required and are present in the code solely so that you can check the event log to see what happened if your code doesn't run properly. There is no error reporting available during execution of the* Application_OnEnd *event because there's no way to display the error to a human— and the errors aren't automatically logged. Therefore, adding log code during the event is the best way to find and fix problems.*

The preceding code writes an entry into the Windows application log when the application starts. It then checks to see if the **counters** directory exists; if not, it creates the directory. One interesting point about the DirectoryInfo.Create method is that it can create a directory even if one or more parent directories in the path don't exist.

If that's confusing, here's a more detailed version. Suppose you want to create the path c:\test1\ test2\test3\test4, but none of the folders exist. In previous versions of VB and ASP, you would have to create the **test1** folder and then create the **test2** subfolder, and so on. Using the Directory-Info object, you can simply call the **Create** method if the folder doesn't exist. The **Create** method begins at the front of the path and follows the tree downward, creating directories as needed until it gets to the end or encounters an error.

Unfortunately, the FileInfo class doesn't have that same capability. If you bind a string to a File-Info object and then call the **Create** method, it follows the tree downward but raises an error as soon as it encounters a missing directory. Therefore, to create a file, you must first ensure that the directory where you want to create the file already exists. That's why the Application_OnStart event code creates the directory.

To write the file in the Application_OnEnd event, the application creates a FileInfo object and opens it with the FileMode.OpenOrCreate enumeration value. If the file doesn't exist, the operating system creates it; otherwise, it just opens the file. To avoid problems, the code disables sharing with the FileShare.None enumeration value.

```
public void Application_End() {
    EventLog.WriteEntry("CSharpASP",
        "CSharpASP application Ending");
    FileInfo fi = null;
    FileStream fs = null;
    int counter  = 0;
    try {
```

```
            fi = new FileInfo
                (@"c:\inetpub\wwwroot\CSharpASP\ch10\counters" +
                "\pagecounter.txt");
            fs = fi.Open(FileMode.OpenOrCreate, FileAccess.Write,
                FileShare.None);
            fs.Seek(0, SeekOrigin.Begin);
            BinaryWriter bw = new BinaryWriter(fs);
            counter = (int) Application["pagecounter"];
            bw.Write(counter);
            bw.Close();
            fs.Close();
        }
        catch (Exception ex) {
            EventLog.WriteEntry("CSharpASP", ex.Message);
            EventLog.WriteEntry("CSharpASP", ex.StackTrace);
        }
    }
```

Writing to Files

The example in the preceding section uses a BinaryWriter to write an integer to a file. There are other ways to accomplish the task. Here's a more flexible way to write to a file. Suppose you want to write a string to a file. First, create a `FileInfo` object instance and open it in writeable mode.

```
String s = new String("Test");
DirectoryInfo di = new DirectoryInfo
    (@"c:\inetpub\wwwroot\CSharpASP\ch10\counters");
FileInfo fi = new FileInfo(di.FullName +
    @"\pagecounter.txt");
fs = fi.OpenWrite;
```

The `OpenWrite` method returns a `FileStream` object. At this point, your options seem limited because the `FileStream` has a `Write` method, but it accepts only an array of bytes, along with an offset and count. Obviously, if you have a byte array, you can write all or part of it easily with the `Write` method; otherwise, you need to convert the data. For example, you *could* convert your string to an array of bytes and write those. But there are simpler options. The example shows one option: Create a StreamWriter and use that to write to the `FileStream`. The StreamWriter has an overloaded `Write` method that accepts `String` objects (as well as many other types).

```
StreamWriter sw = new StreamWriter(fs);
sw.Write(s);
sw.Close();
fs.Close();
```

So you're opening a Stream on another Stream and using that to write the information. Not very intuitive at first, but when it sinks in that you can write almost all data in exactly the same manner, you'll appreciate it.

Writing Text to Files

You can tell that the StreamWriter object is extremely flexible, but just to write some text to a file, there are several other options, depending on exactly what you want to do.

The FileInfo class has an AppendText method that returns a StreamWriter, so you can skip the extra code to create a FileStream and then create a StreamWriter on that. You can also skip using the File and FileInfo objects. The FileStream class has an overloaded constructor that accepts a file path, as well as create/open options and file-sharing restrictions. Finally, if you just want to append text to a file, the StreamWriter constructor itself is overloaded. For example, the following code creates the file test.txt in the current directory if it doesn't already exist and appends the string This is a test to the end of the file. The second parameter (true) in the following code controls whether you're opening the file in append mode. If the parameter is true, the StreamWriter Write or WriteLine method writes to the end of the file. If false, the methods begin writing at the start of the file—overwriting content that may already exist. I've left out error-handling in this example—but you shouldn't.

```
StreamWriter sw = new StreamWriter(Server.MapPath(".") +
    @"\test.txt", true);
sw.WriteLine("This is a test");
sw.Close();
```

It's tough to get much simpler than that.

Reading and Writing Binary Files

Although you've already seen one example of writing to a binary file using a StreamWriter, it's worth noting that the StreamWriter is extremely flexible because it can write so many common types of data. A related class, called a BinaryWriter, handles the rest. There appears to be a lot of crossover between the classes, but the difference is that a StreamWriter inherits from the TextWriter class, so it writes a *string representation* of the data, whereas the BinaryWriter writes the byte values of data. To help you decide which you might use in a given situation, Table 10.2 shows the overloaded Write method parameters for both the StreamWriter and BinaryWriter.

TABLE 10.2: STREAMWRITER AND BINARYWRITER Write METHOD PARAMETER

Write METHOD PARAMETERS	STREAMWRITER	BINARYWRITER
Boolean	X	X
Byte		X
Byte()		X
Byte(), Integer(start), Integer(length)		X
Char	X	X
Char()	X	X
Char(), Integer(start), Integer(length)		X
String	X	X

Continued on next page

TABLE 10.2: STREAMWRITER AND BINARYWRITER Write METHOD PARAMETERS *(continued)*

Write METHOD PARAMETERS	STREAMWRITER	BINARYWRITER
`Char(), Integer(start), Integer(length)`	X	
`Decimal`	X	X
`Double`	X	X
`Short`		X
`Integer`	X	X
`Long`	X	X
`Sbyte`		X
`Single`		X
`Object`	X	
`UInt16`		X
`UInt32`	X	X
`UInt64`	X	X
`String, Object`	X	
`String, ParamArray(Object)`	X	
`String, Object, Object`	X	
`String, Object, Object, Object`	X	

NOTE *The Common Language System (CLS) doesn't support writing unsigned types, so you should avoid this if you want your code to be compliant with CLS.*

NOTE *When you write an object using the StreamWriter, it calls* `ToString` *on the object and writes the resulting string. It does not serialize the object. If you want to serialize the object itself so that you can re-create the object, use the* `BinaryFormatter.Serialize` *method instead, which writes a binary object "graph" to a specified Stream. The overloads that use object parameters are intended for formatting and not for saving objects.*

Writing Data to Memory

Although this chapter deals primarily with files, writing data to memory buffers with .NET is so similar to writing data to files that this is an appropriate place to mention it. In classic VB and ASP, there was no intrinsic way of writing data to a memory buffer except to create an array or a string explicitly and write data into that. In .NET, you can write data to a buffer in memory exactly as if it were a file, which gives you a fast way of writing data. For example, you can create a buffer, write data into it, and then save the buffer to disk in a single operation (now you can see the reason behind the relatively simplistic `Write` method for the FileStream class). For example, the following code fragment creates a MemoryStream, writes some data to it, and displays the result in the browser:

```
Byte b[25];
int i;
MemoryStream ms = new MemoryStream();
for (i = 0; i < 25; i++) {
    b[i] = i + 65;
}
ms.Write(b, 0, b.Length);
ms.WriteTo(Response.OutputStream);
```

The only real difference between the MemoryStream and others you've seen is the `WriteTo` method. Note that you can write directly to the Stream that underlies the `Response` object by retrieving the Stream from the `Response.OutputStream` property. More typically, you would use a StringWriter or StringBuilder to write text to memory, as you've already seen.

Writing HTML

When you need to write well-formed HTML, the .NET framework can assist you. Rather than creating strings, you can use an instance of the HtmlTextWriter class to help format the data correctly. While you *can* use an HtmlTextWriter directly—and you might do that if you were writing a custom control and needed to render the HTML for the control—you would normally let the controls call the HtmlTextWriter for you. In other words, you typically use an HtmlTextWriter indirectly.

For example, suppose you want to write a table of values, where each cell needs to be formatted differently according to the value. Negative values are red, positive values are black, text labels are blue, and so on. I'll show you two examples in this section.

Before you look at the code, here's some information about the HtmlTextWriter class. It has methods to write elements and attributes, and it has fields for every part of the HTML elements and attributes. For example, the class defines fields for the left and right angle brackets that start and end elements; for the equal sign between attributes; for single and double quotes; for the default tab character; for the slash character, and so on. It also defines methods for writing HTML. The class uses a StringWriter that writes to a StringBuilder to output the results. For example, to write the tag `<table align="center">`, you could use the following:

```
//create a StringBuilder with an initial size of 3000 bytes
using System.Text;
StringBuilder sb = new StringBuilder(3000);
HtmlTextWriter htw = new HtmlTextWriter
    (new StringWriter(sb));
htw.WriteBeginTag("table");
htw.WriteAttribute("align","center");
htw.Write(htw.TagRightChar);
```

Other methods let you render a complete tag, write a string, or add style attributes. While you can probably see that writing this code would improve the *accuracy* of complex HTML, it isn't particularly palatable for writing a simple tag.

OK, on to the code. The first example shows how you can format the HTML yourself. The second example creates an HtmlTextWriter instance, creates an `HtmlTable` control, fills the table with data, and then tells the table to render. Note that it's both easier to read and easier to write robust HTML when you let the HtmlTextWriter format the HTML for you.

Both examples create a table containing positive and negative numbers and strings using a two-dimensional object array as the source data (see Figure 10.4).

FIGURE 10.4

Custom
HTML versus
HtmlTextWriter:
two table examples

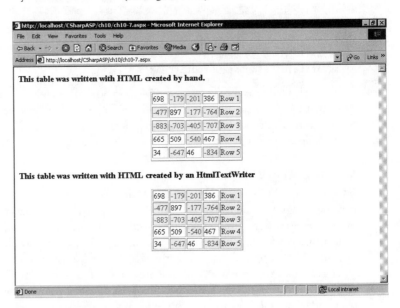

Listing 10.6 shows the code. The Web Form `ch10-7.aspx` creates some randomized data when it loads and then calls the two subroutines `showTable1` and `showTable2` that create the tables.

LISTING 10.6: CREATE TABLE COMPARISON: CUSTOM HTML VERSUS HTMLTEXTWRITER (ch10-7.aspx.cs)

```
public class ch10_7 : System.Web.UI.Page
  {
  private void Page_Load(object sender, System.EventArgs e) {
     Object[,] arrData = getRandomData();
     showTable1(arrData);
     showTable2(arrData);
  }
  private Object[,] getRandomData() {
     String[] strings= {
        "Row 1", "Row 2", "Row 3", "Row 4", "Row 5"};
     Object[,] values = new Object[5,5];
     int aValue;
     Random rand = new Random();
```

```
      int i, j;
      for (i = 0; i < 5; i++) {
         for (j = 0; j < 5; j++) {
            if (j == 4) {
               values[i, j] = strings[i];
            }
            else {
               aValue = rand.Next(-1000, 1000);
               values[i, j] = aValue;
            }
         }
      }
      return values;
}

   private void showTable1(Object[,] values) {
      int i, j;
      Response.Write("<h3>This table was written " +
         "with HTML created by hand.</h3>");
      Response.Write("<table align=\"center\"" +
         "border=\"1\">");
      for (i = 0; i <= values.GetUpperBound(0); i++) {
         Response.Write("<tr>");
         for (j = 0; j <= values.GetUpperBound(1); j++) {
            switch (values[i, j].GetType().Name) {
               case "String" :
                  Response.Write("<td style=\"color:" +
                     "blue; background: lightyellow\">" +
                     values[i, j] + "</td>");
                  break;
               case "Int32" :
                  if ((int) values[i, j] < 0) {
                     Response.Write("<td " +
                        "style=\"color: red;" +
                        "background:lightyellow\">" +
                        values[i, j] + "</td>");
                  }
                  else if ((int) values[i,j] >= 0) {
                     Response.Write("<td " +
                        "style=\"color: black\">" +
                        values[i, j] + "</td>");
                  }
                  break;
            }
         }
         Response.Write("<tr>");
      }
      Response.Write("</table><br>");
```

```
        }

        private void showTable2(Object[,] values) {
            HtmlTable tbl = new HtmlTable();
            StringBuilder sb = new StringBuilder(3000);
            StringWriter sw = new StringWriter(sb);
            HtmlTextWriter htw = new HtmlTextWriter(sw);
            int i, j;
            HtmlTableRow row;
            HtmlTableCell cell;
            tbl.Border = 1;
            tbl.Align = "center";
            Response.Write("<h3>This table was written with " +
                "HTML created by an HtmlTextWriter</h3>");
            for (i = 0; i <= values.GetUpperBound(0); i++) {
                row = new HtmlTableRow();
                tbl.Rows.Add(row);
                for (j = 0; j <= values.GetUpperBound(1); j++) {
                    cell = new HtmlTableCell();
                    switch (values[i, j].GetType().Name) {
                        case "String" :
                            cell.Attributes.Add("style",
                                "color:blue; background:lightYellow");
                            break;
                        case "Int32" :
                            if ((int) values[i, j] < 0) {
                                cell.Attributes.Add("style",
                                    "color:red; " +
                                    "background:lightYellow");
                            }
                            else if ((int) values[i, j] >= 0) {
                                cell.Attributes.Add("style",
                                    "color:black; " +
                                    background:white");
                            }
                            break;
                    }
                    cell.InnerText = values[i, j].ToString();
                    row.Cells.Add(cell);
                }
            }
            tbl.RenderControl(new HtmlTextWriter(sw));
            Response.Write(sb.ToString());
        }
        #region Web Form Designer generated code
        override protected void OnInit(EventArgs e)
        {
            //
```

```
    // CODEGEN: This call is required by the ASP.NET
    // Web Form Designer.
    //
    InitializeComponent();
    base.OnInit(e);
}


/// <summary>
/// Required method for Designer support - do not modify
/// the contents of this method with the code editor.
/// </summary>
private void InitializeComponent()
{
    this.Load += new System.EventHandler(this.Page_Load);
}
#endregion
}
```

The code is rather long because of the code-intensive process for writing HTML, but the code to write the HTML in the showTable1 and showTable2 methods is fairly straightforward. Dealing with the data isn't quite as simple.

Creating random data in .NET is simple: Use the Random class. The Random class seeds itself automatically with a time-based value when you create a new instance. For ex-VB readers, you don't need to use Randomize and supply a value, as was necessary in earlier versions of VB to initialize the randomization engine.

```
    Random rand = new Random();
```

To get random values from the Random object, use the Next method, which returns the next random number in a series. An overloaded version (used in Listing 10.6) returns a number between the parameters lowerBound and upperBound. For example, the following line returns a number between –1000 and 1000.

```
aValue = rand.Next(-1000, 1000);
```

Because one way to create a two-dimensional table with data is to store that data in a two-dimensional array, the getRandomData method fills an array with the random values and returns the array. The array isn't an array of simple numbers; it's a two-dimensional array of objects. Items 1 through 4 are integers, but every fifth item in the array is a string.

```
    private Object[,] getRandomData() {
        String[] strings= {
            "Row 1", "Row 2", "Row 3", "Row 4", "Row 5"};
        Object[,] values = new Object[5,5];
        int aValue;
        Random rand = new Random();
        int i, j;
        for (i = 0; i < 5; i++) {
```

```
        for (j = 0; j < 5; j++) {
           if (j == 4) {
              values[i, j] = strings[i];
           }
           else {
              aValue = rand.Next(-1000, 1000);
              values[i, j] = aValue;
           }
        }
     }
     return values;
  }
```

One problem is that the `Page_Load` method doesn't know the bounds of the array—that's defined inside the `getRandomData` method. When you don't know the bounds of a multidimensional array, you can pass it by placing commas between the array subscripts and leaving the subscripts blank.

```
private void showTable2(Object[,] values) {// code here}
```

To write the data, though, you need to know the data type because the object type determines the formatting. One way is to use the `GetType.Name` method. The code uses this to differentiate integer (`Int32`) values from `String` values.

```
switch (values[i, j].GetType().Name) {
   case "String" :
      // output a formatted string
      break;
   case "Int32" :
      // output a formatted number
      break;
}
```

The ASP.NET server controls render themselves using an HtmlTextWriter. When you need to write HTML at runtime, it's much easier to work with the HTML controls and set properties and methods—especially when you need to change things—than it is to work with the raw HTML. Of course, you aren't limited to tables—you can use any HTML control from the toolbox in a similar manner. So you can see the difference, spend a little time comparing the handwritten HTML code output from the `showTable1` method with the HtmlTextWriter-generated code from the `showTable2` method. The output from both methods is identical, but the code in the second method is (in my opinion) easier to maintain.

Sending and Receiving Files

You've already seen one way to send file *data* in Chapter 6, "Introduction to the System.Web Namespace," but not how to send files themselves. This will be an extremely short section, because you send files by making sure the client's browser receives a file type that it won't open and display. For example, people constantly ask, "How can I send an HTML file? Whenever my users download the file, it opens in their browsers—they don't get a chance to save the file to disk." The answer is this:

Zip the file. When a browser receives a file with a `.zip` extension, it shows the File Save As dialog rather than opening the file directly.

Browsers react differently to file types because users install add-ins and add "helper applications." Some browsers, such as IE, recognize Microsoft Office document extensions and open them as ActiveX documents inside the browser window, merging the application's menus with IE's own menus. Because of these differences and, even more important, because of the numerous viruses present on the Internet, you should always zip your files before letting users download them.

Sending (Downloading) Files

It's important for you to understand that only the client can initiate a file download. You can't write VB.NET code that downloads a file. For Web applications, it's best to forget the term "downloading" or at least, whenever you hear it, twist it in your head so that you think, "Get the client to request the file."

When you approach downloading from the client point of view, it becomes obvious that there are many ways to get the client to request the file. The most common method is to provide a link. For example, the following link will download the text file `FileStaticMethods.zip` that you can find in the `CSharpASP\ch10` folder on `www.sybex.com`. Either use the code below or run `ch10-8.aspx`. You may need to adjust the URL to match your server. Watch for unwanted line breaks in the following URL.

```
<a href="http://localhost/CSharpASP/ch10/
    FileStaticMethods.zip">
    Download FileStaticMethods
</a>
```

When users click the link in IE, they'll see the File Download dialog (see Figure 10.5).

FIGURE 10.5

The IE 6 File
Download dialog

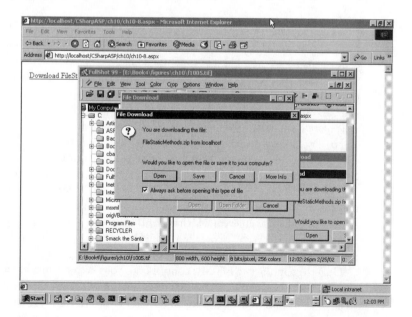

In IE, two dialog boxes actually are open at this point, but the second dialog is hidden behind the File Download dialog. After users select one of the options on the topmost dialog, those who choose the Save option will have an option to save the file. Otherwise, they go directly to this background File Download dialog, which shows a download progress bar. In Figure 10.6, I've dragged the Save As dialog partially out of the way so you can see both dialogs.

FIGURE 10.6

The background IE 6 File Download dialog (progress dialog)

As you've seen, it's easy to create a link that downloads a file, but that may not suit your interface requirements. What if you want to use a button rather than a link? Don't be fooled by the `LinkButton` control's name—it acts like a button, not a link, so you don't want to use that. What if you want to use an image, or a selection from a `ListBox`? You need to write a little client-side script to use these controls to download a file. You haven't seen any client-side script so far in this book, and I'm not going to explain it here, so you'll have to take it at face value for now. Nevertheless, it's going to get a little more complicated than you might like. Bear with me.

For any control type except a `HyperLink`, you call a method in a client-side script to request the file. The event you use to fire the script depends on the control. For example, you would use the `onclick` event for button or image controls, and the `onchange` event for `ListBox`es or `DropDownList` controls.

The problem is that when you use Web Forms server controls, some events *don't fire on the client—* they fire on the server. Fortunately, you can work around this easily. When you need to write client-side script to handle an event *and* that event is one that ASP.NET handles on the server, one solution is this: Don't use a Web Form server control; use an HTML control instead. I'll show you another method in Chapter 20, "Leveraging Browser Clients."

Drag the appropriate HTML control onto your Web Form and set its properties. When you're ready to code the client script, switch to HTML mode. Find the appropriate control tag and insert an attribute for the event you want to respond to. The attribute's value is the name of a function to run when the event occurs—it's a function pointer, in other words.

I recommend you try writing at least one client-side script before you continue. To write a client-side script, create a Web Form and add an HTML `Button` control to the page. Then, switch to HTML mode, find the `Button` control tag—it will be an `<input>` control with a `type="button"` attribute—and add an `onclick="getFile()"` attribute and value (see Listing 10.6).

Paste the `<script>` tag from Listing 10.6 into the HTML. It's best to put the script inside the `<head>` section. Then run the Web Form.

Listing 10.7 contains a slightly more complex example. The Web Form `ch10-8.aspx` (see Figure 10.7) contains three different controls: a HyperLink, an HTML Button, and a ListBox, all of which download the `FileStaticMethods.zip` file.

FIGURE 10.7

Downloading files using various controls

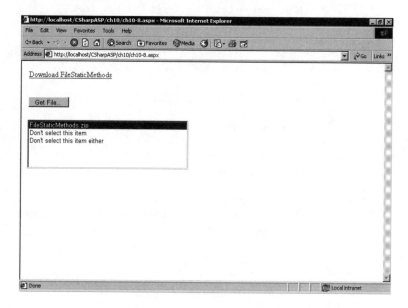

LISTING 10.7: HTML CODE FOR THE ch10-8.aspx FILE (ch10-8.aspx)

```
<%@ Page Language="vb" AutoEventWireup="false"
    Codebehind="ch10-8.aspx.cs"
    Inherits="CSharpASP.ch10_8"%>
<!DOCTYPE HTML PUBLIC "-//W3C//DTD HTML 4.0
    Transitional//EN">
<HTML>
<HEAD>
<title></title>
<meta name="GENERATOR"
    content="Microsoft Visual Studio.NET 7.0">
<meta name="CODE_LANGUAGE" content="Visual Basic 7.0">
<meta name="vs_defaultClientScript" content="JavaScript">
<meta name="vs_targetSchema"
    content="http://schemas.microsoft.com/intellisense/ie5">
</HEAD>
```

```
<body MS_POSITIONING="GridLayout">
<form id="Form1" method="post" runat="server"
   language="javascript">
<asp:HyperLink id="HyperLink1" style="Z-INDEX: 101;
   LEFT: 16px; POSITION: absolute; TOP: 18px"
   runat="server"
   Width="272px" Height="17px" Target="_blank"
   NavigateUrl="FileStaticMethods.zip">Download
   FileStaticMethods</asp:HyperLink> 
<INPUT style="Z-INDEX: 103; LEFT: 15px; WIDTH: 87px;
   POSITION: absolute; TOP: 75px; HEIGHT: 21px"
   type="button" value="Get File..."
   onclick="getFile('FileStaticMethods.zip')">
<asp:ListBox id="ListBox1" style="Z-INDEX: 104; LEFT: 13px;
   POSITION: absolute; TOP: 122px" runat="server"
   Height="102px" Width="344px"
   onchange="getFileFromList(this)"></asp:ListBox>
</form>
<script language="javascript">
<!--
function getFile(fname) {
   window.navigate(fname);
}
function getFileFromList(aList) {
   var fname = aList.options[aList.selectedIndex].text
   window.navigate(fname);
}
//-->
</script>
</body>
</HTML>
```

In this example, the button `onclick` event passes the filename `FileStaticMethods.zip` to the `get-File()` function. When the user clicks the button, the browser calls the highlighted `getFile()` function in the `<script>` tag at the end of Listing 10.7. The function commands the current browser window to request (navigate) to the filename passed in the `fname` parameter.

As an aside, you can navigate to any valid URL using the `window.navigate` method. In other words, the result is the same as when you use the `Response.Redirect` method on the server (although that's not exactly how the `Response.Redirect` method works—see Chapter 6 for details). When you request a URL that returns HTML or some other MIME type that the browser understands, it displays the contents of the file. For all other files, such as the zip file in this example, the browser displays a dialog asking if you want to open the file or save it to disk. If you choose to open the file, the browser will try to run the application associated with the file's extension (or the appropriate Helper application in Netscape browsers). Note that the unrecognized file type doesn't cause the browser to clear the current page.

If you were to use a DropDownList or a ListBox rather than an HTML button, you would use the onchange event. The onchange event is *not* handled on the server, so you can add the event attribute to the <asp:ListBox> tag.

NOTE *If you decide to use an HTML ListBox or DropDownList instead, remember that those controls are* <select> *tags in HTML.*

The ListBox code in Listing 10.7 contains the attribute and value onchange="getFileFromList (this)".

```
<asp:ListBox id="ListBox1" style="Z-INDEX: 104; LEFT: 13px;
    POSITION: absolute; TOP: 122px" runat="server"
    Height="102px" Width="344px"
    onchange="getFileFromList(this)"></asp:ListBox>
```

The this parameter is an object reference to the ListBox control itself, meaning that when the user clicks an item in the list, the onchange event fires, and the page calls the getFileFromList function, passing the select list input control to the function.

First, the script retrieves the selected list item. An HTML select control has an indexed collection of options, each one of which has text and value properties. In that case, you want to retrieve the text property. You can determine the selected item with the selectedIndex property.

```
function getFileFromList(aList) {
    var fname = aList.options[aList.selectedIndex].text
    window.navigate(fname);
}
```

After retrieving the selected item text and assigning it to the variable fname, the script uses the window.navigate method to request the file—exactly the same code as the button onclick event uses.

As a final note to this topic, there are other ways to write the client-side script. In fact, you can pass the selected item directly by using this attribute and value in the <select> tag:

```
onchange="getFile(this.options[this.selectedIndex].text)"
```

The preceding code calls the same function as the button onclick event. By writing the code this way, you could eliminate the need for two separate scripts.

Receiving Files

In contrast to previous versions, ASP.NET makes it relatively easy to receive files uploaded by a client as well as to send files. Request.HttpFilesCollection contains a collection of files sent by the client. To let a client upload a file, place an HTML File Field control on the page. Right-click the control and select Run as Server Control from the context menu. That lets you access the properties of the control in your code-behind class.

There's a small trick involved in getting the File Field control to work properly. Switch to HTML view, find the <form> tag, and add the attribute and value enctype="multipart/form-data" to the tag. The Web Form ch10-9.aspx contains an example. In that Web Form, after adding the attribute, the <form> tag looks like this:

```
<form id="Form1" method="post" runat="server"
  enctype="multipart/form-data">
```

After adding the attribute, you can run the Web Form. The presence of the File Field control in the ASPX file tells the page to create an HtmlFileInput control instance (the difference in the names is confusing). That control is a composite control that contains an input field and a Browse button (see Figure 10.8).

FIGURE 10.8

Uploading files: the File Field control

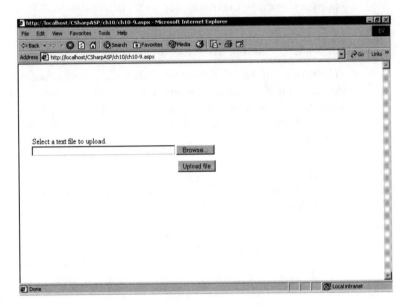

Run the ch10-9.aspx Web Form, click the Browse button, and select a text file. Click the Submit button to upload the file. When you click the Upload File button, the server runs this code:

```
private void cmdUpload_Click(object sender,
    System.EventArgs e) {
    StringBuilder sb = new StringBuilder();
    // Display information about posted file
    sb.Append("<b>Information about your uploaded " +
      "file</b>:<br><br>");
    sb.Append("Name: " + fileInput.PostedFile.FileName +
      "<br>");
    sb.Append("Type: " + fileInput.PostedFile.ContentType +
      "<br>");
    sb.Append("Size: " +
      fileInput.PostedFile.ContentLength.ToString() +
      "<br><br>");
```

```
    divInfo.Visible = true;
    divInfo.InnerHtml = sb.ToString();

    // Save uploaded file to server
    fileInput.PostedFile.SaveAs(Server.MapPath(".") +
        "\\uploadfile.txt");
}
```

The File Field control's name is `fileInput`. Most of the code in the method uses a StringBuilder to concatenate information about the file using the `fileInput` control's properties, which it places into a `Label` control named `divInfo`. The method retrieves the uploaded filename, content type (text/plain), and size (see Figure 10.9).

FIGURE 10.9

Uploading files: information available on the server from the HtmlFileInput control

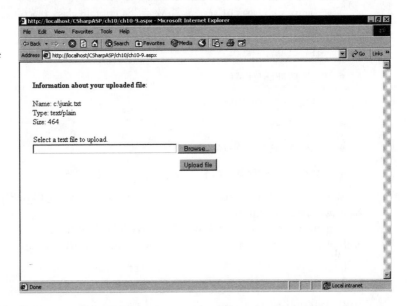

If you look carefully at the preceding example, you'll notice that the `fileInput` variable (the File Field control) has a property called `PostedFile`—which in turn has properties called `Filename`, `ContentType`, and `ContentLength`. This should be a clue that the `PostedFile` property contains an instance of another class, in this case the `HttpPostedFile` class. The last line of the code calls the `HttpPostedFile` object's `SaveAs` method to save the file to a directory on the server. Interestingly, `HttpPostedFile` is part of a collection of files uploaded from a client, called the `HttpFileCollection`, meaning you can upload more than one file at a time from the client. The server parses the data and file meta-information from the `Request` data and creates the `HttpFileCollection` when it receives the request.

The File Field HTML control can upload only one file at a time; but you can place more than one File Field control on a page and send both files at the same time with a Submit button.

Accessing the Windows Registry

Although you didn't have direct access to the Windows Registry using server-side script in classic ASP, several aftermarket controls provided that capability. You could also use some other language such as classic VB, which provided an easy way to read, write, and delete values from the Windows Registry using the `SaveSetting`, `GetSetting`, `GetAllSettings`, and `DeleteSetting` statements—but all the values resided in a specific key. In other words, there was no built-in way to read or write values from any other location in the Registry. But the need was there, so people used the Windows API calls from VB, which was awkward. C and C++ had fewer problems, but reading and writing to the Registry via API calls was not simple. Fortunately, the .NET framework solves that problem. In the Microsoft Win32 namespace, you'll find a Registry class that (as you might expect) wraps and simplifies access to the Registry. It's now child's play to read and write Registry values.

The Registry consists of several "hives" that contain class, machine, user, and configuration data. On a Windows 2000 server, the top-level hive names are as follows:

- `HKEY_CLASSES_ROOT`

- `HKEY_CURRENT_USER`

- `HKEY_LOCAL_MACHINE`

- `HKEY_USERS`

- `HKEY_CURRENT_CONFIG`

- `HKEY_PERFORMANCE_DATA`

Windows 98/ME exposes an additional key, the `HKEY_DYN_DATA` key, which is intended to hold data that changes frequently.

You don't need to create a `Registry` object. The Registry class has no methods. Instead, it exposes each of these root keys as separate static properties that return `RegistryKey` objects:

```
RegistryKey localMachineRoot = Registry.LocalMachine;
RegistryKey classesRoot = Registry.ClassesRoot;
```

In ASP applications, people often used the Registry to store application initialization and configuration values. You no longer need to do this in .NET because you can—and should—use the `Web.config` file `<appSettings>` section instead; I've included this section for people who need to read existing settings from their Registries.

TIP   *I recommend that you use your application's `Web.config` file rather than the Windows Registry to store application initialization and configuration values.*

The Web Form `ch10-10.aspx` shows how to read, write, and update Registry keys. It modifies only the contents of the key `Software\Sybex\CSharpASP` in the `HKEY_CURRENT_USER` hive. The Web Form displays any existing subkeys and values in the `CSharpASP` key and lets you add new values and modify or delete existing values.

WARNING   *The code in the* ch10-10.aspx.cs *Web Form's* Page_Load *method accesses the Registry. You will need to apply sufficient permissions to the Registry key* HKEY_LOCAL_MACHINE\SOFTWARE *on your server to allow the ASP.NET account or your logon account to create, read, and write the* Sybex *subkey. You can set Registry permissions using the* regedt32.exe *program that ships with Windows.*

WARNING   *Modifying the Registry can cause your server to fail if you change critical settings or alter security so that you can't read or write the Registry.*

When you run the Web Form, the Page_Load event first checks to see if the HKEY_CURRENT_USER\ Software\Sybex Registry key exists.

```
private RegistryKey m_keySybex;
m_keySybex = Registry.LocalMachine.OpenSubKey
    ("SOFTWARE\\Sybex", true);
```

The OpenSubKey method returns null if the key does not exist. In this example, if the key doesn't exist, the code creates it:

```
if (m_keySybex == null ) {
    try {
        m_keySybex = Registry.LocalMachine.CreateSubKey
            ("SOFTWARE\\Sybex");
    }
    catch (Exception ex) {
        Response.Write(ex.Message);
        Response.End();
    }
}
```

In contrast, the CreateSubKey method can throw any of several exceptions if the create operation fails.

After creating or opening the HKEY_CURRENT_USER\Software\Sybex\ subkey, the code repeats the test-create operation with the CSharpASP subkey.

```
m_keyCSharpASP= m_keySybex.OpenSubKey("CSharpASP", true);
if (m_keyCSharpASP == null ) {
    try {
        m_keySybex.CreateSubKey("CSharpASP");
        m_keyCSharpASP = m_keySybex.OpenSubKey
            ("CSharpASP", true);
    }
    catch (Exception ex) {
        Response.Write(ex.Message);
        Response.End();
    }
}
```

Because of this code, at the end of the Page_Load routine, the Web Form always has a reference to the CSharpASP key in the m_keyCSharpASP variable.

Each key in the Registry may contain subkeys—much like an XML document. The `fillSubKeys` method reads any subkeys that exist and stores the subkey names in the string array variable `m_subkeys()`.

```
private void fillSubKeys() {
   try {
      m_subKeys = m_keyCSharpASP.GetSubKeyNames();
   }
   catch (Exception ex) {
      Response.Write(ex.Message);
      Response.End();
   }
}
```

The Web Form contains a `ListBox` that displays the keys. When a user clicks a key name in the `ListBox`, the Web Form automatically posts the selection to the server, retrieves the value of the selected subkey, and displays the key name and value in two `TextBoxes` so that the user can view or edit the value for that subkey. The simplest way to fill the `ListBox` is to databind it to the `m_subkeys()` array, which the Web Form does during the initial page load.

```
if (!IsPostBack) {
   ListKeys.DataSource = m_subKeys;
   ListKeys.DataBind();
}
```

The Web Form then is displayed. Because the ListBox's `AutoPostBack` property is set to `true`, the form gets posted each time a user selects an item in the ListBox. That fires the `SelectedIndexChanged` event on the server, which retrieves the key and value for the selected item and sets the contents of the `TextKey` and `TextValue` TextBoxes to the selected key name and value.

```
private void ListKeys_SelectedIndexChanged(object sender,
   System.EventArgs e) {
   RegistryKey aKey;
   int anIndex;
   String aName;
   anIndex = ListKeys.SelectedIndex;
   if (anIndex >= 0) {
      aName = ListKeys.Items[anIndex].Text;
      TextKey.Text = aName;
      // set the subkey
      aKey = m_keyCSharpASP.OpenSubKey(aName);
      // retrieve the default value
      TextValue.Text = (String) aKey.GetValue(null);
      aKey.Close();
   }
}
```

The `GetValue` method in the next-to-last line in the `if` block accepts a value name. Note that the code passes the value `null`, which retrieves the default value of the key. This example uses only the default value for each subkey.

NOTE   *All keys have at least one value—a default, unnamed value, which you can retrieve by passing* `null` *to the* `getValue` *method—but keys may have multiple named values. If you need to access a key with multiple values, you can retrieve the value names using the* `GetValueNames` *method and then retrieve any individual value using the* `getValue` *method.*

There are two buttons on the Web Form—Delete and Add/Update. Clicking Delete posts the form. The Web Form tests to see if the key specified in the `TextKey` field exists. If so, it deletes the key; otherwise, it displays a client-side alert. You'll see more about sending client-side script like this in Chapter 24, "Efficiency and Scalability."

```
private void btnDelete_Click(object sender,
    System.EventArgs e) {
    String aName;
    RegistryKey aKey;
    aName = TextKey.Text;
    if (aName != "") {
        // set the subkey
        aKey = m_keyCSharpASP.OpenSubKey(aName);
        if (aKey != null) {
            aKey.Close();
            m_keyCSharpASP.DeleteSubKey(aName);
            // clear the text boxes
            TextKey.Text = null;
            TextValue.Text = null;
            // reset the listbox
            ListKeys.ClearSelection();
            fillSubKeys();
            ListKeys.DataSource = m_subKeys;
            ListKeys.DataBind();
        }
        else {
            RegisterStartupScript("BadKey",
            "<script type=\"text/javascript\">" +
            "alert('The key you entered does not " +
            "exist.');</script>");
        }
    }
}
```

When the user clicks the Add/Update button, the Web Form fires the `btnAdd_Click` event. That method retrieves the key name from the `TextKey` field and calls the `CSharpASP` key's `Create SubKey` method. If the key already exists, the method retrieves it. If the key does not exist, the method creates it. In either case, the method returns the subkey, which `btnAdd_Click` then uses to set the default value to the text entered by the user in the `TextValue` field.

```
private void btnAdd_Click(object sender,
    System.EventArgs e) {
    RegistryKey aKey;
    String aKeyName;
```

```
        String aValue;
        aKeyName = TextKey.Text;
        aValue = TextValue.Text;
        if (aKeyName != null) {
            aKey = m_keyCSharpASP.CreateSubKey(aKeyName);
            if (aKey != null) {
                aKey.SetValue(null, aValue);
                aKey.Close();
                ListKeys.ClearSelection();
                fillSubKeys();
                ListKeys.DataSource = m_subKeys;
                ListKeys.DataBind();
            }
        }
    }
}
```

In both the btnDelete_Click and btnAdd_Click events, note that the code calls the fillSubKeys method and rebinds the ListKeys ListBox if the event changes the Registry. Otherwise, the ASP.NET engine restores the ListBox from the _VIEWSTATE data. Listing 10.8 shows the full code.

LISTING 10.8: THE WEB FORM ch10-10.aspx.cs CODE

```
using System;
using System.Collections;
using System.ComponentModel;
using System.Data;
using System.Drawing;
using System.Web;
using System.Web.SessionState;
using System.Web.UI;
using System.Web.UI.WebControls;
using System.Web.UI.HtmlControls;
using Microsoft.Win32;

namespace CSharpASP.ch10 {
    /// <summary>
    /// Summary description for ch10_10.
    /// </summary>
    public class ch10_10 : System.Web.UI.Page {
        protected System.Web.UI.WebControls.ListBox ListKeys;
        protected System.Web.UI.WebControls.Button btnAdd;
        protected System.Web.UI.WebControls.Label Label1;
        protected System.Web.UI.WebControls.Label Label2;
        protected System.Web.UI.WebControls.Label Label3;
        protected System.Web.UI.WebControls.TextBox TextKey;
        protected System.Web.UI.WebControls.TextBox
    TextValue;
        protected System.Web.UI.WebControls.Button btnDelete;
```

```csharp
private RegistryKey m_keySybex;
private RegistryKey m_keyCSharpASP;
private String[] m_subKeys;

private void Page_Load(object sender,
   System.EventArgs e) {
   RegistryKey x;
   x = Registry.PerformanceData;
   if (x==null) {
      Response.Write("x is null");
      Response.End();
   }
   m_keySybex =
      Registry.LocalMachine.OpenSubKey
      ("SOFTWARE\\Sybex", true);
   if (m_keySybex == null ) {
      try {
         m_keySybex = Registry.LocalMachine.
            CreateSubKey("SOFTWARE\\Sybex");
      }
      catch (Exception ex) {
         Response.Write(ex.Message);
         Response.End();
      }
   }
   m_keyCSharpASP= m_keySybex.OpenSubKey
     ("CSharpASP", true);
   if (m_keyCSharpASP == null ) {
      try {
         m_keySybex.CreateSubKey("CSharpASP");
         m_keyCSharpASP = m_keySybex.OpenSubKey
            ("CSharpASP", true);
      }
      catch (Exception ex) {
         Response.Write(ex.Message);
         Response.End();
      }
   }
   fillSubKeys();
   if (!IsPostBack) {
      ListKeys.DataSource = m_subKeys;
      ListKeys.DataBind();
   }

}

private void fillSubKeys() {
   try {
```

```csharp
        m_subKeys = m_keyCSharpASP.GetSubKeyNames();
    }
    catch (Exception ex) {
        Response.Write(ex.Message);
        Response.End();
    }
}
public override void Dispose() {
        if (m_keyCSharpASP != null) {
            m_keyCSharpASP.Close();
        }
        if (m_keySybex != null) {
            m_keySybex.Close();
        }
    base.Dispose();
}

#region Web Form Designer generated code
override protected void OnInit(EventArgs e) {
    //
    // CODEGEN: This call is required by the
    // ASP.NET Web Form Designer.
    //
    InitializeComponent();
    base.OnInit(e);
}

/// <summary>
/// Required method for Designer support -
/// do not modify
/// the contents of this method with the code editor.
/// </summary>
private void InitializeComponent() {
    this.ListKeys.SelectedIndexChanged += new
        System.EventHandler
        (this.ListKeys_SelectedIndexChanged);
    this.btnAdd.Click += new
        System.EventHandler(this.btnAdd_Click);
    this.btnDelete.Click += new
        System.EventHandler(this.btnDelete_Click);
    this.Load += new
        System.EventHandler(this.Page_Load);

}
#endregion

private void ListKeys_SelectedIndexChanged
    (object sender, System.EventArgs e) {
```

```csharp
    RegistryKey aKey;
    int anIndex;
    String aName;
    anIndex = ListKeys.SelectedIndex;
    if (anIndex >= 0) {
        aName = ListKeys.Items[anIndex].Text;
        TextKey.Text = aName;
        // set the subkey
        aKey = m_keyCSharpASP.OpenSubKey(aName);
        // retrieve the default value
        TextValue.Text = (String) aKey.GetValue(null);
        aKey.Close();
    }

}

private void btnDelete_Click(object sender,
    System.EventArgs e) {
    String aName;
    RegistryKey aKey;
    aName = TextKey.Text;
    if (aName != "") {
        // set the subkey
        aKey = m_keyCSharpASP.OpenSubKey(aName);
        if (aKey != null) {
            aKey.Close();
            m_keyCSharpASP.DeleteSubKey(aName);
            // clear the text boxes
            TextKey.Text = null;
            TextValue.Text = null;
            // reset the listbox
            ListKeys.ClearSelection();
            fillSubKeys();
            ListKeys.DataSource = m_subKeys;
            ListKeys.DataBind();
        }
        else {
            RegisterStartupScript("BadKey",
                "<script type=\"text/javascript\">" +
                "alert('The key you entered does not " +
                "exist.');</script>");
        }
    }
}

private void btnAdd_Click(object sender,
    System.EventArgs e) {
    RegistryKey aKey;
```

```
String aKeyName;
String aValue;
aKeyName = TextKey.Text;
aValue = TextValue.Text;
if (aKeyName != null) {
    aKey = m_keyCSharpASP.CreateSubKey(aKeyName);
    if (aKey != null) {
        aKey.SetValue(null, aValue);
        aKey.Close();
        ListKeys.ClearSelection();
        fillSubKeys();
        ListKeys.DataSource = m_subKeys;
        ListKeys.DataBind();
    }
}
        }
    }
}
```

Summary

At this point, you should feel reasonably comfortable with file access, with Streams, with writing customized HTML to files and to the client, and with sending files to and from the client. There's no way to cover these topics comprehensively in a book of this size—you could write a small book on the topic of Streams in .NET alone—but you should recognize that Streams let you read and write data generically and that you can use one type of Stream to read or write data to and from an underlying Stream. I hope you also see that the .NET framework uses Streams extensively in its own classes, so your code has the same access (and thus the same speed and efficiency) as the .NET classes do. You've also seen how to write to the server's Event log and how to read, modify, and delete keys and values from the Windows Registry.

In the next chapter, you'll see how to send and receive messages with .NET, both e-mail messages and other types of notification messages, such as communicating between two Web Forms.

Chapter 11

Sending and Receiving Messages with ASP.NET

SOME OF THE MOST common problems when building Web applications involve sending messages. In this chapter, you'll work through a few of the most common messaging-type tasks by solving a few situational problems.

In this chapter:

- Message Types
- Filesystem Messages
- Sending E-mail Messages
- Calling Methods in Another Web Form
- Retrieving Data from Another Web Page

Message Types

You can send and receive several different types of messages with C# Web applications. Here are some examples of situations in which you might want to send messages:

- Salespeople save their order files to a specific directory. Each time a file arrives, you want to add an entry to a report file available via the company intranet. How can you determine when an order arrives?

- You want to create a page that counts the number of requests in the IIS log made over the past 24 hours and sends the total to your boss via e-mail. How do you read the IIS log, and how can you format and send e-mail from a Web Form?

- You've written a method or added code to an event in a Web Form and want to call that method from a different Web Form. How do you make the original Web Form respond to a message from your current Web Form?

- You want to retrieve the contents of a Web page, parse it for some data, and display the data on your own page. How can you perform an HTTP GET request from a Web Form?

All these tasks require sending and receiving messages, yet each presents a different problem or set of problems. For example, to solve these problems, you must be able to respond to messages from the filesystem, send e-mail, send a message to another Web Form, and request data from another site or application. In this chapter, you'll see some ways to solve these problems. A couple of notes before you begin: These are instructional examples, not production code. The examples are meant to be just that—examples—and are by no means the only, or even the best, way to solve the problems. The best way depends entirely on your network, your hardware, and your particular problem.

Filesystem Messages

Problem: Salespeople upload their order files to a specific directory. Each time a file arrives, you want to add an entry to a report file available via the company intranet.

The task requires you to watch a directory and take some action when it changes. For a standard application, you might grab the directory contents and cache them in an array, then using a timer, check periodically to see if the directory contents have changed by comparing the current contents with the cached contents. Unfortunately, doing that is both resource intensive (especially if the directory is large) and prone to error, because if your application shuts down, you run the risk of missing directory changes.

Another way to check would be to create a Web Form that someone could run periodically and that, again, would check to see if the directory contents had changed. But that method is also prone to error, mostly by omission. The person designated to perform the task might be absent, might forget, or might be unable to run the page for some other reason.

You may have questions about the task, such as "Why is this a messaging task? Isn't this a timing and processing task?" The answer is that it is a messaging task because you use an instance of a .NET class called FileSystemWatcher to watch the directory for you. That's a change in perspective. Rather than your checking the directory for changes, the operating system can send a message when the directory changes, at which point you can initiate the appropriate action. You use a FileSystemWatcher to do this.

The FileSystemWatcher can watch for several different types of changes, including deletions and additions, modifications to existing files, attribute changes, file and directory name changes, file date alterations, file size changes, or changes to the file and folder security settings. You can elect to watch an entire directory and all of its subdirectories, a single directory, or a set of files (via a filter) within a directory on a local drive, network drive, or a remote machine. In other words, the FileSystemWatcher is extremely flexible.

But that doesn't answer yet another question: "How can you accomplish this task with an ASP.NET application—which may or may not be running at any given time?" Remember that an ASP.NET application shuts down after the last session times out or is abandoned. Unfortunately, the flexibility of the FileSystemWatcher class doesn't alter the fact that your application may or may not be running. You have to face facts—your application can't perform any work if it's not running; therefore, you need to look outside the ASP.NET framework for this type of functionality. The best way to watch a directory continuously is with a Windows Service, so you need to write a service that interacts with your application by running code when a pertinent directory change event occurs.

Writing a service application is extremely similar to writing any other application type in .NET. I'll run through this briefly because it's not the focus of this book, but it is such a common problem that it's worth including here.

Start a new Windows Service project in VS.NET and call it CSharpDirectoryWatcherService. When you create a new service application, VS.NET automatically creates a `service1.cs` class file, which inherits from `System.ServiceProcess.ServiceBase` and creates two stub event subroutines— `OnStart` and `OnStop among others`. Windows uses the name of the class that defines the service as the service name by default, so you should rename the `service.cs` file `DirectoryWatcher.cs`. Note that both the namespace and the class itself are named CSharpDirectoryWatcherService. You need to edit the code to change the names as well as rename the file. The following code illustrates (but is not a direct copy of) the default code VS.NET creates for the new class.

```
namespace CSharpDirectoryWatcherService

{
    public class CSharpDirectoryWatcherService :
        System.ServiceProcess.ServiceBase {

        protected override void OnStart(string[] args) {
            /// Set things in motion so your service can do its work.
        }

        protected override void OnStop() {
            // Add code here to perform any tear-down necessary
            // to stop your service.
        }
    }
}
```

Assume that the salespeople save their files to the `CSharpASP\ch11\orders_in` folder. On my machine, that directory is `c:\inetpub\wwwroot\CSharpASP\ch11\orders_in`. Whenever a file arrives, the DirectoryWatcher service should move the file to the folder `c:\inetpub\wwwroot\CSharpASP\ch11\orders_out` and log the file arrival and its destination.

Because you know in advance which directory you want to watch, you can hard-code the name of the directory you want to watch into the code.

NOTE *I don't normally recommend that you hard-code the path to any external resource, but in this particular instance, it's better to have the service fail than have an administrator accidentally enter the wrong name.*

The service defines two private variables to hold the names—`m_pathin` and `m_pathout`—a variable called `fsw` that holds a FileSystemWatcher instance, and two `DirectoryInfo` variables that correspond to the file paths.

```
using System.ServiceProcess;
using System.IO;
public class CSharpDirectoryWatcherService :
    System.ServiceProcess.ServiceBase {

    /// <summary>
    /// Required designer variable.
    /// </summary>
    private System.ComponentModel.Container components = null;
```

```
FileSystemWatcher fsw;
private static String m_pathin =
    "c:\\inetpub\\wwwroot\\CSharpASP\\ch11\\orders_in";
private static String m_pathout =
    "c:\\inetpub\\wwwroot\\CSharpASP\\ch11\\orders_out";
DirectoryInfo di_in = new DirectoryInfo(m_pathin);
DirectoryInfo di_out = new DirectoryInfo(m_pathout);

// more code here
}
```

It's worth looking at the autogenerated code. Click the plus (+) sign next to the line Component Designer Generated Code to expand the region. Note that the IDE creates a main method that defines the services to run in this namespace—yes, the plural is correct—you can define more than one service in a namespace.

The ServiceBase class has several events that you can handle to define how your service responds to system events. In particular, you should override or at least consider overriding the OnStart, OnStop, OnPause, and OnContinue events. The DirectoryWatcher service overrides all these events.

Because services don't have a visual interface, you need to create a way for an administrator to know whether the service is running. The easiest way is to write to a log file—this service uses the standard Event log application file. At minimum, you should log an event when the service starts or stops, but you don't have to write the code to do that—the ServiceBase class has a Boolean property called AutoLog that, when true, writes the entries for you automatically. The AutoLog property's default value is true, but in the example I've turned it off because the component writes custom messages when its status changes. You can set the AutoLog property in the OnStart event code.

```
base.AutoLog = false;
```

You wouldn't want your service to fail if the directories don't exist, so the first task is to check the orders_in and orders_out directories and create them if they don't already exist. The code that creates the directories and writes the log entries should look familiar if you read Chapter 10, "File and Event Log Access with ASP.NET." Create a DirectoryInfo object bound to the m_pathin variable that defines the input path. Check to see if the directory exists inside a try block. If not, create the directory. Repeat the operation with the m_pathout directory. If any operation fails, write a message to the Event log. If both directories exist or can be created, you can create the FileSystemWatcher object and set its properties (see the highlighted code, below).

```
protected override void OnStart(string[] args) {
    base.AutoLog = false;
    try {
        // create the orders_in directory if it doesn't already exist
        if (!di_in.Exists) {
            di_in.Create();
        }
        try {
            if (!di_out.Exists) {
```

```csharp
                di_out.Create();
            }
            try {
                EventLog.WriteEntry("CSharpDirectoryWatcherService",
                    "DirectoryWatcher starting.");
                // create a FileSystemWatcher
                fsw = new FileSystemWatcher(m_pathin);
                fsw.Created += new
                    System.IO.FileSystemEventHandler(this.fsw_created);

                // don't watch subdirectories
                fsw.IncludeSubdirectories = false;

                // enable watching
                fsw.EnableRaisingEvents = true;
                EventLog.WriteEntry("CSharpDirectoryWatcherService",
                    "Service started successfully.");
            }
            catch {
                try {
                    EventLog.WriteEntry("CSharpDirectoryWatcherService",
                        "Service starting.");
                }
                catch (Exception ex1) {
                    EventLog.WriteEntry("CSharpDirectoryWatcherService",
                        "Unable to watch the directory: " +
                        m_pathin + System.Environment.NewLine +
                        "Error Description: " +
                        ex1.Message);
                }
            }
        }
        catch (Exception ex) {
            EventLog.WriteEntry("CSharpDirectoryWatcherService",
                "Unable to create the directory " +
            m_pathout + System.Environment.NewLine +
                "Error Description: " + ex.Message);
        }
    }
    catch (Exception ex) {
        EventLog.WriteEntry("CSharpDirectoryWatcherService",
            "Unable to create the directory " + m_pathin +
            System.Environment.NewLine + "Error Description: " +
            ex.Message);
    }
}
}
```

Most of the code consists of error trapping because you don't want to let a service fail without generating some type of error message. The FileSystemWatcher constructor requires a string parameter containing the name of the directory you want to watch.

```
fsw = new FileSystemWatcher(m_pathin);
```

In this case, you don't want to watch subdirectories, so turn off the IncludeSubdirectories property:

```
// don't watch subdirectories
fsw.IncludeSubdirectories = false;
```

You must enable the FileSystemWatcher using the EnableRaisingEvents property before it will raise any events.

```
// enable watching
fsw.EnableRaisingEvents = true;
```

Both the OnStop and OnStart event handlers override ServiceBase class methods. Administrators can pause and continue a service via the Windows Service applet interface. The DirectoryWatcher service pauses the FileSystemWatcher when the overridden OnPause event fires and restarts it when the overridden OnContinue event fires. It logs both events.

```
protected override void OnPause() {
    fsw.EnableRaisingEvents = false;
    EventLog.WriteEntry("CSharpDirectoryWatcherService",
        "Service paused for path " + m_pathin);
}

protected override void OnContinue() {
    fsw.EnableRaisingEvents = true;
EventLog.WriteEntry("CSharpDirectoryWatcherService",
    "Service continued for path " + m_pathin);
}
```

When the service stops for any reason, the service calls the Dispose method and then releases the FileSystemWatcher by setting it to Nothing. The only directory change that this service traps is the created event.

When a salesperson adds a new file to the orders_in directory, the service moves the file to the orders_out directory and then logs the move in a file called report.txt. The FileSystemEventArgs parameter contains the Name and Fullname property values of the file that was just created. I've removed the error-trapping and cleanup code from the snippet below so it's easier to read.

```
private void fsw_created(Object sender, FileSystemEventArgs e) {
    // move the file
    FileInfo fi = new FileInfo(e.FullPath);
    StreamWriter sw;
```

```
    try {
        fi.MoveTo(m_pathout + "\\" +  e.Name);
        // add to processed file report
        try {
            fi = new FileInfo(m_pathout + "\\report.txt");
            if (!fi.Exists) {
                sw = fi.CreateText();
            }
            else {
                sw = fi.AppendText();
            }
            try {
                sw.WriteLine(e.FullPath + "," + m_pathout + "\\" +
    e.Name);
            }
            catch {
                EventLog.WriteEntry("CSharpDirectoryWatcherService",
                    "Unable to write to the file " + fi.FullName);
            }
            finally {
                try {
                    sw.Close();
                }
                finally {
                    // do nothing here
                }
            }
        }
        catch {
            EventLog.WriteEntry("CSharpDirectoryWatcherService",
                "Unable to create or append to the file " + m_pathout +
                "\\" + e.Name);
        }
    }
    catch {
        EventLog.WriteEntry("CSharpDirectoryWatcherService",
            "Unable to move the file " + e.FullPath + " to " +
            m_pathout + "\\" + e.Name);
    }
}
```

After you complete the service code, save and compile it, and then follow this procedure to make it run as a service.

1. Select the `DirectoryWatcher.cs` class and then double-click the class in the Solution Explorer to switch to Design mode.

2. In Design view, below the Properties window, click the Add Installer link. Clicking the link adds two components: a `ServiceProcessInstaller` and a `ServiceInstaller`. There will be one `ServiceInstaller` for each service exposed by your project (see Figure 11.1).

FIGURE 11.1

DirectoryWatcher-
Service project in
Design mode after
clicking the Add
Installer link

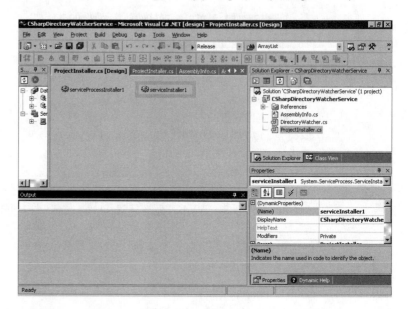

3. Select the serviceInstaller1 item from the Design window. In the Properties window, set the `ServiceName` property to `CSharpDirectoryWatcherService` (the name may already be set). This is the name that appears in the Event log by default.

4. Set the `StartType` property to `Automatic`. The `StartType` property is a ServiceStartMode enumeration that controls whether the service starts automatically when the server boots. Other possible settings are `Manual` (you must start the service through the Services applet) and `Disabled`, which prevents the service from running.

5. Click the ServiceProcessInstaller1 component and set the `Account` property to `LocalSystem`. The `Account` property controls the account under which your service runs.

6. Compile the service. Compiling a service application generates an EXE file.

7. Visual Studio ships with a utility named `InstallUtil.exe` that installs and uninstalls .NET-generated services. Run the `InstallUtil.exe` utility using the full path to the EXE file you generated in step 6. For example, on my machine you would use the following one-line command at a command prompt to install the service (watch out for line breaks in the code below—the command is a single line).

WARNING *Your path will differ from the path shown below. Make sure you enter the correct path. Enter the command on one line in the Command window.*

```
c:\WINNT\Microsoft.NET\Framework\v1.0.3512\InstallUtil.exe
"c:\documents and settings\administrator.RUSSELL-DUAL\
My Documents\Visual Studio
Projects\DirectoryWatcher\bin\Debug\
CSharpDirectoryWatcherService.exe"
```

8. Open the Services applet by clicking Start ➤ Programs ➤ Administrative Tools ➤ Services. Find the CSharpDirectoryWatcherService entry, right-click it, and then select Start from the context menu. Your service will start.

If your service does not start, or if it doesn't work the way you expect, you'll need to debug it. Debugging a service is slightly different from the way you've debugged Web Forms so far. To debug a service, you need to manually attach the debugger to the service process. To do that, load the service project into Visual Studio. Click the Debug menu, and select the Processes entry. You'll see the Processes dialog containing a list of processes running on your server (see Figure 11.2).

FIGURE 11.2

VS.NET debugger
Processes dialog

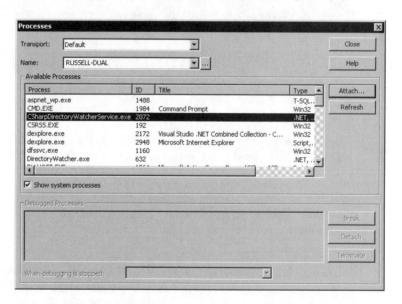

Click the Show System Processes check box to force the dialog to show all the system processes. Select the `CSharpDirectoryWatcherService.exe` entry, then click the Attach button. You'll see the Attach to Process dialog (see Figure 11.3).

FIGURE 11.3

VS.NET debugger Attach to Process dialog

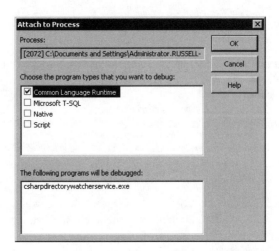

Check the Common Language Runtime entry and then click OK to close the dialog. Click Close to close the Processes dialog. After attaching to the process, you can set breakpoints and debug normally. If you need to make changes, follow these steps:

◆ Stop the service using the Services applet.

◆ Close the Services applet (you won't be able to uninstall the service with the Services applet open).

◆ From a command prompt, run the `InstallUtil.exe` utility with a –u (for uninstall) option:

```
c:\WINNT\Microsoft.NET\Framework\v1.0.3512\InstallUtil.exe –u
    "c:\documents and settings\administrator.RUSSELL-DUAL\
    My Documents\Visual Studio Projects\DirectoryWatcher\
    bin\debug\DirectoryWatcher.exe
```

WARNING   *Your path will differ from the preceding path. Make sure you enter the correct path.*

◆ Start the service.

Listing 11.1 shows the complete code for the `DirectoryWatcherService.cs` class. Unlike many code examples in this book, I've included the generated code in the listing because the comments explain how to generate an assembly that includes more than one service. Note that this code was compiled in Debug mode—you would definitely want to switch this off for a production version and use the `.exe` file generated in the `Release` folder rather than the `Debug` folder.

LISTING 11.1: THE COMPLETE CSHARPDIRECTORYWATCHERSERVICE CODE
             (DirectoryWatcher.cs)

```
using System;
using System.Collections;
```

```
using System.ComponentModel;
using System.Data;
using System.Diagnostics;
using System.ServiceProcess;
using System.IO;


namespace CSharpDirectoryWatcherService
{
    public class CSharpDirectoryWatcherService :
        System.ServiceProcess.ServiceBase {

        /// <summary>
        /// Required designer variable.
        /// </summary>
        private System.ComponentModel.Container components = null;
        private FileSystemWatcher fsw;
        private static String m_pathin =
            "c:\\inetpub\\wwwroot\\CSharpASP\\ch11\\orders_in";
        private static String m_pathout =
            "c:\\inetpub\\wwwroot\\CSharpASP\\ch11\\orders_out";
        DirectoryInfo di_in = new DirectoryInfo(m_pathin);
        DirectoryInfo di_out = new DirectoryInfo(m_pathout);

        public CSharpDirectoryWatcherService() {
            // This call is required by the Windows.Forms
            // Component Designer.
            InitializeComponent();

            // TODO: Add any initialization after the InitComponent call
        }

        // The main entry point for the process
        static void Main() {
            System.ServiceProcess.ServiceBase[] ServicesToRun;

            // More than one user Service may run within the
            // same process. To add
            // another service to this process, change the
            // following line to create a second service object.
            // For example,
            //
            //   ServicesToRun = New System.ServiceProcess.ServiceBase[]
            //        {new Service1(), new MySecondUserService()};
            //
            ServicesToRun = new System.ServiceProcess.ServiceBase[] {
                new CSharpDirectoryWatcherService() };
```

```csharp
        System.ServiceProcess.ServiceBase.Run(ServicesToRun);
    }

    /// <summary>
    /// Required method for Designer support - do not modify
    /// the contents of this method with the code editor.
    /// </summary>
    private void InitializeComponent() {
        //
        // CSharpDirectoryWatcherService
        //
        this.CanShutdown = true;
        this.ServiceName = "CSharpDirectoryWatcherService";

    }

    /// <summary>
    /// Clean up any resources being used.
    /// </summary>
    protected override void Dispose( bool disposing ) {
        if( disposing ) {
            if (components != null) {
                components.Dispose();
            }
        }
        base.Dispose( disposing );
    }

    /// <summary>
    /// Set things in motion so your service can do its work.
    /// </summary>
    protected override void OnStart(string[] args) {
        base.AutoLog = false;
        try {
            // create the orders_in directory if it
            // doesn't already exist
            if (!di_in.Exists) {
                di_in.Create();
            }
            try {
                if (!di_out.Exists) {
                    di_out.Create();
                }
                try {

EventLog.WriteEntry("CSharpDirectoryWatcherService",
                "DirectoryWatcher starting.");
            // create a FileSystemWatcher
```

```
                    fsw = new FileSystemWatcher(m_pathin);
                    fsw.Created += new

System.IO.FileSystemEventHandler(this.fsw_created);
                    // don't watch subdirectories
                    fsw.IncludeSubdirectories = false;
                    // enable watching
                    fsw.EnableRaisingEvents = true;

EventLog.WriteEntry("CSharpDirectoryWatcherService",
                        "Service started successfully.");
                }
                catch {
                    try {
                        EventLog.WriteEntry
                            ("CSharpDirectoryWatcherService",
                            "Service starting.");
                    }
                    catch (Exception ex1) {
                        EventLog.WriteEntry
                            ("CSharpDirectoryWatcherService",
                            "Unable to watch the directory: " +
                            m_pathin + System.Environment.NewLine +
                            "Error Description: " +
                            ex1.Message);
                    }
                }
            }
            catch (Exception ex) {
                EventLog.WriteEntry("CSharpDirectoryWatcherService",
                    "Unable to create the directory " +
                    m_pathout + System.Environment.NewLine +
                    "Error Description: " +
                    ex.Message);
            }
        }
        catch (Exception ex) {
            EventLog.WriteEntry("CSharpDirectoryWatcherService",
                "Unable to create the directory " + m_pathin +
                System.Environment.NewLine + "Error Description: " +
                ex.Message);
        }

    }

    /// <summary>
    /// Stop this service.
    /// </summary>
```

```csharp
        protected override void OnStop() {
            // Add code here to perform any tear-down necessary
            // to stop your service.
            // log a stop event
            try {
                fsw = null;
                fsw.Dispose();
                EventLog.WriteEntry("CSharpDirectoryWatcherService",
                    "Service stopped");
            }
            catch (Exception ex) {
                EventLog.WriteEntry("CSharpDirectoryWatcherService",
                    "Error stopping the CSharpDirectoryWatcherService " +
                    for path: " + m_pathin + System.Environment.NewLine +
                    "Error Description: " + ex.Message);
            }
        }
        protected override void OnPause() {
            fsw.EnableRaisingEvents = false;
            EventLog.WriteEntry("CSharpDirectoryWatcherService",
                "Service paused for path " + m_pathin);
        }
        protected override void OnContinue() {
            fsw.EnableRaisingEvents = true;
            EventLog.WriteEntry("CSharpDirectoryWatcherService",
                "Service continued for path " + m_pathin);
        }
        private void fsw_created(Object sender, FileSystemEventArgs e)
        {

            // move the file
            FileInfo fi = new FileInfo(e.FullPath);
            StreamWriter sw;
            try {
                fi.MoveTo(m_pathout + "\\" +  e.Name);
                // add to processed file report
                try {
                    fi = new FileInfo(m_pathout + "\\report.txt");
                    if (!fi.Exists) {
                        sw = fi.CreateText();
                    }
                    else {
                        sw = fi.AppendText();
                    }
                    try {
                        sw.WriteLine(e.FullPath + "," + m_pathout +
```

```
                  "\\" + e.Name);
                }
                catch {
                  EventLog.WriteEntry("CSharpDirectoryWatcherService",
                    "Unable to write to the file " + fi.FullName);
                }
                finally {
                  try {
                    sw.Close();
                  }
                  finally {
                    // do nothing here
                  }
                }
              }
              catch {
                EventLog.WriteEntry("CSharpDirectoryWatcherService",
                  "Unable to create or append to the file " +
                  m_pathout + "\\" + e.Name);
              }
            }
            catch {
              EventLog.WriteEntry("CSharpDirectoryWatcherService",
                "Unable to move the file " + e.FullPath + " to " +
                m_pathout + "\\" + e.Name);
            }

        }
      }
    }
```

When you start the service, you can see immediately if it worked, because it creates the orders_in and orders_out subdirectories under the ch11 directory.

To test the service, save a file in the orders_in directory. The file should immediately disappear. Look in the orders_out directory. The service will move the file there and create the report.txt file.

The method used for creating the report file is *not* a good example of production-quality work, for at least two reasons. The first reason is that there's not enough security on the service or the report file. For example, what happens if someone deletes the report file? There goes your data. In a production application, you should use an account that has specific rights to the directories and files involved *and no more*. Then you can set the report file permissions so that only administrators and the system account can write to or delete the file, and so that the IIS service can read it. Second, the report itself doesn't contain enough data to be very useful. For example, it doesn't contain the file dates, the ID of the user who created the file in the orders_in folder, or any other useful data besides the filename itself. However, it provides a reasonable example to show how you might begin to go about using the report file to produce a useful report.

Now that the service is working, the last part of the task is to make the data available as a report. It's questionable whether using a flat file for the report data is a good idea. When there are only a few entries in the report, it's no problem to read them, format the data as HTML, and send it to a browser. However, as the number of entries in the report grows, showing all the rows becomes less and less useful. There are several ways to circumvent this problem; perhaps the best way is to log the entries in a database, where you can use the database engine's select capability to select the most recent entries. But databases require a lot of overhead, whereas appending data to a file requires very little.

In a real application, there would be little point in showing all the entries. Typically, you would want to display the entries in reverse order and display only the last 10, 50, or 100 entries—whatever seemed the most reasonable. A simple sequential file, like the report.txt file generated by the service, consists of records delimited by carriage returns. So you could read the file into an array of strings, where each string would contain one record. In this example, the records themselves consist solely of the input filename and the output filename, so you can use the regular expression Split function to isolate the individual data items and generate a report. The Web Form ch11-1.aspx contains a simple report that shows all the data (see Listing 11.2).

LISTING 11.2: REPORT THAT SHOWS ALL DATA COLLECTED BY THE DIRECTORYWATCHER SERVICE (ch11-1.aspx.cs)

```
private void Page_Load(object sender, System.EventArgs e) {
    // Read the report.txt file
    StreamReader sr;
    String s;
    String[] lines, orders;
    sr = File.OpenText(Server.MapPath(".") +
    "\\orders_out\\report.txt");
    s = sr.ReadToEnd().Trim();
    sr.Close();
    lines = s.Split('\n');
    Response.Write("<table border=\"1\">");
    Response.Write("<tr><th>Order In</th><th>Order Out</th></tr>");
    foreach (String aString in lines) {
        orders = aString.Split(',');
        Response.Write("<tr><td>" + orders[0] + "</td><td>" +
            orders[1] + "</td></tr>");
    }
    Response.Write("</table>");
}
```

Obviously, as the number of records grows, this method will quickly become unwieldy. The Web Form ch11-2.aspx contains a better version of the report. It opens the report.txt file in read-only binary mode, grabs the last 2,000 bytes of the file, splits the records, reverses them, and displays those as a table. Listing 11.3 shows the code.

LISTING 11.3: REPORT THAT SHOWS ALL DATA COLLECTED BY THE DIRECTORYWATCHER SERVICE (ch11-2.aspx.cs)

```
private void Page_Load(object sender, System.EventArgs e) {
    // Read the report.txt file
    FileStream fs;
    String s;
    String[] lines;
    String[] orders;
    StreamReader sr;

    fs = File.Open(Server.MapPath(".") + "\\orders_out\\report.txt",
        FileMode.OpenOrCreate, FileAccess.Read, FileShare.ReadWrite);
    if (fs.Length > 2000) {
        fs.Seek(-2000, SeekOrigin.End);
    }
    sr = new StreamReader(fs);
    s = (sr.ReadToEnd()).Trim();
    sr.Close();
    fs.Close();
    lines = s.Split('\n');
    Response.Write("<table border=\"1\">");
    Response.Write("<tr><th>Order In</th><th>Order Out</th></tr>");

    // don't use the first line
    // and show items in reverse
    for (int i = lines.Length - 1; i > 0; i--) {
        orders = lines[i].Split(',');
        if (orders.Length > 1) {
            Response.Write("<tr><td>" + orders[0] + "</td><td>" +
                orders[1] + "</td></tr>");
        }
    }
    Response.Write("</table>");
}
```

Of course, this entire operation would be much easier if the service saved the report data as XML. You'll see more about that later in this book; it's time to move on to other message types.

Sending E-mail Messages

Problem: Every morning, you want to count the number of requests in the IIS log made over the past 24 hours and send your boss an HTML-formatted report via e-mail.

This time, there are two problems to solve. The first involves reading the IIS log, and the second involves sending e-mail. I'll deal with them in order because the first problem is much more involved than the second—sending e-mail in .NET is simple. Understanding and reading the IIS log is vital for tracking your site's usage, finding security attacks and breaches, and generally understanding what's happening with your Web server, so although the task isn't exactly aligned with the goal of this chapter—messaging—it *is* pertinent to the book topic itself.

Before starting on the problem, you should recognize that this solution doesn't *have* to be implemented in a Web application—it could just as easily be a standard application or a service. But as you work through the rest of this book, you're likely to realize that that's true of almost every C# Web application—the main reason to write the user interface as a Web-based application is that you don't have to install code on the client. At the same time, .NET has made installing code on the client much easier, so even that's not as good a reason as it used to be.

READING THE IIS LOG FILE

You've already seen how to write to the IIS log using the `Response.AppendToLog` method. By default, IIS creates a new log file every day in the `WinNT\System32\Logfiles\W3SVC` folder. IIS also logs every request by default; in fact, you may be surprised by how much information the server maintains for each request.

The log file is a comma-delimited text file; each record is a single line. You can read it just like any other text file. Because the log file location is configurable, it's possible that your IIS server logs requests somewhere else. You can check easily. Start the Internet Information Services management application (Start ➤ Programs ➤ Administrative Tools ➤ Internet Services Manager). Right-click your default Web site and select Properties. You'll see the Default Web Site Properties dialog. Click the Web Site tab. The bottom panel on that dialog shows the overall log settings for your server (see Figure 11.4).

FIGURE 11.4

The IIS Default Web Site Properties dialog

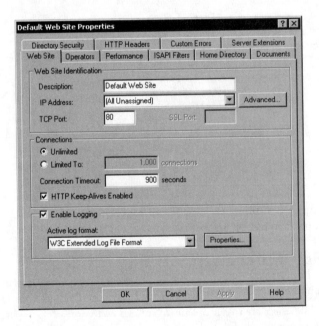

Check the Enable Logging check box if it is not already selected. The rest of this section won't make sense if IIS logging isn't enabled.

On my server, Active Log Format is set to the default, W3C Extended Log File Format; however, the gist of this section applies to any format except ODBC logging, which logs to a database table, not a file. The default format lets you aggregate log data between IIS and any other Web server that supports the standard W3C Extended Log format. The NCSA format and the Microsoft IIS Log format are fixed-field formats; you can't customize the data that IIS logs. In contrast, the delimited W3C format lets you choose the fields you want. IIS inserts the comma delimiters for the fields that you don't need, which facilitates data merges with logs from other servers, but doesn't log the data. Limiting the fields you log can marginally reduce the load on a busy server. Turning off logging altogether, of course, has a much greater effect than limiting the number of fields.

If you have the ODBC logging option set, your server logs data to a database rather than to a file. It's more resource intensive to log to a database, but you can use the database to sort and filter the data for reports. Because of the overhead, I recommend that you log to a file. You can import the data into a database periodically (during off-peak hours) to provide exactly the same report capabilities.

It's interesting to look at the fields that IIS saves for each request. Click the Properties button to view the Extended Logging Properties dialog. The dialog you see depends on which log format you have selected. For the W3C Extended Log format, you'll see the dialog in Figure 11.5.

FIGURE 11.5

The extended log format dialog for the W3C Extended Log format

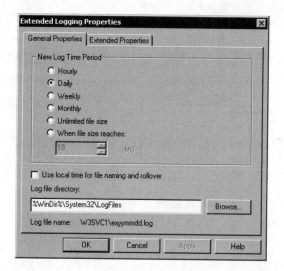

The set of options in the New Log Time Period portion of the dialog controls how often IIS creates a new log file. By default, IIS keeps one log per day (the `Daily` setting). For high-use sites, you might want to use the `Hourly` setting so that the log files remain small enough to process. The Log File Directory field in the bottom panel of the dialog shows the path that IIS will use to create log files. The `%WinDir%` path variable substitutes for the root Windows path on your machine. On most computers, the path resolves to `C:\WINNT`.

The settings you choose affect the frequency of log "rollover"—when IIS creates a new log and the name of the log files. The Use Local Time for File Naming and Rollover check box controls whether IIS uses local time or Greenwich Mean Time (GMT) to control when the log file changes.

You need to know settings for New Log Time Period, Use Local Time for File Naming and Rollover, and Log File Directory to work through this example.

NOTE   *Write down the settings on this page, because you'll need them shortly. The example uses the default settings: daily log rollover, GMT file naming, and the %WinDir%\System32\LogFiles path.*

Next, click the Extended Properties tab (see Figure 11.6).

FIGURE 11.6

IIS Extended
Logging Properties
dialog for the W3C
Extended Log
format

You can select any of the fields. The active fields are those with the check box selected. In addition, several fields save server performance data for each request, among which are Total User Time and Total Kernel Time. Refer to the Help file (click the Help button on the dialog) if you're not familiar with the field names or meanings.

You read the log in the same manner that you read any other sequential file. However, because log files can be extremely large, you probably should not read the entire file into memory. Instead, read the file one line at a time, keeping a running total for the report.

Before you can read the log, you have to find the current log. Fortunately, IIS uses a naming convention of "ex" plus the current date in some form—YYMMDD by default. Unfortunately, it's not quite that easy because the name depends on the log rollover frequency setting and the setting of the Use Local Time... check box. For example, if your server creates a new log daily using local time, you can find the name by formatting the current date in YYMMDD format and concatenating that with "ex". However, if your server creates a new log hourly, you must format the current date and time in YYMMDDHH format. If weekly, the server uses a YYMMON format, where *N* is the week number in the current month. (I haven't explored beyond that because most people would not set log rollover frequency to Monthly or Yearly.)

If your server uses GMT rather than local time, you must obtain the GMT date or date/time value and format that. At any rate, you must know how your server is set up to create a valid log filename. The Web Form ch11-3.aspx shows how to retrieve the log filename when the rollover frequency is set to Daily.

NOTE *You may need to change the date formatting in the example if your server log rollover frequency is not set to Daily.*

Import the System.IO and System.Globalization namespaces:

```
using System.IO;
using System.Globalization;
```

Create an enum that specifies the log rollover frequency, and one for the IIS time setting, which may be GMT or Local.

```
private enum IISLogFrequency {
   Hourly = 0,
   Daily = 1
}


private enum IISTimeSetting {
   GMT = 0,
   Local = 1
}
```

The following code retrieves the log filename, given the log frequency and the time setting.

```
private String getLogFileName(IISLogFrequency logFrequency ,
   IISTimeSetting timeSetting) {
   DateTime aDate = DateTime.Now;
   String sDate="";
   String logFileName;
   String sysFolder;
   sysFolder = System.Environment.GetFolderPath
      (Environment.SpecialFolder.System);
   switch (timeSetting) {
      case IISTimeSetting.GMT :
         aDate = DateTime.Now.ToUniversalTime();
         break;
      case IISTimeSetting.Local :
         aDate = DateTime.Now;
         break;
   }
   switch (logFrequency) {
      case IISLogFrequency.Daily :
         sDate = aDate.ToString("yyMMdd");
         break;
      case IISLogFrequency.Hourly :
         sDate = aDate.ToString("yyMMddhh");
         break;
   }
   logFileName = sysFolder + "\\logfiles\\w3svc1\\ex" + sDate +
   ".log";
   if (File.Exists(logFileName)) {
      return (logFileName);
```

```
        }
        else {
            return null;
        }
    }
```

The method accepts an IISLogFrequency enumeration value (either Hourly or Daily) and an IIS-TimeSetting enumeration value (either GMT or Local). There are a few interesting points. First, you don't need to know where the system folder is on your server—the .NET framework will tell you. Use the System.Environment.GetFolderPath method. The method accepts an instance of the System.Environment.SpecialFolder enumeration, in this case SpecialFolder.System, and returns the associated path:

```
sysFolder = System.Environment.GetFolderPath
    (Environment.SpecialFolder.System);
```

Second, you can obtain the GMT time, also called Universal Time or UTC, using the ToUniversal-Time method:

```
aDate = DateTime.Now.ToUniversalTime();
```

Finally, you format dates by calling ToString with a DateTimeFormatInfo property value or format string. The format strings are similar to, but not the same as, classic VB's Format function. You can create custom formats by combining the format patterns (see Tables 11.1 and 11.2).

TABLE 11.1: STANDARD DATE/TIME FORMATS (FROM THE MSDN .NET DOCUMENTATION)

FORMAT CHARACTER	FORMAT PATTERN	ASSOCIATED PROPERTY/DESCRIPTION
d	MM/dd/yyyy	ShortDatePattern
D	dddd, dd MMMM yyyy	LongDatePattern
f	dddd, dd MMMM yyyy HH:mm	Full date and time (long date and short time)
F	dddd, dd MMMM yyyy HH:mm:ss	FullDateTimePattern (long date and long time)
g	MM/dd/yyyy HH:mm	General (short date and short time)
G	MM/dd/yyyy HH:mm:ss	General (short date and long time)
m, M	MMMM dd	MonthDayPattern
r, R	ddd, dd MMM yyyy HH':'mm':'ss 'GMT'	RFC1123Pattern
s	yyyy'-'MM'-'dd'T'HH':'mm':'ss	SortableDateTimePattern (based on ISO 8601) using local time
t	HH:mm	ShortTimePattern
T	HH:mm:ss	LongTimePattern

Continued on next page

TABLE 11.1: STANDARD DATE/TIME FORMATS (FROM THE MSDN .NET DOCUMENTATION) *(continued)*

FORMAT CHARACTER	FORMAT PATTERN	ASSOCIATED PROPERTY/DESCRIPTION
u	`yyyy'-'MM'-'dd HH':'mm':'ss'Z'`	`UniversalSortableDateTimePattern` (based on ISO 8601) using Universal Time
U	`dddd, dd MMMM yyyy HH:mm:ss`	Sortable date and time (long date and long time) using Universal Time
y, Y	`yyyy MMMM`	`YearMonthPattern`

TABLE 11.2: DateTime CUSTOM FORMATTING PATTERNS (FROM THE MSDN .NET DOCUMENTATION)

FORMAT PATTERN	DESCRIPTION
d	The day of the month. Single-digit days will not have a leading zero.
dd	The day of the month. Single-digit days will have a leading zero.
ddd	The abbreviated name of the day of the week, as defined in `AbbreviatedDayNames`.
dddd	The full name of the day of the week, as defined in `DayNames`.
M	The numeric month. Single-digit months will not have a leading zero.
MM	The numeric month. Single-digit months will have a leading zero.
MMM	The abbreviated name of the month, as defined in `AbbreviatedMonthNames`.
MMMM	The full name of the month, as defined in `MonthNames`.
y	The year without the century. If the year without the century is less than 10, the year is displayed with no leading zero.
yy	The year without the century. If the year without the century is less than 10, the year is displayed with a leading zero.
yyyy	The year in four digits, including the century.
gg	The period or era. This pattern is ignored if the date to be formatted does not have an associated period or era string.
h	The hour in a 12-hour clock. Single-digit hours will not have a leading zero.
hh, hh*	The hour in a 12-hour clock. Single-digit hours will have a leading zero.
H	The hour in a 24-hour clock. Single-digit hours will not have a leading zero.
HH, HH*	The hour in a 24-hour clock. Single-digit hours will have a leading zero.
m	The minute. Single-digit minutes will not have a leading zero.
mm, mm*	The minute. Single-digit minutes will have a leading zero.

Continued on next page

TABLE 11.2: DateTime CUSTOM FORMATTING PATTERNS (FROM THE MSDN .NET DOCUMENTATION) *(continued)*

FORMAT PATTERN	DESCRIPTION
s	The second. Single-digit seconds will not have a leading zero.
ss, ss*	The second. Single-digit seconds will have a leading zero.
t	. The first character in the AM/PM designator defined in AMDesignator or PMDesignator.
tt, tt*	The AM/PM designator defined in AMDesignator or PMDesignator.
z	The time zone offset (hour only). Single-digit hours will not have a leading zero.
zz	The time zone offset (hour only). Single-digit hours will have a leading zero.
zzz, zzz*	The full time zone offset (hour and minutes). Single-digit hours and minutes will have leading zeros.
:	The default time separator defined in TimeSeparator.
/	The default date separator defined in DateSeparator.
% c	Where c is a format pattern if used alone. The % character can be omitted if the format pattern is combined with literal characters or other format patterns.
\ c	Where c is any character. Displays the character literally.

After you obtain the log filename, counting the log entries is easy. Open a StreamReader on the file and loop through it, counting the lines.

```
private int countLogFileEntries(String logfilename) {
    StreamReader sr = null;
    FileInfo fi;
    int lineCount=0;
    String s;
    if (logfilename != null) {
        fi = new FileInfo(logfilename);
        try {
            sr = new StreamReader(fi.Open(FileMode.Open,
                FileAccess.Read, FileShare.ReadWrite));
            do {
        s = sr.ReadLine();
        if (s != null) {
            if (s.Substring(0, 1) != "#") {
                lineCount += 1;
            }
        }
```

```
        }
        while (s != null);

    }
    catch (Exception ex) {
        Response.Write(ex.Message);
    }
    finally {
        if (sr != null) {
    try {
        sr.Close();
    }
    finally {}
        }
    }
}
    return (lineCount);
}
```

As you loop through the lines in the file, skip the lines that begin with a number sign (#), because they aren't valid log entries. Press F5 a few times to refresh the browser. Note what happens to the count. It increases by two (or three), rather than one, each time you refresh the page. That's because the Web Form contains a reference to a style sheet. Using IE5.5, the page makes two calls to the server—one for the page and one for the style sheet. Using IE6, the page makes three calls to the server—one for the page and two for the style sheet. I suspect the difference is that IE6 is still in beta as of this writing. Because only one style sheet reference is in the page, by rights the server ought to receive only one request for it. In any case, if you look at the protocol status, you'll see that for all but the initial request by any given client, the status value is 304—which means "Not Modified," the client has an up-to-date cached copy—so it takes very little time. Logging the request takes more time than returning the status.

The Web Form ch11-3.aspx displays the line count.

AUTOMATING AN E-MAIL MESSAGE

Now that you can see the information, you can automate delivering it to your boss via e-mail. As I said at the beginning of this discussion, that is the easy part. The simplest way to send an e-mail message is to call the static **Send** method of the SmtpMail class with four parameters: the source account; the destination account; a subject, which will appear on the Subject line in the destination account's mail program; and the message body. For example:

```
System.Web.Mail.SmtpMail.Send (
    "myaccount@mydomain.com",
    "toyouraccount@yourdomain.com",
    "This is the subject.",
    "This is the message.");
```

This version of the **Send** method sends a text-formatted message. The **Send** method has an overloaded version that accepts an instance of a MailMessage class. To send HTML-formatted mail, you must use this second version. But it isn't much more difficult. Create a `MailMessage` object and set its properties, then send it via the overloaded `Send` method. Here's a function that sends a `MailMessage` object using the `Send` method:

```
private void sendMail(String fromAccount, String toAccount,
    String title, String msg,
    System.Web.Mail.MailAttachment attachment)
{
    System.Web.Mail.MailMessage mm = new
    System.Web.Mail.MailMessage();
    mm.To = toAccount;
    mm.From = fromAccount;
    mm.Subject = title;
    mm.Body = msg;
    mm.BodyFormat = System.Web.Mail.MailFormat.Html;
    if (attachment != null) {
        mm.Attachments.Add(attachment);
    }
    System.Web.Mail.SmtpMail.Send(mm);
}
```

The code is very straightforward. You'll probably notice immediately that the function handles an attachment as well. To send an attachment, you create a `MailAttachment` object. You can pass the constructor a filename. The Web Form `ch11-3` has two Text controls: an HTML File Field control (see Chapter 10 for information on setting up a Web Form to use the File Field control) and a button (see Figure 11.7).

FIGURE 11.7

Form to send an email message

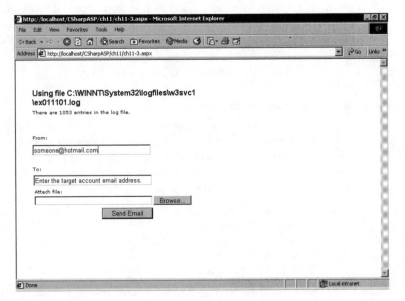

NOTE *To run the Web Form* ch11-3 *successfully, you must have an SMTP server installed on your Web server (installing IIS installs an SMTP server by default).*

When you run the ch11-3 Web Form, it displays the path to the log file used to generate the report and the number of entries in the log and lets you enter a From e-mail address and a To e-mail address. You may also attach a file. When you click the Send E-mail button, the page sends an e-mail message. If you specify a file to attach by selecting or entering a valid filename in the Attach File File Field control, the server sends that file as an attachment. First, it creates a temporary filename, using the Path.getTempPath static class method. Next, it strips the filename from the uploaded file and uses the PostedFile.SaveAs method to save the file. It then sends the e-mail message and deletes the temporary file. Here's the code:

```
private void Button1_Click(object sender, System.EventArgs e) {
    String toAccount, fromAccount, title, msg, attachFile;
    System.Web.Mail.MailAttachment attachment=null;
    String tmpFileName="";
    title = "Hits today!";
    msg = "<html><head></head><body style=\"background:" +
        "lightyellow; color:blue; font-family: Verdana, Arial; " +
        "font-size: 9pt;\">" +
        "<div border=\"1\">We had " + logFileCount.ToString() +
        " hits today.</div></body></html>";
    fromAccount = txtFrom.Text;
    toAccount = txtTo.Text;
    attachFile = attachments.PostedFile.FileName;
    if (attachFile != "") {
        attachFile = attachFile.Substring(
            (int) attachFile.LastIndexOf("\\") + 1);
        tmpFileName = Path.GetTempPath() + attachFile;
        attachments.PostedFile.SaveAs(tmpFileName);
        attachment = new System.Web.Mail.MailAttachment(tmpFileName);
    }
    else {
        attachFile = null;
    }
    sendMail(fromAccount, toAccount, title, msg, attachment);
    if (tmpFileName !=null) {
        File.Delete(tmpFileName);
    }
}
```

So now you know how to read the IIS log (and may have learned something about the .NET framework's date handling capabilities as well) and how to send e-mail messages. Spend a little time looking at all the MailMessage class methods and properties, because I didn't discuss some properties in this section.

Calling Methods in Another Web Form

Problem: You wrote a function in a Web Form that reads a directory and returns a list of subfolders and files in that directory as an `ArrayList` of `DirectoryInfo` and `FileInfo` objects; now you want to use it in another Web Form. Can you call it from the original Web Form or must you move it to a class?

This will be a short section, because it requires only a twist in your point of view. Typically, you work with Web Forms individually. The framework defaults to posting data for a specific form back to the same Web Form, so you can handle control events and user input. But that also tends to coerce people to write code in event handlers—and *that* leads to problems with code reuse. Here's the twist. A Web Form is nothing but a class, so you can instantiate one the same way that you instantiate any other class: by calling the class constructor.

The question isn't so much whether you *can* call functions or raise events in another Web Form; it's whether you *should*. There's a significant overhead involved with creating a Web Form instance as opposed to creating a class instance that doesn't interact with the ASP.NET runtime, which doesn't have to raise all the Web Form events and create the child controls. Therefore, you'll have to decide if the performance hit is more important to you than keeping the code in the original Web Form. If you decide you want to do this, here's an example you can refer to.

The Web Form `ch11-4.aspx` contains a `getFiles` function that accepts a path. If the path exists, the function returns an `ArrayList` filled with `DirectoryInfo` and `FileInfo` objects bound to the subdirectories and files in the specified path.

```
public ArrayList getFiles(String rootpath) {
    ArrayList files;
    DirectoryInfo diRoot = new DirectoryInfo(rootpath);
    if (diRoot.Exists) {
        // get the subfolders and files
        files = new ArrayList();
        files.AddRange(diRoot.GetFileSystemInfos());
        return (files);
    }
    else {
        throw (new DirectoryNotFoundException());
    }
}
```

After obtaining the `ArrayList`, the `ch11-4.aspx` Web Form displays the name of each file or directory in the list by wrapping each item in a `<span>` tag. It formats directories in bold text and all other files in normal text.

```
private void Page_Load(object sender, System.EventArgs e) {
    ArrayList files = getFiles(MapPath("."));
    foreach (Object o in files) {
        if ((o.GetType()).Name == "DirectoryInfo") {
            Response.Write("<span class=\"smallfont\" " +
        "style=\"font-weight:bold\">" +
```

```
          ((DirectoryInfo) o).Name + "</span><br>");
      }
      if ((o.GetType()).Name == "FileInfo") {
          Response.Write("<span class=\"smallfont\" " +
      "style=\"font-weight:normal\">" +
      ((FileInfo) o).Name + "</span><br>");
      }
   }
}
```

The Web Form ch11-5.aspx does exactly the same thing but uses the method from the Web Form ch11-4.aspx. Note that the class name is not the same as the filename—Visual Studio automatically changes the dashes in the filenames to underscores, so the class name for the Web Form ch11-4.aspx is ch11_4.

```
private void Page_Load(object sender, System.EventArgs e)
{
   ch11_4 otherWebForm = new ch11_4();
   System.Web.HttpResponse resp =
      System.Web.HttpContext.Current.Response;
   ArrayList files = otherWebForm.getFiles(MapPath("."));
   foreach(object o in files) {
      if (o.GetType() == typeof(System.IO.DirectoryInfo)) {
          Response.Write("<span class=\"smallfont\" " +
             "style=\"font-weight:bold\">" +
             ((System.IO.DirectoryInfo) o).Name + "</span><br>");
      }
      else if (o.GetType() == typeof(System.IO.FileInfo)) {
          Response.Write("<span class=\"smallfont\" " +
             "style=\"font-weight:normal\">" +
             ((System.IO.FileInfo) o).Name + "</span><br>");
      }
   }
}
```

The only difference between the Page_Load event code for the two Web Forms is that the ch11-5.aspx version creates a new ch11_4 class instance and assigns it to a variable called otherWebForm. The ch11-5 Web Form uses that instance to access the getFiles function. Other than that, the display code is identical. If you run the two Web Forms, you'll see that they produce identical results (see Figures 11.8 and 11.9).

FIGURE 11.8

Output from the
`ch11-4.aspx`
Web Form

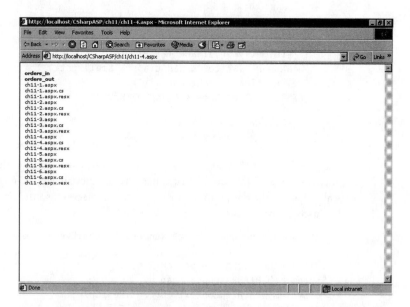

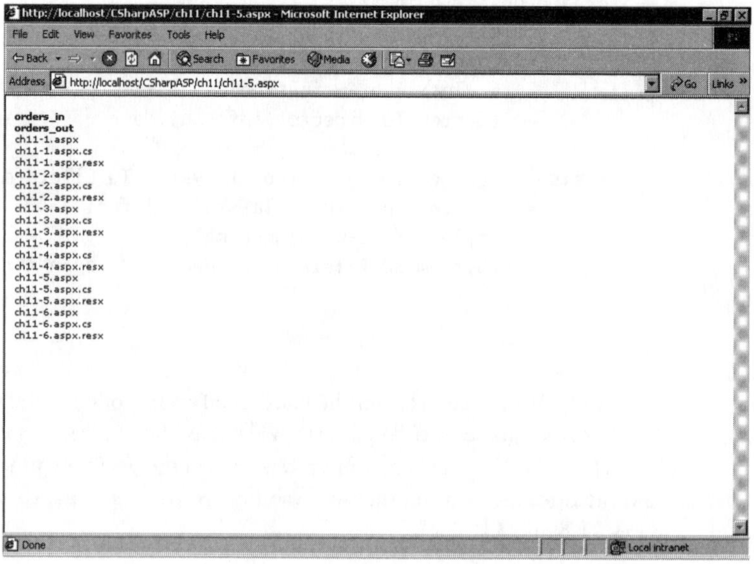

FIGURE 11.9

Output from the
`ch11-5.aspx` Web
Form using the
`getFiles` method
from the class
`ch11_4`

The question that may come to your mind when you see code like this is: Why didn't the programmer wrap the code that displays the lists in a method? Good question! You should try it. Write a subroutine to display an `ArrayList` populated with `FileInfo` and `DirectoryInfo` objects in `ch11-4.aspx`. You could call the subroutine `showFiles`:

```
public void showFiles(ArrayList files) {
    foreach (Object o in files) {
```

```
        if (o.GetType().Name == "DirectoryInfo") {
           Response.Write("<span class=\"smallfont\" " +
        "style=\"font-weight:bold\">" +
        ((DirectoryInfo) o).Name + "</span><br>");
        }
        else if (o.GetType().Name == "FileInfo") {
           Response.Write("<span class=\"smallfont\" " +
        "style=\"font-weight:normal\">" +
        ((FileInfo) o).Name + "</span><br>");
        }
     }
  }
```

NOTE   *The preceding subroutine exists in the CSharpASP project—it's just an example.*

That does clarify things. You could simplify the Page_Load event for ch11-4 so it looks like this:

```
// Simplified Page_Load method for the ch11-4 Web Form
private void Page_Load(object sender, System.EventArgs e) {
   ArrayList files = getFiles(MapPath("."));
      showFiles(files);
}
```

That's certainly easier to read. Now you can also eliminate the display code in the Web Form ch11-5 Page_Load:

```
   // Simplified Page_Load method for the ch11-5 Web Form
private void Page_Load(object sender, System.EventArgs e)
{
   ch11_4 otherWebForm = new ch11_4();
      ArrayList files = otherWebForm.getFiles(MapPath("."));
      otherWebForm.showFiles(files);
   }
}
```

If you enter this code and then compile and run the altered project, you'll get a null reference error because the ch11-4 Web Form doesn't have an instance of the Response object. This is an important point. Instantiating a Web Form using the New constructor does *not* follow the normal ASP.NET initialization procedure.

That's easy to fix. You could rewrite the ch11-4.aspx method showFiles to accept a Response object as a parameter:

```
public void showFiles(ArrayList files, HttpResponse resp) {
   // code here;
}
```

You would then call the method by passing the Response object:

```
otherWebForm.showFiles(files, Response);
```

Alternatively, you could rewrite the method to retrieve the **Response** object from the current context:

```
public void showFiles(ArrayList files) {
    System.Web.HttpReponse resp =
        System.Web.HttpContext.Current.Response
    foreach (Object o in files) {
        if (o.GetType().Name == "DirectoryInfo") {
            resp.Write("<span class=\"smallfont\" " +
        "style=\"font-weight:bold\">" +
        ((DirectoryInfo) o).Name + "</span><br>");
        }
        else if (o.GetType().Name == "FileInfo") {
            resp.Write("<span class=\"smallfont\" " +
        "style=\"font-weight:normal\">" +
        ((FileInfo) o).Name + "</span><br>");
        }
    }
}
```

Using either alternative, you can now use the method from another Web Form. But once more, you have to ask yourself if it's worthwhile to alter the method in the Web Form as opposed to creating a separate class.

Retrieving Data from Another Web Page

You've seen in this chapter that it's generally more trouble than it's worth to call a method in another page. That said, sometimes it *is* useful to call another page. The System.Net namespace contains classes that let you use common Web protocols easily, such as HTTP and FTP.

For example, suppose you have deployed your application and can't change the code for whatever reason. You just *have* to use the code already written in ch11-4 to display the list of files. Here's how you can do that. Create a new Web Form called ch11-6.aspx. In the Page_Load event, create a System .Net.WebClient instance. You can use the WebClient.OpenRead method to request the ch11-4.aspx file. Just as the FileInfo.OpenRead method accepts a path and returns a FileStream, the WebClient .OpenRead method accepts a URL and returns a Stream.

```
private void Page_Load(object sender, System.EventArgs e) {
    // create a WebClient object
    System.Net.WebClient wreq = new System.Net.WebClient();
    System.IO.StreamReader sr;
    // use the WebClient.OpenRead to request the ch11-4 Web Form
    // and open a StreamReader on the returned Stream
    sr = new System.IO.StreamReader(wreq.OpenRead
        ("http://localhost" + Request.ApplicationPath +
        "/ch11/ch11-4.aspx"));
    // write the contents of the Stream
    Response.Write(sr.ReadToEnd());

    // clean up
```

```
    sr.Close();
    wreq.Dispose();

}
```

Looks much like the process to read a file, doesn't it? Of course, that's exactly what you're doing—but rather than using the methods you've seen for opening and reading the file from a local drive, you're opening and reading the file via an HTTP GET request over the network. In this example, the requested page happens to be on the same server, but you can read a file from a server across the world in exactly the same way.

While this particular example works exactly as you would expect, there are a few problems to solve if you are to wrap requests for other servers that include images or other associated files. As you may recall from building the log file example or the DynamicImage.aspx Web Form in Chapter 4, "Introduction to ASP.NET," when a Web page includes references to other files, such as style sheets, images, XML documents, applets, or ActiveX controls, the browser makes multiple requests to the server: one for the main file and one for each associated file. The WebClient class is not a browser; it doesn't make the associated file requests for you. If you want to provide a complete wrapper, you'll need to parse the results returned by the WebClient object's OpenRead method, extract the URLs for the associated files, and make the requests yourself. That's beyond the scope of this book, but here's a hint: Think about *regular expressions*.

Finally, the System.Net classes are extremely powerful. You can perform almost any type of network operation using the classes, and I suggest you study them, especially if you write applications that send and receive files via FTP or you write applications that log into remote applications or networks. Unfortunately (and this is a comment about the .NET framework and C# in general), far too much information exists to put into this book, even at a rudimentary level, so all I can do is recommend that you spend more time reading the namespace documentation so you'll know what's available.

Summary

At this point, you should feel minimally comfortable working with files, whether they're physical files on your server, virtual files created by another Web Form, or remote files returned by another server. You should understand how to handle several different types of messaging tasks, including how to respond to filesystem changes, send e-mail, call code in other classes, and make simple GET requests. If you followed the examples, you've built a large number of Web Forms that display some type of data. However, most Internet and intranet applications don't work primarily with files—they work primarily with relational databases.

There are several reasons why most applications prefer relational databases to files:

◆ Web applications are multiuser. Relational databases already handle the problems associated with multiple users for you.

◆ Web applications are stateless, but most applications require at least some persisted data. Relational databases provide an excellent way to persist and retrieve that data.

◆ Data and the requirements for manipulating that data tend to grow over time. A simple bulletin board application might be easy to create with flat files, but when you have hundreds of thousands of messages and you want to add a search capability, you're in trouble. Modern relational databases scale to millions of records and have powerful sorting and selection mechanisms for retrieving only the data you need.

◆ Relational databases provide a convenient abstraction for building relationships between data items that not only limit the amount of data you must save but also help minimize or eliminate unwanted relationships. For example, a flat file containing customer orders and shipping addresses from multiple customers must repeat the customer information in each row. If the customer's shipping information changes, you would need to find and update every order for that customer. In a relational database, you can put the customer information in a Customers table and the order information in an Orders table. By placing a `CustomerID` value in both tables, you can relate the customer information to the orders without repeating the information.

You use a special language called SQL to access a relational database. SQL is an open standard, and most modern databases implement some variant. In the next chapter, "Introduction to Relational Databases and SQL," you'll see a more detailed explanation of relational databases and the SQL language.

Part 3

Accessing Data with ASP.NET

In this section you will find:

Chapter 12

Introduction to Relational Databases and SQL

THIS CHAPTER CONTAINS AN introduction to relational database technology. The database access code and the discussion in this book center on Open Database Connectivity (ODBC) databases. The examples in this book use SQL Server 2000, which is Microsoft's premier relational database engine, but you can apply the information in this chapter to Oracle, Sybase, or any relational SQL database just as effectively. If you're familiar with relational databases, you can skip this chapter altogether, but if you haven't worked with relational databases before, you should read the information carefully because you need a general understanding of relational databases to work through many of the examples in the rest of this book.

In this chapter:

◆ Databases versus Files

◆ Tables, Indexes, Primary Keys, and Foreign Keys

◆ Set-Based Data Retrieval

◆ Introduction to SQL

Databases versus Files

You've seen how to use sequential files to save data. You probably also realize that sequential files aren't always the most efficient way to store data. Whenever someone begins to discuss data storage and retrieval efficiency, you should immediately be skeptical.

To understand databases, you need to understand why sequential files aren't efficient in some cases. If you're streaming data to a browser, as Web servers stream HTML files, sequential files are *the* most efficient method for storing data long-term. But if you only need a single item of information, sequential files are inefficient. One reason they're inefficient is that you can't jump directly to a single item within the file. You must either read the file sequentially up to the point where the requested data resides for each request or read the entire file at application or session startup and cache the information in memory. When you need to access the data constantly, caching the data in memory is an effective technique, but if you need to access the data only occasionally, caching data in memory just wastes memory. Another reason sequential files are inefficient is that you can't write data to the middle of the file without rewriting the entire file.

In a sequential file, fixed field lengths or delimiters define the separation between individual items, called *fields*, and groups of fields, called *records*. The most common record delimiter is the end-of-line (usually a carriage return/linefeed combination). The most common type of delimited file is the comma-delimited file (also called a comma-separated value (CSV) file), which uses the comma character to separate fields and end-of-line characters to separate records. You don't have to use a comma; although commas are the most common separator character, they're not always the most efficient. Commas appear in most text. Therefore, text fields containing commas always present a problem: How can the computer tell the difference between a comma that acts as a field delimiter and delimits a field and a comma that's part of the data? Typically, delimited fields work around the problem by using quoted strings. Commas that appear between the start and end quotes are part of the data, while commas that appear outside the quotes are delimiters.

Delimiters provide a way to separate the data fields, but they don't specify the length for any particular field. Delimiters separate variable-length fields. But for many field types, you know exactly how long the field needs to be to contain the data. A date/time field, for example, formatted in mm/dd/yyyy hh:mm:ss am/pm form, is always exactly 22 characters long. A name field, on the other hand, may vary between 2 and 20 characters in length. Comma-delimited files work extremely well when you're working with streaming data, but they don't work nearly as well when you need to access or alter individual items in the middle of the file, because there's no way to know in advance exactly where a specific data item is in the file.

Suppose you have a sequential file containing names and addresses, and you need to change the address for the first person in the file. If the new address is longer than the existing address, you can't overwrite the information without also potentially overwriting critical information that follows the address. For example:

```
' Original File contents
Doe,John,15440 St. Paul Ave,Minneapolis,MN,99820

' New Address
98029 Livonia Ave #205,Minneapolis,MN,99820
```

The new address is longer than the old address. If you simply start at the current beginning-of-address position and write the new data, the file will look like this:

```
' Overwritten File contents
Doe,John,98029 Livonia Ave #205,neapolis,MN,99820
```

As you can see, the new address line overwrites part of the city field. Similarly, if the new address were shorter than the old address, overwriting the data would leave extraneous characters from the previous address, and you would need to pad the new data with blanks to erase the old data completely. Therefore, you need to rewrite the entire file to replace the address. Rewriting the entire file to change a value is not a problem when a sequential file contains a small number of items, but as the file grows to hundreds, thousands, or millions of items, it takes longer and longer to write the data. To avoid such problems, programmers invented the concept of *random access* files. With a random access file, you aren't concerned with separator characters; instead, your primary concern becomes field length.

Random access files store data in records. Each record consists of fields, and each field is a preselected size. You can store a date as six text characters in six bytes, for example 041299 (fixed date fields with two-digit years were the root cause of the infamous Y2K problem), as a number that's an offset from a single known date, or as two one-byte values for the month and day combined with a two-byte value for the year. All these date-storing schemes rely on the fact that the program storing the data and the program reading the data both understand and agree on the format in which the dates are stored.

Similarly, you could arbitrarily assume that last names are never longer than 30 characters; therefore, you could create a 30-character field to store last names. Unfortunately, the size you select is critical. Having decided that last names are 30 characters, you may not be able to change that length easily. If you ever find a last name longer than 30 characters, you won't be able to accommodate it. The stability of the data model depends on the accurate assessment and unchanging nature of the data. Similarly, every time you store a last name shorter than the maximum field length, you waste the bytes between the length of the data and the length of the field. For variable-length fields, more often than not the data will be shorter than the field length. In other words, using variable length fields in random access files wastes storage space.

Nevertheless, random access files have a major advantage: You can replace data in the middle of the file without rewriting the entire file. As long as the new data conforms to the field type and size of the existing data, you can overwrite the old data without a problem.

Because all the fields in each record are the same length, all the records are also the same length. You can also think of the data as a set of records, or a recordset. Each recordset consists of an arbitrary number of records, each of which contains the same number and type of fields. That conveniently lets you think of random access files in terms of tables. A table is a set of records in which the data in a given column is always the same type and size. Therefore, a recordset and a table are essentially the same thing.

With a random access file, you can do much more than replace records; you can sort records as well. For example, suppose you have a list of grammar school children. Each child belongs in a specific grade, and several teachers teach each grade. You want to divide the children into classes so that each teacher gets roughly the same number of children. You want a final listing by grade, teacher, and child.

To obtain the final list, you're going to have to sort the data. You need to separate the children into classes and group the class records together. Assume that the records are originally on disk as shown in Table 12.1.

TABLE 12.1: Sample Class Records: Students

ID	GRADE	TEACHER	LASTNAME	FIRSTNAME
1	1	NA	Jones	Barry
2	2	NA	Templeton	Bill
3	2	NA	Jones	Meredith
4	1	NA	McArthur	Isabel
5	3	NA	Said	Mohammed
6	3	NA	Chen	Xiulian
7	2	NA	Barker	Charles

To determine how many teachers you need for each grade, you must first count the number of students in each grade. To do that, you need to loop through the file, reading each record and keeping a separate counter for each grade. At the end of the loop, you'll know the number of students in each grade.

Next, you can assign teachers by desired class size. For example, if you have 160 first-grade students, and you want an average class size of 20 students, you will need 8 teachers, but if you want an average class size of 26 students, you will need only 6 teachers. You can now loop back through the file and assign a teacher to each student, writing the teacher's name into the Teacher field.

The data is complete, but there's still a problem: How are you going to display the data? On disk, the records are still in their original sequence. To display the data in order, you'll need to sort it. You could rewrite the file in the correct sequence, moving each record to its sorted position, but that's inefficient. If you add a student, you'll have to rewrite the data again, and if you have to rewrite all the data to add a record, a random access file provides very little advantage over a sequential file!

Suppose that instead of rewriting the data in the proper sequence, you sort the data in memory and write the list of sorted IDs to a separate, sequential file on disk. Each ID in the separate file is associated with the record number of the complete file. You can now say that the list of IDs is an index into the data file—let's call it the Grade-Teacher-Name (GTN) index. The index file is an extremely powerful concept. You can now determine very quickly if a record exists by looping through the index file rather than reading the records from disk. As long as you maintain the one-to-one relationship of the index file to the data file, if you can find an ID in the index file, you can guarantee that the record exists.

Using the index, you can retrieve the list in GTN sequence without altering the physical position of the data in the data file. Similarly, if you add a new student record to the end of the main file, you can loop through the GTN index to find out where the new student belongs in sorted order and then insert the new student ID number at that location. The index file is a sequential file, but it's relatively small compared to the data file. It's much faster to rewrite the index file than to rewrite the data file.

You still have some problems, though. Suppose a teacher gets married during the school year. You now need to update each student's record with the teacher's new name. Not only that, you probably need to go back to the data from prior years and replace that teacher's name throughout the data set. It would be much simpler if you could keep the teacher names in one file and the student names in another and join them together when you needed a report.

For example, suppose that instead of using up valuable space to put a teacher name in each row, you change the data design so that each row contains a TeacherID column as shown in Table 12.2.

TABLE 12.2: SAMPLE CLASS RECORDS: STUDENTS

ID	GRADE	TEACHERID	LASTNAME	FIRSTNAME
1	1	32	Jones	Barry
2	2	86	Templeton	Bill
3	2	87	Jones	Meredith
4	1	21	McArthur	Isabel
5	3	45	Said	Mohammed
6	3	45	Chen	Xiulian
7	2	86	Barker	Charles

Now, rather than changing each row associated with that teacher, you can change a single row in a related table called Teachers, as shown in Table 12.3.

TABLE 12.3: SAMPLE CLASS RECORDS: TEACHERS

TEACHERID	LASTNAME	FIRSTNAME
32	Franklin	Marsha
86	Barstow	Emily
21	Bannister	Henry
87	McAllister	Ian
45	Pinker	Dorothy

Now, no matter how many teacher changes you make, you can either update a single row in the Teachers table or the `TeacherID` column in the Students table. A data design like this consists of relationships. The `TeacherID` column in the Teachers table is a *primary key*, meaning one and only one row may be associated with a single value. The related `TeacherID` column in the Students table is a *foreign key* because it contains data that originates from outside the table—in other words, from a foreign table. Because one teacher may teach many students, there is a one-to-many relationship between the tables.

Extend this idea a little bit. Imagine that in this school, each student takes many classes during the day and, further, that those classes aren't all the same each day. In other words, each student may have many teachers and classes, which changes the relationship between teachers and students from a one-to-many to a many-to-many relationship. If you can imagine that, then you can also imagine that managing the key relationships and indexes isn't an easy task. You probably wouldn't want to write that code yourself. Well, fortunately, you don't have to. Managing relationships like this is exactly what relational databases were meant to do.

Part of managing data relationships involves ensuring that the data you're putting into the database is the right data. With a file, you must write the data validation code yourself. Databases simplify that process by refusing to store data that doesn't meet the requirements (field types, sizes, and value lists) specified when you created the database. But modern databases go far beyond simple data type validation. You can define complex data types, such as combinations of numeric and string values, as well as rules about how the data in columns must relate. For example, you could create a data type called `ORDER_ID`. An `ORDER_ID` consists of two characters identifying the product, a dash, a four-character product subtype number, a dash, and the order date in MMDDYYYY format. For example:

```
FB-8382-12041999
```

When you assign the `ORDER_ID` data type to a column, the database enforces validity on that column. If your company subsequently changes the rules, you can theoretically revise the `ORDER_ID` data type and change the data in the database to fit the new rules without having to change the code in all the applications that access the data. You may have heard or read experienced developers saying that you should let the database enforce data validity. Unfortunately, many programmers don't do that. Inexperienced programmers write validation code themselves, and because *their* data is already valid, they omit the data validation rules in the database. However, when the rules change, it's much more difficult to find and update the validation code in the production programs than it is to change it in a single place in the database.

In addition to data validity rules, databases can also enforce data-relationship rules. The simplest example involves a one-to-many primary-to-foreign key relationship between two tables. Each row in the table on the many side of the relationship must have a matching row in the table on the one side of the relationship. The database rejects data that doesn't fit those requirements. Similarly, the database would not let you delete a row from the one side that had matching rows on the many side, because that would orphan the data and violate the relationship.

Indexes, primary keys, and foreign key relationships are all part of a larger concept called *constraints*. A constraint is a limitation, a way to prevent error conditions from occurring. For example, a primary key constraint has a unique value for each row in a table. Primary keys may not be null. The database enforces five types of constraints:

Not Null The field may not contain a null value.

Unique The field must be unique within its column.

Primary Key A combination of unique and not null. A table may have only one primary key.

Foreign Key Defines a relationship between two tables: one-to-one, one-to-many, or many-to-many.

Check Enforces rules concerning data values; for example, an `Employee_Age` column must be between 18 and 70.

Databases have one more huge advantage over files—they can run queries. A query is a request to retrieve, alter, or add data to a database. You write queries in a special language called Structured Query Language (SQL, pronounced "sequel"). Because most databases store the database objects themselves in standard tables, you can use SQL not only to modify data, but to modify the database itself, by adding fields, tables, constraints, changing field types, and so forth.

So far, I've approached this subject from a one-program, one-database viewpoint, but Web applications typically have many simultaneous users. The pressure on your server to manage data and index changes grows very rapidly as the number of users increases, because you not only need to retrieve and update the data, but you must do it in such a way that two users don't try to update the same data at the same time. In fact, you usually want to prohibit a user from updating data if it's changed since they saw the original data. Even worse, suppose an update fails for some reason. Imagine that you're updating the Students table. You have to write the values for each field. You write the `ID`, `Grade`, `Teacher`, and `LastName`, then you find that the `FirstName` value is null. But that's a required field. Now you must *roll back* the update operation, because you can't allow the data to change unless it's valid. In other words, each operation that changes data must be complete and verifiable. To meet this requirement, robust relational databases use transactions and logs.

Transactions and Logging

A *transaction* is a unit of work that must either complete successfully or fail completely. For example, when deleting a record with child records in a related table (a one-to-many relationship), you don't want the database to delete only a portion of the child rows; you want it to either delete all the child rows or none of them. Therefore, if any error occurs during the delete operation, you want the database to abandon any deletions it may have already made. You control this by telling the database to start a transaction. Then if any errors occur, you can roll back the transaction—putting the database back into the state it was in before the transaction began.

Modern relational databases such as SQL Server handle all internal operations as transactions. Before a transaction begins, the database logs the current value of all affected data. After the operation finishes, the database logs the operation itself. By logging all data and structure modification to the database, the Relational Database Management System (RDBMS) ensures that you can recover from disasters. For example, if the power should suddenly fail in the middle of an operation, you would be able to recover, or roll back the state of the database to exactly what it was before the power outage. To do that, you would combine the most recent backup with the transaction log. Essentially, the database would replay the transactions in the exact sequence they occurred until it reached the last completely logged operation.

The log file used by databases to maintain the list of transactions is called the *transaction log*. You cannot disable the transaction log, even though disabling it would speed up operations that alter data, because the database would be unable to recover from disasters. Most databases allow some unlogged operations. For example, truncating (deleting all the data from) a table is an unlogged operation. In contrast, using a DELETE statement to delete data is a logged operation—even if you delete all the data in a table. Some databases let you load data from a backup as an unlogged operation.

Although Microsoft Access and most other file-based databases support transactions, they do not maintain a transaction log for each operation. Therefore, their disaster recovery is limited to restoring the database from the latest backup. You cannot recover data changes that occurred since the last backup, a prime reason why they are unsuitable for transactional applications and for applications containing critical data.

Tables, Indexes, Primary Keys, and Foreign Keys

You've already seen a small example of tables, primary keys, and foreign keys in the first section of this chapter. To recap: A table is a collection of rows. Rows consist of fields (or columns), which for any given row are exactly the same size and data type as in any other row. An index is a sorted column that lets a database management system find a row very quickly—much more quickly in most cases than scrolling through the data. A primary key is a number, string value, or combination of field values that uniquely identifies a specific row, and a foreign key is a value inserted in another table to form a relationship with the same value in a different table.

The easiest way to create and maintain tables is with a front-end management system. For example, Visual Studio contains some rudimentary but highly functional tools to help you create tables, indexes, and relationships. Microsoft SQL Server's Enterprise Manager application ships with tools that are much easier to use than most other enterprise-level databases. Commercial tools are available for most popular RDBMSs that can handle almost any type of data management operation. I strongly recommend that you obtain and explore the functionality provided by the management tool(s) provided with your choice of RDBMS. However, with most databases, you can create database objects entirely in SQL.

SQL Server treats tables, indexes, and certain types of relationships as objects. They have properties and methods, and you can create them in code. With most RDBMSs you can also create them with the flavor of SQL supported by that RDBMS.

Your aim in designing a database is twofold: First, you want to define the tables so that you store a specific item in only one place. For example, storing teacher names in both the Teachers table and the Students table (both shown in the previous section) would violate that rule. The process of partitioning information among tables such that the information appropriate to any given row appears only in that row is called *normalization*. Normalization is important because it lets you change information in only one place. Second, you want to be able to retrieve data from the database quickly and/or modify the data quickly. In other words, the second goal is performance.

The two goals of normalization and performance are often in direct opposition. For example, to show a report of students by teachers, it is obviously more work to obtain a set of student records and a set of teacher names and join the two together than it is to read a set of student records where the teacher names are already present in the student rows. Sometimes (but not often) for speed reasons, you may need to denormalize a table. Consider denormalization to be a process of optimization—a process that occurs only after a normalized design has proven to be a bottleneck. In addition, you should think of denormalization as a rare condition—avoid it until you've explored all other performance enhancement solutions.

Every table should have a primary key. That sounds deceptively simple, but it's not always easy finding a meaningful value that is unique to every row. For example, you can't use a LastName field as a primary key, because too many people have the same last name. You can't use a combination of LastName and FirstName values for the same reason. You can't even use a telephone number—what if you have a husband and wife both teaching in the same school? A much better choice would be a Social Security number, which the government guarantees to be unique for each individual. With that said, it's generally a mistake to use *any* meaningful value as a primary key. Even values that people normally presume to be stable tend to change sometimes. For example, 30 years ago, no city used more than a single area code. Now, the term "area code" is rapidly losing its meaning, and almost every major city uses more than one area code. IP addresses are likely to expand in size soon because we're running out of addresses. Even Social Security numbers will need to change eventually.

You aren't limited to using a single value as a primary key; a primary key may consist of multiple fields. Multiple-field keys may have duplicate values in any individual field, but when combined, the fields form a unique value for each row. Multiple-field keys are called *composite* keys. For example, imagine a table that contains car part numbers and descriptions. Sometimes, the parts change slightly, but the part number does not change. For reporting purposes, you want to be able to differentiate between the two different versions of a part—so you need two separate rows—but you also need to be able to continue to refer to the part by its original number. In this case, you might add a revision number field. Neither the revision number field nor the part number field is unique, but the *combination* of the part number and the revision number is unique for each part, and you can use the part number/revision number combination as a primary key.

Because it's often extremely difficult to find a meaningful data field that is both unique and completely stable, you can—and usually should—use an artificial value for your primary key. Most databases support an automatically incrementing field that makes an adequate primary key. The database increments a value—usually a long integer—whenever you add a row. The incremented value ensures that you have a column containing a unique value for each row of the table. In Microsoft SQL Server, this type of field is called an *identity field*. More generally, they're called *synthetic keys*. Identity fields are perfect for differentiating rows in a single database, but they're not perfect if you have several databases and need to merge the data.

For example, suppose your Web application supports a distributed sales force. Each salesperson enters orders into a local database program running on a laptop during the day and then uploads the new or edited rows to a central database whenever they can connect via a dial-up connection. If the database on the laptops uses an identity field, it's highly likely that the central server will eventually receive two rows from separate salespeople that both have the same number. Consider the first row that any salesperson sends. With a fresh database on a laptop, the first row will have an identity value of 1, so each salesperson would tend to send rows with the same numbers. Of course, you could elect to ignore the identity value on the local database and create a new one in the central database when you add the row, but that defeats the purpose of having a unique value because it's no longer unique; the salesperson's row has a different identifier than the central row. A better solution would be to store the salesperson's identity value but create a new one for the central database.

However, suppose your business is global. You may have several "central" databases—one in each region or country. Now you have the same problem when you want to aggregate the rows for global reports.

In such cases, you can take advantage of a Windows concept called a Globally Unique ID (GUID). A GUID is a structure containing values guaranteed to be unique—it uses the time and MAC address of your network card to ensure that no other computer will generate the same ID. You can create a GUID using the .NET framework very easily. This function returns a string representation of a GUID.

```
Private Function getGUID() As String
    GetGUID = "{" & System.Guid.NewGUID().ToString & "}"
End Function
```

Because GUIDs are so useful, Microsoft SQL Server can create them for you. SQL Server versions 7 and higher support GUIDs as a native data type. Using GUIDs, you can merge remote data into a central store without worrying about whether the row IDs might collide, and without the central row ID being different from the local row ID. Unfortunately, GUIDs have one drawback—they're larger and slower than integers (16 bytes versus 4 bytes for an integer). In addition, their length makes them awkward to type and remember, so they're more difficult to work with directly.

A primary key is an index, but not all indexes are primary. A primary key must be a *unique* index. A unique index consists of column values in which each value in the entire column is unique; each row contains a single unique value in that column. Not all indexes are unique—that is, they index columns in which values are repeated from row to row. Often, you need to index a column that does not contain unique values—for example, a list of names. Similarly, you may want to create a unique index on a field that is not a primary key. For example, a Social Security number is unique but doesn't necessarily make a good primary key because it's long. A shorter unique value, such as an identity field, would be faster.

Indexes don't have to consist solely of values from a single column. You can use a combination of columns, called a *composite index*. For example, an application that schedules rooms in a public facility could use a composite index consisting of both the room number and the date it was scheduled as a primary key. The room number isn't unique—a given room may be booked every day; the date isn't unique—many rooms may be booked on the same date, but the combination is unique. A given room may be booked only once on any given date.

You should normally index fields that

◆ Are used to sort data

◆ Are used as foreign keys

◆ Appear as conditional values in queries

If you think about how the database must apply the index to find and sort data, these rules are nothing more than common sense. If you join two tables on a common field—a foreign key relationship—it's obvious that the RDBMS can find matching rows in the tables much faster if you index the columns in both tables. Similarly, sorting an index is considerably faster than sorting an entire table.

An important index type in SQL Server is a *clustered index*. A clustered index controls the physical order of records in the database. A database keeps data in pages. Each page consists of a fixed number of bytes. Typically, databases don't completely fill up a page before beginning to place data into another page. That way, when you add a record, there's an increased chance that it will fit into an existing page. A clustered index forces the database to maintain the data in a specific order, making it much faster to request data sorted in that order—because the data is already sorted. All the RDBMS has to do is retrieve the records in their physical order.

You should create a clustered index on a column that controls the order in which you most often wish to retrieve the data. Note that a table may have only one clustered index. Some types of values aren't suited for clustered indexes. For example, bit fields, which can take only two values, 1 or 0, are unsuitable for clustered indexes. Similarly, columns containing sequential values, such as identity fields, are not good candidates for a clustered index. All indexes other than clustered indexes are called "nonclustered" indexes.

As with many database issues, when you discuss indexes, there are invariably design trade-offs between ease-of-use, speed, and maintainability. For example, a GUID is a large value. It will be slower and use more storage and memory space than a simple identity value; however, you may elect to use a GUID because you need to merge data from many locations. There are no hard and fast rules. You must decide which issues are most important for your application. With that said, there are several considerations that are common to all database applications.

In general, you should try to keep primary keys (and all indexes) as short as possible. Wide values (those that take up many bytes) are slower than narrow values. Numeric values are generally faster than string values.

Index all foreign key columns and columns used to sort data. You need to be able to determine when you should and should not follow this rule, because slavishly following the rule leads to slow databases. Indexes improve data selection operations but slow down data alteration operations. That's because the RDBMS must alter table indexes, deleting, inserting, or re-sorting as needed when you alter data in that table. Therefore, if most of your application's interaction with a table consists of inserting data, such as an application to handle online order processing, you want to minimize the number of indexes on that table. In contrast, if most of your data operations involve selecting data, you want to index every column that might improve the response time. The point is that you should look at the foreign key columns, columns with selection constraints, and columns that control sort order and make a decision as to whether you should index the column based on your application's needs.

Set-Based Data Retrieval

When you access data from a file, you often scroll through data line-by-line, processing values when you find specific values in the line or processing each line. Relational databases, although you may think about them as individual lines containing records, don't work that way. Instead, they work on sets of data. A data set is a combination of one or more rows and columns; in other words, a set of records, also called a recordset or a result set. Note that the columns in the recordset do not have to come from a single table. In fact, with relational databases, most of your queries will not come from a single table—if they do, you're probably making poor use of the relational capabilities of modern databases.

NOTE   When I say relational databases, I'm excluding Microsoft Access and other file-based databases. Although you can use Access for practice, it's not suitable for a full-scale Web application with more than a small number of users. It's not suitable for any users if the data is critical. If you were considering using Access for your production Web application—don't. In fact, I recommend that you not use it at all, even for practice. Consider using the newer MSDE (Microsoft Data Engine) instead. It supports the same syntax as SQL Server, which means you won't have to change your application when you deploy it for use. MSDE is no more suited for a large-scale or critical Web application than is Access, but it is considerably easier to upgrade.

For all discussion of databases throughout the rest of this book, you can assume that I mean both MSDE and SQL Server, even though, for brevity, I will omit the term MSDE. I'm not trying to ignore Oracle, Sybase, Informix, DB2, or any other relational database management system—all the general database information (but not the Transact-SQL code itself) applies equally well to those RDBMSs as to SQL Server. This is, after all, a book about Microsoft technology, so it is Microsoft-centric.

Working with sets requires a different mindset from working with rows of data. It forces you to think in terms of relationships rather than in terms of rows. You also begin thinking about data as collections of records rather than as individual data items. Typically, you join a column from one table with a matching column in another table to retrieve a set of records. A join finds matching values in the columns then selects a specified set of columns from the intersection of the two sets.

For example, consider a teacher-student relationship. One teacher has many students. Conversely, one student may have several teachers. In other words, for any given row on one side of the relationship, many rows may be on the other side—an example of a many-to-many relationship. For your application, you want to select the set of students taught by any given teacher, as well as the set of teachers for any given student. To create this relationship in a database, you must model that many-to-many relationship in table relationships. If the Teachers table contains a unique or primary key index on a `TeacherID` field and the Students table contains a unique or primary key index on a `StudentID` field, you can create a separate table called TeacherStudent that contains only two columns: the `TeacherID` and `StudentID` values.

Using the TeacherStudent table, it's easy to determine which students have which teachers or obtain the set of students taught by any teacher. For example, the teacher Marsha Franklin (`TeacherID=32`) teaches Barry Jones, Meredith Jones, and Mohammed Said. If you query a database for this information, you need to find the intersection of the three tables, as shown in Figure 12.1.

FIGURE 12.1

Teachers-to-students
relationship query

TeacherID	StudentID
32	1
86	5
87	3
21	7
45	2
45	7
86	4
32	3
86	4
32	5
45	1

TeacherID	LastName	FirstName
32	Franklin	Marsha
86	Barstow	Emily
21	Bannister	Henry
87	McAllister	Ian
45	Pinker	Dorothy

StudentID	Grade	LastName	FirstName
1	1	Jones	Barry
2	2	Templeton	Bill
3	2	Jones	Meredith
4	1	McArthur	Isabel
5	3	Said	Mohammed
6	3	Chen	Xiulian
7	2	Barker	Charles

The result of this query is another table—a recordset, shown in Table 12.4.

TABLE 12.4: TEACHERS-TO-STUDENTS RELATIONSHIP QUERY RESULT

TEACHER ID	TEACHER LASTNAME	TEACHER FIRSTNAME	STUDENTID	STUDENT LASTNAME	STUDENT FIRSTNAME
32	Franklin	Marsha	1	Jones	Barry
32	Franklin	Marsha	3	Jones	Meredith
32	Franklin	Marsha	5	Said	Mohammed

To obtain the information from the database, you must frame the question in SQL. In the next section, I'll show you how to do that, but first, you'll need a database with which you can test your SQL statements.

In the remainder of this chapter, you'll work with a database called ClassRecords. You will need MSDE (a time-limited version ships with Visual Studio) or SQL Server 2000 to work through the examples and code in the remainder of this book, although with a little work, you can adapt the examples to any modern relational database. You've already seen a few examples from the database in previous sections in this chapter. The ClassRecords database contains information from an imaginary school in which teachers teach classes to different grades. All the students in the school move from class to class and from teacher to teacher.

Creating the ClassRecords Database

The SQL statements to create the tables, indexes, and data for the ClassRecords database in SQL Server or MSDE are on a file called `CreateClassRecords.sql` on www.sybex,com, in the CSharpASP Ch12 folder. To run the file, click the Tools menu and select SQL Query Analyzer. That opens a new Query window. Click the File menu and select Open. Browse to the `CreateClassRecords.sql` file in the Ch12 folder in your CSharpASP project. Click the Open button to open the file in the SQL Query Analyzer window. Finally, click the run icon (the green arrow) on the toolbar to run the SQL script.

WARNING   *After creating the database by running the script the first time, you can run the script again to restore the database to its original form.*

SQL CODE CONVENTIONS

By convention, SQL keywords appear in uppercase in this book, even though SQL is not case sensitive. SQL doesn't have line termination characters or line continuation characters, so I've broken the lines to fit the layout of this book. You don't have to do that. SQL lets you format the code however you like—including one long line (but don't do that). Indent SQL code as you would indent your VBScript code—make it readable.

SQL has two types of comments: inline comments, which begin with a double-dash (--) and continue to the end of the line, and block comments, which, like Java or C, begin with a slash-star (/*) and end with the reverse, a star-slash (*/). For example:

```
-- This is an inline comment.
/*
This is a block comment.
*/
```

You can freely nest inline comments within block comments. For example:

```
/* The following SELECT statement has been commented out
-- SELECT * FROM SomeTable
*/
```

You may not continue a code line after a comment. For example, the following statement is invalid:

```
SELECT - This is a select statement -- * FROM ...
```
SQL Server ignores all but the first double-dash on any line.

Introduction to SQL

Structured Query Language (SQL) is a straightforward subject, partly because it doesn't do much, and partly because the language is standardized. Most modern databases use a variant of SQL that, for the most part, conforms to the American National Standards Institute (ANSI) 92 standard. That standard means you can use similar—although for some operations not quite identical—SQL code to access many different databases. Fortunately, for basic operations, there's no difference between most common databases.

SQL lets you perform four basic operations on existing tables:

SELECT Retrieve data
INSERT Add data
UPDATE Change data
DELETE Remove data

The SQL *SELECT* Statement

The SELECT statement retrieves data from the database. To retrieve the data, you specify a field list, a table list, a list of fields to sort by, and the sort order. The parts of a SQL statement are called *clauses*. A basic SELECT statement has up to four clauses. For example:

```
SELECT (field1, field2, etc.) FROM (table list) WHERE (condition)
ORDER BY (field1 [ASC|DESC], field2 [ASC|DESC], etc.)
```

The WHERE and ORDER BY clauses are optional. If you omit the WHERE clause, the query returns all rows from the specified tables. If you omit the ORDER BY clause, SQL retrieves rows in an undefined order. In most databases, this is the sequence in which they're stored in a table. By default, when you retrieve data from multiple tables, SQL uses the row order from the first specified field.

At the most basic level, you can obtain all the information from a table using an asterisk (*) as a shorthand way of specifying all fields. For example:

```
SELECT * FROM Teachers
```

The preceding query returns all the columns in all rows of the Teachers table:

TeacherID	LastName	FirstName
32	Franklin	Marsha
86	Barstow	Emily
21	Bannister	Henry
87	McAllister	Ian
45	Pinker	Dorothy

Of course, you don't have to select all fields; you can specify the exact fields and field order that you wish—and you should. For example:

```
SELECT LastName, TeacherID FROM Teachers
```

This query returns a different result:

LastName	TeacherID
Franklin	32
Barstow	86
Bannister	21
McAllister	87
Pinker	45

Programmers moving from file-based databases to relational databases often make the mistake of thinking that the simple SELECT statement is all they need. They are accustomed to scrolling (moving sequentially from field to field) through a set of records to find the ones they need. That's absolutely the wrong way to approach relational databases. Don't search for records yourself—let the database do the work. That's what the WHERE clause does—it limits the returned records to exactly the ones you need. For example, to find only the teachers with last names starting with M, you add a WHERE clause to the SELECT statement:

```
SELECT * FROM Teachers WHERE LastName LIKE 'M%'
```

In T-SQL, the percent sign (%) after the 'M' in the WHERE clause is a wildcard symbol that matches any character. This query returns one row:

TeacherID	LastName	FirstName
87	McAllister	Ian

The ORDER BY clause of the SELECT statement controls the order of the records returned by the query. For example, to select all students by grade, you could use the following SELECT statement:

```
SELECT * FROM Students ORDER BY Grade, LastName, FirstName
```

The fields in the ORDER BY clause do not have to appear in the selected field list. The default sort order is ascending (ASC), but you can retrieve fields in reverse order by specifying the DESC keyword after the appropriate field name. You don't have to select all the fields, and you may select them in any order you desire. The following SELECT statement includes all the basic SELECT clauses:

```
SELECT StudentID, LastName, FirstName FROM Students ORDER BY Grade DESC
```

If you run the query and compare the results to the Grade column in the Students table, you can see that the query does indeed return the data sorted in reverse Grade order.

You aren't limited to using the names of the database columns themselves; you can specify substitute or *alias* column names using the AS option of the SELECT clause. For example:

```
SELECT StudentID AS ID FROM Students
```

The preceding snippet returns a single column consisting of the StudentID values but titled ID. You may create as many aliases as you wish.

INNER and OUTER JOIN Statements

You can use the SELECT statement to retrieve data from more than one table at a time. SQL statements referencing more than one table typically (but not necessarily) use a JOIN statement to connect the tables on a common field or value.

For example, suppose you want a list of all students taught by Marsha Franklin. To obtain the list, you need to join the Teachers table to the Students table on the common TeacherID field. In the Teachers table, the TeacherID field is a primary key; in the Students table, the TeacherID field is a foreign key. Because the primary key in a table is always unique and not null, you know that the TeacherID exists in each row of the Teachers table. For this example, assume you know that every student has been assigned a teacher.

There's a many-to-many relationship between teachers and students. That's because one teacher teaches many students, and each student has several teachers. That relationship appears in the Teacher-Student table. Therefore, you need to join the Teachers table with the TeacherStudent table to find the students assigned to a particular teacher:

```
SELECT StudentID
FROM TeacherStudent INNER JOIN Teachers
ON TeacherStudent.TeacherID=Teachers.TeacherID
WHERE Teachers.LastName='Franklin' AND Teachers.FirstName='Marsha'
```

Note that in SQL you use single, not double, quotes around string values such as `'Franklin'` and `'Marsha'`. When you run the query, the result set is a single column of `StudentID`s:

StudentID

1

5

Although accurate, a list of `StudentID` values is not a satisfactory solution because you still don't know the names of the students assigned to the teacher. The TeacherStudent table contains the `StudentID`s, but not the students' names. To get the names of the students, you need to include the Students table in the query. You can create multiple joins in a single `SELECT` statement.

To retrieve the names, you need two `INNER JOIN` statements because there's no direct relationship between teachers and students. For example:

```
SELECT Students.*
FROM Students INNER JOIN
(TeacherStudent INNER JOIN Teachers ON
    Teachers.TeacherID=TeacherStudent.TeacherID)
ON Students.StudentID=TeacherStudent.StudentID
WHERE Teachers.LastName='Franklin'
ORDER BY Students.LastName
```

The previous statement has several interesting features. First, when you use two tables, you can't use the asterisk shorthand *by itself* to retrieve all the fields from only one of the tables (although you can use it to retrieve all the fields in both tables). When you have more than one table, use the asterisk in conjunction with the table name. In this case, the `Students.*` syntax selects all the columns from the Students table but none of the columns from the Teachers or TeacherStudent tables. Second, the `INNER JOIN` statement requires that you specify which tables and fields the database should join to produce the query. Finally, when you work with more than one table, you must specify the table name as well as the column name for each field where the field name appears in more than one table. The `LastName` and `TeacherID` fields appear in both the Teachers and TeacherStudent tables. In other words, if the column name is not unique among all fields in all tables in the `FROM` clause, the server will raise an error because it can't distinguish the table from which to extract the data.

NOTE   *In general, it's a good idea to get in the habit of specifying your columns using both the table name and the column name. For example, it's better to write* `Teachers.TeacherID` *than just* `TeacherID`. *Specifying the table speeds up your queries because the database doesn't have to check all the table column names to determine the table to which items in the field list belong.*

Now suppose some students haven't been assigned a teacher. In that case, the INNER JOIN clause still works, but the resulting recordset will omit the rows in the Students table for which the TeacherID column value is null. For example:

```
SELECT Teachers.*, Students.*
FROM Students INNER JOIN
(TeacherStudent INNER JOIN Teachers ON
    Teachers.TeacherID=TeacherStudent.TeacherID)
ON Students.StudentID=TeacherStudent.StudentID
ORDER BY Students.LastName
```

When you know that a foreign key may not exist or may not match a key value in the joined table, you can perform a LEFT (OUTER) JOIN or a RIGHT (OUTER) JOIN. The OUTER keyword is optional. Outer joins return all the values from one of the tables even if there's no matching key. For example, if you run the following statement, you'll find that it displays more rows than the previous SELECT example:

```
SELECT Teachers.*, Students.*
FROM Students LEFT JOIN
(TeacherStudent INNER JOIN Teachers ON
    Teachers.TeacherID=TeacherStudent.TeacherID)
ON Students.StudentID=TeacherStudent.StudentID
ORDER BY Students.LastName
```

That's because the LEFT JOIN selects all the students, regardless of whether they have been assigned a teacher. Similarly, you could list all the teachers even if no students had been assigned to them. RIGHT JOIN works the same way but returns all the rows from the right side of the join. One other variation supported by some databases (including SQL Server), the FULL (OUTER) JOIN, retrieves unmatched rows from tables on both sides of the join.

Calculated Values and the *GROUP BY* Clause

Transact-SQL (T-SQL) contains several functions to calculate values. A calculated value is a result of an operation on one or more columns in multiple rows: a sum, an average, or a total, for example. In T-SQL, calculated values are called *aggregates*, and the functions are aggregate functions because they aggregate, or collect a number of values into a single value using a calculation. For example, you can retrieve the total number of rows in any table with the following SELECT statement, substituting an appropriate table name in the FROM clause:

```
SELECT count(*) FROM <tablename>
```

A count of the Students table returns 7. Counting is even more useful when you group results by another column. For example, if you want to know the total number of students taught by each teacher, you could obtain a count of students and group the results by teacher. The result looks like Table 12.5.

TABLE 12.5: COUNT OF STUDENTS BY TEACHER

TEACHERID	LASTNAME	FIRSTNAME	TOTALSTUDENTS
21	Bannister	Henry	1
86	Barstow	Emily	1
32	Franklin	Marsha	3
87	McAllister	Ian	1
45	Pinker	Dorothy	1

The SELECT statement to obtain the results in Table 12.5 includes a new clause, the GROUP BY clause. The syntax is as follows:

```
SELECT (field1, field2, etc.) FROM (table list) WHERE (condition)
GROUP BY (field1, field2, etc.) HAVING (condition) ORDER BY
    (field1 [ASC|DESC], field2 [ASC|DESC], etc.)
```

Here's the statement to select the data in Table 12.5:

```
SELECT Teachers.TeacherID, Teachers.LastName, Teachers.FirstName,
    COUNT(TeacherStudent.StudentID) AS TotalStudents

FROM Students INNER JOIN (TeacherStudent INNER JOIN Teachers
    ON Teachers.TeacherID=TeacherStudent.TeacherID) ON
    Students.StudentID=TeacherStudent.StudentID

GROUP BY Teachers.TeacherID, Teachers.LastName, Teachers.FirstName

HAVING count(TeacherStudent.StudentID) > 0

ORDER BY Teachers.LastName
```

That's an intimidating statement at first, but take each clause separately and it's quite straightforward. The first clause—the column list or field list—simply lists the names of the columns you want the query to return. Note that you can provide a name for the calculated column using the AS keyword followed by the name to use. Calculated values don't belong to a single column—they're not *in* the database, so you can make up your own column names. Actually, the AS keyword lets you rename or provide an *alias name* for any column or table in SQL statements. Experienced SQL programmers use alias names almost all the time because it reduces typing and makes statements easier to read.

The FROM clause lists the table names and the relationships between them, using joins to tell the database how to combine the tables. The GROUP BY clause controls the groupings. You must include all referenced columns in the GROUP BY clause except the calculated columns. Arrange the columns in the GROUP BY clause in the exact sequence in which you want the database to group them. In this case, I put the TeacherID column first because I wanted to obtain the count of students for each teacher.

In this example, the order of the rest of the columns in the GROUP BY clause is immaterial, but they must appear.

The HAVING clause lets you add conditions, just like the WHERE clause. The difference is that the WHERE clause selects records before the grouping occurs, whereas the HAVING clause selects records after the grouping. If you don't include a WHERE clause, the HAVING clause has the same effect as a WHERE clause—but you can have both clauses in one statement.

T-SQL can also perform other, more familiar functions. For example, you can add or concatenate values using the + operator. If you want to retrieve the list of teachers as a single first-last formatted string, you could write a query like this:

```
SELECT Teachers.FirstName + ' ' + Teachers.LastName AS Name FROM Teachers
ORDER BY Teachers.LastName
```

Running the query produces a list of teacher names in first-last format:

Name

Henry Bannister

Emily Barstow

Marsha Franklin

Ian McAllister

Dorothy Pinker

You've seen the rudiments of how to select data. Selecting data doesn't change it, so selecting is a safe operation. All the other statements change data in some way. You'll be happy to know that the other statements are considerably less complex than the SELECT statement. I suggest you make a backup copy of your database before you continue.

The *INSERT* Statement

A SQL INSERT statement adds one or more new rows to a table. The INSERT statement has two variations. The first variation adds one row by assigning values to a specified list of columns in a specified table. The values you want to insert follow a VALUES statement. You put parentheses around both the field list and the values list:

```
INSERT INTO table name (field list) VALUES (values list)
```

You must provide a value for all fields that cannot accept a null value and do not have a default value, with the exception that you do not have to (and are not normally allowed to) provide values for identity columns. For example, to insert a row into the Teachers table, you must provide a last name and a first name:

```
INSERT INTO Teachers (LastName, FirstName)
VALUES('Swarthmore', 'John')
```

The second variation lets you add multiple rows using a SELECT query in place of the VALUES list, as follows:

```
INSERT INTO table name (field list) SELECT query
```

For example, suppose you had a list of students waiting to be enrolled. You could add all the students simultaneously to the Students table. There's a StudentsWaitingList table you can use to test this query. For example:

```
INSERT INTO Students (Grade, LastName, FirstName) SELECT Grade,
    LastName, FirstName FROM StudentsWaitingList
```

If you're inserting data into all the columns in the target table and you specify the values in the same order as the columns appear in the table, you can omit the field list. The SELECT statement you use to obtain the data you want to insert can include any clause or condition discussed in the previous section, including calculated fields and a GROUP BY clause.

The *UPDATE* Statement

UPDATE statements change data in one or more columns and in one or more rows. The UPDATE statement is dangerous because if you forget to specify conditions, your database will happily update all the rows in the table. You should always specify a WHERE condition when updating data, unless you *want* to update all the rows. The UPDATE statement has the following syntax:

```
UPDATE (table name) SET field1 = (value/expression), field2 =
    (value/expression), ... FROM (table/query source) WHERE (condition)
```

The UPDATE statement has four clauses. In the UPDATE clause, you must specify a table name containing the fields to update. You may not update multiple tables simultaneously.

The SET clause contains the list of fields you wish to update. You separate the list with commas. Each item in the list consists of a field name, an equals sign, and a new value. You can use a constant, a variable, a field from another table, or an expression for the value on the right side of the equals sign.

The FROM clause is optional. If you're updating a single row with constant values, you can omit the FROM clause. You need the FROM clause when you're updating data in one table from values stored in a different table (or in another place in the same table). Fortunately, the FROM clause is identical to the FROM clause you saw in the section "The SQL SELECT Statement," earlier in this chapter. You may update from multiple tables using JOIN statements as appropriate.

The WHERE clause (don't forget the WHERE clause!), again, is a condition that identifies the rows in the target table you wish to update. For example, suppose the student Isabel McArthur announces that she is changing her name to Serena McArthur. You can update her student record with the following SQL statement:

```
UPDATE Students SET FirstName = 'Serena' WHERE
    Students.LastName='McArthur' AND Students.FirstName='Isabel'
```

Programmers are tempted to think that an update to a single field alters that field and only that field—as if the row were an array and the update replaced a value in a single index position of the array. While that's a convenient mental picture because the database acts as if it works that way, it doesn't. For example, in SQL Server, the database locks the data page (or row); marks the original row as deleted; inserts the new row, copying values from the original row as needed; and finally deletes the original row and removes the locks, completing the transaction. The implementation details for any specific database may differ. If you need to know exactly how your database works, check your database's documentation.

The *DELETE* Statement

The DELETE statement is the simplest of all, but it is quite powerful. You can use the DELETE statement to delete one or more rows in one or more tables. For example, after inserting all the records from the StudentsWaitingList table, you can delete all the records in the table using the following statement:

```
DELETE FROM StudentsWaitingList
```

As you can see, the DELETE statement is just as dangerous as the UPDATE statement, because it cheerfully deletes data without prompting. If you accidentally run a DELETE statement, it's difficult to recover your data. You should rarely use a DELETE statement without a WHERE clause. If you want to delete all the data from a table, it's much more efficient to use the TRUNCATE TABLE statement, one of a group of statements that alters the database itself. Truncating a table removes all the data and resets the identity column value to its default, usually 1. For example, to delete all the data in the StudentsWaitingList table, you can write the following:

```
TRUNCATE TABLE StudentsWaitingList
```

While, in general, you should rarely use DELETE without a WHERE clause, there is one reason to do so. The TRUNCATE statement is not logged, meaning you can't recover if you use it automatically, whereas the DELETE statement is a logged operation. That's the reason TRUNCATE is so much more efficient—it avoids the log operations—but that also means the data is unrecoverable from the transaction log.

The DELETE statement becomes slightly more complex when you want to delete data based on values from another table. For example, suppose you decide to delete all the students who have no assigned teachers. You need to join the TeacherStudent table to the Students table, find the rows where the TeacherID columns contain null values in the TeacherStudent table, and then delete those rows in the Teachers table. This may sound like a two-step operation, but you can accomplish it in SQL with a single step, as follows:

```
DELETE FROM Students
WHERE StudentID NOT IN
  (SELECT DISTINCT StudentID FROM TeacherStudent)
```

The previous statement uses the NOT IN keywords to test for the existence of a StudentID in a subquery (the portion of the previous query contained in parentheses). A subquery is a separate query that returns data. In this case, the subquery returns the list of all StudentIDs that appear in the TeacherStudent table. Any StudentIDs that do not appear in that table have no assigned teachers and can be deleted. The DISTINCT keyword causes the database to remove duplicate values before returning the data. A StudentID may appear multiple times in the TeacherStudent table. The DISTINCT keyword eliminates the duplicates.

When you want to delete data from one table in a join, you must specify the name of the table after the DELETE keyword. For example, suppose you add all the rows in the StudentsWaitingList table to the Students table, then decide to remove them:

```
DELETE Students
FROM Students INNER JOIN StudentsWaitingList
  ON Students.LastName=StudentsWaitingList.LastName AND
  Students.FirstName=StudentsWaitingList.FirstName
```

Without the DELETE Students clause, the database cannot decide which table to delete the data from.

Generate Unique IDs

You've seen how to create identity fields, but there are other ways to uniquely distinguish one row from another. Identity fields work wonderfully within a table but have serious weaknesses when you're working between tables, or worse, between databases, because the database guarantees the uniqueness of an identity value only for new rows.

For example, suppose your company has a mobile sales force using laptops. Each salesperson generates a few dozen orders per day. The salespeople enter these orders into a local Access database on their laptops. Periodically, the salespeople connect to the central office to upload the orders.

Furthermore, suppose you were given the task of writing both the local order-entry application and an ASP.NET page to accept the orders via a secured connection. You must contrive a means to create a table that can accept the rows from many remote databases—and you're not allowed to change the data from the laptops.

This is a tough problem because you must avoid identical OrderID values from any two machines. To solve it, you can use Globally Unique IDs (GUIDs). A GUID is a string consisting of a sequence of numbers and letters guaranteed to be unique among all computers everywhere. As you can imagine, these numbers are long. Microsoft Windows uses GUIDs to identify COM objects and to provide a COM-compatible ID for exported .NET classes. If you look in the Windows Registry, you'll find that the HKEY_CLASSES_ROOT\CLSID key contains a large number of GUIDs, which look like this:

```
{098f2370-bac0-11ce-b579-08012b30bfeb}
```

GUIDs are globally unique because they depend on the local machine's network card MAC address, the local date and time, and for all I know, the internal ID of your microprocessor and the phase of the moon. It doesn't matter—believe me, the chances of another computer generating a GUID that matches any GUID produced on any other computer in the world is vanishingly small.

SQL Server 7 and higher support GUIDs natively, but earlier versions do not. In previous versions of VB, generating GUIDs was difficult, but you can generate GUIDs in .NET with a single line of code (see the example earlier in this chapter in the section "Tables, Indexes, Primary Keys, and Foreign Keys"), which makes them the most convenient choice when you absolutely have to have a primary key value that's unique between tables, machines, and SQL Server databases.

Summary

There's a great deal more to know about SQL and SQL Server, but the information in this chapter should give you a good start. You may see some SQL constructions and functions in the remainder of this book that you haven't seen so far. I'll try to briefly explain those as they appear. I strongly suggest you spend some more time exploring SQL's capabilities. You should practice writing SQL statements to retrieve and modify data until you're comfortable reading and creating them before you continue. The Transact-SQL help files and the SQL Server Books Online contain an enormous amount of information. In addition, there are many excellent reference and tutorial works on SQL.

In the next chapter, you'll use a database as the data store for information you want to display in Web Forms. To do that, you use a set of objects from the System.Data namespace, collectively known as ADO.NET, which provides the methods you need to connect to a database and retrieve and modify data.

Chapter 13

Introduction to ADO.NET

IF YOU USED ADO in VB6 or ASP 3.0 to retrieve data from a database, you'll be happy to know that many of the concepts you already know apply to ADO.NET as well. There are some major changes, though. First, ADO.NET has much better support for the concept of disconnected data than did ADO. In fact, data you retrieve from a provider with ADO.NET is disconnected by default, although you can create persistent connections if you need to. Second, the main data object in ADO—the recordset—has disappeared entirely in ADO.NET. Before you get worried, the replacement—the data set—is not only much more powerful, but for the most part, easier to use.

In this chapter:

◆ The System.Data Namespace

◆ Working with **Connection** Objects

◆ The ADO.NET Approach to Data Access

The System.Data Namespace

The classes that you use to retrieve data reside in the System.Data namespace. To use them easily, you should use the System.Data namespace in Web Forms that retrieve data.

The first step in retrieving data is to create a connection to the database.

Working with *Connection* Objects

A connection is essentially a pipe through which other objects communicate with the database. The connection takes care of data-translation issues for you according to properties you provide to a **Connection** object, usually at the time you create it. VS.NET ships with two types of connection classes. The OleDbConnection class is a generalized class that works with several popular ODBC databases, including Access (Jet), SQL Server, and Oracle. Microsoft offers a separate download for an OdbcConnection class that works with the OLE DB provider for ODBC databases. An equivalent class, called SqlConnection (pronounced "sequel connection" rather than "S-Q-L connection"), works specifically with SQL Server.

If you're querying a SQL Server database, you should use the SqlConnection class, because it's considerably faster than the generalized OleDbConnection class. This duality—support of both generalized OleDb classes and optimized SQL classes—exists throughout the System.NET namespace. Every applicable OleDb class has an equivalent SQL class counterpart, meaning you can (almost) seamlessly switch to SQL Server and the SQL classes and get a performance boost without changing anything else in your application.

With that said, there *are* some important differences. I'll reiterate these throughout the chapter, so if they don't make complete sense at the moment, bear with me. Briefly, here are the major differences:

◆   You must specify a provider to connect to a database with an `OleDbConnection` object.

◆   `OleDbConnection` objects don't close automatically when they go out of scope. You must explicitly call the `Close` method or the `Dispose` method to close the connection. In contrast, `SqlConnection` objects close automatically when they go out of scope; in other words, `Sql-Connection` objects act like other .NET objects, whereas `OleDbConnection` objects act like COM objects. That's because the `OleDbConnection` object is a .NET wrapper for COM-based OLE DB providers, but the `SqlConnection` object communicates directly with the SQL Server API (which also explains why the SQL classes are faster).

I'll use both versions in the remainder of this chapter, so you'll feel comfortable with either set, but you should keep the SQL Server—only version in mind. Feel free to substitute one for the other in these examples as you wish.

You use a `Connection` object to connect to a specific database. If you're querying multiple databases, you need multiple connections. However, you can reuse a connection to a single database multiple times. If you want to switch your `Connection` object to a different database, you must close it and then open it again. Connecting to a database and "opening" a database are not quite the same thing. You connect to a database by specifying a *connection string*. A connection string, rather obviously, is a string that consists of several fields. Like CSS values, the connection string consists of `key=value` pairs separated by semicolons. For example, the following OleDb connection string contains four `key=value` pairs:

```
Provider=SQLOLEDB; Data source=localhost;
initial catalog=Northwind;user id=sa
```

REQUIRED CONNECTION STRING FIELDS

For every connection string, you *must* specify the following:

The Provider (*OleDbConnection* only)   Here's one difference between the OleDbConnection and SqlConnection classes. When you use an `OleDbConnection` object, you *must* specify a provider. In contrast, when you use a `SqlConnection` object, you don't have to specify a provider because the classes "talk" directly to the SQL Server API.

The Data Source   The location of the database or database server. For example, if your database server is on the same machine as your development environment, you could use the name `local-host`. If the database is remote, you must provide the name or IP address of the database server.

The Initial Catalog   A catalog is the same thing as a database, so all the term *initial catalog* means is that you must specify the name of the database you want to query. Examples are `Northwind` and

pubs. Strictly speaking, the catalog isn't required for SQL Server; but if you don't specify a catalog, SQL Server uses the "master" database, which probably isn't your intention.

Security Information   There are several approaches to security. You can pass an explicit user ID and password, or you can use the `Integrated Security` (a.k.a. `Trusted_Connection`) setting to specify that the connection is secure. The Integrated Security field accepts one of three values: `true`, `false`, or `SSPI` (Security Support Provider Interface). In ADO.NET running on Windows, there's no difference between specifying `Integrated Security=true` and `Integrated Security=SSPI`. SSPI is essentially a buffer between your application and the various security protocols used by data and service providers, such as databases or Web servers. Your application uses SSPI to call a *security support provider* (SSP), which in turn handles the specific security details for each security implementation (such as Kerberos, COM-authenticated RPC, or Secure Channels) for you. Each SSP exposes one or more *security package* that translates generic SSPI function calls into the format required for a specific security implementation. A detailed look at SSPI is beyond the scope of this book. Fortunately, you don't need to know much about it to use it. In fact, you don't even have to call any SSPI functions to use it against SQL Server. On a server running Windows 2000 or Windows XP, the system automatically loads Kerberos and Windows NT Challenge/Response (NTLM) authentication SSPs when you boot the server. Windows NT systems automatically load only NTLM.

In addition to these three required fields (or four if you use an `OleDbConnection` object), connection strings may contain several other optional fields, which are as follows:

Application name   Passes the name of an application to the server, which may accept or reject connections based on that value.

ConnectTimeout   Specifies the length of time the connection will wait for the database server to respond before timing out.

Max Pool Size and *Min Pool Size*   Specify the maximum and minimum number of connections to keep in the connection pool.

Network Library   Specifies how to connect to the server. The default Network Library value is `dbnssocn`, which tells the connection to use TCP/IP, but other values, such as `dbnmpntw` (Named Pipes) and `dbmsrpcn` (Multiprotocol) can connect to databases using those protocols. For most installations and for smaller applications, you won't need to worry about any of these values—the defaults will work just fine.

CREATING A *CONNECTION* OBJECT

There are two ways to create connections: by using the VS.NET Data Connection Wizard and by writing the code yourself. I want you to ignore the availability of the wizard for a few minutes and practice writing the connections in code. Not only will you need to recognize the parameter names and settings when you debug applications, but you can't write quick test code in a text editor unless you're familiar with the code itself rather than the wizard alone.

WARNING   If you're not using SQL Server, you must use the `OleDbConnection` object (and specify the provider) to complete this chapter. Substitute the `OleDb` prefix wherever you see a class that starts with `Sql`—and remember to call `Close` or `Dispose` when you're done with the connection.

WARNING   *In the remainder of this book, I've assumed that you have SQL Server installed on your development server or on a server accessible through your network. If you're using MSDE, you should install the SQL Server Developer edition to gain access to the Enterprise Manager application. You can download the Developer edition from* http://www.microsoft.com/sql/downloads. *The Developer edition is time-limited, but it will serve to introduce you to SQL Server's capabilities and to work with the examples in this book.*

NOTE   *The data-access examples in this book use the server name* localhost *in connection strings. If you're using a remote database server, you won't be able to use* localhost. *In that case, remember to substitute your own server's name wherever you see* localhost *in a connection string.*

The overloaded Connection object constructor lets you create a new Connection object with no parameters or assign the connection string when you create the object. No matter which version of the constructor you choose, for the most part, you must set connection properties *before* you open the connection. For example, you can't change the ConnectionString property while a Connection object is open; you must first close the connection, assign the new connection string, and then reopen it.

Assigning a connection string doesn't open the database, but it can throw errors. For example, syntax errors in the connection string itself cause an error immediately; however, if you assign a connection string with invalid field values, you won't get an error until you try to open the connection.

BUILDING A WEB FORM TO TEST CONNECTIONS

The Web Form ch13-1 lets you create simple connection strings containing the required fields (see Figure 13.1).

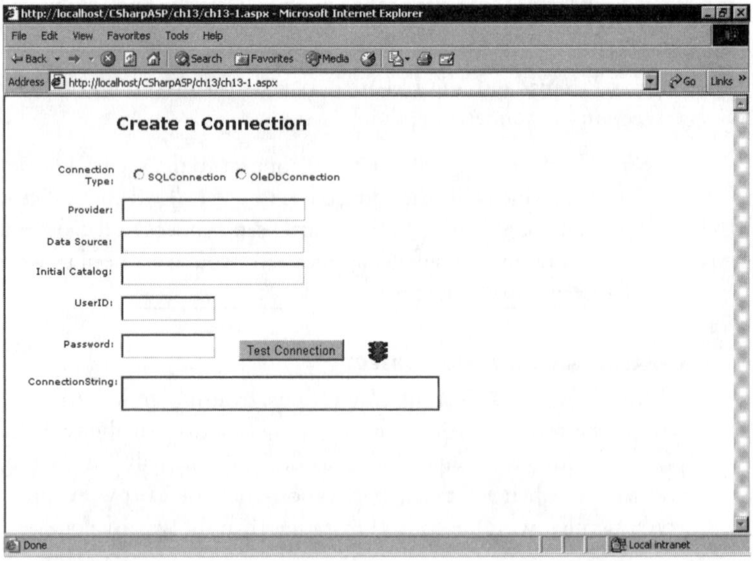

FIGURE 13.1

The Web Form ch13-1 lets you build and test simple connections

To fill out the form, you must select a connection type. The other fields are not required, but you're likely to get an error unless you fill them out. Try clicking the Test Connection button without filling out any of the fields. You'll see an error message stating that the Connection Type field is required. Try filling out the fields as follows:

Field Name	Value
Connection Type	`OleDbConnection`
Provider	Leave blank
Data Source	`localhost`
Initial Catalog	`Northwind`
UserID	*`<your SQL Server User ID>`*
Password	*`<your SQL Server Password>`*

Click the Test Connection button. The `ConnectionString` label displays an error message, and the traffic light icon remains red.

Change the Provider field value to `SQLOLEDB` and click the Test Connection button again. This time, the `ConnectionString` label displays the generated connection string, and the traffic light turns green (see Figure 13.2).

FIGURE 13.2

Web Form `ch13-1` after building a successful connection

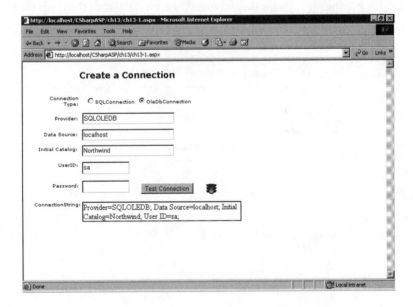

Here's how it works. A `RequiredFieldValidator` checks to ensure that the user has selected a Connection Type, either SqlConnection or OleDbConnection. That validation happens on both the client and the server (remember that the `Validator` controls *always* validate on the server, even if the client supports JavaScript so that the controls can validate on the client).

To simplify the code, the Web Form uses the System.Data.SqlClient and System.Data.OleDb namespaces:

```
using System.Data.SqlClient;
using System.Data.OleDb1
```

When the user posts the form data by clicking the Test Connection button, the Web Form grabs the value (not the text label) of the selected Connection Type radio button to determine whether to use a SqlConnection or an OleDbConnection object.

```
private void Page_Load(object sender, System.EventArgs e) {
    String sConn="";
    SqlConnection sqlconn=null;
    OleDbConnection oledbconn=null;
    if (IsPostBack) {
        sConnectionType = this.connectionType.SelectedItem.Value;
    }
    // more code here
}
```

At this point, the sConnectionType string variable contains either the string SQL or the string OLEDB. Having obtained the desired connection type, the code then calls the makeConnectionString function.

```
String makeConnectionString() {
    String sconn="";
    try {
        if (sConnectionType == "OLEDB") {
            sconn += "Provider=" + txtProvider.Text + "; ";
        }
        // get the server name
        sconn += "Data Source=" + txtServer.Text + "; ";
        sconn += "Initial Catalog=" + txtDatabase.Text + "; ";
        sconn += "User ID=" + txtUserID.Text + "; ";
        if (txtPassword.Text != "") {
            sconn += "Password=" + txtPassword.Text;
        }
    }
    catch (Exception ex) {
        throw ex;
    }
    return (sconn);
}
```

The makeConnectionString function simply concatenates the connection string field names and the user-entered values. If the user selected the OleDbConnection radio button, the function appends the string Provider= and the user-entered provider name. The function always concatenates the Data Source, Initial Catalog, and User ID values, but it ignores blank passwords. Any errors generate an exception.

After obtaining the formatted connection string, the Page_Load method creates the appropriate Connection object (again, by checking the value of the sConnectionType string). Note the use of the overloaded constructor to assign the ConnectionString property during object construction. After creating the appropriate Connection object type, the code attempts to open the connection. If the Open method succeeds, the code sets the imgConnection.ImageURL property to the green traffic light icon and displays the connection string in the lblConnection control. If the Open method fails, the Catch block displays the error message and sets the imgConnection.ImageURL property to display the red traffic light icon.

```
try {
    if (sConnectionType == "SQL") {
        sqlconn = new SqlConnection(sConn);
        sqlconn.Open();
        imgConnection.ImageUrl = "../images/greenlight.gif";
        lblConnection.Text = sConn;
    }
    else {
        oledbconn = new OleDbConnection(sConn);
        oledbconn.Open();
        imgConnection.ImageUrl = "../images/greenlight.gif";
        lblConnection.Text = sConn;
    }
}
catch (Exception ex) {
    imgConnection.ImageUrl = "../images/redlight.gif";
    lblConnection.Text = ex.Message;
}
finally {
    // close the connection
    if (oledbconn != null) {
        oledbconn.Close();
    }
    if (sqlconn != null) {
        sqlconn.Close();
    }
}
```

No matter what happens during the Page_Load event, the finally block forces any open connections to close. Note that you must trap for errors during the finally block just as you would for any other block. Rather than checking to see whether the oledbconn and sqlconn variables are null, an alternate method to ensure the connections are closed would be to put the Close methods in nested try blocks; for example:

```
finally {
    // close the connections
    try {
        oledbconn.Close();
    }
```

```
        catch {}
        try {
            sqlconn.Close();
        }
        catch {}
    }
```

While this takes a little less code, it probably also executes marginally slower. As you can see from the empty `catch` blocks, you don't have to *handle* errors in a `catch` block—you can simply ignore them, but you do have to catch them. Listing 13.1 contains the full code for the ch13-1 Web Form, which lets you build and test simple connections.

LISTING 13.1: CODE FOR THE WEB FORM ch13-1 (ch13-1.aspx.cs)

```csharp
using System;
using System.Collections;
using System.ComponentModel;
using System.Data;
using System.Drawing;
using System.Web;
using System.Web.SessionState;
using System.Web.UI;
using System.Web.UI.WebControls;
using System.Web.UI.HtmlControls;
using System.Data.SqlClient;
using System.Data.OleDb;


namespace CSharpASP.ch13 {
    /// <summary>
    /// Summary description for ch13_1.
    /// </summary>
    public class ch13_1 : System.Web.UI.Page {
protected System.Web.UI.WebControls.Label Label6;
protected System.Web.UI.WebControls.Label Provider;
protected System.Web.UI.WebControls.TextBox txtProvider;
protected System.Web.UI.WebControls.Label Label5;
protected System.Web.UI.WebControls.TextBox txtServer;
protected System.Web.UI.WebControls.TextBox txtPassword;
protected System.Web.UI.WebControls.TextBox txtUserID;
protected System.Web.UI.WebControls.Label Label7;
protected System.Web.UI.WebControls.Label Label1;
protected System.Web.UI.WebControls.TextBox txtDatabase;
protected System.Web.UI.WebControls.Label Label2;
protected System.Web.UI.WebControls.Label Label3;
protected System.Web.UI.WebControls.Label lblConnection;
protected System.Web.UI.WebControls.Label Label4;
```

```
protected System.Web.UI.WebControls.RadioButtonList connectionType;
protected System.Web.UI.WebControls.Image imgConnection;
protected System.Web.UI.WebControls.Button Button1;
protected System.Web.UI.WebControls.RequiredFieldValidator
    RequiredFieldValidator1;
String sConnectionType;

private void Page_Load(object sender, System.EventArgs e) {
    String sConn="";
    SqlConnection sqlconn=null;
    OleDbConnection oledbconn=null;
    if (IsPostBack) {
        sConnectionType = this.connectionType.SelectedItem.Value;
        try {
            sConn = makeConnectionString();
            if (sConn != null) {
        try {
            if (sConnectionType == "SQL") {
                sqlconn = new SqlConnection(sConn);
                sqlconn.Open();
                imgConnection.ImageUrl = "../images/greenlight.gif";
                lblConnection.Text = sConn;
            }
            else {
                oledbconn = new OleDbConnection(sConn);
                oledbconn.Open();
                imgConnection.ImageUrl = "../images/greenlight.gif";
                lblConnection.Text = sConn;
            }
        }
        catch (Exception ex) {
            imgConnection.ImageUrl = "../images/redlight.gif";
            lblConnection.Text = ex.Message;
        }
        finally {
            // close the connection
            if (oledbconn != null) {
                oledbconn.Close();
            }
            if (sqlconn != null) {
                sqlconn.Close();
            }
        }
            }
        }
        catch (Exception ex) {
            lblConnection.Text = ex.Message;
        }
```

```
      }
      else {
         imgConnection.ImageUrl = "../images/redlight.gif";
         lblConnection.Text = "";
      }
   }


   String makeConnectionString() {
      String sconn="";
      try {
         if (sConnectionType == "OLEDB") {
            sconn += "Provider=" + txtProvider.Text + "; ";
         }
         // get the server name
         sconn += "Data Source=" + txtServer.Text + "; ";
         sconn += "Initial Catalog=" + txtDatabase.Text + "; ";
         sconn += "User ID=" + txtUserID.Text + "; ";
         if (txtPassword.Text != "") {
            sconn += "Password=" + txtPassword.Text;
         }
      }
      catch (Exception ex) {
         throw ex;
      }
      return (sconn);
   }


   #region Web Form Designer generated code
   override protected void OnInit(EventArgs e)
   {
      //
      // CODEGEN: This call is required by the ASP.NET Web Form
      Designer.
      //
      InitializeComponent();
      base.OnInit(e);
   }

   /// <summary>
   /// Required method for Designer support - do not modify
   /// the contents of this method with the code editor.
   /// </summary>
   private void InitializeComponent()
   {
      this.Load += new System.EventHandler(this.Page_Load);
```

```
    }
#endregion
    }
}
```

You've seen how to create, open, and close a connection, and you're probably eager to see how to retrieve and display some data. Before leaving this Web Form, there are a few more useful things to learn from the example.

Web Form Tab Order

As I built the Web Form, I added controls in the order that I thought of them and dragged them around a little to create a decent layout. In other words, the controls were not created in their final order. If you use the keyboard to tab between the controls, you'll notice that the tab order is not conducive to easy entry (people who always click to move from control to control—and a few people do that—may not notice).

Unfortunately, you can't set the tab order in a Web Form as you can in a Windows Form—that handy little Tab Order view isn't on the View menu. You can set tab order three ways:

◆ Set the `TabIndex` property for each control in the Properties Window to the appropriate tab order number.

◆ Set the `tabIndex` attribute for each control in the HTML editor to the proper tab order.

◆ Move the control definitions in the HTML so they're created in the appropriate tab order.

All these methods are tedious, so here are a few "tricks" that can help speed things up or improve the result.

1. Don't bother setting the `TabIndex` property until you are otherwise satisfied with the layout and performance of the Web Form. You're likely to have to repeat the operation any time you add or rearrange the controls.

2. Set the tab order manually, incrementing the `TabIndex` value for each control.

3. Unlike Windows Forms, label controls in Web Forms *can* get the focus. The browser shows which control currently has the focus by drawing a dotted line around the control. You don't usually want labels to get the focus, so to leave them out of the tab order, set the `TabIndex` property (or the `tabIndex` attribute) to zero or a negative number.

Finally, you should realize that modern browsers use the z-index style attribute to set the tab order. If you look at the generated HTML after setting the `TabIndex` property, you'll see the text Z-INDEX: *<some integer>* in the generated style attribute. For older browsers (those that don't understand CSS), you *must* create the controls in the desired tab order.

So, no matter what, you must set the tab order either manually or programmatically. Rearranging the controls is a manual—and error-prone—process. If you must deliver Web Forms to downlevel browsers (those for which you use a `pageLayout` property set to `FlowLayout` rather than `GridLayout`), I suggest you build and test the form *first* using GridLayout mode as if you were delivering the page to a modern browser. Then, after everything works exactly the way you want it to, set the `pageLayout` property to `FlowLayout` and test again. It's very difficult to switch the control order in FlowLayout mode.

For example, the listed order of the first few controls in the `ch13-1` Web Form on `www.sybex.com` is as follows:

```
<asp:Label id="Label6" style="Z-INDEX: 116; LEFT: 25px;
    POSITION: absolute; TOP: 70px" runat="server" Width="94px"
    Height="17px" CssClass="smallfontalignright" tabIndex="0">
    Connection Type:</asp:Label>
<asp:Label id="Provider" style="Z-INDEX: 114; LEFT: 24px;
    POSITION: absolute; TOP: 112px" runat="server" Width="94px"
    Height="17px" CssClass="smallfontalignright" tabIndex="0">
    Provider:</asp:Label>
<asp:TextBox id="txtProvider" style="Z-INDEX: 105; LEFT: 127px;
    POSITION: absolute; TOP: 107px" runat="server" Width="196px"
    Height="24px" tabIndex="3"></asp:TextBox>
<asp:Label id="Label5" style="Z-INDEX: 110; LEFT: 24px;
    POSITION: absolute; TOP: 291px" runat="server" Width="39px"
    Height="17px" CssClass="smallfontalignright" tabIndex="0">
    ConnectionString:</asp:Label>
<asp:TextBox id="txtServer" style="Z-INDEX: 104; LEFT: 126px;
    POSITION: absolute; TOP: 141px" runat="server" Width="196px"
    Height="24px" tabIndex="5"></asp:TextBox>
<asp:TextBox id="txtPassword" style="Z-INDEX: 106; LEFT: 126px;
    POSITION: absolute; TOP: 248px" runat="server" Width="101px"
    Height="26px" TextMode="Password" tabIndex="11"></asp:TextBox>
<asp:TextBox id="txtUserID" style="Z-INDEX: 107; LEFT: 126px;
    POSITION: absolute; TOP: 209px" runat="server" Width="101px"
    Height="26px" tabIndex="9"></asp:TextBox>
```

But that's not the ideal tab order. Typically, tab order should move from left to right and top to bottom on the screen. Dragging the fields around visually won't work—you need to alter the order in which the page creates the controls to set the tab order properly—and that means you need to rearrange the code.

TIP   *To set the tab order on a Web Form, ensure that the HTML form creates the controls in the desired tab order.*

I won't force you to do it—although I urge you to try it. The Web Form `ch13-1a` functions identically to the Web Form `ch13-1`, but the controls have the proper tab order.

Web Form Control Accelerator (Access) Keys

Another problem with the `ch13-1` Web Form is that there's no easy way to jump directly to a specific control. In a Windows Form, you typically set an *accelerator* key for each label. When a user presses the Alt key and the label's accelerator key at the same time, Windows sets the focus to the control that *follows* the label in the tab order sequence. For example, you would expect a control labeled `Provider` to have an accelerator key of "P" and, when you press `Alt+P`, you would expect the `txtProvider` control to get the focus. It's not quite that simple in a browser. Each Web Server or HTML control in a browser has its own accelerator key property, called `AccessKey`. The property accepts a single character (you can't create a two-character accelerator for a control).

NOTE   You should get in the habit of assigning the `AccessKey` property when you create a control—just as you should assign the `ID` property to every control you create. It's a tremendous burden for maintenance programmers to find generically named controls on forms, because it makes the code difficult to read.

For some forms, you might find it easier to set the `AccessKey` and `TabIndex` properties in code. You can do that in the `Page_Load` event for the Web Form:

```
Provider.AccessKey = "P";
Provider.Text = "&Provider";
Provider.TabIndex="2";
txtProvider.TabIndex="3";
```

CONNECTION STRING WARNINGS

Connection strings are complicated and often contain sensitive information such as passwords and user account names. Therefore, you need to be particularly careful about keeping that information private and known only to your application.

Check Dynamically Assigned Connection Strings

When you assign a connection string to a `Connection` object, the property code parses the connection string into its associated parts and uses the *last* value for any field occurrence. For example, if you accidentally specify the User ID and Password fields twice, with a specific user ID and password for the first set of values, and `sa` and the system administrator password for the second value, the connection will have system administrator privileges. Therefore, you must be careful if you ever do build a form like the one in Listing 13.1. A user could trick your application by entering extra information in the User ID or Password field.

For example, suppose you have an application that queries a database for sales information. You have programmatically fixed the Data Source and Initial Catalog settings to `localhost` and `Sales-Data`, respectively. But you display a dialog for a user to enter his or her user ID and password. If a malicious user enters the following text into the User ID field, and your application simply concatenates the User ID value with the Data Source and Initial Catalog values, what connection will the server attempt to make?

```
myUserID;Initial Catalog=CompanySalaries
```

Make sure that your code tests to ensure such security breaches can't happen. For example, you might refuse user IDs containing semicolons, or truncate user-supplied information before any embedded semicolon.

Storing Connection Information

Another type of security breach occurs when your application displays sensitive connection information to users. Unfortunately, this can happen in ASP.NET applications entirely by accident. In classic ASP, most developers stored connection information in an Application or Session variable. Do *not* do this in ASP.NET unless you have so severely limited the capabilities of your connection login account that you no longer care if the information is made public. The culprit is tracing. Although you can tell developers never to leave tracing turned on in a production application, people forget. Here's how your connection information can accidentally be made public. Follow this procedure to see it:

1. Create a Web Form that stores connection information in an Application or Session variable.

2. Turn tracing off for the application in the `web.config` file (see Chapter 9, "Debugging ASP.NET and Error Handling," for details).

3. Turn on tracing for the Web Form.

4. Run the Web Form. The `trace` directive displays the values of Application and Session variables—including your entire connection string containing user ID and password values—for anyone to see.

Granted, this may be a little far-fetched, but given the potential security risks, it's better to avoid the problem altogether.

WARNING   *Don't store connection information in Application or Session variables.*

So if you can't store connection information in Application variables, where *should* you store it? The simple answer is this: Store your connection strings in the `web.config` file. You can retrieve the values using the `System.Configuration.ConfigurationSettings.AppSettings` collection. The `AppSettings` collection contains settings from the `<appSettings>` section of your `web.config` file. The collection contains a set of keys. For example, suppose you want to create a fixed connection string to the Northwind database and then use it in multiple pages.

NOTE   *In the rest of this chapter, I'll use the connection strings defined for the Northwind database in the* `web.config` *file. Note that the connections are commented out as the file ships on* www.sybex.com. *Uncomment the connection definitions and modify them as needed for your database server, user ID, and password.*

Find the `<appSettings>` section in your `web.config` file and add the following key and value (you may need to edit the values to apply to your database):

```
<add key="Northwind"
    value="Provider=SQLOLEDB; Data Source=localhost; Initial
    Catalog=Northwind; User ID=sa; Password=;" />
```

The `<add key="name" value="someValue" />` tag adds a key/value pair to the `AppSettings` collection. After you add the key, save the `web.config` file. Now you can access the values from code. Listing 13.2 contains code from the Web Form `ch13-2`. All the code does is use the value stored in the `AppSettings` collection under the key `Northwind` as the connection string to open—and immediately close—a connection, but it serves as an example for accessing `AppSettings` values.

LISTING 13.2: Page_Load EVENT CODE FOR THE WEB FORM ch13-2 (ch13-2.aspx.cs)

```
using System.Data.OleDb;
private void Page_Load(object sender, System.EventArgs e) {
    OleDbConnection conn;
```

```
        conn = new OleDbConnection();
        conn.ConnectionString =
        System.Configuration.ConfigurationSettings.
            AppSettings.Get("Northwind");
        //conn.ConnectionString =
        System.Configuration.ConfigurationSettings.
        //    AppSettings.Get("ConnIntegratedSecurity");
        conn.Open();
        Response.Write("Northwind connection opened successfully<br>");
        conn.Close();
    }
```

Connection String Field Order and Syntax

Every example you've seen so far shows the connection string fields in Provider, Data Source, Initial Catalog, User ID, and Password order, but you should know that there's no required order. You can just as easily reverse the field order or mix the fields in any order you wish.

You must separate the field pairs with semicolons. You do not need to conclude the connection string with a trailing semicolon, although doing so does not affect the validity of the connection string. Optionally, you may surround the field values with single or double quotes. If you must use double quotes within a connection string field value, escape the inner quotes.

```
myConn.ConnectionString = "Data source='localhost'; " +
"user id='sa'; initial catalog=\"Northwind\"; provider='SQLOLEDB';";
```

White space is completely optional. The connection string property accessor ignores all white space except that contained within inner quotes. The accessor also ignores case for all field names, but not for password values. In other words, the following two connection string assignments are equivalent:

```
OleDbConnection myConn = new OleDbConnection();
myConn.ConnectionString = "Provider=SQLOLEDB; " +
    "Data source=localhost; " +
    "initial catalog=Northwind; " +
    "user id=sa";
```

```
myConn.ConnectionString = "DATA SOURCE = localhost  ; " +
"    USER ID=sa;  INITIAL CATALOG=Northwind; PROVIDER=SQLOLEDB; ";
```

However, the following two connection strings are *not* equivalent (note the difference in the Password field capitalization):

```
OleDbConnection myConn = new OleDbConnection();
myConn.ConnectionString = "Provider=SQLOLEDB; " +
    "Data source=localhost; " +
    "initial catalog=Northwind; " +
    "user id=sa; Password="aPassword";
```

```
OleDbConnection myConn = new OleDbConnection();
myConn.ConnectionString = "Provider=SQLOLEDB; " +
    "Data source=localhost; " +
    "initial catalog=Northwind; " +
    "user id=sa; Password="apassword";
```

When you're attaching to file-based databases, such as Microsoft Access, use the provider name `Microsoft.Jet.OLEDB.4.0`. The Data Source field value must contain the location of the database (MDB) file. I'll reiterate here that I don't recommend using Microsoft Access for your Web database.

Integrated Security

So far, the connection strings you've seen all used SQL Server security. You can use integrated security to connect to a database as well. You *can* use integrated security at any time. For example, you can either add permissions to the ASP.NET user account or change the account to one with specific permissions. You *should* use integrated security if

◆ You have a secured Web application that requires authentication.

and

◆ You have individual accounts with different authorizations to access SQL Server data.

Before you can authorize an action by an account, you must know the identity of the account. By default, Web applications run anonymously, and the server uses either the ASPNET account or the System account to serve all pages. In a secured application, the user logs in either explicitly by entering a user ID and password or (with Internet Explorer clients) implicitly via Digest authentication or Integrated Windows authentication (NT Challenge/Response).

Using integrated security, the Web server passes the client's identity to the connected SQL Server instance (both the Web server and the SQL Server may be on the same machine), and SQL Server can grant or deny access to data based on its internal security settings.

I won't go into this in detail, but here's a procedure you can use for a quick test:

1. Add a connection string called `NorthwindSSPI` to your `web.config` file.

   ```
   <add key="NorthwindSSPI" value="Provider=SQLOLEDB;
       Data Source=localhost; Initial Catalog=Northwind;
       Integrated Security=SSPI" />
   ```

2. Using the Web Form `ch13-2`, change the line that assigns the `ConnectionString` property to the following:

   ```
   conn.ConnectionString=System.Configuration.ConfigurationSettings.
       AppSettings.Get("NorthwindSSPI");
   ```

3. Run the Web Form again. The default security settings should allow you to access the database, but if you get an error, you'll need to give the `IUSR_MACHINENAME` or `ASPNET` account on the Web server permission to access the database. You can do that through SQL Server Enterprise Manager by selecting the Security item for your SQL Server instance and adding the `IUSR_MACHINE-NAME` account or `ASPNET` account to the Logins list. Depending on other settings on your SQL Server, you may need to grant the account permission explicitly to access the Northwind database.

Debugging Connections

If you have trouble connecting to your SQL Server, one good debugging technique is to trace connections using the SQL Profiler. An in-depth description of tracing is beyond the scope of this book, but briefly, here's the procedure to set up tracing:

1. Start the SQL Server Enterprise Manager application.

2. Select SQL Profiler from the Tools menu.

3. Click the File menu and select New ➤ Trace. You'll see the Connect to SQL Server dialog (see Figure 13.3).

FIGURE 13.3

The Connect to SQL Server dialog

4. Select your SQL Server and enter your Login Name and Password, then click OK. You'll see the Trace Properties dialog (see Figure 13.4).

FIGURE 13.4

The Trace Properties dialog

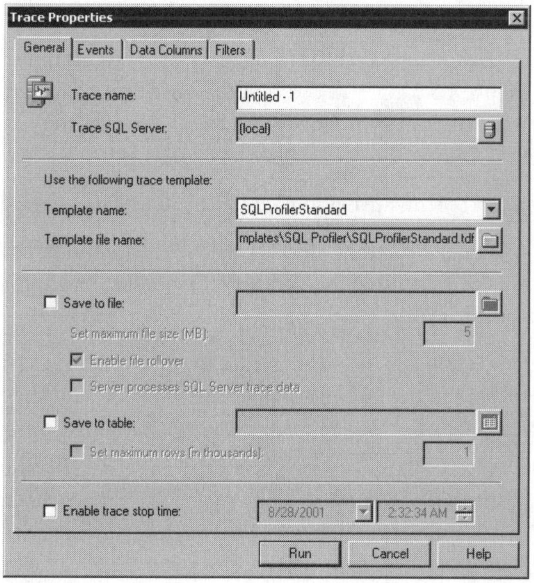

5. Although the dialog has numerous options for tracing, you can accept the defaults; you don't even have to enter a name. However, it's worth exploring just a *little* bit. Click the Events tab.

6. The Events tab displays a list of *available* event classes on the left and a list of *selected* event classes on the right (see Figure 13.5). Note that the default selection includes Security Audit: Audit Login and Audit Logout. You're specifically interested in auditing logins to debug connection problems.

FIGURE 13.5

The Trace Properties dialog Events tab, with default event class selections

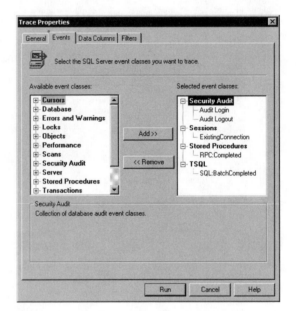

7. Click the Data Columns tab. This tab displays the column list that you'll see in the trace log (refer to Figure 13.5). Scroll through the unselected data list on the left and add any items that you want to trace (you don't need to add any for this exercise) to the selected data list on the right.

8. Click the Run button at the bottom of the dialog to start tracing.

9. To watch the trace in action, browse to a page that connects to SQL Server, such as ch13-1.aspx or ch13-2.aspx. Each time the Web server requests a connection, you'll see an entry in the trace log (see Figure 13.6).

The last event—Audit Login—in the trace log shows a little of the login information. To debug logins, you're interested in the NTUsername field (SYSTEM) and the LoginName field (NT AUTHORITY\ SYSTEM) in Figure 13.6.

The point of this exercise is that it's not always apparent which account is trying to access SQL Server, because the account used by IIS and the mapped SQL Server account depend on the security setup for your Web and SQL servers. Tracing shows you the actual values.

FIGURE 13.6

The trace log set to audit login information

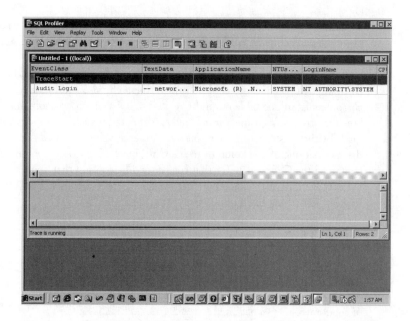

That's enough about connections—time to see the bigger picture.

The ADO.NET Approach to Data Access

If you've used Microsoft DAO or ADO, you're accustomed to dealing with `Recordset` objects. At a basic level, a `Recordset` object contained a two-dimensional arrangement of data, although that's somewhat of an oversimplification. A `Recordset` object contained a set of columns, called "fields," each of which corresponded to an existing or derived column in a database. For example, running the SQL query `SELECT * FROM Customers` against the Northwind database, the server would return the set of all rows and all column values for the existing columns in the Customers table. However, if you run the following query, the server will return a set of rows containing only one *derived* column, named `FullAddress`, consisting of the concatenated values from the three columns named in the query, separated by commas.

```
SELECT Address + ', ' + City + ', ' + PostalCode
    AS FullAddress FROM Customers
```

So, a simple recordset was essentially a table containing rows and columns. The recordset maintained a position pointer set to the current row. Recordsets exposed data through a collection of `Field` objects. A `Field` object represented the intersection of each row and column in the recordset—in other words, a single cell in the table. You could imagine a recordset as appearing like Figure 13.7.

FIGURE 13.7

Simple `Recordset` object

	Column	Column
Row 1	Field	Field
Row 2	Field	Field
Row 3	Field	Field

The Field objects contained the data values. In addition to data values, you could query a Field object to determine its name (the column name or alias name), the data type, its maximum length, its default value, and many other properties.

Later versions of ADO added the capability for a recordset field to contain another recordset. By doing that, recordsets could represent hierarchical or multidimensional data. For example, a list of customers from one table might be related to a list of orders from another table. If you simply combined the two tables using a simple query, the data for each customer would appear once for each order made by that customer in the result set. However, using a shaped query, you could combine the related data so that one of the columns in the Customers table would contain another recordset that in turn contained the Orders data for that customer. The column that contains the Orders recordset is called a *chapter* column. Such shaped queries quickly became complex, but you can imagine a simple version looking something like Figure 13.8.

FIGURE 13.8

Shaped recordset in which each customer record has a chapter column consisting of another recordset containing multiple orders for that customer

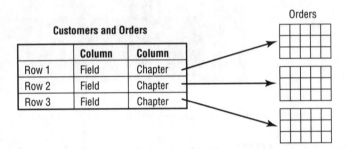

From Recordsets to XML

Shortly before Microsoft introduced shaped recordsets, XML started becoming recognized as an excellent way to represent relationships between data items, particularly parent-child relationships such as those found in most relational databases. XML can represent data ranging from a simple list of values to two-dimensional tables to extremely complex hierarchical sets. So, for example, you can represent the shaped recordset in the preceding section very easily, and in a way that's humanly readable. ADO.NET treats all database data as XML, so it's worthwhile to describe the similarities between XML and recordsets. Listing 13.3 shows some sample customer orders data in XML.

LISTING 13.3: XML FILE CONTAINING CUSTOMER-ORDER-PRODUCT DATA (ch13-3.xml)

```
<?xml version="1.0"?>
<customers>
   <!-- Jan/Feb customers with bolt orders -->
   <customer id="1">
      <orders>
         <order id="1" date="01-12-2001">
            <product id="36ABLT" name="3-inch bolts"
               quantity="2500" unitprice="0.13" />
            <product id="26ABLT" name="2-inch bolts"
```

```
                    quantity="2000" unitprice="0.10" />
            </order>
            <order id="2" date="01-22-2001">
                <product id="36ABLT" name="3-inch bolts"
                    quantity="1000" unitprice="0.14" />
                <product id="26ABLT" name="2-inch bolts"
                    quantity="500" unitprice="0.11" />
            </order>
        </orders>
    </customer>
    <customer id="2">
        <orders>
            <order id="1" date="01-25-2001">
                <product id="26ABLT" name="2-inch bolts"
                    quantity="125" unitprice="0.11" />
            </order>
            <order id="2" date="02-13-2001">
                <product id="26ABLT" name="2-inch bolts"
                    quantity="250" unitprice="0.11" />
            </order>
            <order id="2" date="02-28-2001">
                <product id="26ABLT" name="2-inch bolts"
                    quantity="150" unitprice="0.11" />
                <shipnote><![CDATA[Customer wants these shipped
                    to 4434 Casa la Mer, San Francisco, CA]]>
                </shipnote>
            </order>
        </orders>
    </customer>
</customers>
```

As you can see, the XML represents the same type of relationship as the tables; you have a set of customers, each of which has multiple orders. In this case, each order may consist of multiple products. In fact, it's much easier for most people to see the relationships between the customers, orders, and products in the XML representation than in a relational database representation, where the concept becomes complicated with primary and foreign keys.

An XML file consists of a tree of *nodes*. Each node may be an element, an attribute, a comment, a processing instruction, or a character data (CDATA) section. There are other node types, but these are the five you need to know. Many of the nodes look like HTML tags. The first tag in Listing 13.3 `<?xml version="1.0"?>` is a *processing instruction* that identifies the document as XML. So far, version 1.0 is the only released version. Processing instructions begin and end with a question mark and provide the parser with instructions about the data that follows. This particular processing instruction is also called the *XML declaration*, because it declares that the following data is XML.

The node immediately following the XML declaration is the *root element* or *root node*. Each XML document may have one and only one root element. The root element is the *parent* for all the other nodes in the document.

The third line in the document is a *comment*. Comments need no explanation; they're exactly the same as comments in HTML.

The fourth line, `<customer id="1">`, is an *element node*. An element may contain other elements, text, or both. Inside the first customer element is an *attribute node* (`id="1"`). An attribute consists of a name and a value separated by an equals sign. The value must be quoted. You may use either single or double quotes to delimit a value.

The last `<order>` tag in Listing 13.3 contains a `<shipnote>` element that in turn contains a CDATA node, usually called a CDATA *section*. A parser normally parses (reads and checks) all the text values in a document's nodes, but sometimes you need to include data in the XML document that may contain one or more of the five XML reserved characters. These five characters include the left and right angle brackets (<>), the ampersand (&), and single and double quotes (' "). Common examples of data that you would find in CDATA sections are HTML and binary data, such as base-64 encoded image data.

Two types of character data exist: the parsed character data (PCDATA) in standard elements and attribute values, and the unparsed character data (CDATA) in `CDATA` sections. The parser ignores text placed into `CDATA` sections. You place the unparsed data between the square brackets (`[]`) in the `<![CDATA[unparsed character data]]>` tag:

```
<shipnote><![CDATA[Customer wants these shipped
    to 4434 Casa la Mer, San Francisco, CA]]>
```

Other named tags in XML are also elements. Each element looks like an HTML tag, but unlike HTML, there's no fixed set of XML tags—you're free to name the tags however you like, within the XML naming conventions (see `http://www.w3c.org` for exact naming restrictions). Each tag *must* have a closing tag, and any attribute values *must* be quoted. All tag and attribute names are case sensitive. One of the few variations that XML allows is that you can omit the closing tag by closing the opening tag with a `/>` rather than just the closing bracket.

There are several other advantages to representing data in XML. First, XML consists of text, which, unlike binary data, passes through firewalls with fewer security concerns. Second, you can use a parser to find any data item quickly. Third, you can use an XML Schema Definition (XSD) file or Document Type Definition (DTD) to describe the relationships, data types, and valid data values or ranges within an XML file. An XML schema is an XML document that contains the definitions for a set of XML elements in another document or embedded in the XML document itself. A DTD is an older definition syntax that does much the same thing as schema, but in a less convenient, non-XML format. ADO.NET takes full advantage of XML.

ADO.NET OBJECTS VERSUS ADO OBJECTS

Classic ADO used `Connection`, `Command`, and `Recordset` objects. ADO.NET extends the model somewhat. As you've seen, a `Connection` object connects to a database. A `DataAdapter` object takes care of translating the data to and from the native database format, which serves to isolate your application from back-end data storage and representation changes. A `Command` object, just as in classic ADO, contains the SQL commands and parameter values that you use to retrieve or alter data. The `DataAdapter` uses a `Command` object to query the database. A `DataReader` functions like a forward-only cursor in SQL. You can read rows of data with it but only in a forward direction. Internally, ASP.NET uses `DataReaders` to fill `DataSets`, but you can instantiate and use `DataReaders` directly when you want to process a result set in sequence, such as displaying a table of data. `DataReader`s provide the fastest access to data, because they don't do much but stream the data from the database to your application.

The `Connection`, `Command`, `DataAdapter`, and `DataReader` objects are part of the managed provider for any given type of data source. For example, .NET contains special SqlConnection, SqlCommand, SqlDataAdapter, and SqlDataReader classes that are specifically tuned to work well with SQL Server.

The final new ADO.NET object, the `DataSet`, stands alone. It's not part of the managed provider. `DataSet` objects, in fact, don't need to "know" anything about the data source. `DataSet`s, for those of you familiar with classic ADO, are much like disconnected `Recordset` objects, though much more powerful. Internally, ADO.NET `DataSet` objects represent all data as XML, meaning that `DataSet`s have the capability to represent not only the data but also the relationships and the database schema, so you can work with `DataSet`s as if you were working directly with the database. That capability, as you will see, simplifies data access enormously.

The *Command* Object

A `Command` object contains a SQL command and any required parameters to perform a single SQL SELECT, UPDATE, APPEND, or DELETE command; a stored procedure; or a database-altering command, such as CREATE TABLE. The `Command` object has a `CommandText` property that contains the SQL string or the name of the stored procedure.

For stored procedures that require parameters, the `Command` object exposes a collection of `Parameter` objects containing the name, data type, length, direction, and value of any parameters that you wish to pass to a stored procedure. For example, here's the long version to create a simple `Command` object representing a SELECT statement:

```
// Create a command object
OleDBCommand cmd  = new OleDBCommand();
cmd.CommandText="SELECT * FROM Customers";
```

A `Command` object needs to be connected to a database to do anything useful. You can run the command against the database via a `Connection` object. You might think that a `Connection` would have a collection of `Command` objects, but instead, Microsoft opted to go with the more ADO-compatible solution of giving the `Command` object a `Connection` property. `Command` objects have an overloaded constructor, so you can create one and set its `Connection` property at the same time. For example:

```
// Create a connection object
OleDbConnection conn = null;
OleDBCommand cmd = null;
conn = ew OleDBConnection(
    System.Configuration.ConfigurationSettings.AppSettings.
        Get ("Northwind");
conn.Open();
cmd = new OleDBCommand("SELECT * FROM Customers", conn);
```

At this point, you're ready to get some data. For clarity, I added two more connection string definitions to the `web.config` file:

```
<add key="NorthwindSql" value="Data Source=localhost;
    Initial Catalog=Northwind; User ID=sa; Password=;" />
```

```
<add key="NorthwindSqlSSPI" value="Data Source=localhost;
    Initial Catalog=Northwind; Integrated Security=SSPI;" />
```

The `Sql` at the end of `Northwind` indicates that these connections will use `SqlConnections`, while the ones without `Sql` at the end will use `OleDb` connections.

NOTE   *In the rest of this chapter, I'll use the connection strings defined in the* `web.config` *file. Note that—if you weren't following along before—the connections are commented out as the file ships on* `www.sybex.com`. *Uncomment the connections and modify them as needed for your database server, user ID, and password.*

The simplest and fastest way to get data is to use a `DataReader`, as you'll see in the next section.

The *DataReader* Object

A `DataReader` object is a pointer into a table of rows that can return individual column values for the current row. You can't create a `DataReader` object directly. Instead, use the `Command` object's `ExecuteReader` method; for example:

```
// Create a connection object
OleDbConnection conn = null;
OleDBCommand cmd = null;
OleDBDataReader dr = null;
conn = New OleDBConnection(
    System.Configuration.ConfigurationSettings.AppSettings.
    Get("Northwind");
conn.Open();
cmd = new OleDBCommand("SELECT * FROM Customers", conn);
// create the DataReader
dr = cmd.ExecuteReader(CommandBehavior.CloseConnection);
```

The last line creates the `DataReader`. The `CommandBehavior.CloseConnection` parameter is one of several `CommandBehavior` enumeration options you can select to determine *how* the `DataReader` reads the data from the database. Table 13.1 shows the enumeration options.

TABLE 13.1: CommandBehavior ENUMERATION OPTIONS

MEMBER NAME	DESCRIPTION
CloseConnection	Tells .NET to close the associated `Connection` when you close the DataReader created using the `ExecuteReader` method.
Default	Sets *n*.
KeyInfo	Prevents SQL Server from applying read locks to the selected rows. The query returns column and primary key information as well as the data. Using KeyInfo, the result is identical to appending the FOR BROWSE clause to the query. (See the FOR BROWSE command in SQL Server Books Online for more information.)
SchemaOnly	The query returns column information only. It does not return data. This option is most useful when you need to discover the names and data types of the columns.

Continued on next page

TABLE 13.1: CommandBehavior ENUMERATION OPTIONS *(continued)*

MEMBER NAME	DESCRIPTION
SequentialAccess	The result of the query is read sequentially to the column level. Use this when your query results contain BLOB (binary large objects) or long text binary fields.
SingleResult	Use this option for queries that return a single field. An example is selecting the last name field from a table using a specific primary key value to determine the row.
SingleRow	Use this option for queries that return a single row. For example, you can use the SingleRow option for queries that select a row with a specific primary key value.

When you create a DataReader, the row pointer does *not* point at the first row (see Figure 13.9).

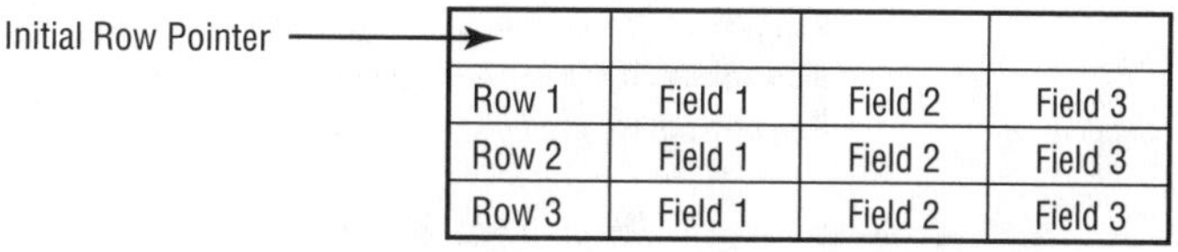

FIGURE 13.9

Initial DataReader state

Initial Row Pointer

Row 1	Field 1	Field 2	Field 3
Row 2	Field 1	Field 2	Field 3
Row 3	Field 1	Field 2	Field 3

To read the first row, you must issue the Read command. Therefore, if you want to process each row of data and display the values in an HTML table, your code for a DataReader might look something like Listing 13.4.

LISTING 13.4: THE WEB FORM ch13-4.aspx CREATES AN OleDbDataReader AND DISPLAYS THE DATA FROM THE CUSTOMERS TABLE (ch13-4.aspx.cs)

```
using System;
using System.Collections;
using System.ComponentModel;
using System.Data;
using System.Drawing;
using System.Web;
using System.Web.SessionState;
using System.Web.UI;
using System.Web.UI.WebControls;
using System.Web.UI.HtmlControls;
using System.Data.OleDb;

namespace CSharpASP.ch13
{
    /// <summary>
    /// Summary description for ch13_4.
    /// </summary>
    public class ch13_4 : System.Web.UI.Page
    {
```

```
private void Page_Load(object sender, System.EventArgs e) {
   OleDbConnection conn  = new
   OleDbConnection(System.Configuration.ConfigurationSettings.
   AppSettings.Get("Northwind"));

   conn.Open();
   OleDbCommand cm = new OleDbCommand
      ("SELECT * FROM Customers", conn);
   OleDbDataReader dr;
   dr = cm.ExecuteReader(CommandBehavior.CloseConnection);
   Response.Write("<table border=\"1\">");
   while (dr.Read()) {
      Response.Write("<tr>");
      for (int i = 0; i < dr.FieldCount; i++) {
         Response.Write("<td>");
         Response.Write(dr.GetValue(i));
         Response.Write(" ");
         Response.Write("</td>");
      }
      Response.Write("</tr>");
   }
   Response.Write("</table>");
   dr.Close();
}
// Web Form Designer generated code omittted
   }
}
```

The Read method returns true as long as the read was successful, so you would typically call the Read method in a loop until it returns false. The dr.GetValue(i) (see highlighted code) retrieves a column value from the current row in its native format. I was able to use this because all the values are strings.

WARNING   *I've left out the error-trapping in this example and upcoming ones in this chapter for clarity, but in production code, you should never try to access outside resources without wrapping the attempt in a* **try** *block and handling any resulting errors.*

In a browser, the result looks like Figure 13.10.

While that type of code will look extremely familiar to those of you who have programmed with classic ASP, it's not at all like most Web Form code because it doesn't take advantage of .NET features such as server controls and data binding.

FIGURE 13.10

Results from Listing
13.4 in Internet
Explorer

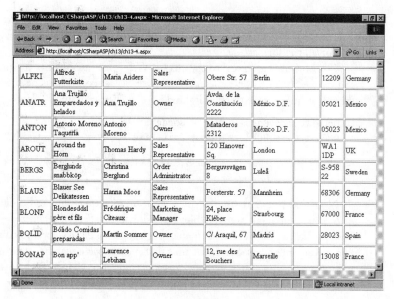

Here's a better example. Create a new Web Form, `ch13-5.aspx`. In Design mode, drag a `DataGrid`
server control onto the form. Name the `DataGrid` control `dgCustomers`. Place the control near the
upper-left corner of the form. Next, switch to the code-behind class and enter this code in the
`Form_Load` event:

```
using System.Data.OleDb;
private void Page_Load(object sender, System.EventArgs e) {
    OleDbConnection conn = new OleDbConnection(
        System.Configuration.ConfigurationSettings.
        AppSettings.Get("Northwind"));
    conn.Open();
    OleDbCommand cm = new OleDbCommand("SELECT * FROM Customers",
    conn);
    OleDbDataReader dr = null;
    dr = cm.ExecuteReader(CommandBehavior.CloseConnection);
    // enable the following two lines to set the outer border
    // dgCustomers.BorderStyle = BorderStyle.Outset
    // dgCustomers.BorderWidth = Unit.Pixel(3)

    dgCustomers.DataSource = dr;
    dgCustomers.DataBind();
    dr.Close();
    conn.Close();

}
```

The big difference between this and the code in Listing 13.4 (other than that it's shorter) is that
you don't have to write the HTML yourself; instead, you can simply bind the `DataGrid` to the

DataReader. The DataSource property assigns the DataReader as the source of the DataGrid's data. The DataBind method causes the control to fill itself with the data when it renders. ASP.NET takes care of all the formatting.

The output is identical to the ch13-4 Web Form except that the table gridlines are different. You can change the outer (perimeter) border for Server controls using the BorderStyle property. Add these lines just before the highlighted lines in the preceding listing:

```
DgCustomers.BorderStyle = BorderStyle.Outset;
DgCustomers.BorderWidth = Unit.Pixel(2);
```

NOTE   *The preceding code lines exist in the* ch13-5.aspx.cs *file on* www.sybex.com *but are commented out. Enable the lines to see the outer border.*

Note that you can't simply assign a constant integer value as border width because several different *units* of measurement are available; instead, you must tell the control which unit you want to use. The System.Web.UI.WebControls namespace exposes a Unit structure containing Pixel, Point, and Percentage members. Select the unit that most closely matches your needs. Remember that specifying measurements in percentages causes the values to change as the user resizes the browser. Typically, you would use the Point or Pixel unit to specify a fixed measurement such as border width.

DataGrid FORMATTING

The DataGrid display that results from the Web Form ch13-5.aspx is functional but not very attractive. With some experimentation, you can format a DataGrid exactly as you like, but at first, it's much easier to use the predefined styles. Go back to Design view. Select the DataGrid and then click the link called Auto Format Builder that appears just below the Properties window. You may recall following this procedure in Chapter 7, "The *SessionState* Object." The Auto Format Builder lets you select among a large number of options to change the DataGrid's appearance. Select one you like and run the Web Form again. The result should be much more attractive.

I'm not going to go deeply into formatting options for Web controls because setting formatting properties corresponds very closely to CSS styles (that's how ASP.NET writes them for the client). The fastest way to get started is to apply an Auto Format to the DataGrid and then look at how that affects the properties of the control. Also, look at the generated HTML after applying an Auto Format. You'll see that the DataGrid consists of three main parts: a header, a body, and a footer. Each part has a distinct CSS style property called HeaderStyle, ItemStyle, and FooterStyle, respectively. In addition, a DataGrid can alternate the styles for neighboring rows. You can see the alternating row styles change as you select different Auto Format styles. You control those styles with the AlternatingItemStyle property. The EditItemStyle and SelectedItemStyle properties control the appearance of the currently selected items in the grid. Because DataGrids can page records, there's a PagerStyle property that controls the appearance of the label controls used to page forward and backward through a set of records, as well as a label for the current page.

Like standard CSS styles, the DataGrid styles are hierarchical and additive—more specialized styles such as AlternatingItemStyle inherit from and override styles from more generalized styles such as the ItemStyle property. All these style properties (except the PagerStyle property, which is a DataGridPagerStyle object) are instances of a TableItemStyle class that has the properties required to format a cell, such as BackColor, BorderColor, BorderStyle, BorderWidth, Font, ForeColor, Height, Width, Wrap, HorizontalAlign, and VerticalAlign.

The *DataSet* Object

While the `DataReader` is the fastest way to get data, the most useful ADO.NET data object is the `DataSet`. Create a new Web Form, `ch13-6.aspx`, drag a `DataGrid` onto the form, and set its ID to `dgCustomers`. The code to retrieve the data and display it in a `DataGrid` is similar to the code for the last Web Form, but you need to create a `DataSet` and a `DataAdapter` object and then populate the `DataSet` using the `Fill` method.

```
private void Page_Load(object sender, System.EventArgs e) {
    OleDbConnection conn = new OleDbConnection(
        System.Configuration.ConfigurationSettings.
        AppSettings.Get("Northwind"));
    conn.Open();
    OleDbCommand cm = new OleDbCommand("SELECT * FROM Customers", conn);
    DataSet ds = new DataSet("customers");
    OleDbDataAdapter da = new OleDbDataAdapter();
    da.SelectCommand = cm;
    da.Fill(ds);
    dgCustomers.DataSource = ds.Tables[0];
    dgCustomers.DataBind();
    da.Dispose();
    conn.Close();
}
```

Note that you can't usually just assign the `dgCustomers.DataSource` property to a `DataSet`, because a `DataSet` contains a collection of tables. Instead, you should bind the `DataGrid` property to one of the tables (there are other collections that you can bind to as well). However, in this case, the `DataSet` contains only one table, so you can reference it as either `ds.Tables(0)`, as shown, or just as `ds`.

The code also makes it clear that the DataSet class isn't part of the managed provider—there is no such thing as an OleDbDataSet class or a SqlDataSet—there's only one DataSet class, and it works with all managed providers.

WARNING   *Because the* `DataAdapter` *uses resources, remember to call the* `Dispose` *method and, with OleDb-type connections, close the connection.*

You've seen the absolute basics of retrieving data from a database by writing the code yourself. Before you continue with Chapter 14, "Accessing Data," you should memorize the sequence of operations required to retrieve data. To use a `DataReader`:

1. Create and open a connection.

2. Create a `Command` object and set its `CommandText` and `Connection` properties.

3. Use the `Command.ExecuteReader` method to create a `DataReader` and populate it with data.

4. Use the `DataReader.Read` method to move the `DataReader` row pointer from one row to the next.

5. Close the `DataReader` when you're done.

6. Close the connection.

To use a DataSet:

1. Create and open a connection.

2. Create a Command object and set its CommandText and Connection properties.

3. Create a DataAdapter object and set its SelectCommand property (you can perform both these steps with the overloaded constructor).

4. Use the DataAdapter's Fill method to fill the DataSet.

5. Remembering that DataSets contain a *disconnected* representation of the data, you should call the DataAdapter's Dispose method to release the resources immediately after filling the DataSet.

6. Close the connection.

There's simply not enough room in a book to give you sufficient practice in using these procedures, so you should plan to spend some time practicing until you can perform both procedures from memory with no example code. It's essential that you understand these basic procedures before moving on to more complex data operations.

Summary

The ADO.NET data model simplifies both data access and data representation by combining the different types of recordsets found in ADO (the disconnected and shaped recordsets) into a single DataSet object. In addition, because the DataSet can contain multiple result tables and a schema, it provides the relationships that were missing in ADO recordsets. In essence, the ADO.NET data set is a miniature database. In the next chapter, I'll show you how to perform common and simple data operations using the Visual Studio drag-and-drop interface, and you'll work with more controls and more complex types of data retrieval, including parameterized stored procedures.

Chapter 14

Accessing Data

IN THIS CHAPTER, YOU'LL see how to retrieve, display, add, delete, and modify data stored in SQL Server. You'll also build a Web Form that performs all these operations. Because database resources, such as connections, are relatively scarce and expensive, you need to understand a little about how .NET frees these objects and what you need to do to ensure that you don't run out of resources as you scale your application.

In this chapter:

◆ Deterministic Finalization

◆ Retrieve Only the Data You Need

◆ Introduction to Stored Procedures

◆ Improving Your Data Access Code

◆ Inserting, Updating, and Deleting Data

◆ How Not to Write an Application

Deterministic Finalization

One of the advantages—or problems, depending on how you approach the subject—of COM-based programming was that every object created had a *reference count*. When you created an object, it had a reference count of 1. As you added additional references to that object, you would call `AddRef` to increment the reference count. Developers using VB and the various scripting languages were spared this manual reference counting because the underlying runtimes called `AddRef` automatically.

Similarly, C and C++ programmers destroying an object reference decremented the reference count manually by calling the `Release` method. When the reference count reached zero, the system could destroy the object and reclaim the memory immediately. Again, classic VB handled this for you. In classic VB and scripting languages, you could destroy the object explicitly by setting the variable reference to `Nothing`. If you used a scripting language such as VBScript or JScript, you could set the variable to `Nothing` (VBScript), `null` (JScript), or some other value. In VB or any scripting language, the runtime destroyed objects implicitly when they went out of scope.

A large number of VB programmers thought that you *had* to set objects to Nothing, and there was a long-running debate over cleaning up—could you trust the system to clean up or should you do it manually? As it turned out, most of the debate was unnecessary as long as you created objects at appropriate scope. However, object creation was an expensive operation in COM (in terms of both time and memory), partly due to the requirement to call AddRef and Release, and partly due to other factors.

Complicating the debate was the fact that VB programmers often used the Windows API to perform memory and graphics operations. The VB runtime did not automatically clean up objects created via Windows API calls. For example, if you performed graphics operations using Graphics Device Interface (GDI) calls, it was your responsibility to remember to free all the objects you used: pens, brushes, device context handles, and so on. Otherwise, the resources would never be freed, and your application would have a *memory leak*. Leaking a little memory with COM-based applications was not uncommon. Because the amount of available memory increased rapidly (from 640KB to 64MB) on most computers over just a few years' span, a small memory leak didn't matter much on desktop and laptop systems, where users tend to turn off the machines fairly often. But on servers, even a slow memory leak would reduce resources, and eventually the machine would run out of memory or slow down to the point of unusability.

Another problem with the reference counting scheme was *circular references.* A circular reference occurs when a child object and a parent object hold references to each other. For example, many collection-type classes had an Add method that created a new item and added the new item reference to the collection. However, sometimes the item itself needed a reference to its "parent" collection object. In other words, the parent held a reference to each child, and each child held a reference to the parent. But that meant you had to be very careful how you destroyed the items. Attempting to destroy the parent directly would fail because the child still held references; therefore, the reference count would never reach zero, and COM would never destroy the object. After destroying the object reference to the parent, the entire collection was orphaned in memory, causing a memory leak. The only way to destroy the parent successfully was to implement a parent object method, often called Clear or something similar, that first destroyed the children, thus decrementing the parent reference count to 1—the reference to the parent held by the application. After calling the Clear method, setting the parent object to Nothing would free the memory. But programmers were often unaware of this problem or forgot to call the Clear method before destroying the parent reference. Companies spent a lot of time and money fixing memory leaks and circular reference problems.

.NET works entirely differently. It doesn't use reference counting to keep track of object references. Instead, the *garbage collector* destroys objects and reclaims memory whenever the managed heap memory fills up. The .NET garbage collector does this by finding all the unreferenced objects in the heap, a process called *tracing*. Before destroying the object, it calls the Finalize method inherited from the root Object class. After destroying the objects, it compacts the memory by moving objects that still have references to the bottom of the heap, creating a contiguous block of free memory for new objects. For any specific object, the process of reclaiming memory is called *finalization.* By now, you've probably seen many .NET classes that have a Finalize method. You may think that such an operation would take a long time, but in practice, the garbage collector is extremely fast.

Garbage collection thus provides a huge advantage. Programmers don't have to remember to destroy object references; unreferenced objects disappear automatically when the garbage collector runs, and the scheme eliminates the circular reference problem altogether. That eliminates an entire class of bugs, simplifies coding, and stops memory leaks at no cost. But there is a problem with garbage collection memory management. Some resources are in such short supply or need to be recycled so fast that the garbage collection scheme can't keep up.

So what does this discussion have to do with data access in ASP.NET applications? One reason for the association is that database connections are usually both scarce (limited) and expensive, both literally and in terms of memory and server cycles. For example, suppose you have a server license for 10 database connections. As requests come in for your pages, you open and close connections exactly as you're supposed to. But with only 10 connections, you can easily use up the connections before the heap memory fills up. Remember, by default the garbage collector runs only when the managed heap runs out of free memory. Despite your having closed the connections, they haven't been freed, because the garbage collector hasn't run yet. The problem is even worse with files. If you open a file and close it in one process, another process may not be able to open the file even though you closed it, because the system doesn't know it's closed, nor has it freed the resource.

Call *Dispose*

As a partial solution to the problem of delayed resource cleanup, objects that use shared resources typically implement a `Dispose` method (they also implement the `IDisposable` interface). If you create an object instance that implements a `Dispose` method, it's a good idea to call it as soon as you no longer need the object. Calling `Dispose` lets the object release shared resources before the garbage collector runs. It then disables the object, leaving in use only the memory used by the object itself until finalization occurs.

WARNING   *Always call* `Dispose` *as soon as possible for any class that implements it so the system can free shared resources.*

The reason that is only a partial solution is that the system doesn't free some types of resources until the garbage collector runs, even if you *do* call the `Dispose` method properly. Unfortunately, there's no good solution to this problem yet, although Microsoft has discussed many ideas for special classes that manage limited resources differently, and you'll probably see the results of that effort in the future. Until then, if you find your applications running out of connections unexpectedly, or if you are unable to open files, you can force the system to free the resources by running the garbage collector manually.

RUNNING THE .NET GARBAGE COLLECTOR MANUALLY

The .NET framework exposes the garbage collector through the GC class. To force garbage collection, use the `System.GC.Collect` method. You can also force garbage collection using the `GetTotalMemory` method. The GC class also has methods for preventing an object from being collected (`KeepAlive`) during a specific section of code and for suppressing finalization indefinitely (`SuppressFinalize`), but those are beyond the scope of this book.

One way to force .NET to clean up references is to implement your own reference counting for objects that use shared resources. By keeping track of resource usage manually, you can run the garbage collector as needed to free the resources. `Collect` is a class method, so you don't need to create a GC instance. Just call it like this:

```
GC.Collect
```

You won't normally need to run the garbage collector if you remember to call Dispose on classes that use shared resources, but if you find yourself running out of resources, the Collect method may help solve the problem.

The Web Form ch14-1.aspx contains a loop that opens 100 connections, closes them, and then calls the GC.Collect method. You may or may not get errors from this code, depending on how many connections your database server allows and how much free memory you have on the server. I created it simply to try to force a resource error. While I *can* force one without the GC.Collect method call by repeatedly refreshing a browser containing a request to the Web Form (eventually the request times out while waiting for an available connection), I have yet to get an error with the call in place. Here's the code:

NOTE *The connection strings in this chapter are stored in the* <appSettings> *section of the CSharpASP project's* web.config *file. You may need to alter the connection string information for your server.*

```
using System.Data.SqlClient
private void Page_Load(object sender, System.EventArgs e) {
    Response.Write(ConfigurationSettings.AppSettings.Get
    ("NorthwindSql")
    + "<br><br>");
    SqlConnection[] conn = new SqlConnection[100];
    try {
        for (int i = 0; i < 100; i++) {
            conn[i] = new SqlConnection();
            conn[i].ConnectionString =
                ConfigurationSettings.AppSettings.Get("NorthwindSql");
            conn[i].Open();
            Response.Write("opened connection " + i.ToString() +
    "<br>");
        }
    }
    catch (DataException dex) {
        Response.Write(dex.Message);
    }
    finally {
        for (int i = 99; i >= 0; i--) {
            if (conn[i] != null) {
            conn[i].Close();
            Response.Write("Closed conn( " + i.ToString() + ")<Br>");;
            }
            conn[i] = null;
        }
    }
    // Disable the following line, and the
    // request will eventually time out when
    // your server runs out of connections.
    //GC.Collect();
}
```

Retrieve Only the Data You Need

One of the most common mistakes that beginning Web programmers make when accessing databases is retrieving too much data. I often get several questions per month e-mailed by people asking how to speed up the display of their 100,000-row data set in a browser. My answer is invariably the same: While there are a few—a very few—valid reasons to send that much data to a client, browsing data is not one of them. People don't browse efficiently through thousands of data items—nor do they like to. That is too much data to assimilate, takes too long to download and display, and makes an otherwise useful program unnecessarily sluggish.

One reason to retrieve only what you need is that you should be considerate of the client. Although the client machine may be able to handle that much data, sending it is not conducive to good interfaces.

Another reason to retrieve only what you need is to reduce the network bandwidth and the time that your application requires to serve pages. Particularly now, when Web Forms maintain state automatically for every control on the page (unless you tell them not to), the page-state process requires the server to send *twice* the volume of data that it needs to simply fill the controls, because it sends the data once for the control and once for the hidden _VIEWSTATE form field. That means it takes nearly twice as long to load the page when you maintain ViewState on controls such as DataGrids or DataLists. Not only are bandwidth and time sucked up during the download, but Web Forms post the data back to the server for *every* client-side event that you're handling on the server. Therefore, you should consider whether you have any *need* to maintain state on those controls.

To see the difference between maintaining state and requerying the database for each request, run the ch13-6.aspx Web Form from Chapter 13, "Introduction to ADO.NET," and then select View Source from the browser context menu. You'll see a page full of _VIEWSTATE text before you see the table tags that display the data. Granted, maintaining state means that you don't have to requery the database to redisplay the page, because the Web Form can re-create the DataGrid from the posted state data. But in return for eliminating a database hit, you have loaded the network by sending the data three times rather than once for every page request.

Despite that, I'm not trying to worry you to the point that you always set the EnableViewState property to false for data controls. The point is this: Now that you're aware of the massively increased request/response data requirements for Web Forms, don't send any more data than you need. If the user must select a name from a table containing names and other data, don't retrieve the other data. Using SQL, you don't have to retrieve unwanted columns. When you write your SQL statements, avoid retrieving entire rows if you need only a few columns from the row. Write your SQL statements so that they retrieve only the data items that you need. By doing that, you automatically improve the page load time and simultaneously make your application less resource intensive and more responsive.

Third, consider the impact of data retrieval on your server and network. Small C# Web applications typically run both IIS and SQL Server on the same machine. This produces extremely fast access to the database, because there's no cross-machine communication, although the effect is mitigated somewhat by the logging requirements for both IIS and SQL Server, which often cause I/O conflicts, slowing down the application. Larger shops typically run IIS and the database server on separate machines. That solves the logging problem but also means that IIS must make a network request to get the data. Therefore, every database operation also increases network traffic, and application bottlenecks can occur due to the volume of data crossing the network. In addition, because modern databases all cache data in memory (as does IIS), retrieving more data than you need wastes memory.

For example, suppose you want to retrieve a specific row from a table. Many programmers who work with file-based databases will open the table and scroll through the data until they find the desired row. But scrolling through unneeded data is not only horrendously slow but also unnecessary. Instead, you should write a stored procedure that selects the row. The difference is that the database must usually retrieve data from disk to scroll through a large table, but it can use an index to find the row using a SQL query.

Finally, consider the database server itself. What happens when you send a SQL query to the server? First, the server must parse the query, separating the various clauses and identifying and validating database names. Next, it compiles the query and builds a *query execution plan*, which identifies the index or indexes that would be most efficient and which tables it must access. Finally, it runs the execution plan, identifying the disk pages or rows that it must read to satisfy the request.

That's a lot of work. I'd wager that, even today, most ASP applications use string SQL queries rather than stored procedures. While modern database servers can cache compiled queries to some degree, subsequently running the cached version rather than reparsing, recompiling, and reexecuting, they can do that only for queries that are *identical* to already cached queries—and only on the same connection. If the connection differs, the server must analyze the query because a different user may not have rights to access the data. If the query differs—even by so much as a changed ID—the server will analyze and recompile the query.

The solution to this problem is stored procedures. A *stored procedure* is a preanalyzed and precompiled query. Using stored procedures can speed up data retrieval dramatically *if* you plan your data retrieval well and store data in such a way that using indexes is faster than *scanning* the tables (searching the table data). In addition, placing your queries in stored procedures moves them out of your application code, which is always a good thing because you can then change and recompile the query to fix errors rather than recompiling and possibly redeploying your application.

If using stored procedures is such a great thing, why don't most ASP developers take advantage of them?

First, modern databases are so fast at analyzing and compiling queries that for infrequent, isolated data retrieval operations, the cost of transferring the data far outweighs the processing power required to compile the query.

Second, classic ASP pages were just text files, and you could replace them on the Web server at any time—in fact, a page could rewrite itself! IIS recognizes ASP page changes and recompiles the changed pages the next time they're requested. Even if IIS has cached the page, it compares the time stamp of the file with the time stamp on the cached version and recompiles the page when the time stamps differ. That made it extremely easy to update an ASP page—just copy the new version to the server. Therefore, putting SQL code in ASP pages wasn't an issue as far as fixing bugs or upgrading the application were concerned.

However, as applications grow, so do the number of queries. Also, a database query may be useful in more than one situation. For example, you may need to run the same query to find customer orders in multiple applications. As a programmer, any time you find yourself writing the same code twice, you should immediately consider isolating (and, if necessary, abstracting) that code so that you can use *one* version. Doing so cuts down on bugs, simplifies development, and makes maintaining or modifying the program much easier and less expensive.

But I think the real reason is that using stored procedures is a tiny bit harder—at first—than writing SQL statements. In the next sections, I'll show you how to eliminate SQL statements from your code by using stored procedures.

One final point is that all database retrieval methods use scarce resources and time. You should use databases only when they're absolutely necessary. For example, if you have a database that holds only a small number of user IDs for authentication purposes, there's little reason to impose the performance overhead of a database. For such situations, consider using an XML file or a simple list read from a text file instead.

Introduction to Stored Procedures

A stored procedure is nothing more than a specially prepared SQL statement stored inside the database itself. You can create stored procedures using the template in the SQL Query Analyzer application or by writing and "running" `CREATE PROCEDURE` statements in Enterprise Manager, among other methods. If you have the Enterprise version of Visual Studio, you can create stored procedures from the Server Explorer. I'll show you these three, then you can decide which one you like best.

The examples in this section all use the `ClassRecords` database, so you should install the database if you didn't do so while reading Chapter 12, "Introduction to Relational Databases and SQL." The SQL statements to create and populate the database in SQL Server or MSDE are on `www.sybex.com` in the Chapter 14 subdirectory, in the file entitled `CreateClassRecords2.sql`.

Creating Stored Procedures

The `ClassRecords` database captures the relationship between Students, Teachers, and Classes. For example, one of the queries you wrote in Chapter 12 selected the `StudentIDs` of students who had Marsha Franklin for a teacher.

```
SELECT StudentID
FROM TeacherStudent INNER JOIN Teachers
ON TeacherStudent.TeacherID=Teachers.TeacherID
WHERE Teachers.LastName='Franklin' AND Teachers.FirstName='Marsha'
```

In the next sections, you'll see several ways to turn the query into a stored procedure named `qryStudentsOfMarshaFranklin`.

NOTE *When you first created it in Chapter 12, the ClassRecords database did not contain the stored procedures that you'll use in this or subsequent chapters, so you need to follow one of the procedures discussed next to create them. Alternatively, you can re-create the entire database (which destroys any changes you might have made) using the* `CreateClass-Records2.sql` *file in the* `Ch14` *folder—which does include the stored procedures used in this chapter.*

CREATING STORED PROCEDURES WITH SQL SERVER QUERY ANALYZER

To create stored procedures with SQL Query Analyzer:

1. Open the SQL Server Enterprise Manager application. Click Start ➢ Programs ➢ Microsoft SQL Server ➢ Enterprise Manager.

2. Select the server where you installed the ClassRecords database, and expand the **Databases** item.

3. Select the ClassRecords database item.

4. Click the Tools menu and then select SQL Query Analyzer.

5. If the Object Browser pane is not visible, click the Object Browser button on the toolbar (see Figures 14.1 and 14.2) to display it.

FIGURE 14.1

SQL Query Analyzer toolbar with the Object Browser button pressed

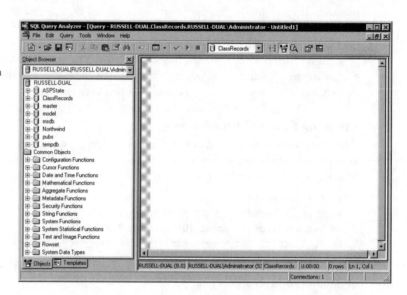

FIGURE 14.2

SQL Query Analyzer with the Object Browser open

WARNING   *Make sure you select the ClassRecords database from the drop-down list on the toolbar before you continue.*

6. Click File ➢ New and select Create Procedure from the New dialog (see Figure 14.3).

7. Click OK. You'll see a second New dialog. Select the Create Procedure Basic Template item (see Figure 14.4).

FIGURE 14.3

SQL Query
Analyzer New dialog

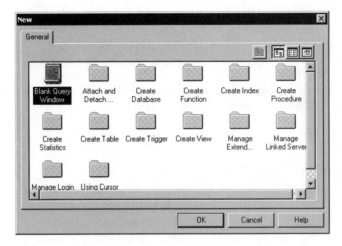

FIGURE 14.4

SQL Query
Analyzer New
dialog, template
selection

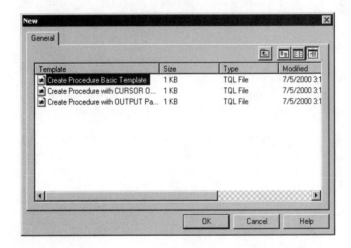

8. Click OK. The template appears in the query window—the right pane (see Listing 14.1).

LISTING 14.1: SQL SERVER 2000 CREATE PROCEDURE BASIC TEMPLATE

```
-- =============================================
-- Create procedure basic template
-- =============================================
-- creating the stored procedure
IF EXISTS (SELECT name
     FROM sysobjects
     WHERE name = N'<procedure_name, sysname, proc_test>'
```

```
        AND type = 'P')
    DROP PROCEDURE <procedure_name, sysname, proc_test>
GO

CREATE PROCEDURE <procedure_name, sysname, proc_test>
    <@param1, sysname, @p1> <datatype_for_param1, , int> =
    <default_value_for_param1, , 0>,
    <@param2, sysname, @p2> <datatype_for_param2, , int> =
    <default_value_for_param2, , 0>
AS
    SELECT @p1, @p2
GO


-- ===============================================
-- example code to execute the stored procedure
-- This code is not part of the stored procedure.
-- ===============================================
EXECUTE <procedure_name, sysname, proc_test> <value_for_param1, , 1>,
    <value_for_param2, , 2>
GO
```

Another way to insert the basic template is to click Edit ➤ Insert Template and then select the Create Procedure Template from the Insert Template dialog. You still need to select the type of template, in this case, Create Procedure Basic Template, from the second Insert Template screen.

NOTE   *Look at the procedure template for a second. It doesn't look much like the standard SQL statements you saw in Chapter 12. That's because it consists largely of DDL—Data Definition Language commands. But you don't need to do much to complete the template. The IF EXISTS test drops (deletes) any existing stored procedure of the same name, if such a procedure already exists.*

To replace the procedure_name, in the template select a name for the procedure. Fill in the template with the SQL statement as follows:

```
-- ===============================================
-- Create procedure basic template
-- ===============================================
-- creating the stored procedure
IF EXISTS (SELECT name
        FROM sysobjects
        WHERE name = N'qryStudentsOfMarshaFranklin'
        AND type = 'P')
    DROP PROCEDURE qryStudentsOfMarshaFranklin
GO
```

SQL Server handles both ASCII and Unicode strings. The N in front of the query name specifies that the string following it is a Unicode string. Data type names follow the same rule, although with slightly different syntax. For example, the char (character) data type has a corresponding nchar (Unicode character) data type.

```
CREATE PROCEDURE QryStudentsOfMarshaFranklin
AS
    SELECT StudentID
    FROM TeacherStudent INNER JOIN Teachers
    ON TeacherStudent.TeacherID=Teachers.TeacherID
    WHERE Teachers.LastName='Franklin' AND Teachers.FirstName='Marsha'
GO
```

You replace the text <procedure_name, sysname, proc_test> with the name of your new stored procedure, wherever it appears. Next, because you don't have any parameters to this stored procedure, you can delete the first part of the CREATE PROCEDURE statement. Delete the highlighted lines below:

```
CREATE PROCEDURE <procedure_name, sysname, proc_test>
    <@param1, sysname, @p1> <datatype_for_param1, , int>
    <default_value_for_param1, , 0>,
    <@param2, sysname, @p2> <datatype_for_param2, , int> =
    <default_value_for_param2, , 0>
AS
    SELECT @p1, @p2
GO
```

Note that you should delete the text that shows how to execute the stored procedure.

```
-- =================================================
-- example code to execute the store procedure
-- =================================================
EXECUTE <procedure_name, sysname, proc_test> <value_for_param1, , 1>,
    <value_for_param2, , 2>
GO
```

Finally, replace the text SELECT @p1, @p2 with the text of your stored procedure:

```
SELECT StudentID
FROM TeacherStudent INNER JOIN Teachers
ON TeacherStudent.TeacherID=Teachers.TeacherID
WHERE Teachers.LastName='Franklin' AND Teachers.FirstName='Marsha'
```

Run the text in the Query Analyzer window by clicking the Run button on the toolbar or pressing F5. Running the text creates the stored procedure. Error messages appear in the bottom pane. If SQL Server was able to create the procedure, the bottom pane will read, "The command(s) completed successfully."

You should check. Expand the Stored Procedures item under the ClassRecords database item in the Object Explorer. You should see an item titled dbo.qryStudentsOfMarshaFranklin. The dbo portion stands for "Database Owner," meaning that the owner of the database also owns this item.

CREATING STORED PROCEDURES WITH ENTERPRISE MANAGER

I find it simplest to create most procedures with Enterprise Manager, primarily because it does some of the work for you.

1. Open the SQL Server Enterprise Manager application. Click Start ➤ Programs ➤ Microsoft SQL Server ➤ Enterprise Manager.

2. Select the server where you installed the ClassRecords database and expand the Databases item.

3. Expand the ClassRecords database item.

4. Right-click the Stored Procedures item and select New ➤ Stored Procedure from the context menu. You'll see the Stored Procedure Properties dialog (see Figure 14.5).

FIGURE 14.5

SQL Server
Enterprise Manager
Stored Procedure
Properties dialog

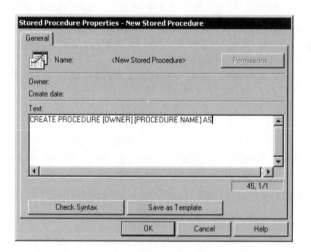

5. The dialog box already contains a little bit of templated text. You'll probably recognize it as the second half of the template text inserted by the Query Analyzer application. Overwrite the [OWNER].[PROCEDURE NAME] portion of the template with your new stored procedure name.

6. Place your cursor after the word AS and insert the SELECT query for this procedure. After doing this, you should have this text in the Text field on the Stored Procedure Properties dialog:

```
CREATE PROCEDURE qryStudentsOfMarshaFranklin AS
SELECT StudentID
FROM TeacherStudent INNER JOIN Teachers
ON TeacherStudent.TeacherID=Teachers.TeacherID
WHERE Teachers.LastName='Franklin' AND
Teachers.FirstName='Marsha'
```

7. Click the Check Syntax button. The dialog warns you if the stored procedure contains any errors, such as misnamed database objects (tables, fields, and so on) or misspelled keywords. If there are no errors, you'll see a Syntax Check Successful message.

8. Click the OK button to save the stored procedure. If you followed the preceding procedure, you'll get an error because the procedure already exists. The warning can save you from overwriting an existing procedure, but if you *want* to overwrite the existing version, here's a trick: Change the CREATE PROCEDURE text to ALTER PROCEDURE. Now you can click the OK button to save your changes.

NOTE   *SQL Server Enterprise Manager has a wizard that can help you build* INSERT, UPDATE, *and* DELETE *queries, as well as views, databases, indexes, logins, full-text indexes, and other database objects. The visual query builder in SQL Server is very similar to the one in the Enterprise version of Visual Studio, so if you don't have the Enterprise version of Visual Studio, you can use the one in Enterprise Manager. Unfortunately, Enterprise Manager Wizard doesn't help you build* SELECT *queries—you'll need to write code to do that. You can access the Enterprise Manager Wizards via the Tools menu.*

CREATING STORED PROCEDURES WITH SERVER EXPLORER (VS ENTERPRISE VERSION ONLY)

This procedure works only with the Enterprise version of Visual Studio. The Professional version lets you browse database items but does not let you create them.

1. Open Visual Studio and show the Server Explorer. Expand the Servers item and select the server that contains the instance of SQL Server containing the ClassRecords database. If the connection isn't already there, you will need to create it as described in Chapter 12.

2. Expand the SQL Servers item and select the SQL Server instance that contains the ClassRecords database. Expand the ClassRecords database item, then right-click the Stored Procedures item and select New Stored Procedure from the pop-up menu.

Following step 2, you'll see yet another template. By now, this should look familiar, so I won't go through the procedure in detail. You can enter the query by hand, but the big advantage of the Enterprise version in this case is that you have access to the Query Builder, which lets you build queries by selecting fields from a visual view of the tables. To access the Query Builder, right-click in the editor window and select the Insert SQL item from the pop-up menu. For complex queries with many joins, the Query Builder can be a great timesaver, especially at first, but for simple queries, there's no big advantage to using the Query Builder.

Retrieving Data Using Stored Procedures

Just this once, I'll show you how to access data using the drag-and-drop method from Visual Studio. First, create a new Web Form named ch14-2.aspx. Next, open Server Explorer and find the stored procedure named qryStudentsOfMarshaFranklin that you created in the preceding section. Drag it onto the design surface. Visual Studio draws a *non-visual* design surface called the Component Designer under the Web Form design surface and adds a SqlConnection and SqlCommand object representation to the non-visual surface.

Open the Toolbox and drag a DataGrid onto the Web Form. All you need to do now is bind the DataGrid to the SqlCommand. But using these controls, you can't do that through the Properties window.

Instead, you must bind the `DataSet` returned by executing the `Command` object to the `DataGrid` control to that in code. For example:

```
using System.Data.SqlClient;
using System.Configuration;

private void Page_Load(object sender, System.EventArgs e) {
    this.sqlConnection1.Open();
    SqlDataReader dr =
    sqlCommand1.ExecuteReader(CommandBehavior.SequentialAccess);
    DataGrid1.DataSource = dr;
    DataGrid1.DataBind();
    dr.Close();
    sqlCommand1.Dispose();
    sqlConnection1.Close();
    sqlConnection1.Dispose();
}
```

There's nothing new in that code, and the results aren't visually impressive, so you can run it yourself to verify that the Web Form displays two `StudentID`s, with values of 1 and 5. But what is impressive is the code that Visual Studio wrote into the code-behind form for you. Find and expand the Web Form Designer Generated Code region in the code-behind class. You'll see the code in Listing 14.2.

LISTING 14.2: VS.NET AUTOGENERATED Connection AND Command OBJECT CODE

```
#region Web Form Designer generated code
override protected void OnInit(EventArgs e)
{
    //
    // CODEGEN: This call is required by the ASP.NET Web Form
        Designer.
    //
    InitializeComponent();
    base.OnInit(e);
}

/// <summary>
/// Required method for Designer support - do not modify
/// the contents of this method with the code editor.
/// </summary>
private void InitializeComponent()
{
    this.sqlConnection1 = new
    System.Data.SqlClient.SqlConnection();
    this.sqlCommand1 = new System.Data.SqlClient.SqlCommand();
    //
    // sqlConnection1
```

```
//
this.sqlConnection1.ConnectionString =
    "data source=localhost;initial catalog=ClassRecords;" +
    "persist security info=False;user id=sa;"
    "workstation id=RUSSELL-DUAL;packet size=4096";
//
// sqlCommand1
//
this.sqlCommand1.CommandText =
"dbo.[qryStudentsOfMarshaFranklin]";
this.sqlCommand1.CommandType =
    System.Data.CommandType.StoredProcedure;
this.sqlCommand1.Connection = this.sqlConnection1;
this.sqlCommand1.Parameters.Add(new
    System.Data.SqlClient.SqlParameter("@RETURN_VALUE",
    System.Data.SqlDbType.Int, 4,
    System.Data.ParameterDirection.ReturnValue, false,
    ((System.Byte)(10)), ((System.Byte)(0)), "",
    System.Data.DataRowVersion.Current, null));
this.Load += new System.EventHandler(this.Page_Load);

}
#endregion
```

The generated code creates a Connection object and builds the connection string for you, a convenient way to find out the correct syntax for a connection string if you aren't sure. Then it creates a Command object, sets the Command's CommandType and Connection properties, and creates a return parameter with an integer value (intended to hold a status code from executing the procedure). That seems like a lot of code compared to the manual version, but sometimes autogenerating the code can be extremely useful.

You'll see more about parameters in the next section. The CommandType property tells the database how to treat the CommandText property value—as one of three enumerated values. The default value is CommandType.Text.

CommandType Enumeration Values

Use the CommandType enumeration values to define the type of command you want to execute.

CommandType.StoredProcedure The CommandText property holds the name of a stored procedure. Strictly speaking, you don't have to specify this value for stored procedures without parameters. SQL Server will look up the type, but you *should* get in the habit of specifying it every time, because it speeds up query execution and because ADO.NET raises an error if you forget to specify it for stored parameters that have parameters.

CommandType.TableDirect Use this command type only when you're retrieving an entire table or view.

CommandType.Text   Use this command type (this is the default) to execute dynamic SQL statements.

For comparison purposes, here's the manual version:

```
using System.Data.SqlClient;
using System.Configuration;

private void Page_Load(object sender, System.EventArgs e) {
    SqlDataReader dr = null;
    SqlConnection conn = new SqlConnection
        (ConfigurationSettings.AppSettings.Get("ClassRecordsSql"));
    SqlCommand cm = new SqlCommand("qryStudentsOfMarshaFranklin",
    conn);
    conn.Open();
    dr = cm.ExecuteReader(CommandBehavior.SequentialAccess);
    DataGrid1.DataSource = dr;
    DataGrid1.DataBind();
    dr.Close();
    conn.Close();
    conn.Dispose();
}
```

It's easier to drag the components onto the form than it is to write the code by hand. There's almost always a trade-off between ease-of-use and power. The question is this: What do you lose in power by using the VS drag-and-drop method of data access? In this case, not much. The trade-off here is between ease of maintenance and ease of development. In my opinion, the second version is much easier to maintain. Granted, with a little work, such as replacing the generic connection names generated by VS and deleting the unnecessary code, you would end up with approximately the same code you'd have to write anyway. Ultimately, it's up to you to decide which you need more—rapid development or simplified maintenance.

As you can see, running a stored procedure is exactly the same as running a standard SQL query. Note that the only difference is that you specify the name of the stored procedure object in the database rather than writing out an explicit query.

However, there are slight differences when you run stored procedures that contain parameters, as you'll see in the next section.

Creating and Using Parameterized Stored Procedures

The qryStudentsOfMarshaFranklin query is not useful except for the single instance where you want to know the IDs of that teacher's students. You certainly wouldn't want to create separate queries for each teacher. If you were creating a SQL string to perform the query, you would probably create the query with a function call. For example, you might create a function that accepts a teacher's first and last names and returns the appropriate SQL query:

```
public String makeStudentsForTeacherQuery(String firstname,
    String lastname) {
    return "SELECT StudentID " +
```

```
    "FROM TeacherStudent INNER JOIN Teachers " +
    "ON TeacherStudent.TeacherID=Teachers.TeacherID " +
    "WHERE Teachers.LastName='" & lastname & "'" +
    "AND Teachers.FirstName='" & firstname & "'";
}
```

Using the preceding function, you could create a query for any teacher.

Parameterized stored procedures work exactly the same way. You define and pass the appropriate parameters, and SQL Server combines the parameters with the query to retrieve the appropriate data.

CREATING A PARAMETERIZED STORED PROCEDURE

To create a stored procedure with parameters, define the parameters and types after the stored procedure name but before the AS clause:

```
CREATE PROCEDURE qryGetStudentIDsFromTeacherName
    @lastname char(20), @firstname char(20)
AS
    SELECT StudentID
    FROM TeacherStudent INNER JOIN Teachers
    ON TeacherStudent.TeacherID=Teachers.TeacherID
    WHERE Teachers.LastName=@lastname AND
        Teachers.FirstName=@firstname
```

You can paste that text into the Enterprise Manager Stored Procedure Properties dialog and click OK to save the stored procedure. SQL Server creates a new stored procedure named qryGetStudent-IDsFromTeacherName.

WARNING   *The SQL script that creates the ClassRecords database does not create the* qryGetStudentIDs-FromTeacherName *stored procedure—you should create it before you continue. You can find the code in the* qryGet-StudentIDsFromTeacherName.sql *file in the* Ch14 *folder of the CSharpASP project on* www.sybex.com.

The new stored procedure accepts two string parameters named @lastname and @firstname. The parameters are required because they don't have a default value, but you can create parameters that have default values.

You can test the new procedure by running it in the Query Analyzer. Select the ClassRecords database and type this text:

```
exec qryGetStudentIDsFromTeacherName 'Franklin', 'Marsha'
```

To run the text, press F5 or click the Run button on the Query Analyzer toolbar. The results look like Figure 14.6.

FIGURE 14.6

Testing a
parameterized
stored procedure in
the Query Analyzer

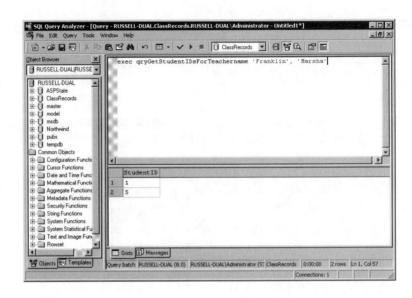

USING A PARAMETERIZED STORED PROCEDURE

To use the qryGetStudentIDsFromTeacherName procedure, you follow the same pattern as you did to run the simple stored procedure *except* that you must add the parameter definitions and values to the Command object's Parameters collection. The Web Form ch14-3 contains an example. Drag a ListBox and a DataGrid server control onto the design surface. You want to display the names of the teachers in the ListBox. When a user clicks a name in the ListBox, you want to return to the server and look up the StudentID values associated with that teacher.

To force the form to submit each time the user clicks a teacher name, set the ListBox.AutoPost-Back property to true. Set the ListBox's ID property to lstTeachers and the DataGrid's ID property to dgStudentIDs.

When the page loads the first time, you need to fill the list of teachers. Because you want any teacher the user selects to remain selected after getting the associated StudentIDs, you should leave the List-Box.EnableViewState property set to true. By doing that, you implicitly agree to send *all* the teacher names back and forth for every request, but it means that you don't have to requery the database to get the teacher names for each request, nor do you have to maintain the ListBox state manually. Because there are only a few teacher names, that's probably a good decision. If there were hundreds of names, you'd want to maintain the state manually and avoid sending hundreds of names back and forth for each request.

You know that you're going to have to open a database connection each time the page loads, so you can define the SqlConnection variable at Page scope.

```
public class ch14_3 : System.Web.UI.Page
{
    protected System.Web.UI.WebControls.Label Label1;
    protected System.Web.UI.WebControls.ListBox lstTeachers;
```

```
    protected System.Web.UI.WebControls.DataGrid dgStudentIDs;
    protected System.Web.UI.WebControls.Label lblSelectedTeacher;
    SqlConnection conn = new SqlConnection
       (ConfigurationSettings.AppSettings.Get("ClassRecordsSql"));
    // more code here
}
```

To fill the ListBox during the initial page load, you need to query the database for the names. Create a Command object and a DataReader. Set the Command properties, retrieve the data, and loop through the values.

```
private void Page_Load(object sender, System.EventArgs e) {
    SqlDataReader dr = null;
    SqlCommand cm = new SqlCommand();
    cm.Connection = conn;
    conn.Open();
    if (!IsPostBack) {
        cm.CommandText = "Select firstname + ' ' + lastname as " +
            "Name from Teachers order by lastname, firstname asc";
        cm.Connection = conn;
        dr = cm.ExecuteReader();
        while (dr.Read()) {
            lstTeachers.Items.Add(dr.GetString(0));
        }
        dr.Close();
    }
}
```

For now, the code uses a dynamic SQL query that tells SQL Server to concatenate each teacher's first and last names, placing a space between the names, and to sort the names by last name and then by first name, in ascending order. You could just as easily retrieve them in lastname, firstname order by concatenating a comma into the string. The AS Name clause tells SQL Server to create an *alias* name. The returned column is a derived column that doesn't exist in the database. SQL Server names virtual columns with automatically generated and nonintuitive names, so you should get in the habit of setting alias names for all derived columns.

Now you've completed the code to display the teacher names. When a user clicks a teacher name, you want to run the qryGetStudentIDsFromTeachername stored procedure and display the Student-IDs associated with the selected teacher. You can place the code into the lstTeachers_SelectedIndex-Changed event, which fires whenever the user changes the ListBox selection.

```
private void lstTeachers_SelectedIndexChanged(object sender,
    System.EventArgs e) {
    String aName;
    String[] names = new String[2];
    SqlCommand cm = new SqlCommand();
    SqlDataReader dr = null;
    if (lstTeachers.SelectedIndex >= 0) {
        cm.Connection = conn;
```

```
aName = lstTeachers.SelectedItem.ToString();
lblSelectedTeacher.Text = "Students of " + aName;
names = aName.Split(' ');
/* One way to define the parameters.
 * comment the following four lines to test the
 * alternate version
 */
cm.CommandType = CommandType.StoredProcedure;
cm.CommandText = "qryGetStudentIDsFromTeachername";
cm.Parameters.Add(new SqlParameter("@lastname", names[1]));
cm.Parameters.Add(new SqlParameter("@firstname", names[0]));


/* An alternate way to define parameters.
 * uncomment the following five lines to test
 * the alternate method.
 *
 * Be sure to comment the first version, above, before
 * testing the alternate method
 */

//SqlParameter param  = null;
//param = cm.Parameters.Add("@lastname",
SqlDbType.Char,20);
//param.Value = names[1];
//param = cm.Parameters.Add("@firstname",
SqlDbType.Char,20);
//param.Value = names[0];

dr = cm.ExecuteReader();
dgStudentIDs.DataSource = dr;
dgStudentIDs.DataBind();
dr.Close();
    }
  }
```

The code first checks to ensure that the user has selected some item from the ListBox. In this case, because the database won't allow either the LastName or the FirstName field to be null, you can be sure that you'll have a valid name for each item. As written, you need to extract the individual names from the selected item. The code uses the Split method to retrieve a string array called names() containing the first and last names.

Next, the code creates a Command object, sets its Connection and CommandType properties (is this becoming familiar?), creates two Parameter objects, and appends them to the Command object's Parameters collection.

```
cm.Parameters.Add(new SqlParameter("@lastname", names[1]));
cm.Parameters.Add(new SqlParameter("@firstname", names[0]));
```

There are several ways to create `Parameter` objects. At minimum, you must specify the parameter name and value. The `Command` object *always* has a `Parameters` collection. Use the `Add` method to add new parameters to the collection. The `Add` method returns a reference to the new `Parameter` object. In this case, because I already know the parameter value, I can create the `Parameter` and set its properties in one step. However, sometimes you want to create the `Command` object in advance and set the `Parameter` values later. To do that, you must specify the parameter name, type, and—for data types that vary in size—the size, in bytes. Here's an alternate version (commented out in the preceding code snippet) that defines and adds the two `parameters` before specifying the value.

```
SqlParameter param  = null;
param = cm.Parameters.Add("@lastname", SqlDbType.Char, 20);
param.Value = names[1];
param = cm.Parameters.Add("@firstname", SqlDbType.Char, 20);
param.Value = names[0];
```

For large applications, it's sometimes useful to define all the `Commands` and cache them. In that case, you'll need to set the `Parameter` values by "finding" the parameters in the `Parameters` collection. For example:

```
// Define Command parameters during application initialization
SqlParameter param = null;
cm.Parameters.Add("@lastname", SqlDbType.Char, 20);
cm.Parameters.Add("@firstname", SqlDbType.Char, 20);

//... later, set the parameters by index or by name
cm.Parameters[0].Value = <last name value>;
cm.Parameters[1].Value = <first name value>;

// or
cm.Parameters.Item[0].Value = <last name value>;
cm.Parameters.Item[1].Value = <first name value>;

// or
cm.Parameters.Item["@lastname"].Value = <last name value>;
cm.Parameters.Item["@firstname"].Value = <first name value>;
```

NOTE *Don't forget to set the* `Command` *object's* `CommandType` *property to* `CommandType.StoredProcedure`.

After appending the parameters to the `Command` object's `Parameters` collection, the `lstTeachers_SelectedIndexChanged` event code creates a `DataReader` and binds the `DataGrid` to it to display the values returned from the stored procedure query.

Finally, remember to close the `Connection` object. You can do that during the `Page_Unload` event.

```
private void Page_Unload(object sender, System.EventArgs e) {
    if (conn! = null) {
        if (conn.State == ConnectionState.Open) {
            conn.Close();
        }
```

```
        conn.Dispose();
    }
}
```

When you run the `ch14-3.aspx` Web Form in a browser, it looks like Figure 14.7.

FIGURE 14.7

The `ch14-3.aspx` Web Form running in a browser

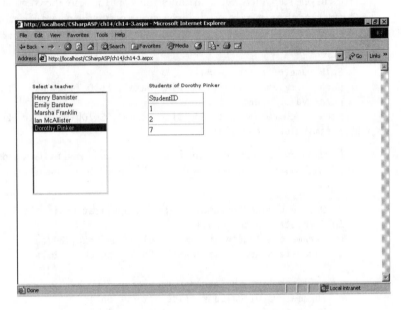

Improving Your Data Access Code

You have to ask yourself at this point whether the code is robust and scalable. Take each portion of the Web Form and ask yourself what would happen if

- The volume of data grows substantially.

- The data values change.

- The display requirements change.

Consider how even this simple application might be used. For a single school, the number of teachers probably wouldn't grow beyond manageable limits. But for a school system or a set of school systems in a state, the volume of data would soon become unmanageable. For example, an administrator would definitely want to filter the list of teachers to show only those associated with a single school. In other words, if the volume of data grew substantially, the database would need to change, as would the interface and display. By simply considering the problem in advance, you can decide whether to add database items such as `School` and `District` to the database and then alter the application plan accordingly. A user might want to view the data in other ways. By anticipating the possible requirements *before* you design the database and write the application, you'll save yourself a great deal of time and effort later.

Suppose the data values change. This application works *only* because each teacher has a unique name. You should *never* use data values as selection criteria that might at some point be duplicated. Fortunately, this is a relatively simple change. Rather than returning the teacher *name* when the form submits, you can submit the `TeacherID` value associated with that name.

Finally, suppose the display requirements change. For example, it's not particularly useful to display the `StudentIDs`—they're meaningless to humans. It would be better to display the students' names. Similarly, what would a user want to do with those names? It's highly likely that administrators would want to create classes and assign teachers and students to those classes, as well as add new students and teachers, change their properties, and remove students, classes, and teachers as the schedule required. In the next section, "Inserting, Updating, and Deleting Data," you'll create a complete application that limits access to authenticated administrators, but because it's so important to use row ID values rather than possibly duplicated data for queries, you'll change the `lstTeachers` `ListBox` to post `TeacherID` values right away.

The first step in altering the `ListBox` is to create a stored procedure that returns the `TeacherID` values as well as the names. Define a stored procedure called `qryGetTeachers` that retrieves the `TeacherID`, `LastName`, and `FirstName` values from the Teachers table. Note that the following query no longer forces the database to concatenate the names as `FirstName LastName`; instead, two parameters determine the way the database returns the names and the sort order. Note that you don't *have* to do this, but it's very convenient and saves you from having to add code at the interface level to sort the returned data. It's much simpler to change or add a parameter value than to add sorting capabilities in code. If you were using `DataGrids` or a third-party `Server` control that can concatenate column values under an alias name, or sort columns, you wouldn't have to do this.

```
CREATE    PROCEDURE qryGetTeachers
    @nameorder char(9) = 'lastfirst',
    @sortorder varchar(4) = 'ASC'
AS
SET @nameorder=lower(@nameorder)
set @sortorder=lower(@sortorder)
IF (@nameorder='firstlast')
    BEGIN
        IF (@sortorder='desc')
            BEGIN
                SELECT TeacherID, FirstName + ' ' + LastName
                AS Name FROM Teachers
                ORDER BY LastName DESC, FirstName
            END
        ELSE
            BEGIN
                SELECT TeacherID, FirstName + ' ' + LastName
                AS Name FROM Teachers
                ORDER BY LastName ASC, FirstName ASC
            END
    END
ELSE
    BEGIN
```

```
        IF (@sortorder='desc')
            BEGIN
                SELECT TeacherID, LastName + ', ' + FirstName
                AS Name FROM Teachers
                ORDER BY LastName DESC, FirstName ASC
            END
        ELSE
            BEGIN
                SELECT TeacherID, LastName + ', ' + FirstName
                AS Name FROM Teachers
                ORDER BY LastName ASC, FirstName ASC
            END
    END
```

This procedure contains some Transact-SQL (T-SQL) code you haven't seen before. First, note that the parameters have *default* values.

```
    @nameorder char(9) = 'lastfirst',
    @sortorder varchar(4) = 'ASC'
```

The calling code does not have to pass these parameters explicitly, meaning that if you're willing to accept the default name order (last, first) and sort order (ASC), you don't have to pass the parameters at all.

Second, T-SQL supports an IF...ELSE construct. You must place the test between parentheses.

```
    IF (@nameorder='firstlast')
```

If you have more than a single statement following the IF test (called a *statement block*), you must place BEGIN and END statements around the statement block. I've found that it's a good idea to always add the BEGIN and END statements.

Finally, note that when you want to sort by multiple columns in different orders, you must explicitly tell the server the sort order for each column. For example, this clause ORDER BY LastName, Firstname DESC doesn't sort the names in descending order as you might expect. Instead, it sorts by LastName ASC, FirstName DESC, which in this particular case has the effect of applying no sort order whatsoever. Instead, use ORDER BY LastName DESC, Firstname ASC.

You'll also need to create a stored procedure to retrieve the students for a particular teacher. Rather than passing the first and last names, which might be ambiguous if the school acquires two teachers with the same name, the altered procedure accepts a TeacherID. The procedure now returns the StudentID, LastName, and FirstName column values for each student. Doing so requires an additional INNER JOIN clause to the Students table to get the names. Finally, the procedure adds @nameorder and @sortorder parameters that work exactly the same as those in the qryGetTeachers procedure. Here's the new procedure, called qryGetStudentsForTeacherID:

```
CREATE PROCEDURE qryGetStudentsForTeacherID
    @TeacherID int, @nameorder char(9)='lastfirst',
    @sortorder varchar(4)='ASC'
AS
set @nameorder=lower(@nameorder)
set @sortorder=lower(@sortorder)
```

```
IF (@nameorder='firstlast')
    BEGIN
        IF (@sortorder='desc')
            BEGIN
            SELECT TeacherStudent.StudentID, Students.FirstName + ' '
                + Students.LastName AS Name
              FROM TeacherStudent INNER JOIN Teachers
              ON TeacherStudent.TeacherID=Teachers.TeacherID
              INNER JOIN Students
              ON TeacherStudent.StudentID=Students.StudentID
              WHERE Teachers.TeacherID=@TeacherID
              ORDER BY Students.Lastname DESC,
              Students.Firstname ASC
            END
        ELSE
            BEGIN
            SELECT TeacherStudent.StudentID, Students.FirstName + ' '
                + Students.LastName AS Name
              FROM TeacherStudent INNER JOIN Teachers
              ON TeacherStudent.TeacherID=Teachers.TeacherID
              INNER JOIN Students
              ON TeacherStudent.StudentID=Students.StudentID
              WHERE Teachers.TeacherID=@TeacherID
              ORDER BY Students.Lastname ASC,
                  Students.Firstname ASC
            END
    END
ELSE
    BEGIN
        IF (@sortorder='desc')
            BEGIN
            SELECT TeacherStudent.StudentID, Students.LastName + ', '
                + Students.FirstName AS Name
              FROM TeacherStudent INNER JOIN Teachers
              ON TeacherStudent.TeacherID=Teachers.TeacherID
              INNER JOIN Students
              ON TeacherStudent.StudentID=Students.StudentID
              WHERE Teachers.TeacherID=@TeacherID
              ORDER BY Students.Lastname DESC,
                  Students.Firstname ASC
            END
        ELSE
            BEGIN
              SELECT TeacherStudent.StudentID, Students.LastName +
                  ', ' + Students.FirstName AS Name
              FROM TeacherStudent INNER JOIN Teachers
              ON TeacherStudent.TeacherID=Teachers.TeacherID
              INNER JOIN Students
```

```
                ON TeacherStudent.StudentID=Students.StudentID
                WHERE Teachers.TeacherID=@TeacherID
                ORDER BY Students.Lastname ASC,
                    Students.Firstname ASC
            END
        END
    GO
```

Finally, you need to change the code a bit to view and select teachers by ID rather than name. The Web Form ch14-4.aspx contains a new version of the ch14-3.aspx Web Form that uses the updated procedures. I won't show the code here, as it's very similar, but when you run it, it looks like Figure 14.8.

FIGURE 14.8

The Web Form ch14-4.aspx contains a modified version for selecting students of a specific teacher

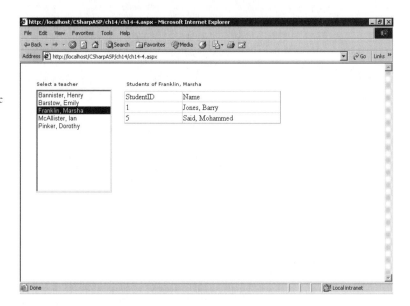

In the next section, you'll work with the DataList and Repeater controls to display data. Then you'll create a Web Form to perform create, update, and delete operations on the student records in the ClassRecords database.

The *DataList* and *Repeater* Web Controls

You've seen a little about how to use a DataGrid control. The DataList control is in some ways even more flexible. A DataList is essentially a repeating list of data items placed into a template. For example, you could write the HTML yourself to repeat items in a DataReader, as you saw in Chapter 13 when you created an HTML table containing the Customers data from the Northwind database:

```
// most database code access code omitted
dr = cm.ExecuteReader(CommandBehavior.CloseConnection);
Response.Write("<table border=\"1\">");
```

```
while (dr.Read()) {
    Response.Write("<tr>");
    for (int i = 0; i < dr.FieldCount; i++) {
        Response.Write("<td>");
        Response.Write(dr.GetValue(i));
        Response.Write(" ");
        Response.Write("</td>");
    }
    Response.Write("</tr>");
}
Response.Write("</table>");
dr.Close();
```

One of the nicest features of classic ASP was that you could easily update the application by changing text files. Now I'll tell you a secret: You haven't lost much of that capability. The ASPX (Web Form HTML definition) files are similar to classic ASP files in that the server recognizes when they change and immediately updates the output—without requiring recompilation of the code-behind classes. You'll see that in action in this section. At the same time, one of the worst features of classic ASP was that if your application depended on COM components (compiled DLLs) and one of the COM components changed, you had to stop the Web server to release the file before you could update it. In .NET, if you *do* need to recompile your application after deploying it, you can simply copy the new DLLs over the old ones, and the server will recognize that change too, and perform a just-in-time (JIT) compile to use the new code. You no longer need to stop the server to replace the DLL files.

At any rate, the server can recognize and serve changes to ASPX files instantly without recompiling the application, because the ASPX files aren't compiled into the application—they're JITed as needed. I'll repeat that, because it's important. The HTML definition of a Web Form, the ASPX file, is not compiled into your application; when you use code-behind classes, the ASPX file acts as a simple HTML file, a template. While a Web Form is one large type of template, the template idea also applies at smaller levels.

TIP   *One convenient side effect is that you can make changes to an ASPX file, save your changes, and immediately rerun the page without recompiling, making it easy to test the effects of template or CSS style modifications.*

There are three types of Web server controls that use templates to define the way the control renders: the `DataList`, `DataGrid`, and `Repeater` controls. I'll concentrate on the `DataList` and `Repeater` controls in this explanation, but there's no substantial difference between the templates for a `DataList` and the templates for the other two controls—in fact, they're often interchangeable. The big difference is that templates for a `DataGrid` apply to columns, whereas templates for the `DataList` and `Repeater` controls apply to rows. The *ideas* in the following section apply to all three controls. Bear in mind that the events they raise are different and have different parameter types, but they are all similar.

Creating a Web Server Control Formatting Template

The `DataList` control isn't just a simple list—it's a way to display multiple rows of items that the user can select and edit. It's actually more like a table than a list box—a table separated into header, item (body), and footer sections. You can provide a separate template for each section. In addition, you can provide four other, not quite so intuitive templates. The `AlternatingItem` template defines how (and whether) rows in the list have alternating formats. For example, you might want every other row to have a light blue background. The `EditItem` template specifies how an item should appear when it's being edited. The `Separator` template defines any items you want to appear between the rows. For example, you might define a custom type of line separator. The `SelectedItem` template controls how selected items appear.

All the templates are optional except the `Item` template. That's easy to remember, because when you drag a `DataList` control onto your Web Form, the designer tells you that you must define an `Item` template.

VS.NET ships with several predefined sets of templates that you can apply, as you've seen with the `DataGrid`, by selecting the control and then clicking the `Auto Format` link that appears below the Properties window. But you don't have to live with the predefined templates. It's not difficult to create your own, and they're reusable, because the template definition can reside in a separate file that's independent from the Web Form and from any specific Web server control. Note that I said *can* reside in a separate file; you can put the template code directly into the ASPX file, although you need to write a little HTML either way.

WRITING TEMPLATES IN THE ASPX FILE

If you decide to write the templates directly into the ASPX file, you must differentiate between the various template types. Each template type (`Header`, `Items`, `AlternatingItems`, `Footer`, and so on) begins and ends with a specific XML tag that controls the type of template being defined. The HTML enclosed in the tag should specify the layout and appearance for the data in the equivalent section of the `DataList`. Table 14.1 shows the template types listed in the first paragraph in this section and the corresponding tag to delimit that template type in the ASPX file.

TABLE 14.1: XML TAGS THAT DEFINE THE TEMPLATE TYPES

TEMPLATE TYPE	TAG	APPLIES TO
Header	<HEADERTEMPLATE>	Repeater, DataList, DataGrid
Footer	<FOOTERTEMPLATE>	Repeater, DataList, DataGrid
Item	<ITEMTEMPLATE>	Repeater, DataList, DataGrid (column)
AlternatingItem	<ALTERNATINGITEMTEMPLATE>	Repeater, DataList, DataGrid (column)
Separator	<SEPARATORTEMPLATE>	Repeater, DataList
SelectedItem	<SELECTEDITEMTEMPLATE>	DataList
EditItem	<EDITITEMTEMPLATE>	DataList
Pager	<PAGERTEMPLATE>	DataGrid

For example, if you place an `Item` template directly into the ASPX file, it might look like this:

```
<Item>
<SPAN class="smallfont" style="COLOR: blue">
<span class="smallfont" style="COLOR: blue">
    <%# DataBinder.Eval(((DataListItem) Container).DataItem,
        "StudentID") %>
</span>  
<span class="smallfont" style="COLOR: blue">
    <%# DataBinder.Eval(((DataListItem) Container).DataItem,
    "Name") %>
</span>
</Item>
```

To insert the data into the template, you bind the `DataList`, `Repeater`, or `DataGrid` control to a data source. For each item, you use a DataBinder class to retrieve the appropriate data. The DataBinder class has one overloaded shared method, `Eval`, which you use to bind a specific data field to the template. One of the overloaded methods takes an object (typically a `DataItem`) and the field name.

WRITING TEMPLATES IN SEPARATE FILES

Another way to use templates is to define them in a separate file. You can load them at runtime and apply them to a Web control by setting one of the Web control's `Template` properties to the loaded `Template` object. You save the template files with an `.ascx` extension.

For example, Listing 14.3 contains the code from the template file `ch14-5ItemTemplate.ascx`. Note that the template contains exactly the same code as the preceding example—but doesn't contain the XML template-type tag (the `<Item>` tag). You don't need the tag because you specify the template type by assigning it to the appropriate Web control property. The properties are named `ItemTemplate`, `AlternatingItemTemplate`, `HeaderTemplate`, and such, so they're easy to remember.

The first line in the template file *must* be the language definition.

LISTING 14.3: A SAMPLE TEMPLATE (ch14-5ItemTemplate.ascx)

```
<%@ Control Language="C#" %>
<span class="smallfont" style="COLOR: blue">
    <%# DataBinder.Eval(((DataListItem) Container).DataItem,
        "StudentID") %>
</span>  
<span class="smallfont" style="COLOR: blue">
    <%# DataBinder.Eval(((DataListItem) Container).DataItem,
    "Name") %>
</span>
```

The code to bind the data items in the template assumes you have a data source containing the fields named `StudentID` and `Name`. The `Container` in the preceding code is the data container—in this case, a `DataReader` object. As the control binds to the data, it extracts the `StudentID` and `Name` values from each row in the `DataReader` and inserts them into the rendered HTML, between the `<span>` tags defined in the template.

Now you need to assign the template to one of the `Template` properties implemented by the `DataList` control. Because the template is in a separate file, you need to load the file, but it's such a common operation that the `Page` object implements a special method called `Page.LoadTemplate` to load the templates into `Template` properties. The method accepts a string containing the virtual path to the template file.

With the `ch14-5ItemTemplate.ascx` file saved in the `ch14` folder in your CSharpASP application, you can load the data and the template, and the control takes care of rendering the HTML for the rows (see Listing 14.4).

LISTING 14.4: THE WEB FORM `ch14-5.aspx` USES AN `ItemTemplate` TO DISPLAY STUDENT DATA FROM THE CLASSRECORDS DATABASE (`ch14-5.aspx.cs`)

```
private void Page_Load(object sender, System.EventArgs e) {
    SqlConnection conn = new
    SqlConnection(ConfigurationSettings.AppSettings.Get
        ("ClassRecordsSql"));
    conn.Open();
    SqlCommand cm = new SqlCommand("Select StudentID,
    Lastname + ', ' " +
        "Firstname AS Name From Students ORDER BY Lastname ASC, " +
        "Firstname ASC", conn);
    SqlDataReader dr = null;
    DataSet ds = new DataSet();
    System.Web.UI.ITemplate template = null;
    dr = cm.ExecuteReader();
    template = Page.LoadTemplate("ch14-5ItemTemplate.ascx");
    DataList1.ItemTemplate = template;
    DataList1.DataSource = dr;
    DataList1.DataBind();
    dr.Close();
    conn.Close();
    conn.Dispose();
}
```

Figure 14.9 shows how the `DataList` renders when you browse to the `ch14-5.aspx` Web Form.

You would follow a similar procedure to add an `AlternatingItemTemplate`, a `Header` or `Footer` template, or any other template.

FIGURE 14.9

`DataList` with an `ItemTemplate` applied

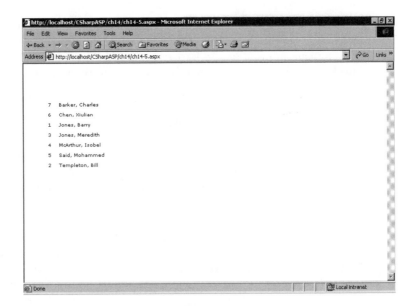

OTHER WAYS TO CREATE TEMPLATES

You can also add a template at design time. Right-click the control and select Edit Template from the context menu, and then select the type of template you want to edit. Fill in the HTML for the template in the designer. Note that you can drag both HTML controls *and Server controls* (see the section "Adding Server Controls to Templates," later in this chapter) into the template editor. For example, you might want to create a `DataList` that contains other controls—such as a "list of lists."

Finally, if you don't need or want to go to quite that much trouble, the simplest possible method is to select the control in the designer and then select a predefined format from the Auto Format link that appears below the Properties window, or build simple templates by clicking the Property Builder link and selecting style properties from the dialogs.

THE BEST WAY TO FORMAT LIST CONTROLS

Because there are so many different ways to create and add templates to the `Repeater`, `DataList`, and `DataGrid` controls, what's the *best* way to do it? That's a tough question, but I think the answer lies firmly in the ASCX template file direction. It's extremely convenient to set properties with property dialogs, and in most cases, the resulting code can show you *how* things work in the background, helping you find the CSS attributes and values you need. But in my opinion, after you understand how things work, you're better off building reusable templates that you can apply quickly at runtime than you are setting multiple properties at design time for each control instance. Not only can you then change templates with a single line of code, you can also ensure that different instances of the controls look and act identically throughout your application or enterprise—and you can modify all the instances at once by updating a single file.

The logic is the same as using CSS styles rather than applying inline styles or worse—using deprecated font tags and formatting attributes to apply font characteristics to your HTML pages. By investing some up-front time to learn how to build and apply templates, you can save a great deal of time later, when you need to repeat the same formats or modify them across an entire application or enterprise.

ADDING SERVER CONTROLS TO TEMPLATES

You aren't limited to pure HTML in templates. The `Repeater`, `DataList`, and `DataGrid` controls can also contain child server controls. For example, suppose you wanted to format each of the items in the Students table as a link. Rather than using an HTML anchor tag, you could use a `LinkButton` control. The `ch14-6.aspx` Web Form contains an example that uses the `Repeater` control rather than a `DataList`.

The `LinkButton` control has `CommandText` and `CommandArgument` attributes. You can take advantage of one or both to send data back to the server when the user clicks the visible link portion of the control. In this case, the template sets the `LinkButton`'s text attribute value to the value of the `Name` field from the query and the `CommandArgument` attribute value to the `StudentID`.

The file `ch14-6ItemTemplate.ascx` contains the template. Here's the template code.

```
<%@ Control Language="C#" %>
<asp:LinkButton
    CommandArgument='<%# DataBinder.Eval(((RepeaterItem)
    Container).DataItem, "StudentID") %>'
    style="Z-INDEX: 101;" runat="server" text='
    <%# DataBinder.Eval(((RepeaterItem) Container).DataItem,
    "Name") %>' />
<br>
```

You can see that the data should display properly, but how can you trap the `LinkButton_Click` event? Because the control isn't part of your Web Form, you can't trap it directly; however, the `Repeater` control has an `ItemCommand` event that provides a way to trap user events. The `ItemCommand` event passes a `RepeaterCommandEventArgument` object that exposes a `CommandSource` property. The `CommandSource` property contains a reference to the control that caused the `ItemCommand` event to fire. For example:

```
private void Repeater1_ItemCommand(object source,
    System.Web.UI.WebControls.RepeaterCommandEventArgs e) {
    Response.Write("You clicked: " +
        ((LinkButton) e.CommandSource).CommandArgument + " ");
    Response.Write(((LinkButton) e.CommandSource).Text);
}
```

The code for the `Page_Load` event retrieves the data, uses the `Page.LoadTemplate` method to load the template as you saw in the preceding section, and fills the `Repeater` control. Because the `Page_Load` method is identical to Listing 14.4, except for the reference to the `Repeater` rather than the `DataList`, I won't repeat it here.

All the Web Form does is display the list of links. When you click a link, it writes `"You clicked "`, along with the `StudentID` and student name that you clicked. Now that you've seen how to display rows of data without writing all the HTML code by hand, how to display data items in lists using the `DataList` and `Repeater` controls, and how to add child controls such as the `LinkButton` example, you can build on those concepts to create a Web Form that lets you update, delete, and insert data.

Deleting, Updating, and Inserting Data

For every nonstatic table you create in your database, it's highly likely that you will need to create a form to delete, update, and insert data in that table. In some simple database applications, you can edit the data in a grid, but more complex applications often present a dialog or new page with a form where users enter data. For many tables, such forms are similar. For readers who have never written database applications where users can change data, here are some guidelines/rules:

1. Never let a user enter freeform data if you can avoid it. Provide choices whenever possible.

2. Choose the input control type based on the column type or contents. For example, use a check box for Boolean fields. Use radio button lists or drop-down lists for selecting single values from a fixed set. Use the `Calendar` control for date entry.

3. Validate all data input, clean it up, and cast it to the correct type before storing it in the database.

You can usually use a single form for all three operations. The user must be able to select an item to edit, meaning that you must provide a way to browse the records and select a row. The user must be able to add a new row or delete a selected one. The Web Form `ch14-5.aspx` lets users modify the contents of the Students table.

I also want to give you an upfront warning—one I'll repeat later in the chapter. In the rest of this chapter, you're going to build a complete but small application to delete, update, and insert data. I've built it this way because it's useful for you to see the "raw" code placed within a Web Form. Here's the warning. What you'll see is *not a good application*; it hasn't been designed properly. Instead, it's representative of applications that are written all too often—you may have even written some yourself. So as you're going through the rest of this chapter, see if you can spot some of the reasons *why* it isn't a good application, and think about what you might do to correct its flaws.

You saw how to use the SQL `INSERT`, `DELETE`, and `UPDATE` commands in Chapter 12. Applying them is straightforward. Most databases update data a row at a time. They delete the existing row, insert the new row, and update the indexes. In SQL Server, updates happen within a transaction, so you can't partially update a row—either the update succeeds completely or it fails completely. Note that just because a data modification process finishes successfully doesn't automatically mean that you got the results you wanted, so you need to test carefully; just as with regular code, it's very easy to code a logic error into T-SQL.

NOTE *In this section and the rest of this chapter, I use dynamic SQL statements. They're easier to see when you're reading examples like this, but you should move them to stored procedures in a production application as soon as you've tested them thoroughly—then test again.*

By extending the formatting template so you have two links associated with each student rather than one, it's easy to provide a way to delete a student record.

NOTE *Don't worry about changing or deleting the data in the ClassRecords database. Whenever you want to recapture the original database, run the* **CreateClassRecords.sql** *file in the Query Analyzer. It will restore the original database tables and values.*

The Web Form ch14-7.aspx displays the student names from the Students table using the template file ch14-7ItemTemplate.ascx. The template uses an ImageButton control to add a small trashcan icon next to each name. An ImageButton is just like a LinkButton except that it displays a clickable image. You can set the CommandArgument property for an ImageButton in exactly the same way as you set the CommandArgument property for a LinkButton. In addition, the template places each name in a <span> tag that provides a fixed width and a border. Because Repeater controls by themselves don't have a position property, a Panel control on the ASP page contains the Repeater control. You can drag the Panel control around the screen to set the layout. Listing 14.5 shows the template code.

LISTING 14.5: ItemTemplate CODE FOR THE Repeater CONTROL IN THE WEB FORM
ch14-7.aspx (ch14-7ItemTemplate.ascx)

```
<%@ Control Language="vb" %>
<span style="border-style:solid; border-width:1; width:180px">
<asp:ImageButton CommandArgument='<%#
    DataBinder.Eval(CType(Container,
    RepeaterItem).DataItem, "StudentID") %>'
    ImageURL="../images/trash.gif" ImageAlign="middle" width="25"
    height="24" runat="server" title="Delete Student">
</asp:ImageButton>
</asp:ImageButton>  
<asp:LinkButton CommandArgument='<%#
    DataBinder.Eval(CType(Container,
    RepeaterItem).DataItem, "StudentID") %>' style="Z-INDEX: 101"
    runat="server" text='<%# DataBinder.Eval(CType(Container,
    RepeaterItem).DataItem, "Name") %>' id="LinkButton2"
    title="Edit
    Student" />
</span>
<br>
```

When you run the ch14-7 Web Form, it looks like Figure 14.10. For now, ignore the radio buttons in the figure that provide delete options; I'll get to that in a minute.

FIGURE 14.10

The list of students
from the Web Form
ch14-7.aspx

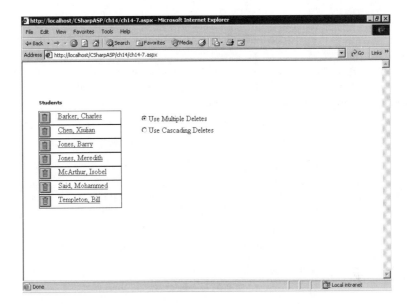

Now all you need to do to delete students is to wire up the click event from the `ImageButton` so that it runs the `Delete` command. You need to add some code to the `Item_Command` event to differentiate between the user clicking the `ImageButton` and the `LinkButton`. Because both controls expose the `CommandArgument` property, the first step is to cast the `RepeaterCommandEventArgs.CommandSource` property to the correct type. Use the `GetType.Name` method to discover the control type name.

For example, if you placed this code in the `Repeater1_ItemCommand` method, you would see the `StudentID` and the student's name when you click a name but only the `StudentID` if you click a trashcan icon.

```
private void Repeater1_ItemCommand(object source,
    System.Web.UI.WebControls.RepeaterCommandEventArgs e) {
    switch (e.CommandSource.GetType().Name) {
        case "LinkButton"  :
            Response.Write("You clicked: " +
                ((LinkButton) e.CommandSource).CommandArgument +
" ");
            Response.Write(((LinkButton) e.CommandSource).Text);
            break;
        case "ImageButton" :
            String aStudentID =
                ((ImageButton) e.CommandSource).CommandArgument;
            Response.Write("You clicked: " +
                ((ImageButton) e.CommandSource).CommandArgument +
" ");
            break;
    }
}
```

DELETING DATA IN A TRANSACTION

When the user clicks one of the `LinkButton` or `ImageButton` controls in the `Repeater` control, the form posts back to the server. Both controls send the `CommandArgument` value. In this example, the `Command-Argument` value is a string object that represents the primary key field (`StudentID`) from the Students table in the `ClassRecords` database. The `StudentID` uniquely identifies a single row in the Students table, so you can use it in the `DELETE` statement to ensure you're deleting the correct row.

Here's the `DELETE` statement:

```
DELETE FROM Students WHERE StudentID=<some StudentID>
```

That seems simple enough. Unfortunately, it won't work. Other tables in the database, specifically the TeacherStudent and StudentClass tables, have *foreign key constraints* defined. You may remember that the foreign key constraint ensures that no one can add a row to the TeacherStudent or Student-Class table if the `StudentID` value for that row doesn't exist in the Students table. The reverse is also true; you can't delete a record from the Students table if that student has been associated with any teachers or classes, because it violates the constraint. There are three ways to solve the problem:

◆ Use multiple `DELETE` statements to delete the rows containing the appropriate `StudentID` from the TeacherStudent and StudentClass tables before deleting the row from the Students table.

◆ Change the relationship between the tables so that deleting a Student record *cascades* the `DELETE` operation to the dependent tables. Cascading deletes is convenient but makes it possible to delete data in tables implicitly by deleting the parent table row.

◆ Write *delete triggers* that delete the dependent table rows. A trigger is an internal database operation that fires when the database takes a specific action. SQL Server supports `INSERT`, `UPDATE`, and `DELETE` triggers. Writing a trigger is very much like writing any other stored procedure.

All three methods are equally valid. Normally, I would probably change the relationship between the tables. Earlier versions of SQL Server did not support cascading deletes, so you *had* to use multiple `DELETE` statements or write delete triggers. Writing database triggers is beyond the scope of this book, but they are an excellent option for performing synchronization operations or enforcing data integrity.

I'll show you how to change the relationship in the upcoming section, "Deleting Data Using Cascading Delete Relationships," but first, I want to explore the multiple `DELETE` statements method because it gives me an opportunity to discuss transactions and how to use them.

The Transaction Class

Whenever you perform multiple dependent operations to a database, you should perform them in the context of a transaction, so if one of the operations fails, you can *roll back* (undo) all the operations, leaving the database in a consistent state. This is extremely important because even with foreign key constraints and cascading deletes, it's possible to delete dependent records (the child side of the relationship) and not delete the parent record. While that may not be critical in any particular case, it can be very difficult to restore the deleted data to put the database back into its original, preoperation state.

In earlier versions of ADO, the `Connection` object managed transactions. In ADO.NET, you begin a transaction similarly, by calling the `Connection` object's `BeginTransaction` method. However, in ADO.NET, the `BeginTransaction` method returns a `Transaction` object. In this case, because the example uses a `SqlConnection` object, the `BeginTransaction` method returns an instance of the

SqlTransaction class. If you're using an OleDbConnection object, the method creates an OleDbTransaction object instead.

After beginning a transaction, you must enlist any Command objects that you subsequently attach to the connection by setting the Command object's Transaction property to the Transaction object returned from the BeginTransaction method. For example:

```
// using statement for the class
using System.Data.SqlClient;
//  other code
SqlConnection conn = new SqlConnection
   (ConfigurationSettings.AppSettings.Get("ClassRecordsSql"));
SqlTransaction trans = null;
SqlCommand cm = new SqlCommand();
conn.Open();
trans = conn.BeginTransaction();
cm.Connection = conn;
cm.Transaction = trans;

// more code here
```

Having begun a transaction, you can subsequently perform multiple operations on the database using that transaction. In the ch14-7.aspx Web Form, the DeleteStudentMultiple method uses multiple DELETE statements to delete a student (see Listing 14.6).

WARNING   *When you run the Web Form* ch14-7.aspx, *don't select the Use Cascading Deletes radio button yet or you'll get an error. Before you can use cascading deletes, you must define a relationship in the database. You'll do that in the next section.*

LISTING 14.6: USING A TRANSACTION TO PERFORM MULTIPLE DEPENDENT DATABASE OPERATIONS (ch14-7.aspx.cs)

```
// at class level
using System.Data.SqlClient;
using System.Configuration;
// other code omitted

private void DeleteStudentMultiple(String StudentID) {
   SqlConnection conn = new SqlConnection
     (ConfigurationSettings.AppSettings.Get("ClassRecordsSql"));
   SqlTransaction trans = null;
   SqlCommand cm = new SqlCommand();
   conn.Open();
   trans = conn.BeginTransaction();
   try {
      cm.Connection = conn;
      cm.Transaction = trans;
      cm.CommandText = "DELETE FROM TeacherStudent WHERE
```

```
          StudentID=" +
              StudentID;
          cm.ExecuteNonQuery();
          cm.CommandText = "DELETE FROM StudentClass WHERE
      StudentID=" +
              StudentID;
          cm.ExecuteNonQuery();
          cm.CommandText = "DELETE FROM Students WHERE
      StudentID=" +
              StudentID;
          cm.ExecuteNonQuery();
          trans.Commit();
      }
      catch (Exception ex) {
          trans.Rollback();
          Response.Write(ex.Message);
      }
      finally {
          trans.Dispose();
          cm.Dispose();
          conn.Close();
          conn.Dispose();
      }
      showStudents();
  }
```

The code is very straightforward. After opening the Connection and beginning the transaction, the method creates three DELETE statements in succession and calls the ExecuteNonQuery method on each one. The ExecuteNonQuery method doesn't return data; instead, it returns an integer value that contains the number of records affected by the command. The example ignores the return value because, in this case, you don't know how many records the DELETE operation might affect *except* for the Students table itself. Even though the example doesn't use the value, it's a good idea to check the return value when you *know* how many records the command should affect. For example, if the ExecuteNonQuery method that deletes the row in the Students table were to return any number other than 1, there's a problem, and you could roll back the transaction.

You've seen one small problem before. The child controls for the Repeater don't exist when the user posts back the page; therefore, the page can't call them unless you create the controls each time. As a result, the Page_Load event calls the showStudents method each time. Doing that creates the controls so that the page can call the Repeater1_ItemCommand method and perform the DELETE operation.

DELETING DATA USING CASCADING DELETE RELATIONSHIPS

You can simplify things considerably by changing the relationships between the Students, Teacher-Student, and StudentClass tables to support cascading deletes. From SQL Server Enterprise Manager, expand the ClassRecords database and right-click the Diagrams item. Select New Database Diagram from the menu. That launches the Create Database Diagram Wizard. Click the Next button to start the wizard. You'll see the dialog in Figure 14.11.

FIGURE 14.11

SQL Server's Create Database Diagram Wizard opened on the ClassRecords database

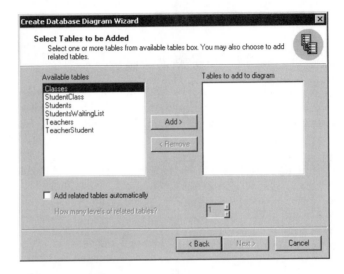

Select the check box titled Add Related Tables Automatically, then select the Students table and click the Add button. The wizard adds three tables to the right list: StudentClass, Students, and TeacherStudent. Click the Next button and then the Finish button to complete the wizard and build the diagram. SQL Server analyzes the tables and their relationships and builds a visual picture showing the tables, fields, and relationships (see Figure 14.12).

FIGURE 14.12

Database diagram for the Students, TeacherStudent, and StudentClass tables

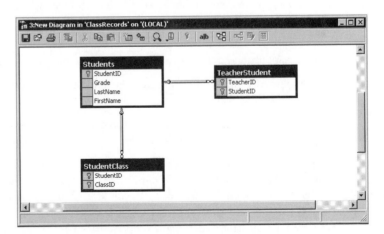

The lines between the tables are the relationships. Right-click the line between the Students and TeacherStudent table and select Properties from the context menu. The Properties dialog shows the details of the relationship between the two tables. I'm not going to explain this dialog in detail, but

near the bottom, you'll see two check boxes. Check the one titled Cascade Delete Related Records. While you're in the dialog, you should also check the Check Existing Data On Creation and Cascade Update Related Fields check boxes. After doing that, click the Close button to close the dialog. Repeat the operation for the relationship between the Students and StudentClass tables. Finally, save the diagram.

WARNING *You must save the diagram for the changes to take effect.*

NOTE *You can also create relationships in SQL Server from the Server Explorer by creating a database diagram, adding tables, and then selecting the relationship lines between the tables. The process is almost exactly the same as the one described for Enterprise Manager. Finally, you can create or change relationships programmatically (see the* ALTER TABLE *statement documentation for details).*

After changing the relationships, you can delete a row in the Students table, and SQL Server will automatically delete the associated rows in the ClassRecords and TeacherStudent tables. That's the reason for the two radio buttons on the ch14-7.aspx Web Form. You can use multiple DELETE statements, as you've already seen or, by checking the Use Cascading Deletes radio button, you can delete the student and the associated rows in the TeacherStudent and StudentClass tables using a single DELETE statement.

NOTE *If you restore the database from the* CreateClassRecords.sql *file, remember to reapply cascading deletes.*

UPDATING DATA

Updating, or changing data, is often more difficult than deleting data because of the need to validate the data. For example, in the Students table, the FirstName and LastName fields may be no longer than 20 characters and may not be null. You have your choice about where to enforce data validity; you can check it on the client, on the server, and in the database itself. In my opinion, you should validate the data in all three places, for the following reasons:

◆ It's best to validate data as close to the user as possible because it improves both the application's responsiveness and the interface; therefore, you should validate data on the client.

◆ A programmer might call your page from a different location, sending unvalidated data; therefore, you should also validate data on the server.

◆ Another programmer might use your stored procedures to insert or update data; therefore, you should always validate data in the stored procedures themselves.

Because this example uses dynamic SQL, I'm not going to show you the T-SQL code to validate the data. In addition, to simplify the example, I'm not going to add Validation controls to validate the data on the client, because you've already seen examples of those. Instead, I'll write a little code to perform the validation on the server.

In this case, it's difficult to determine programmatically that a set of characters submitted by a user is *not* a valid name, but you can check a few things. For example, you can ensure the following:

◆ That the names submitted aren't null

◆ That they don't contain spaces

- ◆ That they are at least two characters long

- ◆ That they don't exceed 20 characters

- ◆ That they don't contain numbers or other non-alphabetic characters

- ◆ That they begin with a capital letter

The Web Form `ch14-8.aspx` has most of the functionality of the Web Form `ch14-7.aspx`, but the controls are slightly rearranged. Clicking a name doesn't just display the name on the server; instead, the Web Form places the name in a `TextBox` control so that the user can edit the selected name. The Web Form tracks the `StudentID` of the selected student by placing it in a `Label` control named `lblStudentID`. The controls to edit the name are invisible (`Visibility=false`) until the user selects a name (see Figure 14.13).

FIGURE 14.13

The Web Form `ch14-8.aspx` editing a student name

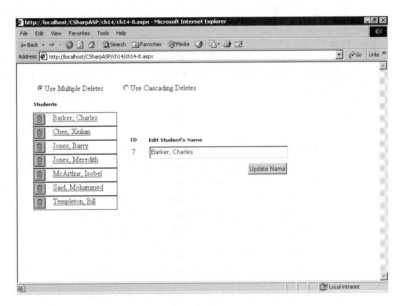

After the user edits the name and clicks the `Update Name` button, the server validates the data. If the data passes validation, an `updateStudent` method updates the database, hides the edit controls, and redisplays the updated list.

WARNING   *Be sure to define the cascading delete relationship in the database before running the* `ch14-8.aspx` *example; otherwise, you'll get an error if you try to use cascading deletes to delete a student. See the section "Deleting Data Using Cascading Delete Relationships," earlier in this chapter for more information.*

Listing 14.7 shows the routines that handle displaying and updating the student name.

LISTING 14.7: THE WEB FORM ch14-8 **LETS YOU EDIT A STUDENT'S NAME AND UPDATES THE DATABASE WITH THE NEW VALUE (**ch14-8.aspx.cs**)**

```csharp
using System;
using System.Collections;
using System.ComponentModel;
using System.Data;
using System.Drawing;
using System.Web;
using System.Web.SessionState;
using System.Web.UI;
using System.Web.UI.WebControls;
using System.Web.UI.HtmlControls;
using System.Data.SqlClient;
using System.Configuration;
using System.Text.RegularExpressions;

namespace CSharpASP.ch14
{
    /// <summary>
    /// Summary description for ch14_8.
    /// </summary>
    public class ch14_8 : System.Web.UI.Page {
        protected System.Web.UI.WebControls.Label Label1;
        protected System.Web.UI.WebControls.Repeater Repeater1;
        protected System.Web.UI.WebControls.Panel Panel1;
        protected System.Web.UI.WebControls.RadioButtonList
            RadioButtonList1;
        protected System.Web.UI.WebControls.Label lblStudentName;
        protected System.Web.UI.WebControls.TextBox txtStudentName;
        protected System.Web.UI.WebControls.Button btnStudentName;
        protected System.Web.UI.WebControls.Label
lblStudentNameError;
        protected System.Web.UI.WebControls.Label lblStudentID;
        protected System.Web.UI.WebControls.Label lblStudentIDLabel;

        private void Page_Load(object sender, System.EventArgs e) {
            showStudents();
            showEditNameGroup(false);

        }
        private void Repeater1_ItemCommand(object source,
            System.Web.UI.WebControls.RepeaterCommandEventArgs e) {
            switch (e.CommandSource.GetType().Name) {
                case "LinkButton"  :
                    showEditNameGroup(true);
                    txtStudentName.Text = ((LinkButton)
                        e.CommandSource).Text;
```

```
                lblStudentID.Text = ((LinkButton)
                   e.CommandSource).CommandArgument;
                lblStudentNameError.Text = "";
                break;
            case "ImageButton" :
                String aStudentID = ((ImageButton)
                   e.CommandSource).CommandArgument;
            switch (RadioButtonList1.SelectedItem.Value) {
                case "Multiple" :
                   DeleteStudentMultiple(aStudentID);
                   break;
                case "Cascading" :
                   DeleteStudent(aStudentID);
                   break;
            }
                break;
        }
    }
    private void showEditNameGroup(Boolean b) {
        lblStudentName.Visible = b;
        txtStudentName.Visible = b;
        lblStudentNameError.Visible = b;
        btnStudentName.Visible = b;
        lblStudentIDLabel.Visible = b;
        lblStudentID.Visible = b;
    }
    private void clearEditNameGroup() {
        txtStudentName.Text = "";
        lblStudentID.Text = "";
    }

    private void showStudents() {
        SqlConnection conn = new SqlConnection

(ConfigurationSettings.AppSettings.Get("ClassRecordsSql"));
        conn.Open();
        SqlCommand cm = new SqlCommand("Select StudentID, " +
          "Lastname + ', ' + Firstname AS Name From Students " +
          "ORDER BY Lastname ASC, Firstname ASC", conn);
        SqlDataReader dr = null;
        DataSet ds = new DataSet();
        dr = cm.ExecuteReader();
        Repeater1.ItemTemplate = Page.LoadTemplate
           ("ch14-7ItemTemplate.ascx");
        Repeater1.DataSource = dr;
        Repeater1.DataBind();
        dr.Close();
        conn.Close();
```

```
            conn.Dispose();
        }

        private void DeleteStudentMultiple(String StudentID) {
            SqlConnection conn = new SqlConnection

(ConfigurationSettings.AppSettings.Get("ClassRecordsSql"));
            SqlTransaction trans = null;
            SqlCommand cm = new SqlCommand();
            conn.Open();
            trans = conn.BeginTransaction();
            try {
                cm.Connection = conn;
                cm.Transaction = trans;
                cm.CommandText = "DELETE FROM TeacherStudent " +
                    "WHERE StudentID=" + StudentID;
                cm.ExecuteNonQuery();
                cm.CommandText = "DELETE FROM StudentClass WHERE " +
                    "StudentID=" + StudentID;
                cm.ExecuteNonQuery();
                cm.CommandText = "DELETE FROM Students WHERE " + "
                    StudentID=" + StudentID;
                cm.ExecuteNonQuery();
                trans.Commit();
            }
            catch (Exception ex) {
                trans.Rollback();
                Response.Write(ex.Message);
            }
            finally {
                cm.Dispose();
                conn.Close();
                conn.Dispose();
            }
            showStudents();
        }

        private void DeleteStudent(String StudentID) {
            SqlConnection conn = new SqlConnection

(ConfigurationSettings.AppSettings.Get("ClassRecordsSql"));
            SqlCommand cm = new SqlCommand();
            try {
                conn.Open();
                cm.Connection = conn;
                cm.CommandText = "DELETE FROM Students WHERE " +
                    "StudentID=" + StudentID;
                cm.ExecuteNonQuery();
```

```
        }
        catch (Exception ex) {
           Response.Write(ex.Message);
        }
        finally {
           cm.Dispose();
           conn.Close();
           conn.Dispose();
        }
        showStudents();
}
#region Web Form Designer generated code
override protected void OnInit(EventArgs e) {
        //
        // CODEGEN: This call is required by the ASP.NET
        // Web Form Designer.
        //
        InitializeComponent();
        base.OnInit(e);
}

/// <summary>
/// Required method for Designer support - do not modify
/// the contents of this method with the code editor.
/// </summary>
private void InitializeComponent() {
        this.Repeater1.ItemCommand += new
           System.Web.UI.WebControls.RepeaterCommandEventHandler
           (this.Repeater1_ItemCommand);
        this.btnStudentName.Click += new
           System.EventHandler(this.btnStudentName_Click);
        this.Load += new System.EventHandler(this.Page_Load);

}
#endregion

private void btnStudentName_Click(object sender,
        System.EventArgs e) {
        String aName;
        String[] names;
        String first, last;
        aName = this.txtStudentName.Text;
        if (aName != null) {
           try {
              names = aName.Split(',');
              if (names.Length < 2) {
              throw new Exception("You must enter a last and " +
                 "first name, for example: Talbert, Melinda.");
```

```
                }
                else if (names.Length > 2) {
                    // too many names
                    throw new Exception("You may only enter a last " +
                        "name, a comma and a first name.");
                }
                else {
                    this.lblStudentNameError.Text = "";

                    last = names[0];
                    first = names[1];
                    if (validateName(ref last, ref first)) {
                    updateName(this.lblStudentID.Text, last, first);
                    }
                    this.showEditNameGroup(false);
                    showStudents();
                }
            }
            catch (Exception ex) {
                this.lblStudentNameError.Text = ex.Message;
                this.showEditNameGroup(true);
            }
        }
    }
    private Boolean validateName(ref String last,
    ref String first) {
        try {
            // trim leading and trailing spaces
            first = first.Trim();
            last = last.Trim();
            // name can't be null
            ensureStringLength(first, 2, 20);
            ensureStringLength(last, 2, 20);
            ensureAlphaOnly(first);
            ensureAlphaOnly(last);
            last = last.Substring(0, 1).ToUpper() +
last.Substring(1);
            first = first.Substring(0, 1).ToUpper() +
                first.Substring(1);
            return(true);
        }
        catch (Exception ex) {
            throw ex;
        }
    }
    private void ensureStringLength(String s, int min, int max)
{
        if ((s.Length < min) | (s.Length > max)) {
```

```
              throw new Exception("String must be between " +
                 min.ToString() + " and " + max.ToString() +
                 " in length.");
           }
       }
       private void ensureAlphaOnly(String s) {
           Regex rx = new Regex("[a-zA-Z']");
           if (rx.Matches(s).Count < s.Length) {
               throw new Exception("A name may only contain " +
                   "alphabetic characters.");
           }
       }
       private void updateName(String StudentID, String last,
           String first) {
           SqlConnection conn = new SqlConnection

   (ConfigurationSettings.AppSettings.Get("ClassRecordsSql"));
           SqlCommand cm = new SqlCommand
            ("UPDATE Students SET LastName='" +
            last + "', FirstName='" + first + "' WHERE StudentID=" +
            StudentID, conn);
           try {
              conn.Open();
              cm.ExecuteNonQuery();
           }
           catch (Exception ex) {
              this.lblStudentNameError.Text = ex.Message;
           }
           finally {
              cm.Dispose();
              conn.Close();
              conn.Dispose();
           }
       }

   }
}
```

INSERTING DATA

Inserting data works much the same way as updating data, but you use an INSERT command. There are many ways of handling the INSERT operation. The Web Form ch14-9.aspx handles it by checking the value of the lblStudentID Label control. In the preceding section, the Web Form ch14-8.aspx set the value of that label to the string value of the selected student's StudentID. In addition, the Update Name button is visible only when the user is adding either a new name or an existing name. Therefore, when the Update Name button Click event fires, if the lblStudentID Label control has no value, the user is adding a new name. There's one other consideration. The Students table has a column called Grade, which you didn't deal with in the preceding sections. To insert a new row, you must have a Grade value, so the Web Form adds a DropDownList control that lets the user select the new student's grade. Of course, that adds one more validation check because you can't provide a default value—there's no such thing as grade 0. Therefore, you must ensure that the user has selected a grade. Figure 14.14 shows how the Web Form looks when you first run it. Note the AddStudent button.

FIGURE 14.14

The Web Form ch14-9.aspx lets a user edit, delete, and insert students

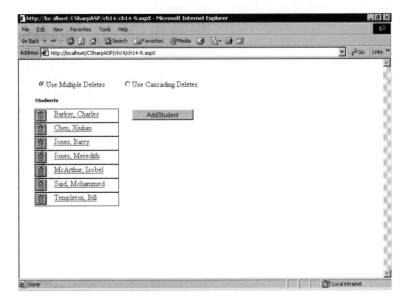

WARNING   Be sure to define the cascading delete relationship in the database before running the ch14-9.aspx example; otherwise, you'll get an error if you try to use cascading deletes to delete a student. See the section "Deleting Data Using Cascading Delete Relationships" earlier in this chapter for more information.

When a user clicks the AddStudent button, the Web Form displays a group of controls for entering a name and selecting the grade for the new student (see Figure 14.15).

Except for the routine that inserts the new student row, I won't display the code for the Web Form here because of its similarity to the ch14-8.aspx example.

```
private void insertName(String last, String first, String Grade) {
    SqlConnection conn = new SqlConnection
        (ConfigurationSettings.AppSettings.Get("ClassRecordsSql"));
    SqlCommand cm = new SqlCommand("INSERT INTO Students " +
        "(LastName, FirstName,Grade) VALUES ('" + last + "','" +
        first + "', " + Grade + ")", conn);
    try {
        conn.Open();
        cm.ExecuteNonQuery();
```

```
        showAddNameGroup(false);
    }
    catch (Exception ex) {
        lblStudentNameError.Text = ex.Message;
    }
    finally {
        cm.Dispose();
        conn.Close();
        conn.Dispose();
    }
}
```

FIGURE 14.15

The Web Form
ch14-9.aspx lets a
user edit, delete, and
insert students

How Not to Write an Application

You've seen the basic operations to insert, update, and delete data from a Web Form, but you may have noticed that as you added each bit of functionality, the code to manage the interface and the data became more and more complicated—and more intertwined. Code like that in ch14-9.aspx is difficult to maintain. Therefore, I wanted to stop here, give you the following warning, and discuss just a little about application design.

WARNING   *Don't write Web Forms like you just saw in the preceding sections! They're easy to create but difficult to maintain or change.*

You may be thinking, "But the application works! Why change it now?" Yes, it does work, but that's about all you can say about it, because it violates many guidelines of good application design. In fact, the application has no design—like many applications, the Web Form grew from the need to provide functionality for users. Like most such applications, what started as a simple display screen quickly became complex and difficult to manage. Worse, it's not reusable. The *ideas* behind updating, inserting, and deleting records are generic, but the *implementation* is entirely specific to the Students table.

The Web Form ch14-9.aspx has three separate functions, but all of them deal with a single type of data—the data from one or more rows in the Students table. Note how complicated it is to maintain the values from one page to another because each function demands slightly different data. Also, look at the amount of code that deals with hiding and showing various elements of the user interface. Admittedly, ASP.NET's built-in page state maintenance (__VIEWSTATE) makes it seem easy, but it can also, as in this case, encourage you to use hidden labels, lists, and other controls to maintain state data rather than planning the application better to begin with.

Here's another way to look at the application. First, you know that you'll be dealing with individual students and lists of students. Wouldn't it be much easier if you built a Student class and a Students collection? By doing that, you would have all the data for any particular student available at any time— whether you wanted to edit, delete, or insert a new student. By creating an object from the data, you can insulate most programmers from having to know exactly how the object stores data. In other words, should every programmer interacting with the Students table have to know the validation rules for names in order to write code that uses the table? Probably not.

Second, as I've already mentioned, it's not a good idea (except during initial application testing) to write dynamic SQL statements. It's better to write stored procedures, which are both faster and reusable. In fact, I'd go so far as to say that you should deny most programmers access to the database *except* through stored procedures and views. By doing that, you minimize problems, simplify the code, eliminate dynamic SQL statements, and isolate errors to a single location, all in one fell swoop.

Third, there's no point in forcing programmers to write the code to open the database, create a Command object, execute a procedure or statement, and clean up for every single statement. In essence, the process of executing a stored procedure is identical *every time*, and the only difference lies in whether the procedure returns data. Therefore, you should abstract that code by creating a single class that retrieves data and executes commands. By doing that, you can create extremely robust applications with Application scope error checking, error logging, and error display capabilities.

Fourth, the application is not network friendly. While it doesn't matter during development or with the tiny amounts of data in the ClassRecords database, it would be much more efficient if the user could make multiple alterations to data without performing as many round trips or requesting the data from the database (sometimes twice) for every click. In the next chapter, you'll see how you can use DataSets and XML to create applications that don't require as much network bandwidth.

Fifth, the application violates data entry rules by letting users edit both the first and last student names in the same field, which in turn leads to some error-prone code to separate the names again to store them into the database. There's no good reason to put both names into a single field—the application might just as well present two fields, one for each name, and avoid the problem.

Finally, rather than writing validation routines into a Web Form, it would be much more efficient to create them in a class that you could reuse. Sure, you could perform data validation in a Student class—and you should—but data object classes are not the proper place for the validation routines themselves unless they're specific to that object. After you realize you're going to be writing validation routines for every alterable field in your table, you'll also see the advantages of creating a `Validator` class that performs all the common validation functions for you.

I'm not going to write a revised version of the code for you. Instead, I'll show you how C# and ASP.NET applications can change the way you think about writing code.

Summary

In this chapter, you've seen how to access databases in C# Web applications using SQL statements and stored procedures, both with and without parameters. You've also seen how to format and display that data using data-bound controls and templates, such as the `DataList`. Finally, you've seen how to delete, update, and insert data; how to create relationships that can delete related records in dependent tables using cascading deletes; and how to perform multiple actions within a transaction. I hope you've also thought a little bit about how deceptively easy it is to create an application that's difficult to maintain or modify. In the next chapter, you'll explore how to access, read, and transform XML documents using the .NET XML classes, and you'll see ways you can use XML in your Web applications.

Chapter 15

Using XML in Web Applications

DESPITE THE RELATIVE YOUTH of the XML specification, it has rapidly become a major focus of Web programming. XML is the underpinning for the newest version of HTML, called XHTML; it's the basis of Web Services, and in combination with the XSLT and XPath recommendations, it's one of the most effective ways to ensure the separation of your data from the interface that displays the data. XML is a crucial part of .NET, so it's not surprising that the framework provides some sophisticated, powerful, and flexible methods for reading, writing, and transforming XML data. You'll find the classes you need to manipulate XML in the System.Xml namespace.

In this chapter:

◆ Introduction to the System.Xml Namespace

◆ Reading XML Documents

◆ Using the XmlDataDocument Class

◆ The XmlException Classes

◆ Performing XSLT Transforms Programmatically

◆ Moving to Applications

Introduction to the System.Xml Namespace

The System.Xml namespace contains all the classes you need to work with XML in .NET. At the most basic level, the XmlDocument class lets you load and save XML documents from disk files or from strings. If you've worked with XML in other systems such as Microsoft's own msxml.dll, you'll recognize XmlDocument as similar to the root object in those systems. An XmlDocument object uses a *parser* to read the XML document and create a node tree: a hierarchical representation of the elements, attributes, and text in the document. For example, to initiate the parsing process for an XML document, you create an XmlDocument instance and pass the file you want to parse to its Load method:

```
XmlDocument xml = new XmlDocument();
Xml.Load(physical filename of XML document);
Response.Write(xml.InnerXml);
```

The code fragment loads an XML document and sends the XML string contents to the client.

What Can You Do with XML?

XML documents, by themselves, are easy for humans to read but aren't that useful to the computer. By themselves, they aren't much better than any other sequential file format—just a wordier, if easier to parse, text file format. To make them useful, you need to add some functionality. In addition to the basic XmlDocument, the System.Xml namespace contains "helper" classes that provide the capability to

◆ Find nodes and values

◆ Define the structure and data for an XML document

◆ Let you traverse a document sequentially without cacheing the data in memory

◆ Transform a document into another form

◆ Move seamlessly between XML and relational data

◆ Read and write XML files

RETRIEVE INDIVIDUAL NODES OR GROUPS OF NODES—*SYSTEM.XML.XPATH*

An XML file consists of a tree of *nodes*. Each node may be an element, an attribute, a comment, a processing instruction, or a character data (CDATA) section, or any of several less common node types. An XML document contains markup that conforms to strict rules. Therefore, you can teach the parser to separate the markup from content easily, but you need to be able to retrieve individual nodes or collections of nodes to find data quickly. You do that using System.Xml.XPath. The XPath specification describes a vocabulary for navigating through the node tree.

DEFINE THE STRUCTURE AND DATA TYPES IN AN XML DOCUMENT—*SYSTEM.XML.SCHEMA*

Over the years, the computer industry has standardized on many file formats for various types of information. For example, each of the many types of image formats (.gif, .bmp, .jpg, and so on) has a specific file format. Only by rigidly adhering to this file format can you create a GIF file and have applications display it correctly. There's no room for customization—the file format is fixed. For those of you who have worked with Windows since version 3 days, another common example is INI (application initialization) files, which—before the Windows Registry—were the premier way to store application-specific information. An INI file had three customizable levels—a set of *sections* enclosed in square brackets, each of which could contain *keys* and *values* separated by an equal (=) sign. You can think of these three items as hierarchical levels, where level one is the sections, which had two child levels—the keys and the values. For example:

```
[section1]
key1=value1
[section2]
key1=value1
key2=value2
```

Unfortunately, without performing customized manipulations on the key or value string, there was no way to go beyond the three fixed items. The equivalent XML document could look like Listing 15.1.

LISTING 15.1: A SIMPLE XML FILE THAT HOLDS INI FILE TYPE INFORMATION (XML-INI.xml)

```xml
<?xml version="1.0"?>
<sections>
   <section name="Section1">
      <key name"key1" value="value1" />
   </section>
   <section name="Section">
      <key name"key1" value="value1" />
      <key name"key2" value="value2" />
   <section>
</sections>
```

In this form, the section name for each section, along with the keys and values, has become an *attribute*. Attributes are fast and easy to read but not as flexible as elements. However, you aren't constrained to using attributes. Listing 15.2 shows an extended version that uses elements rather than attributes. You can extend the number of levels or the number of items associated with a particular key very easily.

LISTING 15.2: THE XML DOCUMENT EXTENDS THE INI FILE FORMAT (XML_INI2.xml)

```xml
<?xml version="1.0" encoding="utf-8"?>
<sections xmlns="http://tempuri.org/XML-INI2.xsd">
   <section>
     <name>Section1</name>
     <keys>
       <key>
         <name>key1</name>
         <value>value1</value>
       </key>
     </keys>
   </section>
   <section>
     <name>Section2</name>
     <keys>
       <key>
         <name>key1</name>
         <value>value1</value>
       </key>
       <key>
         <name>key2</name>
         <value>value2</value>
       </key>
     </keys>
   </section>
</sections>
```

Because XML data can appear in so many forms, you need to be able to describe exactly what any specific XML document can contain. A *schema* lets you do this. I'm not going to go into much depth about schemas in this book because you don't need to know much about them to use XML efficiently. However, it's useful to know what a schema *does*. For each element and attribute, the schema defines the name and the value type. Elements can be simple (they contain only a value) or complex (they may contain a combination of other elements and attributes and a value). For example, in the first XML INI file example, the element <sections> is a complex element that contains one child element— <section>. In turn, each <section> element is a complex element that contains one attribute called name and one complex element named key. Here's a portion of the schema for the XML-INI.xml document that shows the <section> element definition:

```
<xsd:element name="section">
  <xsd:complexType>
    <xsd:sequence>
      <xsd:element name="key" minOccurs="0"
        maxOccurs="unbounded">
      <xsd:complexType>
        <xsd:attribute name="name" form="unqualified"
          type="xsd:string" />
        <xsd:attribute name="value" form="unqualified"
          type="xsd:string" />
        <xsd:attribute name="section_Id" type="xsd:int"
          use="prohibited" />
      </xsd:complexType>
      </xsd:element>
    </xsd:sequence>
    <xsd:attribute name="section_Id" msdata:AutoIncrement="true"
      type="xsd:int" msdata:AllowDBNull="false"
      use="prohibited" />
    <xsd:attribute name="name" form="unqualified"
      type="xsd:string"/>
  </xsd:complexType>
</xsd:element>
```

You can see that the <section> element is a complex element. Look carefully at the attributes for the key element. There are three, even though I only used two: name and value. The VS XML editor defined the section_Id element automatically. In fact, the VS XML editor defined the entire schema automatically by looking at the XML document elements and making a guess as to the types. Letting the IDE generate the schema is extremely convenient. In addition, you can use the schema it creates to define the data in a DataSet. By creating such a schema, you can load your XML directly into a DataSet and then bind it to controls.

TRANSFORM XML DOCUMENTS—*SYSTEM.XML.XSL*

XML data is *mutable*—you can change it from one form of XML into another form, using an XML vocabulary called XSL (Extensible Stylesheet Language) or XSLT (Extensible Stylesheet Language Transformations). The most popular use of XSLT has been to transform it into HTML or, more precisely, XHTML, which is simply HTML cleaned up so that it conforms to the XML specification. The advantage of transforms is that you cleanly separate the data from the markup, because the data is in the XML file, while the markup is in an XSLT file called a *stylesheet*. Using Internet Explorer, you can view the results of a transform simply by loading an XML file. That's because IE contains a *default stylesheet* that it applies to XML documents that don't define their own stylesheets. Listing 15.3 shows a simple XML document called `flexible.xml`.

LISTING 15.3: THE `flexible.xml` XML FILE

```
<?xml version="1.0" encoding="utf-8" ?>
<!--<?xml-stylesheet type="text/xsl" href="flexible.xsl" ?>-->
<items>
    <item>XML </item>
    <item>is </item>
    <item>an </item>
    <item>extremely </item>
    <item>flexible </item>
    <item>data </item>
    <item>format </item>
</items>
```

If you request the file `flexible.xml` in IE, it looks like Figure 15.1.

FIGURE 15.1

The `flexible.xml` file in IE, displayed with the default stylesheet

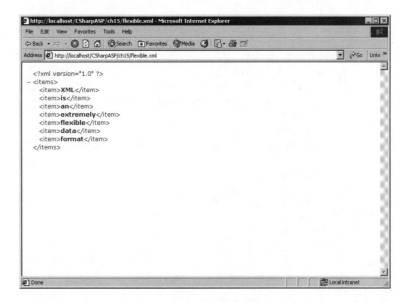

Note that the default stylesheet color codes the various parts of the document and clearly shows the tree structure. It even lets you expand and collapse tags that contain child elements. That's nice, but fortunately, you're not limited to using the default stylesheet. By including a tag that references an XSL or XSLT stylesheet, IE will perform the transform for you and display the results.

For example, the following stylesheet displays the items in an HTML ListBox control (see Listing 15.4).

LISTING 15.4: THE flexible.xsl FILE CREATES AN HTML ListBox CONTAINING THE ITEMS FROM THE flexible.xml FILE (flexible.xsl)

```
<?xml version='1.0'?>
<xsl:stylesheet version="1.0"
    xmlns:xsl="http://www.w3.org/1999/XSL/Transform">

<xsl:output method="html" />

<xsl:template match="/">
    <html>
    <head>
    <title>Simple XSLT Stylesheet</title>
    </head>
    <body>
        <xsl:apply-templates select="items"/>
    </body>
    </html>
</xsl:template>

<xsl:template match="items">
    <form>
    <select id="list1" style="position:absolute; top: 100;
    left: 100; width: 150;
        height: 300" size="20">
        <xsl:apply-templates select="item" />
    </select>
    </form>
</xsl:template>

<xsl:template match="item">
    <option>
        <xsl:value-of select="." />
    </option>
</xsl:template>
</xsl:stylesheet>
```

Performing Client-Side Transforms Using IE5x

Client-side (in-browser) XSLT transforms work only with IE5 and higher; at the time of this writing, no other browser supports XSLT transforms on the client side. In addition, to take maximum advantage of XSLT on the client, you must have the `msxml3.dll` or `msxml4.dll` parser installed on the client computer. Finally, if you're using `msxml3.dll`, you must download and run the `xmlinst.exe` file for IE to recognize the XSLT namespace. IE 6 ships with `msxml3`, so you don't need to install the updated parser if you're running IE 6 or later.

Uncomment the following highlighted line in the `flexible.xml` file:

```
<?xml version="1.0" ?>
<?xml-stylesheet type="text/xsl" href="flexible.xsl" ?>
<items>
    <item>XML </item>
    <item>is </item>
    <item>an </item>
    <item>extremely </item>
    <item>flexible </item>
    <item>data </item>
    <item>format </item>
</items>
```

When you load the file `flexible.xml` into IE, it recognizes the file type and parses the document. The processing instruction you just uncommented instructs the browser to load the stylesheet `flexible` `.xsl`, perform the transform, and display the results of the transform rather than the XML document itself.

If you're not familiar with XSLT, this book won't help you much, but I will briefly walk you through the `flexible.xsl` stylesheet.

```
<?xml version='1.0'?>
<xsl:stylesheet version="1.0"
       xmlns:xsl="http://www.w3.org/1999/XSL/Transform">
```

You can see from the first line that XSLT is an XML vocabulary, not a separate language. You can manipulate XSLT files by loading them into an `XmlDocument` just as you can any other XML file.

The second line of code references the XSLT *namespace* schema URI (Universal Resource Identifier). A URI is different from a URL in that it only needs to be unique. It doesn't need to reference a real file (although it can); it only needs to be a unique identifier. For example, if you enter the XSLT namespace into a browser, you'll see a page that shows the W3C logo and the text, "This is an XML namespace defined in the XSL Transformations (XSLT) Version 1.0 specification" along with some W3C links. You won't see the XSLT namespace schema itself because it isn't there. Instead, IE has an internal reference to the schema—you created that reference when you installed the `msxml3.dll` and ran the `xmlinst.exe` file.

The next line determines the type of output from the transform. Valid values are `html`, `xml`, and `text`. The default output type is `xml`.

```
<xsl:output method="html" />
```

The remainder of the file consists of three templates. A *template* is a block of code that handles a specific tag or group of tags. The `match` attribute in the template definition determines which tags a particular template will handle. For example, the first template matches the root node of the XML document. XSLT works from the concept of a *context node*. Until you select a node, there is no context. In this stylesheet, the root template creates <html>, <head>, <title>, and <body> tags and then tells the stylesheet to select the <items> node and apply a template to it.

```
<xsl:template match="/">
   <html>
   <head>
   <title>Simple XSLT Stylesheet</title>
   </head>
   <body>
      <xsl:apply-templates select="items"/>
   </body>
   </html>
</xsl:template>
```

The stylesheet searches for a template that matches the name items (see the next code fragment). When the stylesheet begins processing the items template, the <items> node becomes the context node, not the root node. Select queries within the items template work from the <items> node by default; in other words, changing templates is one way to change the context.

The template outputs a <form> tag and a <select> tag, then calls xsl:apply-templates again, this time selecting the item nodes first. Note that the select="item" attribute selects *all* the <item> elements, and the xsl:apply-templates method applies the matching item template once for each node in the list of item nodes.

```
<xsl:template match="items">
   <form>
   <select id="list1" style="position:absolute; top: 100;
   left: 100; width: 150;
      height: 300" size="20">
      <xsl:apply-templates select="item" />
   </select>
   </form>
</xsl:template>
```

The item template itself (see the following) writes an <option> tag and outputs the value of the context node—in this case, an <item> element. The highlighted line in the template uses a shortcut notation to select the current node, select=".". The value of a node is the text it contains. Each <item> node in the flexible.xml file contains a single word and a space.

```
<xsl:template match="item">
   <option>
      <xsl:value-of select="." />
   </option>
</xsl:template>
</xsl:stylesheet>
```

The stylesheet "walks the tree" from the root node to the lowest-level node, applying a template at each level. Figure 15.2 shows the result.

FIGURE 15.2

Result from transforming `flexible.xml` using the XSLT stylesheet `flexible.xsl`

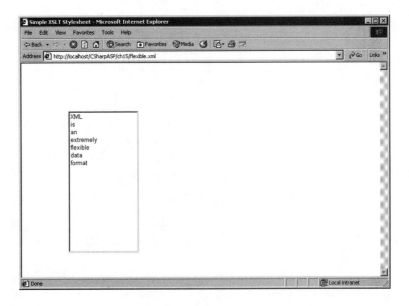

Interestingly, if you view the source in the browser, you'll see only the XML document. You won't see the HTML for the transform results, and you won't see the XSLT stylesheet code.

Performing Server-Side Transforms

As I mentioned in the note at the start of the previous section, client-side automatic transforms are useful only if all your clients use IE. Future browser versions and other client types will no doubt support more XML/XSLT operations, but right now, the only cross-client solution is to perform the transform on the server and send the XHTML result to the client.

NOTE Before you continue, comment out or delete the line that defines the stylesheet reference in the `flexible.xml` *file in the* `ch15` *folder of your CSharpASP project. Remember that XML comments are the same as HTML comments (*`<!-- -->`*). Save the changes, then continue.*

There are several ways to perform XSLT transforms in .NET, but the *easiest* way is to drag an XML Web server control onto your Web Form's design surface. For example, create a new Web Form named `ch15-1.aspx` in the `ch15` folder. Add an XML Server control and click the Custom Property button in the Properties dialog for the `DocumentSource` property. In the resulting dialog, select the `ch15` folder in the `Projects` pane and then select the `flexible.xml` file from the Contents pane. You'll see the dialog in Figure 15.3.

Accept the default settings and click OK to close the dialog. Repeat the process to set the `Transform-Source` property to the `flexible.xsl` file. Now run the Web Form. The result looks identical to performing the client-side transform, but it isn't. You can prove that to yourself by viewing the browser source. This time, rather than the XML file contents, you'll see the HTML resulting from the transform. In other words, the server performed the transform for you and automatically sent the result to the browser.

FIGURE 15.3

The Select XML
File dialog

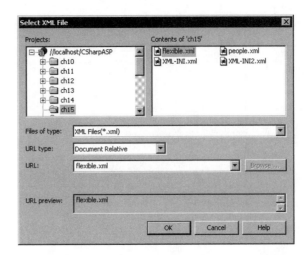

The Xml Web server control is extremely convenient, but what if you need to process an XML document in some other way, such as extracting only some individual data items, saving all or a selected portion of a document to a database, or performing a transform and then modifying the results using C#? To do that, you need to learn a little more about how XML works in .NET and about the classes available in the System.Xml namespace.

Reading XML Documents

As you've seen, the XmlDocument object provides a Read method that reads an XML document and initiates parsing, but underneath, the Read method creates an XmlReader object and uses that to read the document. Of course, underneath the XmlTextReader is a TextReader object. The XmlTextReader wraps the TextReader and implements rules for accessing the content that apply specifically to the process of reading XML. Beyond the physical process of reading the file, there are several different ways of approaching the parse problem.

DOM versus SAX

Until .NET, there were two primary ways to access data in an XML document. The XmlDocument object implements the node tree, as I've already explained. Using an XmlDocument is very efficient when you need to update or extract data from a document multiple times and you don't know in advance *where* the data lies within the document. For example, suppose you have an XML document containing 50,000 usernames and passwords. You can load the document once and then check it repeatedly to search for matches to usernames and addresses. The big advantage of an XmlDocument is that, once loaded, it remains in memory; therefore, operations on loaded documents, especially XPath operations such as finding a matching node, are very efficient. The set of classes implemented to build an in-memory representation of an XML document is called the Document Object Model (DOM).

Unfortunately, the XmlDocument's greatest advantage is also its greatest liability. First, it takes much longer to parse an XML document into a DOM tree than it does to simply scroll through the file contents looking for a specific data item. Therefore, when you only need to make a single pass through the file, looking for specific content, it's much faster *not* to use the DOM model. An alternate way of extracting data from XML documents, called the Simple API for XML (SAX), reads an XML document sequentially, raising events as it encounters the elements and attributes in the file. By handling only the events you need, you can find specific nodes or values very quickly. Second, as you can imagine, building a large DOM in memory takes significant amounts of memory. A rough rule of thumb is that building a DOM requires about three to five times the memory that the XML file requires on disk. In contrast, reading the document with SAX requires very little memory—just the SAX parser and a buffer space.

The SAX model is a push model—SAX always starts at the beginning of the document and reads forward, pushing out events to your application as it encounters nodes and content. In contrast, .NET introduces a new model for reading XML document content—the pull model, implemented by the XmlReader abstract classes and the various `XmlNavigator` objects. The difference lies in where you put the logic. A SAX parser doesn't know whether your application needs to respond to the content available during any individual event, so it makes the data available in string form for every event. In other words, when a SAX parser encounters an element, it reads the element, determines its type, and raises an event, passing the string representation of the element as data to the event handler. In contrast, using an `XmlReader`, you can tell the parser in advance which elements you want to handle, and the reader can skip over all other types of content, making the `XmlReader` pull model much more efficient.

Using XmlReader Classes

Although the XmlReader class is an abstract class, the System.Xml namespace contains three fully implemented versions: the XmlTextReader, XmlNodeReader, and XmlValidatingReader classes. The XmlTextReader and XmlValidatingReader are similar, but the XmlValidatingReader supports document validation from a schema or DTD, whereas the XmlTextReader does not. Note that the XmlValidatingReader's validation capabilities also give it the capability to expand entities and read typed data, which can be a big advantage.

NOTE   The term entities as used in the preceding sentence isn't the same as the character entities already discussed. Using a DTD, you can define a substitute name for a larger block of XML data. It's the same idea as creating a named macro in a word processor that inserts a predefined block of text. Validating parsers must be able to read the DTD and expand or resolve entities whenever they find an entity name in the body of the document. Entity definitions are available only when you use a DTD—the current W3C schema specification does not support entity definitions.

But don't fall into the habit of using the XmlValidatingReader just because it covers all the bases—it's not nearly as efficient as the XmlTextReader.

You use the XmlNodeReader class to iterate through the nodes of a document that's already been loaded and parsed with an `XmlDocument` or `XslTransform` object—either a complete document, the DOM itself, or just a portion of the document, called a *DOM subtree*, or *document fragment*. The XmlNodeReader has no validation capabilities, but it can expand entities. Because this reader works directly in memory only with well-formed and possibly prevalidated nodes, it doesn't have to handle I/O or perform schema/DTD comparisons; therefore, it's extremely fast.

USING THE XMLTEXTREADER CLASS

As you might expect after having seen the set of `Stream` objects available for reading files, XmlText-Reader can read from a file, a string, or an input stream. You provide the input type when you create an XmlTextReader instance, so it has several overloaded constructors. At the simplest level, you can pass the constructor a filename. After constructing the `XmlTextReader` object, you call the `Read` method repeatedly. The `Read` method reads the next sequential node. It returns `true` if the read is successful and `false` if it reaches the end of the data. Be careful. The `XmlTextReader` object isn't a validating parser—it doesn't ensure that a document conforms to a schema—but it does check for well-formedness. In other words, if the XML document violates the XML syntax rules, the reader raises an error. Therefore, you should treat XML documents like any other external resource and trap for potential errors as you're reading them.

The Web Form `ch15-2` shows how to read the `flexible.xml` file and gives you some examples of the type of information available from the `XmlTextReader` for each element it encounters. When the Web Form loads, it creates a new `XmlTextReader` object by passing it the physical path of the `flexible` `.xml` file, then it calls `Read` until it reaches the end, writing various available node properties and values to the browser in a table for each node the reader encountered. The properties and methods used in the Web Form `ch15-2` are as follows:

NodeType **Property**   An enumeration value specifying the *function* of the node in the document. By applying the `ToString` method, you can see a human-friendly version of the `NodeType` property.

IsName(name) **Method**   Returns `true` if the name is a valid XML name—meaning that it conforms to the XML naming specifications, not that the name necessarily even exists in the document. The method returns `true` only for named nodes. For example, `Element` nodes are named nodes, whereas `WhiteSpace` nodes are not.

Name **Property**   The full string name of the node, including any namespace prefix. This is called the *qualified name*. For example, for the node `<xsl:apply-templates>`, the `Name` property would return `xsl:apply-templates`.

LocalName **Property**   When a node has a namespace prefix, such as `<xsl:apply-templates>`, the local name is the portion of the name after the prefix (`apply-templates`). If the node does not have a namespace prefix, the `LocalName` property returns the same value as the `Name` property.

HasAttributes **Property**   Returns `true` if the node has attributes; otherwise, it returns `false`.

AttributeCount **Property**   The number of attribute nodes in the current node. If the node has no attributes, the property returns `0`.

MoveToAttribute **(Overloaded)**   You can supply a string name, a local name and a namespace URI, or an integer value (an index into the list of nodes). The `XmlReader` reads the specified node. Attribute nodes have a `Name` and a `Value`.

ReadString   Reads the text contents of the current node. The text content consists of the text, all white space, and the contents of any child `CDATA` section nodes concatenated together, with no delimiting characters or white space between the values.

Listing 15.5 shows the code to read the XML file and return the properties for node type, name, attributes, and value.

LISTING 15.5: THE WEB FORM ch15-2.aspx **USES AN** XmlTextReader **TO READ THE**
flexible.xml **FILE (ch15-2.aspx.vb)**

```
using System.Xml;
private void Page_Load(object sender, System.EventArgs e) {
    XmlTextReader xr = new XmlTextReader(Server.MapPath(".") +
        "\\flexible.xml");
    Response.Write("Reading file: " + xr.BaseURI + "<br>");
    Response.Write("<table border=\"1\" align=\"center\">");
    Response.Write("<tr>");
    Response.Write("<th>NodeType String</th><th>NodeType</th>" +
        "<th>isName</th><th>Element</th><th>Name</th>" +
        "<th>LocalName</th><th>HasAttributes</th>" +
        "<th>Attributes</th><th>Text</td>");
    Response.Write("</tr>");
    while (xr.Read()) {
        Response.Write("<tr>");
        Response.Write("<td>" + xr.NodeType.ToString() + "</td>");
        Response.Write("<td>" + xr.NodeType + " </td>");
        Response.Write("<td>" + XmlReader.IsName(xr.Name).ToString()
            + " </td>");
        if (XmlReader.IsName(xr.Name)) {
            Response.Write("<td>" + Server.HtmlEncode("<" +
                xr.Name + ">") + "</td>");
        }
        else {
            Response.Write("<td> </td>");
        }
        Response.Write("<td>" + xr.Name + " </td>");
        Response.Write("<td>" + xr.LocalName + " </td>");
        Response.Write("<td>" + xr.HasAttributes.ToString() +
            " </td>");
        Response.Write("<td>");
        if (xr.HasAttributes) {
            for (int i = 0; i < xr.AttributeCount; i++) {
                xr.MoveToAttribute(i);
                Response.Write(xr.Name + "=" + xr.Value);
                if (i < (xr.AttributeCount - 1)) {
                    Response.Write(", ");
                }
            }
        }
        else {
            Response.Write(xr.AttributeCount.ToString());
        }
        Response.Write("</td>");
        if (xr.NodeType == XmlNodeType.Text) {
            Response.Write("<td>" +
```

```
            Server.HtmlEncode(xr.ReadString()) +
                "</td>");
        }
        else {
            Response.Write("<td> </td>");
        }
    }
    Response.Write("</table>");
}
```

Figure 15.4 shows how the Web Form ch15-2.aspx looks in the browser.

FIGURE 15.4

The Web Form ch15-2.aspx uses an XmlTextReader to display node values from the flexible.xml file

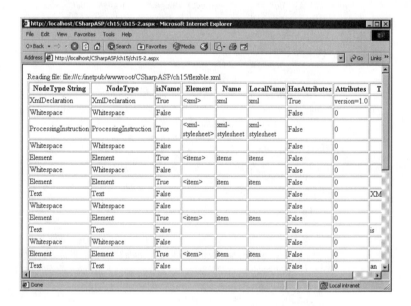

The XmlReader contains several other useful properties and methods not shown in the example Web Form ch15-2.aspx. I'm not going to list all the properties and methods because they're available in the Class Explorer and the documentation, but I've listed the most important ones in the following section.

More XmlTextReader Properties

The following list shows the most important XMLTextReader properties.

Depth   Retrieves the count of ancestor nodes for the current node. Among other things, you can use this property to create indented or "pretty-print" XML output. The property returns 0 for the root node of a document.

LineNumber   Retrieves the line number of the line containing the current node. This property is useful only if the document lines have intrinsic meaning—for example, if the document is stored in human-readable form.

LinePosition   Retrieves the character position of the current node in the current line. Unlike the `LineNumber` property, this property value is useful even when a document is not stored in human-readable form.

NameTable   Retrieves the `NameTable` object used by the reader (see the section "Using the *Xml-NameTable*," later in this chapter, for more information).

There are more properties than I've shown here. I urge you to use the MSDN documentation and the Object Browser to explore the XmlTextReader class thoroughly.

More XmlTextReader Methods

The following list shows the most commonly used `XMLTextReader` methods.

GetInnerXML   Retrieves the markup and content that lie between the start and end tags of the current node.

GetOuterXML   Retrieves the node markup and content, including the start and end tags of the current node.

GetRemainder   Retrieves the remainder of the XML document as a `TextReader`. One use for this method is to open a second `XmlTextReader` to read a different portion of the document while maintaining an existing `XmlTextReader` at a specific position.

IsStartElement   Returns `true` if the current node is the start tag of an element.

MoveToNextAttribute, MoveToPreviousAttribute   Causes the reader to read the attribute after or preceding the current attribute.

MoveToLastAttribute   Causes the reader to skip to the last attribute for the current node.

MoveToElement   When reading attributes, you can move the reader *back* to the parent element. You would use this if you needed to ensure that an attribute or attribute value exists in the document before dealing with the element's contents. For example, if you had the following element structure, you could test the value of the `level` attribute and output only names of the employees at level g5.

```
<employee id="em2930" level="g3">Bob Whitehead</employee>
<employee id="em0830" level="g5">Amanda Criss</employee>
```

MoveToContent   Moves the reader to the next node that contains text content. You can use this to skip over nodes that contain only markup.

Skip   Skips the current element. By skipping elements, you can reduce the processing time for documents that contain content you don't need.

There are more methods than I've shown here. I urge you to use the MSDN documentation and the Object Browser to explore the XmlTextReader class thoroughly.

USING THE XMLNAMETABLE

The XmlNameTable class is an *abstract* class. The table stores string names in a format that provides fast lookups. The implementation of the XmlNameTable class for the XmlTextReader is called `NameTable`, without the `Xml` prefix.

As the reader progresses through the document, it can check the set of names in its NameTable against the current node name. Strings are immutable in .NET; therefore, this scheme is advantageous because as the reader progresses through the document, it doesn't have to perform string comparisons for names it already has in the table; instead, it can simply compare the two strings to see if they reference the same object. The .NET documentation states that because of the difference between string comparison and reference comparison, using an XmlNameTable is faster.

You can retrieve the NameTable object from a reader and add names to it programmatically to improve the speed of node name comparisons, or you can create a new XmlNameTable object, add names to it, and then apply that XmlNameTable object to the XmlTextReader.

For example, suppose you wanted to find a single tag in a reasonably long document. By adding the tag name to the reader's NameTable, you can improve the comparison speed. I tested the theory using a loop. To eliminate the side effects that occur when you load a file from disk, the following example creates an XML string in memory using a StringBuilder, then provides that string to the overloaded XmlTextReader constructor. The overloaded constructor can take a Stream object instead of a file URL, which you can provide by opening a StringReader object on the generated XML string. For example:

```
// open an XmlTextReader on a string (sXML) containing some XML
// using a StringReader to provide the Stream argument.
XmlTextReader xtr = new XmlTextReader(new StringReader(sXML));
```

Here's how you add names to the NameTable:

```
// create a new NameTable
Object itemXObj;
xnt = new NameTable();
itemXObj = xnt.Add("itemX");
```

The XML string the example constructs is a list of 1,000 <item> tags, each of which contains a different value. The last tag in the list is named <itemX>. The code searches for that tag. The generated XML file looks like this:

```
<?xml version="1.0"?>
<items>
    <item>Item1</item>
    <item>Item2</item>
    <item>Item3</item>
    ...
    <item>Item999</item>
    <itemX>Item1000</itemX>
</items>
```

The example code creates the document and then loops through it 1,000 times, hunting for the <itemX> tag. When it finds the tag, it increments a counter, proving that the code found a match for each loop iteration.

Using this test, the results are language dependent. In C#, there's no improvement for the version that uses the XmlNameTable—in fact, the version that does *not* use a NameTable is slightly faster. As each loop searches through 1,000,000 tags, you can see that for most Web application XML documents, the improvement is unlikely to be noticeable.

NOTE *Interestingly, if you translate the code to VB.NET, the* NameTable *version consistently runs about 5 percent faster than the version that doesn't use the* NameTable, *even for this simple document.*

You can run the comparison using the Web Form ch15-3.aspx (see Listing 15.6).

LISTING 15.6: THIS WEB FORM CONSTRUCTS AN XML DOCUMENT IN CODE AND USES AN XmlTextReader BOTH WITH AND WITHOUT A SPECIFIC NameTable TO READ THROUGH THE DOCUMENT (CH15-3.ASPX.CS)

```
using System.Xml;
using System.Text;
using System.IO;
// auto-generated code omitted
private void Page_Load(object sender, System.EventArgs e) {
    XmlTextReader xtr = null;
    String sXML;
    NameTable xnt = null;
    int counter;
    Object itemObj;
    Object itemXObj;
    int startTick, endTick;
    StringBuilder sb = new StringBuilder(50000);
    int tickDuration1, tickDuration2;

    sb.Append("<?xml version=\"1.0\"?>");
    sb.Append("<items>");
    for(int i = 1; i <= 1000; i++) {
        if (i == 1000) {
            sb.Append("<itemX>");
            sb.Append("Item" + i.ToString());
            sb.Append("</itemX>");
        }
        else {
            sb.Append("<item>");
            sb.Append("Item" + i.ToString());
            sb.Append("</item>");
        }
    }
    sb.Append("</items>");
    sXML = sb.ToString();

    // output the method used and the current time
    startTick = System.Environment.TickCount;
    Response.Write("Starting reader without NameTable lookup at: "
+
        System.DateTime.Now.Second + ":" +
        System.DateTime.Now.Millisecond + "<br>");
```

```
// parse the string in a loop
counter = 0;
for (int i = 1; i <= 1000; i++) {
   xtr = new XmlTextReader(new StringReader(sXML));
   while (xtr.Read()) {
      if ((xtr.NodeType == XmlNodeType.Element) &&
         (xtr.Name == "itemX")) {
         counter += 1;
      }
   }
}
endTick = System.Environment.TickCount;
// output the method used and the current time
Response.Write("Ending reader without NameTable lookup at: " +
   System.DateTime.Now.Second + ":" +
   System.DateTime.Now.Millisecond + "<br>" + "Found " +
   counter.ToString() + " instances." + "<br>");
tickDuration1 = endTick - startTick;
Response.Write("Duration in milliseconds = " +
   tickDuration1.ToString());
Response.Write("<br>");

// Now repeat, using a NameTable
Response.Write("Starting reader with NameTable lookup at: " +
   System.DateTime.Now.Second + ":" +
   System.DateTime.Now.Millisecond + "<br>");
// parse the string in a loop
startTick = System.Environment.TickCount;
counter = 0;

// create a new NameTable
xnt = new NameTable();
itemXObj = xnt.Add("itemX");
itemObj = xnt.Add("item");
for (int i = 1; i <= 1000; i++) {
   xtr = new XmlTextReader(new StringReader(sXML), xnt);
   while (xtr.Read()) {
      if ((xtr.NodeType == XmlNodeType.Element) &&
         (xtr.Name == xnt.Get("itemX"))) {
         counter += 1;
      }
   }
}
endTick = System.Environment.TickCount;
// output the method used and the current time
Response.Write("Ending reader with NameTable lookup at: " +
   System.DateTime.Now.Second + ":" +
   System.DateTime.Now.Millisecond + "<br>" + "Found " +
```

```
        counter.ToString() + " instances." + "<br>");
    tickDuration2 = endTick - startTick;
    Response.Write("Duration in milliseconds = " +
        tickDuration2.ToString() + "<br>");
    Response.Write("<br>");
    Response.Write("The NameTable version is " + (((tickDuration1 -
        tickDuration2) / tickDuration1)).ToString("p") +
        " faster than the " +
        "non-NameTable version.");
}
```

Based on this test, I wouldn't bother using the NameTable in C# applications for simple documents. However, it seems likely that as the number of elements and the complexity of the document increases, you would get a corresponding increase in the relative efficiency of NameTables. You should, of course, perform your own tests on your own documents.

Regardless of the NameTable results, if you ran the ch15-3.aspx Web Form, you can see by the timings that the XmlTextReader is extremely fast. When you need to read a document one time to extract values quickly, use an XmlTextReader. But that's not the only way to find nodes and values in a document. You saw a little about how to use XSLT and XPath in style sheets, but you can also use XPath queries in code.

Querying XML Documents for Data

Three classes in the System.Xml namespace let you use XPath to query their contents: XmlDocument, XmlDataDocument, and XPathDocument. I'll discuss the XmlDataDocument in more detail in the upcoming section "Using the *XmlDataDocument* Class," but the only real difference between an XmlDataDocument and the other two DOM document types is that an XmlDataDocument can be synchronized to a DataSet rather than a file. However, regardless of the data source, after parsing the XML data into a DOM tree, the *concepts* for retrieving data from an XmlDataDocument are the same as the ones shown in the following section, although the methods differ slightly.

USING THE *SELECTSINGLENODE* AND *SELECTNODES* METHODS

At the simplest level, all you need to do to retrieve a data item from an XML document is create an XmlDocument object, call its Load method, and then use the SelectSingleNode or SelectNodes method with the appropriate XPath query to retrieve data-specific node or set of nodes. For example, the following code fragment writes the word extremely in the browser, as that word is the text content of the fourth <item> node from the flexible.xml file.

```
XmlDocument xml = new XmlDocument();
xml.Load(Server.MapPath(".") + "\\flexible.xml");
Response.Write(xml.SelectSingleNode("/items/item[4]").InnerText);
```

Similarly, you can use the SelectNodes method to select multiple nodes from a loaded XmlDocument object. For example:

```
XmlDocument xml = new XmlDocument();
xml.Load(Server.MapPath(".") + "\\flexible.xml");
```

```
foreach (XmlNode N in xml.SelectNodes("/items/item")) {
    Response.Write(N.InnerText);
}
```

The preceding code fragment writes "XML is an extremely flexible data format" to the browser.

USING THE XPATHDOCUMENT AND XPATHNAVIGATOR CLASSES

When you're loading a document just to make a few queries, it doesn't matter which XmlDocument type you use, but when you need to query a document repeatedly, it's more efficient to load it into an XPathDocument object than to load and scroll through the document for each query.

The XPathDocument object maximizes the efficiency of XPath queries. Rather than using the SelectNodes and SelectSingleNode methods, you use an object called an XPathNavigator to perform XPath requests. For example:

```
XPathDocument xml = new XPathDocument(Server.MapPath(".") +
    "\\flexible.xml");
XPathNavigator xpn == xml.CreateNavigator();
XPathNodeIterator xpni;
xpni = xpn.Select("/items/item");
while (xpni.CurrentPosition < xpni.Count) {
    xpni.MoveNext();
    Response.Write(xpni.Current.Name + "=" + xpni.Current.Value
        + "<br>");
}
```

The preceding code fragment writes the following output:

```
item=XML
item=is
item=an
item=extremely
item=flexible
item=data
item=format
```

You should explore XPath in detail to make full use of these objects. Unfortunately, a thorough discussion of XPath is beyond the scope of this book, but you'll see more examples later in this book.

Using the XmlDataDocument Class

So far, you've worked exclusively with XML documents stored on disk or created as strings. But the XmlDataDocument class represents a third type of top-level DOM document. The main difference between an XmlDataDocument object and the XmlDocument or XPathDocument object is that an XmlData-Document is closely tied to the DataSet class, so it lets you treat loaded XML data in a relational manner. You can populate the XmlDataDocument object via a DataSet. For example, the Web Form ch15-4.aspx uses a DataSet containing the Students table from the ClassRecords database. I dragged a SqlConnection and a SqlDataAdapter from the Toolbox onto the form design surface and configured the resulting `SqlDataAdapter1` instance with a SQL query that returns all the fields from the Students table. When you right-click the `SqlDataAdapter1` on that Web Form, you see the option to `Generate Dataset`. When you do that, you'll see the Generate Dataset dialog (see Figure 15.5).

FIGURE 15.5

The Generate
Dataset dialog

Click the `New` radio button and enter the name **ch15_dsClassRecords_Students**. Check the Add This DataSet to the Designer option. When you click `OK`, the designer generates a schema for the `DataSet` and a class and adds both to the current folder in the Solution Explorer. Double-click the `Ch15_dsClassRecords_Students.xsd` item in the Solution Explorer to open the schema in the designer. You'll see the schema in Listing 15.7.

LISTING 15.7: GENERATED XSD SCHEMA FOR THE CLASSRECORDS STUDENTS TABLE

```
<xsd:schema id="Ch15_dsClassRecords_Students"
targetNamespace=
   "http://www.tempuri.org/Ch15_dsClassRecords_Students.xsd"
   xmlns="http://www.tempuri.org/Ch15_dsClassRecords_Students.xsd"
   xmlns:xsd="http://www.w3.org/2001/XMLSchema"
   xmlns:msdata="urn:schemas-microsoft-com:xml-msdata"
   attributeFormDefault="qualified"
   elementFormDefault="qualified">
 <xsd:element name="Ch15_dsClassRecords_Students"
    msdata:IsDataSet="true">
  <xsd:complexType>
    <xsd:choice maxOccurs="unbounded">
      <xsd:element name="Students">
        <xsd:complexType>
          <xsd:sequence>
```

```
                    <xsd:element name="StudentID" msdata:ReadOnly="true"
                       msdata:AutoIncrement="true" type="xsd:int" />
                    <xsd:element name="Grade" type="xsd:unsignedByte" />
                    <xsd:element name="LastName" type="xsd:string" />
                    <xsd:element name="FirstName" type="xsd:string" />
                  </xsd:sequence>
                </xsd:complexType>
              </xsd:element>
            </xsd:choice>
          </xsd:complexType>
          <xsd:unique name="Constraint1" msdata:PrimaryKey="true">
            <xsd:selector xpath=".//Students" />
            <xsd:field xpath="StudentID" />
          </xsd:unique>
        </xsd:element>
      </xsd:schema>
```

The schema shows you how the XML representation of the data will look. For example, the root element will be <Students>; each field becomes an element in a sequence that follows the order of the fields in the SQL query for the SqlDataAdapter. Notice that the StudentID element has an attribute with the name and value msdata:AutoIncrement="True", meaning that the schema understands that the StudentID field is marked as an Identity field in SQL Server. Also, look at the constraint definition toward the end of the schema. The schema also captures the fact that the StudentID is a primary key as well as the XPath query to select the <Students> and the name of the primary key field.

WARNING   *XML is case sensitive, so be careful with your SQL and XPath query names.*

The generated class is interesting as well, and I urge you to look at it, although due to its size, I won't show it here. You should *not* alter the generated code manually because the system will overwrite the code if you later regenerate or alter the DataSet.

You can now use the Fill method to fill ch15_dsClassRecords_Students DataSet and print the result to the browser so you can see the XML. For example, the Form_Load method in the ch15-4.aspx Web Form displays the DataSet's XML document contents using very little hand-generated code. One of the reasons it uses so little code is that the SqlDataAdapter.Fill method opens and closes the associated Connection object automatically, so you don't have to do it yourself. However, as you've seen, if you write the code, you have control over what can be seen when page tracing is enabled, whereas when you rely on the designers, you don't.

```
private void Page_Load(object sender, System.EventArgs e) {
    DataSet ds = new ch15_dsClassRecords_Students();
    sqlDataAdapter1.Fill(ds);
    Response.Write(Server.HtmlEncode(ds.GetXml()));
    sqlDataAdapter1.Dispose();
    Response.End();
}
```

You can see from the result that the DataSet does indeed contain the data from the Students table in XML form, but the results aren't very satisfying. Fortunately, the GetXml method's return value already contains line breaks and indentation. If you place the results of the DataSet.GetXml call between <pre></pre> tags, you'll get a better format. Here's another version with better output (see Figure 15.6).

```csharp
private void Page_Load(object sender, System.EventArgs e) {
    DataSet ds = new ch15_dsClassRecords_Students();
    sqlDataAdapter1.Fill(ds);
    Response.Write("<pre>" + Server.HtmlEncode(ds.GetXml()) +
    "</pre>");
    sqlDataAdapter1.Dispose();
    Response.End();
}
```

FIGURE 15.6

Formatted contents of the *Ch15_dsClassRecords_Students1* dataset

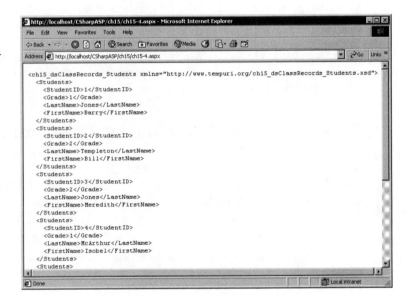

The XmlException Classes

One of the biggest flaws of the msxml.dll parser was that it allowed programmers to call its Load method with a malformed XML document without raising a COM error. Instead, the Load method returned a Boolean value that programmers all too often ignored. The System.Xml classes don't suffer from that particular malady. When you attempt to load a malformed document, compile or perform an XSLT transform, or validate an invalid document against a schema, your code will throw one of the following exceptions:

◆ XmlException

◆ XmlSyntaxException

◆ XmlSchemaException

◆ XsltException

◆ XsltCompileException

There's nothing particularly special about any of these exceptions compared to other Exception objects, but they do provide detailed information about the cause of the error. When an error occurs while loading a document, the XmlException.LineNumber and XmlException.LinePosition properties are particularly important because they can help you pinpoint the location of the error. For Xslt-Exceptions, the SourceUri property contains the path of the stylesheet that generated the error. The XmlSchemaException object has the LineNumber, LinePosition, and SourceUri properties and adds a SourceSchemaObject property containing the XmlSchemaObject that generated the error. The Xml-SyntaxException object has none of these properties, just the common Message property.

As Exception objects may "wrap" other Exception objects, you should always check the Inner-Exception property to see if the Exception contains other, wrapped Exceptions. Particularly when dealing with third-party components, the component vendor may create a component with custom exceptions but include the underlying base exceptions in the InnerException property. Each wrapped Exception object may itself contain wrapped Exceptions. You can either traverse the list of linked exceptions using the InnerException property or use the GetBaseException method to obtain the original Exception directly.

Performing XSLT Transforms Programmatically

Early in this chapter, I promised to show you how to perform server-side transforms programmatically after you learned more about the System.Xml namespace. At this point, you should have at least a tenuous grasp on the various types of DOM objects, how to read XML data, how to find nodes, and how to extract XML from a database. You've also seen how to use the Xml Web server control to perform a transform. Now it's time to use some of the objects you've seen to perform one yourself.

Here's the basic procedure:

1. Load the XML into an XmlDocument, XPathDocument, or XpathNavigator.

2. Load the stylesheet into an XslTransform instance.

3. Call the XslTransform.Transform method.

The Transform method is overloaded. It can do the following:

◆ Send the result of the transform to a TextWriter, Stream, or XmlWriter that you supply as a parameter.

◆ Write the result of the transform to a file.

◆ Return an XmlTextReader object that you can use to process the result.

TIP   The .NET documentation states that you should use an XPathDocument object when possible because it is optimized for XSLT transformations.

The Web Form `ch15-5.aspx` contains an example that's actually a little more complex than it needs to be at this point because it uses client-side script, but it provides a good XSLT sorting example in addition to a simple programmatic server-side transform. You'll see more information about client-side scripting in Chapter 20, "Leveraging Browser Clients."

The example reads an XML document named `people.xml` and an XSLT stylesheet named `people.xsl`. The `people.xml` file contains a last name, first name, telephone number, and e-mail address for several fictional people. Here's a sample:

```xml
<?xml version="1.0"?>
<people>
   <person>
           <last>Jones</last>
           <first>Bob</first>
           <tel>555-666-7777</tel>
           <email>bjones@someco.com</email>
   </person>
   <person>
           <last>Jones</last>
           <first>Fred</first>
           <tel>839-298-7328</tel>
           <email>fjones@anytel.com</email>
   </person>
   <!-- more person tags here -->
</people>
```

The stylesheet transforms the document into an HTML table, creating a row for each person and putting the four data items (`last`, `first`, `tel`, and `email`) in separate columns. It also has two parameters named `sortfield` and `sortorder` that control the way the stylesheet sorts and orders the data. Initially, the `sortfield` parameter is set to `last`, and the `sortorder` parameter is set to `ascending`, so the stylesheet sorts the people by last name in ascending order.

However, the user can change the sort order by clicking on a column header, which fires a client-side function called `sort` that sets a hidden form field to the title of the column the user clicked and then forces the default form (`Form1`) to submit to the server. The `Page_Load` event creates a string containing the client-side code and then "registers" the script with the page using the `RegisterClient-ScriptBlock` method.

```csharp
private void Page_Load(object sender, System.EventArgs e) {
    String sort_script;
    sort_script = "<script type=\"text/javascript\" " +
        "language=\"javascript\">" +
        "function sort(column) {" +
        "document.getElementById(\"Form1\")" +
        ".sortfield.value=column;" +
        "document.getElementById(\"Form1\").submit();}" +
        "</script>";
    this.RegisterClientScriptBlock("sort_script", sort_script);
}
```

The server retrieves the name of the clicked column and uses it to set the stylesheet's `sortfield` parameter. In this example, the server simply alternates between sorting columns in ascending or descending order.

```
if (IsPostBack) {
   mSortfield = Request.Form["sortfield"];
   mSortorder = Request.Form["sortorder"];
   Response.Write("Server sortorder=" + mSortorder +
      "<br>");
   if (mSortorder=="ascending") {
      mSortorder = "descending";
   }
   else if (mSortorder=="descending") {
      mSortorder="ascending";
   }
   else {
      Response.Write("ERROR: sortorder=" + mSortorder);
      Response.End();
   }
}
```

The hidden input fields are a simple way to get the name of the clicked column posted to the server. The hidden fields aren't hard-coded into the HTML (`.aspx`) file; instead, the server creates the controls dynamically and sets their values. So that the form will post the values, you need to place the hidden input controls into the default server form. The `Page` object provides an automatic way to do that with the `RegisterHiddenField` method, which accepts two string arguments: the name of the hidden input and its initial value. The `RegisterHiddenField` method performs the equivalent of this series of steps:

```
// create a hidden input control
HtmlInputHidden hidden_field = new HtmlInputHidden();

// find the default Form control and add the new control to its
// Controls collection
this.FindControl("Form1").Controls.Add(hidden_field);

// set the id and value for the new hidden input control
hidden_field.ID=someIDString;
hidden_field.Value=someValueString;
```

You can perform a similar series of steps to create any type of Web server or HTML control dynamically. The most common error people make while doing this is to add the control to the `Page.Controls` collection rather than the `"Form1"` form's `Controls` collection.

Because adding hidden input controls is such a common operation, you can accomplish the entire procedure in a single step:

```
this.RegisterHiddenField("someID", "someValue");
```

That's extremely convenient. Typically you would add controls in the Page_Load or the PreRender event. The RegisterHiddenField method renders like this:

```
<input type="hidden" name="someID" value="someValue" />
```

Listing 15.8 shows the code for the ch15-5.aspx.cs class.

LISTING 15.8: PROGRAMMATIC SERVER-SIDE XSLT TRANSFORM EXAMPLE (ch15-5.aspx.cs)

```
using System;
using System.Collections;
using System.ComponentModel;
using System.Data;
using System.Drawing;
using System.Web;
using System.Web.SessionState;
using System.Web.UI;
using System.Web.UI.WebControls;
using System.Web.UI.HtmlControls;
using System.Xml;
using System.Xml.Xsl;
using System.Xml.XPath;

namespace CSharpASP.ch15
{
   /// <summary>
   /// Summary description for ch15_5.
   /// </summary>
   public class ch15_5 : System.Web.UI.Page
   {

      private void Page_Load(object sender, System.EventArgs e) {
         String sort_script;
         XPathDocument xml = null;
         XslTransform xslt = null;
         XsltArgumentList param = null;
         String mSortfield = "last";
         String mSortorder = "ascending";
         try {
            if (IsPostBack) {
               mSortfield = Request.Form["sortfield"];
               mSortorder = Request.Form["sortorder"];
               if (mSortorder=="ascending") {
                  mSortorder = "descending";
               }
               else if (mSortorder=="descending") {
                  mSortorder="ascending";
               }
```

```
            else {
               Response.Write("ERROR: sortorder=" +
                 mSortorder);
               Response.End();
            }
         }
         xml = new XPathDocument(Server.MapPath(".") +
            "\\people.xml");
         xslt = new XslTransform();
         xslt.Load(Server.MapPath(".") + "\\people.xsl");
         this.RegisterHiddenField("sortorder", mSortorder);
         this.RegisterHiddenField("sortfield", mSortfield);

         param = new XsltArgumentList();
         param.AddParam("sortorder", "",mSortorder);
         param.AddParam("sortfield", "",mSortfield);
         xslt.Transform(xml, param,Response.OutputStream);
      }
      catch (XsltException exxslt) {
         Response.Write("XsltException: " + exxslt.Message);
      }
      catch (XmlException exxml) {
         Response.Write("XmlException: " + exxml.Message);
      }
      catch (Exception ex) {
         Response.Write(ex.GetType().Name + ": " + ex.Message);
      }

      sort_script = "<script type=\"text/javascript\" " +
         "language=\"javascript\">" +
         "function sort(column) {" +
         "document.getElementById(\"Form1\")." +
         "sortfield.value=column;" +
         "document.getElementById(\"Form1\").submit();}" +
         "</script>";
      this.RegisterClientScriptBlock("sort_script",
   sort_script);
      }

   // autogenerated code omitted
   }
}
```

The XSLT stylesheet (see Listing 15.9, later in this chapter) has several interesting points. First, notice the two `<xsl:parameter>` tags defined near the top of the file, which have default initial values of last and ascending, respectively:

```
<xsl:param name="sortfield" select="last" />
<xsl:param name="sortorder" select="ascending" />
```

The stylesheet first selects the root node of the input XML document:

```
<xsl:template match="/">
```

So that you can see what's happening, the stylesheet then writes the current parameter values to the output:

```
Sorting by <xsl:value-of select="$sortfield"/><br/>
Order = <xsl:value-of select="$sortorder"/><br/>
```

Next, it outputs a `<table>` tag and selects all the child nodes of the `<people>` tag in the input XML document, sorting them by the named parameter values. In XSLT, you reference variables by placing a dollar ($) sign in front of the name, for example $sortfield:

```
<table border="1" align="center">
   <xsl:apply-templates select="people/child::node()[1]"
   mode="thead"/>
   <tbody>
      <xsl:apply-templates select="/people/person">
            <xsl:sort select="*[name(.) = $sortfield]"
         order="{$sortorder}"/>
      </xsl:apply-templates>
   </tbody>
</table>
```

If you were to hard-code the sort field, you could write, for example:

```
<xsl:sort select="last" />
```

The interesting point of the sort is that you can't simply substitute the parameter name:

```
<xsl:sort select="$sortfield" />
```

Instead, you have to select the nodes where the node name is equal to the sortfield parameter's value.

```
<xsl:sort select="*[name(.) = $sortfield]" />
```

The `<xsl:sort>` tag can accept an order attribute that can take either an ascending or descending value. The default is ascending. Again, you can't simply use the variable reference $sortorder because that references the parameter node itself, not its value. By placing the variable name in curly brackets, XSLT substitutes the text value of the node. Therefore, the complete sort tag is this:

```
<xsl:sort select="*[name(.) = $sortfield]"
   order="{$sortorder}"/>
```

Listing 15.9 shows the entire stylesheet.

LISTING 15.9: THE people.xsl XSLT STYLESHEET SORTS THE CONTENTS OF THE people.xml FILE ACCORDING TO THE sortfield AND sortorder PARAMETER VALUES

```
<?xml version="1.0"?>
<xsl:stylesheet xmlns:xsl="http://www.w3.org/1999/XSL/Transform"
    version="1.0">
    <xsl:param name="sortfield" select="last" />
    <xsl:param name="sortorder" select="ascending" />
    <xsl:template match="/">
        Sorting by <xsl:value-of select="$sortfield"/><br/>
        Order = <xsl:value-of select="$sortorder"/><br/>
        <table border="1" align="center">
        <xsl:apply-templates select="people/child::node()[1]"
            mode="thead"/>
        <tbody>
            <xsl:apply-templates select="/people/person">
                <xsl:sort select="*[name(.) = $sortfield]"
                    order="{$sortorder}"/>
            </xsl:apply-templates>
        </tbody>
        </table>
    </xsl:template>


    <xsl:template match="person">
        <tr>
            <xsl:for-each select="child::node()">
            <td>
                <xsl:value-of select="."/>
            </td>
            </xsl:for-each>
        </tr>
    </xsl:template>



    <xsl:template match="person" mode="thead">
        <thead><tr>
            <xsl:for-each select="child::node()">
                <th>
                    <xsl:attribute name="onclick">
                        sort('<xsl:value-of select="local-name()"/>');</xsl:attribute>
                    <xsl:attribute name="style">
                        cursor:hand</xsl:attribute>
                    <xsl:value-of select="local-name()"/>
                </th>
            </xsl:for-each>
```

```
        </tr></thead>
      </xsl:template>

  </xsl:stylesheet>
```

Figure 15.7 shows the output of the `ch15-5.aspx` Web Form running in a browser, sorted by first name in descending order.

FIGURE 15.7

The Web Form
`ch15-5.aspx`
output sorted by
first name in
descending order

Moving to Applications

You've completed Part III of this book. You've seen the basic tools to build dynamic Web pages. In Part IV, you'll apply the knowledge you've gained in the context of building applications. The technologies you've seen—HTML, the `System.Web` classes, Web Forms and Web Controls, XML, and SQL Server—are sufficient to build Web sites. Putting these together as applications requires a different mindset—pages that work together. From planning all the way through development and delivery, an application is different from a set of HTML files or a set of unrelated Web Forms. Applications should have a consistent look-and-feel, store data and metadata, abstract data into classes, and be both scalable and efficient. They should respond to user requests quickly and protect data integrity.

If you're not yet comfortable with the ideas in the first three sections, I urge you to go back and extend the examples. There's no way that a book this size can cover all the properties and methods of even the few namespaces I've shown here; therefore, you'll need to explore those on your own.

Summary

In this chapter, you've seen the rudiments of how to create, modify, search, and transform XML documents using the System.Xml classes. Because XML is so important right now—not just to .NET and Web applications, but to computing in general—if you haven't worked with XML before, you should practice creating XML documents and schema, creating datasets, searching documents using XPath, and writing XSLT transforms until you're comfortable with the basic operations.

Part 4

C# Web Applications

In this section you will find:

Chapter 16

Introduction to C# Web Applications

CHAPTER 3, "BRIEF GUIDE to Dynamic Web Applications," showed that Web applications are distinct from Web sites because they have a defined purpose: Most Web sites are informational, whereas most Web applications are not. IIS makes that difference explicit. In this chapter, you'll see how to set up a Web application in IIS, and you'll explore configuration files in detail.

In this chapter:

◆ Applications versus Web Sites

◆ The `web.config` and `machine.config` Files Revisited

◆ Site Hierarchy versus Directory Hierarchy

◆ Inside Configuration Files

◆ Creating Custom Configuration Sections

◆ Configuration File Location and Lock Settings

Applications versus Web Sites

A Web site is nothing more than a virtual directory associated with a specific server. The simplest way to see that is to create one yourself. Don't use Visual Studio, FrontPage, or your favorite integrated editor; do it by hand, at least this once. Start the Internet Information Services applet on your server. In Windows 2000, click Start ➤ Programs ➤ Administrative Tools ➤ Internet Services Manager to launch the applet. The Internet Services Manager (ISM) applet runs as part of the Microsoft Management Console (MMC).

You'll see the dialog in Figure 16.1 (the dialog and items vary in different Windows versions).

FIGURE 16.1

Internet Services
Manager applet

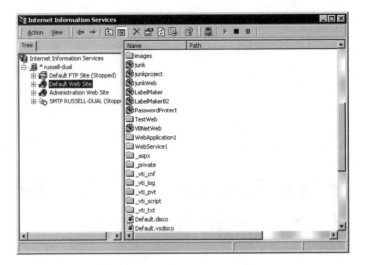

Select the Default Web Site (again, depending on your setup, this item may have a different title; it's configurable, but in my experience, most people leave the name set to the default). Right-click and select New ➢ Virtual Directory from the pop-up menu. You'll see the Virtual Directory Creation Wizard screen (see Figure 16.2).

FIGURE 16.2

Virtual Directory
Creation Wizard

Click the Next button to continue. You'll see the Virtual Directory Alias screen (see Figure 16.3).

FIGURE 16.3

Virtual Directory
Creation Wizard,
Virtual Directory
Alias screen

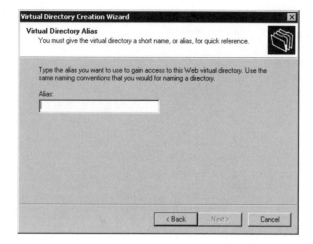

A virtual directory is an *alias* name for a physical directory. Enter the name **CSharpASPTest** into the Alias field and then click Next. You'll see the Web Site Content Directory screen. You need to enter the physical path of the root folder for the new virtual directory. Unfortunately, I usually get this far and *then* decide that I want to create a new directory. No problem. Launch Windows Explorer and create a new directory somewhere named `CSharpASPTest`. After you've created the new directory, return to the Web Site Content Directory Screen and enter the path to the new directory into the `Directory` field. For example, I created the new directory as `c:\inetpub\wwwroot\CSharpASPTest` and entered that path into the Directory field (see Figure 16.4). Click the Next button to continue.

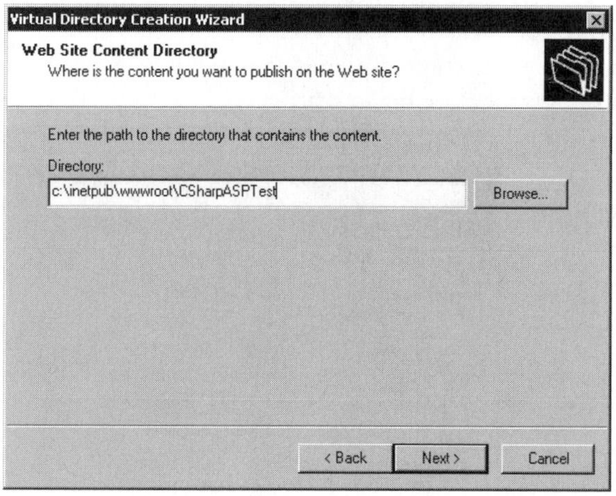

FIGURE 16.4

Virtual Directory
Creation Wizard,
Web Site Content
Directory screen

You'll see the Access Permissions screen (see Figure 16.5).

FIGURE 16.5

Virtual Directory Creation Wizard, Access Permissions screen

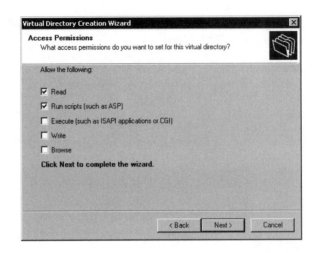

The Access Permissions screen provides a first level of security protection. By default, IIS applies the Read and `Run Scripts` (such as ASP and ASP.NET pages) permissions to the new virtual directory. You have options (unselected by default) to let the application run executable content, let the application write to the directory, and let users browse the content.

WARNING   *Normally, you should not select the Execute, Write, or Browse permissions check boxes. All these options have security ramifications. The only one you need with any regularity is the Write capability, which you should apply only to specific protected files or subfolders. You can do that with the file and directory security options in Windows Explorer at any time. Leave the three options unchecked.*

Click Next to complete the wizard and then Finish to close it. The ISM creates the new virtual directory and applies the selected permissions, but it does something else, too. Look at the icon for the new virtual directory (see Figure 16.6).

FIGURE 16.6

Internet Information Services applet after creating the `CSharpASPTest` virtual directory

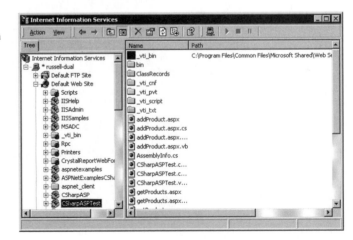

NOTE *Your virtual directory list will look different than mine. The important thing is that you see the new* CSharpASPTest *virtual directory in the list.*

The open box icon denotes an IIS *application* rather than a simple virtual directory.

TIP *If the ISM didn't automatically create an application for you, the icon will not look like a box; it will look like a folder with a globe in one corner, denoting a* World Wide Web *folder. Don't worry about it. You'll see how to create the application manually in this section.*

To understand the difference, you have to go backward in time a little to COM+ technology, or even further, when the name was Microsoft Transaction Server (MTS). A COM+ application runs in a virtual space, isolating it from other applications running on the same server. It's much more difficult for a COM+ application to bring down the entire server if it fails. That's the reason the default virtual directory creation settings for IIS create an IIS application rather than a simple virtual directory.

NOTE *If you don't check the Run Scripts option on the Access Permissions screen, IIS creates a plain virtual directory rather than an IIS application.*

NOTE *Creating a virtual directory in IIS3 on NT4 does not create an IIS application by default.*

It's worth your time to explore this topic just a little further, because there are some things you can't do with the property dialogs for ASP.NET applications.

Right-click your new CSharpASPTest virtual directory and select Properties from the pop-up menu. You'll see the CSharpASPTest Properties dialog (see Figure 16.7). Make sure you're on the Directory tab.

FIGURE 16.7

CSharpASPTest Properties dialog

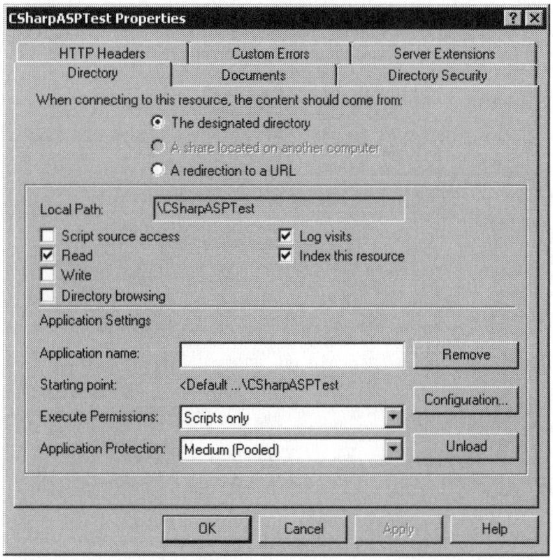

The bottom third of the dialog is titled Application Settings. If the Application Name field is grayed out on your dialog or doesn't contain the name CSharpASPTest, the ISM applet didn't create the application for you automatically. No problem. If that's the case, click the Create button next to the Application Name field.

NOTE *If ISM did create the application, the button caption reads "Remove" rather than "Create."*

Set Execute Permissions to Scripts Only and set Application Protection to Medium (Pooled). Next, click the Configuration button. You'll see the Application Configuration dialog (see Figure 16.8).

FIGURE 16.8

CSharpASPTest
Properties,
Application
Configuration
dialog

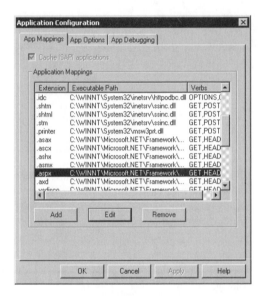

This dialog has three tabs. The App Mappings tab controls how the server treats various types of requests. Scroll down until you see the .aspx entry. Click the Edit button (but don't change anything; you're just exploring). You'll see the path in the Executable field, the .aspx extension in the Extension field, and the four "verbs" GET, HEAD, POST, and DEBUG in the Limit To field. The Script Engine check box lets the executable run in a virtual directory without Execute permissions (one marked Run Scripts in the Virtual Directory wizard or via the Virtual Directory Properties dialog). The Check That File Exists setting tells IIS to return an error message for scripting engines that don't automatically return messages for missing scripts or for requests in which the user doesn't have permission to access the requested file. If you want to add or change application mappings for a specific IIS application, you change them in this dialog. To change application mappings for the entire site, change them in the Default Web Site application properties.

Next, click the App Options tab. While it may look as though you can control some aspects of your application via this dialog, none of the options applies to ASP.NET. The options on this page apply only to classic ASP applications. The options on the last tab, App Debugging, don't apply to ASP.NET either. You configure ASP.NET application settings exclusively through the web.config and machine.config files and through page-level directives or code.

Click Cancel to close the dialogs. Look at the bottom of the CSharpASPTest Properties dialog again. The Application Protection setting should read Medium (Pooled). Click the arrow to drop down the options; with IIS 5 and Windows 2000, there are three of them:

Low (IIS Process) Runs in the same address space as the server itself. Web applications that run in the IIS process address space can crash the server completely; however, Web applications running in this space are faster than those that run as Pooled or Isolated applications.

Medium (Pooled) Runs as part of a group of pooled applications. This setting provides server protection, but one errant application can bring down the entire group. However, the setting provides a good compromise. Although Web applications in this space don't run as fast as those in the IIS process, they can be restarted automatically if they crash. This is the default setting.

High (Isolated) Your application gets its own address space. This setting is the slowest but provides the greatest protection for other applications that may be running on the same server. With classic ASP applications, I recommend that people change the setting to High, but ASP.NET applications seem to be quite stable. When you're worried about the effect of installing a new application on your server, you don't have a dedicated development server, or you're building Web applications that must interoperate with COM components, you should consider changing the setting from Medium to High.

Leave the dialog open for now; you'll change the setting in a minute. If you've never worked with COM+ applications, it's useful to see what effect the setting has.

Click Start ➤ Programs ➤ Administrative Tools ➤ Component Services. That launches the Component Services applet, which runs in the MMC just as the Internet Information Services applet does. In the list in the Tree pane, expand the Component Services item and the Computers item and then expand My Computer. Finally, expand the COM+ Applications item. Exactly what you'll see in the expanded list depends on the installed set of COM+ applications on your server, but one of the items is called IIS In-Process Applications (see Figure 16.9). That's where your application runs when you set the Application Protection property to Low (IIS Process).

FIGURE 16.9

Component Services applet, COM+ Applications

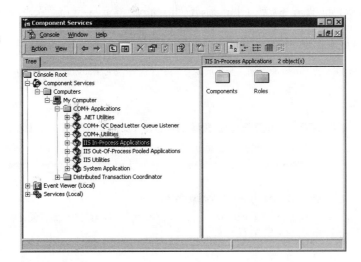

When you run your Web application with the Medium (Pooled) setting, it runs as part of the next item, called IIS Out-Of-Process Pooled Applications. However, when you run your Web application with the High (Isolated) setting, it runs as a separate application. To see that, go back to the CSharpASPTest Properties dialog and change the setting to High (Isolated). Click the Apply button and then close the dialog by clicking OK.

Now switch back to the Component Services applet and shut it down. Reopen it and you'll see an item named IIS-{Default Web Site//Root/CSharpASPTest} in the list (see Figure 16.10).

FIGURE 16.10

Component Services applet, COM+ Applications pop-up menu

The main advantage of running your application separately during development—other than the protection it provides for other applications—is that you can shut down the application, thus releasing all DLLs used by the application. This capability doesn't matter unless you're using COM components as part of your application, but when you are, and you need to make a change to a component, you probably don't want to shut down other applications—or the Web server—just so that you can make that change. You can shut down a COM+ application by right-clicking the application in the list and selecting Shut Down from the pop-up menu.

NOTE   *Before continuing, go back to the CSharpASPTest Properties dialog and change the setting back to Medium (Pooled).*

The *web.config* and *machine.config* Files Revisited

You've explored most of the sections in the config.web file earlier in this book, but there are a few more. You'll continue to use the CSharpASPTest application you created in the preceding section.

Is the *web.config* File Required?

So now, you have a virtual directory but no application. The question is this: Do you need a web.config file to run ASPX files? Let's see.

Launch Visual Studio and select New Project. Select Visual Basic Projects in the Project Types window, and select the ASP.NET Web template. Name the application CSharpASPTest. If the location doesn't reference the root directory of the server where you created the `CSharpASPTest` virtual directory (`http://localhost` if you're running on a stand-alone development machine), change it to the correct server. Click OK. VS creates the application, but it recognizes that the virtual directory already exists, so it attaches the new application to the existing virtual directory. When you create files, that's where the "real" files reside.

The new CSharpASPTest project has a `web.config` file. Rename the file `web_config.txt`.

Next, add a new Web Form. It doesn't matter what you call it. Write a line into the `Page_Load` event or drag some controls onto the Web Form designer so you'll be able to tell if the page finished properly. Compile the project, and then launch a browser instance and type in the URL of the Web Form you just created. If the project compiled, the Web Form should run fine. Obviously, you don't *have* to have a `web.config` file to run Web Forms. However, if you switch back to Visual Studio, set the new Web Form as the start page for the project, and then run the project, you'll get an error. It turns out that although you can *run* Web Forms without a `web.config` file, you can't *debug* them without a `web.config` file. You can launch the project by selecting the Start Without Debugging option from the Debug menu (or pressing Ctrl+F5).

But the application has to get its configuration settings from somewhere, and you've already seen that it doesn't get them from the IIS Application Configuration settings. It turns out that ASP.NET and Visual Studio install several configuration files in the machine configuration directory. You can find the location with a little code. Create a Web Form in the CSharpASPTest application—it doesn't matter what you call it—and write the following code into the `Page_Load` method for the Web Form.

```
Response.Write(HttpRuntime.MachineConfigurationDirectory.ToString());
```

On my computer, that produces the following output, where *n.n.nnnn* is the installed version number of the .NET framework:

```
c:\winnt\microsoft net\framework\v.n.n.nnnn\Config
```

If you look in that directory, you'll see a file called `machine.config`, which contains the default application configuration settings. If you ever forget where the `machine.config` file resides, or if it's in a different location for a particular server, you can use the `HttpRuntime.MachineConfiguration-Directory` property to find it.

The *.config* File Hierarchy

You should explore the `machine.config` file thoroughly because it defines the default settings and behavior for your ASP.NET Web applications. Unless you have a good reason, don't change the `machine.config` file. Some good reasons exist to change it, though. For example, the file contains default time-out (90 seconds), security, compilation, and language settings that you might want to change, default assemblies added to new projects, handlers for various file extensions, and browser definitions (used to set the `HttpRequest.Browser` property) that you will want to update periodically.

The most important thing at this time, though, is that you look through the file and see that a portion of it defines the same settings as the `web.config` file. That's because the CONFIG files form a hierarchy, where the lowest-level setting (the one closest to the executing code) has the greatest effect.

When the .NET runtime looks for a setting, it starts in the currently executing file's directory and works its way up the directory hierarchy. For example, suppose you have the following hierarchical structure, where the Web Forms in the ClassRecords folder access the ClassRecords database and the Web Forms in the Northwind folder access the Northwind database:

```
c:\inetpub\wwwroot\CSharpASPTest
    ClassRecords
        Northwind
```

You could place a different web.config file in the ClassRecords folder, the Northwind folder, or both. It's important to remember that configuration files at *lower* levels take precedence over those at *higher* levels, which is perfectly logical but is exactly the opposite of what some people might expect. Unfortunately, despite the hierarchical nature of CONFIG files, simply copying the web.config file from your application's root directory and placing it in a subdirectory doesn't work, because it turns out that some of the sections aren't allowed at lower levels.

NOTE You can work around this problem using the <location> tag, which lets you specify settings that apply to only a specific location in your application. See the section "Configuration File Location and Lock Settings" at the end of this chapter for an example.

To explore the problem, you'll need to place a web.config file at each level. In the preceding section, you renamed the web.config file web_config.txt. Rename it again, back to web.config. Create the Northwind and ClassRecords subfolders as shown above. Next, copy the file into both the ClassRecords folder and the Northwind folder.

By writing a small test Web Form for each folder, you can find out how the web.config files interact and which sections are not allowed in application subfolders. Create a test.aspx file in each folder, write code in each to display the current folder name, and then use the Server.Transfer command to transfer execution to the next file (see Listing 16.1).

TIP Creating a Web Form in a C# Web project automatically creates the code-behind file, which contains a class definition. But class names must be unique in a namespace; therefore, trying to create two Web Forms with the same name causes problems. VS lets you create the two Web Forms without an error, but the code won't compile. Here's a solution:

The top line of each ASPX file contains an inherits *attribute. You can change the* inherits *attribute value by switching to HTML mode in the designer. Change the value of the attribute. For example, in the* test.aspx *file in the* ClassRecords *directory, change the attribute from* inherits=CSharpASPTest.test *to* inherits= CSharpASPTest.ClassRecords.test, *or some other name unique to your project. Next, change the namespace of the class. For example, change the* namespace *line in the* test.aspx.cs *class in the* ClassRecords *folder to* namespace CSharpASPTest.ClassRecords. *After doing that, your code will compile without problems.*

NOTE Each test.aspx *file on* www.sybex.com *contains a line of code that I purposely left out of this listing. You can see the missing lines in Listing 16.2.*

LISTING 16.1: THE CODE IN THE THREE test.aspx.cs **FILES IN THE** CSharpASPTest, ClassRecords, **AND** Northwind **FOLDERS, USED TO TEST HIERARCHICAL UNMODIFIED** web.config **FILES**

```
// in CSharpASPTest\test.aspx.cs
namespace CSharpASPTest
{
    // autogenerated code omitted

    public class test : System.Web.UI.Page
    {
        // autogenerated code omitted
        private void Page_Load(object sender, System.EventArgs e)
        {
            Response.Write("In ClassRecords folder<br>");
            Server.Transfer("ClassRecords/Northwind/test.aspx");
        }
    }
}
// in CSharpASPTest\ClassRecords\test.aspx.cs
namespace CSharpASPTest.ClassRecords
{
    // autogenerated code omitted

    public class test : System.Web.UI.Page
    {
        private void Page_Load(object sender, System.EventArgs e)
        {
            Response.Write("In ClassRecords folder<br>");
            Server.Transfer("Northwind/test.aspx");
        }
    }
}


// in CSharpASPTest\Northwind\test.aspx.cs
namespace CSharpASPTest.ClassRecords.Northwind
{
    // autogenerated code omitted

    public class test : System.Web.UI.Page
    {
        private void Page_Load(object sender, System.EventArgs e)
        {
            Response.Write("In Northwind folder<br>");
            Response.End();
        }
    }
}
```

Compile the project, and then request the `test.aspx` file in the `CSharpASPTest` root directory with your browser. Unfortunately, that doesn't work. There are several reasons. The first thing that happens is that an error message appears, alerting you that an error occurred while processing a configuration file (see Figure 16.11).

FIGURE 16.11

Nested configuration file error

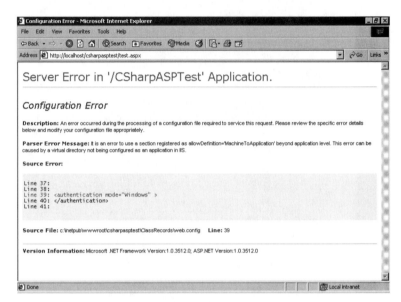

The error occurs because you can't set application-level settings within `web.config` files in subdirectories.

So while `web.config` files may be hierarchical, there are some stated but well-hidden rules. The error occurs in the first-level subdirectory of the `CSharpASPTest` root—the `ClassRecords` directory. Remove the application-level settings. Here are the sections you must remove from `web.config` files in your application's subdirectories:

◆ `<authentication>`

◆ `<sessionState>`

After removing the sections, run the application again. This time, you get a different error when trying to use the `Server.Transfer` method to switch execution to the `Northwind/test.aspx` file. The server can't find the file. The reason is that while the executing file is in the `ClassRecords` folder, the *context* under which the application is running is still that of the original request—the `test.aspx` file in the root folder. If you're going to use the `ServerTransfer`, it's important to understand that it does not work quite the same way as the `Response.Redirect` method. `Response.Redirect` forces the *browser* to request the file; therefore, the context for the next file is appropriate to that file. In contrast, the browser is completely unaware of any `Server.Transfer` command, because when the `Transfer` method occurs, the browser still hasn't received a response.

The other settings in the `web.config` file may not have any effect, but they don't cause errors.

Add this key to the `<appSettings>` section of the `web.config` file in the root directory. Create the `<appSettings>` section if it doesn't already exist.

```
<add key="test" value="root"/>
```

Similarly, add `"test"` keys to the `<appSettings>` section for the `web.config` files in the Class-Records and Northwind folders.

```
<add key="test" value="ClassRecords"/>
<add key="test" value="Northwind"/>
```

Create three new Web Forms, one in each subdirectory of the application, and call them `test2.aspx`. These files are identical to the `test.aspx` Web Forms except that each has an additional line to retrieve and display the value of the `"test"` key in its `web.config` file (see Listing 16.2).

> **LISTING 16.2: THE CODE IN THE THREE `test.aspx.cs` FILES IN THE `CSharpASPTest`, `ClassRecords`, AND `Northwind` FOLDERS, USED TO READ APPLICATION SETTINGS FROM HIERARCHICAL `web.config` FILES**

```csharp
// in CSharpASPTest\test2.aspx.cs
namespace CSharpASPTest
{
    // autogenerated code omitted

    public class test2 : System.Web.UI.Page
    {
        private void Page_Load(object sender, System.EventArgs e)
        {
            Response.Write("In CSharpASPTest folder<br>");
            Response.Write("Application setting \"test\"=" +
                System.Configuration.ConfigurationSettings.
                AppSettings.Get("test") + "<br>");
            Server.Transfer("ClassRecords/test2.aspx");
        }
    }
}

// in CSharpASPTest\ClassRecords\test2.aspx.cs
namespace CSharpASPTest.ClassRecords
{
    // autogenerated code omitted
    public class test2 : System.Web.UI.Page
    {
        private void Page_Load(object sender, System.EventArgs e)
        {
            Response.Write("In ClassRecords folder<br>");
            Response.Write("Application setting \"test\"=" +
                System.Configuration.ConfigurationSettings.
```

```
                    AppSettings.Get("test") + "<br>");
            Server.Transfer("ClassRecords/Northwind/test2.aspx");
        }
    }
}

// in CSharpASPTest\Northwind\test2.aspx.cs
namespace CSharpASPTest.ClassRecords.Northwind
{
    // autogenerated code omitted
    public class test2 : System.Web.UI.Page
    {
        private void Page_Load(object sender, System.EventArgs e)
        {
            Response.Write("In Northwind folder<br>");
            Response.Write("Application setting \"test\"=" +
                System.Configuration.ConfigurationSettings.
                AppSettings.Get("test") + "<br>");
            Response.End();
        }


    }
}
```

Compile the project again and then request the test2.aspx file in the CSharpASPTest root directory with your browser. This time, you'll see the output in Figure 16.12.

FIGURE 16.12

Test hierarchical web.config files— display application settings

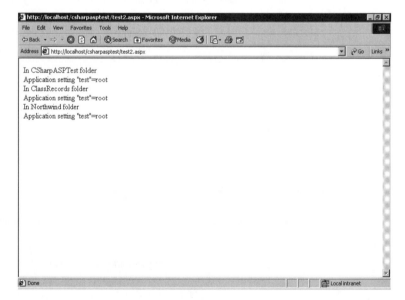

Not exactly what you might expect, but again, the point of this exercise is that you must take into account the context in which a page executes. Despite the fact that the code transfers execution to the `ClassRecords/test.aspx` Web Form and then to the `ClassRecords/Northwind/test.aspx` Web Form, the context for application-level settings is the `web.config` file in the root `CSharpASPTest` folder— that's why you see the output `Application setting test="root"` regardless of which file executes.

At this point, you might think that the `web.config` files in the application subdirectories aren't really valid. If you read the documentation carefully, it seems that `web.config` files apply only to *virtual* directories. However, that's not entirely true. Change the `test2.aspx.cs` file in the `ClassRecords` directory so the `Page_Load` event reads this way:

```
private void Page_Load(object sender, System.EventArgs e)
{
    Response.Write("In ClassRecords folder<br>");
    Response.Write("Application setting \"test\"=" +
        System.Configuration.ConfigurationSettings.
        AppSettings.Get("test") + "<br>");
    Server.Transfer("Northwind/test2.aspx");
}
```

Note the changed `Server.Transfer` line. Recompile the application. Now, request the `CSharpASP-Test/ClassRecords/test2.aspx` file directly from a browser. Hmm. Not only does the file run without errors, but it *does* read the `web.config` file settings in the `ClassRecords` folder, even though the directory is not marked as a virtual directory (you'll see more about that in the next section). That seems unusual because, although config files are supposed to be hierarchical, you might expect that a section named `<appSettings>` would be limited to the application's root directory, but that's not what happens. The output shows that the context, as expected, is the `ClassRecords` directory this time, even after the `Server.Transfer` takes effect and the `test2.aspx` file in the `Northwind` folder executes.

The point here is that *some* `web.config` file settings—even in plain (non-virtual) subdirectories *do* override settings at higher levels, exactly as the documentation (sort of) states.

NOTE   *One quick aside: If you change the* `Server.Transfer` *line in the* `ClassRecords.test2.aspx.cs` *file to* `Server.Transfer("../test2.aspx")`, *transferring execution "up" to the application's root directory, you get a recursion error. In other words, you cannot transfer to another file and then transfer back. In fact, you can't use* `Server.` `Execute(../test2.aspx)` *to do that either, because the root* `test2.aspx.cs` *file transfers execution back—and you still get the recursion error. If you comment out the* `Server.Transfer` *line in the root* `test2.aspx.cs` *file, the code works fine, and the context remains that of the* `ClassRecords/test2.aspx` *file, so there's no problem with transferring execution from a lower to a higher point in the application folder hierarchy.*

Although I haven't yet tested every standard section and setting in the `web.config` file, the only ones that seem to have *any* effect at subdirectory levels are those that deal with application settings, security, and data stored in custom sections. You'll see more about security in Chapter 18, "Controlling Access and Monitoring," and I'll show you how to create custom settings in the "Creating Custom Configuration Sections" section later in this chapter.

Site Hierarchy versus Directory Hierarchy

Go back and look at the error message in Figure 16.11. The message says that this error *can* be caused by forgetting to configure a directory as a virtual directory. In other words, you *can* nest virtual directories.

There's a difference between nesting directories and nesting *virtual* directories. When you create a virtual directory with IIS5, it automatically creates an IIS application, as you've seen. Each application gets its own set of ASP.NET objects, such as `Session`, `Application`, `Request`, `Response`, and `Server`. Unfortunately, that can lead to problems. It's worth exploring briefly, just so that you'll recognize the problems, should they occur in your application.

Launch the Internet Information Services applet, right-click the Default Web Site item in the Tree pane, and select New ➤ Virtual Directory from the pop-up menu. The Virtual Directory Creation Wizard appears. Click Next to begin, and then enter the name **ClassRecords** for the virtual directory alias name on the Virtual Directory Alias screen. Click the Next button and enter the path to the `CSharpASPTest\ClassRecords` subdirectory—normally `c:\Inetpub\wwwroot\CSharpASPTest\ClassRecords`—into the Directory field. Click the Next button and then click Finish to close the wizard.

One more time, change the `test2.aspx.cs` file in the `ClassRecords` folder so that the `Server.Transfer` line looks like this:

```
Server.Transfer("ClassRecords/Northwind/test2.aspx");
```

Compile the application and request the `test2.aspx` file in the `CSharpASPTest` root directory with your browser. It will run. Clearly, creating an IIS application nested inside another IIS application runs without problems when you request files from the top-level application. Next, without changing anything, request the `test2.aspx` file directly from the new virtual `ClassRecords` directory: for example, `http://localhost/ClassRecords/test2.aspx`. The request fails with the following error:

```
The resource cannot be found.
```

That makes sense. When you run the `test2.aspx` Web Form in the `ClassRecords` application directly, it can't find a file that's in the CSharpASPTest application namespace—and the code-behind class (`CSharpASPTest.ClassRecords.test2`) is part of the CSharpASPTest application. Unfortunately, I know of no way to solve the problem entirely. I suspect the lesson to be learned here is that it's perfectly OK to nest directories, but that you should avoid nesting IIS applications.

Inside Configuration Files

A configuration file consists primarily of sections, each of which must be declared at some level within the hierarchy of configuration files. Declaring a section involves creating a section group, within which you declare each section and associate the section with a particular type of *handler*, which provides specific programmatic access to that section.

The `machine.config` file contains the declarations for the standard section groups and sections.

A configuration file begins with the standard XML processing instruction. The configuration file's root element is required and must be called `<configuration>`.

```
<?xml version="1.0" encoding="UTF-8"?>
<configuration>
</configuration>
```

The `<configuration>` element may contain zero or more `<configSections>` elements, each of which may contain zero or more `<sectionGroup>` or `<section>` elements. The `<section>` elements are *not* the sections themselves—they're the *declaration* for the section. For example:

```
<?xml version="1.0" encoding="UTF-8"?>
<configuration>

    <configSections>
        <!-- tell .NET Framework to ignore CLR sections -->
        <section name="runtime"
            type="System.Configuration.IgnoreSectionHandler,
            System, Version=1.0.3300.0, Culture=neutral,
            PublicKeyToken=b77a5c561934e089" allowLocation="false"/>
        <section name="mscorlib"
            type="System.Configuration.IgnoreSectionHandler,
            System, Version=1.0.3300.0, Culture=neutral,
            PublicKeyToken=b77a5c561934e089" allowLocation="false"/>
        <section name="startup"
            type="System.Configuration.IgnoreSectionHandler,
            System, Version=1.0.3300.0, Culture=neutral,
            PublicKeyToken=b77a5c561934e089" allowLocation="false"/>
        <section name="system.runtime.remoting"
            type="System.Configuration.IgnoreSectionHandler,
            System, Version=1.0.3300.0, Culture=neutral,
            PublicKeyToken=b77a5c561934e089" allowLocation="false"/>
    <!--more section declarations-->
    </configSections>
    </configuration>
```

NOTE *The version number in the* `machine.config` *entries may differ on your system, but the information should be essentially the same.*

The `<section>` declaration attributes define the section name, the type, the version, the culture, a `PublicKeyToken` string, and whether the section can contain a `location` attribute (more on that in a second).

The `type` attribute is particularly interesting. In the three section declarations shown previously, the `type` attribute value shows the section handler type (`System.Configuration.IgnoreSectionHandler`); the namespace from which to load the handler (`System`); and the version, the culture, and a `Public-KeyToken` value. However, further down, the file contains section declarations for several standard section handlers. For example, each of the sections below uses a different handler type, most of which are defined in the `System.Configuration` namespace.

```
<section name="system.diagnostics"
    type="System.Diagnostics.DiagnosticsConfigurationHandler,
    System, Version=1.0.3300.0, Culture=neutral,
    PublicKeyToken=b77a5c561934e089"/>
<section name="appSettings"
    type="System.Configuration.NameValueFileSectionHandler,
    System, Version=1.0.3300.0, Culture=neutral,
```

```
        PublicKeyToken=b77a5c561934e089"/>
    <sectionGroup name="system.net">
        <section name="authenticationModules"

type="System.Net.Configuration.NetAuthenticationModuleHandler,
        System, Version=1.0.3300.0, Culture=neutral,
        PublicKeyToken=b77a5c561934e089"/>
    <section name="defaultProxy"
        type="System.Net.Configuration.DefaultProxyHandler, System,
        Version=1.0.3300.0, Culture=neutral,
        PublicKeyToken=b77a5c561934e089"/>
    <section name="connectionManagement"
        type="System.Net.Configuration.ConnectionManagementHandler,
        System, Version=1.0.3300.0, Culture=neutral,
        PublicKeyToken=b77a5c561934e089"/>
    <section name="webRequestModules"
        type="System.Net.Configuration.WebRequestModuleHandler,
        System, Version=1.0.3300.0, Culture=neutral,
        PublicKeyToken=b77a5c561934e089"/>
</sectionGroup>
```

Creating Custom Configuration Sections

The defined handlers are available for you to use for your own custom sections. You need to define a section only once—section definitions are inherited.

For example, suppose you wanted to define a set of product groups containing individual products. You could add a `<productGroups>` section and define a `<product>` section, perhaps using a `System` `.Configuration.NameValueFileSectionHandler` to handle returning individual product values. To see how this works, add a new section definition to the top of the `web.config` file in the root directory of your CSharpASPTest project, just after the `<configuration>` element:

```
<configuration>
    <configSections>
        <section name="product"
            type="System.Configuration.NameValueSectionHandler,
            System" />
    </configSections>
    <!-- rest of the web.config file -->
</configuration>
```

Next, add a `<product>` element at the end of the file, just before the `</configuration>` element.

NOTE *The tags below are commented out in the* `web.config` *file for the CSharpASPTest project on* **www.sybex.com**. *Enable the tags between the comments* `<!-- START Listing 16.3-->` *and* `<!--END Listing 16.3 -->` *to see the code in Listing 16.3 work.*

```
<!-- existing web.config file content-->
<product>
<add key="Flashlights" value="Flashlights description" />
```

```
<add key="Key Rings" value="Key Rings description" />
</product>
```

The `NameValueSectionHandler` type implements a `getConfig` method that returns a `NameValue-Collection` of product element values. The Web Form `getProducts.aspx` retrieves the products and loops through them, displaying the keys and values (see Listing 16.3).

Unfortunately, when you run this code, you get an error stating that `"File or assembly name System, or one of its dependencies, was not found"`. Although the documentation states that you can create custom configuration sections that use the `NameValueSectionHandler` type, you can use it only if you take one of the following steps:

◆ Create a custom configuration handler class.

◆ Add the `<section>` tag to your `machine.config` file rather than to your `web.config` file.

◆ Copy the `system.dll` file from your `Winnt.Microsoft.NET\Framework\<version>` folder to the `bin` folder of your project--in this case, the `CSharpASPTest\bin` folder. While I don't recommend this option, it may be the only way to get your section to work if you don't have access to the `machine.config` file.

The first option is the most flexible because by writing your own class, you can handle anything you like; however, it's also the most trouble. See the section "Creating a Custom Configuration Handler" later in this chapter for more information. However, if you can use one of the existing system handlers, it's much easier to use the first option. For simple key/value pairs such as the `<product>` example, use one of the first two options. Avoid the last option—copying the `system.dll`—unless you have no other choice.

Add the `<section>` tag to your `machine.config` file, and run the Web Form `getProducts.aspx` in the `CSharpASPTest` root folder, which retrieves and displays the information in the `<product>` tag in your `web.config` file. Listing 16.3 shows the code.

LISTING 16.3: RETRIEVING CUSTOM CONFIGURATION SETTINGS (`getProducts.aspx.cs`)

```csharp
using System.Collections.Specialized;
// autogenerated code omitted

private void Page_Load(object sender, System.EventArgs e) {
    NameValueCollection nvc = null;

    nvc = (NameValueCollection) Context.GetConfig("product");
    if (nvc == null) {
        Response.Write("No products defined<br>");
    }
    else {
        foreach (String aKey in nvc.Keys) {
            Response.Write(aKey + "=" + nvc.Get(aKey) + "<br>");
        }
    }
}
```

The output from the code in Listing 16.3 looks like Figure 16.13.

FIGURE 16.13

Output from the
Web Form
`CSharpASPTest`
`.getProducts`
`.aspx`

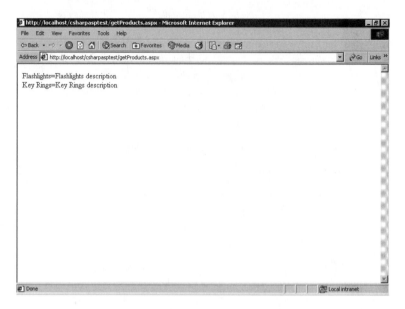

Using the built-in configuration handlers, settings are read-only, so you can't use them to add new settings at runtime. It's not clear why Microsoft chose to make the handlers act in read-only mode, because there's a simple workaround. You *can* add new settings programmatically if you open the file and use the methods in `System.XML` to add nodes. The procedure is as follows:

1. Create an `XmlDocument`.

2. Load the `web.config` file.

3. Retrieve the section node that contains the values you want.

4. Create a new node and add attributes as needed.

5. Append the new node to the section node.

6. Save your changes.

The ASP.NET engine watches the `.config` file hierarchy and reloads the files if they change, so any changes you make in this manner take effect immediately. For example, the Web Form `addProduct` `.aspx` still in the CSharpASPTest application adds a new key and value to the `<product>` section and displays it immediately (see Listing 16.4).

**LISTING 16.4: ADDING A CUSTOM CONFIGURATION SETTING DYNAMICALLY
(addProduct.aspx.cs)**

```
using System.Collections.Specialized;
using System.Xml;

// autogenerated code omitted
private void Page_Load(object sender, System.EventArgs e) {
   NameValueCollection nvc = null;
   XmlDocument xml = new XmlDocument();
   XmlNode node = null, product = null, keys = null;
   xml.Load(Server.MapPath(".") + "\\web.config");
   keys =
   xml.SelectSingleNode("configuration/product/add[@key='Keys']");
   if (keys == null) {
      Response.Write("Adding key<br>");
      product = xml.SelectSingleNode("configuration/product");
      node = xml.CreateNode(XmlNodeType.Element, "add", "");
      node.Attributes.Append(xml.CreateAttribute("key"));
      node.Attributes[0].Value = "Keys";
      node.Attributes.Append(xml.CreateAttribute("value"));
      node.Attributes[1].Value = "Keys description";
      product.AppendChild(node);
      xml.Save(Server.MapPath(".") + "\\web.config");
   }

   nvc = (NameValueCollection) Context.GetConfig("product");
   if (nvc == null) {
      Response.Write("No products defined<br>");
   }
   else {
      foreach(String aKey in nvc.Keys) {
         Response.Write(aKey + "=" + nvc.Get(aKey) + "<br>");
      }
   }
}
```

When you run the Web Form, the output looks like Figure 16.14.

FIGURE 16.14

Output from the
Web Form
CSharpASPTest
.addProduct.asp
x after adding a
custom setting

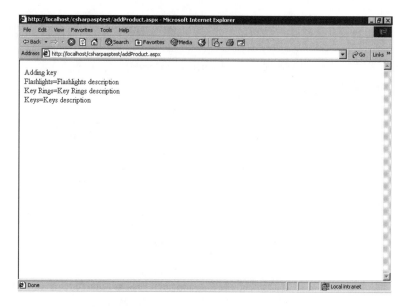

Creating a Custom Configuration Handler

The most flexible option for defining custom configuration sections is to create your own handler.
To do that, you need to create a new project containing a class that implements the IConfiguration-
SectionHandler interface. The custom handler will read a custom section containing the same product information that you already created in the previous section and added to the `web.config` file in
the CSharpASPTest project root folder; however, this time, you can use descriptive names for the tags
and attributes rather than the `"key"` and `"value"` attributes required for the System.Configuration
.NameValueCollectionHandler class. Add the following section to the CSharpASPTest project's
`web.config` file:

```
<products>
   <product name="Tents"
      description="Tents description" />
   <product name="Lanterns"
      description="Lanterns description" />
</products>
```

For this example, create a new Class Library project named CSharpASPCustom. Rename the
default `Class1.cs` file `ProductsNameValueHandler.cs`, and place the code in Listing 16.5 into the file.

LISTING 16.5: THE ProductsNameValueHandler **CUSTOM CONFIGURATION HANDLER CODE**
            (ProductsNameValueHandler.cs**)**

```
using System;
using System.Collections;
using System.Collections.Specialized;
```

```
using System.Xml;
using System.Configuration;

namespace CSharpASPCustom
{
    public class ProductsNameValueHandler :
        IConfigurationSectionHandler {

        public virtual object Create(Object parent,
            Object context, XmlNode node) {
            NameValueCollection products = null;
            int i;
            string key;
            string val;
            products = new NameValueCollection();
            for (i=0; i < node.ChildNodes.Count; i++) {
                key = node.ChildNodes.Item(i).Attributes.
                    GetNamedItem("name").Value;
                val = node.ChildNodes.Item(i).Attributes.
                    GetNamedItem("description").Value;
                products.Add(key,val);
            }
            return products;
        }
    }
}
```

The class has a single function named Create that implements the System.Configuration.
IConfigurationSectionHandler interface's Create method. The function receives three parameters:

◆ A parent object, which can be an object corresponding to the configuration settings for a
parent tag in the config file. You can ignore that parameter for this example.

◆ An HttpConfigurationContext object. You can ignore that object for this example as well.

◆ An XmlNode object, which represents the configuration XML node itself—in this case, the
<product> tag.

The code is simple. It creates a NameValueCollection object and populates it by looping through
each <product> tag in the <products> section, reading the name and description attributes from each
tag. Because the Create method's return value is an Object, you still need to cast the value to the
appropriate type from your Web Form—just as you had to cast it when you used the System
NameValueCollectionHandler.

To test the new handler, add this code to the web.config file in your CSharpASPTest root folder,
just after the <configuration> tag:

```
<configuration>
    <configSections>
```

```
            <section name="products"
                type="CSharpASPCustom.ProductsNameValueHandler,
                CSharpASPCustom" />
        </configSections>
        <!-- rest of the web.config file -->
    </configuration>
```

Note that the tag is identical to the `<configSections>` tag shown in the preceding section except that it references the CSharpASPCustom namespace and the ProductsNameValueHandler class rather than the System.Configuration namespace and the NameValueSectionHandler class. Build the CSharpASPCustom project. Save your changes to the `web.config` file.

Add a reference to the `ProductsNameValueHandler.dll` file. Right-click the References item in the Solution Explorer and select Add Reference. Click the .NET tab, and then click the `Browse` button. You'll find the `CSharpASPCustom.dll` file in the CSharpASPCustom project's bin folder.

Finally, change the line that retrieves the `"product"` configuration in the `getProducts.aspx` Web Form so that it retrieves the `"products"` (note the plural) configuration instead:

```
nvc = (NameValueCollection) Context.GetConfig("products");
```

When you run the `getProducts.aspx` Web Form now, you'll see the values from the new `<products>` section.

Configuration File Location and Lock Settings

Earlier in this chapter, you saw how to nest configuration files in subdirectories. For many purposes, a simpler and more powerful method is to apply a `<location>` tag to values that you want to make available to Web Forms in a particular location. In addition, you can prevent lower-level configuration files from overriding a setting by adding an `allowOverride` attribute to the `<location>` tag.

For example, add the following XML to the `web.config` file in the `CSharpASPTest` directory and then save the file.

NOTE *The XML code is commented out in the* `web.config` *file for the* `CSharpASPTest` *project on* www.sybex.com. *Uncomment the code to run the following example.*

```
<location path="ClassRecords">
    <product>
        <add key="Backpacks" value="Backpacks description
    ClassRecords"
    </product>
</location>
```

The `Backpacks` product is now only available to Web Forms placed in the `ClassRecords` folder. The file `getProductsClassRecords.aspx` in the `CSharpASPTest/ClassRecords` folder is—except for its name—identical to the `getProducts.aspx` file in the root `CSharpASPTest` folder. I simply copied the file and renamed it.

When you run the original `getProducts.aspx` Web Form (`http://localhost/CSharpASP/getProducts.aspx`), you'll see the products defined at the root level, but not the `Backpacks` product.

But when you run the Web Form `http://localhost/CSharpASP/ClassRecords/getProducts.aspx`, you'll see all the products—including the `Backpacks` product.

Location-Specific Tags Override Higher-Level Settings

You can also use the `<location>` tag to override higher-level settings. For example, add a `Flashlights` product to the `ClassRecords` product location. Change the `value` attribute so it differs from the `Flashlights` value already defined. Here's how your `ClassRecords` product location settings might look (I added `"ClassRecords"` to the `value` attribute):

```
<location path="ClassRecords">
   <product>
      <add key="Backpacks" value="Backpacks description" />
      <add key="Flashlights"
         value="Flashlights description ClassRecords" />
   </product>
</location>
```

Now, when you run the `getProducts.aspx` file in the `ClassRecords` folder, you'll see the altered, `ClassRecords`-specific description for the `Flashlights` key rather than the original description.Using the `<location>` tag, you can make a section or set of sections apply to a specific file as well as an entire directory. It's important that you understand the difference between the `<location>` tag and nested `web.config` files. Using the `<location>` technique, you can change the settings that you cannot nest.

You just saw how easy it is to override higher-level settings using the `<location>` tag. That's a potential problem; a lower-level setting might inadvertently change a setting that you *want* to apply to an entire site or set of subdirectories. To solve the problem, add the `allowOverride` attribute to a `<location>` tag. The attribute takes a Boolean value of either `false` or `true`. For example, to prevent a `web.config` file in a subdirectory of the `CSharpASPTest` folder from overriding higher-level settings, add the following `<location>` tag around the products defined for the CSharpASPTest root level. The highlighted lines in the following snippet show the added code:

```
<location path="CSharpASPTest" allowOverride="false">
   <product>
      <add key="Flashlights" value="Flashlights description" />
      <add key="Key Rings" value="Key Rings description" />
   </product>
</location>

<location path="ClassRecords">
   <product>
      <add key="Backpacks" value="Backpacks description" />
      <add key="Flashlights"
         value="Flashlights description ClassRecords" />
   </product>
</location>
```

To test it, run the `getProductsClassRecords.aspx` Web Form. You may recall that you changed the `Flashlights` description in the preceding example, and you saw the changed description when you ran the getProductsClassRecords.aspx Web Form. However, after adding the <location> tag as shown, you will see *only* the ClassRecords-specific settings, which seems odd because if you're not supposed to be able to override the settings, you should *not* see the ClassRecords-specific "Flashlights" item. However, some experimentation shows that if you change the location path for the root items from "CSharpASPTest" to a single period (".") or a blank string (""), it seems to work as advertised:

```
<location path="." allowOverride="false">
   <product>
      <add key="Flashlights" value="Flashlights description" />
      <add key="Key Rings" value="Key Rings description" />
   </product>
</location>
```

Changing the path attribute value to "." and running the getProductsClassRecords.aspx Web Form causes an error stating:

```
Parser Error Message: This configuration section cannot be used at
this path. This happens when the site administrator has locked
access to this section using <location allowOverride="false"> from
an inherited configuration file.
```

As you might expect (although I didn't anticipate that exact result), the error occurs when the page tries to access the <location path="ClassRecords"> products because they have been marked as non-overrideable. I could not force the error to occur with any path setting other than ".". Note that this is a *parse* error—you can't access the values with the root getClassRecords.aspx Web Form either using both <location> tags.

WARNING *The capability to prevent overrides gives administrators the power to control what behavior programmers can and can't override at lower levels. However, if programmers have access to the* Web.config *file in a higher-level directory, they can modify it using straight XML techniques as shown in the preceding example. If you use the* allowOverride *attribute, you should be sure to restrict the change permissions on the* web.config *file.*

Be careful with the sequence! There's an ordering problem as well. If you change the sequence of the entries in the web.config file so that the <location path="ClassRecords"> tag appears before the <location path="" allowOverride="false"> tag, the restriction *will not take effect*. To test the problem, reverse the order of the entries as follows:

```
<location path="ClassRecords">
   <product>
      <add key="Backpacks" value="Backpacks description" />
      <add key="Flashlights"
         value="Flashlights description ClassRecords" />
   </product>
</location>

<location allowOverride="false">
   <product>
      <add key="Flashlights" value="Flashlights description" />
      <add key="Key Rings" value="Key Rings description" />
```

```
    </product>
</location>
```

This time, when you run the `getProductsClassRecords.aspx` Web Form, you'll see three products, and you won't get any errors.

WARNING   *The order of* `<location>` *tags for which you want to disable overrides in lower-level sections is critical. Be sure that the higher-level tags containing the* `allowOverride` *attribute appear first.*

One more note. If you move the `ClassRecords`-specific `<product>` section into the `ClassRecords/Web.config` file instead and remove the `<location>` tag, you no longer need the `path` attribute in the root folder, either. In other words, the whole thing is simpler if the files use this configuration:

```
In CSharpASPTest/Web.config:
<location allowOverride="false">
    <product>
        <add key="Flashlights" value="Flashlights description" />
        <add key="Key Rings" value="Key Rings description" />
    </product>
</location>
In CSharpASPTest/ClassRecords/Web.config:
<product>
    <add key="Backpacks" value="Backpacks description" />
    <add key="Flashlights"
        value="Flashlights description ClassRecords" />
</product>
```

Now you get the error only if you attempt to access the items using the `getProductsClassRecords.aspx` Web Form—the `getProducts.aspx` file still works.

Summary

In this chapter, you've seen how IIS settings determine which virtual directories run as applications and how to create IIS applications manually. You've seen how to use the base `machine.config` file in conjunction with `web.config` files in the various folders of your application to control how that application responds.

The settings you select are critical. The choices you make can have a huge influence on how fast your applications run, how scalable they are, and how easy or difficult it will be to migrate them to another technology. One of the choices you make in configuration files deals with maintaining state. You saw a little about state maintenance in Chapter 7, "The *SessionState* Object," but now that you've worked with Web Forms in more detail, it's time to revisit the subject, because state maintenance is the single most important difference between standard Windows applications and Web applications.

Chapter 17

State Maintenance and Cacheing

STATE MAINTENANCE IS THE process of maintaining a value or an object across page, session, or application boundaries. Because HTTP is a stateless protocol, any objects or values you create for one page are thrown away at the end of the connection, so they're not available for the next request—even to the same page. This is a huge problem in Web applications. In fact, it's the single most intractable problem in writing applications for the Web because you have to make an artificial "application" that sits atop a series of individual requests and responses. In this chapter, you'll explore how you can work with ASP.NET to maintain data across requests, sessions, and applications.

In this chapter:

◆ State Maintenance Options

◆ Using the *Cache* Object

◆ Cacheing ASP.NET Pages

◆ A Multitude of Choices

State Maintenance Options

Suppose you ask users to enter some data—perhaps fill in a product order form. In a Windows application, you would create a screen or dialog containing the appropriate fields. After the user enters the data, you wouldn't allow him to go back and enter the data again for the same record except under your program's control. In other words, you control program flow with the program itself.

In contrast, a Web application has no intrinsic directional flow; there's no way to prevent a person from requesting *any* page in your application, at any time, by entering the appropriate URL. If you imagine our example product order form running in a browser, then after the user clicks the Submit button, there's nothing inherent in Web applications to prevent that user from clicking the browser's Back button, changing some data, and submitting the form again. Because the application code runs on the server but the user interface runs in the browser, you can't prevent the user from clicking the Back button. Instead, you need to prevent multiple form submissions in some other way.

Here's another scenario. Suppose that, in the Windows version of the order form, the user makes a data entry error. A simple solution would be to write the error next to the appropriate field or display a message. The user fixes the error and continues. But in a Web application, the user submits the data to the server. At that point, the user's page disappears. To display an error, you need to redraw the page. Redrawing the form itself is no problem—you already have the HTML code to do that. But you also need to repopulate all the fields with the data that the user entered. That means you not only need to pick that data out of the form data submitted to the server, but you also need to write different HTML back to the browser to redraw the page with the data already entered. This is not only tedious but also time consuming and error prone.

For simple, one-step operations such as registration forms, you need to maintain state for only one form; however, for more complex operations, you need to maintain state *across* forms. For example, you will probably need to maintain directional and positional information as well—information that lets you know where the user is in your application, so you can prevent inappropriate actions, such as moving backward through a forward-only series of forms or resubmitting a form.

There are four different types of state maintenance in Web applications. You've seen some of them already, so I'll be brief with those.

User Page State (ViewState)   This deals with maintaining the state of the user interface between requests—for example, making sure that data the user has entered doesn't disappear after a round trip to the server to perform data validation. When you use Web Forms and Web server controls exclusively, ASP.NET uses ViewState to take care of this type of state maintenance for you. Although ViewState is extremely convenient, you should not use it for controls that hold a lot of data, such as `DataGrids` and `DataLists`, and especially when all you need to do is display the data, unless you simply don't care about moving large volumes of unnecessary data over your network. The most important point to remember is that ViewState is control specific; the `EnableViewState` property is set to `true` by default. You should set the `EnableViewState` property to `false` for every control unless you specifically need ASP.NET to maintain page state information for that control.

User Session State   This type deals with maintaining user data between pages. For many applications, this data is mostly "throwaway" data—it's specific to that particular user and application and applies only during a specific session. When the user leaves the application, you don't need to save the data. For example, you might want to display a special type of advertisement the first and third times a user visits a page in your site, but not for other visits. You could use a `Session` variable to maintain the visit count for each user. You would ensure that the `Session` variable exists and initialize it to 0 during the `Session_OnStart` event in the `global.asax` file. Whenever the user requests the pertinent page, you would increment the counter. Finally, you would display the ad only when the `Session` variable value is 1 or 3. `Session` variables aren't automatic like ViewState, but they are the most convenient way to store user session state data in ASP.NET.

User Application State   This type of state maintenance deals with maintaining data needed by the application for a specific user. This type of data typically moves between long-term storage, such as a database table or file, and temporary storage, such as `Session` variables or cookies. Some examples of user application state data are user preferences, demographic data, and user-entered or selected values such as notes, lists, or uploaded files. During any session, you may want to cache the data locally so that you can access it rapidly when needed; however, unlike user session state data, you can't throw away user application state data, because you will need the data again during the next session. ASP.NET does not handle this type of state maintenance for you automatically.

Application State   Application state deals with data that all users need during the application. For example, at application startup, you might set some global values, such as file paths, URLs, connection strings, and arrays containing frequently used lists, or you might preload XML documents and XSLT stylesheets to enhance your application's performance. For static string values such as connection strings, you have the choice of creating them in the `<appSettings>` section of the `web.config` file, in a custom `web.config` section, or in `Application` variables. For objects, you must store them in `Application` variables if you want them to be globally available, or you must persist them to a file or database table and retrieve them when needed.

None of these state maintenance options are required. You don't *have* to use Web Forms, ViewState, or `Session` or `Application` variables. You can write HTML pages and put your ASP code inline, or you can maintain state with your own code. You can also store session and application information in files or database tables. However, you should normally take advantage of the ASP.NET state maintenance features. There are two exceptions:

◆ When you know before you begin your application that you're going to have to migrate it to some other platform. In this case, use only the features that have parallels on the other platform. For example, if you don't have the equivalent of Web server controls, use HTML controls instead.

◆ When you know that your application must be as efficient as possible and scale to multiple servers with thousands of simultaneous users. In this case, avoid sessions and ViewState. Maintain user page state yourself and use cookies, files, and database tables to maintain user session and application state.

In the remainder of this chapter, you'll implement a short series of three Web Forms that request user information and store that information somewhere so that the application can use the information later. The three forms *must* be presented in forward-only order, and you need to prevent a user from either adding more information or overwriting the information that's already been submitted. To do that, you must let the user alter the information until he's entered a valid value for each page. However, you must not accept invalid input, and you must maintain information about where the user is in the sequence. For example, the first time the user requests any page of the sequence, you must redirect to the first page. After seeing the first page, if a user requests any of the pages, you must reroute him to the second page, and so on. If a user uses the browser's Back button to back up, you must not let him post the information.

Maintaining State in Cookies

Before Microsoft introduced the concept of `Session` variables, Web programmers had to use cookies to manage state. Because `Session` variables slow down the rate at which your server can serve pages and because browsers let users turn off (refuse) cookies, you may find yourself in a situation where you can't use them. Here's how to fulfill the form series requirements with cookies:

◆ For each page, send a sequence cookie containing the page sequence that the browser will return during the next request to the site.

◆ If the sequence cookie is blank, set it to the first page in the sequence and redirect to that page. That way, no matter which page in the sequence users *request* first, they'll always *see* the first page first.

◆ If the sequence cookie is not blank and the request does not match the cookie, redirect to the page specified by the cookie rather than the page requested by the user. This prevents the user from seeing the pages out of sequence.

◆ When the user has completed the last page, set the sequence cookie to **done** or to some other recognizable value. This prevents the user from revisiting the pages after completing the sequence.

You *can* write the logic into each page to manage the cookies, but placing the logic in a class makes the code much simpler. The class should handle creating and reading the cookies, comparing the current request to the *expected* page request (the next one in the series), and redirecting the user. The cookieSequence.cs file in the Ch17 folder of the CSharpASP application contains the definition for the CookieSequencer class.

You've already seen how to set and read cookies, so I won't spend much time there, but the Cookie-Sequencer class has a couple of interesting features. First, it has a custom constructor that overrides the default constructor inherited from Object. The CookieSequencer class contains a private array that holds the master definition of the sequence.

```
private String[] sequence = {"cookiesequence1.aspx",
    "cookiesequence2.aspx", "cookiesequence3.aspx",
    "cookiesequencedone.aspx"};
```

The class obtains a reference to the current `HttpContext` and uses that to set references to the ASP.NET `Request` and `Response` objects, which it needs to retrieve and set cookie values and write content to the browser:

```
// defined at class level
private HttpRequest Request = null;
private HttpResponse Response = null;

// get the current context
HttpContext context = HttpContext.Current;
Request = context.Request;
```

The class also retrieves the lowercase value of the `Request.ServerVariables` item called `SCRIPT_NAME` and saves the name of the current script:

```
// get the current script name
currentScriptName =
    Request.ServerVariables["SCRIPT_NAME"].ToLower();
currentScriptName = currentScriptName.Substring
    (currentScriptName.LastIndexOf("/") + 1);
```

NOTE *IE sends the* SCRIPT_NAME *variable consistently. For some browsers, you must use the* URL *variable instead, which contains the same value. You can test the value quickly using the* showServerVariables.aspx *file in the* Ch17 *folder of the CSharpASP application on* www.sybex.com.

Next, the class attempts to retrieve the sequence cookie. If it's blank, the code creates the cookie and redirects to the first page in the sequence:

```
// get the sequence cookie, if any
cookie = Request.Cookies["sequence"];
if (cookie == null) {
   // first visit
   cookie = new HttpCookie("sequence");
   cookie.Value = sequence[0];
   Response.Cookies.Add(cookie);
   validCookie = true;
}
else {
   // more code here
}
```

The class ensures that the cookie contains some valid value by checking the value against each item in the defined sequence. This isn't strictly necessary, because this code never executes unless the page creates a CookieSequencer object, but it doesn't take much time, and it ensures that test pages or pages removed from the sequence at some point don't affect the sequence itself. If the request matches any of the pages in the sequence, the loop sets the validCookie variable to true, sets a variable named currSequence to the machine index value, and exits the loop.

```
// make sure you have a valid value
for (int i = 0; i <= sequence.GetUpperBound(0); i++) {
   if (cookie.Value == sequence[i]) {
      validCookie = true;
      currSequence = i;
      break;
   }
}
```

If the page request is valid (appears in the defined sequence), the code checks to make sure that the cookie value matches the page request. If so, the request and the cookie match, so you're done and the code exits, letting the page code execute. If not, the page request is invalid in some fashion; perhaps the user is requesting a page out of sequence or a programmer inadvertently created a CookieSequencer object on a page not defined in the sequence. In that case, the method assumes the cookie is correct and redirects to the page defined by the cookie.

```
if (validCookie) {
   if (cookie.Value == currentScriptName) {
      // OK
   }
   else {
      // redirect to appropriate page
      Response.Redirect(cookie.Value, true);
   }
```

```
    }
    else {
        // set the cookie to the first page
        cookie.Value = sequence[0];
        currSequence = 1;
        // append the cookie
        Response.Cookies.Add(cookie);
        // redirect to first page
        Response.Redirect(sequence[0], true);
    }
```

The result of this code is that any page that creates a CookieSequencer object becomes, correctly or incorrectly, part of the sequence and forces the user to see the next appropriate page in the sequence.

CookieSequencer has only two other methods. The setCookie method sets the value of the sequence cookie. The NextPage method increments the currSequence index variable and calls the setCookie method, thus forcing the next request to redirect to the next page in the sequence. If the currSequence index variable value equals or exceeds the number of items in the sequence, CookieSequencer assumes that the user has completed the sequence and redirects to the last page. Listing 17.1 contains the complete CookieSequencer class code.

LISTING 17.1: THE COOKIESEQUENCER CLASS MANAGES THE COOKIES REQUIRED TO FORCE A USER TO TRAVERSE A SPECIFIC SEQUENCE OF PAGES (CookieSequence.aspx.cs)

```
using System;
using System.Web;

namespace CSharpASP.ch17 {
    /// <summary>
    /// Summary description for CookieSequencer.
    /// </summary>
    public class CookieSequencer {
private HttpRequest Request = null;
private HttpResponse Response = null;
private String[] sequence = {"cookiesequence1.aspx",
    "cookiesequence2.aspx", "cookiesequence3.aspx",
    "cookiesequencedone.aspx"};
private int currSequence = 0;
private String currentScriptName = "";
public CookieSequencer() {
    // get the current context
    HttpContext context = HttpContext.Current;
    HttpCookie cookie = null;
    bool validCookie = false;
    Request = context.Request;
    Response = context.Response;
    // get the current script name
    currentScriptName =
```

```
      Request.ServerVariables["SCRIPT_NAME"].ToLower();
      currentScriptName = currentScriptName.Substring
         (currentScriptName.LastIndexOf("/") + 1);
      // get the sequence cookie, if any
      cookie = Request.Cookies["sequence"];
      if (cookie == null) {
         // first visit
         cookie = new HttpCookie("sequence");
         cookie.Value = sequence[0];
         Response.Cookies.Add(cookie);
         validCookie = true;
      }
      else {
         // make sure you have a valid value
         for (int i = 0; i <= sequence.GetUpperBound(0); i++) {
            if (cookie.Value == sequence[i]) {
         validCookie = true;
         currSequence = i;
         break;
            }
         }
      }
      if (validCookie) {
         if (cookie.Value == currentScriptName) {
            // OK
         }
         else {
            // redirect to appropriate page
            Response.Redirect(cookie.Value, true);
         }
      }
      else {
         // set the cookie to the first page
         cookie.Value = sequence[0];
         currSequence = 1;
         // append the cookie
         Response.Cookies.Add(cookie);
         // redirect to first page
         Response.Redirect(sequence[0], true);
      }
   }


   public int CurrentSequence {
      get {
         return(currSequence);
      }
```

```
    }
    private void setCookie(int sequenceIndex) {
        String s="";
        s = sequence[sequenceIndex];
        Response.Cookies["sequence"].Value = s;
    }
    public void NextPage() {
        if (currSequence + 1 < sequence.GetLength(0)) {
            currSequence++;
            setCookie(currSequence);
            Response.Redirect(sequence[currSequence]);
        }
        else {
            Response.Redirect(sequence[sequence.GetUpperBound(0)]);
        }
    }

    public void showCookies() {
        foreach(String aKey in Request.Cookies.Keys) {
            Response.Write(Request.Cookies[aKey].Name +  "=" +
            Request.Cookies[aKey].Value + "<br>");
        }
    }

    }
}
```

Four Web Forms work with this class—three in the sequence, and one to display the results when the user finishes the sequence. Because all three Web Forms in the sequence contain similar code, I'll show only one here. Each Web Form requests a single bit of information. The first page requests a last name; the second, a first name; and the third, a U.S.-formatted telephone number. Each page uses a **TextBox** for the user input, and three **Validator** controls: one **RequiredFieldValidator** to ensure that the user enters *something* in the text field, one **RegularExpressionValidator** to check the input, and one **ValidationSummary**, which displays the validation feedback.

Each form also contains a button to post the form. Each Web Form instantiates a **CookieSequencer** instance. As you've seen, simply creating the object ensures that the user can see the page only in the correct sequence (see Listing 17.2).

LISTING 17.2: CODE FOR THE CookieSequence1.aspx *WEB FORM* (CookieSequence1.aspx.cs)

```
private void Page_Load(object sender, System.EventArgs e) {
    CookieSequencer cookieSequencer = new CookieSequencer();
    // NOTE, you'll never process this page if the
        // cookie is not valid
    if (IsPostBack) {
        Page.Validate();
```

```
    if (Page.IsValid) {
        // save the last name
        HttpCookie ln = new HttpCookie("lastname");
        ln.Value = txtLastName.Text;
        Response.Cookies.Add(ln);
        cookieSequencer.NextPage();
    }
  }
}
```

Here's how to test the sequence. First, request the CookieSequence1.aspx file into your browser and enter a last name (see Figure 17.1).

FIGURE 17.1

The first page of the CookieSequence Web Form sequence

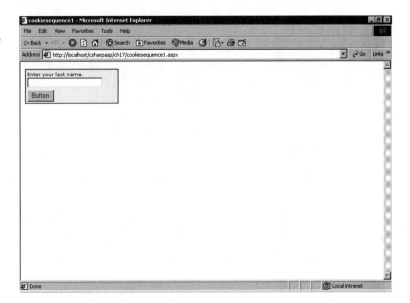

Click the button or press Enter to submit the form.

TIP *Whenever you have a page with a form containing a single text field, with or without a submit button, IE submits the form automatically when you press Enter. You can leave the field without submitting it by pressing the Tab key.*

The Web Form posts back to itself and validates the input. When the input is valid, the code calls the CookieSequencer.NextPage method, which redirects the user to the next page in the sequence.

After entering a last name, you'll see the CookieSequence2.aspx page. Move back up to your browser's address field and change CookieSequence2.aspx to CookieSequence1.aspx. The server accepts the request. The CookieSequence2.aspx page creates a CookieSequence object, which compares the request to the value of the sequence cookie. Because they don't match, it immediately redirects the browser back to the CookieSequence2.aspx page.

The same thing happens if you request the CookieSequence3.aspx page. When you reach the end of the sequence, any request for any page in the sequence redirects you to the CookieSequenceDone.aspx page. After submitting valid data for a page in the sequence, you can still browse back to that page using the Back button, (because the browser caches the page), but any data you submit will not be accepted, because the CookieSequencer class automatically redirects you to the next page before processing occurs.

Try using your browser's Back button to back up, change the information in one of the forms, and click the button to resubmit the form. Doing so doesn't change the data you already submitted; in other words, the solution also solves the problem of repeated posts for the same page. Again, the reason reposting doesn't alter the results is that the CookieSequencer object redirects the request *before* the page processes any information.

While you can prevent people from backing up at all with some extra work, it's *very* difficult to override the browser's cache completely. In other words, you have to write client-side code to prevent people from revisiting a visited page. In this case, it doesn't matter if people revisit a page earlier in the sequence by backing up—they can't change the data anyway.

As you can see, the results are good, and you don't have to have Sessions enabled for this method to work, which makes it a good choice for a large Internet application. In this particular instance, because the information is short, cookies work well. If the information were longer, you'd have to use a database table or a file to store the information between requests.

Maintaining State in *Session* Variables

The three Web Forms SessionSequence1, SessionSequence3.aspx, and SessionSequenceDone.aspx function identically to the CookieSequence Web Forms, but they save information about the user's progress through the sequence in Session variables instead. Again, I've used a class called Session-Sequencer, which ensures that the sequence exists, handles updating the array pointer (NextPage method), and displays the final results (showSessionVars method). The class creates the sequence if it doesn't already exist and maintains a Session("sequenceIndex") variable that points to the correct position in the sequence. Although the code is quite similar, it's smaller because you don't have to set and retrieve the cookies each time. Also, using Sessions would work even if the information were large because you don't have to pass the information back and forth for each request as you do with cookies. Listing 17.3 shows the code for the SessionSequencer class.

LISTING 17.3: CODE FOR THE SESSIONSEQUENCER CLASS (SessionSequencer.cs)

```
using System;
using System.Web;
using System.Net;
using System.Web.SessionState;

namespace CSharpASP.ch17 {
    /// <summary>
    /// Summary description for SessionSequencer.
    /// </summary>
```

```
public class SessionSequencer {
    private String expectedPage;
    private String requestedPage;
    private int sequenceIndex;
    private String[] sequence = {"sessionsequence1.aspx",
        "sessionsequence2.aspx", "sessionsequence3.aspx",
        "sessionsequencedone.aspx"};
    private HttpRequest Request;
    private HttpResponse Response;
    private HttpSessionState Session;
    public SessionSequencer() {
        Request = HttpContext.Current.Request;
        Response = HttpContext.Current.Response;
        Session = HttpContext.Current.Session;
        if (Session["SequenceIndex"] == null) {
            Session["SequenceIndex"] = 0;
        }
        sequenceIndex = (int) Session["SequenceIndex"];

        requestedPage = Request.ServerVariables
            ["SCRIPT_NAME"].ToLower();
        requestedPage = requestedPage.Substring
            (requestedPage.LastIndexOf("/") + 1);
        if ((sequenceIndex < 0) ||
            (sequenceIndex > sequence.GetUpperBound(0))) {
            sequenceIndex = 0;
        }
        expectedPage = sequence[sequenceIndex];
        if (requestedPage != expectedPage) {
            Response.Redirect(expectedPage);
        }
    }

    public void showSessionVars() {
        foreach(String aKey in Session.Keys) {
            Response.Write(aKey + "=" + Session[aKey] + "<br>");
        }
    }

    public void NextPage() {
        if (sequenceIndex + 1 < sequence.GetLength(0)) {
            sequenceIndex++;
        }
        else {
            sequenceIndex = sequence.GetUpperBound(0);
        }
        Session["sequenceIndex"] = sequenceIndex;
```

```
            Session["sequence"] = sequence[sequenceIndex];
            Response.Redirect(sequence[sequenceIndex]);
        }
    }
}
```

Except for the field names, the three code-behind classes for the input pages contain identical code. Again, I'll show only the code for the first page (see Listing 17.4).

LISTING 17.4: Page_Load **EVENT CODE FOR THE WEB FORM** SessionSequence1.aspx
(SessionSequence1.aspx.cs)

```
private void Page_Load(object sender, System.EventArgs e) {
    SessionSequencer SessionSequencer = new SessionSequencer();
    // NOTE, you'll never process this page if the session variable
    // Session("sequenceIndex") doesn't match this page name
    if (IsPostBack) {
        Page.Validate();
        if (Page.IsValid) {
            // save the last name
            Session["lastname"] = this.txtLastName.Text;
            SessionSequencer.NextPage();
        }
    }
}
```

Maintaining State in Files

You can make up your own file format to hold whatever data you want, but just to reiterate how convenient XML files are, the example in this section uses an XML-formatted file to hold the data. The FileSequencer class handles loading and saving the file based on a GUID value stored in a permanent cookie created the first time a user requests any page in the sequence.

NOTE *You must give the account used by IIS read/write permission to the directory where you want to save the files before this example will work. The example saves the XML files in a subdirectory of the* **CSharpASP/Ch17** *folder named* **XMLData**.

There are several interesting points about using files to maintain state. First, you can see that you need some way to associate a user with his file. This solution uses a permanent cookie. This dovetails nicely with the second point, which is that, unlike the session and cookie examples you saw in the preceding sections, files can manage data not only across requests but across browser sessions and instances, as long as the user requests the sequence from the same server. For Web farms with multiple servers running the same application, where load balancing software apportions requests to the server with the lowest load, the file in which the data is stored must be accessible from any server the user can reach.

To test this, browse to the `FileSequence1.aspx` page and enter a last name. Then, before you enter anything into the `FileSequence2.aspx` page, close your browser. At this point, the FileSequencer class has already written the cookie. If you're using IE, you'll find the cookie in the `c:\Documents and Settings\<your user name>\cookies` folder on your hard drive. Netscape browsers store permanent cookies in a `cookies.txt` file in a subdirectory of the directory where Netscape is installed. The cookie contains a GUID that matches the name of an XML file written to the `CSharpASP\ch17\XMLData` subdirectory on the Web server. The filename will be something like `784a524f-67f0-470a-8588-17e278cf9a83.xml`, although the GUID will be different. If you're testing more than once, look for the latest copy.

TIP   To reset the sequence, delete the cookie file from your hard drive, then exit and reload your browser.

Double-click the XML file. It should open in IE. If it doesn't, drag the file onto an open instance of IE to view it. The file's contents look like Figure 17.2 except that the `<lastname>` element will have a different value.

FIGURE 17.2

The `File-Sequencer` object writes an XML file containing the sequence, the current sequence index, and the data entered by the user

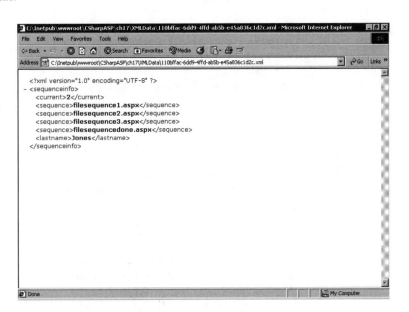

The file contains everything you need to maintain the user's state—the sequence index `<current>`, the sequence of filenames, and the user-entered data. The `FileSequencer` object code handles almost everything (see Listing 17.5).

LISTING 17.5: THE FILESEQUENCER CLASS HANDLES USER SEQUENCING (`FileSequencer.cs`)

```
using System;
using System.Web;
using System.IO;
```

```csharp
using System.Xml;

namespace CSharpASP.ch17 {
    /// <summary>
    /// Summary description for FileSequencer.
    /// </summary>
    public class FileSequencer {
        private String m_filename;
        private String m_path;
        private System.Xml.XmlDocument xml = null;
        private int currSequenceIndex;
        private HttpRequest Request = null;
        private HttpResponse Response = null;
        private HttpServerUtility Server = null;
        private String expectedPage;
        private String requestedPage;

        public FileSequencer() {
            HttpContext Context = HttpContext.Current;
            FileInfo fi = null;
            String sGUID;
            HttpCookie sequenceCookie = null;
            Response = Context.Response;
            Request = Context.Request;
            Server = Context.Server;
            // get the current page name
            requestedPage = Request.ServerVariables
                ["SCRIPT_NAME"].ToLower();
            requestedPage = requestedPage.Substring
                (requestedPage.LastIndexOf("/") + 1);

            // create the output filename
            m_filename =
                Request.ServerVariables["SCRIPT_NAME"].ToLower();
            m_filename = Server.MapPath(m_filename);
            m_filename = m_filename.Substring
                (0, m_filename.LastIndexOf("\\"));

            // get the sequence cookie
            sequenceCookie = Request.Cookies.Get("sequencefile");
            if (sequenceCookie != null) {
                sGUID = sequenceCookie.Value;
            }
            else {
                sGUID = getGUID();
            }
            m_filename = m_filename + "\\XMLData\\" + sGUID + ".xml";
```

```
// read the xml document if it exists
fi = new FileInfo(m_filename);
xml = new XmlDocument();
try {
    if (!fi.Exists) {
        // ensure the directory exists
        m_path = m_filename.Substring
            (0, m_filename.LastIndexOf("\\"));
        DirectoryInfo di = new DirectoryInfo(m_path);
        if (!di.Exists) {
            di.Create();
        }
        // write the default state of the document
        xml = new XmlDocument();
        xml.LoadXml("<?xml version=\"1.0\" " +
            "encoding=\"UTF-8\"?><sequenceinfo>" +
            "<current>1</current>" +
            "<sequence>filesequence1.aspx</sequence>" +
            "<sequence>filesequence2.aspx</sequence>" +
            "<sequence>filesequence3.aspx</sequence>" +
            "<sequence>filesequencedone.aspx</sequence>" +
            "</sequenceinfo>");
        // write the GUID as a permanent cookie
        sequenceCookie = new HttpCookie("sequencefile",
        sGUID);
        // set the expiration date
        sequenceCookie.Expires = new DateTime
            (2010, 12, 31, 23, 59, 59);
        Response.Cookies.Add(sequenceCookie);
    }
    else {
        xml.Load(m_filename);
    }
    // get the current sequence
    currSequenceIndex = XmlConvert.ToInt32
        (xml.SelectSingleNode("//sequenceinfo/current")
         .InnerText);
    // get the name of the expected page
    expectedPage = xml.SelectSingleNode
        ("sequenceinfo/sequence[" +
        currSequenceIndex.ToString() + "]").InnerText;
    if (expectedPage != requestedPage) {
        Response.Redirect(expectedPage);
    }
}
catch (Exception e) {
    Response.Write(e.Message);
```

```
            Response.End();
        }
    }
    private String getGUID() {
        return System.Guid.NewGuid().ToString();
    }
    public void addNode(String nodename, String nodevalue) {
        XmlNode N = null;
        N = xml.SelectSingleNode("sequenceinfo/" + nodename);
        if (N != null) {
            N.InnerText = nodevalue;
        }
        else {
            N = xml.CreateElement(nodename);
            N.InnerText = nodevalue;
            xml.DocumentElement.AppendChild(N);
        }
    }
    public void NextPage() {
        if (currSequenceIndex <
xml.SelectNodes("//sequence").Count) {
            currSequenceIndex++;
            xml.SelectSingleNode("sequenceinfo/current").
                InnerText = currSequenceIndex.ToString();
            xml.Save(m_filename);
            Response.Redirect(xml.SelectSingleNode
                ("sequenceinfo/sequence[" +
currSequenceIndex.ToString() +
                "]").InnerText);
        }
    }
    public void showFileVars() {
        // just show the XML file contents
        Response.ContentType = "text/xml";
        Response.Write(xml.InnerXml);
    }
}
}
```

As with the other sequence management classes you've seen in this chapter, the constructor handles the sequence operation. The code creates references to the Request, Response, and Server objects and retrieves the current filename in the same way as the preceding code examples.

Next, the code creates an XmlDocument object and checks for the GUID cookie. If it finds the cookie, it constructs a filename and attempts to read the file. If it doesn't find the cookie, it creates a new GUID. The XmlDocument object updates nodes in memory during page execution but uses the XmlDocument.Save method to persist the altered XML to disk when the page calls the FileSequencer object's NextPage method. You can find the full code for the FileSequencer.cs class on www.sybex.com and in Listing 17.5.

```
// get the sequence cookie
sequenceCookie = Request.Cookies.Get("sequencefile");
if (sequenceCookie != null) {
   sGUID = sequenceCookie.Value;
}
else {
   sGUID = getGUID();
}
```

The code uses the sGUID variable to construct a filename and write the initial file values:

```
// read the xml document if it exists
fi = new FileInfo(m_filename);
xml = new XmlDocument();
try {
   if (!fi.Exists) {
      // ensure the directory exists
      m_path = m_filename.Substring(0,
   m_filename.LastIndexOf("\\"));
      DirectoryInfo di = new DirectoryInfo(m_path);
      if (!di.Exists) {
         di.Create();
      }
      // write the default state of the document
      xml = new XmlDocument();
      xml.LoadXml("<?xml version=\"1.0\" encoding=\"UTF-8\"?>" +
         "<sequenceinfo><current>1</current>" +
         "<sequence>filesequence1.aspx" +
         "</sequence><sequence>filesequence2.aspx</sequence>" +
         "<sequence>filesequence3.aspx</sequence>" +
         "<sequence>filesequencedone.aspx</sequence>" + "
         "</sequenceinfo>");
      // write the GUID as a permanent cookie
      sequenceCookie = new HttpCookie("sequencefile", sGUID);
      // set the expiration date
      sequenceCookie.Expires = new DateTime(2010, 12, 31, 23,
   59, 59);
      Response.Cookies.Add(sequenceCookie);
   }
   else {
      xml.Load(m_filename);
   }
   // get the current sequence
   currSequenceIndex = XmlConvert.ToInt32
      (xml.SelectSingleNode("//sequenceinfo/current").InnerText);
```

```
      // get the name of the expected page
      expectedPage = xml.SelectSingleNode("sequenceinfo/sequence[" +
         currSequenceIndex.ToString() + "]").InnerText;
      if (expectedPage != requestedPage) {
         Response.Redirect(expectedPage);
      }
   }
}
catch (Exception e) {
   Response.Write(e.Message);
   Response.End();
}
```

NOTE *Internet Explorer shows the XML file using its default XSLT stylesheet. Netscape browsers show only the content. To show the markup in Netscape browsers, you will need to create a stylesheet, "borrow" the IE default stylesheet, or use the* Server.HTMLEncode *method to encode the markup so that it appears properly. If you want an indented look, use an XML-TextReader (hint: see the* Depth *property).*

To finish the test, open a new browser instance and browse to the FileSequence1.aspx page again. This time, the code redirects you to the FileSequence2.aspx page.

The code in the FileSequence(x).aspx pages is much the same as in the previous examples in this chapter. Each page creates a FileSequencer object, which prevents the page from completing unless it's the proper page in the sequence. Here's the Page_Load event code for the first page in the sequence:

```
private void Page_Load(object sender, System.EventArgs e) {
   FileSequencer fileSequencer = new FileSequencer();
   // The FileSequencer object redirects the request
   // if it's not a valid request in the sequence
   if (IsPostBack) {
      Page.Validate();
      if (Page.IsValid) {
         // save the last name
         fileSequencer.addNode("lastname", txtLastName.Text);
         fileSequencer.NextPage();
      }
   }
}
```

The only new code here is the FileSequencer.addNode method, which creates or updates the <lastname> node in the XML data file.

So, using files to maintain state extends your state management technique across browser instances on the same machine. That's considerably more robust than forcing the user to start over again if he accidentally closes the browser or loses his connection. However, that's still not robust enough, because cookies only identify *machines* and individual browser types, not users. The application would break if any of the following conditions occurred:

◆   A user moved from one machine to another. The cookie resides only on one machine. The user would have to start the sequence over.

◆ A user opened a different type of browser and browsed to one of the sequence pages. Browsers from different manufacturers don't usually share cookies. The user would have to start the sequence over.

◆ There are multiple people using the same computer under the same username or account. For example, a shared computer in a manufacturing control room might easily have multiple users. In that case, the application works properly for the *first* user but not for subsequent users, because the local machine sends the same cookie for each user.

◆ A user erases the cookie file either intentionally or unintentionally.

While cookies work to identify a machine, even across sessions, they won't work by themselves to identify a user and are useless across machine and browser boundaries. Nonetheless, permanent cookies are often good enough for applications where there's no security involved, you don't really care *who* the user is, and the work or task performed by the application is not critical. The biggest problem for most of the failure scenarios is that you lose the connection (the cookie) between the machine and the data.

That loss leads to yet another potential problem—or advantage, depending on how you look at it. Files are more or less permanent on a backed-up server. Therefore, they tend to accumulate rapidly. If you test the FileSequence sample several times, perhaps with different browsers, from different client machines, or by erasing the cookie between tests, you'll see that the program has no way to delete the XML files holding the data. Even though the files exist, no user will ever be able to use them again. Whenever you create a scheme that uses files, you must consider the problem of how to archive or destroy older files. Finally, because files use relatively slow IO, reading and writing too many files can become a performance bottleneck for busy sites.

Maintaining State in Database Tables

Here's another "permanent" method for saving the data. Create a new SQL Server database named CSharpASP and create one table named ch17. The T-SQL script CSharpASP_Database.sql contains the SQL script to create the database and the table. Give the System or ASPNET account permission to access and write to the database.

WARNING   *Be sure to update the file paths in the T-SQL script before you run it.*

The table itself has five columns: an id column that holds a GUID for identification, a sequence-Index column that holds the current user position in the sequence, and three columns for the Lastname, Firstname, and Telephone data entered by the user. You still need some way to connect a user (or in this case, a browser instance) to a row of data; I've used a Session variable named GUID in this example. As you probably expect by now, the DBSequencer class handles sequence management. Each Web Form instantiates a DBSequencer object during the Page_Load event, which causes the browser to redirect if the user did not request the proper page in the sequence.

As with the database code in Chapter 13, "Introduction to ADO.NET," the DBSequencer class reads an <appSettings> value from the web.config file to retrieve the connection string. Add the following code to your web.config file in the <appSettings> section:

```
<add key="CSharpASP" value="Data Source=localhost; Initial
    Catalog=CSharpASP; Integrated Security=SSPI" />
```

WARNING *You must add the preceding code to the* `<appSettings>` *section to define the database connection used by the DBSequencer class.*

The code itself is straightforward but uses a public inner class to manage the user data. While this is not a requirement, it is convenient. The class is simply a collection of public variables. You can find the code for the DBSequencer and the DBSequenceUser classes in the `DBSequencer.cs` file on www.sybex.com.

```
public class DBSequenceUser {
   public String id, lastname, firstname, telephone;
   public int sequenceIndex;
}
```

When a user first requests one of the Web Forms in the `DBSequenceX.aspx` sequence, the constructor code creates a new private class-level `DBSequenceUser` object named `mUser`, sets its `id` field to a new GUID, inserts a new row in the database containing the new `id` value, and ensures that the user sees the first form in the sequence. If the current request is *not* the first request from a user, the constructor retrieves the user data from the ch17 table in the CSharpASP database by calling the `getUserData()` method.

```
using System.Data;
using System.Data.SqlClient;
using System.Configuration;
private DBSequenceUser mUser = new DBSequenceUser();
public DBSequencer() {

   Response = context.Response;
   Request = context.Request;
   Session = context.Session;

   // get the Session GUID
   mUser.id = (String) Session["GUID"];
   if (mUser.id == null) {
      mUser.id = Guid.NewGuid().ToString();
      insertUser();
   }
   else {
      getUserData();
   }
   requestedPage =
   Request.ServerVariables["SCRIPT_NAME"].ToLower();
   requestedPage = requestedPage.Substring
      (requestedPage.LastIndexOf("/") + 1);

   if (sequence[mUser.sequenceIndex] != requestedPage) {
      Response.Redirect(sequence[mUser.sequenceIndex]);
   }
}
```

For new users, the first request for any of the sequence pages calls the insertUser method, which inserts the new GUID into the id column of the ch17 table.

```
private void insertUser() {
    // insert a new row
    SqlConnection conn = new SqlConnection
        (ConfigurationSettings.AppSettings.Get("CSharpASP"));
    SqlCommand cm = new SqlCommand("INSERT INTO ch17
    (id, SequenceIndex, LastName,
        FirstName, Telephone) VALUES('" + mUser.id +
        "',0,' ',' ', ' ')", conn);
    try {
        conn.Open();
        cm.ExecuteNonQuery();
        Session["GUID"] = mUser.id;
    }
    catch (Exception e) {
        Response.Write(e.Message);
    }
    finally {
        try {
            cm.Dispose();
            conn.Close();
            conn.Dispose();
        }
        catch (Exception e) {
            Response.Write(e.Message);
        }
    }
}
```

Subsequent calls retrieve the existing user row via the getUserData method, which populates the mUser DBSequenceUser object.

```
private void getUserData() {
    // retrieve the user's data
    SqlConnection conn = new
    SqlConnection(ConfigurationSettings.AppSettings.Get
        ("CSharpASP"));
    SqlCommand cm = new SqlCommand("SELECT sequenceIndex, " +
        "lastname, firstname, telephone FROM Ch17 WHERE id='" +
        mUser.id + "'", conn);
    SqlDataReader dr = null;
    try {
        conn.Open();
        dr =
    cm.ExecuteReader(System.Data.CommandBehavior.SingleRow);
        if (dr.Read()) {
            mUser.sequenceIndex = (int) dr["sequenceIndex"];
```

```
          mUser.lastname = (String) dr["lastname"];
          mUser.firstname = (String) dr["firstname"];
          mUser.telephone = (String) dr["telephone"];
        }
      }
      catch (Exception e) {
        Response.Write(e.Message);
      }
      finally {
        try {
          dr.Close();
          cm.Dispose();
          conn.Close();
          conn.Dispose();
        }
        catch (Exception e) {
          Response.Write(e.Message);
        }
      }
    }
```

The inner class variables are public, making the code much shorter than if you had to write public properties, but in a production application, you would not normally want to create or expose an inner class in this manner because someone might put inappropriate data into one of the fields. At any rate, in this example, the Web Forms update the mUser fields, which is not a good design. A better design would let the Web Forms pass data to the DBSequencer instance, where you can validate it and prepare the data for the database.

Whenever one of the sequence forms calls the NextPage method, the code updates the database from the current values in the mUser fields and redirects the browser to the next page in the sequence:

```
public void NextPage() {
    if (mUser.sequenceIndex < sequence.GetUpperBound(0)) {
        mUser.sequenceIndex++;
        updateUser();
        Response.Redirect(sequence[mUser.sequenceIndex]);
    }
}

private void updateUser() {
    SqlConnection conn = new
    SqlConnection(ConfigurationSettings.AppSettings.Get("CSharpASP"));
    SqlCommand cm = null;
    try {
        mUser.lastname = mUser.lastname.Replace("'", "''");
        mUser.firstname = mUser.firstname.Replace("'", "''");
        cm = new SqlCommand("UPDATE ch17 SET sequenceIndex = " +
            mUser.sequenceIndex + ", LastName='" + mUser.lastname +
            "', FirstName='" + mUser.firstname + "', Telephone='" +
```

```
        mUser.telephone + "' WHERE id='" + mUser.id + "'", conn);
    conn.Open();
    cm.ExecuteNonQuery();
}
catch (Exception e) {
    Response.Write(e.Message);
}
finally {
    try {
        cm.Dispose();
        conn.Close();
        conn.Dispose();
    }
    catch (Exception e) {
        Response.Write(e.Message);
    }
}
}
```

The highlighted lines in the preceding code point out one reason why you would not normally expose the inner class fields; if the user enters an apostrophe for either the last or first name, you *must* replace the apostrophe with two apostrophes or the database insert fails because T-SQL uses single quotes (apostrophes) to delimit strings. If a string you're inserting contains a single quote character that's not followed immediately by a *second* single quote, the database's SQL parser assumes that the embedded quote character marks the end of the string. When the database returns the data, it returns it with a single quote—you don't have to change double quotes back to singles after retrieving the data.

When the user reaches the end of the sequence, the DBSequenceDone.aspx form calls the show-Values method:

```
public void showValues() {
    Response.Write("id=" + mUser.id + "<br>");
    Response.Write("sequenceIndex=" + mUser.sequenceIndex +
        "<br>");
    Response.Write("Lastname=" + mUser.lastname + "<br>");
    Response.Write("Firstname=" + mUser.firstname + "<br>");
    Response.Write("Telephone=" + mUser.telephone + "<br>");
}
```

Using the *Cache* Object

In addition to all the ways you've already seen to cache data for Web applications, ASP.NET supports yet another—the Cache object. Each Page object exposes a Cache object. Cached data is not specific to an individual user, page, or session; cached data belongs to the application. The cache, like the Application object, contains pairs of keys and values, but it also contains methods that let you determine exactly when and how long to cache the data, to specify the priority of those items (which ones the server recycles first if memory becomes scarce), and how long a cached item remains valid. You can also create dependencies between items in the Cache and another resource, such as a file or another cached item, so that changes to the dependent object let you refresh the cache.

For example, suppose your application uses an XSLT stylesheet that changes fairly frequently because of variations in advertisement size and placement. You could read the stylesheet from disk for every request, but that's much slower than reading the stylesheet from memory. However, if you cache the stylesheet, you need to be able to refresh it whenever the disk copy of the stylesheet file changes. You could write code to ensure that the file date and size have not changed since cacheing the copy in memory, but creating a file dependency between the cached copy of the XSLT and the disk file solves the problem without your having to write custom code. You can use a dependency between cached items as a "trigger" to ensure that the items stay synchronized.

You cache items by calling the Cache.Insert or Cache.Add method. Both methods let you specify the expiration time, refresh interval, and dependencies. The Add method requires the parameters shown in Table 17.1.

TABLE 17.1: THE Cache OBJECT's Add METHOD PARAMETERS

PARAMETER NAME	DESCRIPTION
Key	A string value used as the key for retrieving, refreshing, or removing an object from the Cache.
Value	The object you want to place into the Cache.
Dependencies	A filename, a directory name, an array of files, or an array of cache keys. The CacheDependency monitors the items for changes. You can also create a CacheDependency object that depends on another CacheDependency object. Finally, you can specify when monitoring should begin.

For example, the Web Form cacheExample1.aspx (see Listing 17.6) caches the contents of a text file named items.txt and creates a dependency on the source file. If you change the source file, the cache updates automatically.

LISTING 17.6: THE WEB FORM CacheExample1.aspx **CREATES A Cache OBJECT WITH A FILE DEPENDENCY (**cacheExample1.aspx.cs**)**

```
using System;
using System.Collections;
using System.ComponentModel;
using System.Data;
using System.Drawing;
using System.Web;
using System.Web.SessionState;
using System.Web.UI;
using System.Web.UI.WebControls;
using System.Web.UI.HtmlControls;
```

```csharp
using System.IO;
using System.Web.Cacheing;

namespace CSharpASP.ch17
{
    /// <summary>
    /// Summary description for cacheExample1.
    /// </summary>
    public class cacheExample1 : System.Web.UI.Page
    {
        protected System.Web.UI.WebControls.Label Label1;
        protected System.Web.UI.WebControls.ListBox lstItems;
        private void Page_Load(object sender, System.EventArgs e) {

        String[] aList;
        aList = (String[]) Cache.Get("items");
        if (aList == null) {
            Response.Write("Reading from file.<br>");
            String aFilename = Server.MapPath(".") + "\\items.txt";
            FileInfo fi = new FileInfo(aFilename);
            StreamReader sr = null;
            sr = fi.OpenText();
            aList = sr.ReadToEnd().Split('\n');
            sr.Close();
            Cache.Add("items", aList, new CacheDependency(aFilename),
                DateTime.MaxValue, new TimeSpan(1, 1, 1),
                CacheItemPriority.Normal,
                new CacheItemRemovedCallback(removingItems));
        }
        else {
            Response.Write("Read from cache.");
        }
        lstItems.DataSource = aList;
        lstItems.DataBind();

    }

    private void removingItems(String key, Object value,
        CacheItemRemovedReason reason) {
        Response.Write("Item has been removed from the cache.");
    }

    // autogenerated code not shown
    }
}
```

For this example, the item's text file itself can have any content in it as long as it's a carriage-return/linefeed delimited list—in other words, each item appears on a single line. I started with a file containing the following:

```
Item 1
Item 2
Item 3
Item 4
Item 5
```

When you run the Web Form, the code reads the `items.txt` file whenever the `Cache` item named `"items"` is `null`. That condition occurs the first time you run the Web Form, and—because of the file dependency—whenever the `items.txt` file changes. In that case, the code creates a string array object and stores the string array in the `Cache` object with a dependency on the text file (see Figure 17.3).

FIGURE 17.3

The Web Form `cacheExample1` `.aspx` displays the text `Reading from file.` whenever the cache is refreshed

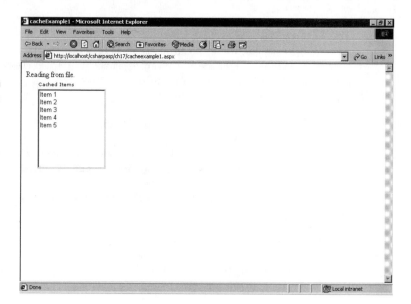

Subsequent requests for the page display the data from the cache (see Figure 17.4).

Set the `cacheExample1.aspx` file as the start page for the application, and refresh the page so that you're sure the request reads the data from the cache. Now, without halting the application, open the `items.txt` file and make some changes. I added two extra items to the bottom of the file.

```
Item 6
Item 7
```

FIGURE 17.4

The Web Form `cacheExample1` `.aspx` displays the text **Read from cache.** when the cache is current

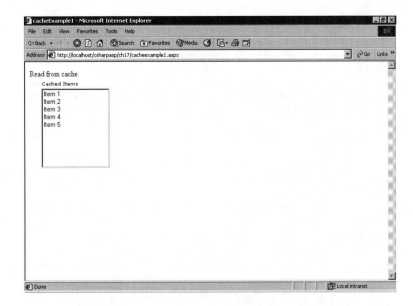

After saving your changes to the `items.txt` file, refresh the page again. The change to the file forces the `Cache` to refresh the `"items"` object for the next request, so the code to read the text file executes again, and you'll see the added data in your browser (see Figure 17.5).

FIGURE 17.5

The Web Form `cacheExample1` `.aspx` displays the text **Reading from file.** after refreshing the cache

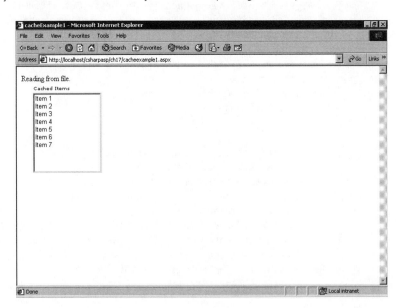

The `Cache.Add` and `Cache.Insert` methods are similar but not identical. First, the `Add` method returns the newly cached object, while the `Insert` method does not. Second, if an item with the specified

key already exists in the Cache, the Insert method replaces it, but the Add method does not. The Web Form cacheExample2.aspx illustrates this second difference between the two methods (see Listing 17.7). Both methods take the same parameters.

LISTING 17.7: THE Cache.Add AND Insert METHODS PERFORM DIFFERENTLY (cacheExample2.aspx.cs)

```
private void Page_Load(object sender, System.EventArgs e) {
   /*
    * Uncomment the following code to see all the data
    * cached by the system.
    */
   //Response.Write("Cache count before clearing is: " +
      //Cache.Count + "<br>");
   //Response.Write("<b>Cached items</b>:<br>");
   //foreach(DictionaryEntry de in Cache) {
   //    Response.Write("Removing key:" + de.Key + "<br>");
   //    }
   foreach(DictionaryEntry de in Cache) {
      Cache.Remove((String) de.Key);
   }
   Cache.Add("AddString", "Add1", null, DateTime.MaxValue,
      TimeSpan.FromMinutes(60),
      System.Web.Cacheing.CacheItemPriority.Default,null);
   Cache.Add("AddString", "Add2", null, DateTime.MaxValue,
      TimeSpan.FromMinutes(60),
      System.Web.Cacheing.CacheItemPriority.Default, null);
   Response.Write("Cache count after two Add methods=" +
      Cache.Count + "<br>");
   Response.Write("Cache item AddString=" +
      Cache.Get("AddString") + "<br>");


   Cache.Insert("InsertString", "Insert1", null,
      DateTime.MaxValue, TimeSpan.FromMinutes(60),
      System.Web.Cacheing.CacheItemPriority.Default, null);
   Cache.Insert("InsertString", "Insert2", null, DateTime.MaxValue,
      TimeSpan.FromMinutes(60),
      System.Web.Cacheing.CacheItemPriority.Default, null);
   Response.Write("Cache count after two Insert methods=" +
      Cache.Count + "<br>");
   Response.Write("Cache item InsertString=" +
      Cache.Get("InsertString") + "<br>");
}
```

The output from the Add method call displays Add1, meaning that the second Add call did *not* replace the value—but it doesn't generate an error either, which means you must be very careful when using this method. In contrast, the output from the Insert method displays Insert2, meaning that it did replace the value.

WARNING   *The Cache keys are case sensitive. For example, the keys myvalue and myValue are not identical and may refer to different objects. There's no option to change the case sensitivity of the keys, making it very easy to accidentally create additional keys.*

The ASP.NET engine itself uses the Cache extensively. The reason for the clear Cache code in Listing 17.7 is primarily to clear the Cache of all the system-generated values so that the example numbers make sense. To see how the system uses the Cache, uncomment the commented code in Listing 17.7 that appears *before* the loop that clears the Cache.

NOTE   *The following code exists on www.sybex.com but is commented out. Enable the code to see the output.*

```
Response.Write("Cache count before clearing is: " & _
    Cache.Count & "<Br>")
Response.Write("<b>Cached items</b>:<br>")
For Each de In Cache
    Response.Write("Removing key: " & de.Key & "<br>")
Next

' clear the cache
For Each de In Cache
    Cache.Remove(de.Key)
Next
```

NOTE   *I generated this sample immediately after clearing the Cache object during the preceding request. If you run several other ASPX files before requesting this sample, you'll see that the system caches a lot of data in the Cache object. Knowing that the system relies on the Cache object should affect how you think about using the feature—in other words, it's extremely robust.*

You're not limited to watching a single file for changes. You can create a list of files and use the entire list as a dependency. Thus, you can go far beyond this simple example using the Cache object. For example, you can cache database data based on a file dependency. By writing a trigger in your database that alters a file, your code can update the Cache. Because the Cache object has Application scope, you can cache objects on one page and use them as dependencies that, when changed, control other pages in your application. The sky's the limit. I'm certain you'll see innovative uses of the Cache object in the near future.

Cacheing ASP.NET Pages

So far, you've worked with only part of ASP.NET's cacheing capability. In addition to placing objects into the Cache, you can tell ASP.NET to cache the output from your pages. There's a huge performance advantage to doing this—after cacheing the result from one request for a page, the ASP.NET engine doesn't have to format the output for subsequent identical requests repeatedly; instead, it can read the preformatted output directly from the cache. Obviously, cacheing won't help you in situations where every page request is different, but for most sites, that isn't much of a problem.

There are two ways to cache pages. The simplest way is to edit the HTML directly. To enable cacheing, add an output directive to the HTML content of the page in the ASPX file:

```
<% OutputCache Duration="20" VaryByParam="None" %>
```

Place the directive on a separate line below the <%@ Page%> directive. For those of you familiar with classic ASP syntax, which allowed only one directive per page, there are several new directives, and you can place them in any order, anywhere on the page. But don't do that. Put them at the top of your pages where you and programmers after you can see them easily.

The OutputCache directive shown above causes the cache to store the page output for 20 seconds before refreshing it (by letting the code run rather than taking the output directly from the cache). Each time the page code runs, ASP.NET caches the output for another 20 seconds.

To see this in action, try running the Web Form cacheExample3.aspx in the Ch17 directory. The Web Form creates a Session scope counter variable and increments it in the Page_Load event each time the page runs. It displays the results in a Label control. A Button control lets you submit the page quickly. Because this page doesn't send much data for each request, I overrode the Page.onPreRender method and switched the Form1 method attribute value to GET rather than POST. Switching the method to GET causes the form to submit the data using QueryString values instead of Form variables. However, in this case, I don't care about the submitted values at all—I switched the method so I could refresh the page quickly without getting those irritating "This page cannot be refreshed..." messages.

The point of the example code is that you need to think carefully before cacheing a page. Cacheing subverts the point of dynamic pages because it circumvents the ASP.NET code altogether; in other words, *cacheing causes your code not to run*. Here's the proof. The example Web Form simply shows the value of the counter variable. When you run it the first time, the counter increments to 1 and caches the page for 20 seconds. During that time, the counter does not increment, no matter how many times you request the page. After reaching the cache Duration time limit, the ASP.NET engine runs the code to refresh the cache, and the counter will increment to 2.

```
//autogenerated code omitted
private void Page_Load(object sender, System.EventArgs e)
{
   int counter;
   if (Session["counter"] == null) {
      Session["counter"] = 1;
   }
   else {
      counter = (int) Session["counter"];
      counter += 1;
      Session["counter"] = counter;
   }
}

private void Label1_Load(object sender, System.EventArgs e) {
   Label1.Text = "This page has been seen: " +
```

```
      Session["counter"].ToString() + " time(s)";
}

private void cacheExample3_PreRender(object sender, System.EventArgs e)
   {
     HtmlForm f = (HtmlForm) this.FindControl("Form1");
     f.Method = "GET";
}
```

The OutputCache directive attributes Duration and VaryByParam are *required*. The Duration attribute takes any integer value greater than zero. The VaryByParam attribute can be None, as you've seen, but it can also take one or more values delimited with semicolons. The values should correspond to the names of QueryString or Form variable sent via the GET or POST method. For example, suppose you had a list of states in a drop-down list on your page. When the user selects a state, you post the state abbreviation back to the server in a Form variable named StateCode, so you can display a map displaying the locations and numbers of product sales in that state. These product sales figures change at irregular intervals based on data posted to a central server. You don't want to query the server every time someone selects a state, but you do want to refresh the data after 30 minutes. You also don't want to loop through the cache refreshing unrequested data; instead, you want to refresh the data only when someone requests that particular state and the data is uncached or the cached data has exceeded the 30-minute Duration limit. To do this, use the VaryByParam attribute with a value of StateCode and set the Duration attribute value to 1800 (remember, you specify the cache Duration in seconds).

The OuputCache directive can take any or all of several optional attributes as well. Most of the attributes accept a single value or a semicolon-delimited list of values. When you supply a list, the ASP.NET engine caches a separate version of the page for each item in the list.

TIP OutputCache *directives are not case sensitive when placed in an ASPX file.*

Cache *Location* Attribute

When a browser requests a page, the result may come from the browser's own local cache, from a proxy server on the local network, from a proxy server anywhere between the browser and the source server represented by the URL, or directly from the source server. In other words, it's difficult to be absolutely sure that you're getting the latest page. However, in your applications, you can use the OutputCache-Location attribute value to tell these intermediate caches how or whether to cache your page. The attribute controls the value of the HTTP Cache-Control header. The values are as follows:

Any   Let the requesting browser, the originating server, or any proxy cache the page. Any is the default value, which leads to problems with dynamic pages. Use this value only for static pages that never change.

Client   Let the requesting browser cache the page.

Downstream   Let the client or any proxy cache the page, but not the originating server.

None   Disable cacheing for this page.

Server   Let only the originating server cache the page.

Cache *VaryByCustom* Attribute

You can control cacheing with any custom string. For example, you might use a custom string to refresh the cache after a specific time or a certain number of hits, or based on average page usage in a specific section of the application. To use this method, you must override the `HttpApplication.GetVaryBy-CustomString` method in the `global.asax` file. You can control cacheing based on client type by setting the `VaryByCustom` attribute to `Browser`. That forces the cache to maintain a separate copy of the page output for each client name *and* major client version number. For example, using this method on a public Internet site means you won't have one copy for IE browsers; instead, you'll probably have three or four, one for each version of IE (IE3/4 through IE6).

Cache *VaryByControl* Attribute

The `VaryByControl` attribute applies only to user controls (custom-built controls). It accepts a semicolon-delimited list of user control properties. You must fully qualify the names of the properties. In other words, if your user control is named `NameInputControl` and has properties named `LastName` and `FirstName`, you could set the cache to change whenever either property changed (the user entered a different name) by setting the `VaryByControl` attribute value to the following string:

```
NameInputControl.LastName;NameInputControl.FirstName
```

Cache *VaryByHeader* Attribute

You can control cacheing using the standard HTTP headers sent by clients. For example, you might want to cache pages based on the domain or IP address of the clients.

Cacheing Data Programmatically

You don't have to alter the HTML and insert an `OutputCache` directive to cache `Page` object output; instead, you can control output cacheing in your code. If you explore the `Page` methods, you'll find one named `Page.InitOutputCache`. This method *looks* like the one you would use to control cacheing from code because the names match the `OutputCache` directive attribute names—but it isn't. The .NET documentation states, "The member is not intended to be used directly from your code." Fortunately, there's an alternative. The HttpCachePolicy class lets you set cache options. Unfortunately, the property and method names for the HttpCachePolicy class don't directly correspond to the attribute values you just learned for the `OutputCache` directive—and there are more of them. Most control HTTP 1.1 cache header values. Table 17.2 shows the ones you need to match some of the functionality of the `Output-Cache` directive.

TABLE 17.2: PROPERTY AND METHOD NAMES FOR THE HTTPCACHEPOLICY CLASS AND THEIR EQUIVALENT `OutputCache` DIRECTIVE ATTRIBUTES

PROPERTY/METHOD	EQUIVALENT OR SIMILAR `OutputCache` DIRECTIVE ATTRIBUTE
SetExpires	Duration is not quite equivalent because the Duration attribute accepts an integer value that controls the number of seconds until the Page cache expires, whereas the SetExpires method takes a DateTime value specifying exactly *when* the cache expires. You can get around that easily by using the syntax DateTime.now().addSeconds(*n*), where *n* is the number of seconds before the cached copy expires.

Continued on next page

TABLE 17.2: PROPERTY AND METHOD NAMES FOR THE HTTPCACHEPOLICY CLASS AND THEIR EQUIVALENT **OutputCache** DIRECTIVE ATTRIBUTES *(continued)*

PROPERTY/METHOD	EQUIVALENT OR SIMILAR OutputCache DIRECTIVE ATTRIBUTE
SetVaryByCustom	VaryByCustom works the same way as the VaryByCustom attribute value for the OutputCache directive.
SetCacheablity	Close to but not exactly the same as the Location attribute. The method takes a System.WebHttpCacheability enumeration value, which is one of the following: NoCache, Private, Public, or Server.
VaryByHeaders	Equivalent to the VaryByHeader attribute. The VaryByHeaders property returns an HttpCacheVaryByHeaders object. The object has three custom properties that you can set to add HTTP header types to the list of headers that vary the cache. The AcceptTypes property adds or removes the HTTP Accept header, the UserAgent property adds or removes the User-Agent header, and the UserCharSet property adds or removes the Accept-Charset header. You can add custom headers to the list or retrieve specific values with the HttpCacheVaryByHeaders.Item property.
VaryByParams	Equivalent to the VaryByParam attribute. The VaryByParams property returns an HttpCacheVaryByParams object. That object has an IgnoreParams property. Setting that property to true is the equivalent of setting the VaryByParam attribute to None. Use the HttpCacheVaryByParams.Item property to add or retrieve individual parameter names.

For example, here's the OutputCache directive you saw earlier:

```
<% OutputCache Duration="20" VaryByParam="None" %>
```

Here's the equivalent using the Response.Cache object:

```
Response.Cache.SetExpires(DateTime.Now.AddSeconds(20))
Response.Cache.SetCacheability(System.Web.HttpCacheability.Public)
Response.Cache.VaryByParams.IgnoreParams=True
```

While it's convenient and sometimes necessary to apply cache settings in code, you may need to adjust these after deploying. Therefore, I recommend that you use the OutputCache directive, because you can change the directive in the ASPX HTML template file *without* changing your compiled code-behind files.

Partial Page Cacheing

There's no special trick to cacheing part of a page—the system won't do it automatically; it only caches the output from complete ASPX or ASCX files. But that *is* the trick. You can cache the output from custom server controls that you place in your page. You'll see more about this in Chapter 23, "Build Your Own Web Controls." Until then, just remember that you can cache only a portion of a page. It's not difficult, and it's often far more efficient to cache most of a page and let selected dynamic sections remain dynamic than it is to either attempt to cache the entire dynamic page but refresh it often or forego cacheing altogether.

A Multitude of Choices

Now that you've seen various methods for maintaining application state for a browser instance, both within a single session and across multiple sessions, you can make decisions about which method is most appropriate for your application.

Cookies   Cookies are the least capable, but they're widely available. On the other hand, cookies must accompany every request, and they reside on users' machines, where they're liable to disappear at any time.

Session **Variables**   These are the simplest but are technology specific. For example, you can't share `Session` data between a classic ASP page and an ASP.NET page. `Session` variables depend on either cookies or `QueryString` data (`HttpSessionState.Mode=IsCookieless`) to maintain a connection with the user, but with the Enterprise version of ASP.NET, they're scalable across multiple servers and can hold more data than cookies. In addition, when you set the `HttpSessionState.Mode` property to `SQLServer`, you can store `Session` data in a database to maintain state across sessions.

Files   Files are relatively slow because they require disk I/O, but they are permanent, almost unlimited in size, and completely customizable to hold any type of data in any arrangement you prefer. As you've seen, some kinds of files, such as XML files, can act as mini-databases themselves. For some applications, it's appropriate to cache a user's entire file in memory, giving you very fast access to the data. Files are also appropriate for unstructured data.

Database Tables   These are like files but are very flexible. They have one huge advantage over files, which is that you can easily compare data across many users. For the most part, database tables are also faster than files. Despite the overhead of creating `Connections`, `Commands`, and `DataReaders` or `DataSets` to hold the data, modern databases use memory caches and indexes to reduce data retrieval time. Databases are highly scalable, and you can use them in a server farm containing multiple servers. However, when you need to store unstructured data, databases lose many of their advantages.

The *Cache* **Object**   The `Cache` object, like the `Application` object, stores Application scope data, but because of the expiration, refresh, and dependency settings, it can save you a great deal of code.

Output Cacheing   This improves response time and reduces the load on your server but can have side effects, such as not updating variable values, because your code doesn't run when the server serves a cached page.

In addition to all these state maintenance and cacheing options, there are others that I didn't show you. For example, in this section I didn't discuss using `QueryString` variables or hidden form variables to maintain state. That's because I'm not a big fan of using `QueryString` variables to maintain state. A user can see—and change—the values in his browser's Address field. In addition, most browsers limit `QueryString` data to somewhere between 1,024 and 2,056 bytes. However, for non-critical applications where you don't need much data and where the user viewing and changing the data doesn't affect security or the application itself, `QueryString` variables are convenient and easy to use—and they're also the easiest method to debug. I didn't discuss maintaining state using hidden form variables because the easiest way to handle this in an ASP.NET application is to create an invisible control that contains the data, such as a `Label` control, and let the built-in ASP.NET form and ViewState operations handle the data-cacheing tasks for you. Although I don't normally advocate using invisible controls to maintain values, in this particular instance, there's no significant difference between writing the code to maintain state yourself by creating hidden form variables (`<input type=hidden">`) and letting ASP.NET do it for you with an invisible `Label` control.

Finally, any of these methods works—in the appropriate setting—and you can and should combine them as your applications require. For example, combining databases and XML/XSLT is an extremely powerful and flexible technique that gives you the capability to provide customized data and customized data display. If you combine that with the `Cache` object's capability to store results and update them whenever required, you can create high-performance applications without much effort.

Summary

You've seen a number of ways to maintain state and cache data on the server. Unfortunately, the biggest problem with all the solutions you've seen so far is that they connect stored data to a browser instance (with `Session` variables and in-memory cookies), to a specific machine (with permanent cookies), or to an application (with the `Cache` object), but they don't connect data the way applications often need it the most—to individuals. Associating data with an individual presupposes that you can identify that individual. To do that, you need to be able to *authenticate* and *authorize* the people who use your application. Authentication is the process of determining a user's identity, for example, with a username and password, and authorization is the process of determining what permission levels an authenticated individual has. Fortunately, ASP.NET has some built-in features that help automate authentication and authorization. You'll explore those in the next chapter.

Chapter 18

Controlling Access and Monitoring

As you've seen, there's a difference between restricting access to a site based on *machine* identification, which you can enforce with a permanent cookie, and restricting access based on *user* identification, which requires a token that can be associated unambiguously with a specific person.

You can look at the need for security from two perspectives. From the client perspective, users want to know that their private information is adequately protected. From the application perspective, you need to know who's accessing the application and what their level of access should be. The user perspective is slightly easier because users can be relatively sure that the application they're accessing actually *is* the application they intended to access. Unfortunately, the reverse is not true. There's currently no good method for ensuring that the client *is* the client.

The most commonly used security method is a combination of usernames and passwords—and that's a weak method of security. People lose and forget their usernames and passwords; they write them down; they put them in desk drawers and notebooks where they can be seen by others; they give them to administrators and friends; they create multiple logins; they use poorly chosen passwords—the problems are well known. Better methods of security exist, particularly biorecognition, which uses tokens derived from difficult-to-duplicate physical characteristics to represent a specific individual. For example, fingerprints, "voiceprints," retinal scans, and facial recognition are all becoming more common.

The cost of the technology needed to implement biorecognition has dropped recently to reasonable levels—for example, I log on to my desktop computer using a fingerprint identification system that cost less than $100. Even though the cost of implementing such technology over an entire organization may be considerable, when compared to the maintenance and security costs for using username/password security, it begins to sound worthwhile. I expect biorecognition to replace usernames and passwords entirely as identification methods over the next decade, but for now, we have to work with username/password security and accept its limitations.

In this chapter:

◆ Implementing Username/Password Security

◆ Securing Your Server with SSL

◆ Monitoring Your Site—Beyond Page Counting

◆ Disabling an Application for Maintenance

Implementing Username/Password Security

There are several levels of username/password security. Some require you to write code; others are more or less automatic. The simplest way to authenticate individuals in an intranet application is to capitalize on Windows' own security. Microsoft calls this type of authentication Integrated Windows authentication.

For example, if all the users have to log in to a Windows domain, then the client workstation already has the client's account information—because the user typed it in to log onto Windows. If you can get the client to provide that account information to the server, where the server is also a member or has trusted access to the client's domain, the server can authenticate the request transparently.

To implement Integrated Windows authentication, you must deny anonymous access. To do that, open the Properties dialog for the CSharpASP application using the Internet Services Manager application. Click the Directory Security tab, and then click the Edit button. You'll see the Authentication Methods dialog shown in Figure 18.1.

FIGURE 18.1

IIS Authentication
Methods dialog

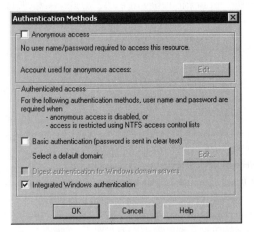

Uncheck the Anonymous Access item, and check the Integrated Windows Authentication item. Click OK to close all the dialogs and apply your changes. Now, when a user requests any page in the CSharpASP application, the server will attempt to authenticate him transparently. If the server cannot authenticate the client, it will return an access denied header value, and the user will see an Enter Network Password dialog (see Figure 18.2), where he can attempt to provide valid information.

FIGURE 18.2

Enter Network
Password dialog

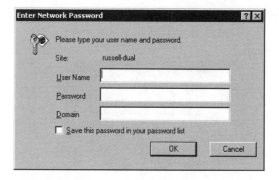

If the user enters invalid information in the Enter Network Password dialog, the server will deny access, the browser will redisplay the dialog, and the user can retry. Every time the user's attempt at access fails, the server returns an access denied error code, and the browser stops parsing the response as soon as it receives the request for authentication. Most servers have a default count for the number of tries they allow before simply returning the access denied message, without the authorization header. On IIS, you can attempt to log in three times before the server denies the attempt. When the user gives up trying to authenticate and presses the Cancel key, the browser parses the remainder of the server's response, which displays the access denied message returned by the server. Figure 18.3 shows the default IIS access denied page.

FIGURE 18.3

Access denied page

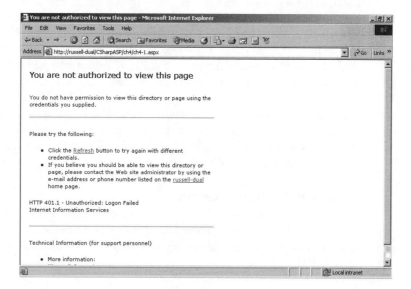

NOTE *Netscape browsers do not support Integrated Windows security. If you attempt to access a site with Integrated Windows security with a Netscape 6 browser, you won't get any reply. With Netscape 4, you get a Username and Password Required dialog. Note that it's a different dialog than you see when using IE (see Figure 18.4).*

The server does not generate the Enter Network Password dialog itself. Each browser has its own built-in dialog. For example, Figure 18.4 shows the dialog generated by Netscape 4.

FIGURE 18.4

Netscape 4
Username and
Password Required
dialog

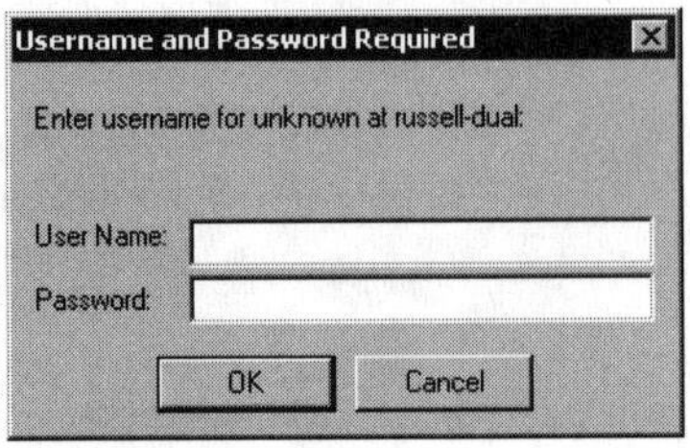

In previous versions of ASP, you had to implement your own username/password security. Although that's not difficult, it is tedious. Nevertheless, you should know how it works so you will understand what .NET and IIS/IE can do for you to simplify the process.

When you uncheck the Anonymous Access option in IIS for your application, you're telling IIS that it must receive a value in the HTTP LOGON_USER request header variable. Browsers send that value only when challenged by the server to provide authentication information. You can tell IIS to send the challenge by checking any other security option. When you check the Basic Authentication option, IIS challenges the browser for authentication information, and the browser displays a dialog so the user can log on. The username and password sent via Basic Authentication are encoded into base-64, but that's not secure—in fact, it's not true encryption at all. Encoding simply translates characters from one representation to another, while encryption uses various schemes to change the content to make it from mildly to extremely difficult to retrieve the original value without the correct decryption code.

Similarly, when you check the Integrated Windows Authentication option, you're telling IIS to go through a specific series of actions to force IE to provide the user's identity. IE doesn't provide the actual username and password; instead, it provides a hashed token that the server can verify. The entire process is transparent to both the user and the developer, but because Integrated Windows authentication doesn't work with Netscape browsers, it's suitable only for intranet applications.

In the next section, you'll implement authentication using several different methods—including the "old" way using Basic authentication—and explore different ways of accomplishing authentication that are built in to ASP.NET.

Using Basic Authentication

Although you should not use Basic authentication with .NET or in any public Web application except in conjunction with Secure Sockets Layer (SSL) encryption or some other strong encryption mechanism, it's a useful exercise so that you understand the benefits of the authentication methods that IIS, IE, and .NET provide.

NOTE *Before you start, open the CSharpASP Properties dialog using the Internet Services Manager application and make sure that Anonymous Access and Integrated Windows Authentication are disabled, and Basic Authentication is enabled. You must have at least one authentication method enabled or IIS will deny all access to the application. However, you may have more than one authentication method enabled simultaneously. After doing this you may need to authenticate to open or edit the project in VS.NET.*

NOTE *In your* `web.config` *file, make sure the authentication mode is set to* `"Windows"` *(*`<authentication mode="Windows">`*).*

WARNING *When you turn off Integrated Windows Authentication, you may no longer be able to debug your application by running it in Debug mode. However, you can debug by writing output messages or by attaching to the running* **asp-net_wp.exe** *process. To do that, click the Debug menu, select Processes, highlight the* **aspnet_wp.exe** *process, and click the Attach button. Run the project, and then launch a browser and make the request, and ASP.NET will break into the debugger at any breakpoints you set.*

The process to set up Basic authentication is simple.

1. When the server receives a request, it sends an access denied message. The user must log on with a valid domain account and password to get entry to the application.

2. When the user has been authenticated, you can further restrict access by checking the value of the `Request.ServerVariables["AUTH_USER"]` variable, which will contain the username for the authenticated account. The `Request.ServerVariables["AUTH_PASSWORD"]` variable contains the user's password. By comparing the username to an access list, you can deny access to specific individuals.

The Web Form `ch18-1.aspx` contains an example. When you request the page for the first time, you'll see the username/password dialog and a custom message. Enter the name and password of a valid network account. If the values you enter map to a valid account, you'll see the `ASPSessionID` for this session and the message `User authorized`, followed by the information in the `AUTH_USER`, `AUTH_PASSWORD`, and `LOGON_USER` variables in the `Request.ServerVariables` collection. I've included these three variables so you'll understand why Basic authentication is dangerous. Remember that anyone along the route from the client to the server can intercept the request and steal the username and password information. You should not use this method to secure your site.

The Web Form `ch18-1` contains very little code (see Listing 18.1). It creates a user variable, assigns it the contents of the `Request.ServerVariables["LOGON_USER"]` variable, and then checks to see if the user variable contains a null string. If so, it denies access by returning a 401 (access denied) status code and a custom error message. Some browsers, such as IE, use the custom error message in the username/password dialog.

LISTING 18.1: DOMAIN AUTHENTICATION WITH BASIC AUTHENTICATION BASED ON THE LOGON_USER HTTP VARIABLE VALUE (ch18-1.aspx.cs)

```
// autogenerated code omitted
public class ch18_1 : System.Web.UI.Page
{
    protected System.Web.UI.WebControls.Label lblAuthorized;
    protected System.Web.UI.WebControls.Label lblResult;

    private void Page_Load(object sender, System.EventArgs e) {
        String s="";
        s = Request.ServerVariables["HTTP_AUTHORIZATION"];
```

```
s = s.Substring(6);
Response.Write(s);
if (!this.User.Identity.IsAuthenticated) {
    Response.Status = "401 Unauthorized";
    Response.AddHeader("WWW-Authenticate",
        "BASIC REALM=\"You are not authorized to " +
        "access this resource.\"");
    s = "LOGON_USER=" + this.User.Identity;
    s += "AUTH_USER=" + Request.ServerVariables.Get
        ("AUTH_USER") + "<br>";
    s += "AUTH_PASSWORD=" + Request.ServerVariables.Get
        ("AUTH_PASSWORD") + "<br>";
    lblResult.Text = s;
    this.lblAuthorized.Visible=false;
    foreach(String aKey in Request.ServerVariables.Keys) {
        Response.Write(aKey + "=" +
            Request.ServerVariables[aKey] + "<br>");
    }
}
else {
    s = "LOGON_USER=" + Request.ServerVariables.Get
        ("LOGON_USER") + "<br>";
    s += "AUTH_USER=" + Request.ServerVariables.Get
        ("AUTH_USER") + "<br>";
    s += "AUTH_PASSWORD=" + Request.ServerVariables.Get
        ("AUTH_PASSWORD") + "<br>";
    lblResult.Text = s;
    this.lblAuthorized.Visible=true;
}
}
}
```

Figures 18.5 and 18.6 show the authentication sequence.

Because you have no control over how a user reaches a page in your application, you must check authentication for *every* page in your application for which you want to restrict access. Therefore, the simplest place to perform the check is in the global.asax file in the Application_BeginRequest event. However, you don't need to perform the full check for every request, and rather than displaying some information after authenticating the client, you don't need to do anything—ASP.NET automatically continues the request with the code in the requested page.

Although I'm not going to show you a working example, it's easy to understand, based on the code you saw in the last chapter, that you can set an in-memory cookie (for sessionless applications) or a Session variable after the user has authenticated the first time. If the cookie or Session variable has a value, then the user is authenticated, and you don't need to perform any more checks.

FIGURE 18.5

Initial request for
the Web Form
ch18-1.aspx.
Request denied;
browser displays
login dialog

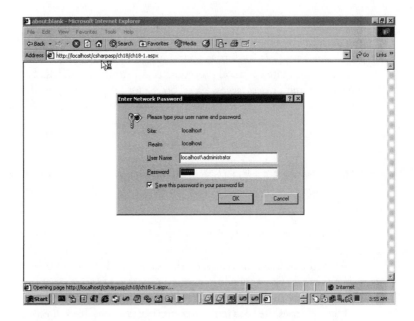

FIGURE 18.6

The user entered
a valid
username/password
combination

Using Custom Authentication

You don't have to rely on Windows domain account information to authorize users. In fact, that's neither practical nor possible for Internet applications that may have thousands or hundreds of thousands of users. A much more common procedure is to provide an HTML-based username and password dialog and then permit or deny access based on the user-supplied values. To do this, you normally need to be able to look up the name and password information in a database or file.

NOTE   *In this example, you can log on only with the username* admin *and the password* admin.

NOTE   *Before you start, open the CSharpASP Properties dialog using the Internet Services Manager application and make sure that Anonymous Access is enabled, Integrated Windows Authentication is disabled, and Basic Authentication is disabled.*

The Web Form ch18-2.aspx displays a form containing Username and Password Text controls and a Log In button. The title bar over the form provides directions and feedback. When the user submits the form, the code simply compares the values of the txtUsername and txtPassword fields with admin. When the user successfully logs in, the code sets a Session variable named "authenticated" to true and displays the message User Authenticated.

The code uses the Session["authenticated"] variable value as a flag to determine what to do. After successfully being authenticated, the user no longer sees the form.

Figure 18.7 shows the initial form state.

FIGURE 18.7

Custom authentication form before successful authentication

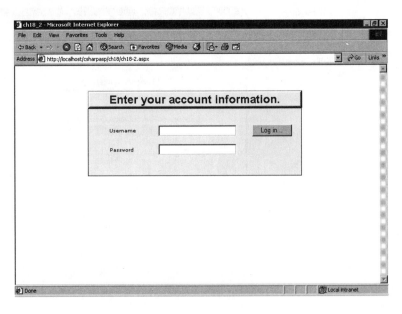

After authentication, the page returns a success message (see Figure 18.8).

FIGURE 18.8

Custom
authentication form
after successful
authentication

Requesting the page again brings up the message User *Already* Authenticated. The `Session["authen-ticated"]` variable serves as both evidence of the user's authentication state and a means to prevent the user from resubmitting the form. With the form controls hidden, the user cannot submit the form (see Figure 18.9).

FIGURE 18.9

Custom
authentication form
after attempting to
authenticate more
than once

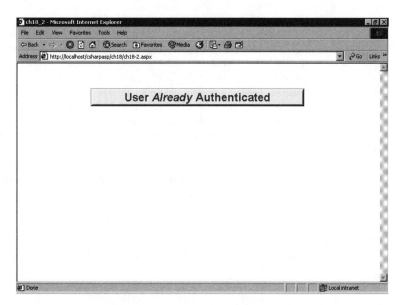

Note that the code that displays the User *Already* Authenticated message uses embedded HTML to set the Label's Text property. In other words, the browser interprets the embedded HTML as markup. If you want a Label or other control to display markup instead—for example, to place the phrase Use a <b> tag to start displaying bold text, and a </b> tag to stop displaying bold text. into a Label—you need to use the Server.HTMLEncode method to encode the text or manually substitute the character entities < and > for the left and right angle brackets, respectively.

Listing 18.2 contains the full code for the Web Form ch18-2.aspx.

LISTING 18.2: THE WEB FORM ch18-2 USES CUSTOM AUTHENTICATION (ch18-2.aspx.cs)

```
using System;
using System.Collections;
using System.ComponentModel;
using System.Data;
using System.Drawing;
using System.Web;
using System.Web.SessionState;
using System.Web.UI;
using System.Web.UI.WebControls;
using System.Web.UI.HtmlControls;

namespace CSharpASP.ch18 {
    /// <summary>
    /// Summary description for ch18_2.
    /// </summary>
    public class ch18_2 : System.Web.UI.Page {
        protected System.Web.UI.WebControls.Label lblTitle;
        protected System.Web.UI.WebControls.TextBox txtPassword;
        protected System.Web.UI.WebControls.Label lblPassword;
        protected System.Web.UI.WebControls.TextBox txtUserName;
        protected System.Web.UI.WebControls.Label lblBackground;
        protected System.Web.UI.WebControls.Label lblUsername;
        protected System.Web.UI.WebControls.Button btnLogin;
        protected System.Web.UI.HtmlControls.HtmlGenericControl
    divForm;

        private void Page_Load(object sender, System.EventArgs e) {
            if (Session["authenticated"] == null) {
                Session["authenticated"] = false;
                lblTitle.ForeColor = Color.Blue;
                lblTitle.Text = "Enter your account information.";
                this.FindControl("divForm").Visible = true;
            }
            else if ((bool)Session["authenticated"]) {
                lblTitle.ForeColor = Color.Green;
                lblTitle.Text = "User " + "<font color=\"red\"><i>" +
                    "Already " + "</i></font>" + "Authenticated";
```

```csharp
            this.FindControl("divForm").Visible = false;
        }
    }

    #region Web Form Designer generated code
    override protected void OnInit(EventArgs e) {
        //
        // CODEGEN: This call is required by the ASP.NET Web
        // Form Designer.
        //
        InitializeComponent();
        base.OnInit(e);
    }

    /// <summary>
    /// Required method for Designer support - do not modify
    /// the contents of this method with the code editor.
    /// </summary>
    private void InitializeComponent() {
        this.btnLogin.Click +=
            new System.EventHandler(this.btnLogin_Click);
        this.Load += new System.EventHandler(this.Page_Load);

    }
    #endregion

    private void btnLogin_Click(object sender, System.EventArgs
e) {
        if (!(bool)Session["authenticated"]) {
            if (txtUserName.Text.ToLower().Trim() != "admin") {
                lblTitle.ForeColor = Color.Red;
                lblTitle.Text = "Invalid Username";
            }
            else if (txtPassword.Text.ToLower().Trim() != "admin")
{
                lblTitle.ForeColor = Color.Red;
                lblTitle.Text = "Invalid Password";
            }
            else {
                lblTitle.ForeColor = Color.Green;
                lblTitle.Text = "User Authenticated";
                Session["authenticated"] = true;
            }
        }
    }
}
}
```

Obviously, in a real application, you would normally want to look up the username and password values in a database table, and you might provide a button for new users to create a username and password, depending on *why* you're authenticating users. For example, in an Internet application where you're using authentication only to set news link preferences, you would let new users register themselves. You can think of this type of authentication as *identification*, because you need only to identify users rather than truly authenticating them. In contrast, in an online banking application, you may not want to let users register themselves—you might set up your security so that only bank employees may register new users.

When an unauthenticated user requests a page that requires authentication, you would redirect him to your login page. After successfully authenticating, you would redirect him back to the initially requested page. For example, suppose the user launches a browser and immediately requests the page `somePage.aspx`. You want the `somePage.aspx` page to be accessible only to authenticated users. Therefore, upon receiving the request for `somePage`, you would check the `Session["authenticated"]` variable value and, finding it to be `false`, you would redirect the user to the login page (`ch18-2.aspx`). After the user is authenticated successfully, you would redirect back to `somePage.aspx`.

Don't worry, I won't make you write that code. Instead, I'll show you in the next section how ASP.NET performs those tasks automatically.

Using ASP.NET Forms Authentication

Now that you've seen how to perform a custom authorization process manually, here's a simpler method. ASP.NET has a concept called *Forms authentication* that does exactly what you just saw in the preceding section. However, all you need to do is create a Web Form containing your login screen and set up the `web.config` file properly.

With Forms authentication enabled, ASP.NET redirects unauthenticated users to a login Web Form of your choice. Here's the procedure:

1. When a browser sends a request, ASP.NET checks for an authorization cookie.

2. If ASP.NET doesn't find the authorization cookie, it redirects the browser to the login Web Form.

3. After a successful authentication, ASP.NET sets the authorization cookie and redirects to the page originally requested.

As you can see, the process is essentially identical to the one you just saw—but it's somewhat more automatic. The next section presents a generalized procedure.

IMPLEMENTING ASP.NET FORMS AUTHENTICATION

To implement ASP.NET Forms authentication:

1. Create the login page. When the user is authenticated successfully, call the `System.Web.Security` `.FormsAuthentication.RedirectFromLoginPage` method to redirect the user back to the page originally requested (see Listing 18.3, later in this section).

2. In your `web.config` file, change the authentication mode to `"Forms"`:

```
<authentication mode="Forms">
```

3. Add an element called `<forms>` as a child of the `<authentication>` element in the web `.config` file.

4. Add a `loginUrl` attribute to the `<forms>` element. The value of the `loginUrl` element is the relative URL of your login page. For the example in this section, the `<forms>` element would look like this:

```
<forms loginUrl="ch18/ch18-3.aspx" />
```

5. Add a `name` property to the `<forms>` element. The `name` property controls the name of the cookie that ASP.NET sets when a user is authenticated successfully. For example:

```
<forms
    loginUrl="ch18/ch18-3.aspx"
    name="CSharpASPAuthorization" />
```

WARNING   Be sure to select a name that's unique to your application because, by default, ASP.NET creates the cookie so that the browser will send it to every application running on your server. If the name you select is the same as the name selected for some other application, it's possible to authenticate a user in only one application but for ASP.NET to treat the user as authenticated for both applications (see the path attribute in Table 18.1 for more information).

There are several other attributes that you can add to the `<forms>` element, but they're all optional. Table 18.1 lists the optional attributes.

TABLE 18.1: Optional Attributes That Can Be Added to the `<forms>` Element

ATTRIBUTE	VALUE(S)	DESCRIPTION
path	The cookie path	By default, ASP.NET creates a cookie with a / path, meaning the browser will return the cookie for all applications. You can limit the cookie by setting a more restrictive path.
protection	All, None, Encryption, Validation	Determines what type of encryption, if any, ASP.NET uses to protect the cookie.
		All: Encrypts and validates the cookie.
		None: No encryption. The cookie is sent in plain text.
		Encryption: Uses DES or TripleDES encryption on the cookie but does not perform validation.
		Validation: Compares the received cookie with a hashed value to ensure that the cookie received is the same as the one that was originally created.
		The default protection is All. Unless you have some reason to want *less* protection, don't change this value.
timeout	Number of minutes	The cookie expires after the specified number of minutes. The default is 30 minutes.

Microsoft used cookies rather than `Session` variables to ensure that sessionless applications can use Forms authentication. However, as you can see, using cookies causes security risks because the cookies must be transmitted over the network for each request. Unfortunately, there's no option for using `Session` variables to maintain the authorization status in this release.

After you make the modification to the CSharpASP `web.config` file, the `<authentication>` section should look like this:

```
<authentication mode="Forms" >
   <forms
      loginUrl="ch18/ch18-3.aspx"
      name="CSharpASPAuthorization"
      timeout="3" />
</authentication>
```

For testing purposes, I've set the timeout value to just three minutes. After being authenticated, if you allow three minutes to pass without requesting a page in the application, you'll have to log in again. Shorter timeout values are more secure because they minimize the chance of authenticated users accidentally leaving their browsers open, thus potentially letting an unauthorized user access the application. On the other hand, shorter timeout values force users to authenticate more frequently. You can probably find a good balance for your application. If you're interested primarily in identification rather than authentication, you can try to make the cookie permanent. That way, users need to authenticate only once from any given machine. They will be authorized for subsequent accesses until the cookie expires.

The login page can contain any custom code you want for authentication. This example simply checks that the username and password are both `"admin"`. When authentication fails, you don't have to do anything special (although you should inform the user *why* authentication failed, even though this simplistic test page doesn't do so), but when authentication succeeds, you call the

```
System.Web.Security.FormsAuthentication.RedirectFromLoginPage
```

method to redirect the user to the originally requested page. To use the method, add a `using System.Web.Security;` line to the class file. You don't have to know *what* page was originally requested. Listing 18.3 shows the `btnLogin_Click` event code for the login Web Form `ch18-3.aspx`.

LISTING 18.3: THE WEB FORM `ch18-3.aspx` DISPLAYS A LOGIN FORM AND AUTHENTICATES USERS

```
// using System.Web.Security;
private void btnLogin_Click(object sender, System.EventArgs e) {
    if ((txtUserName.Text.ToLower().Trim() == "admin") &&
        (txtPassword.Text.ToLower().Trim() == "admin")) {
        FormsAuthentication.RedirectFromLoginPage("admin", false);
    }
    else {
        lblFeedback.Text = "Authentication failed.";
    }
}
```

The call to the `RedirectFromLoginPage` method takes two parameters—the authorized username and a Boolean value that controls whether ASP.NET should create an in-memory cookie or a permanent cookie. In a real application, you typically would look up the username and password in a database, and you would use the authorized username rather than a hard-coded value as the first `RedirectFromLoginPage` parameter.

You need to make one more modification to the `web.config` file before running the test. By default, the `web.config` file `<authorization>` section allows access to all users. You want to constrain access to authenticated users only. Delete the `<allow users="*" />` element in the `<authorization>` section and replace it with a `<deny users="?"/>` element. The question mark is a wildcard that represents authenticated users. In other words, after making the change, the application denies access to all unauthenticated users.

```
<authorization>
   <deny users="?" />
</authorization>
```

After making the changes to the `web.config` file, you can test Forms authentication as follows:

1. Rebuild the CSharpASP application.

2. Open a browser and request the Web Form `ch18-4.aspx`. ASP.NET will redirect you to the login form `ch18-3.aspx`.

3. Log in using `admin` for both the username and password. ASP.NET will redirect you to the page originally requested, `ch18-4.aspx`.

The Web Form `ch18-4.aspx` displays a message stating that you have been authenticated and have access to the page. If you close the browser and re-request the page, you will need to log in again because the cookie isn't permanent. After being authenticated and viewing the `ch18-4.aspx` page, wait several minutes and then refresh the page. You will have to log in again because the authentication cookie expires after three minutes.

NOTE *You would normally place your login form in the root directory of your application. By default, if you don't specify a form but you have the authentication method set to* **Forms**, *ASP.NET attempts to redirect to a Web Form called* `login.aspx` *in the root directory. You can change the default by altering the* `machine.config` *file for your server, although I recommend that you avoid doing so, because it's likely that the* `machine.config` *file will change in the future.*

If you want to restrict access to a small, previously identified set of users, you can even eliminate the tiny bit of code to perform the authentication. In the `<authorization>` section of your `web.config` file, you can create a list of authorized usernames and passwords. Place the list inside a `<credentials>` element as follows:

```
<authentication mode="Forms">
   <forms loginUrl="ch18/ch18-3.aspx"
      name="CSharpASPAuthorization" timeout="3">
      <credentials passwordFormat="SHA1" >
         <user name="admin" password="GASDFSA9823598ASDBAD"/>
         <!- more <user> elements here ->
      </credentials>
```

```
        </forms>
    </authentication>
```

NOTE *The <user> tag specified in the preceding code snippet is just an example—no such user exists. Add usernames and passwords as appropriate for your server.*

The `<credentials>` section accepts a set of `<user>` elements, each of which contains `name` and `password` attributes. You can see that the password is encrypted (actually, it's a hash value). It doesn't have to be, although I highly recommend that you use encrypted passwords. You specify the type of password hashing with the `passwordFormat` attribute in the `<credentials>` attribute. Possible values are `None`, `SHA1` (Secure Hash Algorithm), and `MD5` (Message Digest algorithm); the values are case sensitive.

The problem is, how do you get the hashed password to store in the `<credentials>` section to begin with? Fortunately, the FormsAuthentication class has a method that accepts a password string and a string that specifies the hashing algorithm to use. It returns the hashed string. You can store that in the `<user>` element as the value of the `password` attribute. There's no automatic way to store the hashed value, but you can use the `FormsAuthentication.HashPasswordForStoringInConfigFile` method to create the hashed value, and then store it yourself. The Web Form `ch18-5.aspx` accepts a username and password and automatically creates the `<credentials>` and `<user>` tags if they don't already exist. Listing 18.4 shows the code.

LISTING 18.4: THE WEB FORM ch18-5 CREATES <credentials> AND <user> TAGS IF THEY DON'T ALREADY EXIST (ch18-5.aspx.cs)

```
Imports System.Xml
Imports System.Web.Security
' autogenerated code omitted
    Private Sub Page_Load(ByVal sender As System.Object, _
        ByVal e As System.EventArgs) Handles MyBase.Load
        Dim lbl As System.Web.UI.WebControls.Label
        lbl = Me.FindControl("lblTitle")
        lbl.Text = "Enter a username and password"
    End Sub


    Private Sub btnCreateUser_Click(ByVal sender As System.Object,
    _
        ByVal e As System.EventArgs) Handles btnCreateUser.Click
        Dim xml As XmlDocument
        Dim NCredentials As XmlElement
        Dim NForms As XmlElement
        Dim NUser As XmlElement
        Dim username As String
        Dim password As String
        Dim hashedPassword As String
        Dim configFilename As String
        Dim hashmethod As String = "SHA1"
        username = txtUserName.Text.Trim.ToLower
        password = txtPassword.Text.Trim.ToLower
        xml = New XmlDocument()
```

```
    FormsAuthentication.Initialize()
    configFilename = Server.MapPath("..") & "\web.config"
    Try
        xml.Load(configFilename)
        NForms = xml.SelectSingleNode("//authentication/forms")
        If Not NForms Is Nothing Then
            NCredentials = NForms.SelectSingleNode("credentials")
            If NCredentials Is Nothing Then
                NCredentials = xml.CreateElement("credentials")
                NCredentials.SetAttribute("passwordFormat", _
                  hashmethod)
                NForms.AppendChild(NCredentials)
            End If
            ' do you already have this user?
            If FormsAuthentication.Authenticate _
              (username, password) Then
                ' no changes needed
                Exit Sub
            Else
                hashedPassword = _

FormsAuthentication.HashPasswordForStoringInConfigFile _
                (password, hashmethod)
            End If
            ' see if you have this username already
            NUser = NCredentials.SelectSingleNode _
              ("user[@name='" & username & "']")
            If NUser Is Nothing Then
                ' add a new user
                NUser = xml.CreateElement("user")
                NUser.SetAttribute("name", username)
                NUser.SetAttribute("password", hashedPassword)
                NCredentials.AppendChild(NUser)
                xml.Save(configFilename)
            Else
                ' just update the password
                NUser.SetAttribute("password", hashedPassword)
                xml.Save(configFilename)
            End If
        Else
            Me.lblTitle.Text = "Forms authentication is not " & _
            enabled in your web.config file. You must have a " & _
            " &lt;forms&gt; element to create users."
        End If
    Catch ex As Exception
        lblTitle.Text = ex.Message
    End Try
End Sub
```

> **WARNING** *The Web Form* `ch18-5.aspx` *changes the* `web.config` *file in the CSharpASP root directory. Changing the* `web.config` *file relaunches your application, so don't change it while you have users attached to the application.*

REMOVING FORMS AUTHENTICATION FROM THE *WEB.CONFIG* FILE

Before you continue, you should undo the changes you made earlier to the `web.config` file. Follow this procedure to restore the defaults:

1. In the `<authentication>` section, change the `mode` attribute back to `"Windows"`.

   `<authentication mode="Windows" />`

2. Delete or comment out the `<forms>` element you added in the preceding section.

3. Change the `<authorization>` section so that it contains an `<allow users="*" />` element. Delete or comment out the `<deny users="?" />` element you added in the preceding section.

> **WARNING** *Before continuing, be sure to follow the instructions preceding this warning to remove Forms authentication from the CSharpASP application.*

Securing Your Server with SSL

Controlling access (implementing authentication and authorization) is one part of having a secured site. To secure your site fully, you need to encrypt the transmission of information between the client and the server. The .NET framework supports a large and growing set of cryptographic methods. The most common methods are RSA, named after Ronald Rivest, Adi Shamir, and Leonard Adelman, who first published the algorithm in April 1977. RSA is an *asymmetric* encryption. It uses a public key/private key algorithm whereby encrypting a message with the public key creates a message that can be unencrypted only by the private key. Therefore, as an individual or entity, you can freely release your public key, knowing that by maintaining the secrecy of your private key, you are the only one who can unencrypt messages encrypted with your public key. The most popular implementations of RSA encryption include Pretty Good Privacy (PGP), the GNU Privacy Guard (GnuPG or GPG), and Secure Sockets Layer (SSL), supported by most modern browsers.

To use SSL, you need a public key. You can obtain a public key from various *certificate authorities*, which can verify that a key actually belongs to an individual or organization. SSL does not require the client to have a certified public key; instead, when you browse a site using SSL, the server provides its public key to the browser, which verifies the key with the certificate authority.

RSA does have one drawback—it's relatively slow, too slow to support sustained Internet server-browser communications. Therefore, the browser generates a new encryption value that both the server and the browser will use to encrypt subsequent messages using a faster encryption algorithm, typically a *symmetric* encryption algorithm in which both the message sender and the message recipient must know the encryption key. The browser encrypts the new symmetric key value with the server's public key and returns the symmetric key to the server. The server uses its private key to decrypt the symmetric key provided by the browser. Then both server and browser have a symmetric encryption key that they can use to encrypt subsequent messages.

If you're involved in transactions such as e-commerce, medical, or financial, in which people provide credit card numbers, Social Security numbers, private medical data, or any other data that must remain private, you should obtain an encryption key from a recognized certificate authority and use SSL for the pages in your site that transmit sensitive information. You *must* combine SSL with authentication and authorization techniques to ensure the privacy of the information—it does you no good to encrypt information if you can't be reasonably sure of the client's identity.

Certificate authorities can provide SSL certificates on a per-server or per-site basis. Some prominent authorities are Verisign (`http://www.verisign.com`) and Thawte (`http://www.thawte.com`). Pricing is based on the number of certificates and servers. At the time of this writing, Thawte provides a test certificate good for 30 days that makes it easy to test SSL with your server. After installing the certificate, you can enforce SSL by changing the IIS security settings for any application, or for the root Web (all applications).

NOTE *Using SSL slows down your server and your application to some degree because the server (and the browser) must encrypt and decrypt requests and responses.*

The first step in obtaining a certificate is to generate a certificate request. IIS 5 or higher can generate the request for you. Launch the Default Web Site Properties dialog, select the Directory Security tab, and click the Server Certificate button. Follow the IIS Certificate Wizard's directions to generate the certificate request. Although the screens differ in IIS 6, you'll have little trouble following the procedure in either version.

The first time through the wizard, select the Create a New Certificate option (see Figure 18.10).

FIGURE 18.10

IIS 5 Certificate Wizard options

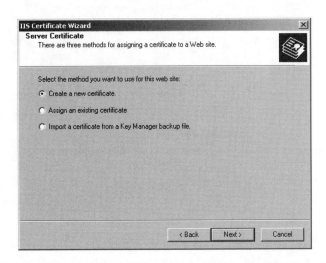

The request itself creates a text file that you'll need to get a certificate from your selected certificate authority. In turn, the authority provides a text file that contains the certificate (see Figure 18.11). Select the delayed request option on the next wizard screen.

FIGURE 18.11

IIS 5 Certificate
Wizard, Delayed or
Immediate Request
screen

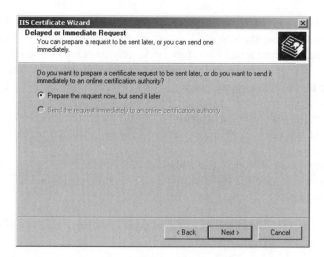

You must provide a name and select the bit length for the certificate request. Shorter bit lengths are faster, but longer bit lengths are more secure (see Figure 18.12). Don't leave the default name—pick a specific name.

FIGURE 18.12

IIS 5 Certificate
Wizard, Name and
Security Settings
screen

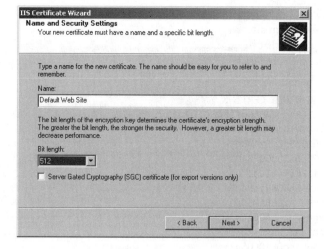

There are U.S. government restrictions on the bit length you can use for overseas installations. If you're developing in the U.S. and you deal with international clients, you should become familiar with these restrictions.

The next three screens ask for your organization, organizational unit, server or site's fully qualified domain name, and location. When users view your certificate, they'll see some of the information you enter into these wizard screens, so make sure the information is correct and reflects your company policies.

The final screen requests that you enter a filename for the new certificate request. Give the request a name identifying it as a request for this server (requests are not transferable), and click the Next button to create the request and finish the wizard (see Figure 18.13).

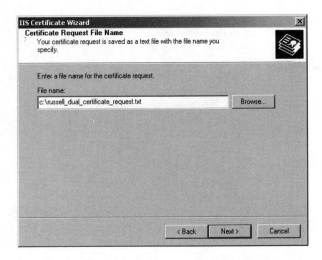

You'll see a summary screen. Check the information carefully. Certificates are expensive, and you can't change them after making the request.

The text file that the wizard saves contains your certificate request. Your selected certificate authority will process the request and return another text file containing the certificate—typically via e-mail or on site in a text field. Both the request and the certificate look similar to the following:

```
---BEGIN NEW CERTIFICATE REQUEST---
MIICkTCBAjsCAQAwgYAxFTATBgNVBAMTDHJ1c3NlbGwtZHVhbDEVMBMGA1UECxMM
UlVTU0VMTC1IT01FMRUwEwYDVQQKEwxSVVHTRUxMLUhPTUUxEzARBgNVBAcTCkhp
Z2ggUG9pbnQxFzAVBgNVBAgTDk5vcnRoIENhcm9saW5hMQswCQYDVQQGEwJVUzBc
MA0GCSqGSIb3DQEBAQUAA0sAMEgCQQDJuapg3wwkoXzwK00//n3vICKyhOnGb6EF
a/kPi5FK8MAHILb37PfwVdd4zT46If39eY+FlwA8/PThp+cOT85bAgMBAAGgggFT
MBoGCisGAQQBgjcNAgMxDBYKNS4wLjIxOUTuMjA1BgorBgEEAYI3AgEOMScwJTAO
BgNVHQ8BAf8EBAMCBPAwEwYDVR01BAwwCgYIKwYBBQUHAwEwgf0GCisGAQQBgjcN
CgIxge4wgasCAQEeWgBNAGkBigyxBG8AcwBvAGY2dAAgAFIAUwBBACAAUwBDAGgA
YQBuAG4AZQBsACAAQwByAHkAcAB0AG8AZwByAGEAcABoAGkAYwAgAFAAcgBvAHYA
aQBkAGUAcgOBiQCO5g/Nk+1suAJZideg15faBLqe4jiiytYeVBApxLrtUlyWEQuW
dPeEFvOGWvsjQGwn+WC5m9kVNmcLVsx41QtGDXtuETFOD6dSi/M9wmEy8bsbcNHX
s+sntX56AcCxBXh1ALaE4YaE6e/zwmE/O/Cmyje3a2olE5rlk1FFIlKTDwAAAAAA
AAAAMA0GCSqGSIb3DQEBBQUAA0EAWhylMc/CBYcTSnQRMrwXv97xuWEqFhQReXnS
nNo/VvBygne9nLqfWqCE/XU/9bCQwjzVDxYrSk5BWtUkVDRHOg==
---END NEW CERTIFICATE REQUEST---
```

You cut and paste the returned certificate to a text file on your server. By convention, certificate files have a `.cer` extension, even though they're simple text files.

To install the new certificate, restart the IIS Certificate Wizard. The wizard tracks pending requests. This time, select the Process the Pending Request and Install the Certificate option (see Figure 18.14).

FIGURE 18.14

IIS 5 Certificate
Wizard, Pending
Certificate Request
screen

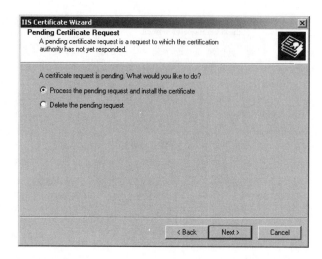

The wizard will ask for the name of the certificate file. Enter the name of the CER file you saved from the certificate authority, *not* the name of the certificate request file.

After installing the certificate on your server, you can make any virtual directory use SSL by requesting pages using the HTTPS protocol rather than the HTTP protocol.

WARNING *Make sure you keep a copy of the returned certificate. The process of installing the certificate alters the CER file. You cannot install the same CER file twice.*

You should use SSL for any pages that transfer sensitive information such as account numbers, passwords, financial information, or Social Security numbers over the network. For example, you should use SSL for login pages. If you don't, the transmission may be intercepted by anyone between you and the client.

Monitoring Your Site—Beyond Page Counting

Any Web site or application that has commercial value—and even many that don't—eventually begin tracking usage. For very small sites, simple page counts are enough, but larger sites and almost all sites that sell advertising need more sophisticated tracking mechanisms. In this section, I'll show you the rudiments of tracking by reading the server logs, but you should be aware that there are both commercial and free programs that perform much more sophisticated tracking and reporting, such as Site-Tracker (www.sitetracker.com), WebTrends (www.webtrends.com), Analog (http://www.analog.cx/), and others.

Tracking Usage

One of the main goals of modern Internet applications is *personalization*. Personalization, beyond simple tasks such as saving a user's preferences for an application, involves monitoring the user's frequency of use, input, position, and—perhaps most important—the user's patterns. The sites use this information to improve future browsing experiences.

For example, past usability studies found that people tended to use Microsoft Word's menus more frequently when they were shown only common features, such as text selection and formatting, cut-and-paste, and copy operations at first, and when the program adapted the menus to suit each user's patterns. In modern versions of Word, menu items that you frequently use remain visible. Others migrate to a hidden portion of the menu. The hidden features are still available, but they're not in the way.

Some Internet sites have begun to use personalization to increase sales. For example, Amazon stores a list of the pages individuals visit and the purchases they make. Amazon can then compare the lists with each other, allowing them to make highly accurate predictions about what people would like to read. If you and 50 other people all buy the same book, and 30 people of that group also buy a second book, it's highly likely that some of the remaining 20 people would like to buy that second book also. Not only that, but some of the people in the original group of 50 probably also bought some other books. It's likely that some of those books would be interesting to the people in the remainder of the group.

Over time, you can see that the predictive value of monitoring goes far beyond simple page counting or even knowing who's using your application. Nevertheless, that's where you should start. After you create a program, simple monitoring is absolutely essential in marketing, extending, and justifying the development costs of that program. I've been involved in numerous projects where the expenditure stopped just as the program was finished, leaving no money or development resources for monitoring the programs—and they almost invariably fail. In contrast, where monitoring was built into the project from the beginning, the end users received more attention, problems were fixed more rapidly, and the programs were well received and used often.

Advanced Page Counting

In Chapter 10, "File and Event Log Access with ASP.NET," you saw a simple example of how to count pages in an application. In some cases, simply knowing that your application has logged 30,000 visits may be sufficient feedback or justification for the application. In other cases, you'll want to know a great deal more than a simple count. For most applications, you should at least save the following:

The Number of Visits to Each Page This is a difficult problem unless your application requires a username and password because there's no absolute way to know whether a visit is unique, and the numbers you'll get depend on how you count visits. If the same user opens two separate browser instances to your application, are those unique visits? If a user twice visits a page with the same browser instance, should you count both visits?

The User's IP Address Some people have fixed IP addresses that never change, but most Internet users have dynamically assigned IP addresses. Therefore, two different IP addresses may be the same user—or two different users may appear with the same IP address. You can often look at the time between visits or the value of the `ASPSessionID` cookie to attempt to determine whether the duplicate IP addresses represent two separate individuals or the same individual visiting twice.

The Time when the Request Occurred   You can use this to sort pages in browse order later, when you're analyzing browse patterns. You can also use the difference between two successive requests as an indication of how long the user spent on any given page (and thus how interesting the information on that page was).

The Referring Page   Strictly speaking, if you're saving every page visit for every user within your own application, you don't need to save the referring page; you can find it by looking at the preceding request. However, the referring page can be useful in letting you know how people find or browse to your site from related sites. For example, if 10 percent of your users reach your page from a particular search engine, you may increase the number of visits by placing advertising on that search engine or by changing the metatags on your page so that the search engine places your site higher in the search hit list. Obviously, this information is crucial for placing ad resources most efficiently.

The User's Identity or Any Cookie Values That Can Help Identify the User   For secured sites, you can use a unique user ID associated with the authenticated user. For ASP.NET applications that use sessions, you can use the `Session` cookie. For sessionless applications, you may want to create a unique cookie for each user.

IIS can track most of this information for you in the IIS log files, and numerous commercial programs can perform sophisticated log file analyses—most large sites find that buying one of these programs is less expensive than writing their own. However, for smaller sites, you can easily generate your own logging method that stores exactly the information you need. The Web Forms `ch18-6.aspx`, `ch18-7.aspx`, and `ch18-8.aspx` all use the same code-behind class (`ch18-6.aspx.cs`), so they all do exactly the same thing; they save information in the CSharpASP database in the `ch18` table using an instance of a class named Ch18Counter that the ch18_6 class instantiates when each page loads. The class saves the information listed in this section, the URL, the IP address, the request time, the referring page, and the user's `SessionID`. Finally, the Web Form `ch18-9` reads the information and creates a summary information page for application administrators.

To let you see what's going on, each page displays the number of visits to that page, but it displays the count by counting the number of rows for that URL. Although it is absolutely generic, it will work with any Web Form. You would not normally use this method to display a page count; instead, you'd use a trigger to update a summary page count in a separate table whenever you inserted a new record for the given URL. In fact, you wouldn't normally use this simple table structure at all, but it suffices for an example.

Here's the SQL statement to create the table. You can run the script `CSharpASP_ch18Table.sql` in the `ch18` folder on `www.sybex.com` to create the table automatically:

```
USE CSharpASP
if exists (select * from dbo.sysobjects where
    id = object_id(N'[dbo].[ch18]') and
    OBJECTPROPERTY(id, N'IsUserTable') = 1)
drop table [dbo].[ch18]
GO

CREATE TABLE [dbo].[ch18] (
```

```
    [ID] [uniqueidentifier] NULL ,
    [URL] [nvarchar] (150) COLLATE SQL_Latin1_General_CP1_CI_AS
        NOT NULL ,
    [IP] [nvarchar] (15) COLLATE SQL_Latin1_General_CP1_CI_AS
        NOT NULL ,
    [TimeOfRequest] [datetime] NOT NULL ,
    [Referrer] [nvarchar] (150) COLLATE
    SQL_Latin1_General_CP1_CI_AS
        NULL ,
    [SessionID] [nvarchar] (50) COLLATE
    SQL_Latin1_General_CP1_CI_AS
        NOT NULL
) ON [PRIMARY]
GO
```

The ID (`uniqueidentifier`) field ensures that each row is unique. SQL Server generates values for this field via the T-SQL `NEWID()` function. The `Referrer` page can be null because the value can be blank. All other fields are required.

When any of the three example Web Forms load, they create an instance of the `Ch18Counter` object and call its `countPage` method. The `countPage` method retrieves the appropriate information and uses a stored procedure called `ch18_CountPage` to log the request (see Listing 18.5). The `CSharp-ASP_ch18Table.sql` script in the `ch18` folder on www.sybex.com creates this stored procedure as well as the `ch18` table.

LISTING 18.5: THE STORED PROCEDURE ch18_countPage LOGS PAGE REQUESTS TO THE CH18 TABLE IN THE CSHARPASP DATABASE (CSharpASP_ch18Table.sql)

```
CREATE PROCEDURE ch18_CountPage
    @URL nVarChar(150),
    @IP nVarChar(15),
    @Referrer nVarChar(150)=NULL,
    @SessionID nVarChar(50)
AS

INSERT INTO ch18 ([ID], URL, IP, TimeOfRequest, Referrer,
    SessionID)
VALUES (NEWID(), @URL, @IP, getDate(), @Referrer, @SessionID)
GO
```

The procedure accepts input parameters specifying the URL, IP address, referring page, and `SessionID`. It generates the row ID value using the built-in T-SQL `NEWID()` function and the current date/time with the T-SQL `getDate()` function. Finally, it appends the data to the end of the table.

Next, each Web Form calls the `Ch18Counter` object's `getPageCount` method, which accepts a URL input parameter and returns the number of rows in the `ch18` table with matching URL values (see Listing 18.6).

LISTING 18.6: THE STORED PROCEDURE ch18_getPageCount **RETURNS THE TOTAL NUMBER OF REQUESTS FOR A SPECIFIED URL (**CSharpASP_ch18Table.sql**)**

```
CREATE PROCEDURE ch18_getPageCount @URL nVarChar(150),
    @count int output
as
select @count =  count(URL) FROM ch18 WHERE URL=@URL
GO
```

You can use similar techniques to count anything you want; however, you should probably set up the table structure in a different way. For example, repeatedly writing the URL for every request is foolish when there is a limited number of URLs available in your application. A better method might be to create a URL table containing unique URLs and a shorter URL_ID column. When inserting a row, you would use the URL_ID value from that table that matches the URL, thus considerably limiting the size of the data (and speeding up searches and sorts). For greater efficiency, you could add an integer URL_COUNT field and increment the field value for each request.

Finally, be careful when dealing with URLs. URLs that contain query string data may be "unique" for every user—even though the page request itself is identical except for the query string. A better database design would have a separate field for query string data. A custom design might save only specific query string values or form values.

The Ch18Counter class doesn't require any parameters—it gets all the information directly from the current HttpContext (see Listing 18.7).

LISTING 18.7: THE CH18COUNTER CLASS INSERTS DATA INTO A DATABASE TABLE FOR EACH COUNTED PAGE AND RETURNS PAGE COUNTS (Ch18Counter.cs**)**

```
using System;
using System.Data;
using System.Data.SqlClient;
using System.Web;


namespace CSharpASP.ch18
{
    /// <summary>
    /// Summary description for ch18Counter.
    /// </summary>
    public class ch18Counter
    {
        public ch18Counter()
        {
            //
            // TODO: Add constructor logic here
            //
        }
```

```csharp
public void CountPage() {
   HttpContext context = HttpContext.Current;
   SqlConnection conn = new SqlConnection
     (System.Configuration.
      ConfigurationSettings.AppSettings.Get("CSharpASP"));
   SqlCommand  cm = new SqlCommand("ch18_CountPage", conn);
   SqlParameter p = null;
   cm.CommandType = CommandType.StoredProcedure;
   // set the URL info
   p = new SqlParameter("@URL", SqlDbType.NVarChar, 150);
   p.Value = context.Request.RawUrl;
   cm.Parameters.Add(p);

   // set the IP
   p = new SqlParameter("@IP", SqlDbType.NVarChar, 15);
   p.Value = context.Request.UserHostAddress;
   cm.Parameters.Add(p);

   // set the Referrer
   p = new SqlParameter("@Referrer", SqlDbType.NVarChar,
     150);
   if (context.Request.UrlReferrer == null) {
     p.Value = null;
   }
   else {
     p.Value = context.Request.UrlReferrer.AbsoluteUri;
   }

   cm.Parameters.Add(p);

   // set the SessionID
   p = new SqlParameter("@SessionId", SqlDbType.NVarChar,
     50);
   p.Value = context.Session.SessionID;
   cm.Parameters.Add(p);

   // open the connection
   conn.Open();

   // execute the insert
   cm.ExecuteNonQuery();

   cm.Dispose();
   conn.Close();
   conn.Dispose();

}
public int getPageCount() {
```

```
HttpContext  context = HttpContext.Current;
SqlConnection  conn = new
  SqlConnection(System.Configuration.
   ConfigurationSettings.AppSettings.Get("CSharpASP"));
SqlCommand  cm = new SqlCommand("ch18_getPageCount",
  conn);
SqlParameter p = null;
int count;
cm.CommandType = CommandType.StoredProcedure;
// set the URL info
p = new SqlParameter("@URL", SqlDbType.NVarChar, 150);
p.Value = context.Request.RawUrl;
cm.Parameters.Add(p);

// create an output parameter
p = new SqlParameter("@count", SqlDbType.Int);
p.Direction = ParameterDirection.Output;
cm.Parameters.Add(p);
// open the connection
conn.Open();

// execute the insert
cm.ExecuteNonQuery();

// get the output parameter value
count = (int) cm.Parameters["@count"].Value;
cm.Dispose();
conn.Close();
conn.Dispose();
return count;
    }

  }
}
```

The code is straightforward; however, it does use a few interesting properties to obtain the request data:

Request.RawUrl   Contains the portion of the request *after* the domain, which is appropriate for a counter scheme running within a single domain. In other words, for this application, it leaves out the portion of the request containing `http://www.localhost` or `http://www.csCSharpASP`. Note that the `RawUrl` property value also contains any query string data. Because this application uses none, I haven't split that into a separate field, but you should consider doing so for a production application.

Request.UserHostAddress   Contains the requester's IP address.

Request.UrlReferrer   Contains the URL visited by the client before requesting your page. Many people use software that suppresses this information, so you may not be able to retrieve it from all clients. Just because a URL appears in the UrlReferrer doesn't mean there's an explicit link between that URL and your page—all it means is that the user visited that site just prior to requesting your page.

The `getPageCount` method uses an output parameter to retrieve the page count for any particular URL and returns that value.

Each of the Web Forms `ch18-6.aspx`, `ch18-7.aspx`, and `ch18-8.aspx` has a single label for displaying the page count, and all have identical code—as I mentioned earlier, they all reference the same code-behind class:

```
private void Page_Load(object sender, System.EventArgs e) {
    ch18Counter counter = new ch18Counter();
    counter.CountPage();
    Label1.Text = "This page has been visited " +
        counter.CountPage().ToString() + " times.";
}
```

Knowing Who's in Your Application

If you have a login page, or you're using Windows Integrated Security and you're using sessions, you can track who's using your application at any particular time. Override the `Session_OnStart` and `Session_OnEnd` events in the `global.asax` file to store an object containing the `SessionID` and username for each user. After the user is authenticated, you can update the username field. Store the objects as a custom `Collection` object at Application scope. You can then write code that accesses your collection to perform various tasks such as these:

◆ Creating a report showing logged-in users

◆ Intercepting the next request for any specific user to display customized advertisements or messages

◆ Adding the user's login information to the `<credentials>` section of a `web.config` file

◆ Letting users see (and potentially communicate with) other logged-in users in the application

Disabling an Application for Maintenance

In older versions of ASP, many developers hesitated to use components because IIS locked the DLL at runtime. Therefore, updating a component meant you had to stop the application or the entire Web server, depending on whether your components ran in Microsoft Transaction Server (MTS). For critical and public applications, that was a severe restriction because, by halting the application or the server, you could affect an unknown number of users.

ASP.NET does not lock the source DLL files containing your code-behind classes—it "shadows" them. Therefore, you can update the code simply by replacing it at runtime. The .NET framework recognizes that the code source has changed and reloads and compiles the code on demand, beginning with the next request.

Despite this welcome improvement, you may still need to close down an application completely—perhaps for server maintenance or for applications that use COM interop to access legacy COM components. While public schedules and home page announcements help, people tend to ignore those. You still need a way to warn users using the application that it will shut down for maintenance.

You can implement this by writing a little code in the `global.asax` file, creating an application-level variable, and creating a `Session` variable or cookie for each active user. Here's how it works.

When you decide to shut down the site, you set an `Application` variable, perhaps named `Application["shutdownTime"]`, to the date/time you want to shut down. At the start of each request, the code in your `global.asax` file (in the `Application_BeginRequest` event) checks the current time against the stored `Application["shutdownTime"]` variable value. You can use the result to display a message to the user stating that the application will shut down. For example, sending the following JavaScript client-side script will display a warning alert message:

```
<script language="JavaScript" type="text/JavaScript">
    alert("This application will shut down at " & _
        Application("shutdownTime").ToString("F") & "." &
        " Please save any information and exit this application.")
</script>
```

Similarly, you can use the stored `Application["shutdownTime"]` variable to prevent users from starting the application beginning at some interval before the scheduled shutdown time.

Summary

No matter what type of application you have, you should plan security and monitoring into the design from the beginning. Beyond any other advantage that monitoring may give you, it provides the critical difference between saying to management, "Well, the users *seem* to like the application—we're not getting complaints," and being able to provide real information, such as, "Use of the application has increased from an initial 1,200 hits per day to 12,000 per day over the last four-week period. Currently, 150 employees are using the application…" You get the picture.

Unfortunately, most of us, as programmers, are eager to get to the code. It's more fun to write an application than to plan one, but planning often makes the difference between a smooth, successful project and one that has problems. In the next chapter, you'll see how to plan your application to minimize such problems.

Chapter 19

Planning Applications

THE TASKS OF APPLICATION developers run the gamut from extremely specific to extremely general. Some programmers work in shops where they're given detailed specifications for individual portions of a program; their job is to create and debug functions, classes, or components that meet those specifications. Others are given a general description of a task and are expected to plan and document the code they write to meet the description. Still others are given a general description of an entire application; they must design, write, and test the application, either by themselves—in which case they have final control over every facet of the application—or as part of a team, where the entire team makes decisions about the application. Finally, because they're close to the process, developers often imagine applications that could simplify or streamline a business process (often a tedious part of their own jobs). In such a case, the task is to sell that application idea, taking it from conception to fruition; document the business need for the application; perform a cost/benefit analysis; create and sell the vision, the way users would interact with the application, and the database; code; test; and finally, perform deployment, delivery, and maintenance.

No single situation applies to everyone. In some cases, an individual might perform all the tasks; in other cases many different individuals or teams may cooperate to perform the tasks. The point of this chapter is, don't skip steps. Even if you think that the task doesn't apply to the application you're developing, it does to some degree. Although it may not be *your* job to handle that task, someone should at least consider the relationship of the application to each of the tasks in this chapter.

In this chapter:

- ◆ Imagine Something

- ◆ Determine the Audience

- ◆ Determine the Application Requirements

- ◆ Create and Sell a Vision

- ◆ Plan the User Interface

- ◆ Plan Data Storage and Retrieval

- ◆ Plan Object Responsibilities and Interfaces

◆ Plan Administrative Functions

◆ Create the Database

◆ Create Data-Access Components

◆ Create Business Components

◆ Build the User Interface

Imagine Something

All applications begin with imagination. Somewhere, someone thinks, "Wouldn't it be great if we had an application that could do [something]." That something may be impossible, too expensive, trivial, unnecessary, impractical—or it may be the next killer app. That doesn't matter. All that matters is that the person or group imagining the application feels strongly enough about the idea to take it in hand, think about it realistically, and mold it into a finished, *presentable* idea. Ideas are legion; presentable ideas are rare. An idea is a thought that produces a reaction in the individual who has it, whereas a presentable idea is a thought communicable to others in such a way that it produces a (preferably) similar reaction in them. Therefore, the first requirement for an application is the creation of a presentable idea—and that means you must consider the application from the aspects presented in the remainder of this chapter.

Determine the Audience

All applications have an intended audience, but when you initially conceive of an application, you're often unclear exactly who the audience is. For example, suppose you imagine the perfect search engine, one that not only finds relevant information but also contains links to every piece of related information across the entire Internet. By paying a small fee, users could improve their search experience. But wait—who's the audience? Is there an audience for a pay-per-search service when there are so many free search services already available? It turns out that people *are* willing to pay for search services, but only when those services are extremely targeted.

While that may be an extreme example, you can apply the same thought process to almost any program. For example, suppose your company's salespeople fill out orders by hand when they're on the road and then enter them into a mainframe application when they return to the office. The data-entry process is error prone, not only because the salespeople don't type very well, but also because they're removed from the customer when they actually fill out the order. You think, wouldn't it be more efficient if the salespeople filled out the order interactively when they're actually speaking with the customer? That way, when questions arise, they could ask the customer right away, rather than having to call or e-mail the customer later, when the transaction isn't fresh, and also avoid the inevitable delays caused by this. But who's the audience? Who benefits from the salespeople being able to fill out the orders immediately? The business and the customer may benefit from the reduced turnaround time between order placement and order fulfillment. The data processing department may benefit by not having to maintain as many mainframe terminals. However, giving the salespeople laptops may not benefit the IT department, because they would have to load and maintain many more computers.

Finally, the program may not benefit the salespeople themselves, because they don't *want* to fill out the order in front of the customer—they want to talk, to increase the sale amount, to build a relationship so they can return and be reasonably assured of future sales. They may tell you that calling customers back with questions provides additional sales opportunities that they wouldn't have if they filled out the order immediately.

As you can see, it's not immediately obvious who the audience is in this example. It may turn out that the reduced error rate and faster sales turnaround *increase* sales and overcomes the salespeople's initial reluctance to use the program. It may turn out that the salespeople are more than willing to accept the solution once they see that filling out the order, rather than being an onerous handwritten process, has become an automated point-and-click operation that they can perform not only at the point-of-sale, but with equal ease back in the office after the sale, just as they do now.

Finally, you should recognize that this example is a rare application that affects primarily the direct audience. Most applications affect several groups—sometimes they end up affecting people or groups who initially had no direct interest in the application itself. For example, the hypothetical sales application obviously affects the salespeople, but it may also affect the central data operations group because they must now acquire data in some way other than through the mainframe terminals. It may affect managers, who find they can use the data to track dates and times of sales appointments more closely. As you determine the audience, try to keep in mind the direct beneficiaries, but also try to anticipate how the application will affect the organization as a whole.

Determine the Application Requirements

It's very difficult for people to describe how a computer program works. In fact, for computer programs with interfaces, as soon as the program grows beyond a few screens, it's usually very difficult for people even to describe exactly what the program should look like and what it should do. That's partly because different people have different visions, partly because it's relatively rare for a single individual to know *all* the ins and outs of the business, and partly because people react to existing programs much more readily and accurately than they do to the *idea* of a program in the planning stages.

Choose a Design Methodology

Despite the numerous names for application design methodologies, there are only two basic approaches to application design: top-down and bottom-up. A top-down approach concentrates on the planning stage, ensuring the existence of a detailed plan for each portion of the application before coding begins, whereas a bottom-up approach begins coding sooner but spends more time making changes during the debugging and testing phases.

There is no one "right" way. I prefer to mix the two, spending considerable time and effort planning the database operations, noninteractive data, and business rule components of the application. That's because it's relatively easy to determine in advance which tables and fields you'll need, how to get the data in and out, and how to massage the data to fit the business rules. In addition, these types of components are relatively easy to test because they have well-defined inputs and outputs. Finally, if you can't get these components right, there's no point in working on the interface, because the program will never work correctly.

In contrast, for the interactive portion of the application—the user interface—I prefer to build and test it interactively. Facets of application development that matter very little in back-end processing are critical in user interface design. For example, in a well-planned back-end system, it doesn't matter much whether you have a few hundred or a few thousand rows in a table; for most applications the difference isn't sufficient to change the program design. However, the difference between *displaying* a few hundred and a few thousand rows is significant; users don't need, don't want to scroll through, and often can't use all the data at one time.

Use Terminology Appropriately

Different users and groups prefer and understand different terminology. For example, programmers quickly become comfortable with using abbreviated field names such as `CU_ORD` or `ORDNUM`, but end users would rather see `Customer Order` and `Order Number`. Programmers are comfortable with reading technical explanations of what a field does, but a help file containing information suitable for programmers may not be suitable for end users.

Test Often

The people who use a program may see the process very differently from the people who build it. Sometimes, especially for large programs, that's because each end user group might use a different part of the program and not be interested in the other parts. Other times, it's because the people using the program may not use—or be able to use—all the data fields at one time. In some cases, end user comments will necessitate back-end program changes even late in the program creation cycle. You should plan to test interfaces often with a minimum of five representative end users. You should do this very early in the program cycle, using static screens or even paper drawings if necessary, so that you can capture as much of the program's data requirements as possible and also iteratively, capturing progressive levels of information at each repetition as you build the user interface.

People's ideas often change as they become familiar with the capabilities of a program. They almost invariably think of additional features that could be added or ways that a program should interface with other applications or systems that they're using. The more exposure you can give the target audience before the program design is complete, and the more realistic that exposure is, the more likely you are to build a successful program. For example, I've seen numerous examples of programs that violated almost every rule of good interface design but were extremely successful programs because the people who used them had a large influence over how they looked and acted and chose that particular interface because it suited their business processes.

Consider All Facets of the Application

A program doesn't start and end with the program designer. I've seen many programs, especially those designed and coded by a single individual, that had extreme "quirks." The programs work in their original configuration, but the person forgot to consider several ancillary—and critical—parts of the application cycle. The most commonly missed parts are these:

Security People create an application and then try to tack the security requirements on at the end of the application development cycle.

Versioning   If you think you may need to deliver multiple versions of your program (and even if you don't), think about versioning. For example, your application may acquire data from flat files. If you should ever need to change the file format, you'll want to ensure that you can differentiate between the original file format and any changed file format. Add versioning support to tables, resources, the application itself, and any components that the application requires. Writing the version support code in the *first* release of the application will save you considerable time when you want to create the next version. For example, when you're reading a file, create a separate component to import and parse the file. To change file versions, you need to update only that component, not the entire application.

Installation   Installation programs are often forgotten until the end of the development cycle and are often the source of huge problems during the deployment phase. Several powerful commercial installation-building programs are available; take advantage of them. Unlike a custom installation, these programs help ensure that users can uninstall the program as well, which is often just as important as installing it properly in the first place. You should develop the installation program as soon as you begin testing the application. Don't fix test installations manually by copying files and registering components; instead, add any missing components and files to the installation program and then uninstall and reinstall the application.

Deployment   Despite knowing that the application must be deployed to machine configurations that might be widely different, developers often pay attention to deployment only when the application is ready to be deployed, which usually leads to problems and sometimes a complete reworking of the application. During the testing phase, insist that the application be deployed to a significant fragment of the intended audience so that you can uncover problems before the official rollout. There may be several different deployment tracks. For example, the desktop support group might initially install a Windows application that consumes Web Services. Subsequent installations might be delivered on a CD or DVD, via an install from a network share, delivered via an application management system such as MS SMS, or via the intranet or VPN.

Training   Even simple tasks often require training, but new applications are often dumped on the target audience without any training whatsoever. Begin planning the training requirements early in the development cycle, in tandem with the user interface. If the program is complicated enough to require training, you will also want to prepare overheads, handouts, and printed manuals.

Help   Help can be as simple as pop-up windows when a user hovers over a field, or it can include online help files, paper manuals, quick reference guides, online audio and video, or offline support materials. In large organizations, you should alert the desktop support group well in advance of the program rollout, train them if necessary, and help them set up support procedures for the application. At the very least, such support procedures should include a list of possible problems and workarounds, including any unfixed problems that you uncover during testing. Find or create a procedure for the support group to follow to track or log ongoing or repeated problems so that they can be fixed for the next application release. Make sure the support group can contact the people responsible for maintaining the program. For mission-critical applications, you'll need to designate people from the maintenance group. For round-the-clock critical applications, at least one person from the support group must be available 24/7.

Maintenance   I'm using the term "maintenance" to mean everything related to keeping the application running in its current form. For example, data backups, solving problems related to network hardware or configuration changes, adding additional servers to scale the application, optimization, and solving problems experienced by end users are all part of application maintenance.

Ongoing Development   Few programs are "finished" when first deployed. Sometimes, people suggest changes that everyone agrees would be useful, but they're too big or too difficult to fit into the initial budget or schedule. For most programs, you should plan for ongoing development to incorporate the best or the most critical suggestions. Don't react to every suggestion by updating the current application version; instead, save the suggestions, prioritize them, and add features to subsequent versions. If you get this far, you'll appreciate the versioning features you built into the first version of the application.

Troubleshooting   As used in this context, troubleshooting means the process of figuring out why an application isn't working *after* it's been debugged and deployed, even though it isn't causing an error. You'll find that this process is much easier if you build in a switch that lets you turn logging on and off for the application. This process goes hand-in-hand with error trapping and error logging, but it isn't exactly the same. You should *always* log application errors, but you don't want to log every application action except when you're trying to troubleshoot the application. However, you *do* want to be able to log application actions so that you can pinpoint the source of problems while the application is running. With server-based ASP.NET applications, tracing can handle most of your needs, but not all of them. Consider adding a switch that logs each application action, with checks after each action to confirm that the action took place. I recommend you add this switch as an administrative and maintenance-level option only. You should be able to turn logging on and off for an individual user or for the application as a whole.

Create and Sell a Vision

All the planning in the world won't help you create a program unless you have a clear vision of how that program will help people accomplish a task more easily, increase their power, save them time, or give them new capabilities. Further, unless you're a one-person operation, you probably need to get other people to share your vision.

At the beginning of the application creation cycle, you need to be a salesperson as well as an inventor. It doesn't matter how good your application is if you can't get other people to understand how it can help them. Whether you're creating the next killer app or a manufacturing workflow application, you'll need to convince others that your idea is viable. The goal is to create a vision that others can share; if they can share your vision, they can help you make the application a reality. Without a shared vision, you'll be hard pressed to get others to work with you effectively.

You'll find that as you determine the audience and application requirements, you'll also build a vision of the application that you can communicate to the various people involved. Not everyone needs exactly the same vision, and not everyone wants or needs to know about the application in its entirety. You'll probably want to articulate the vision differently to different individuals, depending on their interests. For example, describing to a senior manager how the network architecture of your application will reduce resource contention doesn't constitute a shared vision, but the same language may greatly interest a network administrator. Discussions of database relationships with a database administrator may win you friends, but the same vision, when shared with a high-level manager, a salesperson, or a data-entry clerk, may only tag you as a consummate bore.

In some cases, you may be competing with other application creators; these may be other in-house groups, commercial vendors, or consultants. Your job during this stage is to make sure you have a clear idea of how to describe the application—not necessarily a screen-by-screen slide show, an object diagram, or a flowchart, but a way to make sure that the people who can approve and fund the project understand the intent of the program and how it will help the company, the audience, and in some cases, the bottom line. You need a reasonable estimate of what the program will cost or, at a minimum, how long building it will take and what human resources it will require. But just as a good salesperson doesn't list the price of every possible feature, you should try not to get dragged into a financial or resources discussion at this time. Also, try to stay away from any implementation details. At this stage, it's usually not important to present exactly how the program will work, what technology you're planning to use, or whether the application will require one server or many. Instead, try to maintain focus on the *purpose* of the application and to build excitement, enthusiasm, or at least a reasonable level of support.

While you should aim to avoid detailed discussions of program implementation at this stage, you must *personally* have a clear idea of how the application will work, so that if you do find yourself drawn into a discussion of hardware or technology requirements, you'll be able to provide reasonably specific answers. Most applications require buy-in from one or more people or groups; you have to convince them that your idea is the best, or that you're the best person to build the application—one or the other, preferably both.

With each group, you should share the portion of your application's vision that will gain a champion for the application. Champions are people in each area who can influence others. Focus on the people who can help or authorize your application, then communicate your vision so they'll *want* to help. They'll only want to help if it solves a problem. Perhaps the application saves money or time. Perhaps it simplifies a task through automation. Perhaps it does none of these things, but it provides integration with other applications they already have or grafts an aesthetic face onto an existing unappealing application. The point is that each group has different interests, and it's your task to create a vision that appeals to each group.

Plan the User Interface

Although many application-planning methodologies start with the data and work forward from there, I usually start with the interface because that's the public persona of your application. Also, at this stage, you often can uncover requirements that aren't part of the back-end program data. For example, a few minutes with paper and pencil drawing screens will let you see immediately that the order form you want to put online can't be directly transferred from the paper form; it will have to be broken into several parts. Also, you may discover that some data is repeated on almost every screen. While people may be *used* to writing or typing the data for paper versions, there's no reason that they have to do the same in an online version. By saving a unique set of past entries, you can probably give them a drop-down list or a set of preferences or…you get the picture.

Some applications have no visual interface requirements—in fact, parts of your C# Web applications, as you begin writing data-access components, business components, and Web Services, won't need a visual interface. However, those portions that do require a visual interface are the ones that people see. You need to groom and plan them artistically and aesthetically because if people don't like the interface, they're unlikely to use the application.

You shouldn't try to plan every detail of the user interface at this point—you probably can't, because you're unlikely to *know* all the details yet—but you should be able to gain a good sense of how you want end users to interact with the program. If you're not intimately familiar with the audience, you should take the time to find out *now* what they do and don't like about a current program, or how they'd prefer to work with a new one. You don't have to translate every suggestion that end users make into a program requirement. Often, the process of getting a good picture of the user interface is a learning process on both sides; you learn what end users want and need, and they learn what's possible, what's expensive, and what they can reasonably expect given the time and budget constraints of the project.

Goals for User Interface Planning

The output from this stage should be a rough mental picture of how the screens that make up the application should look, a basic set of features, and a sense of how users reach those features, for example, via a button, a menu, a keystroke combination, or all three. You should understand the various paths a user might take through the application, and you need to envision what happens when a user quits the application, and how or whether the application lets them go "backward." As you've seen, controlling the sequence of an application can be a critical part of Web application design. In addition, you need to have a good idea of security and how the various security levels (if any) affect the screens and features of the application. Try to keep these goals in mind as you design the user interface:

Make the application time sensitive. By that I mean to make the most common actions both easy to perform and as responsive as possible.

Spend your efforts on the 30 percent of the application that people use every day.

Minimize difficult input. Gather the information you'll need for pick lists and consider ways to program intelligence into the application. A program that responds rapidly and consistently is much more pleasant to learn and use.

Remember that many people don't like computers. Try to make the computer adjust to suit the humans. If people want to see spreadsheet-like applications and reports, provide them. If some people would rather fill out forms, provide an alternative interface.

Have the application remember its state from one session to another. Little is more irritating to users than having to reset preferences because a program designer forgot to save them.

In short, before you begin writing code, you must refine your vision of the end product until it begins to take a clear shape. Write down what you decide upon or agree to. You don't have to make professional-quality screen-design documents for every application—rough sketches usually suffice—but try to capture the main features and get a sense of how people will use the program, what tools they will need, and how you'll build those into the final screens.

Building Prototypes

If you want to build a prototype to see how the application will work, this is a good time to do that, but don't let the prototype mutate into the first release of the application. Negotiate the time and budget to build a minimal prototype, show it off to management, and use it to demonstrate the application to the target audience if you like, but remember that it's a prototype and not production code. Plan to throw the entire program away before you continue.

Prototypes can be dangerous because they set expectations that you may not be able to meet. Showing a prototype is analogous to agreeing to an unwritten contract. You're stating that the application actually *will* look and act exactly like the prototype. After a prototype has been approved, it's that much more difficult to explain to management and the potential audience why changes are needed. Also, because the user interface is all that most people ever see of your application, if you show them a prototype, they immediately jump to the conclusion that the application's almost finished—even when the prototype consists of only the interface and doesn't deal with real data.

Plan Data Storage and Retrieval

Now that you know how the program looks and how you want it to act, you can design how the program should store and retrieve data. If you intend to use a database, plan the tables, relationships, and indexes. I typically do this twice, once to "play" with the data model, and then later to build a final database. For example, your application may get data in XML form, from a mainframe in a flat file, from user input as large text strings, or from uploaded binary files. You need to decide *how* you're going to handle the various data requirements, but not necessarily create the details. For example, it's overkill to begin writing every stored procedure at this point, but it's perfectly logical to create some tables and experiment with the relative efficiency of storing XML as complete documents (long text strings or blobs), separated into individual fields, translated into the appropriate data types or left as text, or some combination. For binary files, you must decide if you want to store the data itself in the database or store the data as files and have the database reference the file location.

If you're not using a database, you need to plan the file structures and folder hierarchy; select names and locations; and consider security, backup plans, and how you can avoid contention for resources.

If you get data from other sources, such as mainframe flat files, decide how you want to get the data into a form (such as XML) usable by your application. Decide when that should occur. For example, mainframes often send text files to a specific directory at intervals. You need a scheduled process to read those files and get them into a form appropriate for your application.

Plan to Archive or Delete Unwanted Data

Consider how you plan to eliminate or archive unwanted data. For example, if you're saving user preferences or intermediate form data, what do you plan to do with preferences when a user quits or never returns to your application? How long should you maintain intermediate form data? If you never purge obsolete data, you'll most definitely want to take your application down at some point to archive unneeded records. Most (but not all) data has a reasonably useful lifetime, after which you can discard it without problems. Some types of data can never be discarded but can be moved to where they don't hinder operations on current data but can be retrieved if needed. For example, people working with a medical records application need fast access to current patient data, in addition to recent patient data such as last quarter's patients and next week's appointments, but they don't need immediate access to non-current patients or data from five years ago. However, you can't ever delete the information altogether. In contrast, if you have an application that provides online registration services for a conference, you might elect to keep incomplete registrations until the start of the conference, after which you can safely delete them, or you may decide not to store incomplete registrations at all.

Just as with the user interface stage, by the end of this stage you should have a clear idea of each major data input, output, and transfer required by your application, but not necessarily the details, such as individual field names or filenames. Whatever you decide, write it all down.

Plan Object Responsibilities and Interfaces

C# is an object-oriented language, so you should build an object model for your application. Because you've been working with the user interface and the data requirements, by this time you will have a fair idea of the *things* that your users and application must manipulate. You don't have to match these up exactly with either the user's expectations or the back-end data model. For example, despite the fact that a given application works with sales data from a mainframe and stores each order in a table row, it may or may not be useful to have an `Order` object—you might not care about individual orders because the application identifies sales trends. The goal is to discover—and that's the watchword here, *discover*—the discrete parts of the application and the data.

Find the discrete parts and differentiate between the *attributes* of those parts and the *variations* on the parts. That's often difficult and is the subject of much discussion and argument among even the best OOP application designers. For example, is it better to have a `User` object that has a `PermissionLevel` property, or to have an abstract `User` object and subclasses for the various permission levels, such as `Administrator`, `Manager`, and `Employee`? Only you can decide, and now is the time to do that, *before* you start writing code.

Plan Administrative Functions

Even for programs with no built-in differentiation among various security levels, you need to plan administrative functionality. For example, suppose you want to be able to shut down your application at odd intervals for maintenance. Certainly, you can just shut down the server, but that may not be the best method. Instead, you might want to create a warning message that would begin displaying a warning—perhaps 24 hours in advance—that the site is unavailable. You might be able to leave one server running and redirect users to another site or to a message page that states why the application is unavailable and when it will become available again.

To do this, you'll need a way to intercept all requests and redirect them to some new location—and unless you want to write custom code each time, you need a way for an application administrator to create the messages and specify times. In other words, you need an administrative interface into the application itself, one or more Web Forms that are not part of the normal user interface.

Similarly, you may want to build in ways to switch detailed logging or state message levels on or off for debugging purposes. You may want a way to purge obsolete or expired data, to archive data, or to change values in static tables. If your application doesn't use integrated Windows security but requires users to log in, you'll definitely want a way to clear passwords and fix misspelled usernames. If you collect metadata, such as page counts, application usage times, or user paths through your site, you'll want to be able to analyze the data and create reports.

No general statement fits all applications, but I would venture to say that if you read this section and *don't* find ideas applicable to your situation, you should probably rethink your application. I cannot imagine a Web application that couldn't benefit from some type of administrative interface. At the very least, you should be able to track application usage, because collecting metadata about an application is one of the best ways to discover whether the money required to create it was well spent.

Create the Database

Finally, you're ready to code something. Armed with the results of all the interface planning, data requirements, object modeling, and administrative planning, you should have enough requirements to build the database. At this stage, you *do* create the tables, relationships, indexes, triggers, stored procedures, and functions. You build the database before writing the program because you can (and should) test it exhaustively without writing any user interface code. Populate the tables with sample data. When you're done, make sure you can re-create the database in its entirety by saving the SQL DDL statements that create the database objects.

The database is the backbone of your application; therefore, it should be bulletproof. That means it should not accept information that doesn't meet requirements. It's easy to write code that tests for information validity, but you can't be sure everyone will write bulletproof code. While *you* would never allow an invalid value to slip through, you can be sure that eventually one will slip through someone else's code.

Databases on the Web must service all the application's users and, because of the stateless nature of the Web, they must provide more information more often than in a standard client-server situation. Because database operations are inherently machine and network intensive, it's your job to minimize the volume of data that must traverse the network for any given request. That means you must take advantage of SQL's capability to select only the required data. But that's only the beginning.

Plan Data Relationships Carefully

The relationships you build into your database during this stage will grow deep roots. For example, the way you plan to store something as simple as a phone number has major ramifications. Not all phone numbers are alike: Some phone numbers require area codes. Some have extensions. Foreign phone numbers are completely different from U.S. phone numbers. In addition, many people would prefer to dial numbers using their phone card to transfer charges. Consider all the phone numbers a person may have.

You might put the phone numbers in a Contacts table using fields such as `HomePhone`, `WorkPhone`, `FaxPhone`, and `CellPhone`, but how many fields are sufficient? Those four may meet your application's needs today, but it's almost certain that someone will require more eventually. You can circumvent this problem by normalizing the database. Put the telephone numbers in a separate table with `ContactID` as a foreign key and use `JOIN` operations to retrieve the telephone numbers associated with an individual. Add a field such as `TelephoneType` to the telephone table. Index the `ContactID` field and the `TelephoneType` field because you're most likely to use these fields to look up values. After a database enters production—and especially after other programs (other than this application) begin using the database—it becomes much more difficult, if not impossible, to change the database structure. If you anticipate changes, you'll be much better off putting your data access logic in stored procedures or in data-access classes so that you can then (sometimes) modify only the procedures or those specific classes rather than the entire application when the data model changes—and there are *always* changes.

Plan a Data Programming Interface

Plan the interface to the database as carefully as you plan the names and arguments of your class methods and properties. You can control *access* to the database through security, but your primary methods for controlling *content* are through stored procedures, triggers, and views. You can (and often should) deny direct access to any database table. Instead, you provide SELECT access through views and stored procedures and INSERT and UPDATE operations through stored procedures, defaults, and triggers. For example, if you have a CreatedOn field, you don't have to trust programmers to update the field. Write a default value or a trigger to insert the value. Create a rule or constraint that protects the field from invalid or out-of-range values. Don't expose the field for direct update. If other database values depend on the field, write a trigger to update them when the field value changes—don't rely on application code to do that for you. Maintain relationships between data values within the database automatically, if possible.

Consider Database Administration

Plan time for administrative pages. The rule of thumb is that you need to create at least four procedures for each top-level database table for administration purposes. These are as follows:

- A way for the administrator to select records to modify

- A way to add new records

- A way to edit existing records

- A way to delete records

If you have username and password fields in your database, the administrator will need to be able to clear passwords and modify usernames. You'll need a form where administrators can select an individual and a ClearPassword stored procedure. If any database processes must be run on a schedule, such as archiving or deleting obsolete records, you need to create a mechanism that will launch the processes. You also need a way to let the appropriate people know when the process started and whether it finished successfully.

Data Size Matters

Plan your data size requirements. Databases tend to grow over time. A SELECT query on an unindexed field may perform adequately when the database has a few hundred records. But when the database grows to hundreds of thousands of records, that same query will bog down the application. You need to plan for the future. Does the data expire or become obsolete? How will you remove obsolete data from the database? Manually? Automatically? What will you do with the records you remove? Discard them? Archive them?

The size of the data at any given time may also affect the application code. You should cringe whenever you see a query such as SELECT * FROM <Tablename>. Unless you know the table contains a fixed number of rows, such queries are an invitation to disaster. The first few hundred rows won't matter, but when the code needs to display or winnow through thousands of records, it will make a huge difference in the responsiveness of your code. Populate the tables with sample data that approaches the maximum expected size and test your application. Doing that will also let you test the application's performance realistically under load and help you optimize the database.

How many servers will it take to service the total anticipated number of users? If it takes more than one, how will you split up or replicate the data? Test the queries using the database server's analysis tools. If the database doesn't have such tools built in, obtain them. Database design and analysis tools can help you find and anticipate problems. For example, the SQL Server Query Analyzer tool can show you the query plan for any query—the SQL, the indexes used, any other columns used in the query, the output, and the time required. When using the Query Analyzer, you should look especially for table scans because those indicate columns for which the database was unable to find an appropriate index to use for the query and therefore has to read the entire column.

Create Data-Access Components

As part of the database testing, you create the components and objects you'll use to get data into and out of the database. The goal is to be able to SELECT, INSERT, UPDATE, and DELETE every table in the database. There are two major approaches.

One approach is to write just a few stored procedures that perform those operations on entire rows. The other approach is to write many smaller stored procedures that return or update just the data you want. Although I believe the second approach is better because you have pinpoint control and can write stored procedures with names appropriate to their individual functions, there's little difference in speed between the two approaches. There is an efficiency gain using small specific procedures, especially for wide tables or for those that store long text or binary values, but there's a corresponding increase in the amount of time you spend testing the procedures, and there's a larger penalty for changing the database, because you have more procedures to update and retest. With larger row-oriented procedures, you retrieve and maintain extra data—either on the server or by maintaining the values through cookies, hidden form variables, or ViewState.

To minimize the problem, you can create "business objects" that handle calling the queries. But don't make the mistake of combining the business object functionality and the pure database operations. You can often create just one data-access component that accepts a stored procedure name, an optional list of parameter values, and some optional transaction information. The component should either return data (SELECT) or perform an operation that alters data.

Create Business Components

A business component contains rules for manipulating the data you retrieve from and insert into the database. You should build the business components as classes—usually a single class and often a collection class for each type of object in your application. Sometimes, the objects' properties mirror a database table, but often they don't. You want to isolate the business rules in a separate layer, or application tier, because the rules usually change more often than either the user interface or the database itself. The usual example is a tax-calculating application. There are many rules for calculating taxes, and they change often; however, neither the interface for entering the data nor the data storage needs to change as often as the rules.

Another example might be an application that arranges route patterns for salespeople. The route data—the customer lists and locations—resides in a database. Although the data changes constantly, the format of the data does not. On the other hand, the rules for calculating the routes change constantly, depending on pricing, product availability, salesperson availability, changing customer lists, the potential size of orders from different customers, and many other business factors.

The application must be able to adapt to the changing route rules. You do that by adding or changing the business components. For example, one rule might be that salespeople must visit each customer a minimum of once each month unless the customer has been inactive for three or more consecutive months. Another might be that customers with total orders exceeding $1,000,000 per year receive a discount of 15 percent on all orders over $10,000, whereas customers with total orders between $500,000 and $999,999 receive a 10 percent discount. Customers with yearly orders totaling less than $500,000 get discounts on a sliding scale, depending on the size of each individual order.

If (or rather, when) these rules change—perhaps the business focus changes to acquire new customers, so discounts to smaller customers increase—the business logic must also change. Therefore, the main purpose of a business component is to isolate business rules so you can replace the logic inside the component without disturbing any other parts of the application.

This isn't as simple as it sounds, although it is simpler with C# than it was with classic VB or other procedural languages. The challenge is to design the components so you can change the logic *inside* the components without changing the external programmatic interface.

In COM programming, changing an interface also required you to recompile any other parts of the application that used the interface. To work around this, people often created "generic" methods that accepted `Variant` arrays. You no longer need to do this. You can use overloading to add new methods that accept additional parameters, or you can subclass existing components and add new methods to those. Also, replacing the component no longer breaks the application. The .NET runtime recognizes that the class has been changed and handles JIT recompilation of other parts of the application that use the updated class. Another common workaround was to create data access methods that could accept any *ad hoc* SQL statement and a command type. Doing that "covers" for missing stored procedures. Unfortunately, unless people were very careful, such workarounds quickly led to errors and unmaintainable code.

Although .NET makes it much easier to update the components of an application, try to anticipate the kinds of changes that are likely to occur and plan for them in advance. For example, you may have started the application with browser clients in mind, but maybe it's worthwhile to expose some of the data as Web Services or to ensure that you can deliver in multiple languages or to other client types. Don't forget to build in security as you create the application—it's much harder to add it later.

Finally, test everything thoroughly. You should be able to perform all the data manipulation *without* building the user interface (not without *planning* the interface, though). I know it's tempting because it's very satisfying to put controls on the screen and work backward from the user interface—and you can often change the way you think about the application by doing that. Unfortunately, I've seen several projects fail because the people coding it began mixing up the business rules and data access with the user interface. Later, after the original development group left, the maintenance programmers, not understanding the ramifications of their actions, were unable to make even simple changes quickly without causing other problems.

In addition, the development time went way up because the programmers concentrated on the quirks and problems of the user interface rather than testing the back-end code, leading to cascading change lists and lots of bugs. If you're the kind of developer who *must* see and "feel" the user interface first, build a prototype project. When you're satisfied with that, throw away all the code and start over, following the steps listed here. The prototype project will uncover most of the big problems you'll face, so you won't lose much time by building it, as long as you recognize that almost all the code you write during the prototype phase is throwaway code.

Build the User Interface

After you can manipulate the data and you have a well-defined interface to the business objects, putting the user interface together is often very straightforward. Even if you do find additional data requirements because of changes during the user interface development, they're often much easier to implement because you can add items to a well-tested back-end model with fewer problems than if you were trying to make changes to both tiers simultaneously.

As you build the user interface, keep these points in mind:

- Try to keep the interface uncluttered.

- Use applications as models that you and the potential audience admire.

- Use controls appropriately.

- Make the application functional first, and then make it aesthetically pleasing as well.

- Use graphics effectively, as aids to help people locate and place information rather than as pure decoration.

- Use high-contrast color schemes.

- Avoid small font sizes.

- Try to minimize the interdependence of controls.

- Consider the state of the application at all times. Hide or disable controls that people shouldn't use during that state. For example, you've probably seen numerous forms on the Internet that have required fields—and also have an enabled Submit button before those fields contain valid data.

- For browser-based applications, use client-side script when possible to avoid server round trips.

- Use directions liberally, and word them carefully.

- If you plan to internationalize your application, create database tables and resource files containing the text, and test the application in the languages you'll support. Different languages require differing amounts of space for equivalent meanings. Try to avoid embedding text within graphics; otherwise, you'll need to change the graphics whenever you change languages.

- Keep control placement consistent. If you have navigation controls that appear on most pages, consider putting them on every page and disabling the ones that aren't applicable.

- Try to avoid scrolling forms (it's OK to deliver content pages that scroll). Unless you have an extremely homogenous client base, you'll probably need to consider the client's screen resolution. If you have many downlevel clients, you may also need to consider the color depth, although that restriction has largely disappeared over the past few years because most modern computers support "true" color.

Although you can't test a user interface in the same way that you can test back-end components, there are test suites that let you program in action patterns; if you have the resources, it's probably a good idea. If you can borrow members of the target audience, they will give you useful feedback. Try to plan at least two tests with potential end users.

For other testing, consider dedicating one or more people to a quality assurance (QA) process. It's very difficult to test an event-driven interface exhaustively, but a good rule of thumb is that it takes five individuals to find 95 percent of the problems. Don't be complacent—test thoroughly and find and fix bugs during development.

Summary

In this chapter, you've seen that Web application development goes far beyond learning the ASP.NET framework and writing code. You can build an application and hope that it gets adopted merely because it's useful, but most successful applications require more planning than that. Not every application needs every step discussed here, but by following the guidelines in this chapter, you can ensure that your applications won't be ignored—they'll be eagerly anticipated. More than that, management, the help desk, network and database administrators, and maintenance programmers will welcome and support them. Finally, and perhaps most important, the applications themselves will work better and last longer than if you just sit down and start coding.

As you're planning applications and thinking about efficiency and the user interface, consider how you might improve the interface and responsiveness of your Web applications. Writing client-side code lets you minimize the number of server round trips. In addition, by manipulating content dynamically with script using the Document Object Model (DOM) built into modern browsers, you can create smooth, easy-to-use interfaces. In the next chapter, you'll see how to take advantage of client-side script in your ASP.NET applications.

Part 5

Advanced Visual C# Web Applications

Chapter 20

Leveraging Browser Clients

AT THIS POINT, YOU'VE completed the core task of learning about the server end of C# Web applications. The rest of this book is devoted to raising your awareness of peripheral technologies that can affect the depth and quality of your applications. The first and probably most important of these is client-side scripting. Through your server-side code, you have the capability to write code that executes within the client—in other words, you can use code to write code. The code you write can be dynamic, and you can write browser-specific code. That's often a difficult concept for beginning Web programmers to master—that you can write client-side code using text generated from server-side code. Nevertheless, in this chapter you'll see how client-side code can improve the effectiveness and efficiency of your ASP.NET applications.

In this chapter:

◆ Which Client-Side Script Makes Sense?

◆ Sending Script to the Browser

◆ The Document Object Model

◆ Accessing the DOM from Script

◆ Using ActiveX Controls

Which Client-Side Script Makes Sense?

Unfortunately, different browsers support different types of script. ECMAScript, JScript, and JavaScript are all variants of the same language. While all three variations support the core JavaScript language features, there are some differences, but for most purposes, you can treat them as identical. Unless you're an ex-VB or ASP VBScript programmer, you won't care about the other major in-browser scripting language—VBScript. As far as I can tell, Internet Explorer (IE) is the only browser that supports VBScript, but almost all browsers support JavaScript. Therefore, unless you have some special reason to use VBScript, you should write your client-side script in JavaScript.

Not all browsers support all versions of JavaScript; the various versions of JavaScript differ in functionality, and the browsers themselves have different object models. That's equally true for IE-only shops. Even if everyone has the same browser version, not everyone may have the same version of the scripting runtime. Therefore, code that runs perfectly well in one browser may not execute or may execute differently in another. You should plan to test extensively with a good sample of your potential browser clients if you decide to use client-side script. Finally, you need to decide how your application should respond when script simply doesn't work, either because clients are using browsers that don't support JavaScript or because a client has disabled JavaScript.

Most classic ASP programmers wrote server-side VBScript, which had the advantage that, if you *were* able to use client-side VBScript, the syntax for client- and server-side script was identical, with the exception that the ASP intrinsic objects such as the `Request` and `Response` objects weren't available through client-side script. Therefore, using VBScript on the client cut the learning curve. Using C# (or J# or JScript) on the server, you're in essentially the same position, but with different languages, and you won't have any trouble with the syntax of client-side JavaScript. Eventually, when Windows clients (and perhaps others) have a .NET framework runtime installed, you'll be able to take advantage of the entire .NET framework to program on the client. Unfortunately, that's at least two (and probably more) years away from being generally available except in intranet situations.

In this chapter, I'll provide examples almost exclusively in JavaScript (JScript). Don't confuse Microsoft's client-side JScript-interpreted scripting language with JScript.NET; they're not the same language, even though they have a similar syntax and some of the same intrinsic functions. Also, I'll use the term *JavaScript* from now on rather than *JScript*, which may help make the difference clear. IE doesn't differentiate between *JScript* and *JavaScript*, but most browsers recognize only *JavaScript*.

If you're running a non-IE browser, you will be able to run only the JavaScript examples. You won't be able to run the examples that demonstrate COM functionality. If you're using IE 6, all the examples will work properly. I used IE 6 during the writing of this book, but most of the examples will work with IE 4 and 5 as well.

As you can see from this discussion, adding client-side script introduces an entirely new level of complexity. In addition, it limits the set of clients that can see the full functionality of your pages. By some estimates, when writing applications for the Internet, you eliminate up to 20 percent of all potential clients when you begin using frames, JavaScript, Cascading Style Sheets (CSS), and the DOM. That's because a significant percentage of people use obsolete or less-capable browsers. However, the true percentage is probably less than 10 percent because even Netscape 4 was capable of dealing with frames, running JavaScript, and supporting a minimal level of CSS and DOM functionality. In addition, most reports count hits from spiders, newsgroup browsers, and people using text-only browsers. These clients don't expect and won't miss any advanced features you may add. If you *must* support these "downlevel" browsers, you'll need to either create two versions of your pages—one that uses HTML 3.2 (*not* HTML 4) and one that uses the more advanced features supported by modern browsers—or write all your UI code so that it runs on the server. The Web Form `targetSchema` property can help you support older browsers. By setting the `targetSchema` property to `Internet Explorer 3.02 / Navigator 3.0` or to `Navigator 4.0`, the built-in server controls will render in a form that those browsers can fully understand. Note that if you build custom server controls, you're responsible for changing the rendering to support the `targetSchema` setting in effect at render time.

Personally, I feel that the development community should do everything in its power to *stop* supporting these (in Internet terms) ancient browsers, because they cost everyone money in added design, testing, and support time. You can even argue that they cost their owners money because they don't deliver modern user-interface features, such as drop-down menus and absolute positioning; therefore, at best they slow down interactivity and, at worst, make it impossible to deliver timesaving features. If at all possible, try to limit the clients supported by your Web applications to version 5 and higher browsers.

In intranet situations, you may have much more control over the set of clients. For example, if everyone in your company uses IE 5.5 or higher, you can freely use JScript, the DOM, ActiveX controls, DHTML, XML, and CSS to improve your interfaces and make your applications more attractive.

Why Use Client Script?

Now that Visual Studio provides the ASP.NET server control model, why should you even bother writing client script? If you can react to events, gather data, perform validation, and move items on the client's screen from the server, why suffer through learning yet another language and worrying about the client environment?

The answer, of course, is that there are things you can do on the client that are impossible or too time-sensitive to handle from the server. Also, it's a matter of being attentive to network bandwidth, user connection speeds, and the responsiveness of your application, and of presenting the smoothest possible user interface. Here are some tasks that you *cannot* accomplish without client-side script:

◆ Display a message box on the client

◆ Open a new browser window

◆ Communicate between frames

◆ Perform simple animations

◆ Write custom client-side validation scripts

These are all common Web application tasks.

Sending Script to the Browser

There are at least five ways to create script that executes within a browser. I'll show you these five, and then you can decide which method is most appropriate for your application at any given time:

◆ The simplest way is to modify the ASPX file in HTML mode and add the script. You can place script anywhere in the file, although you should avoid placing it inside the VS-generated `<form>` tag because the designer rewrites the contents of that tag as you add, move, and modify items on the Web Form. I've found that the best places are in the `<head>` section and at the end of the file.

◆ You can create a script as a string in your server-side code. From your code-behind class, you send script to the browser in much the same way you send dynamically generated HTML.

◆ You can send a script tag to the client with a `src` attribute that references a server-based file containing `JavaScript`. The advantage of this method is that you can reference the same script from many different Web Forms, thus letting you maintain and modify the script in a single file. The disadvantage is that the browser must make a separate request for the file. However, because most script files are relatively small, and because the browser caches the script files just as it does other files, the time consumed by this extra request is (usually) unnoticeable.

◆ Using IE, you can create XML-formatted HTML extensions called *HTML behaviors*, which run code placed in special files that have an `.htc` extension on the server. I won't cover HTML behaviors in this book, because they don't have anything to do with .NET, but if you're interested, you can find articles on the Web that explain the techniques.

◆ Finally, just to complicate things, you can write client-side script with client-side script. The point to remember here is that you can think of script as executable text. Because the browser *interprets* the code at runtime, you can force the script engine to execute any valid code string at any time. Writing script with client-side script is useful primarily as a method for simplifying the process of writing cross-browser–compatible scripts, for creating short scripts for windows that you open from the client, and for executing code when you don't know what the code should be at design time.

Writing Client Script Directly into an ASPX File

You place client-side script inside a `<script>` tag. Early in this book you saw how to place C# server-side inline code directly into an ASPX file. Client-side script looks similar, but it doesn't contain the `runat="server"` attribute. For example:

```
<script type="text/javascript">
   // your code goes here
</script>
```

The `</script>` tag can accept several attributes, but you should normally include *at least* a `language` or `type` attribute. The `language` attribute, which had only a few possible values, such as `JavaScript`, `JScript`, `VBScript`, and `VBS`, has been "deprecated" in favor of the `type` attribute, which accepts a MIME-type string specifying the language. For example, the following code is identical to the preceding `<script>` snippet and executes in any script-aware browser:

```
<script language="JavaScript">
   // your code goes here
</script>
```

TIP   VS.NET can insert a script block for you. Place the insertion point where you want the script to start and select Edit ➢ Insert Script Block ➢ Client/Server to insert a client-side script or a server-side script block.

You place functions, subroutines (VBScript-only syntax for a "void" function), and global code and definitions between the `<script>` tags. Code executes within subroutines and functions only when called, whereas global code—code within the `<script>` tag—executes immediately after the script engine on the browser compiles it. Listing 20.1 shows an HTML file containing a client-side script to display two `alert`s (an `alert` is a modal dialog box that displays a message). `alert`s are essentially the equivalent of the familiar Windows MessageBox, but somewhat less functional.

LISTING 20.1: CLIENT-SIDE SCRIPT TO DISPLAY `alert`s (ch20-1.htm)

```
<html>
<head>
</head>
```

```
<body>
This script creates two "alert" boxes that execute on the client
using JavaScript.
<script type="text/javascript">
   function showAlert() {
      alert("Hello from the showAlert function!");
   }
   alert("Hello world");
   showAlert();
</script>
</body>
</html>
```

The first `alert` displays `Hello World`, and the second `alert` displays `Hello from the showAlert` `function!`. That may seem odd because if you look at the preceding script, you'll see that the two `alerts` are displayed in a different order than they appear in the script. The script defines the `showAlert()` function *before* the `alert` that displays the `Hello World` code. Remember, code placed at Global scope (inside a `<script>` tag, but outside any function definition) executes immediately. Functions and subroutines execute only when called. Global code executes in the same order in which it appears in the script.

Writing Client Script with Server Script

There's a difference between `<script>` tags intended for server-side script and `<script>` tags for client-side script. The ASP.NET framework assumes you want the script to execute on the client unless you specifically mark it as server-side script using the `runat="server"` attribute. You can include both server- and client-side `<script>` tags in the same ASP file, but there's a trick. Listing 20.2 shows an example.

LISTING 20.2: COMBINING SERVER AND CLIENT `<script>` TAGS (ch20-2.aspx)

```
<%@ Page Language="vb" AutoEventWireup="false"
   Codebehind="ch20-2.aspx.cs" Inherits="CSharpASP.ch20.ch20_2"%>
<html>
   <head>
      <title>ch20_2test</title>
      <meta name="GENERATOR" content="Microsoft Visual Studio.NET
   7.0">
      <meta name="CODE_LANGUAGE" content="Visual Basic 7.0">
      <meta name="vs_defaultClientScript" content="JavaScript">
      <meta name="vs_targetSchema"
         content="http://schemas.microsoft.com/intellisense/ie5">
      <script language="C#" runat="server">
         void writeShowAlertScript() {
            Response.Write( "<scr" + "ipt
   language=\"JavaScript\">" +
               System.Environment.NewLine);
            Response.Write("function showAlert() {"  +
```

```
                    System.Environment.NewLine);
               Response.Write("alert('Hello from showAlert
        function!'); "
                    + System.Environment.NewLine);
               Response.Write("}" + System.Environment.NewLine);
               Response.Write( "alert('Hello world');" +
                    System.Environment.NewLine);
               Response.Write( "showAlert();"  +
                    System.Environment.NewLine);
               Response.Write("</scr" + "ipt>");
            }
        </script>
    </head>
    <body MS_POSITIONING="GridLayout">
        <form id="Form1" method="post" runat="server">
            <asp:Label id="Label1" style="Z-INDEX: 101; LEFT: 41px;
            POSITION: absolute; TOP: 26px" runat="server"
            Width="439px" Height="58px">The script that shows the
            alerts on this page was written dynamically with
            inline server-side code.</asp:Label>
            <asp:Label id="lblMessage" style="Z-INDEX: 102; LEFT:
        41px;
            POSITION: absolute; TOP: 147px" runat="server"
            Width="605px"></asp:Label>
        </form>
        <% writeShowAlertScript();%>
    </body>
</html>
```

When you run the file, the first thing you see is the two `alerts`. Which one do you see first? Note that the server script between the code (`<% %>`) tags at the *bottom* of the file calls the server-side `write-ShowAlertScript` function that generates the client script. Where does the client script appear in the output sent to the browser? Hint: Browse to the file, close the `alerts`, and then view the browser source code.

The file shows you a trick. The `writeShowAlertScript` method breaks the client-side `<script>` tag itself into separate parts. If you don't do this, the ASP engine tries to compile the `<script>` tag meant for the client and generates an error. To see this in action, change the first and last lines to recombine the word `script` into a single word:

```
void writeShowAlertScript() {
    Response.Write( "<script language=\"JavaScript\">" +
        System.Environment.NewLine);
    Response.Write("function showAlert() {"  +
        System.Environment.NewLine);
    Response.Write("alert('Hello from showAlert function!'); "
        + System.Environment.NewLine);
```

```
        Response.Write("}" +  System.Environment.NewLine);
        Response.Write( "alert('Hello world');" +
            System.Environment.NewLine);
        Response.Write( "showAlert();" +
            System.Environment.NewLine);
        Response.Write("</script>");
    }
```

Execute the file by requesting it from the browser. You'll see a compilation error stating that the line containing the closing </script> has a newline character in a constant. Of course that's not true—it's a spurious error that occurs when the parser encounters the second <script> tag (see Figure 20.1).

FIGURE 20.1

If you don't "break up" the <script> tag when you write script with inline code, you'll get a spurious error

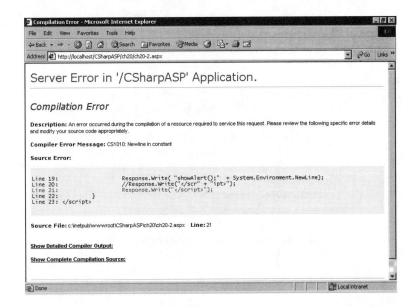

After each line of the client-side script, the server script writes a carriage return/linefeed character combination by calling the System.Environment.NewLine method. The call to NewLine produces two characters in Windows: the ASCII characters 13 and 10. The NewLine calls are optional with JavaScript, which uses semicolons to delimit the ends of code lines, but they're required for VBScript, which relies on the end-of-line character to delimit the code lines. I usually write them for both languages because, in the browser, the NewLine character makes the code easier to read for debugging purposes.

NOTE *If you've been recompiling between making changes to the HTML (ASPX) files in this chapter, you can stop. The ASP.NET framework automatically detects changes to text file resources such as ASPX files and CONFIG files. Interestingly, when the framework detects such a change, not only does it refresh the cached HTML, but it also parses and JITs any server-side code that appears in the file. Therefore, you can save yourself a little time. You don't have to recompile when you alter HTML files, even those containing server-side scripts; let the framework handle the changes. Of course, you should also recognize that forcing the server to JIT inline code is slower than using precompiled code in a code-behind class, but it's a very useful technique for writing debugging code in the field.*

Writing Client Script from a Code-Behind Class

There's a second label on the ch20-2.aspx Web Form. If you look at the code-behind class, you'll see some code in the lblMessage_Init event (see Listing 20.3).

LISTING 20.3: THE CODE-BEHIND FILE ch20-2.aspx.cs WRITES A CLIENT-SIDE SCRIPT

```
public class ch20_2 : System.Web.UI.Page
{
    protected System.Web.UI.WebControls.Label Label1;
    protected System.Web.UI.WebControls.Label lblMessage;

    private void Page_Load(object sender, System.EventArgs e)
    {
        // Put user code to initialize the page here
    }

    // autogenerated code omitted
    private void lblMessage_Init(object sender, System.EventArgs e)
    {
        System.Web.UI.WebControls.Label lbl =
          (System.Web.UI.WebControls.Label) sender;
        lbl.Text = "This label changes color when you move your " +
            "mouse over it.";
        lbl.Style["color"] = "#0000FF";
        lbl.Attributes.Add("onmouseenter",
    "this.style.color='#FF0000';");
        lbl.Attributes.Add("onmouseleave",
    "this.style.color='#00FF00';");
    }
}
```

Just as the inline code in the preceding section writes script to the client, this code does the same thing from the code-behind class. The two calls to the lbl.Attributes.Add method add style attributes to the control that contain the code.

MIXING CODE-BEHIND AND INLINE CODE

I put this code into the ch20-2.aspx.cs file specifically to remind you that you can mix code-behind code and inline code freely. The ASP.NET framework handles the entire process for you. In this example, the code doesn't write a complete <script> tag (although it could); instead, it adds some event-driven script to the lblMessage Web control that causes it to change color as you move your mouse into and out of the control area.

NOTE   While experimenting with this file, I found that one thing you can't mix is inline code and dynamic controls. If you attempt to use the Page_Load event to add a new Web control, you'll get an error. That's one more reason to avoid inline code.

Passing Values from Server Code to Client Code

You can use script to pass information from the server to the client. One of the most common ASP.NET questions is how a client-side script can gain access to the values of Session and Application variables. Although there's more than one way to pass server values to the client, the simplest way is to write the *values* of the server-side variables and assign those values to client-side variables in a script. For example, Listing 20.4 shows how to assign Session.SessionID to a variable in a client-side script.

LISTING 20.4: TRANSFERRING SERVER-SIDE VARIABLES TO CLIENT-SIDE SCRIPTS (ch20-3.aspx.cs)

```
private void Page_Load(object sender, System.EventArgs e) {
   String s = "<script language=JavaScript>";
   Response.Write("When you load this page, you'll see an alert
   containing your SessionID.");
   s += "var sessionID='" + Session.SessionID + "';" +
      System.Environment.NewLine;
   s += "alert('Your SessionID is: ' + sessionID);";
   s += "</script>";
   RegisterClientScriptBlock("script1", s);
}
```

Another way to write a client-side script is to use the Page object's RegisterClientScriptBlock method. The method accepts two arguments: a String object containing an identifying String key for the script and a second String object containing the script code, including the opening and closing <script></script> tags.

When this code executes, it adds the following script to the browser (although not formatted in quite this way, and with the client's SessionID rather than the one shown below):

```
<script language=JavaScript>
   var sessionID='dzlgjyuuxar342ncewfex545';
   alert('Your SessionID is: ' + sessionID);
</script>
```

Here's how it works. On the server, the code in the Page_Load event writes the *value* of the Session .SessionID to the client-side script string. The call to the RegisterClientScriptBlock method writes the script to the output immediately after the hidden __VIEWSTATE control. The browser parses the page and passes the script to the scripting engine, which compiles the script and then displays the alert.

A similar Page class method called RegisterStartupScript inserts a client script at the *end* of the default form, just before the closing </form> tag. For both the RegisterClientScriptBlock and the RegisterStartupScript methods, you can use the key parameter to avoid inserting duplicate scripts. For example, if you had two custom server controls that shared a client-side script, you wouldn't want to insert two copies. Similarly, if you had a shared server method that registered a script and the method might be called multiple times, you would need to prevent VS from generating multiple script copies. Using the key value, you can test to see if a script is already registered:

```
if (!Me.IsClientScriptBlockRegistered("yourScriptKeyHere")) {
    // register the script using Me.RegisterClientScriptBlock
}
```

or

```
if (!Me.IsClientStartupScriptRegistered("yourScriptKeyHere")) {
    //register the script using Me.RegisterClientStartupScript
}
```

You can use client-side script transparently to force the browser to request other pages, to submit forms, or to display alternate content. For example, suppose you want to display different pages based on the client's screen resolution. The `Request.Browser` class gives you the capability to determine which browser a client is using and which scripting engine the browser supports, but it doesn't provide the client's screen resolution. You can work around that problem by writing a client-side script to obtain the screen resolution and send it back to your ASP program.

NOTE   When you write client-side script from within an inline server code block, you have to break up the `<script>` tags to avoid errors, as you saw earlier in this chapter. However, when you write script from a code-behind code method, you have no such restriction. That's because the ASP.NET engine does not have to parse the code-behind class code for HTML.

Listing 20.5 uses a script written (purposely) in VBScript to determine the screen resolution width and height; it displays that information using the VBScript `MsgBox` function and then directs the browser back to the originating ASP page with the screen resolution information embedded in the query string data. The server retrieves the screen resolution from the `Request.QueryString` and then writes it to the screen.

LISTING 20.5: OBTAINING THE SCREEN RESOLUTION OF THE CLIENT COMPUTER (ch20-4.aspx.cs)

```
private void Page_Load(object sender, System.EventArgs e) {
    String s = null;
    if (Request.QueryString["Width"] != null) {
        Response.Write("Your screen resolution is: " +
            Request.QueryString["Width"] + "x" +
            Request.QueryString["Height"] + "<br>");
        Response.End();
    }
    s = "<script language=VBScript>" + System.Environment.NewLine;
    s += "    " + "Dim x,y" + System.Environment.NewLine;
    s += "    " + "x=window.screen.width" +
    System.Environment.NewLine;
    s += "    " + "y=window.screen.height" +
    System.Environment.NewLine;
    s += "    if MsgBox('Your screen resolution is: ' & x & ', ' &
```

```
    y, " +
       "vbOkCancel ,'Screen Resolution') = vbOK Then" +
       System.Environment.NewLine;
    s += "       window.location.href='ch20-4.aspx?Width=' & x & " +
       "'&Height=' & y" + System.Environment.NewLine;
    s += "   end if" + System.Environment.NewLine;
    s += "</script>";
    s = s.Replace("'", "\"");
    RegisterClientScriptBlock("script1", s);
}
```

The script first tests to see if the `Request.QueryString("ScreenWidth")` variable has a value. If not, it writes a client-side script to obtain the screen dimensions. The client side script (formatted) looks like this:

```
<script language=VBScript>
   Dim x,y
   x=window.screen.width
   y=window.screen.height
   if MsgBox("Your screen resolution is: " & x & ", " & y, _
      vbOkCancel ,"Screen Resolution") = vbOK Then
      window.location.href="ch20-4.aspx?Width=" & x & "&Height="
   & y
   end if
</script>
```

The script obtains the browser screen width and height and assigns them to the x and y variables, respectively. Next, it displays a VBScript message box. VBScript message boxes are more flexible than JavaScript `alerts` because you can control the number and content of buttons and display a title (see Figure 20.2), whereas JavaScript `alerts` have no programmable title or button control capabilities. In addition, VBScript's `MsgBox` function returns a value indicating which button the user clicked, which can be extremely useful. VBScript contains built-in constants for the buttons. This example uses the constant vbOKCancel, which displays OK and Cancel buttons. The example also checks the return value to see if the user clicked the OK button, using the vbOK constant.

When the user clicks the OK button, the script formats a URL containing `Width` and `Height` query string values and then sets the `document.location.href` property. The `document.location` object has properties containing information about the browser's location. For example:

```
window.location.href="ch20-4.aspx?Width=" & x & "&Height=" & y
```

Setting the `document.location.href` property causes the browser to load the requested document. In this case, setting the property reloads the same page.

The rest of the line appends the page request with the screen width and height that the script obtained from the `Screen` object to create a URL. After concatenation, the URL looks like this (of course, your resolution may be different):

```
ch20-4.aspx?Width=800&Height=600
```

FIGURE 20.2

VBScript message
boxes are more
flexible than
JavaScript `alert`s

When the browser submits the request to the server, the ASP.NET engine populates the `QueryString` collection with the query string key/value pairs appended to the URL—in this case, `Width=800` and `Height=600`.

The `Page_Load` event checks the `Request.QueryString("Width")` variable. When it has a value, the other portion of the form must have been sent to the browser already; therefore, the server-side code displays the user's screen resolution and exits; otherwise it writes the script, causing the browser to display the message box.

The most important point to remember from this example is that you can use client script to perform some action on the client and immediately return that information to the server—without the user seeing anything. For example, if you suppress the `MsgBox` call by deleting it or commenting it out, you'll see that, to the user, the request appears to write the screen resolution immediately, when in fact what's happened is an extra round trip. The server responds to the original request with a script that executes and immediately returns the screen resolution values to the server, which then responds with some visible information. You can use this technique in many ways.

For example, suppose you have two sites, both secured and running on different servers in different domains: `http://www.mySite1.com` and `http://www.mySite2.com`. Whenever a user successfully logs on to one of those sites, you want that browser instance to have seamless access to the other site. After a successful authentication at either site, you set a cookie to prove authentication for future requests to that site. But cookies are domain specific. A browser holding a cookie from `Site1` won't send it to `Site2`. By redirecting the authenticated browser from `Site1` to `Site2` by submitting a form containing the authentication cookie to `Site2`, that site can set its own cookie and redirect the browser back to `Site1`. You can use the concepts shown in this section—of client-side code that executes automatically behind the scenes—to do exactly that.

Referencing Script Files on the Server

The techniques you've seen so far are page specific. When you have generic client-side scripts, it's not a good idea to place them into individual pages, because if you need to modify them for any reason, you have to perform error-prone search-and-replace operations on all your pages. It's much more efficient, from a maintenance point of view, to place generic scripts in separate files on the server and reference them from multiple pages.

For example, suppose you want to scroll the contents of a `<div>` tag that periodically displays a different "special offer" from a list of offers that are updated at irregular intervals on the server. Each item consists of the duration (in seconds) that the offer should be displayed; an optional expiration time; the font, size, and color in which to display the offer text; and a string containing the offer text itself. Here's the logic:

1. A marketing representative updates the list of items and the display time for each item in an XML file stored on the server using an administrative page (not shown in this example).

2. Whenever a page is displayed, you need to obtain the current list of items and show them one at a time in a `<div>` tag on the page, changing the displayed items at specified durations.

3. Your Web Form reads the items from the XML file and places them in a client-side JavaScript array.

4. A client-side script loops through the items, displaying them in round-robin sequence and changing the items based on an interval value, also obtained from the database.

The code for this example resides in four different files. Listing 20.6 shows the XML file that defines the special offers.

LISTING 20.6: XML FILE CONTAINING THE DATA FOR THE SPECIAL OFFERS (SpecialOffers.xml)

```xml
<?xml version="1.0" encoding="utf-8" ?>
<offers>
<offer>
   <duration>3</duration>
   <text>Housewares on sale until 4:00</text>
   <font name="Microsoft Sans Serif" size="12" bold="false"
      italic="true" color="#0000ff" />
   <url>ch20-6.aspx?item="Housewares"</url>
   <backgroundimage>images/acindstr.gif</backgroundimage>
</offer>
<offer>
   <duration>6</duration>
   <text>Quick Sale on all CDs! Click Now!</text>
   <font name="Arial" size="16" bold="true" italic="false"
      color="#ff0000" />
   <url>ch20-6.aspx?item="CDs"</url>
   <backgroundimage>images/stone.bmp</backgroundimage>
</offer>
```

```
<offer>
   <duration>4</duration>
   <text>Visit our Garden Center for special end-of-summer
      deals!</text>
   <font name="Times New Roman" size="14" bold="true"
   italic="true"
      color="#00ff00" />
   <url>ch20-6.aspx?item="Garden"</url>
   <backgroundimage>images/acbluprt.gif</backgroundimage>
</offer>
</offers>
```

The `ch20-5.aspx` file itself is straightforward. Other than the standard HTML template that VS creates when you add a Web Form to your project, it contains only two extra bits of code. First, I added a `<div>` tag with an `id` attribute of `divOffer`:

```
<div id="divOffer"></div>
```

That `<div>` will act as a container for the special offers. Second, I added an `onload` attribute to the `<body>` tag that calls a `showOffer` function defined in the `specialoffers.js` file (more about that in a second) to show the first special offer when the page finishes loading:

```
<body onload="showOffer(0);"
```

The code-behind `ch20-5.aspx.cs` file loads the `specialoffers.xml` file into an `XmlDocument` object. Using the `XmlDocument.selectNodes` method, the code retrieves an `XmlNodeList` of `<offer>` elements and loops through them. For each `<offer>` element, the code performs a series of `select-SingleNode` calls and uses the data contained in those nodes to write a client-side script containing a global array named `offers[]` (see Listing 20.7). Each item in the `offers[]` array corresponds to a single item in the XML file.

LISTING 20.7: THE WEB FORM `ch20-5.aspx.cs` CREATES ONE CLIENT-SIDE SCRIPT CONTAINING AN ARRAY AND CREATES A SCRIPT REFERENCE TO A SEPARATE FILE CONTAINING JAVASCRIPT (`ch20-5.aspx.cs`)

```
using System.Text;
using System.Xml;
// autogenerated code omitted
private void Page_Load(object sender, System.EventArgs e) {
   XmlDocument doc = new XmlDocument();
   XmlNodeList offers = null;
   StringBuilder sb = new StringBuilder(1000);
   string newline = System.Environment.NewLine;
   int i = 0;
   try {
      // load the specialoffers.xml document
      doc.Load(Server.MapPath(".") + "\\specialoffers.xml");
```

```
// get a list of all the offers
offers = doc.SelectNodes("offers/offer");
sb.Append("<script type=\"text/JavaScript\">" + newline);
sb.Append("var offers= new Array();" + newline);
foreach (XmlElement offer in offers) {
    sb.Append("offers[" + i.ToString() + "]=" +
        offer.SelectSingleNode("duration").InnerText +
        ";" + newline);
    i++;
    sb.Append("offers[" + i.ToString() + "]='" +
        offer.SelectSingleNode("text").InnerText + "';" +
        newline);
    i++;
    sb.Append("offers[" + i.ToString() + "]='" +
        offer.SelectSingleNode("font/@name").Value +
        "';" + newline);
    i++;
    sb.Append("offers[" + i.ToString() + "]=" +
        offer.SelectSingleNode("font/@size").Value +
        ";" + newline);
    i++;
    sb.Append("offers[" + i.ToString() + "]=" +
        offer.SelectSingleNode("font/@bold").Value +
        ";" + newline);
    i++;
    sb.Append("offers[" + i.ToString() + "]=" +
        offer.SelectSingleNode("font/@italic").Value +
        ";" + newline);
    i++;
    sb.Append("offers[" + i.ToString() + "]='" +
        offer.SelectSingleNode("font/@color").Value +
        "';" + newline);
    i++;
    sb.Append("offers[" + i.ToString() + "]='" +
        offer.SelectSingleNode("url").InnerText +
        "';" + newline);
    i++;
    sb.Append("offers[" + i.ToString() + "]='" +
        offer.SelectSingleNode("backgroundimage").InnerText
        + "';" + newline);
    i++;
}
sb.Append("</script>" + newline);
RegisterClientScriptBlock("dynamicScript", sb.ToString());
RegisterClientScriptBlock("serverScript",
    "<script type=\"text/javascript\" " +
    "src=\"specialoffers.js\"></script>");
}
```

```
    catch (Exception ex) {
        Response.Write(ex.Message);
        Response.End();
    }
}
```

The last line in the `try` section of the code in Listing 20.7 registers a client script block with no code in it. Instead, the code gives the `<script>` tag a `src` attribute that specifies the file `special-Offers.js`. The `specialOffers.js` file contains the static part of the JScript code that the server sends to the client. Notice that it doesn't have `<script></script>` tags because the server inserts those when it creates the reference to the file. The server writes

```
<script type="text/javascript" src="specialoffers.js"></script>
```

The browser requests the file and inserts the contents between the `<script>` tags when it parses the response. Listing 20.8 shows the referenced JScript file. Note the `.js` extension.

LISTING 20.8: REFERENCED JSCRIPT FILE (SpecialOffers.js)

```
var itemCount = offers.length + 1;
    var offerCount = parseInt(itemCount / 9);

    function showOffer(offerNumber) {
        offerNumber = parseInt(offerNumber);
        // the server creates a list of special offers
        // in a global array named "offers".
        // each item in array dimension contains one item
        // of information
        var s;
        var index = offerNumber*9
        var duration = offers[index];
        var text = offers[index+1];
        var fontname= offers[index+2];
        var fontsize= offers[index+3];
        var fontbold= offers[index+4];
        var fontitalic= offers[index+5];
        var fontcolor= offers[index+6];
        var url= offers[index+7];
        var backgroundImage=offers[index+8];

        s = "<a href='" + url + "' style='cursor: hand'>";
        s += "<span style=" + "'" + "height: 80; width: 400;
padding-top:
        20; border: 3 inset blue; text-align: center; font-name:
" +
        fontname + "; ";
        s += "font-size: " + fontsize + "; ";
```

```
    if (fontbold) {
        s += "font-weight: bold; ";
    }
    if (fontitalic) {
        s += "font-style: italic; ";
    }
    s += "color: " + fontcolor + "; ";
    s += "background-image: url(" + backgroundImage + ")";
    s += "'>"
    s += text + "</span></a>"

    if (offerNumber + 1 >= offerCount) {
        offerNumber = 0;
    }
    else {
        offerNumber += 1;
    }
    window.setTimeout("showOffer(" + offerNumber +
        ")",1000 * duration)
    document.getElementById("divOffer").innerHTML = s;
}
```

This file has two global variables that retrieve the number of items in the offers[] array written by the ch20-5 code-behind class (refer to Listing 20.7). It uses those values to cycle through the items. The file expects the server to set up the array—you'll see that in the next listing. The showOffer function expects an integer value specifying the item number to show. There are nine array items for each special offer. The script calculates the index offset into the array by multiplying the offerNumber parameter value by nine:

```
var index = offerNumber*9
```

Next, it reads the values from the global array and assigns the values to local variables—purely to make the code easier to read:

```
var duration = offers[index];
var text = offers[index+1];
var fontname= offers[index+2];
var fontsize= offers[index+3];
var fontbold= offers[index+4];
var fontitalic= offers[index+5];
var fontcolor= offers[index+6];
var url= offers[index+7];
var backgroundImage=offers[index+8];
```

It uses the local variables to construct an anchor (<a>) tag containing a <span> with a style attribute containing the font characteristics, background image, and color specified in the global `offers` array (which was built from the XML file). Although it changes for each special offer, the resulting anchor tag always looks much like this:

```
<a href='ch20-6.aspx?item="Housewares"'>
   <span style='height: 80; width: 400; padding-top: 20; border: 3
      inset blue; text-align: center; font-name: Microsoft Sans
   Serif;
      font-size: 12; font-style: italic; color: #0000ff;
      background-image: url(images/acindstr.gif)'>
      Housewares on sale until 4:00
   </span>
</a>
```

When you run the `ch20-5.aspx` Web Form, the resulting page displays three special offers. Each one has a different background and display characteristics, and it is displayed for a different length of time. Figures 20.3 and 20.4 show the first and second of the special offer displays.

FIGURE 20.3

First special offer from the Web Form `ch20-5.aspx`

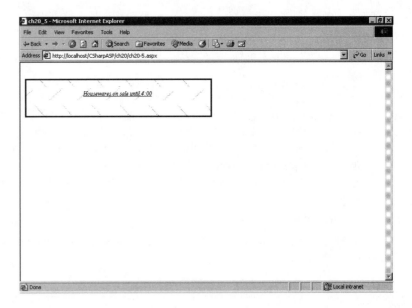

Clicking on the link in any of the offers formats a URL and requests the `ch20-6.aspx` Web Form with an `item` parameter that contains the name of the special offer. The `ch20-6.aspx` Web Form reads the `item` parameter from the query string. This page doesn't do much except serve as a target for the link, but it shows how you can obtain a `QueryString` value, do something with it, and still return the user to the calling page. In this case, the `ch20-6.aspx` Web Form just displays the selected special offer name and presents a link so the user can return to the calling page. Rather than explicitly linking back to the `ch20-5.aspx` Web Form, the link has a client script as well:

```
<a href="JavaScript: window.history.back(1);">
```

FIGURE 20.4

Second special offer from the Web Form ch20-5.aspx

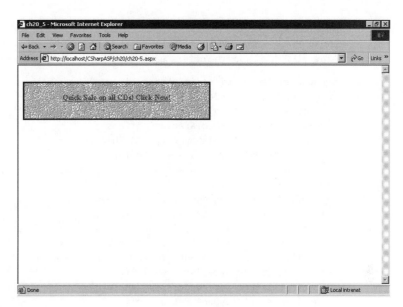

The `window.history` object has `back`, `forward`, and `go` methods that accept an integer value containing the number of items to move forward or backward. The browser moves forward or backward the specified number of pages. For example, the following two commands are identical and are *the equivalent of a user clicking the Back button*:

```
window.history.back(1);
window.history.go(-1);
```

This example is a much more substantive illustration of your capability to send data from the server to the client, but it's formidably complicated to coordinate complex client scripts using two different methods that must work together. Not only that, but it's both error prone and difficult to maintain. For example, using arbitrary "magic numbers" such as the number 9 that the client script uses to get the index into the array of values created by the server is not generally a good programming technique. You'd be much better off if you could send the XML file to the client and use XSLT to transform it there (see the section "Special Offers Example Using a Data Island," later in this chapter). While that's certainly possible with modern Internet Explorer browser clients, it isn't an option for all Internet applications.

Simplifying the Special Offers Example

The special offers example you've just seen is an older way of doing things—and it works—but it certainly isn't the only way. This section contains some ideas and examples that have much the same result but use some .NET helper functions and different client-side techniques to display the special offers from the preceding section.

ASP.NET can help you write complex client scripts. The first change you can make is to use a Page class method called `RegisterArrayDeclaration`. For example, you can condense the `For...Next` loop in Listing 20.7 that builds the `offers` array string for the client to these few lines of code:

```
foreach(XmlElement offer in offers) {
    this.RegisterArrayDeclaration("offers", "'" +
        offer.SelectSingleNode("duration").InnerText + "'");
    this.RegisterArrayDeclaration("offers", "'" +
        offer.SelectSingleNode("text").InnerText + "'");
    this.RegisterArrayDeclaration("offers", "'" +
        offer.SelectSingleNode("font/@name").Value + "'");
    this.RegisterArrayDeclaration("offers", "'" +
        offer.SelectSingleNode("font/@size").Value + "'");
    this.RegisterArrayDeclaration("offers", "'" +
        offer.SelectSingleNode("font/@bold").Value + "'");
    this.RegisterArrayDeclaration("offers", "'" +
        offer.SelectSingleNode("font/@italic").Value + "'");
    this.RegisterArrayDeclaration("offers", "'" +
        offer.SelectSingleNode("font/@color").Value + "'");
    this.RegisterArrayDeclaration("offers", "'" +
        offer.SelectSingleNode("url").InnerText + "'");
    this.RegisterArrayDeclaration("offers", "'" +
        offer.SelectSingleNode("backgroundimage").InnerText + "'");
}
```

See the Web Form `ch20-7.aspx` for an example. `RegisterArrayDeclaration` accepts the name of the client-side array variable (in this case, `offers`) and the value to place into the array. It outputs a `<script>` tag containing a JScript array declaration. In the browser, the script generated by the preceding code looks like this:

```
<script language="javascript">
<!--
    var offers =  new Array(
        '3', 'Housewares on sale until 4:00', 'Microsoft Sans
    Serif',
        '12', 'false', 'true', '#0000ff', 'ch20-6.aspx?item=
    Housewares',
        'images/acindstr.gif', '6', 'Quick Sale on all CDs!
    Click Now!',
        'Arial', '16', 'true', 'false', '#ff0000',
        'ch20-6.aspx?item=CDs', 'images/stone.bmp', '4',
        'Visit our Garden Center for special end-of-summer deals!',
        'Times New Roman', '14', 'true', 'true', '#00ff00',
        'ch20-6.aspx?item=Garden%20Center', 'images/acbluprt.gif');
    // -->
</script>
```

Although this is slightly less readable than the handcrafted version, it's just as functional and much easier to code and maintain. Note that the code creates each array item as a string by surrounding it with quotes. That's not strictly necessary, because not all the items are strings, but it does illustrate the point that client-side JavaScript, being typeless, converts data types as needed.

SPECIAL OFFERS EXAMPLE USING FRAMES

Frames are irritating beasts at best. They slow down page loads, cause multiple requests to your server, and cause you to lose control of the order in which content is displayed. Browsers treat each frame as a separate window. They *request* content for each frame in the order in which you define the frames, but that doesn't mean the data *appears* in that order. To create a frames-based application, you need to define the frameset—the set of frames that your application uses to display the content.

For example, in this application, you might define two frames: a narrow top frame to display the special offers and the remainder of the screen, dedicated to other site content. A frameset page may not contain content other than the frames definition and a message for browsers that don't support frames (not much of a consideration these days).

A frameset page is not a Web Form, it's an HTML page; Visual Studio does not automatically treat framesets as Web Forms. With that said, you are free to create a new Web Form, remove its content, and treat it as a frames page if you like. To create a frameset the Visual Studio way, right-click the project name in Solution Explorer, then add a new frameset item. You get a choice of some predefined frameset templates (see Figure 20.5).

FIGURE 20.5

Predefined frameset templates

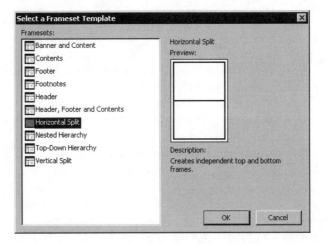

You can find an example in the specialOffersFrameset.htm file in the Ch20 folder of the CSharpASP project on www.sybex.com. For the example, I used the "horizontal split" layout, which creates two independent frames. You can change the split—the area occupied by each frame—using the HTML designer (see Figure 20.6).

FIGURE 20.6

Horizontal split
frameset template

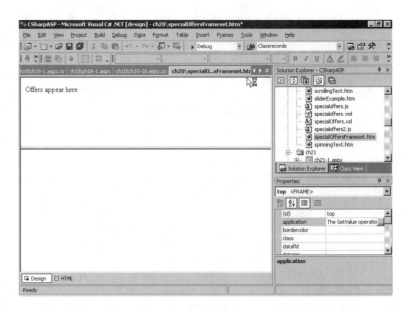

In the designer, click each frame and set its `id` property and `name` property to the same value. You'll need the `id` property to refer to the frame in script. Each frame accepts the name of a file to request for the frame's contents. You can use the designer to assign an initial file for each frame. Set the `src` property for each frame to assign the initial file. In this example, the top frame (named `top`) gets its content from the `ch20-8.aspx` file, which is identical to `ch20-7.aspx` except that it adds a second query string parameter `Back=false` that prevents the `ch20-6.aspx` file from displaying the `Click here to return` message. It does that because there's no need to return—the content appears in the bottom frame when you click an offer.

This version also uses a slightly altered version of the `specialOffers.js` file, called `special-Offers2.js`, which sets the `target` property of the anchor tag in the ad to `main`.

SPECIAL OFFERS EXAMPLE USING A DATA ISLAND

The frames version was somewhat simpler than the original, but if you didn't have to extract the data from the XML file and place it into a client-side array, it would require much less code. In addition, if you could perform an XSLT transform on the client, you wouldn't have to run the rather involved included script (`specialOffers.js`). You can accomplish both these tasks using data islands.

A *data island* is an XML document (or an XSLT stylesheet—remember that those are XML documents, too) placed inline in an HTML stream sent to the client. You surround each XML document with `<xml id="someID"></xml>` tags that you can access and manipulate from script. The `<xml>` tag can read a file directly using an `src` attribute. For example, the following tag creates a data island containing the contents of the `specialOffers.xml` file:

```
<xml id="specials" src="specialOffers.xml"></xml>
```

Internet Explorer exposes the XML document as an ActiveX `DOMDocument` object that's similar to the `XmlDocument` and `XPathDocument` objects in .NET. For example:

```
<xml id="specials" src="specialOffers.xml"></xml>

<script type="text/javascript">
   var doc = document.getElementById("specials").XMLDocument;
   alert(doc.xml);
</script>
```

The preceding script loads and parses the XML in the `specialOffers.xml` file into a `DOMDocument` object. The script sets a variable named `doc` to refer to the `DOMDocument` object and then uses the JavaScript `alert` method to display the contents in a message box.

When the browser parses the `<xml>` tag, it requests the document content from the server. By placing two `<xml>` tags on the page, you can load an XML document and a corresponding XSLT stylesheet and then perform the transform on the client side with the help of a little JavaScript.

NOTE *Unfortunately, browsers—even IE—aren't quite up to .NET standards yet. IE ships with the COM-based MSXML parser. Even more unfortunately, not all versions of IE ship with the same parser. For example, IE 5x ships with a very early version of MSXML that doesn't understand the XSLT namespace. IE 6x ships with the MSXML3 parser, which works fine with the XSLT namespace. The most current version is MSXML4 (sp1), which adds XML Schema support and improves the performance of parsing and transformation operations somewhat. To use XSLT client-side transforms with versions of IE earlier than IE 6, you must install the MSXML parser (downloadable for free from the MSDN XML Developer Center). For some versions of the parser, you must also download and run a small program named* `xmlinst.exe`*, also downloadable from MSDN, which lets IE use the XSLT namespace.*

The Web Form `ch20-9.aspx` shows an example using the client-side transform technique. In this version, there's no code in the code-behind class at all; all the code is HTML and script placed directly into the ASPX file. Listing 20.9 shows the `ch20-9.aspx` file code.

LISTING 20.9: THE WEB FORM ch20-9.aspx USES A CLIENT-SIDE XSLT TRANSFORM TO DISPLAY THE SPECIAL OFFERS (ch20-9.aspx.cs)

```
<%@ Page Language="c#" AutoEventWireup="false"
   Codebehind="ch20-9.aspx.cs" Inherits="CSharpASP.ch20.ch20_9" %>
<!DOCTYPE HTML PUBLIC "-//W3C//DTD HTML 4.0 Transitional//EN">
<html>
   <head>
      <title>ch20_9</title>
      <meta name="GENERATOR" content="Microsoft Visual Studio.NET
   7.0">
      <meta name="CODE_LANGUAGE" content="C#">
      <meta name="vs_defaultClientScript" content="JavaScript">
      <meta name="vs_targetSchema"
         content="http://schemas.microsoft.com/intellisense/ie5">
```

```
<script type="text/javascript" language="javascript">
    var xml;
    var xsl;
    function XMLloaded() {
        // load the DOMDocument object for the XML document
        xml = document.getElementById("specialsXML").XMLDocument;
    }
    function XSLTloaded() {
        // load the DOMDocument object for the stylesheet
        xsl = document.getElementById("specialsXSLT").XMLDocument;
    }
    function showSpecial(offerNumber) {
        var s;
        var duration;
        // set the stylesheet parameter value that controls
        // which offer to show.

    xsl.selectSingleNode("//xsl:param[@name='offerNumber']").text =
            offerNumber;
        s = xml.transformNode(xsl);
        document.getElementById("specialOffer").innerHTML = s;
        duration = xml.selectSingleNode("offers/offer[" +
          (offerNumber - 1) + "]/duration").text;
        duration = parseInt(duration);
        offerNumber = parseInt(offerNumber);
        offerNumber += 1;
        if (offerNumber > (xml.selectNodes("offers/offer").length))
    {
            offerNumber = 1;
        }
        window.setTimeout("showSpecial(" + offerNumber + ")",
            duration * 1000);
    }
</script>

    </head>
    <body MS_POSITIONING="GridLayout" onload="showSpecial(1)">
        <xml id="specialsXML" src="specialOffers.xml"
            ondataavailable="XMLloaded();"></xml>
        <xml id="specialsXSLT" src="specialOffers.xsl"
            ondataavailable="XSLTloaded();"></xml>
        <form id="Form1" method="post" runat="server">
        <div id="specialOffer"></div>
        </form>
    </body>
</html>
```

Here's what happens. Look at the last part of the listing, after the `</head>` tag. When the browser parses the first `<xml>` tag, it retrieves the `specialOffers.xml` file from the server. Immediately after that file is completely loaded, it fires the `ondataavailable` event, which is bound to the `XMLloaded()` JavaScript function at the top of the listing. The browser loads the XSLT `specialOffers.xsl` file the same way but calls the `XSLTloaded()` function instead.

```
<script type="text/javascript" language="javascript">
    var xml;
    var xsl;
    function XMLloaded() {
        xml = document.getElementById("specialsXML").XMLDocument;
    }
    function XSLTloaded() {
        xsl = document.getElementById("specialsXSLT").XMLDocument;
    }
```

Note that the script defines two global (page-level) variables named `xml` and `xsl`. These variables will hold XML `DOMDocument` objects corresponding to the XML document and the XSLT stylesheet. Both functions perform the same task—they retrieve a `DOMDocument` object instance from the `<xml>` tag.

After instantiating these objects, the `<body>` tag fires the `onload` event. That event is bound to the `showSpecial(offerNumber)` JavaScript function:

```
<body MS_POSITIONING="GridLayout" onload="showSpecial(1)">
```

You can translate this as "When the document finishes loading, call the `showSpecial` function to show the first special offer (the parameter 1)."

The `showSpecial()` function sets a parameter value in the XSLT file—also named `offerNumber`—to the value passed in the `offerNumber` parameter to the `showSpecial()` function. The XSLT stylesheet uses the `offerNumber` parameter value to extract the appropriate `<offer>` node from the XML document.

```
xsl.selectSingleNode("//xsl:param[@name='offerNumber']").text =
    offerNumber;
```

Next, the script performs the transform by calling the `transformNode()` method of the `DOMDocument` object and saves the string output from that transform in the variable `s`. The output is the HTML to display the special offer:

```
s = xml.transformNode(xsl);
```

The script assigns the results of the transform to the `innerHTML` property of the `<div id="special-Offer">` tag toward the bottom of Listing 20.9:

```
document.getElementById("specialOffer").innerHTML = s;
```

That displays the special offer, but you still need to retrieve the duration—the number of seconds to display that offer—from the `DOMDocument`:

```
duration = xml.selectSingleNode("offers/offer[" +
    (offerNumber - 1) + "]/duration").text;
duration = parseInt(duration);
```

The script retrieves the value and assigns it to the `duration` variable. When retrieved, the variable is a string; therefore, the script transforms it into an integer using the `parseInt()` method.

Finally, the script needs to call itself to display the next special offer. Therefore, it must increment the `offerNumber` variable and then call the `window.setTimeout()` function, passing its own name and the duration in milliseconds. It also needs to ensure that `offerNumber` doesn't exceed the number of offers in the XML document; otherwise, you'll get an error. To increment `offerNumber`, first ensure that it's an integer value:

```
offerNumber = parseInt(offerNumber);
offerNumber += 1;
if (offerNumber > (xml.selectNodes("offers/offer").length)) {
    offerNumber = 1;
}
```

Finally, it calls the `window.setTimeout()` function using the incremented `offerNumber` and the `duration` value multiplied by 1,000 to turn it into milliseconds:

```
window.setTimeout("showSpecial(" + offerNumber + ")",
    duration * 1000);
```

As you can see, you have a multitude of choices for doing almost anything. Other options involve running the transform on the server. For example, you could write a Web Service that returns the special offer HTML given the offer number. You could use an `<iframe>` tag to display the offers rather than a `<div>`. Doing it that way, you could use a standard ASPX file to deliver the HTML and just set the `src` property of the `<iframe>` to change the contents from one special offer to another.

The Document Object Model

At this point, it should be apparent that there's another object model you need to learn if you want to work effectively with the objects exposed by the browser. The W3C Document Object Model (DOM) specification describes how browsers should expose the objects they contain. Although no current browser completely meets the W3C DOM specifications, IE, starting with version 4, was far closer than Netscape and other browsers, although Netscape 6.2 and Mozilla are very close. IE's implementation of the DOM and, most recently, its capability to use XML efficiently, have made it the most popular browser for development. I'll show you more about the DOM throughout the remainder of this chapter.

You should begin thinking of *all* HTML as describing objects that have properties and methods rather than as tags with attributes, because the DOM describes all HTML tags as objects. For example, a `<p>` paragraph tag has properties describing its position, width, and height. It has border and background properties and contains both HTML (all the markup between the `<p>` and `</p>` tags) and text (all the text between the `<p>` and `</p>` tags not inside angle brackets).

The Document Object Model (DOM) contains two central rules:

◆ All the tags in an HTML document must be accessible as objects.

◆ It must be possible to retrieve those objects' HTML source.

As you can see, that means you should be able to use the DOM to obtain a reference to *any* object on an HTML page, change its properties, and call its methods (assuming it has any). You should also be able to delete DOM objects and create new DOM objects, thus dynamically changing the collection of objects on the page. These capabilities are at the heart of Dynamic HTML (DHTML). If you can change the properties of objects on the page, delete objects, and add new objects, then you can change the look and action of the page dynamically with script without reloading the entire page.

As the browser HTML-parsing engine reads the incoming page, it creates objects and collections of objects. The top-level objects in this model are the `Navigator` object (browser), the window object, the `frames` collection, and the document object. A window contains a document. Even if the browser hasn't fulfilled an HTML request, the window still contains a document—albeit one with no contents. A window may contain several child windows, each of which corresponds to a frame. The window object bundles the child windows together in a `frames` collection. Each frame is itself a window, with its own `frames` collection and its own document.

In the rest of this chapter, you'll work primarily with the document object, which contains the HTML on the page. You may remember from Chapter 2, "HTML Basics," that some tags are `block` elements, which can contain other tags. For example, a `<div>` tag may contain font, paragraph, and other formatting tags, as well as other `<div>` tags. These tags contained inside a `<block>` tag translate to *collections* in object parlance. You can obtain the contained collections using the `all` property, which returns all elements that start within the block, and the `children` property that returns only the child elements contained entirely within the block.

WARNING *Not only is the* `document.all` *property IE specific but it also (unfortunately) was not adopted as part of the W3C recommendations. Although* `document.all` *still works—even in current IE versions—and is useful in differentiating between browsers in some cases, you should use the* `children` *method in most cases because it is part of the W3C recommendation and is supported in Netscape.*

The difference is that `all` refers to all contained tags, even tags in which the end tag overlaps the containing tag's end tag. For example:

```
<p><b>This is bold text</p></b>
```

The `all` collection would include the first `<b>` tag. The `children` collection contains only tags entirely contained between the start and end tags of the `block` element. The `children` collection, in the preceding example, would not contain the `<b>` tag because it's an overlapped tag (and bad HTML practice, I should add).

Each tag has attributes, which translate to properties, although not always directly. For example, the `<p align="center">` tag has one attribute. The difference between the attributes of an HTML element and the properties of a DOM object is that the DOM object always has *all* its properties, even if they aren't explicitly set. Attributes that set visible characteristics, such as `align`, `color`, `size`, `visibility`, and so on, can be subsumed under the `style` property for each object. The `style` property itself is a character string (which translates to a `style` object) containing the `style` attributes. So `style` is an example of an attribute that doesn't translate directly. An example that does translate directly is the `bgcolor` attribute of a `<body>` tag. The body DOM object has a `bgColor` property whose value is the same type of value—a hex color string or named color—as the `<body>` tag itself.

In addition, some attributes translate into the equivalent of .NET delegates. For example, when you assign a JavaScript function to an event, you *bind* the event to the function.

As you work with the DOM, you'll begin to memorize the properties and capabilities of each object. Because these properties and methods are generally similar to the attributes you used in HTML, you'll find that your HTML experience translates easily into the DOM objects and properties.

In general, you can think of the object model for the DOM in DHTML as a hierarchy, with a few outlying objects accessible from script that are *not* part of the document and, thus, not part of the DOM. For example, the `Navigator` object—the browser or client itself—is an important part of writing interactive client applications, but it is not part of the DOM. The DOM concepts apply equally well to HTML documents and XML or XHTML documents, but because HTML documents may not be well formed, you may not be able to use a parser to load and query them. The loose specifications for HTML are a good part of the reason the W3C has moved the focus of Web page creation toward XHTML, which *is* well formed and can be queried and manipulated with the full DOM.

Accessing the DOM from Script

To manipulate the DOM, you need to be able to reference the various element types. The root element in the DOM hierarchy is the `Document` object. You can think of the `Document` object in much the same way as you might think of the `DocumentElement`—the root element—of an XML document. The `Document` object contains all the other elements in the document, as well as methods to create new elements or remove existing elements.

Because there may be many tags of the same type on a page, you need a way to identify the specific tag you want to reference. You can reference a tag by `name`, which is a translation from the `name` attribute in HTML 3.2, or you can reference it by `id` (the preferred method). You can also reference objects by index. All DOM objects can have an `id`. You can create a specific `id` by writing it into the HTML or assigning it from code, but if an element doesn't contain an explicit `id`, you may not be able to differentiate it from similar elements except by its position in the document (its index).

Browsers expose an automatic reference to the document element through the `Document` object. You can then use the DOM methods of the `Document` element to obtain references to other elements in the document.

The primary way to obtain a reference to an element is via the `document.getElementById` function. For example, suppose the HTML page contains this `<div>` tag:

```
<div id="div1"><This is the div content</div>
```

Using JavaScript, you can get a reference to the `<div>` using its `id` value:

```
var div1 = document.getElementById("div1");
```

After obtaining the reference, you can change the properties (remember, they correspond roughly to the attributes) of the element using the reference. For example, to create a `<div>` with a blue background in HTML, you would use the `style` property:

```
<div id="div1" style="background-color: #0000FF">This is the div
    content</div>
```

Now, to change the background color of the <div> to green from script, you obtain a reference to the <div> element itself, and then to its `style` object, which exposes the `backgroundColor` property. Note that the script property name (`backgroundColor`) and the CSS attribute name (`background-color`) are not identical. If you're not sure of the property name, you can look up the property corresponding to any CSS attribute on the Microsoft Developer Network (MSDN) on the Web or enter the index term `CSS Attributes Reference` using the MSDN documentation that ships with .NET:

```
var div1 = document.getElementById("div1");
div1.style.backgroundColor = "#00FF00"
```

Here's an interactive example. The following script changes the background color of the page using the VBScript `InputBox` function. The `InputBox` function displays a dialog at a specified location containing a prompt, a title, and a text field and returns a user's input. I've used VBScript for this example because JavaScript has no equivalent to VBScript's `InputBox` function. The last two arguments to the `InputBox` function below contain the x and y positions for the upper-left corner of the dialog. Note that you specify the location in *twips* (a twip equals 1/1440 inch), not pixels. The script assigns the user's input to the `document.bgColor` property. In this example, the default value for the `InputBox` is the current background color of the document. Listing 20.10 contains the code for an HTML file example.

LISTING 20.10: USING THE Document OBJECT (documentObject.htm)

```html
<html>
<head>
</head>
<body bgcolor="lightblue">
</body>
</html>
<script language="VBScript">
   dim s
   s = Inputbox("Enter the background color for the " & _
      "document.","Background Color", _
      document.bgColor,3000,2000)
   document.bgColor = s
</script>
```

When you run this script, you may enter either a hex-formatted color number, such as #ffffff, or a named color, such as red. You'll see the background color of the document change instantly.

NOTE *It's important to understand that changes you make to the document's contents with script are not reflected in the background HTML for the document.*

After changing the background color, if you right-click and select View Source from the context menu, you won't see the color value you entered in the <body> tag of the HTML; you'll see the original color value. In other words, DOM manipulations occur in memory, and users can't see the source code changes.

You can obtain references to child elements of the document using the `document.getElementsById` (`"ID/name"`) method, which returns a collection, or the `document.getElementById` method, which returns an individual object. Alternatively, you can omit the parentheses and quotes and use `document.ID`, where `ID` is the value of the `ID` attribute for the element you want to reference. Listing 20.11 shows how to change the text of a paragraph.

LISTING 20.11: CHANGING PARAGRAPH CONTENTS WITH SCRIPT (`paragraphText.htm`)

```
<html>
<head>
</head>
<body bgcolor="lightblue">
<p id="p1">This is a paragraph tag.</p>
</body>
</html>
<script language="JavaScript">
   el = document.getElementById("p1");
   el.innerText = "The text of this paragraph was " +
      "changed via script";
</script>
```

The paragraph tag has an `id` of `p1`. The code inside the `<script>` tag sets a reference to the paragraph element using the following code:

```
Set el = document.getElementById("p1")
```

The `el` variable refers to the paragraph. Next it changes the `innerText` property of the paragraph. When the property changes, IE instantly updates the text on-screen so that it reflects the new property value. Until IE 4, such client-side content changes were limited to the contents of input controls. With DHTML, you can control the content and appearance of every element on the screen.

You can scroll the text across the screen by using absolute positioning. For example, Listing 20.12 extends the previous script by changing the `left` position attribute of the paragraph element's `style` property. To control the speed, the script uses a window method called `setTimeout`. The `setTimeout` method accepts three arguments: the name of a function or subroutine, a time interval specified in milliseconds (thousandths of a second), and an optional language argument. You can use the language argument to call a JScript function from a `window.SetTimeout` method called from VBScript, or vice versa. When the specified interval has elapsed, the scripting engine calls the routine specified in the first argument.

LISTING 20.12: MOVING OBJECTS ON-SCREEN (`scrollingText.htm`)

```
<html>
   <head>
   </head>
   <body bgcolor="lightblue">
```

```
    <p id="p1" style="position: absolute; left: 800;
        font-size: 20">This text will move
        from right to left across the screen.</p>
  </body>
</html>
<script language="JavaScript">
   window.setTimeout("moveText()", 50);
   function moveText() {
       el = document.getElementById("p1");
       pos = el.style.left;
       if (pos.substr(pos.length - 2, 2) == "px") {
           pos = pos.substr(0, pos.length - 2);
       }
       el.style.left = pos - 10;
       if (pos >= -300) {
           window.setTimeout("moveText()", 50);
       }
   }
</script>
```

A proposed W3C specification called HTML+TIME and an existing specification called SMIL both address the problems of coordinating multiple simultaneous actions for on-screen elements. For example, if you wanted to coordinate the movement of a cartoon character's mouth with an audio clip and at the same time coordinate the wind moving through computer-generated trees, you would have a difficult time doing it with timed scripts. Both the SMIL and HTML+TIME specifications provide a specialized syntax to perform complex positioning and coordination actions.

If all you could do with client-side script were to change colors and text in the browser, it wouldn't be a subject for this book; however, from an application perspective, client-side script can do much more than that. For example, you've seen how the .NET framework uses client-side script to prevalidate user input, thus saving a round trip to the server. You've also seen (in the client-side XSLT special offers example) how script can move server-side processing to the client, effectively partitioning your application.

Using ActiveX Controls

Sometimes, even with DHTML, the capabilities available through HTML and a browser just aren't enough. For example, suppose you wanted to use a slider control to let a user control audio volume. You could create your own slider using lines or images and a lot of code, but in doing so you would have re-created functionality that's already available on every Windows computer in the form of ActiveX controls. Recognizing this problem, Microsoft did two things to IE that made it the premier browser for development. First, IE is an ActiveX host. That means you can *site* (place) ActiveX controls within the browser and control them via script. Second, Microsoft made IE itself an ActiveX control. That means you can site IE within a window and instantly gain access to a custom browser for your own programs. In this section, you'll see how to use ActiveX controls inside IE.

WARNING *The examples in this section work only in Internet Explorer.*

You've already seen how to instantiate ActiveX components on the server. The client-side analogues of ActiveX components are ActiveX objects or ActiveX controls. All three—ActiveX components, objects, and controls—are COM objects. The only difference is that ActiveX controls are usually visible, and users may be able to interact with them directly, whereas components and objects are usually invisible. To instantiate ActiveX controls within the browser, you use an `<object>` syntax that's similar to the syntax you've seen to create global Application and Session-scope components in the `global.asax` file. For example:

```
<object
   classid="clsid:25bdf09d-ec8b-11cf-bd97-00aa00575603"
   codebase="/Controls/MyContrl.cab#version=1,0,0,0"
   id=myControl left: 40px; top: 10px; width: 385px;
   height: 42px; >
   <param name="property1">
   <param name="property1">
   <param name="property1">
</object>
```

NOTE *The `<object>` tag in this example does not represent a real control.*

The `<object>` tag tells the browser to

1. Look up the `classid` in the Registry.

2. Find the Registry child key called `InProcServer32`, which contains the name of the OCX or DLL file that contains the code for the control.

3. If the control is not registered on the local computer, or if the version installed on the local computer is lower than the version specified in the optional `codebase` attribute, the browser can download and install the control from the URL specified in the `codebase` attribute.

4. The browser instantiates the control, sites it, resizes it, and finally displays the control.

5. The browser doesn't use the optional `<param>` tags—the control itself obtains the property values specified in the `<param>` tags and uses them to initialize its own properties.

The advantages of using ActiveX controls are as follows:

◆ You gain instant access to a wide range of prebuilt and tested code.

◆ You can perform tasks with ActiveX controls that are difficult or impossible through any other technology.

The disadvantages are as follows:

◆ Only IE browsers can use ActiveX technology natively. Netscape users can obtain a third-party plug-in that extends Netscape so it can use ActiveX controls—with mixed results. Therefore, avoid building solutions that require ActiveX controls and components on the client unless you *know* that all the clients have IE.

◆ ActiveX controls and objects have full access to the local machine; therefore, *they are a security risk.* To help alleviate this problem, Microsoft introduced code signing, which lets you know the code producer. Code signing uses a third party to provide a code authentication certificate stating that the code actually comes from the code producer. When the browser downloads an unknown ActiveX control, it warns you that the page is trying to download new code. If the code is signed, you can follow a URL to the authentication site to read about and verify the code. You can then choose to continue or to ignore the download.

◆ Users can set IE to block ActiveX controls as part of the browser security settings. If you plan to use ActiveX controls in your application, you need to be certain that the clients support their use.

Sending ActiveX Objects to the Client

To instantiate an ActiveX control on the client, you simply include the `<object>` tag in the response. For example, the angledText.html file code in Listing 20.13 shows a `Label` control that displays angled text (see Figure 20.7).

LISTING 20.13: ACTIVEX CONTROL EXAMPLE FOR IE (angledText.htm)

```html
<html>
<head>
</head>
<body bgColor=#c0c0c0>
<OBJECT
    classid="clsid:99B42120-6EC7-11CF-A6C7-00AA00A47DD2"
codebase="http://activex.microsoft.com/controls/iexplorer/
    ielabel.ocx#Version=4,70,0,1161"
    id="spinner"
    width=250
    height=250
    align=left
    hspace=20
    vspace=0
>
<PARAM NAME="Angle" VALUE="45">
<PARAM NAME="Alignment" VALUE="4">
<PARAM NAME="BackStyle" VALUE="0">
<PARAM NAME="Caption" VALUE="Angled Text">
<PARAM NAME="FontName" VALUE="Arial, Verdana, Helvetica, Sans
    Serif">
<PARAM NAME="FontSize" VALUE="30">
<PARAM NAME="FontBold" VALUE="1">
<PARAM NAME="FrColor" VALUE="0">
</OBJECT>
<div id="junk"></div>
</body>
</html>
```

FIGURE 20.7

The ActiveX Label control lets you display angled text on the page.

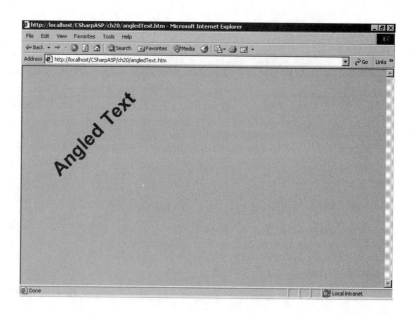

The browser uses the `classid` attribute of the `<object>` tag to find and instantiate the `Label` object on the client. Because the `Label` control may not be installed on all clients, the preceding example includes an optional `codebase` attribute. If the control is not installed, the browser will use the `codebase` attribute value (a URL) to download it and then—depending on the user's security settings—ask the user whether to install the control.

Accessing ActiveX Objects from Client-Side Script

Sending ActiveX controls to the browser would be of little use if you couldn't access their properties and respond to their events. You can bind script to ActiveX control events in the same way you bind code to HTML elements. For example, Listing 20.14 instantiates the same `Label` control as the preceding example, but then it uses the `<body>` tag's `load` event and a timer to "spin" the control on-screen using DHTML.

LISTING 20.14: COMMUNICATING WITH CLIENT-SIDE ACTIVEX CONTROLS (spinningText.htm)

```
<html>
<head>
<script type="text/javascript" language="JavaScript">
    var angle=0;
    function spin() {
        angle += 4;
        if (angle > 360) {
            angle=0;
        }
        document.getElementById("spinner").Angle=angle;
```

```
        window.setTimeout(spin, 60);
    }

</script></head>
<body bgColor=#c0c0c0 onload="spin()">
<OBJECT
    classid="clsid:99B42120-6EC7-11CF-A6C7-00AA00A47DD2"
    id="spinner"
    width=200
    height=200
    align=left
    hspace=40
    vspace=20
>
<PARAM NAME="Angle" VALUE="45">
<PARAM NAME="Alignment" VALUE="4">
<PARAM NAME="BackStyle" VALUE="0">
<PARAM NAME="Caption" VALUE="Spinning Text">
<PARAM NAME="FontName" VALUE="Arial, Verdana, Helvetica, Sans
    Serif">
<PARAM NAME="FontSize" VALUE="20">
<PARAM NAME="FontBold" VALUE="1">
<PARAM NAME="FrColor" VALUE="0">
</OBJECT>
</body>
</html>
```

The `<body>` tag's `onload` attribute calls the `spin()` function when the page loads. The `spin()` function obtains a reference to the `spinner` object, increments a variable called `angle` that controls the angle at which the `Label` draws text, and then sets the `Label` control's `Angle` property, which causes the `Label` to invalidate its rectangle and repaint. The code then calls the `window.setTimeout()` function, passing its own name as the function to call when the interval expires. The entire process repeats every 60 milliseconds, thus making the text appear to spin.

So far, you've seen how to use the `<object>` tag to create controls from the ASP page, but you can also use client-side script directly to create non-visual ActiveX objects.

NOTE   *You can create ActiveX controls as well as ActiveX objects without errors, but you can't site them with client-side code, so unless you need an invisible control for some reason, it won't do you much good.*

For example, Listing 20.15 creates a `Dictionary` object, stores a few hundred items, and then displays the dictionary contents in a `<div>` tag. Of course, you need to ensure that the Microsoft Scripting Runtime (`scrrun32.dll`) is installed and registered on the client computer before trying to create a `Dictionary` object, but because it's installed with IE, normally it shouldn't be an issue.

LISTING 20.15: CREATING CLIENT-SIDE ACTIVEX OBJECTS WITH JSCRIPT (dictionaryExample.htm)

```
<html>
<head>
</head>
<body>
<script language="JScript">
   var d, i, V, aDiv, s="";
   window.setTimeout("docComplete();",100);
   function docComplete() {
      while (document.readyState != "complete") {
         window.setTimeout("docComplete",100);
      }
      showDictionary();
   }
   function showDictionary() {
      var keys;
      var items;
      d = new ActiveXObject("Scripting.Dictionary");
      for (i=1; i <= 500; i++) {
         d.Add("Item" + i, i);
      }
      aDiv = document.all("dictionaryDiv");
      keys = new VBArray(d.Keys());
      keys = keys.toArray();
      for (i=0; i < keys.length; i++) {
         s = s + keys[i] + "=" + d.item(keys[i]) + "<br>";
      }
      aDiv.innerHTML = s;
      return("");
   }
</script>
<div id="dictionaryDiv"></div>
</body>
</html>
```

In this script, because the code references a <div> tag that appears *after* the script, you must wait until the document has created the <div>. This time, the code uses the window.setTimeout method to test the document readyState property repeatedly rather than binding a routine to the onReady-StateChange event. Which do you think is more efficient?

I've written this script specifically to show you a few differences. Microsoft has extended its version of JScript to access ActiveX objects—the script will not work in any browser other than IE because the scripting language is IE specific, even if it does look like JavaScript.

The script creates the variable `d` to hold the `Dictionary` reference. In JScript, you create the reference as follows:

```
d = new ActiveXObject("Scripting.Dictionary");
```

You add objects to the `Dictionary` using the `Add` method. For example:

```
d.Add("Item" + i, i);
```

The major difference is how you gain access to the `Dictionary`'s collections. JScript doesn't have a direct way of accessing ActiveX arrays or collections, such as the `keys` collection. Instead, you must create a `VBArray` object and assign it to a variable. For example:

```
keys = new VBArray(d.Keys());
```

After you have a reference to the `VBArray` object, you can convert it into a JScript array using the `toArray` function. For example:

```
keys = keys.toArray();
```

After conversion, you use the array normally. The remainder of the script concatenates a string (the variable `s`) and sets the `innerHTML` property of the `<div>` to the contents of the string variable, thus displaying all the keys and values contained in the `Dictionary` object.

To end this section, here's a short observation on the relative merits of using the `<object>` tag syntax versus the `createObject` function in client-side script. The `<object>` syntax, while awkward and time consuming, lets you specify the `codebase` from which the client can download the control if it's not already installed. You can use `createObject` only if you're delivering to clients and you know the ActiveX controls and objects you're using have already been installed and registered on the client machines.

Summary

You've seen how to leverage your scripting language knowledge by partitioning your application—putting some of the logic on the client. As you increase your DHTML knowledge and improve your client-side scripting abilities, you'll begin to appreciate the power of a DOM-based client document model. There are many more opportunities to use your knowledge. In the next chapter, you'll see how to build Web Services, which let you access server resources—anywhere in the world—and use the resulting data on the server, at the client, and even using Windows Forms clients. Web Services make Web applications much more important than they have been in the past because they can serve data to *any* client that can form and parse simple XML documents.

Chapter 21

Web Services

WEB SERVICES ARE, IN the simplest terms, class methods exposed via an HTTP call. In other words, just as you can call a method in a class in your application, you can call a method that exists on your own or some other server. In this chapter, you'll explore Visual Studio's built-in support for Web Services, and you'll create and consume a Web Service from several different client types.

In this chapter:

◆ Introduction to Web Services

◆ Build a Web Service

◆ Consume a Web Service

◆ SOAP (Simple Object Access Protocol)

◆ Finding Web Services (UDDI)

Introduction to Web Services

In C#, creating a Web Service is as simple as adding a few attributes to your class and to each method in the class that you want to expose to remote computers. The exposed methods are the public interface to your Web Service. A single Web Service may have many exposed methods, just as a class may have many public methods and properties. The difference is that a Web Service is stateless. The server instantiates an instance of the Web Service on demand and then destroys that instance after it finishes servicing a call—just as it does with the Web Form classes. In fact, the *only* conceptual differences between a Web Form and a Web Service are that a Web Form returns HTML, whereas a Web Service returns XML.

Remote Method Calls and XML

XML is at the heart of Web Services and provides several huge advantages over existing methods for calling code running on remote servers.

Standardized File Format   XML has a simple syntax, readable (with some effort) by human beings. Best of all, the XML file format has been standardized by the W3C. Despite the relative newness of XML, parsers are already available for every major programming and scripting language, so you can read XML regardless of which platform or language you need to use. XML parsers check whether documents are "well-formed" and can raise errors when reading a document that contains errors. The error messages and properties tell you exactly where an error occurred, greatly reducing the number of errors that occur due to malformed data.

Self-Describing Unlike simple delimited or fixed-width field text file formats, XML files use tag markup to describe the type of data included in each field. Well-chosen tag names add to legibility in both programming code and when viewing raw XML documents.

Hierarchical Unlike flat-file delimited or fixed-width field text file formats, XML documents can represent an arbitrary number of hierarchical relationships. The capability to model relationships also means that you can use a tag name appropriately, even if it duplicates a tag name that appears elsewhere in the document. For example, the following document uses the `<name>` tag to represent several different types of information: a person's name, his children's names, a book title, and the name of a country; but due to the hierarchical placement of the `<name>` tags, they aren't ambiguous. For example, it's easy to see that the `<name>` tag in the `<child>` element belongs to the child, and the `<name>` tag in the `<book>` element belongs to the book.

```
<?xml version="1.0"?>
<items>
    <person>
        <name>John Smith</name>
            <children>
                <child>
                    <name>Joyce</name>
                </child>
            <children>
    </person>
    <book>
        <name>Wicked</name>
    </book>
    <country>
        <name>United States</name>
    <country>
</items>
```

Can Hold Both Structured and Unstructured Data Relational databases already provide a common way to store hierarchical *structured* data, but they're not ideal for storing unstructured data because a relational database works best when you can clearly define the relationships between different items and groups of items. XML documents can model relational schema very easily, so they're eminently suited for hierarchical structured data, but because there's no *requirement* to model hierarchical relationships, XML documents work just as well for unstructured data.

Supports Queries Using a standardized grammar called XPath, you can query an XML document, finding or counting XML elements, attributes, and values. In contrast, there's no standardized way to find a data item in a text file. Databases also support queries, and they're optimized for large data sets, whereas XML is not optimized for large data sets. Using a combination of the two, you can model the relationships in a larger database within a much smaller data subset in XML. That's the idea behind ADO.NET data sets.

Passes Through Firewalls   XML is composed of plain text; therefore, it can easily pass through firewalls and let companies expose internal code to external clients without affecting security.

Supports Schema and Validation   Until recently, you could use only Document Type Definitions (DTDs), an older method for specifying the schema of a document (the element and attribute names, data types, possible data values and ranges, occurrence ranges, and relationships). However, the W3C recently released the XML schema recommendation (usually called XSD or XSDL schema, for XML Schema Definition Language), which uses a second XML document to describe an XML document. Because XSD schemas are XML documents, you can read them programmatically, making machine-to-machine communications possible even when the communicating computers don't know the full protocol in advance. In addition, you can use an XML schema to *validate* the contents of a document. While parser checking for well-formedness catches only syntax errors, validation catches *content* errors. Using a validating parser, you can check the contents of a document against a schema, ensuring that the document contains all the elements and attributes that it *should* contain; that the relative positions, and thus the hierarchy of the document, are correct; and that the values associated with validated elements and attributes are the correct types, ranges, and/or values. The advent of schema, XML, robust parsers, and of course ubiquitous HTTP connections and the Internet makes Web Services possible.

Interoperate Across Applications/Platforms

The common file format and the simple text base of XML documents mean that you can create, parse, and transfer XML documents very easily, not only between applications running on one platform, but also between applications running on disparate platforms. For example, it's just as easy to create an XML document in Java as it is in .NET; therefore, a Java application running on a Unix workstation can call a Web Service running on a Windows platform and receive a return value as long as both applications pass properly formatted XML. In other words, any server can service any client that can create and parse XML.

A Web Service is *not* a specific type of application—it's a way to *expose* application functionality via (usually, but not necessarily) an HTTP interface. There's no special language requirement and no special platform requirements.

Although I won't attempt to show you cross-platform Web Services in this book (it's a .NET book, after all), you should keep in mind that when you build a Web Service, you're building generic code that any application or platform can consume. Web Services are the *first* true cross-platform code, because they require nothing but a parser, some string-handling capabilities, and HTTP connection capabilities on the part of the client.

When Should You Use Web Services?

In Web applications, Web Services are particularly useful for updating specific areas of the page *without* redrawing the entire page. By doing this, you can avoid the "flash" that typically occurs when the browser requests a page.

For example, suppose you have a list of customers in a listbox, and you want to display customer details when the user selects a customer from the list. For a small number of customers, you could download the entire set of details and handle all the display logic on the client. But that becomes less and less palatable as the number of customers increases. Eventually, you'll have to let the user select a customer, return to the server, get the details for that customer, and display the details on the client. But when the browser makes the request for the details, if you're keeping the list on the page at the same time, the server will have to resend the customer list as well as the details and any other items on the page. Not only is that inefficient and slow, but it also means that you have to add logic to maintain the selected list item. Finally, the page flashes when it redraws.

Obviously, it would be better if you could just fill the detail fields with the selected customer data. A Web Service is ideal for such situations because it accepts a request and returns the data in an easy-to-use form. You can use an XML parser to extract the individual data values and display them in the appropriate fields.

Another reason to use Web Services is when you need to provide data to clients both inside and outside your company firewall. Because the XML data traverses firewalls freely via a standard HTTP connection, you don't have to open extra ports (potential security hazards) to your servers.

By default, Web Services are stateless, which makes them highly scalable. You can run Web Services in a multiserver (server farm) environment. Clients initiate Web Service requests using standard HTTP GET and POST methods, so you can use the same Web farm setup to handle Web Service requests as you do to handle ASP.NET or HTML requests. If you *must* maintain state in a Web Service, you can derive it from the WebService class, which gives you access to the .NET framework HttpContext objects, so that you can use Cookies, Session, and Application variables just as you would in a Web Form.

How Does VS.NET Help?

To create a Web Service, you add class and method attributes that identify a class as a Web Service and identify the publicly exposed methods (called WebMethods). When you do that, VS.NET automatically creates XML documents that help you find and consume the Web Service. Using these documents, VS.NET also automatically creates a Web Service Description page that shows you the title of the Web Service as well as the set of operations it supports (see Figure 21.1).

When you click the operation links, VS.NET provides a Web Form you can use to test each operation. For example, if you click the getPayment link shown in Figure 21.1, you'll see the page in Figure 21.2.

The page also shows you sample Simple Object Access Protocol (SOAP) request and response documents. You'll see how to use SOAP with Web Services later in this chapter. Finally, the Web Method Operation page shows GET and POST requests and responses for the WebMethod.

For example, the getPayment WebMethod shown in Figure 21.2 calculates a mortgage payment. The WebMethod requires three parameters—the APR (AnnualPercentageRate), the amount of the loan (TotalCost), and the mortgage duration in years (DurationInYears). If you look at the bottom of the Web Form, you'll see that a GET request generates a simple XML document that returns a string element containing the monthly payment amount (see Figure 21.3).

ch21_payment Web Service - Microsoft Internet Explorer
File Edit View Favorites Tools Help
Back Search Favorites Media
Address http://localhost/csharpasp/ch21/ch21-payment.asmx
Go Links
ch21_payment
The following operations are supported. For a formal definition, please review the Service Description.
getPayment
totalPaymentAmount
Done
Local intranet

FIGURE 21.1
Web Service Description page generated automatically by VS.NET

ch21_payment Web Service - Microsoft Internet Explorer
File Edit View Favorites Tools Help
Back Search Favorites Media
Address http://localhost/csharpasp/ch21/ch21-payment.asmx?op=getPayment
Go Links
ch21_payment
Click here for a complete list of operations.
getPayment
Test
To test the operation using the HTTP GET protocol, click the 'Invoke' button.
Parameter
Value
AnnualPercentageRate:
TotalCost:
DurationInYears:
Invoke
SOAP
The following is a sample SOAP request and response. The placeholders shown need to be replaced with actual values.
POST /csharpasp/ch21/ch21-payment.asmx HTTP/1.1
Host: localhost
Content-Type: text/xml; charset=utf-8
Done
Local intranet

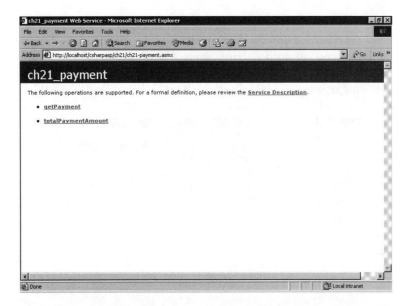

FIGURE 21.2
Test Web Method Operation page generated automatically by VS.NET

HTTP GET
The following is a sample HTTP GET request and response. The placeholders shown need to be replaced with actual values.
GET /csharpasp/ch21/ch21-payment.asmx/getPayment?AnnualPercentageRate=string&TotalCost=string
Host: localhost
HTTP/1.1 200 OK
Content-Type: text/xml; charset=utf-8
Content-Length: length
<?xml version="1.0" encoding="utf-8"?>
<string xmlns="http://CSharpASP/ch21/">string</string>

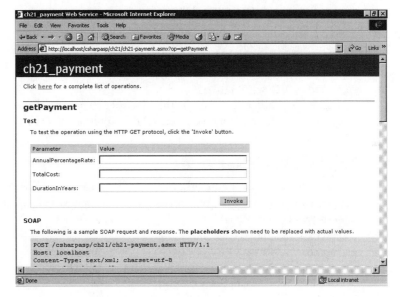

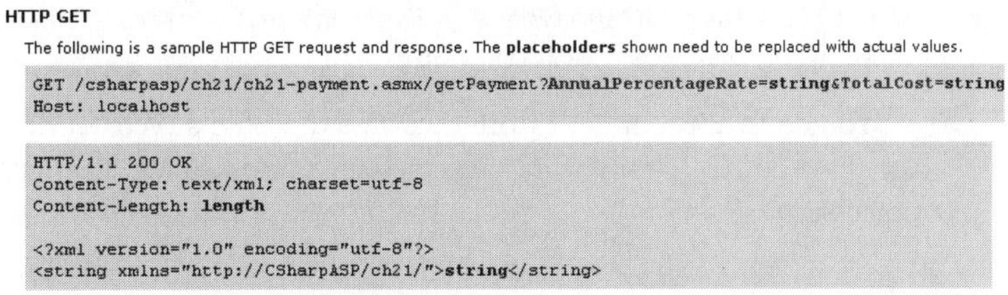

FIGURE 21.3
VS-generated sample `GET` request and response for the `getPayment` WebMethod

The bottom half of the second box in Figure 21.3 shows the response XML. When you fill in the fields and post the form, you can quickly test the return values from your Web Service methods using the GET method. For example, when you send 6.5 as the annual percentage rate, $200,000 for the loan amount, and 30 as the mortgage duration, the Web Service calculates the monthly payment and returns the XML document shown in Figure 21.4.

FIGURE 21.4

XML response from the GET request for the getPayment WebMethod

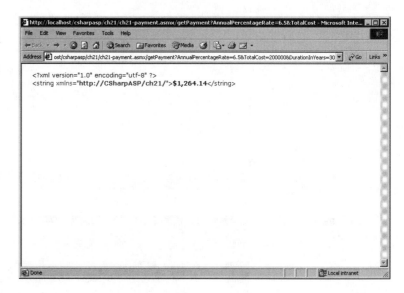

In the next sections, you'll create the Mortgage Payment Calculator Web Service and consume it from a browser, from a Windows Forms .NET application, and from a VB6 client application.

Build a Web Service

VS.NET takes care of most of the details for you. To create a Web Service, simply add a new Web Service item to your project. Web Services use an .asmx extension. For this project, name the service ch21-payment.asmx. VS adds three files to your project: the ASMX file, a code-behind VB file, and a resources RESX file.

Switch to Code view. Notice that VS automatically creates the code-behind file with a reference to the System.Web.Services namespace and that the ch21_payment class inherits from the System.Web.Services.WebService class.

```
using System.Web.Services;
public class ch21_payment : System.Web.Services.WebService {
}
```

You don't *have* to inherit from this class to create a Web Service, but doing so makes it very easy to use the ASP.NET framework objects, such as the Request, Response, Session, and Application objects.

You should provide a WebService namespace attribute for each Web Service you create. Strictly speaking, this isn't necessary, but VS warns you to provide a namespace before using your Web Service in production mode, so you might as well get in the habit of adding the namespace at the beginning.

A namespace is nothing more than a unique identifier. It doesn't have to be globally unique—just unique for your server. A namespace doesn't have to refer to anything in particular, and it has nothing to do with the physical location of the Web Service itself, even though it's formatted as a URI. In other words, the namespace does *not* have to point to a physical location. Here's the WebService attribute and the namespace used in the Mortgage Payment Calculator Web Service class:

```
[WebService(Namespace="http://CSharpASP/ch21/")]
public class ch21_payment :
    System.Web.Services.WebService {
}
```

The WebService attribute is *part of the class definition line*. You're perfectly free to write the entire class definition line in a single code line, but you'll find that it's better to wrap the code, because the length of the WebService attribute usually causes the class name to disappear off the right side of the screen, making the code difficult to read on-screen.

The Visual Studio Web Service template inserts the new constructor, the InitializeComponent method, and the Dispose method. I'll show that code here—once (see Listing 21.1). For subsequent listings I'll omit that code (because it's essentially the same every time) and insert a line such as ...autogenerated code omitted at the top of the listings.

LISTING 21.1: VS AUTOGENERATED CODE FOR THE ch21-payment.asmx WEB SERVICE (ch21-payment.asmx.cs)

```
using System;
using System.Collections;
using System.ComponentModel;
using System.Data;
using System.Diagnostics;
using System.Web;
using System.Web.Services;
using Microsoft.VisualBasic;

namespace CSharpASP.ch21
{
    /// <summary>
    /// Summary description for ch21_payment.
    /// </summary>
    [WebService(Namespace="http://CSharpASP/ch21/")]
    public class ch21_payment : System.Web.Services.WebService
    {
        public ch21_payment()
        {
            //CODEGEN: This call is required by the ASP.NET Web
            //Services Designer
```

```
        InitializeComponent();
    }

    #region Component Designer generated code

    //Required by the Web Services Designer
    private IContainer components = null;

    /// <summary>
    /// Required method for Designer support -
    /// do not modify
    /// the contents of this method with the code editor.
    /// </summary>
    private void InitializeComponent()
    {
        //
        // ch21_payment
        //

    }

    /// <summary>
    /// Clean up any resources being used.
    /// </summary>
    protected override void Dispose( bool disposing )
    {
        if(disposing && components != null)
        {
            components.Dispose();
        }
        base.Dispose(disposing);
    }

    #endregion

    // custom code here
    }
}
```

Add the following two methods to the Web Service's code-behind class. The getPayment method accepts two doubles for the AnnualPercentageRate and TotalCost parameters, and an integer for the DurationInYears parameter. Interestingly, the Microsoft.VisualBasic namespace contains a Financial function called Pmt, which calculates a monthly payment given an annual percentage rate, the total amount financed, the future worth of the loan amount, and a constant that represents whether payments are made at the beginning or end of the payment period. You can reference the namespace, add a using line, and then use the Pmt method to calculate the payment and total amounts (see Listing 21.2).

LISTING 21.2: THE MORTGAGE PAYMENT CALCULATOR WEB SERVICE'S getPayment METHOD (ch21-payment.asmx.cs)

```
[WebMethod()] public String getPayment
   (Double AnnualPercentageRate, Double TotalCost,
   int DurationInYears) {
   Double payment;

   // divide the APR by 100 to get a decimal
   // percentage, if necessary
   if (AnnualPercentageRate > 1) {
      AnnualPercentageRate /= 100;
   }

   // and then divide by 12 for the number of months
   // in a year to get the percentage interest rate
   // per payment. Multiply the DurationInYears
   // by 12 to get the total number of payments.
   payment = Microsoft.VisualBasic.Financial.Pmt
      (AnnualPercentageRate / 12, DurationInYears * 12,
      TotalCost,0,
      Microsoft.VisualBasic.DueDate.EndOfPeriod);

   // the Pmt function returns the payment as
   // a negative number
   payment = System.Math.Abs(payment);
   return payment.ToString("$###,###,##0.00");
}
```

You need to make only *one* alteration to a `Public` method to expose it through a Web Service: add the `[WebMethod()]` attribute to the front of the method declaration. However, you *must* add the `[WebMethod()>]` attribute to methods you want to expose or else the method won't be included in the Web Service's list of operations.

While it's useful to know what the monthly payment is for a proposed mortgage loan, it's also enlightening to see how altering the percentage rate, the loan amount, or the mortgage duration affects the total amount that you'll have to pay to satisfy the mortgage. The `totalPaymentAmount` function in Listing 21.3 lets you calculate that value.

LISTING 21.3: THE MORTGAGE PAYMENT CALCULATOR WEB SERVICE'S totalPaymentAmount METHOD (ch21-payment.asmx.cs)

```
[WebMethod()] public String totalPaymentAmount
   (Double MonthlyPayment, int DurationInYears) {

   return (MonthlyPayment *
```

```
        (DurationInYears * 12)).ToString("C");
    }
```

There are three ways to call a WebMethod function from a client:

Use a GET Request   The first way is to use a special URL that identifies the Web Service, names the method, and includes any parameter values. The Web Service will attempt to cast the parameter values to the correct types, then it returns an XML-formatted message. For example, to find the monthly payment for a 30-year mortgage on a $200,000 house at an annual percentage rate of 6.5 percent, you can call the Web Service with the following URL:

```
http://localhost/CSharpASP/ch21/ch21-
    payment.asmx/getPayment?
    AnnualPercentageRate=6.5&
    TotalCost=200000&DurationInYears=30
```

NOTE   *I've broken the URL into separate lines in the code, but you would enter it as a single line in a browser.*

You can easily type the URL to call a Web Service from IE, which simply displays the returned data XML document (see Figure 21.4 again for the returned XML).

Use a POST Request   Using a POST request, you place the individual data values into named fields in the form. By default, ASP.NET uses the GET method in the WebMethod test form that it creates automatically (see Figure 21.3). However, you can easily test the page using the POST method by saving the output from the automatically generated test page (right-click in the browser and select View Source to get the HTML), finding the <form> tag in the page, changing the METHOD attribute value to POST, and saving the page. There's no difference between the output from the GET and POST methods. The WebMethod test page shows a sample request and response using a POST method (see Figure 21.5).

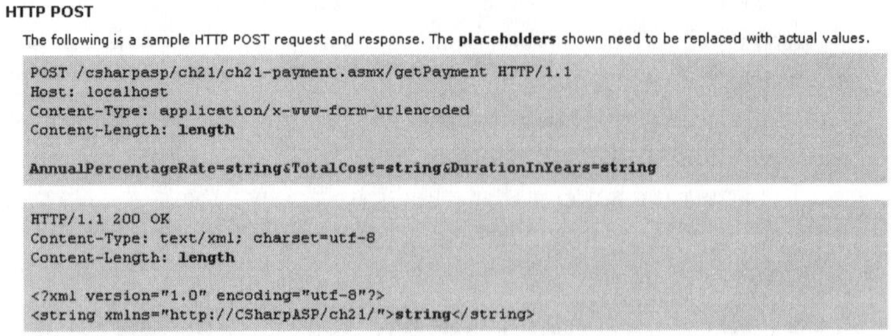

FIGURE 21.5

VS-generated sample POST request and response for the getPayment WebMethod

HTTP POST

The following is a sample HTTP POST request and response. The **placeholders** shown need to be replaced with actual values.

```
POST /csharpasp/ch21/ch21-payment.asmx/getPayment HTTP/1.1
Host: localhost
Content-Type: application/x-www-form-urlencoded
Content-Length: length

AnnualPercentageRate=string&TotalCost=string&DurationInYears=string
```

```
HTTP/1.1 200 OK
Content-Type: text/xml; charset=utf-8
Content-Length: length

<?xml version="1.0" encoding="utf-8"?>
<string xmlns="http://CSharpASP/ch21/">string</string>
```

Use a SOAP Request   The GET and POST methods work only for Web Services that use simple data types. For more complex request and return types, and for the best performance, you should use SOAP messaging to handle the requests and responses. SOAP messages are XML-formatted documents. The .NET framework transparently handles serializing complex objects and data to and from SOAP requests and responses. Again, the WebMethod test page shows you sample SOAP request and response messages (see Figures 21.6 and 21.7). You'll see more about using SOAP messages with Web Services later in this chapter.

FIGURE 21.6

VS-generated sample SOAP request for the getPayment WebMethod

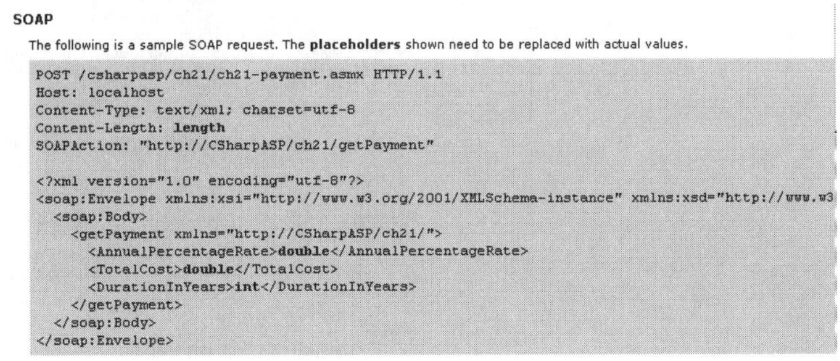

SOAP

The following is a sample SOAP request. The **placeholders** shown need to be replaced with actual values.

```
POST /csharpasp/ch21/ch21-payment.asmx HTTP/1.1
Host: localhost
Content-Type: text/xml; charset=utf-8
Content-Length: length
SOAPAction: "http://CSharpASP/ch21/getPayment"

<?xml version="1.0" encoding="utf-8"?>
<soap:Envelope xmlns:xsi="http://www.w3.org/2001/XMLSchema-instance" xmlns:xsd="http://www.w3
  <soap:Body>
    <getPayment xmlns="http://CSharpASP/ch21/">
      <AnnualPercentageRate>double</AnnualPercentageRate>
      <TotalCost>double</TotalCost>
      <DurationInYears>int</DurationInYears>
    </getPayment>
  </soap:Body>
</soap:Envelope>
```

FIGURE 21.7

VS-generated sample SOAP response for the getPayment WebMethod

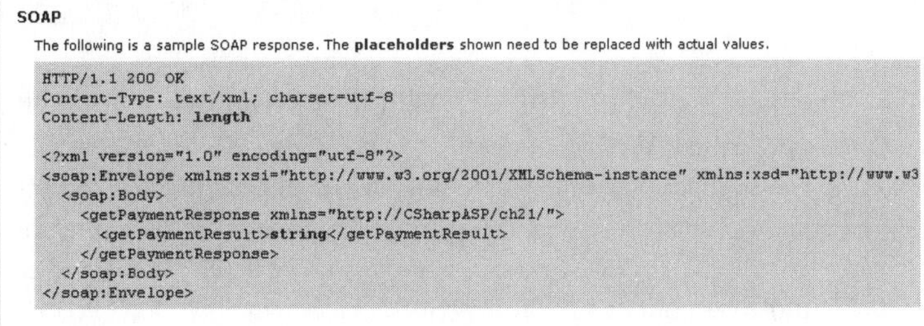

SOAP

The following is a sample SOAP response. The **placeholders** shown need to be replaced with actual values.

```
HTTP/1.1 200 OK
Content-Type: text/xml; charset=utf-8
Content-Length: length

<?xml version="1.0" encoding="utf-8"?>
<soap:Envelope xmlns:xsi="http://www.w3.org/2001/XMLSchema-instance" xmlns:xsd="http://www.w3
  <soap:Body>
    <getPaymentResponse xmlns="http://CSharpASP/ch21/">
      <getPaymentResult>string</getPaymentResult>
    </getPaymentResponse>
  </soap:Body>
</soap:Envelope>
```

Testing WebMethods with IE using the autogenerated information and test pages is useful for quick-and-dirty testing, but it's not particularly useful in real-world applications. After you know that the WebMethod works, you can use client-side code to request the data, process the data, and then display it.

Web Service Description Language (WSDL)

You may be wondering how VS.NET generates the test pages. The answer is that the framework uses the classes in the System.Reflection namespace, which "reflects" runtime information back to the running code, to discover the Web Service's name, methods, and parameter types dynamically. It uses this information to create a Web Service Description Language (WSDL) file automatically. The WSDL file is—as you probably expect by now—an XML document containing a complete description of the Web Service. WSDL is a W3 specification that defines an XML format for describing automated network services.. Internally, VS.NET uses the WSDL document to perform an XSLT transform that creates the HTML for the test pages. In other words, the WSDL document and the HTML test pages aren't static pages—they're created on demand.

You can see the WSDL file by clicking the Service Description link on the page generated when you request the ch21_payment.asmx file with no parameters (see Figure 21.8 for a partial view of the file).

FIGURE 21.8

Partial view of the ch21_payment WSDL XML document in IE

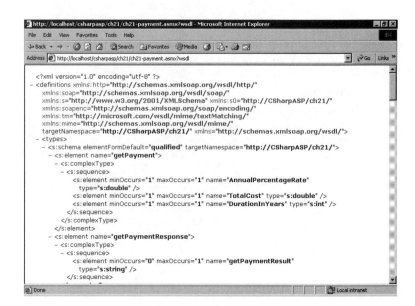

Although a full discussion of WSDL is beyond the scope of this book, the W3C has issued a note describing WSDL in detail at `http://www.w3.org/TR/wsdl`. Even a rather cursory look at the file shows that you can use a WSDL document to discover everything you need to know to call the service it describes from another program, including the name, location, methods, parameter types, supported call types (this Web Service supports GET, POST, and SOAP calls), and return types. Listing 21.4 contains the full WSDL document.

LISTING 21.4: THE WSDL DOCUMENT FOR THE MORTGAGE PAYMENT CALCULATOR WEB SERVICE (ch21_payment.asmx)

```xml
<?xml version="1.0" encoding="utf-8"?>
<definitions xmlns:s="http://www.w3.org/2001/XMLSchema"
    xmlns:http="http://schemas.xmlsoap.org/wsdl/http/"
    xmlns:mime="http://schemas.xmlsoap.org/wsdl/mime/"
    xmlns:tm="http://microsoft.com/wsdl/mime/textMatching/"
    xmlns:soap="http://schemas.xmlsoap.org/wsdl/soap/"
    xmlns:soapenc="http://schemas.xmlsoap.org/soap/encoding/"
    xmlns:s0="http://CSharpASP/ch21/"
    targetNamespace="http://CSharpASP/ch21/"
    xmlns="http://schemas.xmlsoap.org/wsdl/">
  <types>
    <s:schema attributeFormDefault="qualified"
      elementFormDefault="qualified"
      targetNamespace="http://CSharpASP/ch21/">
      <s:element name="getPayment">
        <s:complexType>
```

```
        <s:sequence>
          <s:element minOccurs="1" maxOccurs="1"
            name="AnnualPercentageRate" type="s:double" />
          <s:element minOccurs="1" maxOccurs="1"
            name="TotalCost"
            type="s:double" />
          <s:element minOccurs="1" maxOccurs="1"
            name="DurationInYears" type="s:int" />
        </s:sequence>
      </s:complexType>
    </s:element>
    <s:element name="getPaymentResponse">
      <s:complexType>
        <s:sequence>
          <s:element minOccurs="1" maxOccurs="1"
            name="getPaymentResult" type="s:string" />
        </s:sequence>
      </s:complexType>
    </s:element>
    <s:element name="totalPaymentAmount">
      <s:complexType>
        <s:sequence>
          <s:element minOccurs="1" maxOccurs="1"
            name="MonthlyPayment" type="s:double" />
          <s:element minOccurs="1" maxOccurs="1"
            name="DurationInYears" type="s:int" />
        </s:sequence>
      </s:complexType>
    </s:element>
    <s:element name="totalPaymentAmountResponse">
      <s:complexType>
        <s:sequence>
          <s:element minOccurs="1" maxOccurs="1"
            name="totalPaymentAmountResult"
            type="s:string" />
        </s:sequence>
      </s:complexType>
    </s:element>
    <s:element name="string" type="s:string" />
  </s:schema>
</types>
<message name="getPaymentSoapIn">
  <part name="parameters" element="s0:getPayment" />
</message>
<message name="getPaymentSoapOut">
  <part name="parameters"
     element="s0:getPaymentResponse" />
</message>
```

```
<message name="totalPaymentAmountSoapIn">
  <part name="parameters"
    element="s0:totalPaymentAmount" />
</message>
<message name="totalPaymentAmountSoapOut">
  <part name="parameters"
    element="s0:totalPaymentAmountResponse" />
</message>
<message name="getPaymentHttpGetIn">
  <part name="AnnualPercentageRate" type="s:string" />
  <part name="TotalCost" type="s:string" />
  <part name="DurationInYears" type="s:string" />
</message>
<message name="getPaymentHttpGetOut">
  <part name="Body" element="s0:string" />
</message>
<message name="totalPaymentAmountHttpGetIn">
  <part name="MonthlyPayment" type="s:string" />
  <part name="DurationInYears" type="s:string" />
</message>
<message name="totalPaymentAmountHttpGetOut">
  <part name="Body" element="s0:string" />
</message>
<message name="getPaymentHttpPostIn">
  <part name="AnnualPercentageRate" type="s:string" />
  <part name="TotalCost" type="s:string" />
  <part name="DurationInYears" type="s:string" />
</message>
<message name="getPaymentHttpPostOut">
  <part name="Body" element="s0:string" />
</message>
<message name="totalPaymentAmountHttpPostIn">
  <part name="MonthlyPayment" type="s:string" />
  <part name="DurationInYears" type="s:string" />
</message>
<message name="totalPaymentAmountHttpPostOut">
  <part name="Body" element="s0:string" />
</message>
<portType name="ch21_paymentSoap">
  <operation name="getPayment">
    <input message="s0:getPaymentSoapIn" />
    <output message="s0:getPaymentSoapOut" />
  </operation>
  <operation name="totalPaymentAmount">
    <input message="s0:totalPaymentAmountSoapIn" />
    <output message="s0:totalPaymentAmountSoapOut" />
  </operation>
</portType>
```

```xml
<portType name="ch21_paymentHttpGet">
  <operation name="getPayment">
    <input message="s0:getPaymentHttpGetIn" />
    <output message="s0:getPaymentHttpGetOut" />
  </operation>
  <operation name="totalPaymentAmount">
    <input message="s0:totalPaymentAmountHttpGetIn" />
    <output message="s0:totalPaymentAmountHttpGetOut" />
  </operation>
</portType>
<portType name="ch21_paymentHttpPost">
  <operation name="getPayment">
    <input message="s0:getPaymentHttpPostIn" />
    <output message="s0:getPaymentHttpPostOut" />
  </operation>
  <operation name="totalPaymentAmount">
    <input message="s0:totalPaymentAmountHttpPostIn" />
    <output message="s0:totalPaymentAmountHttpPostOut" />
  </operation>
</portType>
<binding name="ch21_paymentSoap"
  type="s0:ch21_paymentSoap">
  <soap:binding
    transport="http://schemas.xmlsoap.org/soap/http"
    style="document" />
  <operation name="getPayment">
    <soap:operation
      soapAction="http://CSharpASP/ch21/getPayment"
      style="document" />
    <input>
      <soap:body use="literal" />
    </input>
    <output>
      <soap:body use="literal" />
    </output>
  </operation>
  <operation name="totalPaymentAmount">
    <soap:operation        soapAction=
      "http://CSharpASP/ch21/totalPaymentAmount"
      style="document" />
    <input>
      <soap:body use="literal" />
    </input>
    <output>
      <soap:body use="literal" />
    </output>
  </operation>
</binding>
```

```xml
<binding name="ch21_paymentHttpGet"
  type="s0:ch21_paymentHttpGet">
  <http:binding verb="GET" />
  <operation name="getPayment">
    <http:operation location="/getPayment" />
    <input>
      <http:urlEncoded />
    </input>
    <output>
      <mime:mimeXml part="Body" />
    </output>
  </operation>
  <operation name="totalPaymentAmount">
    <http:operation location="/totalPaymentAmount" />
    <input>
      <http:urlEncoded />
    </input>
    <output>
      <mime:mimeXml part="Body" />
    </output>
  </operation>
</binding>
<binding name="ch21_paymentHttpPost"
  type="s0:ch21_paymentHttpPost">
  <http:binding verb="POST" />
  <operation name="getPayment">
    <http:operation location="/getPayment" />
    <input>
      <mime:content
        type="application/x-www-form-urlencoded" />
    </input>
    <output>
      <mime:mimeXml part="Body" />
    </output>
  </operation>
  <operation name="totalPaymentAmount">
    <http:operation location="/totalPaymentAmount" />
    <input>
      <mime:content
        type="application/x-www-form-urlencoded" />
    </input>
    <output>
      <mime:mimeXml part="Body" />
    </output>
  </operation>
</binding>
<service name="ch21_payment">
  <documentation>Mortgage Payment Web Service
```

```
      Calculator</documentation>
    <port name="ch21_paymentSoap"
       binding="s0:ch21_paymentSoap">
      <soap:address
        location=
        "http://localhost/CSharpASP/ch21/ch21-payment.asmx"
        />
    </port>
    <port name="ch21_paymentHttpGet"
      binding="s0:ch21_paymentHttpGet">
      <http:address
        location=
        "http://localhost/CSharpASP/ch21/ch21-payment.asmx"
        />
    </port>
    <port name="ch21_paymentHttpPost"
      binding="s0:ch21_paymentHttpPost">
      <http:address
        location=
        "http://localhost/CSharpASP/ch21/ch21-payment.asmx"
        />
    </port>
  </service>
</definitions>
```

Consume a Web Service

Now that you've created and tested a Web Service, you can use it in your applications. In this section, you'll see how to create a Web Form that calls the Mortgage Payment Web Service from a browser, using IE and the equivalent Windows Form application that consumes the same Web Service using SOAP messages.

Consuming Web Services from IE

This example uses a browser client—IE version 6—to call the Mortgage Payment Web Service and display the results. Because Mortgage Payment is a simple Web Service, this example uses the GET method to simplify the process.

The ch21-1.aspx Web Form uses the MSXML.DLL COM parser, which exposes an XMLHTTPRequest-Object object, to make a background GET request and parse the results for display in the page.

NOTE   You can use the XMLHTTPRequest object to make HTML requests as well as XML requests, or even to retrieve plain text or binary files; therefore, think of this example as a more-or-less generic way to retrieve information in the background from a Web page in IE.

ch21-1.aspx contains a form that users can fill out. They click the Get Payment button to contact the Web Service and display the results in the area below the form (see Figure 21.9).

FIGURE 21.9

The Mortgage
Calculator Web
Service interface

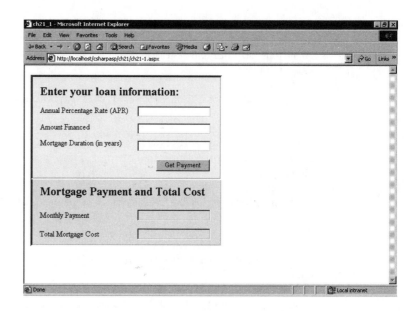

The form contains standard Web Server Control Label, TextBox, and Validation controls except for the Get Payment button, which is an HTML `<input type="button">` control. The reason the form uses an HTML button rather than a Web Server Control Button control is that the Web Server Button control always submits the form—and in this case, you don't *want* to submit the form. In contrast, the HTML button does only what you tell it to do. In this case, it calls a client-side JScript function called getPayment(), which makes sequential requests to the getPayment and totalPayment-Amount Web Service methods (see Listing 21.5).

**LISTING 21.5: THE JSCRIPT getPayment FUNCTION CALLS THE getPayment AND
totalPaymentAmount WEB SERVICE METHODS AND DISPLAYS THE RESULTS
(ch21-1.aspx.cs)**

```
function getPayment() {
   if (!Page_ClientValidate()){
      return;
   }
   var s="";
   var apr = document.getElementById("txtAPR").value;
   var total = document.getElementById("txtTotal").value;
   var duration = document.getElementById("txtDuration").value;
   var doc = new ActiveXObject("MSXML2.DOMDocument.3.0");
   var xhttp = new ActiveXObject("MSXML2.XMLHTTP");
   var url = "http://localhost/CSharpASP/ch21/ch21-payment.asmx/
      getPayment? AnnualPercentageRate=" + apr + "&TotalCost="
      + total + "&DurationInYears=" + duration;
   xhttp.Open("GET", url, false);
   xhttp.Send();
```

```
    doc.load(xhttp.ResponseXML);
    s = doc.selectSingleNode("//string").text;
    document.getElementById("lblPaymentResult").innerHTML = s;

    // get the total payment
    // strip the dollar sign from the monthly payment amount
    s = s.substr(1);
    url = "http://localhost/CSharpASP/ch21/ch21-payment.asmx/
        totalPaymentAmount?MonthlyPayment=" + s +
    "&DurationInYears="
        + duration;
    xhttp.Open("GET", url, false);
    xhttp.Send();
    doc.load(xhttp.ResponseXML);
    s = doc.selectSingleNode("//string").text;
    document.getElementById("lblCostResult").innerHTML = s;
}
```

Because the ch21-1.aspx Web Form contains Validation controls, ASP.NET automatically includes a reference to a JScript that performs validation. However, ASP.NET performs that validation only when you submit the form—and in this case, you're not going to submit the form. But it's useful to hook into the validation script anyway, so you can take advantage of the generic client-side validation code and the Validation Web Server controls. The first lines in the script force validation. If validation fails, the function exits without calling the Web Service methods. The validation process displays any validation error messages.

```
if (!Page_ClientValidate()){
    return;
}
```

TIP *Take advantage of ASP.NET's client-side validation process by calling the* Page_ClientValidate() *method included in the validation script.*

Next, the script creates a DOMDocument object and an XMLHTTPRequest object:

```
var doc = new ActiveXObject("MSXML2.DOMDocument.3.0");
var xhttp = new ActiveXObject("MSXML2.XMLHTTP");
```

NOTE *I'm using the release version of the MSXML.DLL parser, version 3, downloadable from MSDN. To use version 3 in IE 5 or 6, you must also download and run a small program named* xmlinst.exe; *otherwise, you won't be able to create the* DOMDocument *or* XMLHTTPRequest *object.*

The script creates the GET request by appending the user-entered values to the base Web Service URL.

```
var url = "http://localhost/CSharpASP/ch21/" +
  "ch21-payment.asmx/getPayment?AnnualPercentageRate="
  + apr + "&TotalCost=" + total + "&DurationInYears=" +
  duration;
```

To send the URL, use the XMLHTTPRequest object's Open method. The first parameter, GET, specifies the request method; the second parameter specifies the URL; and the third (optional) parameter specifies whether the object makes a synchronous or asynchronous call. Because the default is asynchronous, and you don't want the script to continue until it gets the values, the call explicitly passes false. For secured requests, two other optional parameters (not shown) accept a username and password. After setting up the request with the Open method, you must call the Send method to begin the request process:

```
xhttp.Open("GET", url, false);
xhttp.Send();
```

When the Send method returns, the ResponseXML property holds the return XML document. The script loads that into the DOMDocument object.

```
doc.load(xhttp.ResponseXML);
```

The returned XML for both methods looks like this (although, of course, the value of the <string> element changes based on the user input values):

```
<?xml version="1.0" encoding="utf-8" ?>
  <string xmlns="http://CSharpASP/ch21/">$1,264.14</string>
```

The script then selects the contents of the <string> element and displays the result value in the Monthly Payment field in the second half of the form.

```
s = doc.selectSingleNode("//string").text;
document.getElementById("lblPaymentResult").innerHTML
    = s;
```

The script follows an identical process to call the getPaymentTotal method. When the user enters valid values, the result looks like Figure 21.10.

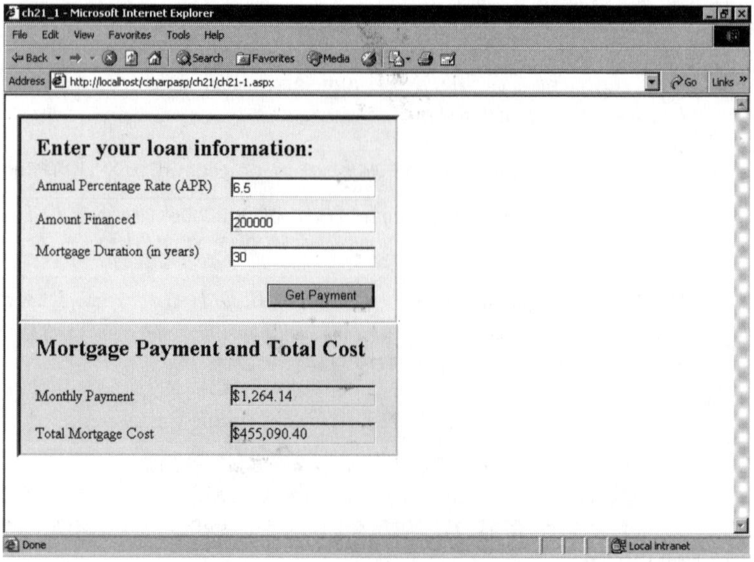

FIGURE 21.10

The Mortgage Payment response after executing successfully

There are other ways to access a Web Service from IE. If you're building an intranet application in which all the clients have IE 5.5 or later, you can download and use an HTML behavior (`.htc`) file from Microsoft at

```
http://msdn.microsoft.com/downloads/samples/internet/
    default.asp?url=/downloads/samples/internet/behaviors/
    library/webservice/default.asp
```

An HTML `behavior` is a referenced script file with an `.htc` extension that runs on the client. Behavior files have access to the DOM for the page, which means you can write very abstract behavior logic that works generically for almost any HTML page.

The `webservice` behavior lets you use SOAP requests rather than HTTP `GET` or `POST` requests to access a Web Service. Because the audience for pure IE 5+ applications is considerably smaller than the audience for a wider range of browsers, and because you're about to see two other ways to consume Web Services using SOAP messages, I haven't included an example. However, if you *do* have exclusively IE 5+ clients, HTML behaviors are extremely powerful, and I recommend that you investigate the topic thoroughly.

Consuming Web Services from a .NET Windows Forms Application

In this section, you'll create a C# Windows application that uses the Mortgage Calculator Web Service to display calculated payments. The code for this project is separate from the CSharpASP ASP.NET project you've been working with in most of this book.

First, create a new Windows Application project and name it MortgageCalculator. Although the interface uses Windows Form controls, it's essentially identical to the Web Form interface you just saw in the preceding section (see Figure 21.11).

FIGURE 21.11

The Mortgage Payment Windows Form application interface

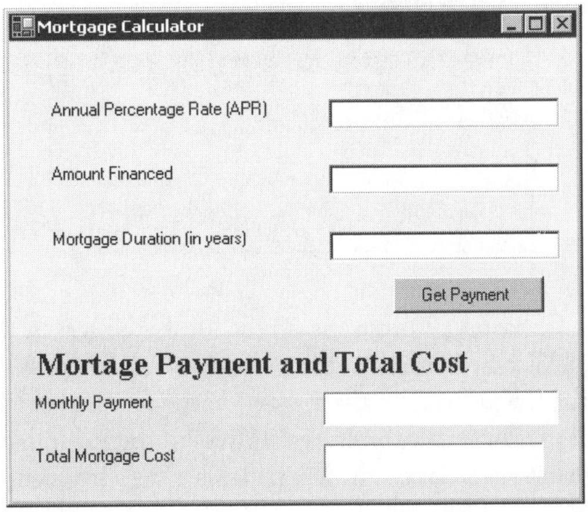

The major differences are that `Validation` controls aren't (yet) available in the System.Windows .Forms namespace, so you have to code your own validation. Most of the code for the project does exactly that—checks the user-entered values to make sure they meet the Web Service requirements.

For example, you must ensure that you can cast the APR and Amount Financed to doubles and the Mortgage Duration to an integer as well as ensure that the values are within some reasonable range.

Just as with the IE-based UI, the button on the form makes two calls to the Mortgage Calculator Web Service: one to the `getPayment` method to obtain the monthly payment, and one to retrieve the total cost of the mortgage. It places the results into the two labels (that look like text boxes) in the lower panel of the form. The form acts just like the IE interface, but it communicates with the Web Service via SOAP messages rather than with an HTTP GET request.

ADD A WEB REFERENCE

The .NET framework makes the process extremely simple. All you need to do is add a Web Service reference to the form. To do that, right-click the `References` item in the Solution Explorer and select the `Add Web Reference` menu item from the pop-up menu. You'll see the `Add Web Reference` dialog shown in Figure 21.12.

FIGURE 21.12

The Add Web Reference Wizard

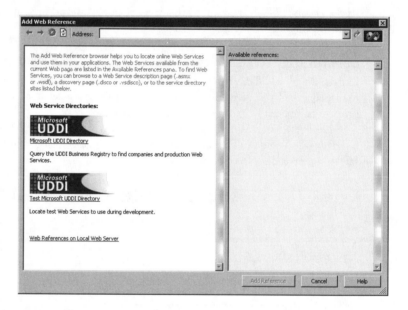

In my setup, the CSharpASP project is on the local Web server; therefore, I was able to use the Web References on Local Web Server link at the bottom of the left panel to find the reference. If the Web server containing the CSharpASP project is *not* on the same machine as your VS.NET development environment, you'll need to enter the server address in the Address field at the top of the dialog in the form `http://yourServerName`. The left panel is a WebBrowser, so you can navigate to the correct location if links are available to do so.

If you can't find the reference, enter the following name, substituting your server name for `local-host` if you aren't using your local machine server:

```
http://localhost/CSharpASP/ch21/ch21-payment.asmx/wsdl
```

When the Add Web Reference Wizard finds the server, it requests a discovery file called `default` `.vsdisco`, which is an XML file containing locations to look in (and to avoid looking in) for Web Services available on that server. The left panel of the dialog displays the results of the search, while the wizard reads the file and fills the right panel with links to the various Web Services available on that server. Each .NET project on the server also has a `.vsdisco` file containing a similar list of locations in which the server can find Web Services exposed by that project. Find the CSharpASP project and select it. You'll see the `ch21-payment.asmx` Web Service shown in the right panel and the `.vsdisco` file that describes the location of the Web Service in the left panel (see Figure 21.13).

FIGURE 21.13

The CSharpASP `ch21-payment` `.asmx` Web Service in the Add Web Reference Wizard dialog

Click the Add Reference button at the bottom of the dialog window to add the reference to your project. When you do this, VS.NET creates a proxy that your project can use to call the Web Service just as you call any other class methods.

WARNING *If your Web server is not on the same machine as your VS.NET development environment, you'll need to delete the Web Reference to the* `ch21-payment.asmx` *Web Service and then add it back using the correct server.*

VS.NET adds a Web References item to your Solution Explorer window containing one item that has the same name as the selected server. That item, in turn, contains a WSDL file describing the Web Service interface (see Listing 21.4 for details), a `.disco` file containing location information for files related to the Web Service, and a `Reference.map` file that maps URLs to the local cached file location and contains references to the discovery (`.disco`) file and the WSDL files.

After adding the Web Reference, using the referenced Web Service is straightforward. For example, after validating the user input, the button click event for the Get Payment button on the form calls a `runWebMethods` method that calls the Web Service methods and updates the two `Label` controls in the bottom half of the form (see Listing 21.6).

> **LISTING 21.6: THE MORTGAGECALCULATOR FORM'S runWebMethods METHOD**
> **(MortgageCalculator.frmMortgageCalculator.cs)**

```
private void runWebMethods(Double apr, Double totalCost,
   int durationInYears) {
   String payment;
   String cost ;
   try {
      this.Cursor = Cursors.WaitCursor;
      localhost.ch21_payment ws = new
         localhost.ch21_payment();
      payment = ws.getPayment(apr, totalCost,
         (Int16) durationInYears);
      this.lblPaymentResult.Text = payment;
      payment = payment.Substring(1);
      cost = ws.totalPaymentAmount(Double.Parse(payment),
         (Int16) durationInYears);
      lblCostResult.Text = cost;
   }
   catch (Exception ex) {
      this.Cursor = Cursors.Default;
      MessageBox.Show("An error occurred: " + ex.Message,
         "An Error Occurred", MessageBoxButtons.OK,
         MessageBoxIcon.Error,
         MessageBoxDefaultButton.Button1,
         MessageBoxOptions.DefaultDesktopOnly);
   }
   finally {
      this.Cursor = Cursors.Default;
   }
}
```

The highlighted lines create an instance of the Web Service proxy and call its methods. Use the syntax `servername.WebServiceName` to create the proxy object. Note that after obtaining the proxy object, calling its methods is identical to calling methods for any other class. VS.NET uses the WSDL file to provide IntelliSense for method names and parameters.

Visual Studio's transparent use of the WSDL and `.disco` files makes consuming Web Services from a Windows client much easier than consuming the same Web Services from IE and has two ramifications that will have a huge effect on future application development—and probably on *your* Web application development tasks as well.

The first is that, until now, it's been relatively difficult to provide a rich-client UI because HTML, while it has many strengths as a data *display* markup language, has many weaknesses as an interactive GUI interface. In contrast, Windows, Mac, and other windowing client interfaces support superior GUI interfaces but lack a means for generically displaying information, lack intrinsic support for network communications, are bound to specific platforms and hardware configurations, and are often difficult to distribute and install.

Many attempts have been made to solve this problem. Initially, Java was touted as the answer to cross-platform problems. Browsers were able to host Java *applets*, small binary programs that used all or a portion of the browser window to provide capabilities that HTML was incapable of providing, such as dynamic graphics, background server communications, and complex GUI controls. As long as the host machine had a platform-specific Java runtime package installed, the browser could download and launch applet code on command. The runtime constrained the actions that applets could take by running them in a "sandbox" that prevented the applet, for example, from writing files or launching local applications. Despite an initial flurry of interest when applets first appeared, poor runtime implementations, restricted bandwidth, and the slower machines available at the time caused users to categorize applets as "slow." Although all these problems have been solved or (in the case of bandwidth) ameliorated, the technology never recovered its initial allure. A similar, more powerful, but much more dangerous Microsoft-specific technology used COM components called ActiveX controls or ActiveX documents hosted in Internet Explorer. To avoid IE displaying default security warnings about such components, they had to be "signed," thus letting you trace the author of malevolent code (after the damage was done) before IE would let them run (although users can defeat the warnings via the security settings). Unfortunately, they also had to be installed and registered like any other COM component, with all the attendant versioning and portability problems. ActiveX controls delivered with Internet Explorer or distributed inside intranets have enjoyed widespread use, but the Internet at large eschewed and vilified the technology because of its potential for abuse.

The Java applet and ActiveX control efforts focused on improving browser interfaces and capabilities through hosted code add-ons. At the same time, a third effort, Dynamic HTML (DHTML), focused on improving the browser's intrinsic capabilities. DHTML is a good idea that has never quite managed to come to fruition because browser manufacturers' support for DHTML varies widely. In addition, because DHTML was (and is) a work in progress, developers face many problems supporting even different versions of browsers from the *same* manufacturer.

Web Services help solve this problem by letting you create platform-specific rich-client interfaces that communicate relatively transparently with servers through a simple XML-based format. In other words, Web Services give platform-specific applications many of the networking capabilities that browsers provide—without being version specific (although it remains to be seen how robust and stable SOAP and other protocols will be); bound to individual manufacturers like IE, Netscape, and Java are; or dependent on complex, specific binary implementations, like DCOM and CORBA. In my opinion, the advent of Web Services is one step toward the end of the browser era. Browsers will remain important as generalized display applications but will rapidly diminish in importance as application delivery platforms, because using a robust native environment to build interactive data-driven applications provides a better user experience than general-purpose browsers can provide.

The second way Web Services will affect your Web application development is that, because they give you a clean way to abstract program logic and data from the interface, the demand for that separation will inevitably grow. Despite this book's emphasis on Web development and browsers, the future reality is much broader. Browsers are *not* the only clients, and Internet/intranet development is highly likely to become even more important than it already is. HTTP-based communications are part of the new application infrastructure not because they're more efficient or easier to develop, but because they're standardized and widely available. As the number of devices increases, the pressure to develop centralized ways of delivering the same data to multiple types of devices also increases. It's just not efficient—from either the user or the business point of view—to create multiple applications that store or consume the same types of data in different ways.

For example, many applications use contact lists, but I'm sure you're well aware of the difficulties involved in transferring data from one application to another, because most applications use proprietary formats to store the lists. Typically, the most popular programs buy or reverse-engineer the file formats of other popular programs so that they can "import" or "export" data. However, now XML and schema remove the necessity for programs to create proprietary binary formats for common data. That means you'll see increasing interoperability and simplified data sharing between different applications. However, the concept reaches further than that. If you can share data between the various applications, then there's no need to maintain multiple *copies* of that data other than for speed and for use when the applications can't connect to a central server.

Again, Web Services hold the promise of a solution. By making it easy for applications of all types to communicate with and retrieve data from a central server via common and ubiquitous network protocols, they also increase the probability that common data will be stored as "master files" in a centrally located store.

Web Services also help solve the real and increasing problems within and between organizations that have incompatible hardware and software. An entire branch of programming, called Enterprise Application Integration (EAI), has grown up around writing software that enables these incompatible systems to exchange data. Because it's much easier and faster to write Web Services wrappers for the applications than to write custom code to translate from one format to another, EAI's future probably lies almost entirely within Web Services.

Finally, because any type of application can read and process XML without much effort, you can write programs that can find or "discover" and consume Web Services without knowing in advance where those services are or knowing the details of communicating with those services. Until such capabilities become so commonplace that they're part of the background infrastructure, it's useful to know a little bit about the technologies involved. From the .NET viewpoint, you should be aware of two public standards: the Universal Description, Discovery, and Integration (UDDI) specification, which lets programs find Web Services, and the Simple Object Access Protocol (SOAP), which lets them communicate. You've already seen the third piece of this puzzle, WSDL, which describes the requirements that you need to create properly formatted SOAP messages.

SOAP (Simple Object Access Protocol)

Even though XML reduces the process of remote communication to simple XML-formatted text files, for programs to interoperate, you must have a standard that specifies a request and response format. Several different formats have been proposed, but the current standard is the Simple Object Access Protocol (SOAP).

To understand why SOAP is important, it's useful to compare it to existing remote access methods such as Microsoft's Distributed COM (DCOM), the Object Management Group's Common Object Request Broker Architecture (CORBA), and Java's Remote Method Invocation (RMI). All three (DCOM, CORBA, and RMI) use binary messages to communicate between the client and server. All three address security, garbage collection, activation, and state management. SOAP addresses none of these things—it's just a wire protocol. But that simplicity makes it extremely portable—each platform or machine can use different methods for state maintenance, activation, security, and garbage collection.

Unfortunately, there are some serious tradeoffs when using SOAP:

♦ You lose the capability to maintain state easily between method calls. Using DCOM, CORBA, or RMI, you can call servers that remember state between calls, which is a huge advantage with small numbers of clients because it simplifies development. As the number of clients increases, the stateless model becomes more and more attractive because, with stateless calls, you can route client requests to any available server. In contrast, maintaining server state means you must route clients to the specific server that maintains that specific client's state. The only way to combine the two approaches is to store state on yet another server, which is exactly what Web farm applications using database tables to store state do, and it's exactly what Microsoft's State Server does, running in StateServer mode (out-of-process) or SQLServer mode (using a SQL Server database). In the end, state maintenance problems with Web Services are no different from the state maintenance problems you've already explored with C# Web applications, and they can be solved the same way.

♦ The SOAP messages themselves are rather bulky. XML, while very generic, is also a "heavy" format compared to binary representations of the same data. The increased message size increases network traffic and slows the process of sending and receiving the data.

♦ You must cast SOAP data values to the correct types. A SOAP message contains a string representation of the data values. The cast requirements contribute to the increased size because the message must also contain a representation of each data type in the message. Using XSD schema improves the speed and reduces the message size, but it does not absolve the receiving code from casting (and checking) each data value.

♦ SOAP doesn't have built-in security, compression, activation, or garbage collection. Microsoft's Web Service implementation handles garbage collection, and efforts are well under way to provide standardized methods for handling security needs and compression.

♦ There is no support for asynchronous processing. Because clients don't typically run a Web server, a Web Service has no way to initiate communications with the client; therefore, you can't invoke a Web Service asynchronously (or rather, you can't receive any status or completion messages from the server). However, in some situations, you can use messaging queues (such as MSMQ) to help solve the problem. Using a message queue, the client would post the request and then continue with other processing. The queue would deliver the request, and the server would queue the response message. The queue would notify the client when the response was available. Message queues have proven to be very scalable and effective. Unfortunately, there's no generic worldwide support for any specific type of message queue. Until that occurs, all solutions will be custom code.

What Is SOAP?

SOAP consists of two types of messages—requests and responses—and both are XML documents. The request XML document contains the following:

♦ An *envelope* element that surrounds the SOAP *payload* (the message). The envelope is the root element of a SOAP XML document.

- ◆ A *header* (optional) that describes the type of SOAP message.

- ◆ A *body* (mandatory) that carries the method call name and parameter names and values. For example, suppose you have a Web Service that provides mortgage payment information. Given an interest rate, a total cost, and the number of years in the mortgage, the Web Service returns the payment amount per month.

Listing 21.7 shows a simple SOAP request message for the `getPayment` method of the Mortgage Calculator Web Service.

LISTING 21.7: SOAP REQUEST MESSAGE FOR THE MORTGAGE CALCULATOR WEB SERVICE'S getPayment METHOD

```xml
<?xml version="1.0" encoding="utf-8"?>
<soap:Envelope
   xmlns:xsi="http://www.w3.org/2001/XMLSchema-instance"
   xmlns:xsd="http://www.w3.org/2001/XMLSchema"
   xmlns:soap="http://schemas.xmlsoap.org/soap/envelope/">
  <soap:Body>
    <getPayment xmlns="http://CSharpASP/ch21/">
      <AnnualPercentageRate>6.5</AnnualPercentageRate>
      <TotalCost>200000</TotalCost>
      <DurationInYears>30</DurationInYears>
    </getPayment>
  </soap:Body>
</soap:Envelope>
```

The server can parse this message and determine the data types using the WSDL schema generated by the Web Service on demand. After obtaining the correctly typed data values, it calls the requested method and creates a response SOAP message containing the return value from the method, which it returns to the client (see Listing 21.8).

LISTING 21.8: SOAP RESPONSE MESSAGE FOR THE MORTGAGE CALCULATOR WEB SERVICE'S getPayment METHOD

```xml
<?xml version="1.0" encoding="utf-8"?>
<soap:Envelope
   xmlns:xsi="http://www.w3.org/2001/XMLSchema-instance"
   xmlns:xsd="http://www.w3.org/2001/XMLSchema"
   xmlns:soap="http://schemas.xmlsoap.org/soap/envelope/">
  <soap:Body>
    <getPaymentResponse xmlns="http://CSharpASP/ch21/">
      <getPaymentResult>string</getPaymentResult>
    </getPaymentResponse>
  </soap:Body>
</soap:Envelope>
```

Notice that the `<soap:Body>` element return uses the name of the Web Service method plus the term Response: `<getPaymentResponse>`. That element contains a similarly named element with the postfix Result: `<getPaymentResult>`. All standard .NET-generated SOAP messages follow this convention, but you're not at all constrained by the SOAP specification to follow it in your applications. By defining the element names and types yourself, you can create SOAP messages that are specific to your particular application.

MORE COMPLEX SOAP MESSAGES

The simple Web Service envelope has a simple response body that returns a string, but you aren't limited to returning strings. For example, the following SOAP return message returns a `DataSet` object. Interestingly, if you look at the return type sample SOAP message, it's coded as an `<xsd:schema>` type. That makes sense because a `DataSet` serialized to XML for transport via SOAP—or any object, for that matter—consists of nothing more than a schema and some supporting XML data needed to reinstantiate the object at some other point. By default, .NET objects serialize by writing out their public properties. For example, suppose you define a simple NameObject class that has `LastName` and `FirstName` properties:

```csharp
using System;
namespace CSharpASP.ch21 {
    /// <summary>
    /// Summary description for NameObject.
    /// </summary>
    public class NameObject {
        private String mFirstName="NA";
        private String mLastName="NA";
        public NameObject() {
        }
        public NameObject(String first, String last) {
            mFirstName=first;
            mLastName=last;
        }
        public String FirstName {
            get {
                return mFirstName;
            }
            set {
                mFirstName=value;
            }
        }
        public String LastName{
            get {
                return mLastName;
            }
            set {
                mLastName=value;
            }
```

```
        }
    }
}
```

If you were to create a WebMethod that returned an instance of the NameObject class, it would return SOAP messages similar to this:

```xml
<?xml version="1.0" encoding="utf-8"?>
<soap:Envelope
    xmlns:xsi="http://www.w3.org/2001/XMLSchema-instance"
    xmlns:xsd="http://www.w3.org/2001/XMLSchema"
    xmlns:soap="http://schemas.xmlsoap.org/soap/envelope/">
  <soap:Body>
    <getNameObjectResponse
      xmlns="http://CSharpASP/NameObject">
      <getNameObjectResult>
        <LastName>string</LastName>
        <FirstName>string</FirstName>
      </getNameObjectResult>
    </getNameObjectResponse>
  </soap:Body>
</soap:Envelope>
```

Note that the response carries the public properties needed to instantiate a copy of the object on the client. Also note that returning a simple object type is one way to return more than a single value. You can return arrays of values or collection objects as well. For example, you can easily alter the Mortgage Calculator so it returns both the monthly payment and the total cost of the loan, either as an object or as a two-item array. Whether you would want to do that depends on how you use the Web Service. In the Mortgage Calculator, creating a single method that returns both values would eliminate a round trip for the example applications, which would be much more efficient.

SECURED WEB SERVICES

The examples shown in this chapter don't use the optional SOAP header element, which carries information such as versioning, security, identification IDs, and so forth. SOAP messages work fine over SSL, so if you're simply interested in encrypting the content of the messages themselves, access your Web Services via SSL. However, if you also need to build in authentication and authorization, you have two choices: You can use ASP.NET's built-in authentication methods, or you can specify custom security options in the SOAP header.

The built-in choices are similar to those you can use with Web Forms, except that you can't use Forms authentication (because they use redirection and an HTML-based user interface to provide authentication credentials and, thus, can't be automated easily). You can use Basic encryption to pass (lightly) encrypted username and password information data between the client and the server. Except in low-security intranet environments, you should avoid Basic authentication because it transmits usernames and passwords in plain text. If you *must* use Basic authentication, combine it with SSL, which provides much better security. For Windows clients, you can also use Windows Digest, Integrated Windows, or Client certificates authentication.

Finding Web Services (UDDI)

Unless you're exclusively building and consuming your own Web Services, you'll need to find and reference Web Services created by others. Interestingly, you can use a Web Service to find other Web Services. The Universal Description, Discovery, and Integration (UDDI) service acts as a centralized directory of available Web Services, and you can use it either manually or programmatically to find out what services are available at a given UDDI registry.

Discovery may seem like a rather trivial operation, but in fact it's crucial to the automatic workings of Web Services. For example, suppose you're a corporate buyer and you want to buy 300 laptop computers. You know exactly what model and features you want; now you're searching for the best price. Today, the only way to compare prices is to compile a list of possible vendors and then either call them or visit their Web sites individually. For some products, sites exist that perform such tasks for you, but there's no generally available solution. In contrast, if enough businesses register their services in UDDI registries, you can create an automated price-hunting program that would find and query laptop vendors, comparing prices until it found the best price. For some tasks, this might save days or weeks of human effort.

In version 1.0, UDDI contains four types of information; each defines part of the business:

businessEntity   Contains general information about the business itself. Each `businessEntity` contains one or more `businessService` descriptions.

businessService   A general description of the services available at a business.

tModel   A unique type ID that identifies a single type of service. For example, time services would be one `tModel`; credit card validation would be another. Multiple services may use the same `tModel`. A large number of generic `tModel` identifiers already exist, so most Web Services should be able to use one of the existing `tModels`.

bindingTemplate   A way to map Web Services to `tModels`. When you find a company that exposes services belonging to the particular `tModel` you're looking for, you use the `bindingTemplate` information to get an exact location for the Web Service detailed description. Although the description is usually a WSDL file, you should know that while a UDDI location *might* store Web Service descriptions as WSDL, that's not a requirement. You may find Web Services that are *not* described with WSDL.

There are huge advantages for businesses and individuals to being able to find and interact with exposed business services programmatically. You probably can also see that a truly useful UDDI registry must contain a huge amount of information. To gather industry support for UDDI, Microsoft, Ariba, and IBM are spearheading UDDI registries, providing online help, developer information, and integration services to combine multiple UDDI registries into a global directory for Web Services. You can find more information about UDDI at

```
http://uddi.microsoft.com/default.aspx
```

and

```
http://www-109.ibm.com/cgi-bin/dWsearch.pl?selScope=dW&UserRestriction=UDDI
```

Summary

You've seen how to create and consume a simple Web Service from Internet Explorer and a C# Windows Forms application. However, it's important that you realize exactly how ubiquitous this way of handling application data is likely to become, and what the ramifications are for you as a developer. In the next chapter, you'll build a more complex set of Web Services that supplies data to a front-end Windows Forms application and updates any user changes to that data.

Chapter 22

Web Services, COM Components, and the SOAP Toolkit

IN CHAPTER 21, "WEB Services," you saw how to create a Web Service that returns single values and consumes them with Internet Explorer (IE) and a C# Windows Forms application. But Web Services can reach even further. In fact, in many environments, Web Services and XML are most useful as integration services, letting newer applications obtain and update data from older applications. As a developer, by planning stand-alone functionality as Web Services, you can update existing client applications and machines that don't have the .NET platform installed and let them take advantage of those services. In other words, even if you can't deploy .NET to every machine in your organization yet, you can still begin building and using Web Services from existing technology.

In this chapter, you'll build a VB6 application that uses the Microsoft SOAP Toolkit, version 2, to access the Mortgage Payment Calculator Web Service you created in the last chapter. You could just as easily use the SOAP Toolkit to connect a C++ Windows application to the Web Service. For those of you moving to C# from Java, the solutions aren't quite as simple, but there are Java APIs that let you consume Web Services from Java without too much effort, so the concepts are similar, even though this particular example doesn't specifically apply.

NOTE   *I've chosen to use a VB6 client for this book, first because VB6 was—and still is—ubiquitous; therefore it was the language that was most likely to be readable by the majority of readers. Second, I expect a large percentage of this book's audience to be migrating from VB6 (or VB.NET). If you're not familiar with VB code, I apologize and advise you simply to skim this chapter, paying particular attention to the parts that show and explain the WSDL format and the (minimal) logic involved in calling the client or server. The most important concept from this chapter is that, with little effort, you can use ASP.NET to integrate XML Web Services into your applications as wrappers for existing code. If you already understand that, you can skip the chapter altogether.*

Why Worry about Older Technology?

Many organizations have a large number of existing client-server or three-tier database applications that have been developed, debugged, and deployed to good effect. Many of these applications use Windows application front-ends connected either directly to back-end databases or to server-based components that retrieve and update data. While these applications might benefit marginally from a full rewrite as .NET Windows Forms applications, there's little need or desire to rewrite them immediately. However, often there *is* a need to update the business components or to give employees access to the applications from outside the corporate firewall. In those cases, it makes sense to update the applications so that they can take advantage of Web Services' capability to pass through firewalls rather than opening outside ports and increasing the risk of security breaches.

In addition, many organizations have large numbers of older computers that either will not work with the .NET runtime, such as Windows 95, or would need significant memory and disk upgrades to be .NET compatible. By moving program logic to a server and writing Windows front-ends, you can enable these machines to benefit from .NET technology. In many cases, you can use browser clients, but for complicated data manipulation, when you don't want the code to be accessible to the users, or when you need more control over the interface than you can achieve with browsers, using Web Services coupled with Windows applications running on the clients is the easiest way to expose server-based data to these older computers.

Finally, there are a huge number of businesses that need to connect disparate legacy applications— so many, in fact, that an entire industry, called Enterprise Application Integration (EAI), has sprung up to create such connections. Web Services provide benefits to these organizations because it's much easier, faster, and less expensive in many cases to expose parts of the functionality of these legacy applications through Web Services, thus letting them communicate using XML, than it is to modify, rewrite, or replace the applications entirely. Many of these applications run on hardware or OSs for which the .NET framework is not yet available. Fortunately, any programmable client that can perform string handling can consume Web Services.

Of course, the flip side of that statement is that any executable code that can perform string handling can be invoked by a Web server and act as a Web Service—and that's almost everything. Microsoft and .NET have no claims to Web Service exclusivity; they're in the pot with everyone else. With that said, Microsoft has made it extremely easy for older code to communicate with Web Services.

You've seen how easy it is to create a proxy object in a C# Windows Forms class that the client uses to communicate with the server. Fortunately, it's not much harder to accomplish the same thing from a VB6 application.

The Microsoft SOAP Toolkit

Microsoft provides a SOAP Toolkit that contains everything you need to get Web Services installed and running both on VB6 clients and on IIS servers using ASP. You can download the SOAP Toolkit free from MSDN. The example code uses the SOAP Toolkit, version 2. When you download and install the Toolkit, it also installs the release version 3 (sp1) of the Microsoft XML parser.

The SOAP Toolkit makes the process of connecting to a Web Service relatively painless. It follows the same model as the Windows Forms method, reading the WSDL file to create a proxy object that you can then use just like any other component to access the methods exposed by that particular Web Service.

Create a Client Application

In this section, you'll create a Visual Basic 6 client application to consume the Mortgage Payment Calculator Web Service. Start a new Visual Basic 6 application and create a new Standard EXE project. Name the project MortgageCalculatorClient, and rename the default form frmMain. Build the user interface as shown in Figure 22.1.

NOTE   *You must download and install the Microsoft SOAP Toolkit before you can create or run this project in the development environment.*

NOTE   *If you simply want to see the project run and don't have Visual Studio 6, you can install the Visual Basic runtime, the redistributable files for the SOAP Toolkit, and the* MortageCalculatorClient.exe *executable file from* www.sybex.com.

FIGURE 22.1

VB6 Mortgage-Payment Calculator-Client application interface

The background panels on the frmMain form in this example are PictureBox controls with their BorderStyle property set to None. The PictureBoxes resize to fill the width of the form when the form loads.

```
Private Sub Form_Load()
    Unload frmInit
    pnl1.Move 0, 0, Me.Width
    pnl2.Move 0, pnl1.Top + pnl1.Height, Me.Width
End Sub
```

Select the Project ➤ References menu item and add the references required for the SOAP Toolkit: the Microsoft SOAP Message Object Generator and the Microsoft SOAP Type Library. After adding the references, you can access the objects and methods in the Toolkit components.

When the user clicks the Get Payment button, the project must validate the user-entered values, contact the server, and retrieve the results, just as the browser and Windows Forms clients did in the last chapter. The SOAP Toolkit handles generating the SOAP request and parsing the SOAP response. All you need to do is create a SOAP client proxy object.

```
Dim wsClient As MSSOAPLib.SoapClient
Set wsClient = New soapClient
```

The preceding lines create the client, but it isn't "attached" to a specific Web Service instance. To do that, you must initialize the `SoapClient` object, as discussed in the next section.

Initializing the *SoapClient*

Initialization lets the `SOAPClient` read the Web Service's WSDL file so that it can create and parse the SOAP wrappers required to access the service. To initialize the `SOAPClient`, you specify the location of the Web Service by calling the `soapClient.mssoapinit` method. The method takes four arguments. The first (required) argument is the URL of the WSDL file for the Web Service you want to use. The other three arguments are optional—and you may not know any of them immediately:

♦   The public Web Service identifier name—needed only if you want to access a service other than the *first* service identified in the WSDL file.

♦   The *port identifier*—needed only if the `<portType>` element specifying the SOAP port does not appear first in the WSDL file.

♦   A URL specifying the Web Service's WSML file location (not applicable to .NET-generated Web Services—you need this only if you're generating a Web Service from a COM object).

As mentioned, the first parameter to the `SoapClient.mssoapinit` method accepts the URL for the Web Service's WSDL file. Unfortunately, you might not *have* a WSDL static file (and you might not want one either, because if you change the Web Service, clients using an older copy of the WSDL file might break). Instead, you can retrieve the WSDL file from .NET Web Services in the same way that the automatic Web Service test file does—by requesting it dynamically. Use the full URL of the Web Service, but append a query string parameter of `WSDL` to the URL. For example:

```
http://localhost/CSharpASP/ch21/ch21-payment.asmx?WSDL"
```

Using this method, you know the WSDL file is always up to date.

The WSDL file location is relatively easy, but how do you find the name and the port identifier? The answer is to look at the WSDL file. Remember, you can use the URL with the `?WSDL` query string parameter to display the WSDL file in IE. To find the name string you should use for the `name` parameter, look for a `<binding>` element in the WSDL that has a `<soap:binding>` element. The `name` attribute of the `<binding>` element contains the name you should use.

```
<binding name="ch21_paymentSoap" type="s0:ch21_paymentSoap">
  <soap:binding transport="http://schemas.xmlsoap.org/soap/http"
    style="document" />
  <operation name="getPayment">
    <soap:operation
  soapAction="http://CSharpASP/ch21/getPayment"
```

```
      style="document" />
    <input>
      <soap:body use="literal" />
    </input>
    <output>
      <soap:body use="literal" />
    </output>
  </operation>
  <operation name="totalPaymentAmount">
    <soap:operation
      soapAction="http://CSharpASP/ch21/totalPaymentAmount"
      style="document" />
    <input>
      <soap:body use="literal" />
    </input>
    <output>
      <soap:body use="literal" />
    </output>
  </operation>
</binding>
```

The WSDL file may contain multiple `<binding>` elements. For example, the Mortgage Payment Calculator WSDL file contains a `<binding>` element for each operation type—GET, POST, and soap—but only the soap binding element contains a `<soap:binding>` element as its first child.

Note that, although the Mortgage Payment Calculator Web Service file in the CSharpASP project is named ch21-payment.asmx, the WSDL file turns the dash into an underscore (ch21_payment). In other words, it uses the .NET class name, not the filename.

You must also extract the port identifier string from the WSDL file. You'll find the correct port identifier in the appropriate `<portType>` element. For example, the WSDL file for the Mortgage Payment Calculator defines three portType names:

```
<portType name="ch21_paymentHttpPost">
<portType name="ch21_paymentHttpGet">
<portType name="ch21_paymentSoap">
```

In this case, because you're using SOAP to communicate with the service, use the name ch21_paymentSoap for the port identifier parameter to the SoapClient.mssoapinit method:

```
<portType name="ch21_paymentSoap">
  <operation name="getPayment">
    <input message="s0:getPaymentSoapIn" />
    <output message="s0:getPaymentSoapOut" />
  </operation>
  <operation name="totalPaymentAmount">
    <input message="s0:totalPaymentAmountSoapIn" />
    <output message="s0:totalPaymentAmountSoapOut" />
  </operation>
</portType>
```

You need the fourth parameter—the WSML file URL—only if you're accessing a Web Service exposed by a COM object, so it doesn't apply to this example. However, to be complete, you can generate WSDL and WSML files using a utility that the SOAP Toolkit installs called the WSDL Generator. After installing the SOAP Toolkit, you can find the WSDL Generator utility at Start ➢ Programs ➢ Microsoft SOAP Toolkit ➢ WSDL Generator.

The soapClient.mssoapinit method to initialize the Mortgage Payment Calculator Web Service looks like this:

```
Dim wsClient As MSSOAPLib.SoapClient
Set wsClient = New soapClient
Call wsClient.mssoapinit( _
  "http://localhost/CSharpASP/ch21/ch21-payment.asmx?WSDL"), _
  "ch21_payment", "ch21_paymentSoap")
```

The code for the project is shown in Listing 22.1. Although Web Services are relatively fast once initialized, just like DCOM or any other remote invocation mechanism, they take a little while to load and execute the first time you call them. Therefore, the project uses a Sub Main routine to load a small initialization form that displays a Contacting Server... message when you first load the project. Depending on your setup, your network speed, and how long it's been since you tested or ran the Mortgage Payment Calculator Web Service from the test pages or the other sample applications, the initialization form may be visible only as a brief flash, or for several seconds.

The Main routine loads the initialization form, retrieves the Web Service initialization values from an instance of a class named InitServiceXMLReader, which reads the Web Service WSDL file URL, the service name, and the PortID from an XML file and then exposes the values as public properties. The Main routine uses those property values to call the initialization form's initService method, passing the necessary parameters. The initialization form performs the initialization, and then the Main routine hides it and displays the main form (see Listing 22.1).

NOTE *You will need to change the URL for the* initService *call. To do that, open the* MortgageCalculator-Client.xml *file in the project folder and modify the* WSDLFileURL *value so that it points to the correct server and path for the* ch21-payment.asmx *file on your server.*

LISTING 22.1: MAIN SUBROUTINE FOR THE VB6 MORTGAGE PAYMENT CALCULATOR CLIENT APPLICATION (modMain.bas)

```
Public InitServiceReader As InitServiceXMLReader
Sub main()
restart:
    On Error GoTo ErrMain
    Load frmInit
    frmInit.Show
    DoEvents
    Set InitServiceReader = New InitServiceXMLReader
    InitServiceReader.InitService
    With InitServiceReader
        Call frmInit.InitService(.WSDLFileURL, .ServiceName,
```

```
            .PortID, .WSMLFileURL)
        End With
        frmInit.Hide
        Unload frmInit
        frmMain.Show vbModal
    ExitMain:
        Exit Sub
    ErrMain:
        ' log the error (not shown)
        ' hide any forms still showing
        Unload frmInit
        Unload frmMain
        ' display the error
        If MsgBox("The application encountered a fatal error: "
          & Err.Description & vbCrLf & vbCrLf &
          "Do you want to try again?", vbCritical + vbYesNo,
          "Unable to Continue: Try Again?") = vbYes Then
            Resume restart
        Else
            Resume ExitMain
        End If
    End Sub
```

The initialization form (see Figure 22.2) creates a `SOAP client` object, calls the `soapClient`
`.mssoapinit` method, raising an error if it can't initialize the Web Service properly, and then exits. The
form functions as both a splash screen and a way to prevent the application from running if the Web
Service can't be properly initialized. It's useful to set up and check all application initialization *before*
users enter any values; that way, you can warn them of problems before they spend time entering data.

FIGURE 22.2

The initialization
form acts as a splash
screen and initializes
the SOAP client

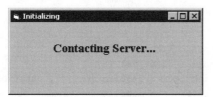

The main form (`frmMain`) contains code to validate the input, call the Mortgage Payment Calculator
Web Service, and display the results—it's very similar to the Windows Forms client you saw in the
preceding chapter. As before, most of the code is in the method named `Validate,` which checks the
user input, stripping dollar signs, percent signs, and commas from the numbers entered by the user.
The interesting action happens in the highlighted section of code in Listing 22.2, which calls the
Web Service and displays the results.

**LISTING 22.2: VB6 CODE IN frmMain TO CALL AND DISPLAY THE MORTGAGE PAYMENT
CALCULATOR WEB SERVICE (frmMain.frm)**

```
Const AppTitle = "MortgageCalculator"

Private Sub Form_Load()
   Unload frmInit
   pnl1.Move 0, 0, Me.Width
   pnl2.Move 0, pnl1.Top + pnl1.Height, Me.Width
End Sub

Private Sub cmdGetPayment_Click()
   Dim apr As Double
   Dim total As Double
   Dim duration As Integer
   Dim wsClient As MSSOAPLib.soapClient
   Dim sPayment As String
   Dim dPayment As Double
   Dim sTotalResult As String
   Set wsClient = New soapClient
   On Error Resume Next
   Me.MousePointer = vbHourglass

   'initialize the Web Service
   Call wsClient.mssoapinit( _
      "http://localhost/CSharpASP/ch21/ch21-payment.asmx?WSDL", _
      "ch21_payment", "ch21_paymentSoap")
   If Err <> 0 Then
      Me.MousePointer = vbDefault
      Debug.Print "initialization failed " + Err.Description
      Exit Sub
   End If

   ' validate user input
   If Validate(apr, total, duration) Then
      sPayment = wsClient.getPayment(apr, total, duration)
      Me.lblPaymentResult = sPayment
      ' strip the dollar sign from the payment string
      ' and get a double for the call to getTotalAmount
      dPayment = CDbl(Mid$(sPayment, 2))
      sTotalResult = wsClient.totalPaymentAmount _
         (dPayment, duration)
      Me.lblTotalResult = sTotalResult
   End If
   Me.MousePointer = vbDefault
End Sub

Private Function Validate(apr As Double, total As Double, _
```

```
duration As Integer) As Boolean
Dim sAPR As String
Dim sTotal As String
Dim sDuration As String
Dim sMsg As String
Const validationError = 50000

On Error GoTo ErrValidate

' get the APR
sAPR = txtAPR.Text
' ensure user entered a value
If Len(Trim$(sAPR)) = 0 Then
    sMsg = "You must enter an APR."
    Err.Raise validationError, AppTitle, sMsg
End If
' strip percent sign if present
sMsg = "You entered an invalid value in the APR field."
sAPR = Replace(sAPR, "%", "")
sAPR = Trim$(sAPR)
apr = CDbl(sAPR)
sMsg = "The APR must be between .01 and 100"
If apr < 0.01 Or apr > 100 Then
    Err.Raise validationError, AppTitle, sMsg
End If


' get the total
sTotal = txtTotal.Text
If Len(Trim$(sTotal)) = 0 Then
    sMsg = "You must enter the Amount Financed."
    Err.Raise validationError, AppTitle, sMsg
End If
' strip dollar sign, and commas, if present
sMsg = "You entered an invalid value in the " & _
  "Amount Financed field."
sTotal = Replace(sTotal, "$", "")
sTotal = Replace(sTotal, ",", "")
sTotal = Trim$(sTotal)
total = CDbl(sTotal)
If total < 1000 Or total > 20000000 Then
    sMsg = "The Amount financed must be between " & _
  "1000 and 20,000,000"
    Err.Raise validationError, AppTitle, sMsg
End If

' get the duration
sDuration = txtDuration.Text
If Len(Trim$(sDuration)) = 0 Then
```

```
        sMsg = "You must enter the Mortgage Duration."
        Err.Raise validationError, AppTitle, sMsg
    End If
    sMsg = "You entered an invalid value in the " &
        "Amount Financed field."
    duration = CInt(sDuration)
    If duration < 1 Or duration > 100 Then
        sMsg = "The Mortgage Duration must be between " &
            "1 and 100."
        Err.Raise validationError, AppTitle, sMsg
    End If
    Validate = True
ExitValidate:
    Exit Function
ErrValidate:
    Me.MousePointer = vbDefault
    Debug.Print Err.Description
    MsgBox sMsg, vbOKOnly, AppTitle
    Resume ExitValidate
End Function
```

Create a Server Application

Just as you've seen how you can create VB6 applications that use .NET functionality through Web Services, the reverse is also true: You can expose COM component functionality through Web Services and consume them from .NET applications. If you're migrating existing applications to .NET, it may be easier to add Web Service functionality to existing components than to rewrite and retest all the logic in those components. It's also possible that you may already have COM-based Web Service components, so it's good to know that you can consume them from .NET applications.

Build a VB6 ActiveX DLL

In this example, you'll build a VB6-based ActiveX DLL (a COM component) that functions as a Web Service. For example, the VB6 DLL MortgageCalculatorWS functions in exactly the same way as the Mortgage Payment Calculator Web Service—it exposes two methods, called getPayment and totalPaymentAmount, that accept the same parameter types as the ch21_payment Web Service class methods. The VB6 code is shown in Listing 22.3. To create the DLL, open a new VB6 ActiveX DLL project, rename the project MortgageCalculatorWS (the WS stands for Web Service, but the extra text makes the fully qualified method names too long for COM), and rename the default class ch22_payment. I translated most of the code from the ch21-payment.asmx.cs class, changing syntax as needed to create equivalent VB6 code.

LISTING 22.3: THE VB6 MORTGAGECALCULATORWS PROJECT'S ch22_payment CLASS CONTAINS THE MORTGAGE PAYMENT CALCULATOR getPayment AND totalPaymentAmount METHODS (ch22_Payment.cls)

```vb
Public Function getPayment _
   (ByVal AnnualPercentageRate As Double, _
   ByVal TotalCost As Double, _
   ByVal DurationInYears As Integer) As String

   Dim payment As Double
   ' divide the APR by 100 to get a decimal percentage, if
   necessary
   If AnnualPercentageRate > 1 Then
      AnnualPercentageRate = AnnualPercentageRate / 100
   End If

   ' and then divide by 12 for the number of months
   ' in a year
   ' to get the percentage interest rate per payment.
   ' Multiply DurationInYears by 12 to get the total
   ' number of payments.
   payment = Pmt(AnnualPercentageRate / 12, DurationInYears * 12, _
      TotalCost)

   ' the Pmt function returns the payment as a
   ' negative number
   payment = Abs(payment)

   ' format the result and return it
   getPayment = Format$(payment, "$###,###,##0.00")
End Function

Public Function totalPaymentAmount _
      (ByVal MonthlyPayment As Double, _
      ByVal DurationInYears As Integer) As String

      totalPaymentAmount = Format$(MonthlyPayment *
      (DurationInYears * 12), _
         "$###,###,##0.00")
End Function
```

Compile the DLL and save your work.

Build a .NET Web Service Wrapper

To use the DLL from .NET, you must do the following:

◆ Register the `MortgageCalculatorWS.dll` on your server (you can skip this step if your VB6 development environment is on the same computer as your .NET test environment and you compiled the MortgageCalculatorWS project on that computer). Otherwise, run the command `regsvr32.exe` *pathToDLL*, replacing *pathToDLL* with the full path and filename of the `MortgageCalculatorWD.dll` file.

◆ Add a new COM reference in the CSharpASP project to the `MortgageCalculatorWS.dll` file.

◆ Write a Web Service wrapper for the COM DLL's methods as shown in Listing 22.4.

Create a new Web Service named `ch22-1.asmx`. The class will expose the `getPayment` and `total-PaymentAmount` methods as WebMethods, but they'll just be wrappers for the VB6 COM component call (see Listing 22.4).

LISTING 22.4: THE `ch22-payment.asmx` WEB SERVICE IS JUST A WRAPPER FOR A VB6-GENERATED COM DLL (`ch22-payment.asmx.cs`)

```
using System;
using System.Collections;
using System.ComponentModel;
using System.Data;
using System.Diagnostics;
using System.Web;
using System.Web.Services;

namespace CSharpASP.ch22
{
    /// <summary>
    /// Summary description for ch22_payment.
    /// </summary>
    [WebService(Namespace="http://CSharpASP/ch22/")]
    public class ch22_payment :
        System.Web.Services.WebService
    {
        private MortgageCalculatorWS.ch22_Payment mc=null;
        public ch22_payment()
        {
            //CODEGEN: This call is required by the ASP.NET
            // Web Services Designer
            InitializeComponent();
        }

        #region Component Designer generated code

        //Required by the Web Services Designer
```

```csharp
        private IContainer components = null;

        /// <summary>
        /// Required method for Designer support -
        /// do not modify
        /// the contents of this method with the code editor.
        /// </summary>
        private void InitializeComponent()
        {
        }

        /// <summary>
        /// Clean up any resources being used.
        /// </summary>
        protected override void Dispose( bool disposing )
        {
            if(disposing && components != null)
            {
                components.Dispose();
            }
            base.Dispose(disposing);
        }

        #endregion

            [WebMethod]
            public string getPayment(double APR ,
          double AmountFinanced , int DurationInYears ) {
          String payment="";
          mc = new MortgageCalculatorWS.ch22_Payment();
          payment = mc.getPayment(APR, AmountFinanced,
                (Int16)DurationInYears);
          mc = null;
          return payment;
        }
        [WebMethod]
        public string totalPaymentAmount
            (Double MonthlyPayment , int DurationInYears ) {
            String paymentAmount="";
            mc = new MortgageCalculatorWS.ch22_Payment();
            paymentAmount = mc.totalPaymentAmount
                (MonthlyPayment, (Int16) DurationInYears);
            mc = null;
            return paymentAmount;
        }
    }
}
```

TIP *There is one slight change between the parameter types in the .NET version of the Web Service and the VB6 COM component version. The COM component used an* `Integer` *keyword to define the* `DurationInYears` *parameter type. In VB6, the* `Integer` *keyword denotes a 16-bit integer, whereas in VB.NET, the* `Integer` *keyword denotes a 32-bit variable. Therefore, to call the COM component successfully, you must cast the 32-bit* `Integer` *parameter exposed by the* `ch22_payment` *Web Service to a 16-bit integer (*`Int16`*). If the VB6 component had used the keyword* `Long` *for the* `DurationInYears` *parameter, this cast would not be necessary.*

Save and compile the CSharpASP application.

Testing the COM-Based Web Service

To test the new Web Service using the Mortgage Payment Calculator Windows Forms project, you need to add a Web Reference to the project so that the Mortgage Payment Calculator project can "see" the new Web Service and change the line that creates the proxy in the `runWebMethods` method in the `frmMortgageCalculator.cs` form class.

To update the Web Reference, right-click the server name (`localhost`, in my case) in the Web References section of the Solution Explorer for the Mortgage Payment Calculator Windows Forms project and select Add Web Reference from the pop-up menu. If your Web server is on your development machine, select the Web References on Local Web Server link in the left pane, and then select the `http://localhost/CSharpASP.vsdisco` file from the Discovery Documents list in the right pane. If your Web server is elsewhere, you'll need to type the address into the Address field at the top of the Add Web Reference dialog.

Next, open the Mortgage Payment Calculator project you created in Chapter 21. In the `frmMorgage-Calculator.cs` form file, find the `runWebMethods` method. Comment out the line that creates the proxy for the `ch21_paymentSoap` Web Service and replace it with a new line that creates a proxy for the equivalent COM-driven `ch22_paymentSoap` Web Service. After doing that, your code should contain these lines:

```
// use the following line for chapter 21
// localhost.ch21_payment ws = new
    // localhost.ch21_payment(); */
//use the following line for chapter 22
localhost1.ch22_payment ws =
    new localhost1.ch22_payment();
```

Now recompile and run the project. It should act *exactly the same* as it did before, although now it accesses the COM component through the .NET Web Service wrapper.

At this point, you should understand that Web Services form the backbone of a network world view in which any platform and any language can provide services or use services exposed by any other platform using code written in any other language—no matter where the two machines are physically located. That's powerful stuff. Although the process is still a bit slow, the speed will improve automatically as bandwidth and machine speed improve. Web Services are changing the face of computing.

Finally, the SOAP Toolkit is *far* more comprehensive than the SOAP client calls you've seen in this chapter. The SOAP Toolkit contains everything you need to read, write, and parse WSDL files, to expose COM-based DLL functionality via a Web Service interface, to serialize and deserialize objects from the SOAP XML-based format, and to debug Web Services either used by or driven by COM components. In other words, it makes creating and consuming Web Services from older C++ and VB technology about as straightforward as possible without .NET's intrinsic support.

Summary

So far in this book, you've used the Web Server controls that arrive packaged with Visual Studio, but you aren't limited to those controls. Just as you could build custom ActiveX controls in classic VB, you can build custom Server controls in C# and use them in your Web Forms. In the next chapter, you'll see how to build custom controls that you can use to create specialized types of content and cache data.

Chapter 23

Build Your Own Web Controls

IN ADDITION TO THE Web Forms Server controls and HTML controls that you get with ASP.NET, you can build your own controls that work in any of three different ways. First, User controls are essentially stand-alone Web Forms; you can design them almost exactly like a Web Form, placing controls on a form, or you can create controls at runtime. Second, you can create controls that tie two or more Server controls together as a *composite* control. Finally, you can build Custom controls in which you can define everything about the control. This is the equivalent of creating a brand-new control.

In this chapter, you'll build a User control, a Composite control, and a Custom control and see the relative advantages and disadvantages of each type.

In this chapter:

◆ Build a User Control

◆ Build a Composite Control

◆ Build a Custom Control

◆ Transferring Data Between ASP.NET Web Forms and Components

Build a User Control

The simplest type of control you can build is a User control, which is essentially an ASPX page changed to have an `.ascx` extension. When you install .NET, it prevents IIS from displaying files with an `.ascx` extension directly, so users can't request your User controls by themselves.

So that you can see all the differences, it's useful to attempt to change a Web Form into a User control (that is, change an ASPX page into an ASCX page). For example, create a Web Form called `testChange.aspx`, place a Button control on it, and set the button's `Text` property to `My Button`.

Add a client-side script to display an `alert` when a user clicks the button. For example:

```
private void Button1_Click(object sender,
    System.EventArgs e) {
    this.Page.RegisterStartupScript("msg",
```

```
      "<script language='JScript'>" +
      "alert('My Button clicked!');</script>");
}
```

Next, right-click the `testChange.aspx` file and select the `Rename` item from the pop-up menu. Change the file's extension to `.ascx`. You'll see a warning about changing file extensions. Answer Yes to accept the change. When you save your changes, the code-behind class and the RESX file also are renamed to reflect the changed extension, but just renaming the file isn't quite enough. After renaming the file, you have just four manual changes to make to change the Web Form into a User control:

1. User controls inherit from System.Web.UI.UserControl rather than System.Web.UI.Page. In the code-behind file, change the class definition

   ```
   public class testChange : System.Web.UI.Page
   ```

   to

   ```
   public class testChange : System.Web.UI.UserControl
   ```

2. Although Visual Studio changes the *name* of the associated code-behind file, it doesn't change the *reference* to it in the ASPX file. Open the `testChange.ascx` file in the HTML editor, then change the `Codebehind` attribute in the top line from

   ```
   Codebehind="testChange.aspx.cs"
   ```

   to

   ```
   Codebehind="testChange.ascx.cs"
   ```

3. Change the `Page` attribute in the top line to `Control`. Now, you no longer have a `Page` object; you have a `Control` object.

4. Remove the `<form>` tag but not the `<asp:Button>` tag. Actually, this last step is not really required—the rule is, you can't have two `<form>` tags in a Web Form *that run at the server*, so it's perfectly OK to leave the `<form>` tag in place, but you must remove the `runat="server"` attribute. However, for simple controls, it's easier not to deal with the added complexity of forms embedded in forms; normally you should remove the `<form>` tag. In this particular case, it doesn't matter.

Now test the new User control in a Web Form. Create a new Web Form in the `ch23` folder and name it `ch23-1.aspx`. In HTML mode, change the `id` attribute of the `<form>` tag to `Form1`. In the code-behind file, add this line to the `Form_Load` method:

```
this.FindControl("Form1").Controls.Add
   ((ch23.testChange) this.LoadControl("testChange.ascx"));
```

When you compile and run the Web Form, you'll see the button from your User control in the browser window. When you click it, you'll see the JavaScript alert (see Figure 23.1).

FIGURE 23.1

The `ch23-1.aspx` Web Form contains an instance of the User control `testChange.ascx`, which displays an alert when you click the button

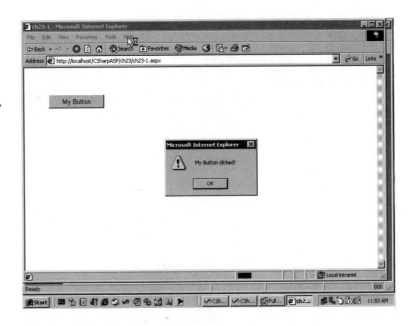

Creating a Web Form and then changing it to a User control is one easy way to create a User control. You may be thinking, "But there's a User control file type in the Add Item dialog!" That's true—I'll show you that in a minute. But changing a Web Form into a User control shows you how few differences there are between the two types. Also, after you've built a Web Form, you may at some point realize that it would be better implemented as a User control. Now you know how to accomplish the change.

To compare the two approaches, you should try building a User control directly. Add a new User control to your CSharpASP project in the `ch23` folder. Name the control `prettyXML.ascx`.

TIP   You can't create a User control with a name like `23-1`—VS doesn't allow dashes in class names.

This time, you'll create a read-only control that can display any XML file in "pretty-print" form in a TextBox control on any Web Form. You can control the XML file URL and the size and position of the TextBox. The User control itself is very simple: It contains one TextBox Web Server control named `txtXML`. It doesn't matter where you place the control on the Web Control design surface because it won't appear in that position anyway—you can provide an absolute position if you wish, or use FlowLayout mode to position the TextBox as you would any other HTML control.

Listing 23.1 contains the HTML for the `prettyXML.ascx` file.

LISTING 23.1: HTML FOR THE `prettyXML.ascx` FILE (`prettyXML.ascx`)

```
<%@ Control Language="c#" AutoEventWireup="false"
   Codebehind="prettyXML.ascx.cs"
   Inherits="CSharpASP.ch23.prettyXML"
   targetSchema="http://schemas.microsoft.com/intellisense/ie5"%>
<!DOCTYPE HTML PUBLIC "-//W3C//DTD HTML 4.0 Transitional//EN">
```

```
<HTML>
    <HEAD>
        <title>ch23_2</title>
        <meta content="Microsoft Visual Studio.NET 7.0"
    name="GENERATOR">
        <meta content="Visual Basic 7.0" name="CODE_LANGUAGE">
        <meta content="JavaScript" name="vs_defaultClientScript">
        <meta
    content="http://schemas.microsoft.com/intellisense/ie5"
            name="vs_targetSchema">
    </HEAD>
    <body MS_POSITIONING="GridLayout">
        <form id="Form1" method="post">
            <asp:TextBox id="txtXML" TextMode="MultiLine"
                EnableViewState="False" ReadOnly="True"
                runat="server">
            </asp:TextBox>
        </form>
    </body>
</HTML>
```

All the code in Listing 23.1 is VS generated except for the `<asp:textbox>` Web control tag. I included it here so that you can see that the control is absolutely plain; it has no `style` attribute and no `rows` or `cols` attributes—no layout attributes whatsoever. The only attributes it contains are `Read-Only="True"`, `EnableViewState="False"`, and `TextMode="MultiLine"`. These three attributes enforce the control's purpose: to display (not to provide editable) XML documents in read-only mode. When designing a control, you should change hats: Stop thinking in Web Form designer mode and start thinking in control author mode. As a control author, your job is to expose as much functionality to the potential users of your control as possible. At the same time, you want to set reasonable defaults. In this case, because you want the control to be read-only, it's reasonable to enforce that at the control level. But the control doesn't contain style attributes or other display settings because it's reasonable to use the default TextBox control settings unless the user overrides them.

When developers use your control, they need to be able to pass the filename of an XML file to display, so you must add a property. Add a private string variable named `mXMLFile` and a public property named `XMLFile` to the code-behind class file.

```
// private class level member variable
private String mXMLFile="";

// public property
public String XMLFile {
    get{
        return mXMLFile;
    }
```

```
    set {
        mXMLFile = value;
    }
}
```

When the Web Form runs, you want the control to open the XML file, read it, and format it as a string that you can place into the TextBox. The `getPrettyXML` method accepts an XML filename and returns the formatted string containing the document formatted with indented elements—much as you'd see the document if you loaded it into IE:

```
public String getPrettyXML(String aFilename ) {
    if (aFilename != null) {
        FileInfo aFile = new FileInfo(aFilename);
        if (aFile.Exists) {
            StringBuilder sb = new StringBuilder((int)
                aFile.Length * 2);
            XmlDocument doc = new XmlDocument();
            const int indent = 3;
            doc.Load(XMLFile);
            XmlTextWriter writer = new XmlTextWriter
                (new StringWriter(sb));
            writer.Formatting = Formatting.Indented;
            writer.Indentation=indent;
            doc.WriteContentTo(writer);
            return sb.ToString();
        }
        else {
            return null;
        }
    }
    else {
        return null;
    }
}
```

The preceding code snippet creates a StringBuilder to hold the formatted XML, creates a DOM-Document, loads the file, and then creates an `XmlTextWriter` object named `writer` that formats and writes the content. The last three lines do all the work. The first tells the `XmlTextWriter` to create indented XML output:

```
writer.Formatting = Formatting.Indented;
```

Next, the code uses a Microsoft-specific DOM extension called `WriteContentTo` that writes the XML content of an XmlDocument to an XmlTextWriter:

```
doc.WriteContentTo(writer);
```

Finally, because the `XmlTextWriter` object writes the content to a StringBuilder (the variable `sb`), the method just returns the StringBuilder's text contents:

```
return sb.ToString();
```

TIP   *This code illustrates a very convenient trick, because it's not as easy as you might think to format and indent an XML file with custom code.*

Finally, you should override the Render method to call the getPrettyXML routine and fill the TextBox with the results. In addition, you want to "pick up" any style attributes that the control user set in the ASPX file and apply them to the TextBox control. By adding the style attributes at render time, you give the control user the capability to set the look and position of your control. When you override a control method, you should normally call the base method as well.

```
protected override void Render(System.Web.UI.HtmlTextWriter
   writer)
{
   String aValue;
   if (this.XMLFile != null) {
      txtXML.Text = getPrettyXML(XMLFile);
      // allow style attributes override
      if (this.Attributes.CssStyle != null) {
         foreach(string key in this.Attributes.CssStyle.Keys) {
            aValue = this.Attributes.CssStyle[key];
            txtXML.Attributes.CssStyle.Add(key, aValue);
         }
      }
   }
   base.Render(writer);
}
```

The last line calls base.Render, passing the HtmlTextWriter object received by the Render event. That's a specific decision. I decided that the TextBox control should render even if the control user doesn't set the XMLFile property, which gives the user a visual clue (because the control renders an empty TextBox) that the XMLFile property is missing. However, it's equally valid to decide that the control shouldn't render anything. You can accomplish that by moving the base.Render method call inside the first if block, as in the following altered version:

```
protected override void Render(System.Web.UI.HtmlTextWriter
   writer)
{
   String aValue;
   if (this.XMLFile != null) {
      txtXML.Text = getPrettyXML(XMLFile);
      // allow style attributes override
      if (this.Attributes.CssStyle != null) {
         foreach(string key in this.Attributes.CssStyle.Keys) {
            aValue = this.Attributes.CssStyle[key];
            txtXML.Attributes.CssStyle.Add(key, aValue);
         }
      }
      base.Render(writer);
   }
}
```

Now you need to create a Web Form to test the control. Create a new Web Form named `ch23-2`
`.aspx`, change the default form `id` attribute to `Form1`, and drag the `prettyXML.ascx` item from the
Server Explorer to the design surface. It should look like Figure 23.2.

FIGURE 23.2

Web Form designer
surface with
`prettyXML.ascx`
User control

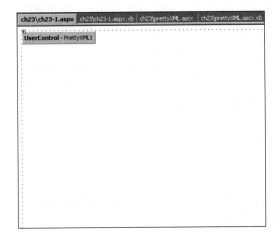

Note that you can't drag a User control and place it where you want, and the representation of the
User control in the Web Form doesn't *look* like the control you just built. That's a User control limitation. Don't worry about the look of the control in the designer. Click the User control and then look
at the Properties box. You won't see the `XMLFile` property for the User control either, despite the fact
that the property is public—that's another limitation. Rather than setting properties in the property
browser and defining the look and position of the User control in the designer, you must work directly
with the HTML. Change the designer to HTML mode. The HTML for the completed Web Form
looks like Listing 23.2.

NOTE   *Be sure to correct the hard-coded path in Listing 23.2 if it doesn't match that required for your server.*

**LISTING 23.2: HTML CODE FOR THE `ch23-2.aspx` WEB FORM THAT DISPLAYS THE `prettyXML`
USER CONTROL (`ch23-2.aspx`)**

```
<%@ Page language="c#" Codebehind="ch23-2.aspx.cs"
    AutoEventWireup="false" Inherits="CSharpASP.ch23.ch23_2" %>
<%@ Register TagPrefix="ucl" TagName="prettyXML"
    Src="prettyXML.ascx" %>
<!DOCTYPE HTML PUBLIC "-//W3C//DTD HTML 4.0 Transitional//EN" >
<HTML>
    <HEAD>
        <title>ch23-2</title>
```

```
        <meta name="GENERATOR" Content="Microsoft Visual Studio 7.0">
        <meta name="CODE_LANGUAGE" Content="C#">
        <meta name="vs_defaultClientScript" content="JavaScript">
        <meta name="vs_targetSchema"
          content="http://schemas.microsoft.com/intellisense/ie5">
    </HEAD>
    <body MS_POSITIONING="GridLayout">
        <form id="Form1" method="post" runat="server">
          <ucl:prettyXML id="PrettyXML1" runat="server"

XMLFile="c:\inetpub\wwwroot\CSharpASP\ch23\people.xml">
          </ucl:prettyXML>
        </form>
    </body>
</HTML>
```

The highlighted lines define, insert, and format the prettyXML User control. The first highlighted line defines the tag and code location for the control:

```
<%@ Register TagPrefix="ucl" TagName="prettyXML"
    Src="prettyXML.ascx" %>
```

The @ Register directive defines the XML tag (ucl:prettyXML). TagPrefix controls the portion of the tag before the colon; TagName controls the portion of the tag after the colon. The names you see here are the default names (ucl stands for User control 1) inserted by VS when you drop a User control onto a Web Form, but you are free to change them to anything you like. Similarly, the Src attribute, in this case, contains only a filename because the control is in the same project folder as the Web Form, but the Src attribute accepts a relative URL for any location *in the same project.*

TIP *User controls must be in the same project as the Web Form that references them. If you want to reuse a User control, copy it into your current project.*

When you run the Web Form, you'll see a small multiline text (a <textarea>) control containing the people.xml file contents. That doesn't look very nice. Try making the control bigger by creating a style attribute for the <ucl:prettyXML> tag. For example, change the tag so it looks like this:

```
<ucl:prettyXML id="PrettyXML1" runat="server"
    XMLFile="c:\inetpub\wwwroot\CSharpASP\ch23\people.xml"
    style="position: absolute; left: 50: top: 50;
    width: 500; height: 500;">
</ucl:prettyXML>
```

The highlighted code shows the added style attribute. Save the changes and request the Web Form again from your browser. This time, the generated <textarea> tag is large enough for you to see the XML contents clearly. Note that the contents are read-only as defined in the User control itself. In addition, the control doesn't maintain ViewState because the `EnableViewState` attribute in the `prettyXML.ascx` file is set to `false`.

Loading User Controls at Runtime

You don't have to site User controls on a Web Form at design time; you can load them dynamically. For example, suppose you wanted to load one of two User controls based on a user's identity. You *could* put them both on the Web Form and then hide one with client-side script, but that wouldn't be particularly efficient. A better way is to load the appropriate control using program logic. The `Page` `.LoadControl` method accepts a filename and returns a `UserControl` object or a `PartialCaching-Control` object (more about that later). For example, the following code shows how to load an instance of the `prettyXML.ascx` control, set its properties and display characteristics from code-behind code, and add the control to the default `<form>` tag's child controls. The code in Listing 23.3 is equivalent (other than the control size) to the preceding example, where you created the User control instance in the HTML file.

LISTING 23.3: LOADING A USER CONTROL DYNAMICALLY (ch23-3.aspx.cs)

```
private void Page_Load(object sender, System.EventArgs e)
{
    prettyXML ctl = (prettyXML) this.LoadControl("prettyXML.ascx");
    ctl.XMLFile = @"c:\inetpub\wwwroot\CSharpASP\ch23\people.xml";
    ctl.Attributes.Add("style","left: 10; top: 10; " +
        "width: 500; height: 500;");
    this.FindControl("Form1").Controls.Add(ctl);
}
```

Remember to cast the generic object returned from the `LoadControl` method to the correct type, add all attributes (even style attributes) for a User control via the `Attributes` collection property, and place the control inside the server-side form tag. To do that, use the `FindControl` method to obtain a reference to the control, and then add the new User control instance to the form's `Controls` collection.

Partial Page Caching and User Controls

Even if you don't need User controls, you should seriously consider creating them for those parts of your pages that don't change often, because they let you cache a portion of a page at the server level. Most site designs have static page portions around the edges and change the center of the page to display page content. For example, navigation bars, headers, and footers are often static or contain only one or two dynamic portions, such as ad tags and counters. However, most sites also created these mostly static portions by using #INCLUDE directives, which referenced files containing the dynamic code for ads and counters. Although IIS did cache these pages in memory, the classic ASP engine still had to run the contained code to create each request for the page.

In contrast, in ASP.NET applications, you can create User controls for the dynamic parts of the page and cache them based on query string or form parameters, custom strings, file dependencies, or duration—in exactly the same way that you saw in Chapter 17, "State Maintenance and Cacheing." To cache a User control, add an `OutputCache` directive to the page:

```
<%@ OutputCache Duration="20" VaryByParam="None" %>
```

This directive caches the User control for 20 seconds.

TIP   *You can speed up pages and reduce server load dramatically by implementing partial page caching in the form of User controls.*

Build a Composite Control

User controls are sufficient for building simple UI collections of controls, but they have several limitations that make them unsuitable for commercial products, for repeated use in multiple projects, and for handing off to HTML authors.

◆ User controls must reside in the same project as the Web Forms that use them. That's a serious limitation because it means you can't create a single User control and then reference it in projects; instead, you must have multiple copies of the User control files—one for each project where you want to use it.

◆ User control properties don't appear in the property browser; the control users must know what they are in advance and write them into the HTML tag manually or set them via code. That's OK for controls you build for your own use, but it isn't suitable for controls you build for others.

◆ User controls in design mode don't look like they do at runtime; therefore, from a designer's viewpoint, they can be difficult to align, size, and control.

Instead, ASP.NET supports two other types of custom controls, termed Composite controls and (confusingly) Custom Server controls. These types of controls are exactly the same as the ASP.NET intrinsic Web Server controls, except that you must define them yourself, in code.

A Composite control, unlike a User control, compiles to an assembly and has design-time support for letting control users set properties in the Properties window and move and size the control at design time. A Composite control combines controls by creating the child controls programmatically. To the control user, a Composite control, like a User control, is a single entity. The user of a Composite control adds one item to a Web Form, but that single action may create any number of controls contained *inside* the Composite control. The user may or may not have direct access to the control properties; as the control author, you can decide. The ASP.NET framework contains several examples; the data-bound controls such as Repeater, DataList, and DataGrid are Composite controls that contain child controls.

One common task when building input forms of almost any kind is the addition of paired Label and TextBox controls (see Figure 23.3). You can create the Label and the TextBox as a single composite control.

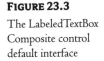

FIGURE 23.3

The LabeledTextBox Composite control default interface

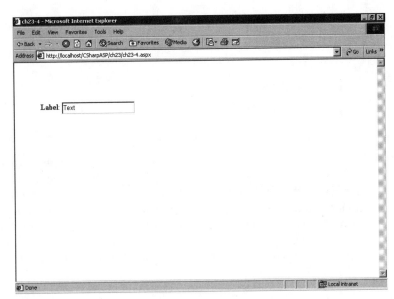

In this section, you'll build a Composite control named `LabeledTextBox`. A Composite control consists of a single class in which you must do the following:

◆ Inherit the Control or WebControl class

◆ Override the `CreateChildControls` method

◆ Implement the INamingContainer interface

◆ Optionally, override the `Render` method

The base Control or WebControl class handles events such as rendering ASP.NET or HTML controls, manages ViewState for the child controls, and supports ASP.NET events. The `CreateChild-Controls` method fires when the framework signals the control to create its child controls. The method fires only once for any instance of the control.

The INamingContainer interface tells the framework to create a new naming scope, ensuring that the child controls within the naming scope have unique names. In other words, if there is already a ListBox on the Web Form, the framework encounters your control and changes the naming scope. Then when you add the child ListBoxes, the new name scope ensures that they aren't named `ListBox1` and `ListBox2`, which would otherwise be the default names.

You can build the Composite control in your Web application project namespace, but it's usually best to create generic controls in a separate namespace because you may need them again, and it's much easier to reference and load them if they're in a separate control collection namespace. Therefore, you'll build the `LabeledTextBox` control in the CSharpASPCustom project you created in the preceding section of this book.

To begin building the control, load the CSharpASPCustom project and add a new class to the project. Add `using` statements to include these namespaces:

- System
- System.Web
- System.Web.UI
- System.Web.UI.WebControls

Create the class name—this is the name that will appear in the Toolbox for control consumers. In this case, name the class `LabeledTextBox`. You can inherit from either the System.Web.UI.Control or the System.Web.UI.WebControls.WebControl base classes. To choose, consider how much support your control needs at design time. If you're building a visible control, you might want to expose UI properties such as `Width`, `Height`, and `Font`. In that case, inherit from WebControl; otherwise, just inherit from the Control class. Implement the INamingContainer interface. Because the LabeledTextBox control is a visible control that designers should be able to size and place on the page, it inherits from the WebControl class.

The code for the LabeledTextBox control resides in the CSharpASPCustom project.

```
using System;
using System.Web;
using System.Web.UI;
using System.Web.UI.WebControls;
namespace CSharpASPCustom
{
    public class LabeledTextBox :
        System.Web.UI.WebControls.WebControl, INamingContainer
    {
        // more code here
    }
}
```

Although you don't have to predefine variables for the child controls, it's convenient and prevents you from having to refer to them later using an index into your control's child controls. In this project, there are three controls: two Labels and one TextBox:

```
private System.Web.UI.WebControls.Label lbl = null;
private System.Web.UI.WebControls.Label lblSpacer = null;
private System.Web.UI.WebControls.TextBox tx = null;
```

The `lbl` control displays the label text for the control. The `lblSpacer` control acts as a spacer between the Label containing the text and the TextBox. The TextBox lets users input data.

You override the `CreateChildControls` method to create the controls:

```
protected override void CreateChildControls() {
    lblSpacer = new Label();
    lblSpacer.Height = Unit.Pixel(25);
    lbl = new Label();
```

```
    lbl.Height = Unit.Pixel(25);
    tx = new TextBox();
    tx.Height = Unit.Pixel(25);
    Controls.Add(lbl);
    lblSpacer.Text = "";
    Controls.Add(lblSpacer);
    Controls.Add(tx);
}
```

You can expose custom properties by adding public properties to your control. Public control properties appear in the Properties window by default. For example, the LabeledTextBox class exposes five public properties. Their names are self-explanatory: Text, LabelText, LabelWidth, TextWidth, and SpaceBetweenControls. The call to the EnsureChildControls method in each property setting ensures that the child controls exist—if you forget this call, you'll get an error stating that the control doesn't exist when it tries to site itself.

```
public String Text {
    get {
        EnsureChildControls();
        return tx.Text;
    }
    set {
        EnsureChildControls();
        tx.Text = value;
    }
}
public String LabelText {
    get {
        EnsureChildControls();
        return lbl.Text;
    }
    set {
        EnsureChildControls();
        lbl.Text = value;
    }
}
public Unit TextBoxWidth {
    get {
        EnsureChildControls();
        return tx.Width;
    }
    set {
        EnsureChildControls();
        tx.Width = value;
    }
}
public Unit LabelWidth {
    get {
```

```
            EnsureChildControls();
            return lbl.Width;
        }
        set {
            EnsureChildControls();
            lbl.Width = value;
        }
    }
    public Unit SpaceBetweenControls {
        get {
            EnsureChildControls();
            return lblSpacer.Width;
        }
        set {
            EnsureChildControls();
            lblSpacer.Width = value;
        }
    }
}
```

Exposing the LabelWidth, TextBoxWidth, and SpaceBetweenControls properties as the type System .Unit lets users enter any of several specific unit types for that property. The ASP.NET engine translates the string representation to the appropriate value. For example, 30px, 1in, and 10pt are all valid Unit measurements. Because the control inherits from System.Web.UI.WebControls.WebControl, it also inherits several public properties such as Width, Height, Font, BackColor, ForeColor, BorderStyle, and a few others. Listing 23.4 shows the full code.

LISTING 23.4: THE LABELEDTEXTBOX COMPOSITE CONTROL CODE
   (CSharpASPCustom.LabeledTextBox.cs)

```
using System;
using System.Web;
using System.Web.UI;
using System.Web.UI.WebControls;

namespace CSharpASPCustom
{
    [ToolboxData("<{0}:LabeledTextBox runat='server'
        style='position:absolute; width:300px; height: 30px'
        Text='Text' LabelText='<b>Label</b>:'
        SpaceBetweenControls='5px'/>")]
    public class LabeledTextBox :
        System.Web.UI.WebControls.WebControl, INamingContainer
    {
        private System.Web.UI.WebControls.Label lbl = null;
        private System.Web.UI.WebControls.Label lblSpacer = null;
        private System.Web.UI.WebControls.TextBox tx = null;
        public LabeledTextBox() {
```

```
    }
    public String Text {
       get {
          EnsureChildControls();
          return tx.Text;
       }
       set {
          EnsureChildControls();
          tx.Text = value;
       }
    }
    public String LabelText {
       get {
          EnsureChildControls();
          return lbl.Text;
       }
       set {
          EnsureChildControls();
          lbl.Text = value;
       }
    }
    public Unit TextBoxWidth {
       get {
             EnsureChildControls();
             return tx.Width;
          }
       set {
             EnsureChildControls();
             tx.Width = value;
          }
    }
    public Unit LabelWidth {
       get {
          EnsureChildControls();
          return lbl.Width;
       }
       set {
          EnsureChildControls();
          lbl.Width = value;
       }
    }
    public Unit SpaceBetweenControls {
       get {
          EnsureChildControls();
          return lblSpacer.Width;
       }
```

```
                set {
                    EnsureChildControls();
                    lblSpacer.Width = value;
                }
            }
            protected override void CreateChildControls() {
                tx = new TextBox();
                lbl = new Label();
                lblSpacer = new Label();
                lbl.Height = Unit.Pixel(25);
                lbl.Text = "Label";
                tx.Height = Unit.Pixel(25);
                tx.Width = Unit.Pixel(200);
                tx.Text = "Text";
                Controls.Add(lbl);
                lblSpacer.Text = "";
                Controls.Add(lblSpacer);
                Controls.Add(tx);
            }
        }
    }
```

The full code listing contains one item I haven't yet explained—the ToolboxData attribute.

```
[ToolboxData("<{0}:LabeledTextBox runat='server'
    style='position:absolute; width:300px; height: 30px'
    Text='Text' LabelText='<b>Label</b>:'
    SpaceBetweenControls='5px'/>")]
```

By default, when you drag and drop a control from the Toolbox to the design surface, VS.NET inserts a "blank" tag—in other words, the default control tag won't have the properties you might want. You'll find that even setting the properties in code won't help because those properties won't appear in the designer, but the properties you set in the ToolboxData attribute will appear. The value of the ToolboxData attribute is the full tag that you want the control to have. VS.NET replaces the {0} placeholder at the front of the tag with the tag prefix for the control class. The ToolboxData attribute for the LabeledTextBox control sets every custom property to a default value. Build the control and save it. Be sure to compile the project before attempting to add an instance of the control to the project.

Customize the Toolbox

One of the advantages of Composite and Custom controls is that you can add them to the Toolbox, where they then act just like any other ASP.NET Server control. To add the controls, right-click the Toolbox and select the Customize Toolbox item. Note that you can add both COM components and components that reside within .NET assemblies to the Toolbox (see Figure 23.4).

FIGURE 23.4

The Customize
Toolbox dialog

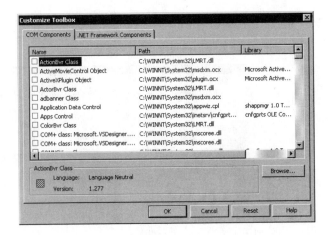

Click the .NET Framework Components tab. You won't find custom assemblies in the list. Click the Browse button, find the `CSharpASPCustom` folder (if you don't know where the project resides, you can find it in the Project Properties dialog), navigate to the `bin` subfolder, and select the compiled `CSharpASPCustom.dll` file.

Selecting the file adds all the public classes in the file to the .NET Framework Components tab. Find the LabeledTextBox item and make sure it's checked, and then click OK to close the dialog.

NOTE *If you have multiple public classes in an assembly, VS adds them all to the list visible from the .NET Framework Components tab in the Customize Toolbox dialog.*

Any components you add to the Toolbox appear at the bottom of the Toolbox. You may have to scroll down to see your added item(s).

How to Add a Custom Toolbox Bitmap for Your Control

By default, VS.NET uses a "gear" bitmap for your custom controls. You can assign a specific bitmap using the `ToolboxBitmap` attribute. The bitmap should be 16×16 pixels in size. You need to add a `using System.Drawing` statement to the top of your class to use the attribute. The attribute has an overloaded constructor that can load an image from a file or from a resource in the same or a different assembly. Add the `ToolboxBitmap` attribute above the class declaration.

Test the LabeledTextBox Composite Control

Add a Web Form named `ch23-4.aspx` to test the LabeledTextBox Composite control. Change the default form tag ID to `Form1`. Find the LabeledTextBox component in the Toolbox and drag it onto the design surface. VS adds a new instance of the control to the designer. You should immediately see that it's much easier to work with Composite controls than with User controls. Click the added LabeledTextBox item and look at the Properties window. You will find the control's properties (`Text`, `LabelText`, `LabelWidth`, `TextBoxWidth`, and `SpaceBetweenControls`) under the `Misc.` category (sort the Properties window entries by category using the leftmost button on the Properties window toolbar to see this).

For example, if you set the control's BackColor, BorderStyle, and BorderWidth properties and add some LabelText and Text values, the control might look similar to Figure 23.5.

FIGURE 23.5

LabeledTextBox Composite control with custom property settings

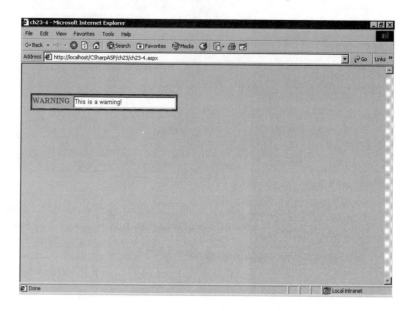

NOTE   *The control's properties change at design time, just like any other ASP.NET Server control.*

Build a Custom Server Control

In this section, you'll build a basic control called DateTable and see how you can use it in multiple projects. The difference between a Custom Server control and a Composite control is that with a Custom Server control, you handle drawing the interface yourself by overriding the Render method rather than creating controls during the CreateChildControls method. The control displays a date within a table tag. You can control all the UI features—colors, the border, font characteristics, and the date itself from the Web Form that hosts the control.

Create the DateTable Custom Control

The DateTable Custom control displays a date of your choice in an HTML table cell. By default, the control looks like Figure 23.6 in the designer. I took this screenshot after double-clicking in the Tool-Box to add the control without sizing it or setting any properties.

Not too exciting, is it? But it's a powerful concept. Even with this plain example, you can immediately see that a major difference between a Custom control and a User control is that you can provide a customizable design-time user interface for a Custom control, but you can't for a User control. The control displays the current date by default. For this example, the control *always* displays the date in LongDateTime format—that's easy enough to change if you want to extend the control.

FIGURE 23.6

DateTable Custom
control default UI
characteristics

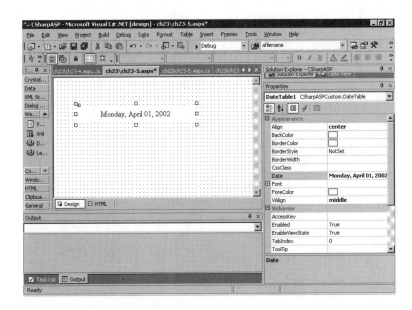

Next, here's the Properties window for the DateTable control (see Figure 23.7).

FIGURE 23.7

DateTable Custom
Control Properties
window

The default property for the control is called Date, and it has a default date value (the current date) as soon as you add the control. Custom controls inherit a reasonable set of properties from the System.Web.UI.WebControl class—most of the properties shown are inherited. You control which properties you want to display in the Properties window via Property attributes.

Because the control supports design-time properties, by setting those properties, you can radically alter the look of the control (see Figure 23.8).

FIGURE 23.8

DateTable Custom
control after
setting design-time
properties

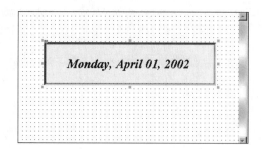

Despite the fact that Custom controls inherit some default design-time features, such as BackColor, BorderColor, BorderWidth, Font, CssClass, and so forth, you do have to write some other common properties. Listing 23.5 shows the code for the DateTable class.

LISTING 23.5: CODE FOR THE DATETABLE CUSTOM CONTROL (CSharpASPCustom.DateTable.cs)

```csharp
using System;
using System.Web.UI;
using System.Web.UI.HtmlControls;
using System.ComponentModel;
using System.Drawing;

namespace CSharpASPCustom
{
   /// <summary>
   /// Summary description for DateTable.
   /// </summary>
   public enum TextAlign {
      left = 1,
      right = 2,
      center = 3,
      justify = 4
   }
   public enum TextVAlign {
      top = 1,
      middle = 2,
      bottom = 3,
      baseline = 4,
      subscript = 5,
      superscript = 6,
      text_top = 7,
      text_bottom = 8
   }

   [ Description("Exposes a Date in an HTML Table tag")]
   [ DefaultProperty("Date"), ToolboxData("<{0}:DateTable " +
```

```
      "runat=server style='position: absolute; width:300: " +
      "height: 100;' />")]
public class DateTable : System.Web.UI.WebControls.WebControl,
    INamingContainer {
    private DateTime mDate = new DateTime();
    private String mNow = DateTime.Now.ToLongDateString();
    private TextAlign mAlign = TextAlign.center;
    private TextVAlign mVAlign = TextVAlign.middle;

    [Bindable(true), Category("Appearance"),
        DefaultValue("Monday, January 1, 0001")]
    public String Date {
        get {
            if (mDate.Year == 1) {
                return DateTime.Now.ToLongDateString();
            }
            else {
                return mDate.ToLongDateString();
            }
        }
        set {
            mDate = DateTime.Parse(value);
        }
    }
    [Bindable(true), Category("Appearance"),
DefaultValue("center")]


    public TextAlign Align {
        get {
            return mAlign;
        }
        set {
            mAlign = value;
        }
    }


    private String AlignText {
        get {
            return TextAlign.GetName(mAlign.GetType(), mAlign);
        }
    }


    [Bindable(true), Category("Appearance"),
DefaultValue("middle")]
    public TextVAlign VAlign {
```

```
        get {
            return mVAlign;
        }
        set {
            mVAlign = value;
        }
    }


    private String VAlignText {
        get {
            if (mVAlign == TextVAlign.subscript) {
                return "sub";
            }
            else if (mVAlign == TextVAlign.superscript) {
                return "super";
            }
            else {
                return TextVAlign.GetName(mVAlign.GetType(),
mVAlign);
            }

        }
    }


    protected override void Render
        (System.Web.UI.HtmlTextWriter output) {
        HtmlTable tbl = new HtmlTable();
        HtmlTableRow row = new HtmlTableRow();
        HtmlTableCell cell = new HtmlTableCell();
        String aValue;
        tbl.Style.Add(" color",

System.Drawing.ColorTranslator.ToHtml(this.ForeColor));
        tbl.Style.Add(" background-color",

System.Drawing.ColorTranslator.ToHtml(this.BackColor));
        tbl.Style.Add(" border-color",

System.Drawing.ColorTranslator.ToHtml(this.BorderColor));
        tbl.Style.Add(" border-style",
this.BorderStyle.ToString());
        tbl.Style.Add(" border-width",
this.BorderWidth.ToString());
        tbl.Style.Add(" width", this.Width.ToString());
        tbl.Style.Add(" height", this.Height.ToString());
        tbl.Style.Add(" text-align", this.AlignText);
```

```
cell.Style.Add(" vertical-align", this.VAlignText);
if (this.Font != null) {
    if (this.Font.Names.Length > 0) {
        tbl.Style.Add(" font-family",
            ArrayJoin.Join(this.Font.Names));
    }
    tbl.Style.Add(" font-size",
        this.Font.Size.ToString());
    if (this.Font.Bold) {
        tbl.Style.Add(" font-weight", "bold");
    }
    if (this.Font.Italic)  {
        tbl.Style.Add(" font-style", "italic");
    }
    if (this.Font.Overline)  {
        tbl.Style.Add(" font-decoration", "overline");
    }
    if (this.Font.Strikeout) {
        tbl.Style.Add(" font-decoration", "line-through");
    }
    if (this.Font.Underline) {
        tbl.Style.Add(" font-decoration", "underline");
    }
}
if (this.Attributes.CssStyle != null) {
  foreach (String key in this.Attributes.CssStyle.Keys) {
      aValue = this.Attributes.CssStyle[key];
      tbl.Attributes.CssStyle.Add(" " + key, aValue);
  }
}
cell.InnerText = this.Date;
tbl.Rows.Add(row);
row.Cells.Add(cell);
tbl.RenderControl(output);
        }
    }
}
```

You can see that the class implements only three public properties: Date, Align, and VAlign. It defines text Align and text VAlign enumerations and uses those as the property type values for the private Align and VAlign properties, respectively.

Note that (other than the Property attributes) there's no special code to support design-time properties or any Property Window special code or types; all that is built into the .NET framework. For string properties, all you need to do is make sure the properties you want to expose to the designer are defined as public properties.

TIP *The default designer handles simple types such as strings, but for more complex property types such as arrays of strings or custom property types, you'll need to set the* `Designer` *attribute to the proper type or create a custom designer class or interface—but that's beyond the scope of this book.*

In fact, most of the code is in the overridden `Render` method. The `Render` method creates `HtmlTable`, `HtmlRow`, and `HtmlCell` objects and then assigns style attributes and values based on the properties the user set in the HTML tag in the Web Form, or using the Properties window to render the HTML for the control. After setting up the table, the method writes the table using the `RenderControl` method, passing the HtmlTextWriter received by the overridden `Render` method as the only parameter.

The `RenderControl` method writes an HTML string containing a single-row/single-column HTML `<table>` tag.

MORE ABOUT ATTRIBUTES

Attributes are classes in .NET. Each of the built-in attribute class names ends with the word "Attribute," but in the shorthand version shown, you don't have to include the *Attribute* portion. For example, as shown in Listing 23.5, the class attribute list looks like this:

```
[DefaultProperty("Date"), ToolboxData("<{0}:DateTable " +
    "runat=server style= position: absolute; width:300: " +
    "height: 100;' />")]
```

TIP *To search for an attribute in Help or the Object Browser, remember to append the word "Attribute" to the end of the class name.*

If you used the full attribute class names rather than the default shorthand version, you could write this:

```
[DefaultPropertyAttribute("Date"), ToolboxDataAttribute("<{0}:DateTable " +
    "runat=server style='position: absolute; width:300: " +
    "height: 100;' />")]
```

The `DefaultProperty` attribute declares that the class DateTable has a default property called `Text`. Just as in the LabeledTextBox control code you saw earlier in the chapter, the `ToolboxData` attribute controls the initial tag that the designer places into the Web Form HTML when you drop a control onto the design surface.

NOTE *If you have a VB background, the* `DefaultProperty` *attribute replaces the rather quirky (and well-hidden) method used in classic VB to define a default property for a class. That's true for all classes in .NET, not just classes created as Web controls.*

It's worth noting that attributes aren't required for Custom controls—they're all optional. You can delete all the default attributes without adverse effects.

You can add as many tag attributes as needed to the `ToolboxData` class attribute.

The property attributes affect both design-time and runtime aspects of the control. Design-time properties are those that appear in the Properties window when a user adds your control to a Web Form at design time. Again, the designer uses the shorthand form of the attribute class names by default. Remember that the full names of these attribute classes are `BindableAttribute`, `Category-Attribute` and `DefaultValueAttribute`.

The `Bindable` attribute controls whether you can bind the property to a data value. The `Category` attribute controls in which area or category of the Properties window a property appears. It's not always clear which area you should specify. For example, does the `Date` value belong in the `Appearance` category or the `Data` category? At any rate—you get to choose. Although the built-in categories usually suffice, you can create custom categories if necessary.

The `DefaultValue` attribute, of course, is the default value of the control. That property accepts only hard-coded values. For example, you can't call a function to set a derived value as the default control value using a property attribute. In other words, this `DefaultValue` attribute is acceptable:

```
[DefaultValue("This is some text")]
// property declaration here
```

In contrast, the following version is not acceptable and will not compile:

```
[DefaultValue(getDefaultValue())]
// property declaration here


private String getDefaultValue() {
    return "This is some text";
}
```

Despite that, you can work around it by creating an "impossible" default value and then handling that condition explicitly in code. For example, the default `Date` property specifies a date of `"Monday, January 1, 0001"`.

```
[Bindable(true), Category("Appearance"),
DefaultValue("Monday, January 1, 0001")]
public String Date {
    // implementation here
}
```

However, as you can see in the figures, the default date that *appears* in the control is the current date. This is the workaround for not being able to specify a `DefaultValue` and run the `DateTime.Now.ToLongDateString` method. The `Date` property implementation explicitly checks for the condition `Year == 1`. When that evaluates to `true`, the property returns the current date. It's true that that means users wouldn't be able to use the control to set an explicit date in the year 0001—but that's an acceptable risk.

```
public String Date {
    get {
        if (mDate.Year == 1) {
            return DateTime.Now.ToLongDateString();
        }
        else {
            return mDate.ToLongDateString();
        }
    }
```

```
set {
    mDate = DateTime.Parse(value);
}
}
```

Although you won't see any more information about attributes in this book, attributes are an extremely powerful concept. .NET contains a large number of predefined attribute classes, which you should explore thoroughly. If the built-in attribute classes don't meet your needs, you can define your own custom attribute classes. Attributes aren't limited to classes and properties; you can apply attributes to assemblies, constructors, delegates, enums, events, fields, interfaces, parameters, return values, and structs.

There are several interesting features related to using the control in the designer. First, look at the Web Form ch23-5.aspx in the VS designer. The Web Form has a single DateTable control. Try selecting the DateTable control and then entering an invalid date for the **Date** property. You'll see an error message, but it doesn't stop the program. The error message (see Figure 23.9) is automatic—you get property value type-checking and conversion for free.

FIGURE 23.9

Automatic property error dialog appears after an invalid date is set.

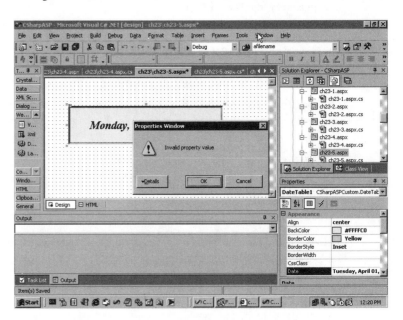

Another interesting feature is that the Properties window seamlessly accommodates the enumeration types. Click the **Align** or **VAlign** property, and you get a list of values corresponding to the appropriate enumeration names. Again, this feature is free—you don't have to add special code to make it work.

In the **Render** method, you access properties set by the control user by retrieving them from the class itself, using the **this** keyword. The .NET framework helps a great deal by being able to transform color selections to their HTML equivalents using the ColorTranslator class's static **ToHtml** method. The

ColorTranslator changes the colors either to common color names, such as red, or to the HTML color representation, such as #C0C0C0.

```
tbl.Style.Add(" color", _
    System.Drawing.ColorTranslator.ToHtml(this.ForeColor))
```

Because the font-family CSS attribute can accept a list of font names, the Properties window lets you enter more than one font name. If a client browser can't display the first font in the list, it tries subsequent font names in sequence until it finds one it can use. If none of the named fonts are available, the browser displays the control's text content in the browser's default font. The font names the control user enters appear as a Font property called Names, which returns an array of string objects. You need to turn that array into a comma-delimited string. In classic ASP, using VBScript, you could use the Join method to accomplish that. In .NET, the Array class doesn't have a Join method, but you can write a small helper class to iterate through the array and accomplish the task:

```
If Me.Font.Names.Length > 0 Then
    tbl.Style.Add(" font-family", _
        ArrayJoin.Join(Me.Font.Names))
End If
```

The ArrayJoin class (in the CSharpASPCustom project) accepts an array and returns a comma-delimited string object containing a string representation (using the ToString() method inherited from Object) of each element in the array (see Listing 23.6).

LISTING 23.6: CODE FOR THE ARRAYJOIN HELPER CLASS (CSharpASPCustom.ArrayJoin.cs)

```csharp
using System;
using System.Text;
using System.Collections;

namespace CSharpASPCustom
{
    public class ArrayJoin
    {
        public ArrayJoin()
        {
        }

        public static String Join(Array arr) {
            StringBuilder sb = new StringBuilder(arr.Length *
                (arr.GetValue(0).ToString().Length + 1));
            for (int i = 0; i < arr.Length; i++) {
                if (i < arr.Length - 1) {
                    sb.Append(arr.GetValue(i).ToString() + ",");
                }
                else {
                    sb.Append(arr.GetValue(i).ToString());
                }
```

```
        }
        return sb.ToString();
      }
    }
  }
```

Transferring Data Between ASP.NET Web Forms and Components

One of the more commonly asked questions about ASP.NET is how to transfer or share data between an ASP.NET Web Form and other components, such as Custom controls and Web Services. The simplest answer is to set parameters for the methods you want to call that accept the data you need to share. For example, to set the text of a Custom control to the value of a TextBox entered by the user, you would post the Web Form from the browser and then, on the server, create or reference the Custom control instance and call the method you want to set.

If passing the data around between multiple objects becomes too onerous, you can cache the data at Session or Application scope. You can also create custom classes to hold the data and cache them at Session or Application scope, which often makes using the data much easier than using raw scalar values stored in Session or Application variables.

As you've seen, any component activated during the process of running a Web Form or Web Service has access to the user's context, via the `System.Web.HttpContext.Current` property. In turn, the `Current` context exposes the `Response`, `Request`, `Server`, and other objects, the same objects that you have available through the Web Form itself, so you can access `Request` data or values stored in Application or Session variables from *any* .NET component you create—not just ASP.NET specific classes, such as the Custom control, but any .NET class.

Summary

In this chapter, you've seen how to create several types of custom controls. This capability is particularly important for ASP.NET applications because you can use the controls to cache data and HTML, which can improve the efficiency and scalability of your applications. In the last chapter of this book, I'll discuss scalability and efficiency in more detail and give you some thoughts about how you can speed up your applications and make them easier to maintain.

Chapter 24

Efficiency and Scalability

As you write more ASP.NET applications, or write them for larger audiences, you'll find that most of the material covered in this book will become second nature. However, this topic will remain fresh because you'll always have to make trade-offs between efficiency and scalability, time, and resources.

The terms "efficiency" and "scalability" themselves need some definition. Efficiency can mean "human efficiency"—for example, reducing development time—or it can refer to "machine efficiency," as in "it's more efficient to create long strings with the StringBuilder class than by concatenating string objects." I'll discuss both aspects in this chapter.

Scalability can refer to "scaling up" by improving throughput speed via hardware, architectural, or program changes and also to "scaling out" by adding additional servers. Again, both types of scalability have relevance, depending on your application's requirements, your hardware setup, and your ability to change either or both. For example, it does you little good to plan and build an application for a Web farm situation if you know in advance that the application will never run in that environment. However, if you plan to expand the application to multiple servers at some point, it's worthwhile making the extra effort to ensure that the application will scale out as seamlessly as possible. Similarly, there's little point in worrying about how efficient your code is if it's running on a stand-alone server and serving a couple of dozen people intermittently (unless, of course, it's so slow as to cause problems for the users). However, if that application suddenly begins serving more people, perhaps through a merger or consolidation, and the server use climbs steadily, you might want to go back and see which parts of the application you can optimize so that you can avoid having to scale the application across multiple servers.

In this chapter:

◆ Always Consider Efficiency

◆ Response Time versus Development Cost

◆ Hardware versus Software

◆ Tips for Efficiency and Scalability

Always Consider Efficiency

Visual Studio and ASP.NET reduce the human cost of developing Web applications. By supporting multiple languages, strong typing, visual design tools, inheritance, managed code, and a good debugger, in addition to having fairly consistent framework syntax, .NET saves designers and programmers time, which is one type of efficiency. But that concept is not in question in this book. The better question is whether the code is efficient. With Web applications, you can answer that question by asking only a few more:

◆ Am I using the framework appropriately?

◆ Am I retrieving appropriate amounts of information to service the request?

◆ Am I caching data appropriately?

◆ Am I maintaining state appropriately?

I can't answer any of these questions for you, but I can give you some things to think about that may help you answer the questions for yourself.

Am I Using the Framework Appropriately?

The ASP.NET framework is extremely easy to learn and use because it hides the complex processes of maintaining page state and generating HTML from developers behind the dual screens of Server controls and ViewState. Unfortunately, both of these have performance penalties.

SERVER CONTROLS AND EFFICIENCY

Suppose you create a ListBox Server control. When the page executes, the ASP.NET framework reads the `<asp:ListBox>` tag, parses the attributes, style information, and enclosed `<asp:ListItem>` tags, and writes HTML to the browser. While that's a very convenient process, it's obviously slower than writing a `<select>` tag in code. *Every* programming process that removes burdens from developers has performance and resource implications. That's not to say that you shouldn't use them, but you *should* be aware that, by using them, you're implicitly accepting the performance penalty that accompanies their use. So the real question becomes whether you are using them *appropriately*.

For most intranet sites, which generally have rather light use (thousands of page hits per day compared to some Internet sites with millions of hits per day), using ASP.NET server tags for basically all tasks is appropriate. It's not a difficult translation process to move from an XML representation of an ASP.NET server tag to an HTML representation of that server tag. However, you can produce fairly dramatic speed improvements by *not* using them in certain situations. Specifically, where pages aren't dynamic, you introduce processing inefficiencies by forcing the translation from the ASP.NET XML tag to the equivalent HTML tag.

With that in mind, you can see why creating User controls for static pages becomes so important, because they let you minimize the translation process and *still* take advantage of the ASP.NET programming model. Using the `VaryByParams` and `VaryByCustom` output caching mechanisms, you can serve that content to many different types of clients and be assured that, for most requests, you're serving the content from cache, which is an order of magnitude faster than creating it anew for each request.

VIEWSTATE AND EFFICIENCY

ViewState (page state management) is a huge timesaver for developers, saving untold thousands of hours of development time and avoiding code errors caused by manually round-tripping values from the client to the server and back. Unfortunately, it also has a cost. First, ViewState is "on" by default for Server controls. (I think it should be "off" by default, but I won't argue the point.) It's unfortunate because ViewState makes it easy to be lazy—to persist ViewState for *every* control on the page. The ASP.NET framework is relatively new, but I've already seen *numerous* instances of programmers creating long lists of values for ListBoxes or creating large DataSets and binding them to DataGrids and then blithely letting the automatic ViewState mechanism encrypt the data and send it to the client (along with the HTML, which *already* contains the list items, so they're sending it twice), even when they don't need to manage page state for the data. Remember that by default, ASP.NET will also have the browser send the data back in the __VIEWSTATE hidden field, so the cost of ignoring the problem is significant—there's a performance penalty due to sending the data twice: a performance penalty for encrypting the data into ViewState; a bandwidth cost for sending more information than is required, in both directions; and an additional performance penalty required to decrypt the View-State information and create the Server controls when the user posts the page back to the server.

Again, I'm not advocating that you turn off ViewState and manage all page state yourself. Instead, for each control, you should evaluate the *appropriateness* of using ViewState. For example, there's a good argument for using ViewState on very short lists, where you have to maintain the user's selection over several posts back and forth to the page. There's also a good argument for using it in editable controls of all types. The argument for using it is much weaker when you don't have to maintain the user's selection, when you won't ever redisplay the page, or when the data size increases. In those cases, it makes much more sense to write and test the few lines of code required to build and maintain the lists. You can cache the HTML required to build the list, eliminating or reducing database lookups. Finally, it makes *no sense at all* to use ViewState for read-only controls. Doing so sends the data three times when you need to send it only once.

I've also talked to a few people who *misunderstood* ViewState; they thought that turning it off meant that they wouldn't be able to determine user-entered values on the server. For example, one person thought that the ViewState data encoded the ListBox values selected by the user and the TextBox entries entered by the user.

ViewState has *nothing* to do with the form data sent by the client. ViewState consists of *static* content. The ASP.NET framework does use ViewState to determine if the state of a control has changed; by looking for posted form data and comparing the form data with the information stored in the __VIEW-STATE hidden form variable, the server can unambiguously know whether the user changed the value of a control. But the changed data itself—the user selections, text entries, and so on, are sent by the browser automatically because of the <form> tag, and you can retrieve them and interact with them manually using the Request.Form collection methods even if you turn off ViewState for every control on the page.

OUTPUT CACHING AND EFFICIENCY

If you've developed ASP pages, you'll recognize that the ASP.NET model produces huge efficiency increases without your having to do *anything* except migrate the code to ASP.NET. Typically, you can serve twice as many pages from the same server. I won't list the reasons why—you can find those in many places. But that's not the only efficiency improvement that the ASP.NET framework has to offer. The best way to improve the efficiency of your pages is to cache data in memory. However, doing that efficiently requires that you take a good hard look at the set of pages you're planning to deliver and begin thinking of them as collections of items rather than as single entities.

For example, ask yourself if the page header is always the same. If not, how many versions are there? That drop-down menu may change according to the user's location in your site, but can you abstract the logic and cache the different versions based on the directory or a query string value? The large dataset that displays orders—do you really have to retrieve it from the database for *every* request? Perhaps you could cache it using a database trigger to notify the cache to refresh the data whenever the underlying data changes. You may be able to cut the number of database lookups by several hundred percent using techniques like these—and that will not only increase the efficiency of your pages but also reduce the load on your database server.

CLIENT-SIDE SCRIPT AND EFFICIENCY

Learn to take advantage of client-side script to improve page efficiency. One of the most common ASP.NET (and for that matter, classic ASP) questions is how to transfer values from the server to the client. With ASP.NET, it isn't quite as clear how to launch client-side script from an event as it is in pure HTML or classic ASP. You can't simply add the `onclick=someFunction()` attribute to the HTML in the ASPX file—ASP.NET generates an error when you do that because the schema for Server controls doesn't include the attribute definitions for client-side script. Therefore, I'll reiterate here. Use the `Attributes` collection of any ASP.NET tag to add a call to a client-side script function. For example, if you have a button, which normally causes a postback to the server, you can call a client-side script first with this code:

```
myButton.Attributes.Add("onclick",
   "someClientSideScriptFunction()");
```

You see, ASP.NET lets you use server-side code to handle client-side events, but that's *not* efficient in many cases. Any time you can write client-side code to handle client-side events, consider doing so. Here are the times when you should *not* always use client-side code to handle client-side events:

♦ When your application delivers data to a wide range of clients, some of which may not be able to run JavaScript. Even then you can take advantage of the `Request.Browser` property (the HttpRequestBrowserCapabilities) class methods to determine whether the browser accepts ECMAScript (remember, that's the equivalent standard name for JavaScript/JScript) and deliver pages accordingly.

♦ When you have to validate values on the server side anyway. Even then, you may find it worthwhile to validate values on the client and then perform one final validation on the server, just in case someone sends you bad data via an HTTP POST or GET request.

♦ When your application delivers data through one or more Web Services. In that case, the client could be a Windows application or Linux application, and those applications (mostly) don't support JavaScript. Therefore, for Web Services applications, you (usually) must write to the lowest common denominator and assume that the client will not support script.

To get server values into client-side script, you can take advantage of the `RegisterClientScript-Block`, `RegisterStartupScript`, `RegisterHiddenField`, and `RegisterArrayDeclaration` methods, all of which let you write client-side script from server-side code. The `RegisterClientScriptBlock` and `RegisterStartupScript` methods let you send entire scripts to the client and place them either immediately after the `__VIEWSTATE` tag (`RegisterClientScriptBlock`) or just before the closing `</form>` tag (`RegisterStartupScript`). The `RegisterHiddenField` method lets you place server-side data in a hidden field that you can access with script on the client. Finally, if you need to build an array of values, don't forget the `RegisterArrayDeclaration` method, which makes it very easy to build client-side arrays.

Although you often can find performance efficiency gains by writing client-side code, clients change very quickly—as does their support for script versions, object models, CSS, XML, and other client-side technologies. Often you can't control client environments as closely as you can control server environments, so in some cases, migrating code to the client may cause long-term maintenance problems. For example, if you rely on extensive client-side code with an all-IE base when you create an application, but later you find that you must extend the application to other client types, you may have problems. Similarly, as the clients change versions, you may find that the weakest link in your application code is the client-side script.

CSS AND EFFICIENCY

You've seen numerous examples in this book that use CSS to define styles for client display. Unlike some of the other efficiency suggestions, there's no significant tradeoff for CSS between development-time and runtime efficiency; CSS is a godsend for making large sites both consistent and easy to change. It does take some time and thought to produce a capable and reusable set of CSS classes for your specific content; however, once done, you often can reuse the same CSS styles across many applications, particularly in intranet situations or where you're building multiple sites with common element types. Even if you change the look of the styles defined by your classes, often you can name them consistently according to function. For example, if you create a set of header, body, program font, footer, and link style classes and train people to use the names consistently, you can completely change the styles defined by the class names, but everything will still work properly.

You must be aware that downlevel browsers don't always understand CSS tags—and don't always implement them consistently across platforms—and that simply checking the browser manufacturer is insufficient; browsers implement CSS styles differently even between different versions of the same browser. You should test thoroughly with all the client types (and versions) that you intend to support.

CSS is efficient at design time because after defining the classes once, you can include them in any Web Form by simply dragging the CSS file onto the Web Form design surface. After that, the styles appear even at design time in VS—all but eliminating the code-browse cycle that, up to now, has been a hallmark of Web page development. Using the class names cuts the number of tags required to define a specific look-and-feel, which saves time and reduces maintenance.

CSS is also efficient at runtime, particularly if you reference styles in an external style sheet, because the browser caches CSS style sheets in the same way it caches other downloaded files, meaning that the browser can retrieve the CSS file from cache rather that having to retrieve the file from the server for each request. In addition, the reduction in file size and number of tags speeds up the process of downloading and parsing the file. Finally, it's considerably faster to apply a preparsed set of attributes to an element via a CSS class reference than it is to parse an unknown number of individual inline style attributes or older style elements and apply those to an element.

DHTML AND EFFICIENCY

Most of the tasks you need to accomplish with script require accessing the Document Object Model (DOM), which gives you the power to manipulate the positions, display characteristics, CSS class and style attributes, and content of any element on the page.

There are many situations where using DHTML is much more efficient than round-tripping to the server. For example, consider the classic multiple-list problem (usually associated with databases), where the user "drills down" into content by selecting an item from one list. The user's selection in the first list causes the content in a second, subordinate list to change. Imagine two lists, one containing states and the other containing cities. When you select a state, the content of the city list changes. When you know that a user needs data for both lists, you can deliver the contents of the second list in a client-side array and use the array data to fill the second list whenever the user changes the selection in the first list.

Obviously, you need to use some common sense when deciding whether that scenario is appropriate for your application. If there are 50 items in the first list, each of which has an average of 10 subordinate items in the second list, then you'll have to download about 500 items to manage the display of the second list entirely on the client. In contrast, if each of the items in the first list has 100 subordinate items, you'll need to download 5,000 items, which may be an onerous burden. Nevertheless, you may be able to download the items in blocks, using a combination of a Web Service on the server and DHTML scripting on the client to make the data appear without redrawing the page.

You've seen how client-side script and DHTML can help improve the responsiveness of a UI by validating data on the client (for example, with ASP.NET's built-in validation control scripts). In some cases, it's simply not possible to validate data fast enough on the server. For example, if you want to limit the characters that a user can enter in a TextBox, you must check the entries when the user presses the key—*before* the character actually appears. The process must be nearly instantaneous to be effective; there's no time to send the current TextBox contents to the server, process the information, and return a result.

Using DHTML in conjunction with remote scripting or the `XMLHttpRequest` object lets you query the server for data without refreshing the entire browser page. The example for the Web Services Mortgage Payment Calculator browser client in Chapter 21, "Web Services," used that technique.

DHTML lets you add complex UI elements that aren't directly available through HTML. One common example is the *rollover button*, where the browser changes an image or changes the style settings for one or more elements on the page as the user moves the mouse cursor into and out of some element's on-screen rectangle. You can find many useful rollover button scripts on the Web by searching for the term "rollover button JavaScript" in any good search engine.

XML/XSLT AND EFFICIENCY

XML is not a particularly efficient way to *store* information, but in conjunction with XSLT it can be an extremely efficient way to *format* that information. For example, it's faster to transform a database result set stored in XML into HTML with a compiled and cached XSLT template than it is to create the same output by writing loops to concatenate a string containing the HTML tags. When you combine the capability to perform cached transforms with the capability (for IE clients) to offload the transform onto the client using data islands (so far, available with IE clients only), XML/XSLT becomes an extremely efficient way to deliver and format information because your server needs only to serve the files rather than performing complex transformations.

Response Time versus Development Cost

There's almost always a way to increase efficiency. As a long-time developer, I've learned that very few programmers write the most efficient code the first time. As a manager, I've learned that finishing the project is often much more important than writing elegant code. Finally, as an admitted programming addict, I've realized that you can approach a problem from many different viewpoints—and you're likely to get very different results. While this is easy to say and may seem obvious to you, I don't think it's at all obvious when you're actually programming a project. Getting something to work correctly can be a horrendous battle because your initially clean code inevitably becomes cluttered with exceptions, error-trapping code, code to handle the quirks of multiple operating systems, code for multiple languages, different resolutions, color depths, folder preferences, user preferences, missing files, upgrade checks, advertisements, browser version alternatives, and so on. Over time, you may find that all the added code has changed your fast, clean Web pages into an unusable and unmaintainable morass and increased the download time to the point that you may be losing customers. From a business point of view, you don't want to spend money and time on optimization until it becomes apparent that you're reaching this point, but you *must* optimize before you actually reach it.

When you begin an optimization process, try to find out exactly where your efforts will do the most good. Although the exact problems will differ between applications, here are some good places to start.

HTML

Check your HTML files, especially older templates that you may have "inherited" from classic ASP projects or that were originally developed as pure HTML and later integrated into your application. I can recommend HTML Tidy, a free program you can find by searching the Web. Make sure that the files are XHTML compatible; close all the tags, change them to lowercase, and quote all attributes. Get rid of obsolete `<font>` `<kbd>` and other deprecated tags by changing them to CSS class references, combined if necessary with inline styles. Note that doing this will not speed up your program on the server side, but it can improve rendering time and help prepare your files for use with XSLT style sheets, which you can use to offload processing to the client, reduce the load on your server, and simplify further maintenance and changes.

Database Access

Many older client-server programs, when converted to Web applications, still used individual database connections, with a distinct username and password for each person. But typically, an application needs only a few levels of access; for example, administrative, supervisor, and user access levels are common distinctions. By creating one account for each permission level and mapping users to one of those accounts when they access the application, you can reduce the number of connections required and greatly improve the efficiency of connection pooling.

Make sure that each database access retrieves only the necessary data. Many programmers are used to opening individual tables rather than using queries and joins to select data. That's extremely inefficient and becomes more inefficient as the volume of data in the tables increases. Scrolling through rows to select data is not a good way to find data when you're working with relational databases. Unless you need the entire table, use a query to retrieve the rows and columns you need.

Similarly, you're likely to find numerous instances of dynamic SQL statements embedded in the code. Dynamic SQL has a place (a small place) in Web applications, but the database must parse and compile the query each time it runs. In contrast, stored procedures are precompiled, so they execute much faster. Use parameterized stored procedures to replace concatenated SQL statements embedded in the code.

In addition, check your indexes. Create an index for *every* column that you use to select data, not just the primary and foreign key columns. If your database has native optimization tools, use them, or find aftermarket analysis and optimization tools and use those.

Particularly in larger projects, you'll find numerous instances of static tables, which hold lists of options used either by the program or as user selections for lists. Rather than retrieving the data each time, retrieve it once and store the lists in a more usable form. For example, to compare entered values with a list of possible values, you can create a `HashTable` or `Dictionary` object and store that at Application scope. Don't be content with caching the DataSets themselves; when possible, create User controls, populate them with data, and cache the output as discussed in Chapter 23, "Build Your Own Web Controls."

Use the SQL Server optimized SqlClient classes rather than the more generalized OleDb classes to interact with SQL Server. Use the forward-only SqlDataReader class rather than DataSets when you don't need the more robust capabilities of the DataSet class.

Tuning your data access to your application has many facets, and there are no perfect recommendations that fit all projects, but these general principles will definitely help speed up your application's data access code. As you build your application, keep these goals in mind:

- Minimize the number of times you must connect to the database to retrieve data.

- Minimize the volume of data that you retrieve.

- Maximize your use of that data after retrieving it.

There's little point in running the same query for every user if you can retrieve the data once, massage it for presentation, and then cache the results.

Web Forms

Although Web Forms are very convenient and can save you a great deal of development time, they're not particularly efficient at runtime. A complex Web Form may need to create several dozen controls for every postback to the server. If all you need is to grab a few bits of data from the posted form, creating the controls is overkill. Once more: watch out for overuse of ViewState. Turn off ViewState for every control except those where you truly need it. When you can replace Web Server controls with HTML controls, do so. In fact, if you're aiming for efficiency, you should consider Web Server controls to be something you use only where *not* using them would cause development time to balloon. As you can see by the recommendations for Custom Server controls in the documentation, it's faster to render your own HTML than to rely on the `Render` method built into the intrinsic controls.

Replace complete pages with collections of cached User controls when possible. In fact, next to reducing database lookups (and hand in hand with it), look to caching as the most important way to improve efficiency.

Session Data

The fastest way to serve pages is to serve static pages from an in-memory cache. Obviously, one of the reasons you've selected C# and ASP.NET is because they simplify the process of serving dynamic pages. But often, not all pages in an application are dynamic. For example, many sites let users browse, search, or drill down to static pages such as technical articles, forms, or documentation. The interactive pages may well need to be dynamic pages because you build them based on user input, but the static pages do *not* need to be dynamic. You can often turn off SessionState maintenance `<%@ Page EnableSessionState="False"%>` for these pages and gain by eliminating the processing required to maintain Session data.

Sometimes, you must look elsewhere to improve your application's performance. For example, when a program is working well but is outgrowing its hardware, it may be much less expensive to "throw hardware at the problem" than to reprogram, retest, and re-debug the application, attempting to optimize it to work better on the current hardware setup.

Hardware versus Software

Improving the efficiency of software can be extremely effective. The combination of writing tighter code, tuning databases, and partitioning applications can often improve throughput by several hundred percent. Unfortunately, in most cases, working on software-only solutions provides diminishing returns. At some point, it makes more economic sense to upgrade the hardware rather than spend money to try to squeeze more performance out of the existing hardware. You can do this in two ways: by scaling up or scaling out.

Scaling Up

Scaling up involves improving the existing application architecture by making it faster. For example, one of the best ways to speed up your application is to cache data that has already been processed and perhaps already formatted for display; therefore, it's extremely important that you have enough server memory to hold the cached data. As with all Windows programs, the caching mechanism will spool data to disk when it has insufficient RAM available. This causes "disk thrashing," where the server must continually swap data in and out of memory to retrieve the data. Caching without sufficient memory available is actually worse than not caching at all. You can use the Performance Monitor to track memory use on your server. Whenever you find the server consistently using over 90 percent of the available RAM, consider adding more memory.

Beyond adding memory, you can add processors to your existing server or replace your existing server with a multiple-processor configuration. Windows 2000 out of the box supports up to four processor configurations, and you can buy servers that support up to 36 processors. The speed improvement is not linear—a four-processor server is not four times as fast as a one-processor server, because task-switching, bus sharing, and memory sharing use up an increasing amount of time as the number of processors increases. But you can get a significant increase in throughput by adding processors and memory, buying faster disk controllers and drives, and using RAID. From a programming point of view, anything you can do to improve performance with hardware alone is cheap because you don't have to change the program at all. There are some ancillary costs. For example, many software packages have licensing agreements that charge on a per-processor basis. You should check to discover the licensing costs of adding more processors and compare that with estimates for reprogramming to increase efficiency.

Scaling Out

Another way to increase efficiency is to "scale out." For example, many small applications start with IIS and SQL Server running on the same machine. That configuration has a high degree of contention for resources. While SQL Server is busy fulfilling a data request, IIS must block until SQL Server finishes processing the request. SQL Server itself runs better when you separate the log portion of the database from the data portion, so just adding a second disk can give you a marginal improvement. A better configuration is to give SQL Server its own separate server, with a fast disk controller and a RAID configuration. By physically separating IIS and SQL Server, you can nearly double the page per minute (ppm) throughput for database-intensive applications.

You can scale out by moving Session data to a separate server. In classic ASP, you needed special software to accomplish that, but with ASP.NET, as you've seen, changing the method used to store Session data is as simple as switching the `<SessionState>` mode to `StateServer` in your `web.config` file. Doing this changes the performance characteristics of your application; it makes retrieving Session data *slower* overall because retrieving the data becomes a cross-server call rather than a local object method, but it also lets you add additional servers. In other words, the benefit from moving Session state onto a separate server increases as you add servers to the application. There's essentially no benefit in moving Session data to a separate server when your application runs on only one IIS server, unless you've run out of room to expand the memory on the IIS server *and* your application consistently spools data to disk.

After moving Session data to a separate server, you can scale out by adding multiple IIS servers, creating a server farm. Multiple IIS servers backed by a single SQL Server installation can cause problems eventually, but you can solve those in most cases by distributing data across multiple SQL Server instances.

Note that, in most cases, you'll get the best bang for the buck by looking at both hardware and software bottlenecks and, often, improving both.

Tips for Efficiency and Scalability

The following sections present these tips for ensuring application efficiency and scalability:

◆ Move processing into components.

◆ Avoid large pages.

◆ Remove dead code.

◆ Avoid extra trips to the server.

Move Processing into Components

You can increase application efficiency by moving processing into components and running those components as COM+ applications in Microsoft Transaction Server (MTS). A description of that process is beyond the scope of this book but, basically, MTS lets you instantiate a pool of stateless components and then use that pool to service requests. The efficiency gain occurs because—unlike your Web Forms—MTS doesn't have to instantiate a new component for each request; it instantiates components on demand but then keeps them in memory, ready for use, for a defined period of time. With that said, you may find a greater speed increase by caching .NET classes in memory at Application scope than in building MTS components.

Bear in mind that there's a performance penalty for running the components in a separate process, particularly the first time your application instantiates a component. For example, when your application uses a component only rarely, it may not be worth moving that component into MTS, because the performance and startup penalty may be greater than the delay associated with using the component to begin with. Also, remember that an instantiated component uses server resources. If you only need the component periodically, you may not want to waste server resources on it during the bulk of the application time, when the application isn't using the component anyway. You can set a timeout value for MTS applications. MTS destroys component instances when they haven't been used for a specified amount of time. In contrast, for components that your application uses often, the penalty for initially instantiating an object becomes trivial in comparison to the time savings you realize by keeping copies of the object instantiated and ready for use.

Avoid Large Pages

Try to avoid creating large pages unless you can cache the entire page. Instead, break the page logic up into smaller chunks—particularly if you can reuse those chunks in other pages in your application.

Try to design pages that require user interaction so that they fit on a single screen without scrolling. Although most users have become inured to long pages for reading information, it's extremely irritating to fill out a form only to find that the Submit button—and perhaps a few "hidden" fields—can be found only by scrolling around the page.

Remove Dead Code

As applications grow, you'll often find that older, unused code remains in the application. Even though your application may never use the code, the server must still compile it. Find and remove unused methods, variable declarations, components, Web Forms, Web Services, and client-side code blocks.

Avoid Extra Trips to the Server

As a final note, the greatest performance bottleneck in a Web application is usually the Web itself. This isn't as great a problem for intranet applications as it is for Internet applications; nonetheless, performing an action on the local machine is almost always faster than making a call to the server. Therefore, try to plan your applications so that you perform as much processing as possible locally, between server round trips.

One way you can do that is by downloading the interface to the local machine in advance and then retrieving just the data from the server itself. Of course, that's what Web applications were all about; by using a browser to draw the UI, you could maintain the entire application centrally, with no deployment or installation required. But another model is equally powerful and even better suited for many types of applications—the Windows UI running in conjunction with Web Services.

Like browser applications, .NET Windows applications can download a very small amount of user-interface code at runtime; in other words, you can deploy your application dynamically, on demand, via HTTP to remote clients. You can even deploy the .NET framework on demand, although that requires broadband clients because the framework itself is (in the first release) approximately 15 megabytes in size. However, with many if not most corporate applications, businesses can ensure that the client machines have the .NET framework installed in advance. With the framework in place, downloading the Windows Forms and logic required for an application's user interface is usually a very small download—in the thousands of bytes rather than the megabyte range.

That combination means that it's now both possible and efficient to deliver Web applications with Windows Forms front-ends that use Web Services to supply the data. By doing this, you gain more control over the application's interface, and the application looks, feels, and acts like the familiar applications people use on a daily basis. After all, there's little point in transmitting UI content over and over again via the browser if the user can run a similar but more powerful interface in native code.

Finally, as you've seen, planning your application around Web Services means you can get the customized UI available with Windows .NET-capable clients, take nearly instant advantage of your existing COM components, and *still* deliver the same application to browser-based clients or clients running customized user interfaces on other platforms. My advice is this: If you have any inkling that you may ever need or want to deliver an application to non-browser clients, plan the dynamic portions of your applications as Web Services whenever practicable, starting immediately.

Summary

Congratulations on completing this book. I hope you've had as much fun working through the examples and exploring C# Web applications as I've had writing them. .NET is an enormous subject, and ASP.NET is only one part. Because of the nature of Web applications, which as you've seen, require you to know something about HTML, DHTML, database technology, ADO.NET, XML, XSLT, Web Services, SOAP, WSDL, and even how to create Windows Forms applications that consume those Web Services, there's no way to provide a deep exploration of ASP.NET in a book this size. Each of those topics is sufficiently broad to be worthy of a complete book. But my hope is that you've seen a few of the advantages each technology can provide. More than that, I hope you've seen and appreciated this book's *approach* to exploring technology—by writing small test programs that exemplify the core problems and then writing variations until you understand what happens.

Afterword

WHERE SHOULD YOU GO from here? That requires a little bit of prognostication about where Web technology is headed, and *that* depends on your situation, to some degree. In my opinion, browsers are not a particularly effective technology for delivering distributed applications. That opinion may surprise you, having worked through all the examples in the book; nevertheless, I feel it is true. Unfortunately, browsers are currently the most important and, in some cases, the *only* viable delivery platform for Web-centered applications. But that's likely to change, and here's why.

Web Development Is Time Intensive

You can whip up a Windows Forms C# application such as the MortgageCalculator used in Chapter 22, "Web Services, COM Components, and the SOAP Toolkit," in just a few minutes: build a few Web Services on your server, copy the client files onto any machine with the .NET runtime installed, and have a working application. In contrast, the Web Form designer and the ASP.NET API, while they provide huge improvements over writing raw HTML and managing page state manually, simply have not evolved to the same level of sophistication. It takes longer to create a Web Form than it does to create an equivalent Windows Form. Even when you do, Web Forms don't quite act, look, or respond quite like native applications.

Browser Incompatibilities Cause Problems

There are large and significant differences between the capabilities of browsers, both between products from different browser manufacturers and between versions of the same browser. There are even subtle and not-so-subtle differences between the *same browser versions* running on different platforms. Inevitably, those differences cause problems for developers. While .NET will not solve all platform differences (exactly how much remains to be seen, based on Open Source implementations underway), the overwhelming majority of desktops run Windows—and .NET *does* help solve that problem.

Although modern browsers differ less than their predecessors, the differences aren't likely to disappear altogether anytime in the near future. Even though browsers are mostly free, each manufacturer feels pressure to distinguish its browser from the others, so there may always be differences that lead to cross-browser development problems.

Browsers Are Great—But Not Always

Browsers made HTML important, and HTML has huge advantages, but it also has many disadvantages as a display mechanism—it's slow and bulky, interacting with browser-based controls is awkward, and you don't have fine control over the interface. For the past several years, browsers have enjoyed a near monopoly as a platform for building Web-based applications that run on remote clients, but they are no longer the only game in town.

Even in the early days of the Web, browser makers recognized that their products needed some help. Netscape browsers introduced the concept of "helper" applications, such as the common PDF viewer and Flash. Helper applications provided a way to handle code sent from the server other than HTML. Some of these applications run inside the browser window, and some run as separate applications. Either way, there's a problem with delivering *safe* code to distributed clients—code that users trust to run on their computers.

An early attempt at delivering safe code to distributed clients—Java applets—has been cited as a failure due to slow downloads and slow execution speed. That failure was due primarily to lack of bandwidth and the available CPU speed of the time. Java applets are making a comeback in games, graphical applications, and even some business and development applications. That trend will increase as bandwidth and CPU speed continue to increase.

But Java isn't the only way to distribute executable code. As the .NET runtime becomes ubiquitous, you'll be able to deliver and update .NET applications to distributed clients as well. With their built-in support for Web Services, Windows Forms–based .NET applications can supplant browsers quite easily—not for general surfing, but for applications. You can download them initially using a browser or any program that can download and save files; after that, you can update such applications via HTTP just like Java applets. However, .NET-distributed applications have at least two major advantages over Java applets. First, they run in native, processor-specific code, so they're fast. Second, you can apply security restrictions directly to .NET applications, so that rather than running in a "sandbox," users can control the permission levels, making them much more useful for building applications. Such applications will also become more common as bandwidth and processor speed increase—and you'll be a step ahead, having already learned how to build the Web Services that drive the applications.

XML Is Important

You've seen a little about how important XML is to the .NET framework. The framework uses XML for configuration, for remoting, for Web Services, for object serialization, for data, for Server Controls, for form layouts—for almost everything. At this point, you should have realized that XML data combined with schema is *the* universal file format, are becoming increasingly important, and will become even more important in the future.

Despite XML's drawbacks (it's bulky, it's not well suited for holding binary data, it's not as easy to sort and query as a relational database), its benefits are so overwhelming that such drawbacks fade into insignificance. All of XML's drawbacks, by the way, are being solved. Compressed XML will become more common. For example, in the wireless world, Wireless Binary XML (WBXML) is already winning converts. Back-end XML-specific databases offer the promise of RDBMS-like speed and query power, without the fixed-schema relationship restrictions. Overall, the benefits accruing to both businesses and developers from placing data in a universal format will necessarily far outweigh the performance difficulties arising from the format itself.

What Should You Study Now?

What should you study now? First and foremost, you should learn XML, schema, and XSLT thoroughly. Even if you eventually decide not to work with .NET, the time you spend on XML will be useful.

Second, you should explore more of the .NET framework. Specifically, practice caching until the ideas are second nature, practice using ADO.NET and the DataGrid, DataList, and Repeater controls. Learn about remoting, reflection, serialization, threading, the .NET TCP and UDP Listener and Client classes, and the Socket class and practice building more complex Web services, user controls, and custom controls. These topics are extremely important for building advanced Web applications with VB.NET, but they're a little beyond the level of suitable topics for this book. Nevertheless, they provide ways to build and supplement applications that ASP.NET alone does not provide. Third, look at the HttpHandler classes, which can be extremely useful in handling special request types or providing "filters" that perform actions on particular request types. Finally, you should acquire and study the Microsoft Mobile Internet Toolkit, which lets you build Web applications suitable for handheld and small form-factor clients in much the same way as you build Web Forms. Opportunities for building such applications are increasing rapidly, and that trend is likely to continue as technological advances shrink devices while extending their power. That should keep you busy for a while. I know it will keep *me* busy. Good luck to you all.

Part **6**

Appendices

In this section you will find:
- **Appendix A: Quick HTML Reference**
- **Appendix B: JScript 5.5 Reference**

Appendix A

Quick HTML Reference

THIS REFERENCE COVERS THE most commonly used tags for HTML 4. The most current working version of the W3C recommendation is HTML 4.01, issued in December 1997. Although end tags are not always required for compliance with HTML, you should get in the habit of explicitly ending all tags so that your HTML will be Extensible Hypertext Markup Language (XHTML) or Extensible Markup Language (XML) compliant. You should bear in mind that the XHTML 1.0 specification is intended to *replace* HTML as the standard markup language for the Web. The W3C is no longer working to extend HTML. In this case, the standard is ahead of common practice—HTML is still the only common markup language understood by most client devices. Nevertheless, HTML itself is obsolete, in a sense. The XHTML specification uses the HTML 4.01 specification to define the set of HTML tags; while HTML is not exactly disappearing, it's being subsumed in a larger, more flexible context.

HTML is not case sensitive, but the W3C initially recommended that people use uppercase for tags and lowercase for attributes. XML is case sensitive. The XHTML specification requires all tags to be lowercase. Therefore, I recommend you use lowercase for all tags, which is the only method that meets the requirements of all three specifications.

Unfortunately, there's no specification or common standard for attribute names, so you'll need to select your own naming conventions. If it helps, all-uppercase attribute names are rare. Much recent use keeps attribute names in all-lowercase, but that becomes less practical as the names get more complex.

In XML files, Microsoft's current practices use "camel" case for both element and attribute names, with the first letter of the name in lowercase but the first letter of subsequent concatenated words capitalized. Microsoft recommends using Pascal case for attribute values, in which names begin with a capital letter, but is subsequently identical to camel case.

Camel-cased name	`myVeryLongName`
Pascal-cased name	`MyVeryLongName`
Microsoft's recommendation for XML	`myVeryLongName="SomeVeryLongValue"`

No matter which naming convention you choose, you should acquire the habit of quoting all attribute values. Both single and double quotes are acceptable, but double quotes currently are the most common by far. At times, you'll find that you're forced to use single quotes because of the syntax of the surrounding code—and you'll also find that when you're writing HTML programmatically, it's often simply easier to write single quotes than to embed escaped double quotes.

Quick Tag Reference

This reference shows the HTML 4 tags in alphabetical order. Some of the tags have been *deprecated*, which means they are no longer recommended (although they still work). Some tags are marked *obsolete*, which means they are no longer part of the HTML recommendation, and you should not use them. To prevent your HTML pages from becoming obsolete, use the recommended alternative tag or style definition instead.

TAG	DESCRIPTION
`<!=`	Begins a comment section.
`=>`	Ends a comment section.
`!doctype`	Specifies the Document Type Definition (DTD) of the document. For example, `<!DOCTYPE HTML PUBLIC "-//W3C//DTD HTML 4.0 Strict//EN">` specifies strict compliance with the W3C HTML 4 specification.
`a`	Defines an anchor tag (a hyperlink, usually shortened to "link"). When given a `name` attribute, the link acts as a destination for a hyperlink. When given an `href` attribute, the link acts as the point of departure for a hyperlink.
`abbr`	Specifies an abbreviation.
`acronym`	Specifies an acronym.
`address`	Formats text as an address.
`applet`	Deprecated. Embeds a Java applet into the page. *Substitute*: Use an `<object>` tag instead.
`area`	Defines a clickable shape within a graphic. The `area` tag can define rectangular, circular or oval, and irregularly shaped areas.
`b`	Formats text as bold. There's considerable support for the idea of using `<strong>` rather than `<b>` because the bold tag is specifically related to print, whereas the `<strong>` tag means "apply emphasis in some way relative to the surrounding content." For example, documents being read out loud via an audio interface could easily render `<strong>`, but it's unclear how they might render bold. Despite that support, the `<b>` tag is not deprecated.
`base`	Sets the base URL for the page.
`basefont`	Deprecated. Sets the base font for the page. Subsequent font settings are relative to the `<basefont>` tag. You should use this tag before any text rendered in the document. *Substitute*: Use CSS styles to set document font defaults.
`bdo`	Specifies a different character rendering order for Unicode text. You must include a `dir=` attribute (*deprecated*) specifying the character rendering direction with the `<bdo>` tag.

bgsound	IE-specific. Specifies a background audio file. The file begins loading after the remainder of the page. This tag is not part of the W3C 4.01 recommendation.
big	Formats text larger than the surrounding text.
blockquote	Indents text.
body	Encloses the body of the document.
br	Inserts a carriage return/linefeed.
button	Displays a button.
caption	Specifies a table caption.
center	Deprecated. Centers content.
	Substitute: Use CSS styles to center content.
cite	Indicates a citation.
code	Displays code in a small, fixed-width font.
col	Specifies default settings for a table column.
colgroup	Groups columns with similar formatting needs.
comment	Obsolete. Do not use. Use <– to start a comment and –> to end a comment.
dd	Used for the definition portion of a definition list.
del	Indicates text that has been deleted from the document.
dfn	Used for the first instance of a term in a document, called the *defining* instance.
dir	Deprecated. Begins a directory listing. The items in the directory listing must begin with an <li> (list item) tag.
	Substitute: Use the <ul> tag instead.
div	Indicates a document division. In Netscape, these are called *layers*. Use the <div> tag to separate a document into individually programmable sections.
dl	Begins a definition list.
dt	Used for the term portion of a definition list.
em	Emphasizes text. Most browsers italicize text with this tag.
embed	Netscape-specific. Embeds a document or binary file (such as a sound file) into an HTML page. The browser must have the appropriate application or viewer to view or process the content. This tag is not part of the W3C 4.01 recommendation.
fieldset	Groups fields within a form, placing a border around them with a title—much like the border around related elements on a Windows dialog box.
font	Deprecated. Sets the font size, face, and color.
	Substitute: Use CSS styles to set font characteristics.

`form`	Begins a form.
`frame`	Defines a frame within a <frameset> tag.
`frameset`	Defines a frameset—a group of related frames. You define frame sizes within the <frameset> tag.
`h1`	Heading 1 text (largest).
`h2`	Heading 2 text.
`h3`	Heading 3 text.
`h4`	Heading 4 text.
`h5`	Heading 5 text.
`h6`	Heading 6 text (smallest).
`head`	Denotes the head section of a document. You place header information between the <head></head> tags.
`hr`	Inserts a horizontal rule (a line).
`html`	Required start/end tag for an HTML document.
`i`	Formats text in italics. There's considerable support for the idea of using <em> (emphasis) rather than <i> because the italics tag applies a visual emphasis—it's specifically related to print—whereas the emphasis tag means "apply emphasis in some way relative to the surrounding content." For example, documents being read out loud via an audio interface could easily render <em>, but it's unclear how they might render <i>. Despite that support, the <i> tag is not deprecated.
`iframe`	Defines an inline frame. The frame appears as an embedded browser window within the document. The embedded browser does not display a frame or toolbars.
`img`	Places an image into the document.
`input`	Defines an <input> tag. There are several types:

`Text`

`Password`

`Button`

`Submit`

`Reset`

`Radio`

`Checkbox`

`Hidden`

`Image`

`File`

These input controls are scriptable even in earlier HTML versions. In some browsers these input controls must appear inside a <form> tag. Some browsers don't support the `type=file` <input> tag attribute.

ins	Formats text as having been inserted into a document.
isindex	Deprecated.
	Substitute: Use the <input> tag instead.
kbd	Formats text as if it were input from a keyboard—in a monospaced font.
label	Displays a label and associates the label with an element.
layer	Netscape-specific. Essentially the same as the <div> tag. Netscape 6 browsers no longer support the <layer> tag. Use <div> instead for modern browsers.
legend	Adds a legend for a <fieldset> tag. The <legend> tag must appear immediately after the <fieldset> tag.
li	Adds an item to an <ol> ordered or <ul> unordered list.
link	Used in the <head> section of a document to specify a typed link to another document. Most often seen with style sheet references. For example, <LINK REL="stylesheet" HREF="styles.css" TYPE="text/css">.
listing	Obsolete. Use the <pre> tag instead. Formats text in a fixed-width font for a code listing.
map	Defines a collection of hotspots for a client-side image map. The tag contains a collection of <area> tags. You can apply a defined map within an <img> tag with the usemap= attribute.
marquee	IE-specific. Defines a scrolling text area. The text for the marquee appears between the start and end tags.
menu	Deprecated. Begins a menu list. Place the menu items between <li></li> tags.
	Substitute: Use the <ul> tag instead.
meta	Contains meta-information about the document. Place <meta> tags in the head section of the document.
nobr	Obsolete. Specifies that you don't want to break text to fit within the boundaries of its container.
noframes	Use this tag with the <frameset> tag to provide content to downlevel browsers that can't render frames. Place the <noframes> tag within the <frameset></frameset> tags.
noscript	Defines text that appears for downlevel browsers that can't run script.
object	Inserts an object, such as an image, ActiveX control, or document, into the HTML document.
ol	Defines an ordered list. The list items appear numbered. Place items in the list between <li></li> tags.
option	Defines an item in a <select> list.
optgroup	Defines a subgroup of items within a <select> list.
p	Defines a paragraph.
param	Defines an initial setting or value for an <object> or <embed> tag.
plaintext	Obsolete. Use the <pre> tag instead. Specifies that the browser should render the following text without processing tags. The browser displays the closing </plaintext> tag, if present.

pre	Specifies that the browser should render the following text exactly as it appears—the text is "pre" formatted.
q	Formats text as a quotation. Use only with short quotations. Use <blockquote> for longer quoted sections.
s	Deprecated. Renders text in strikethrough characters.
	Substitute: Use CSS styles to apply character formatting.
samp	Renders text in a small, fixed-width font.
script	Specifies that the following text is script, not HTML. To avoid problems with downlevel browsers, place the script within this tag inside a comment. For example, <script><- script code here -></script>.
select	Defines a list of selectable items—equivalent to a VB listbox or combobox, depending on the value of the height= attribute. Appears as a list when the height= attribute is greater than 1.
small	Renders text in a font smaller than the surrounding text.
span	Like a <div> tag, the <span> tag defines a section of a document. You may use it to apply special CSS formatting to individual items on the page.
strike	Deprecated. Renders text in strikethrough font.
	Substitute: Use CSS styles to apply character formatting.
strong	Renders text in bold print.
style	Defines a style sheet for a document.
sub	Renders text as a subscript.
sup	Renders text as a superscript.
table	Defines a table.
tbody	Optional tag—serves to separate the body of a table from the head and footer sections.
td	Defines a cell—stands for *table data*.
textarea	Defines a multiline text input control. Unlike the <input type="text"> tag, you place the text for the <textarea> tag between the start and end tags.
tfoot	Optional tag—defines the footer area of a table.
th	Use this in the <thead> section of a table in place of the <td> tag.
thead	Defines the header section of a table.
title	Defines the title of the document. The title appears in the browser title bar. Used in the <head> section of a document.
tr	Defines a table row.
tt	Renders text in a fixed-width font like a teletype terminal.
u	Deprecated. Renders underlined text.
	Substitute: Use CSS styles to apply character formatting.

ul	Creates an unordered list. The list items appear as bullets. Place items in the list between `<li></li>` tags.
var	Defines text that specifies a variable name. For example, `<var>filename</var>=c:\someFile`.
wbr	Inserts a soft line break in a line of `<nobr>` text.
xmp	Obsolete. Use the `<pre>` tag instead. The `<xmp>` tag renders the text of an example in a small, fixed-width font.

HTML 4 Attribute Reference

This section contains a complete listing of the W3C-approved attributes for HTML 4, including those attributes termed *deprecated* (which means they are no longer recommended and you shouldn't use them). In general, the deprecated attributes assigned style information to their parent elements. In HTML 4, you should use style sheets or inline styles to define style information. Not surprisingly, all attributes that apply exclusively to deprecated tags have also been deprecated. I have noted deprecated attributes and deprecated tags with (d).

Unfortunately, no browser currently implements *all* the possible attribute values. Check the browser manufacturer's documentation for specific information about individual browsers.

The HTML 4 specification provides seven main attributes that are common to nearly all elements and have the same meaning for all elements. These elements are as follows:

id   Should identify a single item explicitly and uniquely. In previous versions of HTML, you could link only to anchor tags. In this version, you may create a link to any element with a unique id. You should avoid setting a tag's id and its name attribute to the same value if you must deliver content to downlevel browsers.

name   Provides an identifying name for the element. In HTML 4, you should use the id attribute in preference to the name attribute.

class   Defines the class name for the tag and determines which CSS class styles apply to the tag element. This is unimportant until you want to begin programming the tag elements from script. It becomes important then because you can easily change the look-and-feel of the tag by changing its class affiliation.

style   Contains a string specifying style settings for that element. Style settings specified in the `<style>` tag are called inline styles, as opposed to style settings an element inherits from a Cascading Style Sheet (CSS). Inline styles always take precedence over CSS styles.

title   Defines the tool-tip text that appears when you place your cursor over the element. You may leave this attribute blank.

lang   Defines the language for the element. The value is any valid language code. You will find the language codes at `http://msdn.microsoft.com/workshop/author/dhtml/reference/language_codes.asp#language_codes`.

language   Defines the scripting language used to handle element events. The valid values are VBScript, VBS, JavaScript, and JScript.

Most elements that reference other documents do so via a Uniform Resource Identifier (URI), as opposed to a Uniform Resource Locator (URL). The change in terminology reflects the reality that not all references refer to a file.

ATTRIBUTE	APPLIES TO	VALUE OR DESCRIPTION
abbr	td and th	Designates an abbreviation for a table header cell.
accept-charset	Form	Contains a list of supported character sets.
accept	Form input	List of MIME types for file upload.
accesskey	A	Specifies a shortcut key.
	area	
	button	
	input	
	label	
	legend	
	textarea	
action	form	Specifies the URI to which to submit form data.
align	applet (d)	Specifies alignment. In some cases, the alignment may be relative to a containing parent tag; in others it specifies the alignment of content within the tag.
	caption (d)	
	col	
	colgroup	
	div (d)	
	h1 (d)	
	h2 (d)	
	h3 (d)	
	h4 (d)	
	h5 (d)	
	h6 (d)	
	hr (d)	
	iframe (d)	
	img (d)	

	input (d)	
	legend (d)	
	object (d)	
	p (d)	
	tbody	
	td	
	tfoot	
	th	
	thead	
	tr	
alink (d)	body	Color of selected links.
alt	applet (d)	Contains a short text description. This text appears when a user hovers over an element.
	area	
	img	
	input	
archive	applet (d)	Specifies a list of archive locations.
	object	
axis	td	Contains a comma-separated list of related headers.
	th	
background (d)	body	Specifies a background tiled image for the document.
bgcolor (d)	body	Specifies the background color for the element.
	table	
	td	
	th	
	tr	
border (d)	img	Specifies the width of the element's border.
	object	
	table	
cellpadding	table	Specifies the white space between the outer edge of content and the inner edge of a table cell border.
cellspacing	table	Specifies the spacing between table cells.

char	col	Specifies a character that controls alignment. Used in conjunction with the `align="char"` attribute. For example, if you specify the decimal point as the alignment character, numbers should appear aligned by the decimal point.
	colgroup	
	tbody	
	td	
	tfoot	
	th	
	thead	
	tr	
charoff	col	The offset for the alignment character from the containing element margin.
	colgroup	
	tbody	
	td	
	tfoot	
	th	
	thead	
	tr	
charset	a	Specifies the character encoding of the content specified in the anchor, link, or script.
	link	
	script	
checked	input	Controls whether a check box or radio button appears selected.
cite	blockquote	URL for the source of a quote or block quote. For deleted or inserted text, this attribute states the reason for the change.
	del	
	ins	
	q	
class	All elements except the following:	Space-separated list of classes to which this element belongs.
	base	
	basefont (d)	

	head	
	html	
	meta	
	param	
	script	
	style	
	title	
classid	object	Specifies the URL for the implementation of a class.
clear (d)	br	Specifies where the line following the ` ` tag should begin. Use style sheets and classes to implement this behavior in HTML 4.
code	applet (d)	Specifies the path to an applet's class file.
codebase	applet (d)	Determines the base URI for an applet object. After specifying the codebase, you may specify all subsequent URIs relative to the codebase URI.
	object	
codetype	object	Specifies the content type of an `<object>`.
color (d)	basefont (d)	Determines the text color. To change the color of other elements, use the `style` attribute.
	font (d)	
cols	frameset	Specifies the width of a frameset in pixels, or of a `textarea` in characters.
	textarea	
colspan	td	Controls the number of columns spanned by a table cell.
	th	
compact (d)	dir	Reduces the spacing between items.
	dl	
	menu	
	ol	
	uldir	
	dl	
	menu	
	ul	
content	meta	Specifies the content of a `<meta>` tag.

coords	area	Contains a comma-separated list of coordinates (points) for use with client-side image maps.
	a	
data	object	Contains a URI specifying the location of an object's data.
datetime	del, ins	Contains the date and time the content was changed.
defer	script	UA may defer execution of script.
dir	All elements except the following:	Specifies the direction for text when the direction information is lacking in Unicode. For the \<bdo\> tag, the dir= attribute overrides Unicode directionality.
	applet (d)	
	base	
	basefont (d)	
	br	
	frame	
	frameset	
	iframe	
	param	
	script	
disabled	button	Specifies that the input control may not receive focus, does not generate events, and is removed from the control tab order.
	input	
	optgroup	
	option	
	select	
	textarea	
enctype	form	Specifies the type of content the form will submit to the server. The default value is application/x-www-form-urlencoded. For file uploads (input type=file), use the value multipart/form-data.
face (d)	basefont (d)	Specifies a font face name or, optionally, a comma-delimited list of alternative face names.
	font (d)	
for	label	Determines the field to which a label belongs.
frame	table	Controls which parts of the table border the browser should render.

`frameborder`	`frame`	Specifies whether the browser should render a separator (usually a pixel) between one border and another.
	`iframe`	
`headers`	`td`	Contains a comma-delimited list of column titles. Use this attribute so that nonvisual browsers (such as speech-enabled browsers for the blind) can deliver information about table contents.
	`th`	
`height`	`applet` (d)	Specifies the height of the element/object in pixels.
	`iframe`	
	`img`	
	`object`	
	`td` (d)	
	`th` (d)	
`href`	`a`	Contains a URL specifying either a content source (`base`) or a destination (`a`, `area`, `link`).
	`area`	
	`base`	
	`link`	
`hreflang`	`a`	Contains the language code of the language for the destination specified by the `href` attribute.
	`link`	
`hspace` (d)	`applet` (d)	Determines the amount of horizontal space added around the element.
	`img`	
	`object`	
`http-equiv`	`meta`	HTTP response header name.
`id`	All elements except the following:	Specifies a unique ID for the element.
	`base`	
	`head`	
	`html`	
	`meta`	
	`script`	

	`style`	
	`title`	
`ismap`	`img`	Specifies a server-side image map. This attribute does not take a value.
	`input`	
`label`	`option`	Short text content for display.
	`optgroup`	
`lang`	All elements except the following:	Contains the language code for the element.
	`applet` (d)	
	`base`	
	`basefont` (d)	
	`br`	
	`frame`	
	`frameset`	
	`iframe`	
	`param`	
	`script`	
`language` (d)	`script`	Contains a scripting language name. Use a `<meta http-equiv="Content-Script-Type" content="VBScript|VBS|JScript|JavaScript">` tag instead. Despite this attribute having been deprecated, it is still in common use throughout the Web.
`link` (d)	`body`	Specifies the initial color of links—the color before they're visited.
`longdesc`	`img`	Specifies a link to a `long` description. Use the `alt` attribute for short descriptions.
`longdesc`	`frame`	Link to `long` description (complements `title`).
	`iframe`	
`marginheight`	`frame`	Determines the top and bottom inside margin height in pixels.
	`iframe`	
`marginwidth`	`frame`	Determines the left and right inside margin width in pixels.
	`iframe`	
`maxlength`	`input`	Specifies the maximum number of characters allowed in an `input` field.

media	link	Contains a comma-delimited list of media where the content should be rendered. The possible values are screen, tty, tv, projection, handheld, print, braille, aural, and all. The default value is screen.
	style	
method	form	Specifies the HTTP method used to submit a form. Values are get and post. Unfortunately, get is the default, which appends form content to the URL, where it's visible.
multiple	select	Specifies that the user may select more than one value in a select list. This attribute does not take a value.
name	a	Provides a means of identifying elements.
	applet (d)	
	button	
	form	
	frame	
	iframe	
	img	
	input	
	map	
	meta	
	object	
	param	
	select	
	textarea	
nohref	area	Specifies that an area on an image map has no target URL.
noresize	frame	Determines whether the user may resize a frame.
noshade (d)	hr	Specifies a flat rule rather than a raised rule.
nowrap (d)	td	Disables automatic text wrapping within the cell.
	th	
object (d)	applet (d)	URI of serialized applet code.
onblur	a	Event raised when an element loses focus.
	area	
	button	
	input	

	label	
	select	
	textarea	
onchange	input	Event raised when the value of an input element changes.
	select	
	textarea	
onclick	All elements except the following:	Event raised when the user clicks a visible element.
	applet (d)	
	base	
	basefont (d)	
	bdo	
	br	
	font (d)	
	frame	
	frameset	
	head	
	html	
	iframe	
	isindex (d)	
	meta	
	param	
	script	
	style	
	title	
ondblclick	All elements except the following:	Event raised when the user double-clicks a visible element.
	applet (d)	
	base	
	basefont (d)	
	bdo	
	br	
	font (d)	

	`frame`	
	`frameset`	
	`head`	
	`html`	
	`iframe`	
	`isindex` (d)	
	`meta`	
	`param`	
	`script`	
	`style`	
	`title`	
onfocus	`a`	Event raised when an element receives the focus.
	`area`	
	`button`	
	`input`	
	`label`	
	`select`	
	`textarea`	
onkeydown	All elements except the following:	Event raised when the user presses a key while an element has the focus.
	`applet` (d)	
	`base`	
	`basefont` (d)	
	`bdo`	
	`br`	
	`font` (d)	
	`frame`	
	`frameset`	
	`head`	
	`html`	
	`iframe`	
	`isindex` (d)	

	meta	
	param	
	script	
	style	
	title	
onkeypress	All elements except the following:	Event raised when the user presses and releases a key while an element has the focus.
	applet (d)	
	base	
	basefont (d)	
	bdo	
	br	
	font (d)	
	frame	
	frameset	
	head	
	html	
	iframe	
	isindex (d)	
	meta	
	param	
	script	
	style	
	title	
onkeyup	All elements except the following:	Event raised when the user releases a pressed key while an element has the focus.
	applet (d)	
	base	
	basefont (d)	
	bdo	
	br	
	font (d)	

	`frame`	
	`frameset`	
	`head`	
	`html`	
	`iframe`	
	`isindex` (d)	
	`meta`	
	`param`	
	`script`	
	`style`	
	`title`	
`onload`	`frameset`	Event raised when the browser has loaded all frames (for the `<frameset>` tag) or the complete document (for the `<body>` tag).
	`body`	
`onload`	`body`	Event raised when the browser has loaded the document.
`onmousedown`	All elements except the following:	Event raised when the user presses a mouse button while the mouse pointer is over a visible element.
	`applet` (d)	
	`base`	
	`basefont` (d)	
	`bdo`	
	`br`	
	`font` (d)	
	`frame`	
	`frameset`	
	`head`	
	`html`	
	`iframe`	
	`isindex` (d)	
	`meta`	
	`param`	
	`script`	

	style	
	title	
onmousemove	All elements except the following:	Event raised when the user moves the mouse pointer while over the screen area defined by a visible element.
	applet (d)	
	base	
	basefont (d)	
	bdo	
	br	
	font (d)	
	frame	
	frameset	
	head	
	html	
	iframe	
	isindex (d)	
	meta	
	param	
	script	
	style	
	title	
onmouseout	All elements except the following:	Event raised when the user moves the mouse pointer out of the area defined by a visible element.
	applet (d)	
	base	
	basefont (d)	
	bdo	
	br	
	font (d)	
	frame	
	frameset	
	head	

	`html`	
	`iframe`	
	`isindex` (d)	
	`meta`	
	`param`	
	`script`	
	`style`	
	`title`	
onmouseover	All elements except the following:	Event raised when the user moves the mouse pointer into the area defined by a visible element.
	`applet` (d)	
	`base`	
	`basefont` (d)	
	`bdo`	
	`br`	
	`font` (d)	
	`frame`	
	`frameset`	
	`head`	
	`html`	
	`iframe`	
	`isindex` (d)	
	`meta`	
	`param`	
	`script`	
	`style`	
	`title`	
onmouseup	All elements except the following:	Event raised when the user releases a pressed mouse button while the mouse pointer is over a visual element.
	`applet` (d)	
	`base`	
	`basefont` (d)	

	bdo	
	br	
	font (d)	
	frame	
onmouseup	frameset	Event raised when the user releases a pressed mouse button while the mouse pointer is over a visual element.
	head	
	html	
	iframe	
	isindex (d)	
	meta	
	param	
	script	
	style	
	title	
onreset	form	Event raised when the user presses a Reset button (input type=reset).
onselect	input	Event raised when the user selects some text.
	textarea	
onsubmit	form	Event raised when the user submits a form.
onunload	frame	Event raised when the browser has removed all frames (for the \<frameset\> tag) or the document (for a \<body\> tag).
	setbody	
profile	head	Contains a comma-delimited list of URIs that contain meta-information about the document.
prompt (d)	isindex (d)	Contains the input prompt message.
readonly	input	Specifies that the input field is not editable.
	textarea	
rel	a	Specifies the relationship between this document and a forward link.
	link	
rev	a	Specifies the relationship between this document and backward links.
	link	

rows	frameset	For a <frameset> tag, the attribute value is a comma-delimited list of values that specify the width of frames defined by the <frameset> tag. For a <textarea> tag, the rows attribute value specifies the width of the textarea in characters.
	textarea	
rowspan	td	Controls the number of rows spanned by a table cell.
	thtd	
	th	
rules	table	Controls whether a table contains inner grid lines (rulings).
scheme	meta	Specifies how to interpret tag content.
scope	td	Specifies the columns or rows to which a table header applies. The valid values are row, col, rowgroup, and colgroup.
	th	
scrolling	frame	Determines whether a frame or iframe displays scroll bars.
	iframe	
selected	option	When present, this attribute controls whether an item in a select list initially appears selected. The attribute has no value.
shape	a	Specifies the shape of a server- or client-side image map area. The possible values are rect, circle, poly, and default.
	area	
size	hr (d)	This attribute takes on different meanings, depending on the tag.
		For the <hr> (horizontal rule) tag, the size attribute controls the width of the rule.
	font (d)	For the <font> tag, the size attribute controls the relative size of text. The default value is 3.
	input	Each <input> tag specifies this attribute differently.
	select	For the <select> tag, the size attribute controls the number of visible rows in the control.
	basefont (d)	For the <basefont> tag, the size attribute controls the size of the base font used in the document.
span	col	For a <col> tag, the span attribute specifies the number of columns in a colgroup. For a <colgroup> tag, the span attribute determines the default number of columns in the group.
	colgroup	
src	frame	For a <script> tag, the src attribute specifies the URI for an external script.
	iframe	For <frame> and <iframe> tags, the src attribute specifies the URI from which to obtain the document content.

	img	For `<input>` and `<img>` tags, the `src` attribute specifies the URI for an associated image.
	input	
	script	
standby	object	Specifies a text message to display while the browser loads the content.
start (d)	ol	Controls the starting number for numbered items.
style	All elements except the following:	Contains style settings for an element.
	base	
	basefont (d)	
	head	
	html	
	meta	
	param	
	script	
	style	
	title	
summary	table	Contains a short description of the table's content for nonvisual rendering, such as rendering to audio-enabled browsers or Braille readers.
tabindex	a	Controls the position of an element in the document tab order sequence.
	area	
	button	
	input	
	object	
	select	
	textarea	
target	a	Specifies the frame in which to render content.
	area	
	base	
	form	
	link	

text (d)	body	Controls the default color in which the browser will render a document's text.
title	All elements except the following:	For most browsers, this controls the tool-tip text that appears when you hover your mouse over an element. Some browsers render this text while waiting for content (such as an image) to load.
	base	
	basefont (d)	
	head	
	html	
	meta	
	param	
	script	
	title	
type	a	For <li>, <ol>, and <ul> tags, the type attribute controls the style of the list item.
	button	For the <button> tag, the type attribute specifies the type of button: button, submit, or reset.
	li (d)	
	link	For <a>, <link>, <object>, <param>, <script>, and <style> tags, the value is the MIME type of the referenced content or item.
	object	
	ol (d)	
	param	
	script	For script tags, use the MIME type for the enclosed script; for example, text/javascript or text/vbscript.
	style	
	input	For <input> tags, the value of the type attribute controls the type of control, such as button, text, password, and so on.
	ul (d)	
usemap	img	Specifies the named image map associated with the element.
	input	
	object	
valign	col	Determines the vertical alignment of tag content.
	colgroup	

	tbody	
	td	
	tfoot	
	th	
	thead	
	tr	
value	button	For all the tags in the Applies To list, except the `<li>` tag, the `value` attribute specifies the value both for initial display and the value sent to the server when the user submits the containing form.
	input	
	li (d)	For the `<li>` tag in an ordered list, the `value` attribute overrides the default number.
	option	
	param	
valuetype	param	Specifies how to interpret the `value` parameter of an element.
version (d)	html	Specifies the HTML version number.
vlink (d)	body	Specifies the color of visited links.
vspace (d)	applet (d)	Determines the amount of vertical space added around the element.
	img	
	object	
width	applet (d)	Specifies the width of an element.
	col	
	colgroup	
	hr (d)	
	iframe	
	img	
	object	
	pre	
	table	
	td (d)	
	th (d)	

Appendix B

JScript 5.5 Reference

THIS JSCRIPT REFERENCE IS *not* a JScript.NET reference; it's a reference for the scripting language JScript, version 5.5, as implemented in Internet Explorer and also delivered with other Microsoft products such as Internet Information Server. Most ASP.NET programmers use JScript for client-side script because most browsers support JavaScript/ECMAScript. JScript contains many Microsoft specific extensions so that JScript can interact with COM and VBScript. Still, although JScript is a proprietary version (superset) of ECMAScript, it *does* contain all the ECMAScript-compatible keywords. However, you should bear in mind that only Microsoft products support JScript's proprietary extensions. See the section "JScript Microsoft-Specific Extensions" in this appendix for a list of the JScript features that are not ECMA compliant.

JScript Intrinsic Objects

JScript's intrinsic objects are built into the language; you don't have to include special code or reference external files to use them.

OBJECT	DESCRIPTION
ActiveXObject	Creates and returns references to ActiveX (COM) objects. You provide the class identifier of the object you want to create; for example: `var myOjb = new ActiveXObject ("Scripting.Dictionary")`
Array	Contains arrays of any data type. JScript can also handle COM (VBScript-type) arrays via special language extensions.
arguments	Contains a list of arguments passed to a function or method.
Boolean	Creates a Boolean value.
Date	JScript object for manipulating date and time values.
Dictionary	Object that holds key/value pairs. You can look up a value if you know the key name. The Dictionary object also supports iteration over either the keys or the values.
Enumerator	Object for enumerating or iterating over collections.

Error	Object to hold runtime error information. This object is essentially the equivalent of the VBScript Error object, but it has only number and description properties.
FileSystemObject	Object used to manipulate the file system.
Function	Creates a new function.
Global	A JScript object that holds globally available functions.
Math	A JScript intrinsic object used to perform math operations and retrieve constants.
Number	Used to hold numeric values and constants.
Object	Parent object for all object variables.
RegExp	Contains the results of a regular expression search.
Regular Expression	Contains the patterns for a regular expression search.
String	Object that contains text and exposes methods and properties to manipulate that text.
VBArray	Used to contain and manipulate COM safe-array arrays, known as VBArrays.

JScript Properties

This section contains a list of JScript object properties arranged alphabetically.

PROPERTY	DESCRIPTION
$1 through $9	Contain values from the result of the RegExp function.
arguments	Contains an array of the arguments passed to the currently executing function.
caller	Provides a reference to the function that called the current function. In other words, the caller property gives you access to the item immediately preceding the current item on the call stack.
callee	Provides programmatic access to the name of the currently executing function.
constructor	The function that creates an object.
description	Holds a description of a runtime error.
E	Returns Euler's constant, the base of natural logarithms, approximately 2.718.
index	For a RegExp object, returns the index of the first successful search for a regular expression.
global	Contains a Boolean value corresponding to the presence (true) or absence (false) of the global (g) flag in a regular expression.
ignoreCase	Contains a Boolean value corresponding to the presence or absence of the ignore case (i) flag in a regular expression.
index	The character position of the first successful match in a string searched with the RegExp object.
Infinity	Number object property that contains an initial value of POSITIVE_INFINITY.

input	For a RegExp object, the input property returns the string that was searched.
lastIndex	Property of a RegExp object that returns the index of the last matching substring within a string.
lastMatch	Returns the set of characters matched last in a regular expression search.
lastParen	Returns the last parenthesized submatch from a regular expression search.
length (Arguments)	Returns the number of arguments passed to a function.
length (Array)	Returns the size of an array or collection.
length (Function)	Contains the number of arguments defined for a function.
length (String)	Returns the length of the text for the String object.
LN2	Returns the natural logarithm of 2.
LN10	Returns the natural logarithm of 10.
LOG2E	Returns the base 2 logarithm of e (Euler's constant).
LOG10E	Returns the base 10 logarithm of e (Euler's constant).
MAX_VALUE	The largest number you can use in JScript, approximately $1.79E+308$.
message	Contains an Error object's error message string.
MIN_VALUE	The smallest number you can use in JScript, approximately $2.22E-308$.
multiline	Contains a Boolean value corresponding to the presence (true) or absence (false) of the multiline (m) flag in a regular expression.
name	Contains an Error object's name (the name of the error). Usually one of the intrinsic Error types; for example, SyntaxError or ConversionError.
NaN (Global)	Contains the global initial constant for NaN (Not a Number).
NaN (Number)	NaN is a special value meaning Not a Number.
NEGATIVE_INFINITY	A value that represents negative infinity.
number	Contains a numeric value for a runtime error.
PI	Returns the value of pi (approximately 3.14159).
POSITIVE_INFINITY	Returns a value representing positive infinity.
propertyIsEnumerable	Returns true if a property both exists and is enumerable (is a collection or array). The property checks only directly owned properties, not prototype properties.
prototype	Returns a reference to a prototype object. New instances of that object type inherit the behavior of the prototype. For example, String.prototype.hasVowels = has_vowels; adds a prototype function called has_vowels to String objects. The has_vowels function tests a string expression for the presence of any vowel. After defining the function and the prototype, you can use it with *any* string, for example, var vowels="thwactpzp9579902";alert(novowels.has_Vowels());

`rightContext`	Returns characters from a string searched with a regular expression. The property returns all the characters in the string that appear *after* the last match.
`source`	Returns the text of a regular expression pattern.
`SQRT1_2`	Returns the square root of 0.5, or 1 divided by the square root of 2.
`SQRT2`	Returns the square root of 2.
`undefined`	The value of a declared but uninitialized variable.

JScript Methods

This section contains a list of JScript object methods, arranged alphabetically.

METHOD	DESCRIPTION
`abs`	Returns the absolute value of a numeric expression.
`acos`	Returns the arc cosine of a numeric expression.
`anchor`	Surrounds the text of a `String` object with an `<a>` anchor tag.
`apply`	Lets you call an object method substituting a different object for the current object.
`asin`	Returns the arcsine of a numeric expression.
`atan`	Returns the arctangent of a numeric expression.
`atan2`	Returns the angle (in radians) from the x-axis to a specified point (x, y).
`atEnd`	Returns `true` if an `Iterator` object has reached the end of its associated collection.
`big`	Surrounds the text of a `String` object with `<big>` tags.
`blink`	Surrounds the text of a `String` object with `<blink>` tags.
`bold`	Surrounds the text of a `String` object with `<b>` tags.
`call`	Calls an object method, substituting a different object for the current object.
`ceil`	Returns the smallest integer value greater than the value of the argument passed to the method.
`charAt`	Returns the character at a specified offset within a string.
`charCodeAt`	Returns the character code for the character at a specified offset within a string.
`compile`	Compiles a regular expression. Used to improve the speed of loops and repeated code.
`concat (Array)`	Concatenates two arrays.
`concat (String)`	Concatenates two strings.
`cos`	Returns the cosine of a numeric expression.

decodeURI	Unencodes an encoded Uniform Resource Identifier (URI). This method is the equivalent of the Server.URLDecode method in ASP.NET. Use this Global object method rather than the obsolete unescape method.
decodeURIComponent	Unencodes a portion (a component) of a Uniform Resource Identifier (URI). This method is the equivalent of the Server.URLDecode method in ASP.NET.
dimensions	Returns the number of dimensions in a VBArray array.
encodeURI	Encodes a Uniform Resource Identifier (URI) string. This method is the equivalent of the Server.URLEncode method in ASP.NET. Use this Global object method rather than the escape method to encode URI strings.
encodeURIComponent	Encodes a portion (a component) of a Uniform Resource Identifier (URI). This method is the equivalent of the Server.URLEncode method in ASP.NET. Use this Global object method rather than the escape method to encode portions of URI strings.
escape	HTTP-encodes strings. This method is obsolete. Use the Global encodeURI and encodeURIComponent methods instead.
eval	Evaluates JScript code. You use this to execute code strings you build at runtime.
exec	Searches a string for a regular expression.
exp	Returns e to the power you supply as an argument to the method.
fixed	Surrounds the text of a String object with <tt> teletype tags. The browser renders this text in a fixed-width font such as Courier.
floor	Returns the largest integer value less than the value of the argument passed to the method.
fontcolor	Surrounds the text of a String object with <font> tags where the starting tag includes a color attribute.
fontsize	Surrounds the text of a String object with <font> tags where the starting tag includes a size attribute.
fromCharCode	Creates a string from a list of Unicode values.
getDate	Returns the integer (1-31) value for the current day of the month stored in a Date object.
getDay	Returns the integer (0-6) value for the current day of the week stored in a Date object.
getFullYear	Returns the year as a four-character integer (for example, 2001) for the date stored in a Date object.
getHours	Returns the hour of the date stored in a Date object.
getItem	Returns the item at a specified position in a VBArray.
getMilliseconds	Returns the milliseconds past the current second for the time stored in a Date object.

getMinutes	Returns the number of minutes past the hour for the time stored in a Date object.
getMonth	Returns the month as an integer (1-12) for the current month stored in a Date object.
getSeconds	Returns the number of seconds past the minute for the time stored in a Date object.
getTime	Returns the time stored in a Date object.
getTimezoneOffset	Returns the difference (in minutes) between the local time on the computer and Universal Coordinated Time (UTC).
getUTCDate	These methods are identical to the getDate, GetDay, and such methods, except that they perform all calculations using Universal Coordinated Time (UTC) rather than the date and time on the local computer. Note that, because the computer must calculate UTC dates and times as an offset of the local computer's date/time, your date/time operations are still only as accurate as the local computer's time.
getUTCDay	
getUTCFullYear	
getUTCHours	
getUTCMilliseconds	
getUTCMinutes	
getUTCMonth	
getUTCSeconds	
getVarDate	Returns a JScript date from the date stored in a Date object in COM VT_DATE format. You need to use this method only if you're working with date or time arguments received from a VBScript or ActiveX control function or object.
getYear	Returns the two-digit year from the date stored in a Date object.
indexOf	Returns the starting position of the first matching substring within a String object.
isFinite	Returns true if the argument supplied is a finite number.
isNaN	Returns true if the argument supplied is NaN (Not a Number).
italics	Surrounds the text of a String object with <i> italics tags.
item	Property of an Enumerator object. Returns the current item in an enumerated collection.
join	Returns a string consisting of all the elements in a string array joined into a single string with an optional separator character between the values.
lastIndexOf	Returns the starting position of the last matching substring within a String object.

lbound	Returns the lower bound of a VBArray.
link	Surrounds the text of a String object with an `<a>` anchor tag containing an HREF attribute.
log	Returns the natural logarithm of a numeric value or expression.
match	Performs a search for a substring using a RegExp object.
max	Returns the larger of two arguments.
min	Returns the smaller of two arguments.
moveFirst	Resets the current item of an Enumerator object to the first item of its associated collection.
moveNext	Moves the current item of an Enumerator object to the next item of its associated collection.
parse	Parses the text of a String object. Returns the elapsed number of milliseconds between a string or date and the constant date January 1, 1970.
parseFloat	Parses the text of a String object and returns a floating-point value if the String contains a text representation of a number.
parseInt	Parses the text of a String object and returns an integer value if the String contains a text representation of a number.
pop	Removes the element from the array and returns it.
pow	Returns the value of a numeric expression to the power of an argument you supply to the function.
push	Appends new elements to an array. The method returns the number of elements in the array after adding the new elements. You can push multiple items onto an array using the push method.
random	Returns a pseudo-random number between 0 and 1.
replace	Replaces substrings found by a regular expression search with other substrings.
reverse	Reverses the order of elements in an array.
round	Returns a number rounded to the nearest integer value.
search	Searches a string for matches to a regular expression.
setDate	Sets the date value of a Date object.
setFullYear	Sets the year of the date value of a Date object.
setHours	Sets the current hour of a time value contained in a Date object.
setMilliseconds	Sets the number of milliseconds past the second for the time value contained in a Date object.
setMinutes	Sets the minutes past the hour for the time value contained in a Date object.

setMonth	Sets the current month of the date value contained in a Date object.
setSeconds	Sets the number of seconds past the minute for the time value contained in a Date object.
setTime	Sets the time value of a Date object.
setUTCDate	These methods are identical to the setDate, SetFullYear, and other such methods except that they perform all calculations using Universal Coordinated Time (UTC) rather than the date and time on the local computer. Note that, because the computer must calculate UTC dates and times as an offset of the local computer's date/time, your date/time operations are still only as accurate as the local computer's time.
setUTCFullYear	
setUTCHours	
setUTCMilliseconds	
setUTCMinutes	
setUTCMonth	
setUTCSeconds	
setYear	Sets the year of the date value contained in a Date object.
shift	Removes the first element from an array and returns the removed element.
sin	Returns the sin value of a numeric value supplied as an argument.
slice (Array)	Returns a portion of an array. You supply the starting and ending indexes.
slice (String)	Returns a portion of a string. You supply the starting and ending indexes.
small	Surrounds the text of a String object with <small> tags.
sort	Returns a sorted array.
splice	Removes a specified number of items from an array starting from a specified offset. Optionally, you can insert new items in place of the deleted items. The method returns the deleted items as a new array.
split	Splits the text of a String object into an array of strings separated at the delimiter value you supply.
sqrt	Returns the square root of a numeric argument.
strike	Surrounds the text of a String object with <strike> strikethrough tags.
sub	Surrounds the text of a String object with <sub> subscript tags.
substr	Returns a substring from the text of a String object beginning from a specified offset with a specified length.
substring	Returns a substring from the text of a String object beginning from a specified start offset and extending to a specified end offset.

sup	Surrounds the text of a String object with <sup> superscript tags.
tan	Returns the tangent of a numeric value or expression.
test	Returns true if a specified pattern exists in a string; otherwise, returns false.
toArray	Converts a VBArray to a JScript array.
toDateString	Returns the string representation of a Date object.
toExponential	Returns a string containing the exponential notation representation of the number.
toFixed	Returns a string containing the fixed-point representation of the number.
toGMTString	Obsolete. Use the toUTCString method instead.
toLocaleDateString	Returns a locale-appropriate string version of a Date object.
toLocaleLowerCase	Returns the lowercase locale-appropriate version of a string.
toLocaleString	Returns the locale-appropriate string representation of a date in long-date format.
toLocaleTimeString	Returns the string representation of a time.
toLocaleUpperCase	Returns the uppercase locale-appropriate version of a string.
toLowerCase	Returns a string with all the characters converted to lowercase.
toPrecision	Returns a string representation of the number with a specified number of digits in either exponential or fixed-point notation.
toString	Returns a string representation of an object.
toTimeString	Returns a string representation of a time.
toUpperCase	Returns a string with all the characters converted to uppercase.
toUTCString	Returns a string representation of a date in Universal Coordinated Time (UTC).
ubound	Returns the upper bound of a VBArray.
unescape	Accepts an escaped (HTTP-encoded) string. Returns the string converted to normal text. Do not use this method to unescape URI strings; use the decodeURI and decodeURIComponent methods instead.
unshift	Inserts a specified list of elements at the front of an array and returns the full array, including the inserted elements.
UTC	Returns the number of milliseconds between the constant January 1, 1970 and the supplied date. Uses UTC time to make the calculation.
valueOf	Returns the primitive value of the object argument. The method returns arrays as comma-separated strings; Boolean values as strings; dates and times as milliseconds (see UTC method); functions as the text of the function; numbers as a numeric value; objects as themselves; and strings as text.

JScript Functions

This section contains a list of JScript's built-in functions, arranged alphabetically.

FUNCTION	DESCRIPTION
GetObject	Returns a reference to a COM or OLE object stored in a file.
ScriptEngine	Returns a string containing the name of the scripting language in use.
ScriptEngineBuildVersion	Returns a string containing the build version of the scripting language in use.
ScriptEngineMajorVersion	Returns a string containing the major version number of the scripting language in use.
ScriptEngineMinorVersion	Returns a string containing the minor version number of the scripting language in use.

JScript Statements

This section contains a list of JScript statements, arranged alphabetically.

STATEMENT	DESCRIPTION
break	Used to end processing in a loop or code block. Processing starts at the code line following the code block.
@cc on	Turns on conditional compilation.
catch	Begins a block containing code to run when a try statement fails.
Comment (//); single-line version	Used to place a comment on a single line. You may place the slashes anywhere in the line. The compiler ignores any text on that line following the slashes. Use the multiline /*...*/ syntax for multiline comments.
Comment (/*...*/); multiline version	Used to surround comment lines. The compiler ignores all text between the starting /* characters and the ending */ characters.
continue	JScript does not process code following a continue statement in a loop. Instead, it begins processing again at the top of the loop.
do...while	Loop structure that always executes at least once.
for	Used at the start of a for loop structure. The syntax is for (value; test; increment) statement or block. Equivalent to VBScript's For...Next statement block.
for...in	Executes a statement or block for each item in a collection or array. Equivalent to a C# foreach...in block.
function	Declares a new function.
@if	Conditional if structure. Used to compile code conditionally where the host-scripting environment may not be able to interpret the code correctly.

`if...else`	Code block. Performs a Boolean test on an expression and executes the code within the block if the expression evaluates to `true`.
`Labeled`	A unique identifier that marks a position or label in code. To create a label, append a colon (`:`) to the end of the label text, such as `myLabel:`. The code line following the label is called a `Labeled` statement. If you include a label after a `continue` statement in a loop, execution continues at the code line following the label.
`return`	Exits a function and (optionally) returns a value.
`@set`	Conditional variable-creation statement.
`switch`	A code block that conditionally executes one of a group of statements according to the value of the condition.
`this`	Contains a reference to the current object.
`throw`	Raises an error.
`try...catch...finally`	Sets up error handling. Requires two code blocks: a `try` block and a `catch` block. If an error occurs in the `try` block, execution resumes at the start of the `catch` block. Statements in the `finally` block always execute regardless of whether an error occurs. You can handle a trapped error locally or raise it to the calling method using the `throw` statement.
`var`	Used to declare a variable.
`while`	Begins a conditional code block. The block executes if the condition following the `while` statement evaluates to `true`.
`with`	Sets the default object for the following statement or group of statements. Equivalent to the `With` statement in VBScript.

JScript Operators

This section contains a list of JScript operators, arranged alphabetically.

OPERATOR	DESCRIPTION
Addition Assignment (+=)	Adds the value on the right side of the operator to a variable on the left side and assigns the result to the variable on the left side.
Addition (+)	Adds values. In JScript, you use the addition operator for both addition and string concatenation.
Assignment (=)	Assigns a value to the variable on the left side of the equals sign.
Bitwise AND Assignment (&=)	Performs a Boolean AND operation on a variable on the left side of the operator and a value on the right side and assigns the result to the variable on the left side.
Bitwise AND (&)	Performs a Boolean AND operation on two values.

Bitwise Left Shift (<<)	Shifts the bits of a value one position to the left.
Bitwise NOT (~)	Negates a value by flipping all the bits from 1 to 0 or from 0 to 1.
Bitwise OR (|=) Assignment	Compares the bit pattern of a variable on the left side of the operator with the bit pattern of a value on the right side and produces 1 if either or both bits in a column are 1 and 0 otherwise. It assigns the result to the variable on the left side.
Bitwise OR (|)	Compares two bit patterns and produces 1 if either or both bits in a column are 1.
Bitwise Right Shift (>>)	Shifts the bits of a value one position to the right.
Bitwise XOR (^=) Assignment	Compares the bit pattern of a variable on the left side of the operator with the bit pattern of a value on the right side and produces 1 if only one of the bits, but not both, in a column is 1. It assigns the result to the variable on the left side.
Bitwise XOR (^)	Compares two bit patterns and produces 1 if only one of the bits, but not both, in a column is 1.
Comma (,)	Causes multiple expressions to be evaluated in sequence as if they were a single expression. It returns the value of the rightmost expression in the list.
Comparison	Less than (<).
	Greater than (>).
	Less than or equal to (<=).
	Greater than or equal to (>=).
	Equal (==).
	Not equal (!=).
	Identity equality—same object (===).
	Identity inequality (!==).
Compound Assignment	Addition (+=).
	Bitwise AND (&=).
	Bitwise OR (|=).
	Bitwise XOR (^=).
	Division (/=).
	Left Shift (<<=).
	Modulus (%=).
	Multiplication (*=).
	Right Shift (>>=).

Subtraction (-=).

Unsigned Right Shift (>>>=).

Conditional Compilation Variables These are built-in variables that either are `true` or evaluate to NaN.

`@_win32`—`true` if running on a Win32 system.

`@_win16`—`true` if running on a Win16 system.

`@_mac`—`true` if running on an Apple Macintosh system.

`@_alpha`—`true` if running on a DEC Alpha processor.

`@_x86`—`true` if running on an Intel processor.

`@_mc680x0`—`true` if running on a Motorola 680x0 processor.

`@_PowerPC`—`true` if running on a Motorola PowerPC processor.

`@_jscript`—Always `true`.

`@_jscript_build`—Contains the build number of the JScript scripting engine.

`@_jscript_version`—Contains the JScript version number in `major.minor` format.

Conditional (Ternary) (?:) Used to execute one of two statements based on an expression. If the expression evaluates to `true`, JScript executes the first statement. If the expression evaluates to `false`, JScript executes the second statement. The syntax is `expression ? statement1 : statement2`.

Decrement (–) Decrements a value by 1. There are several syntax variations.

`–variable` decrements a variable before an operation.

`variable–` decrements a variable after an operation

`var = –variable`.

`delete` Deletes a property or an `array` element.

Division Assignment (/=) Divides a variable on the left side of the operator by a value on the right side and assigns the result to the variable on the left side.

Division (/) Divides two numbers.

Equality (==) Tests for equality between two values or expressions.

Greater than (>) Compares the relative size of two numeric values or expressions. Returns `true` if the value of the expression on the left side of the operator is larger than the value of the expression on the right side.

Greater than or equal to (>=) Compares the relative size of two values or expressions. Returns `true` if the value of the expression on the left side of the operator is larger than or equal to the value of the expression on the right side.

Identity (===)	Compares two variables containing object references and returns true if both variables refer to the same object.
Increment (++)	Increments a value by 1.
Inequality (!=)	Compares two values or expressions for nonequality (read the operator as "not equal"). Operations using the inequality operator evaluate to true if the value on the left side of the operator is not equal to the value on the right side.
instanceOf	Returns true if the object is an instance of the specified class argument.
Left Shift Assignment (<<=)	Shifts the bits of a value on the right side of the operator one position to the left and assigns the result to a variable on the left.
Left Shift (<<)	Shifts the bits of a value one position to the left.
Less than (<)	Compares the relative size of two numeric values or expressions. Returns true if the value of the expression on the left side of the operator is smaller than the value of the expression on the right side.
Less than or equal to (<=)	Compares the relative size of two values or expressions. Returns true if the value of the expression on the left side of the operator is less than or equal to the value of the expression on the right side.
Logical AND (&&)	Performs a Boolean AND operation.
Logical NOT (!)	Performs a Boolean NOT operation.
Logical OR (||)	Performs a Boolean OR operation.
Modulus Assignment (%=)	Performs modulo arithmetic (returns the remainder of a division operation) between a variable on the left side of the operator and a value on the right side and assigns the result to the variable on the left side.
Modulus (%)	Performs modulo arithmetic (returns the remainder of a division operation).
Multiplication (*)	Multiplies numeric values.
new	Creates a new object variable.
Nonidentity (!==)	Returns true if the operand on the left side of the operator does not refer to the same object as the operand on the right side.
Right Shift Assignment (>>=)	Shifts the bits of a value on the right side of the operator one position to the right and assigns the result to a variable on the left.
Right Shift (<<)	Shifts the bits of a value one position to the right.
Subtraction Assignment (-=)	Subtracts the value on the right side of the operator from the value of a variable on the left side and assigns the results to the variable on the left side.
Subtraction (-)	Subtracts numeric values.

typeof	Returns the type of an object or expression as a string. The return value is number, String, Boolean, Object, Function, or undefined.
Unary Negation (-)	Negates a value or expression.
Unsigned Right Shift Assignment (>>>=)	Shifts the bit pattern of a value on the right side of the operator to the right, zero-fills the bits on the left, and assigns the results to a variable on the left side of the operator.
Unsigned Right Shift (>>>)	Shifts the bit pattern of a value to the right and zero-fills the bits on the left.
void	Used to evaluate an expression. The void operator returns the value undefined.

JScript Microsoft-Specific Extensions

The features listed in this table are not ECMA compatible; they work only with Microsoft JScript.

EXTENSION TYPE	DESCRIPTION
Array operations	The array methods concat, slice, dimensions, getItem, lbound, toArray, ubound, the VBArray object.
Conditional compilation	Use in situations where non-Microsoft browsers or servers may not be able to compile the code. You begin conditional compilation using the @cc_on statement or the @if or @set statement. See the Conditional Compilation Variables entry in the previous section in this appendix, "JScript Operators," for a full list.
Control Flow	do...while, Labeled, switch.
Dates and Time	getVarDate.
Enumeration	Enumerator, atEnd, item, moveFirst, moveNext.
Error Handling	Error object, description, number, throw, try...catch.
Function Creation	caller.
Operators	Identity (===), nonidentity (!==).
Objects	Enumerator, RegExp, Regular Expression, VBArray, ActiveXObject, GetObject.
Regular Expressions and Pattern Matching	RegExp, index, input, lastIndex, $1...$9, source, compile, exec, test, Regular Expression syntax.
Script Engine Identification	ScriptEngine, ScriptEngineBuildVersion, ScriptEngineMajorVersion, ScriptEngineMinorVersion.
Strings	The String methods concat, slice, match, replace, search, anchor, big, blink, bold, fixed, fontcolor, fontsize, italics, link, small, strike, sub, sup.

JScript Constants

This section contains a list of JScript compile-time error numbers and messages, arranged alphabetically by message.

ERROR NUMBER	DESCRIPTION
5029	Array length must be a finite positive integer.
5030	Array length must be assigned a finite positive number.
5028	Array or arguments object expected.
5010	Boolean expected.
5003	Cannot assign to a function result.
5000	Cannot assign to 'this'.
5006	Date object expected.
5015	Enumerator object expected.
5022	Exception thrown and not caught.
5020	Expected ')' in regular expression.
5019	Expected ']' in regular expression.
5023	Function does not have a valid prototype object.
5002	Function expected.
5008	Illegal assignment.
5021	Invalid range in character set.
5014	JScript object expected.
5001	Number expected.
5007	Object expected.
5012	Object member expected.
5016	Regular Expression object expected.
5005	String expected.
5017	Syntax error in regular expression.
5026	The number of fractional digits is out of range.
5027	The precision is out of range.
5025	The URI to be decoded is not a valid encoding.
5024	The URI to be encoded contains an invalid character.
5009	Undefined identifier.

5018	Unexpected quantifier.
5013	VBArray expected.

JScript Runtime Error Constants

This section contains a list of JScript runtime error constants, arranged in numerical order.

ERROR NUMBER	DESCRIPTION
5	Invalid procedure call or argument.
6	Overflow.
7	Out of memory.
9	Subscript out of range.
10	This array is fixed or temporarily locked.
11	Division by zero.
13	Type mismatch.
14	Out of string space.
17	Can't perform requested operation.
28	Out of stack space.
35	Sub or Function not defined.
48	Error in loading DLL.
51	Internal error.
52	Bad filename or number.
53	File not found.
54	Bad file mode.
55	File already open.
57	Device I/O error.
58	File already exists.
61	Disk full.
62	Input past end of file.
67	Too many files.
68	Device unavailable.
70	Permission denied.
71	Disk not ready.

74	Can't rename with different drive.
75	Path/File access error.
76	Path not found.
91	`Object` variable or `With` block variable not set.
92	`For` loop not initialized.
94	Invalid use of `Null`.
322	Can't create necessary temporary file.
424	Object required.
429	Automation server can't create object.
430	Class doesn't support automation.
432	Filename or class name not found during automation operation.
438	Object doesn't support this property or method.
440	Automation error.
445	Object doesn't support this action.
446	Object doesn't support named arguments.
447	Object doesn't support current locale setting.
448	Named argument not found.
449	Argument not optional.
450	Wrong number of arguments or invalid property assignment.
451	Object not a collection.
453	Specified DLL function not found.
458	Variable uses an automation type not supported in JScript.
462	The remote server machine does not exist or is unavailable.
501	Cannot assign to variable.
502	Object not safe for scripting.
503	Object not safe for initializing.
504	Object not safe for creating.
507	An exception occurred.
5000	Cannot assign to `'this'`.
5001	Number expected.

5002	Function expected.
5003	Cannot assign to a function result.
5004	Cannot index object.
5005	String expected.
5006	Date object expected.
5007	Object expected.
5008	Illegal assignment.
5009	Undefined identifier.
5010	Boolean expected.
5011	Can't execute code from a freed script.
5012	Object member expected.
5013	VBArray expected.
5014	JScript object expected.
5015	Enumerator object expected.
5016	Regular Expression object expected.
5017	Syntax error in regular expression.
5018	Unexpected quantifier.
5019	Expected ']' in regular expression.
5020	Expected ')' in regular expression.
5021	Invalid range in character set.
5022	Exception thrown and not caught.
5023	Function does not have a valid prototype object.
5024	The URI to be encoded contains an invalid character.
5025	The URI to be decoded is not a valid encoding.
5026	The number of fractional digits is out of range.
5027	The precision is out of range.
5028	Array or arguments object expected.
5029	Array length must be a finite positive integer.
5030	Array length must be assigned a finite positive number.

JScript Syntax Error Constants

This section contains a list of JScript syntax error constants, arranged numerically.

ERROR NUMBER	DESCRIPTION
1001	Out of memory.
1002	Syntax error.
1003	Expected ':'.
1004	Expected ';'.
1005	Expected '('.
1006	Expected ')'.
1007	Expected ']'.
1008	Expected '{'.
1009	Expected '}'.
1010	Expected identifier.
1011	Expected '='.
1012	Expected '/'.
1013	Invalid number.
1014	Invalid character.
1015	Unterminated string constant.
1016	Unterminated comment.
1018	'return' statement outside of function.
1019	Can't have 'break' outside of loop.
1020	Can't have 'continue' outside of loop.
1023	Expected hexadecimal digit.
1024	Expected 'while'.
1025	Label redefined.
1026	Label not found.
1027	'default' can only appear in a 'switch' statement.
1028	Expected identifier or string.
1029	Expected '@end'.
1030	Conditional compilation turned off.
1031	Expected constant.

1032	Expected '@'.
1033	Expected 'catch'.
1034	Expected 'var'.
1035	'throw' must be followed by an expression on the same source line.

JScript Feature Availability, by Version

Because JScript has evolved over time, the different versions available in the various releases of Internet Explorer support different feature sets. This table shows the features available by IE version.

	IE VERSION					
JSCRIPT FEATURE	**1**	**2**	**3**	**4**	**5**	**5.5**
0...n Property						X
$1...$9 Properties			X			
abs Method	X					
acos Method	X					
ActiveXObject Object			X			
Addition Operator (+)	X					
anchor Method	X					
apply method						X
arguments Property		X				
Array Object		X				
asin Method	X					
Assignment Operator (=)	X					
atan Method	X					
atan2 Method	X					
atEnd Method			X			
big Method	X					
Bitwise AND Operator (&)	X					
Bitwise Left Shift Operator (<<)	X					
Bitwise NOT Operator (~)	X					
Bitwise OR Operator (|)	X					
Bitwise Right Shift Operator (>>)	X					

		IE VERSION				
JSCRIPT FEATURE	**1**	**2**	**3**	**4**	**5**	**5.5**
Bitwise XOR Operator (^)	X					
blink Method	X					
bold Method	X					
Boolean Object		X				
break Statement	X					
call Method						X
callee Property						X
caller Property		X				
catch Statement					X	
@cc_on Statement			X			
ceil Method	X					
charAt Method	X					
charCodeAt Method						X
Comma Operator (,)	X					
// (Single-line Comment Statement)	X					
/*..*/ (Multiline Comment Statement)	X					
Comparison Operators	X					
compile Method			X			
concat Method (Array)			X			
concat Method (String)			X			
Conditional Compilation			X			
Conditional Compilation Variables			X			
Conditional (ternary) Operator (?:)	X					
constructor Property		X				
continue Statement	X					
cos Method	X					
Data Type Conversion			X			
Date Object	X					
decodeURI Method						X
decodeURIComponent						X

JSCRIPT FEATURE	IE VERSION					
	1	2	3	4	5	5.5
Decrement Operator (−)	X					
delete Operator			X			
description Property					X	
dimensions Method			X			
Division Operator (/)	X					
do...while Statement			X			
E Property	X					
encodeURI Method						X
encodeURI Component						X
Enumerator Object			X			
Equality Operator (==)	X					
Error Object					X	
escape Method	X					
eval Method	X					
eXec Method			X			
eXp Method	X					
fiXed Method	X					
floor Method	X					
fontcolor Method	X					
fontsize Method	X					
for Statement	X					
for...in Statement					X	
fromCharCode Method			X			
Function Object		X				
function Statement	X					
getDate Method	X					
getDay Method	X					
getFullYear Method			X			
getHours Method	X					
getItem Method			X			

			IE VERSION			
JSCRIPT FEATURE	**1**	**2**	**3**	**4**	**5**	**5.5**
getMilliseconds Method			X			
getMinutes Method	X					
getMonth Method	X					
GetObject Function			X			
getSeconds Method	X					
getTime Method	X					
getTimezoneOffset Method	X					
getUTCDate Method			X			
getUTCDay Method			X			
getUTCFullYear Method			X			
getUTCHours Method			X			
getUTCMilliseconds Method			X			
getUTCMinutes Method			X			
getUTCMonth Method			X			
getUTCSeconds Method			X			
getVarDate Method			X			
getYear Method	X					
Global Object			X			
global Property						X
Greater than Operator (>)	X					
Greater than or equal to Operator (>=)	X					
hasOwnProperty Method						X
Identity Operator (===)	X					
@if Statement			X			
if...else Statement	X					
ignoreCase Property						X
Increment Operator (++)	X					
indeX Property			X			
indeXOf Method	X					
Inequality Operator (!=)	X					

JSCRIPT FEATURE	1	2	IE VERSION			
			3	4	5	5.5
Infinity Property			X			
input Property			X			
instanceof Operator					X	
isFinite Method			X			
isNaN Method	X					
isPrototypeOf Method						X
italics Method	X					
item Method			X			
join Method		X				
Labeled Statement			X			
lastIndeX Property			X			
lastIndeXOf Method	X					
lastMatch Property						X
lastParen Property						X
lbound Method			X			
leftConteXt Property						X
length Property (Arguments)						X
length Property (Array)		X				
length Property (Function)		X				
length Property (String)	X					
Less than Operator (<)	X					
Less than or equal to Operator (<=)	X					
link Method	X					
LN2 Property	X					
LN10 Property	X					
localeCompare Method						X
log Method	X					
LOG2E Property	X					
LOG10E Property	X					
Logical AND Operator (&&)	X					

JSCRIPT FEATURE	1	2	IE VERSION 3	4	5	5.5
Logical NOT Operator (!)	X					
Logical OR Operator (||)	X					
match Method			X			
Math Object	X					
maX Method	X					
MAX_VALUE Property		X				
message Property						X
min Method	X					
MIN_VALUE Property		X				
Modulus Operator (%)	X					
moveFirst Method			X			
moveNeXt Method			X			
multiline Property						X
Multiplication Operator (*)	X					
name Property						X
NaN Property (Global)			X			
NaN Property (Number)		X				
NEGATIVE_INFINITY Property		X				
new Operator	X					
Nonidentity Operator (!==)	X					
Number Object		X				
number Property					X	
Object Object			X			
Operator Precedence	X					
parse Method	X					
parseFloat Method	X					
parseInt Method	X					
PI Property	X					
pop Method						X
POSITIVE_INFINITY Property		X				

JSCRIPT FEATURE	1	2	3	4	5	5.5
			IE Version			
pow Method	X					
prototype Property		X				
propertyIsEnumeramble Property						X
push Method						X
random Method	X					
RegEXp Object			X			
Regular Expression Object			X			
Regular Expression Syntax			X			
replace Method	X					
return Statement	X					
reverse Method		X				
rightConteXt Property						X
round Method	X					
ScriptEngine Function		X				
ScriptEngineBuildVersion Function		X				
ScriptEngineMajorVersion Function		X				
ScriptEngineMinorVersion Function		X				
search Method			X			
@set Statement			X			
setDate Method	X					
setFullYear Method			X			
setHours Method	X					
setMilliseconds Method			X			
setMinutes Method	X					
setMonth Method	X					
setSeconds Method	X					
setTime Method	X					
setUTCDate Method			X			
setUTCFullYear Method			X			
setUTCHours Method			X			

			IE VERSION			
JSCRIPT FEATURE	**1**	**2**	**3**	**4**	**5**	**5.5**
setUTCMilliseconds Method			X			
setUTCMinutes Method			X			
setUTCMonth Method			X			
setUTCSeconds Method			X			
setYear Method	X					
shift Method						X
sin Method	X					
slice Method (Array)			X			
slice Method (String)			X			
small Method	X					
sort Method		X				
source Property			X			
splice Method						X
split Method			X			
sqrt Method	X					
SQRT1_2 Property	X					
SQRT2 Property	X					
strike Method	X					
String Object	X					
sub Method	X					
substr Method			X			
substring Method	X					
Subtraction Operator (-)	X					
sup Method	X					
switch Statement			X			
tan Method	X					
test Method			X			
this Statement	X					
throw Statement					X	
toArray Method			X			

JSCRIPT FEATURE	1	2	3	4	5	5.5
			IE VERSION			
toDateString Method						X
toEXponential Method						X
toFiXed Method						X
toGMTString Method	X					
toLocaleDateString Method						X
toLocaleLowercase Method						X
toLocaleString Method	X					
toLocaleTimeString Method						X
toLocaleUppercase Method						X
toLowerCase Method	X					
toPrecision Method						X
toString Method		X				
toTimeString Method						X
toUpperCase Method	X					
toUTCString Method			X			
try Statement					X	
typeof Operator	X					
ubound Method			X			
Unary Negation Operator (–)	X					
undefined Property						X
unescape Method	X					
unshift Method						X
Unsigned Right Shift Operator (>>>)	X					
UTC Method	X					
valueOf Method		X				
var Statement	X					
VBArray Object			X			
void Operator		X				
while Statement	X					
with Statement	X					

Index

Note to the Reader: Throughout this index **boldfaced** page numbers indicate primary discussions of a topic. *Italicized* page numbers indicate illustrations.